PUBLIC OPINION AND THE COMMUNICATION OF CONSENT

THE GUILFORD COMMUNICATION SERIES

PUBLIC OPINION AND THE COMMUNICATION OF CONSENT
Theodore L. Glasser and Charles T. Salmon, *Editors*

COMMUNICATION RESEARCH MEASURES: A SOURCEBOOK
Rebecca B. Rubin, Philip Palmgreen, and Howard E. Sypher, *Editors*

PERSUASIVE COMMUNICATION
James B. Stiff

MESSAGE EFFECTS RESEARCH: PRINCIPLES OF DESIGN AND ANALYSIS
Sally Jackson

REFORMING LIBEL LAW
John Soloski and Randall P Bezanson, *Editors*

COMMUNICATION AND CONTROL: NETWORKS AND THE NEW ECONOMIES OF COMMUNICATION
G. J. Mulgan

CRITICAL PERSPECTIVES ON MEDIA AND SOCIETY
Robert K. Avery and David Eason, *Editors*

THE JOURNALISM OF OUTRAGE: INVESTIGATIVE REPORTING AND AGENDA BUILDING IN AMERICA
David L. Protess, Fay Lomax Cook, Jack C. Doppelt, James S. Ettema, Margaret T Gordon, Donna R. Leff, and Peter Miller

MASS MEDIA AND POLITICAL TRANSITION: THE HONG KONG PRESS IN CHINA'S ORBIT
Joseph Man Chan and Chin-Chuan Lee

STUDYING INTERPERSONAL INTERACTION
Barbara M. Montgomery and Steve Duck, *Editors*

CASE STUDIES IN ORGANIZATIONAL COMMUNICATION
Beverly Davenport Sypher, *Editor*

VOICES OF CHINA: THE INTERPLAY OF POLITICS AND JOURNALISM
Chin-Chuan Lee, *Editor*

PUBLIC OPINION AND THE COMMUNICATION OF CONSENT

Edited by

THEODORE L. GLASSER
Stanford University

CHARLES T. SALMON
Michigan State University

Introduction by

ELIHU KATZ

THE GUILFORD PRESS
New York London

A Division of Guilford Publications, Inc.
72 Spring Street, New York, NY 10012

Printed in the United States of America

This book is printed on acid-free paper.

Last digit is print number: 9 8 7 6 5 4 3 2 1

Library of Congress Cataloging-in-Publication Data

Public opinion and the communication of consent / edited by
Theodore L. Glasser, Charles T. Salmon.
p. cm. — (The Guilford communication series)
Includes bibliographical references and index.
ISBN 0-89862-405-3. — ISBN 0-89862-499-1
1. Public opinion—United States. 2. Mass media and public opinion—United States. 3. Public opinion polls—United States. 4. Communication—United States—Psychological aspects. 5. Communication—Social aspects—United States. I. Glasser, Theodore Lewis. II. Salmon, Charles T. III. Series.
HM261.P835 1995
303.3′8—dc20 94-49154
CIP

Contributors

Lee B. Becker, Ph.D., School of Journalism, Ohio State University, Columbus, Ohio

James R. Beniger, Ph.D., Annenberg School for Communication, University of Southern California, Los Angeles, California

Harry C. Boyte, Ph.D., The Center for Democracy and Citizenship, Humphrey Institute of Public Affairs, University of Minnesota, Minneapolis, Minnesota

James W. Carey, Ph.D., Graduate School of Journalism, Columbia University, New York, New York

Clifford G. Christians, Ph.D., The Institute of Communications Research, University of Illinois, Champaign, Illinois

Lucig Danielian, Ph.D., International Research and Exchanges Board, Armenia

George A. Donohue, Ph.D., Department of Sociology, University of Minnesota, St. Paul, Minnesota

Murray Edelman, Ph.D., Department of Political Science, University of Wisconsin-Madison, Madison, Wisconsin

Theodore L. Glasser, Ph.D., The Graduate Program in Journalism, Department of Communication, Stanford University, Stanford, California

Carroll J. Glynn, Ph.D., Graduate Studies, Department of Communication, Cornell University, Ithaca, New York

Jodi A. Gusek, Doctoral Candidate, Annenberg School for Communication, University of Southern California, Los Angeles, California

Susan Herbst, Ph.D., Departments of Communication Studies and Political Science, Northwestern University, Evanston, Illinois

Elihu Katz, Ph.D., The Annenberg Scholars Program, The Annenberg School for Communication, University of Pennsylvania, Philadelphia, Pennsylvania; Guttman Institute, Hebrew University of Jerusalem, Jerusalem, Israel

Elliot King, Ph.D., Media Studies Program, Loyola College, Chicago, Illinois

Maxwell McCombs, Ph.D., Department of Journalism, University of Texas at Austin, Austin, Texas

Daniel G. McDonald, Ph.D., Department of Communication, Cornell University, Ithaca, New York

Jack McLeod, Ph.D., Mass Communications Research Center, School of Journalism and Mass Communication, University of Wisconsin-Madison, Madison, Wisconsin

Peter V. Miller, Ph.D., Department of Communication Studies and Journalism, Northwestern University, Evanston, Illinois

Elisabeth Noelle-Neumann, PhD., The Institut für Demoskopie Allensbach and Department of Communication Research, University of Mainz, Allensbach, Germany

Clarice N. Olien, M.A., Department of Rural Sociology, University of Minnesota, St. Paul, Minnesota

Hayg Oshagan, Ph.D., Department of Communication, University of Michigan, Ann Arbor, Michigan

Ronald E. Ostman, Ph.D., Department of Communication, Cornell University, Ithaca, New York

Zhongdang Pan, Ph.D., Annenberg School for Communication, University of Pennsylvania, Philadelphia, Pennsylvania

John Durham Peters, Ph.D., Department of Communication, University of Iowa, Iowa City, Iowa

Vincent Price, Ph.D., Department of Communication, University of Michigan, Ann Arbor, Michigan

Gertrude J. Robinson, Ph.D., Graduate Program in Communications, McGill University, Montreal, Canada

Dianne Rucinski, Ph.D., Department of General Studies, National Opinion Research Center, Washington, DC

Charles T. Salmon, Ph.D., Department of Advertising, Michigan State University, East Lansing, Michigan

Klaus Schoenbach, Ph.D., Department of Journalism and Communication Research, University of Music and Theater, Hannover, Germany

Michael Schudson, Ph.D., Department of Communication, University of California-San Diego, La Jolla, California

Phillip J. Tichenor, Ph.D., School of Journalism and Mass Communication, University of Minnesota, Minneapolis, Minnesota

Wayne Wanta, Ph.D., School of Journalism, University of Oregon, Eugene, Oregon

Acknowledgments

Any edited volume is indebted to the authors whose work it contains. Ours especially. The 30 friends and colleagues who prepared 17 of the chapters in *Public Opinion and the Communication of Consent* were gracious and patient, particularly patient, as they waited and waited for it to finally appear in print. Some waited for literally years. Every author had to contend with our request for revision; almost everyone responded quickly and expertly. It was in many ways an easy volume to edit; we began with an excellent cast of contributors. If the ensemble has its problems, only the editors can be faulted.

We are indebted as well to the editorial (notably, but not only, Peter Wissoker), production, and marketing staff at The Guilford Press. They, too, endured intolerable delays.

Thanks also to others who pitched in, including Hyun-yi Cho, Margaret Morrison, Nurit Guttman, Johnna Tuttle, and Peggy Bowers.

Preface

This project represents the culmination of a dialogue that began in the early 1980s at the University of Minnesota. Schooled in different intellectual traditions, we nonetheless soon found ourselves on common ground, intrigued by the elusive nature of public opinion. In particular, we were struck by the degree of methodological homogeneity which seemed to characterize the area of study even as copious reviews of the literature cautioned that "public opinion" was a term with a multiplicity of meanings (e.g., Childs, 1965).

The infant field of public opinion research benefitted from an unusually strong consensus concerning how to conceive and study the phenomenon of public opinion. In a seminal article in the inaugural issue of *Public Opinion Quarterly*, for example, Floyd Allport (1937) closed off what he considered to be "blind alleys," that is, conceptualizations which he believed would impede the formation of a scientific approach to public opinion and hence were unworthy of scholarly attention. Mainstream public opinion research needed to be refined methodologically, of course, but intellectually it was comparatively unproblematic and uncontroversial. Philip Converse (1987) made just this point in his review of 50 years of changing conceptions of public opinion: "For the most part, we feel there is a closer fit between our concept of public opinion and its conventional operationalization than is true in much of social science, and we are grateful for this fact (p. 514)."

If we do not fully agree with Converse's assessment of the study of public opinion, it is in part because we define the field in broader terms. But it is also because we are now witnessing important and exciting changes in the conceptualization of public opinion and a concomitant dimunition of the consensus that prevailed only a decade ago.

By design, then, there is no single theme or overarching perspective that binds together the chapters in this book. We have not tried to reconcile contrasting—even competing—conceptions of public opinion, nor have we insisted on any conceptual or intellectual orthodoxy with regard to the study of communication. Rather, we have solicited work that represents what we believe to be the full range of contemporary discussion on public opinion and what communication portends for its study.

REFERENCES

Allport, F. H. (1937). Toward a science of public opinion. *Public Opinion Quarterly*, 1, x–xx.

Childs, H. L. (1965). *Public opinion: Nature, formation, and role*. Princeton: Van Nostrand.

Converse, P. E. (1987). Changing conceptions of public opinion in the political process. *Public Opinion Quarterly, 51* [4 (part 2)], S13–S24.

Contents

V. PUBLIC OPINION AND THE PROMISE OF DEMOCRACY

PUBLIC OPINION AND THE COMMUNICATION OF CONSENT

Introduction

Taken together, the essays in this collection accomplish four big things and make a start at a fifth. (1) They treat public opinion and mass communication as elements in a single system, rather than as two separate systems. (2) They explore some of the connections between individual-level opinion and public opinion, refusing the facile assumption that public opinion is the simple aggregation of private opinions. (3) They redress the balance between the predominantly normative theories of influence and effect in favor of more cognitive theories of information processing and reality-testing. (4) They try to explain how the media work as institutions, refusing to give credence either to simplistic theories of capitalist conspiracy or mimetic dreams of mirroring reality. (5) What is largely left undone is the exploration of the missing links between opinion and action. We know something about the dynamics of participation in movements of social and political protest. We also know something about the extent of participation—or better, nonparticipation—in such activities as voting, contacting one's congressman, participating in demonstrations, etc. What we know too little about, on the micro side of participation, are the incidence and the conditions for conversation about public affairs—the most elementary building block of political efficacy. At the macro end of the process, we know too little about how public opinion affects the process of governance—how it is anticipated, noticed, depicted, negotiated, incorporated, and internalized. The reader will find these essays full of hints and assumptions about how the system of public opinion and mass communication constrain policy-making. But policy-making should be inside the system, not outside. It is not enough to lament romantically about how far we fell from town-meeting democracy. What we need to know is how and whether participatory democracy is at all possible in a complex, pluralistic, fragmented mass society, and where we stand in this respect. I would like to introduce this book with a brief elaboration on each of these themes.

PUBLIC OPINION IMPLIES COMMUNICATION

It is difficult to imagine how the study of public opinion and the study of mass communication could have gone off in different directions. But they did, even though both grew up in the context of social psychology and political science, and even though both took an individualistic turn in adopting the methodology of survey research (Neuman, 1986). Yet, they went their separate ways as if in agreement that communications research had charge of messages that move from top to bottom, and opinion research had charge of messages that move from the bottom up.

These obviously siamese twins were separated not only from each other but also from their shared theoretical parentage. They lost their grounding, it seems, in their preoccupation with the empiricistic reporting of the distribution of agree/disagree and in the measurement of media effects. Ironically, there was symbiosis so long as the mass media were thought to exert direct, immediate, and powerful influence on the formation and change of political opinions and attitudes, as in studies of voting behavior (which are conducted even today). But when these processes were seen to be more complex, the two lost sight of each other. Academic opinion research turned back to psychology to better understand the structure and stability of opinions and beliefs, while students of the mass media—surprised by the ostensible ineffectiveness of the media in changing attitudes—began the quest for more subtle and more powerful effects.

This book documents the reunion of the two strands in terms of these more complex processes. The "agenda-setting" tradition in communication research, for example, has established that the media tell us not what to think but what to think about. In Chapter 11 of this book, McCombs reports that the five to seven issues that occupy citizens' minds at any given time are, on the whole, a reflection of the prominence of these issues in the media. This focusing of attention is prerequisite to the formation of public opinion via the arousal of shared interest and the stimulation of conversation. Similarly, the "spiral of silence" theory proposes that the media are used as a map to read the distribution of opinion, on the basis of which some people participate in political conversation when they find their ideas supported, while others withdraw, perceiving themselves shamefully outnumbered. As a result, Noelle-Neumann suggests in Chapter 2 of this book that the mass media create and accelerate an ostensible consensus of public opinion—by claiming (often falsely) to represent reality.

That public opinion implies mass communication is a point also made by Peters in Chapter 1. Like Noelle-Neumann, Peters argues that public opinion is formed in response to the inevitable "representation" of public opinion in the press. In other words, it is not only agenda-setting that engages and focuses our attention; it is also our image of the distribution of opinion. However much Habermas (1962/1989) shuns the irrationality of representation in favor of reasoning, knowledge of what others think has bearing on making one's mind up—even among rational and free men in small groups.

Robinson, too, understands news discourse as integral to the process of Public opinion formation, except that the causal process is the other way round: public opinion dictates to the press what it wants to see and hear. Robinson argues in Chapter 14 that we can glimpse the "consensus view of society" through the analysis of the "forms" of news discourse which represent the "common stock of knowledge." Robinson's study, therefore, concentrates not on the content of the news media in French and English Quebec, but on their differing styles of speech, narrative devices, and story formats. Her assumption is that these special forms of news discourse stem from the "audience" rather than the other way around.

These examples make evident that mass communication and public opinion are part of an interactive system involving also private opinions and interpersonal communication. Far from separate disciplines, it can be argued—as Hans Speier (1950) did 50 years ago—that public opinion, in effect, *is* communication. Differentiating private or clandestine opinions from opinions "disclosed to others or at least noted by others," he conceives of public opinion as consisting of (1) citizens deliberating with each other over issues of public concern, and (2) the upward communication of such deliberation to the powers that be. Like Habermas some years later, he adds that the persons deliberating should not themselves be officials of the state, and that their deliberations must be anchored in a shared belief in freedom of expression and the right to exert influence.

As such, Speier is reminding us that public opinion is one of the constituents of a democratic order which postulates that public policy should rest not only on the consent of the governed, but on their active participation in its formation and change. He does not tell us how this works out in practice, of course, nor does he pay much attention to mass communication. He does not elaborate on the channels that transmit citizen opinion upward. His point is that the process of public opinion, by definition, implies communication—mass and interpersonal.

Even earlier, the French social-psychologist, Gabriel Tarde (1898/1969, see also Katz, 1992b), said this, and more. Writing in 1898, he proposed a model that links press-conversation-opinion-action in a causal chain. Influenced, perhaps, by the Dreyfus trial, when an entire society was talking politics, he suggests (1) that the press stimulates and sets the agenda (2) for myriad conversations (3) from which considered opinions emerge, and (4) are translated into social and political action. He suggests, as Speier does, that conversation is prerequisite to public opinion. He proposes that far from being the most ancient of the communication arts, conversation is modern (!), and came into being *because* of the press; on another occasion, Michael Schudson (1978) has made a similar observation. Tarde further proposes that opinion is not worth much unless it has been tested in the crucible of conversation. The present book is testimony to Tarde's empirical, if impressionistic, effort to link the media and public opinion, although much needs to be done to reincorporate conversation and action more explicitly into the system.

INDIVIDUAL OPINION AND PUBLIC OPINION

In addition to linking mass communication and public opinion, the essays in this book explore the connections between individual-level opinion and public opinion. They take for granted that opinion polls collect the private, often ill-considered opinions of individuals. They are aware that this is a widely accepted definition of public opinion, and that it fits, ostensibly, with the democratic idea of one-person-one-vote.

But they are uneasy—from the vantage points both of participatory democracy and of social psychology—over the popular tendency to equate the aggregate of such opinions with the idea of public opinion. The models of participatory democracy imply involved citizens—informed, motivated, communicative—who join together with others to forge their opinions about public affairs. The American model of the public sphere probably does not expect its citizens to live up to the Habermassian ideal of setting aside group interests and personal identities in order to achieve a reasoned consensus about the best course for the commonweal. It would be satisfied if respondents could say to survey researchers that they had heard about an issue before being asked, and that they had occasion to discuss it with others. But, on the whole, the essays in this book are pessimistic even about this much participation—at the individual level, at the interpersonal level, at the level of social institutions such as pubs and union halls, and at the level of political parties and other forms of political organization. Carey, in Chapter 15, laments the demise of localism—the "group of strangers who met in Philadelphia taverns to discuss the news." In 18th- and 19th-century America, says Boyte in Chapter 7, there were reform movements, political associations, and an overall view of the citizenry as a deliberative body, while today's citizens are overwhelmed by bigness (drowned by information, says Christians in Chapter 7), engaged—when they are—not by a sustained politics of reason and judgment but by an occasional "manichean" politics of uprising against perceived evil or injustice which does only little good for the public sphere.

Thus, there is widespread despair over dignifying the uninformed, unprocessed opinions of the majority, adding them up, and calling it public opinion (Herbst, 1993; Neuman, 1986). There is almost equal despair expressed over the likelihood of active political participation, except for the several case studies highlighted by Boyte. Nevertheless, there is some intermediate ground which we are invited to explore. In Chapter 3, McLeod, Rucinski and Pan, in particular, seek to explicate some of the connections that link private and public opinion as well as the micro sphere of small groups with the sphere of institutional politics. One of their illustrations is drawn from the mobilization of opinion for and against the nomination of Robert Bork to the United States Supreme Court. These authors argue that a passing news item about the nominee would have found its way—at least among those motivated to do so—into a larger mental compartment which gives it meaning in ideological or other terms (conservative/liberal, pro-choice/pro-life, etc.) to which the contestants will ultimately appeal for support. As the issue gains momentum in the press and table talk, this process of constructing meaningful associations motivates some individuals to speak up and thus contribute to the formation of public opinion on the issue.

McLeod et al. propose a set of tools or a model with which to examine the ways in which the individual and institutional levels interact. There is a storehouse of data on how and why interpersonal influence works when an individual finds himself in a small group of others who matter to him. The aim is to observe and model the links that connect the process of opinion formation and change at the level of group dynamics with the dynamics of how public opinion emerges, about which we know only very little so far.

INFORMATION VERSUS INFLUENCE

Beniger and Gusek in Chapter 9, align themselves with McLeod et al.—and also with Price and Oshagan in Chapter 8, and Glynn, Ostman and McDonald in Chapter 10—in reorienting our thinking about opinion and communication. These essays argue that the classic social psychology that nurtured early research on opinion and communication has been superseded by the turn toward information processing and away from the concept of influence. They show that early theorizing—from outside the black box—gave primacy to overt, ostensibly unambiguous influence attempts aimed at converting the opinions and attitudes of passive individuals. This held true, they demonstrate, for both interpersonal communication in small groups and for mass communication. Conformity and compliance were the supposed results of these persuasive efforts.

A parallel tradition emphasizing information, not influence, began to take shape rather early—but has blossomed only recently into what is known as cognitive theory. In an earlier paper, Beniger (1987) pointed out the "shift" toward a new tradition in communication research—from attitude change (influence) to cognitive processing (information):

> This "shift" toward is perhaps most succinctly summarized as a change in dependent variables from attitudes to cognition, as a shift in independent variables from persuasive communication to less directed media processes ranging from "framing" through "discourse" to the social construction of reality, or as a refocusing of interest from simple change (like political conversion) to the structuring or restructuring ("structuration") of cognitions and meaning, with stability now no less interesting than change. (pp. S52–S53)

This tradition postulates an individual actively attempting to make sense of ambiguous social reality, and actively seeking direction and meaning in a world full of complex and contradictory messages. Inside the heads in which messages are processed and opinions are formed, there seems to be an elaborate machinery of frames of reference, schemata, and scripts in terms of which perceptions are structured and restructured until they fit together and take on meaning. The emphasis is on stability, consonance, and reintegration, rather than on change. Beniger and Gusek show how this new orientation made its way into opinion and communication research such that individuals are seen to be rational strivers for understanding, consistency, and control, and where information is more effective than persuasion. They illustrate the working of these assumptions by reference to studies of viewer decodings of the media, to agenda-setting research, and to theories such as the spiral of silence. Like Gamson (1992), they show how schema may be deployed for an understanding of how opinions are constructed on persistent social issues such as atomic energy, international tension, industrial strife, and the like. The Arab-Israel conflict, for example, may evoke the isolationist schema of "feuding neighbors" or the interventionist schema of "global responsibility." Issues associated with the use of atomic energy may be given the Frankenstein frame of "runaway technology" or the modernist frame of "harnessing nature," depending on the orientations of senders and receivers.

Such differences in orientation, say Price and Oshagan, may underlie not only the reception of information but the desire to communicate. Thus, in line with McLeod et al., they argue that the mass media locate different mappings of an issue in differing social groups—pro-life, for example—in response to which a public may arise as an organized collectivity to take sides in the ideological and group-anchored debate.

THE MEDIA AS SOCIAL INSTITUTIONS

The book places heavy emphasis on the role of the media of mass communication—newspapers and television—in calling attention to issues on the public agenda. Nobody—least of all the authors of these essays—thinks that this service is value-free. That the media favor the rhetoric of conflict—Olien, Donohue, and Tichenor remind us in Chapter 12—is itself evidence that journalism is guided by rules of selection. People who want "good news" or "happy news" do not understand that the Western concept of news deals, by definition, with deviation from the normal, and especially with crisis and misbehavior. As Carey points out, public misunderstanding and mistrust of the press is not the least of the problems of democracy.

Journalism was supposed to be our "watchdog"—to represent our right to know about things that are too shielded, or too complex, or too far away for us to observe directly. Instead, says Carey, there is distrust of the press, which is gradually manifesting itself as talk shows. The media are no longer our fiduciaries, he says. They are "guard dogs" of special interests, say Olien et al. and Edelman. They are fragmented into multiple channels which undermine a shared focus and a shared agenda.

Thus, in reading the group of essays on the ways in which bias and interest infiltrate the press—more unwitting than not—one should keep in mind that the democratic duty to watch the watchdog is not a license to kill it, but to make certain that the job gets done. That holds equally for both critics of the press and critics of public opinion. There is an urgent need, says Carey, to defend the professionalism and the freedom of the press.

Still, there is an impressive array of legitimate criticism of the performance of the press in these essays, and the ways in which they constrain and bias opinion and public perception of public opinion.

Analyzing the debate over separatism in Canada, Robinson shows how the rhetorical routines of the French and English broadcasts manage to reinforce the inclinations of both sides. Edelman, in Chapter 16, warns that the trendy language of rational-choice policy-making has made the journalist an unwitting partner to narrow constructions of rationality and cost-effectiveness that serve upper-class interests (low inflation), more than lower-class ones (high employment).

Schoenbach and Becker, in Chapter 13, question whether media defined crises coincide in timing and in content with the real-life crises they purport to represent. Noelle-Neumann, Schudson and King, (in Chapter 6), and Peters each question news media representations of the distribution of opinion on an issue, while acknowledging that this is certainly a central part of the journalist's job. Schudson and King present an amusing aspect of this dilemma in their puzzlement over how the press misperceived Ronald Reagan's popularity—personal and political—by projecting their own fascination with him onto the people.

Shanto Iyengar (1991) deserves mention here for trying to illuminate the subtle ways in which media shape the criteria for evaluating public issues. His recent paper (with Simon, 1993), for example, is an attempt to capture three types of media effects on public opinion (agenda setting, priming, and framing). Iyengar and Robinson share the same fundamental assumptions, though they use somewhat different language: Both concentrate on how news discourse is "framed." Their units of content analysis focus on the different formats of news stories rather than on their different messages. Robinson, however, believes that dominant opinion is the "cause" of news discourse while Iyengar assumes (and tries to verify) that public opinion is the "result" of news framing.

From the essays on the cognitive approach, we learn how the encoding of issues by the media as well as their decoding by viewers and readers may move opinion and evaluation in one direction or another. Olien et al. argue, for example, that the presentation of conflict itself tends to benefit the status quo, presumably because the public is tired of conflict and would rather trust its leaders than the press.

Even more macroscopic are the warnings of writers like Carey, Christians, and Peters, that participatory democracy is threatened by the endless barrage of instant information, by "stupefying spectacle," by the confusion of news and entertainment, by the segmentation of media channels, by the privatization and commercialization of both media and citizens, and by isolated news consumers the vestige of whose political power is being "aggregated" in the voting booth and in the polls. Lazarsfeld and Merton (1948) long ago, dubbed this last the "narcotizing dysfunction" of the news.

From my point of view, these essays understate the "liberating" aspects of mass communication. True, we are dependent on the media—and on language, and on myth—to give us access to reality, and we must therefore put up with the bias of their rhetorics, their hegemonics, their genres, their scripts, their technologies. But sometimes—bias and all—they give us glimpses of possible worlds; sometimes they let us see ourselves as others see us, or see others as they seem themselves as Meyrowitz (1985) has observed. Sometimes they show us the vulnerabilities of those who dominate us in ways that make action thinkable. Thus, for better and for worse, East Germans could contemplate West German freedoms and living standards thanks to the electronic media; the Eastern bloc could perceive how the USSR was not going to intervene in 1989; Yeltsin could push Gorbachev (Gerbner, 1993), Egypt could push Arafat because the broadcasts were live; the Israelis could come to believe that Sadat really meant peace when he risked coming to Israel in 1977 (Katz, Dayan, & Motyl, 1983); the world could come to pressure South Africa to abandon apartheid; the Vietnam War could possibly end more abruptly because of how the press interpreted it (Hallin, 1993); Nixon could be deposed consensually (Lang & Lang, 1983); American women could reconsider their roles in the workplace after Anita Hill made the subject of sexual harassment speakable (Fraser, 1992); the UN could finally decide to act against the Serbs after seeing the bomb explode in the Sarajevo market, just as the massacre in Tiananmen Square influenced U.S. policy toward China. Some of these examples are difficult to research, admittedly, though there have been some very good attempts. And there are the easier ones, like watching presidential debates, which make a difference—with all their flaws—to millions of Americans (Jamieson, 1988). To repeat, the media do not make such events magically "transparent" (Ezrahi, 1990); like the Gulf War, they need encoding and critical decoding (Katz, 1992a; Liebes & Bar-Nachum, 1994). But they are part of what is right about freedom of the press, and deserve the kind of attention that is given to what is "wrong." Analysis of both kinds gives us insight into how the system works (Ezrahi, 1990).

Edelman (1988) disagrees, and would have us look elsewhere for the real news. Fortunately for this argument, most of the authors in this collection agree that the media are not omnipotent. In this connection it is useful to refer to Gamson's (1992) analysis of the different frames deployed by the establishment, by the media, and by political discussion groups to discuss the same issues. Sometimes the discussants adopted media frames—when the media portrayed anti-nuclear demonstrations, for example, but sometimes they called on experience—in discussions of "troubled industry" issues, for example. It is important to note that in spite of its cumbersomeness, this method of narrative analysis of frames has virtually displaced the traditional kind of content analysis.

MISSING LINKS: CONVERSATION, ORGANIZATION, AND POLITICAL ACTION

There are at least two missing links in these essays. Using the Tarde formula of media-conversation-opinion-action, one of them is conversation, the other is action. There is probably another link worth interpolating between opinion and action that might be called organization.

For Tarde, Speier, Habermas and many others, the elementary building block of participatory democracy is conversation. Conversation is the crucible in which opinion is tested and shaped; it is the rehearsal hall for political action. We know, historically, how central were the enclaves of conversation for the development of participatory democracy in England, France, Germany, and the United States (Tarde, 1898/1969; Coser, 1966; Herbst, 1993; Carey, 1989), and from the tradition of research on opinion leadership we know something about how the media make their way into the networks of talk. But we know all too little about the extent of political talk in contemporary society and the conditions that nourish it. Certain surveys—especially the GSS and NES—routinely ask about the frequency of talking politics, but this evokes a too generalized self-portrait that gives little insight into the dynamics of everyday talk about politics. Even focus group methodology can tell us only about how people talk about something when asked to, not whether and how they actually do so (Gamson, 1992; Liebes & Katz, 1990; Delli Carpini & Williams, 1994). What we need is empirical research on how the media stimulate talk and on what talk does to crystallize opinion.

An effort to chart the effect of talk on various measures of "considered opinion"—especially on the consistency of opinion in the spirit of Converse (1964)—is being made by Kim (1994). The political talk shows on radio and television and the various experiments with so-called "electronic town meetings" have been much criticized both for their pretentiousness and for their populism (Livingstone & Lunt, 1993), but some admire their potential (Abramson, 1992). It is ironic that talk of such electronic democracy should follow the shattering of the television audience into fragments and fractions. Ironically, when "everybody" still gathered for the nightly network news, nobody wondered how citizens could be gotten together to give shared and simultaneous attention to some issue or value of public concern. The only occasions on which this happens nowadays is during the live broadcasting of historic events such as the appearance of Anita Hill at the Senate hearings on the nomination of Clarence Thomas (Morrison, 1992), the fall of the Berlin Wall (Loshitzky, 1993), and presidential debates (Dayan & Katz, 1992; Jamieson, 1988; Kraus, 1962).

Even more notable by its absence is the link between opinion and action. Some of the essays make allusions to this interface—without which the entire system of mass communication and public opinion would be empty from the point of view of democracy. The definition of action implicit in Tarde anticipates modern studies of political marketing: The press stimulates and focuses conversation on matters of common concern; conversation generates opinion; opinion leads to choice (which Tarde calls "reputation") whether of heroes, or candidates, or products. Sounds familiar, perhaps, but also inadequate. More to the point are the series of studies that consider the conditions under which public opinion finds expression in more direct political action such as pressuring congress, lobbying, demonstrating, protesting, etc. Perceptions of injustice are prerequisite to such action, says Gamson (1992), as is the perception that change can be achieved through such action, and that many others feel the same way. Case studies in this tradition are Taylor (1986), Eliasoph (1993) and Wolfsfeld (1988).

We need to know much more about how politicians and civil servants take account of public opinion both in day-to-day functioning and in policy-making, as well as the kinds of actions that bring opinion and public opinion out of privacy, out of public space, onto the agendas of the powerful. Schoenbach and Becker properly note that elites read the media as representatives of public opinion. Going a step further, Molotch, Protess, and Gordon (1987) point out that investigative journalism moves office-holders to act because they believe that public opinion has been aroused by the exposed—whether or not this is actually the case.

But are the media the representatives of public opinion? Should they be—and how? What about the reporting of opinion polls in the media? What about the use of survey results in political lobbying? Peter Miller, in Chapter 5, gives us a good introduction to these issues while Herbst (1993) and Ezrahi (1990) intimate what it feels like for a president or politician to have to be elected day after day. For one thing, it certainly undermines that brand of representative democracy that would give free rein to elected officials to do their best during the period of their tenure—because no lay public is capable of understanding the problems with which they are grappling—even when the problems are themselves.

Election campaigns, wars, and taxes—now maybe health reform—are the areas in which politicians anxiously scan public opinion for signs of dissent, mistrust, or demoralization. Intimations of corrupt practices are another perennial. But as studies in the cognitive tradition have shown, there is an intricate interaction between the framing of realities by establishments, by the media, and by public opinion, and nothing like a direct stimulus-response relationship. As Lang and Lang (1983) have shown, the Watergate hearings affected public opinion only slowly and very indirectly—via the idea that impeachment was thinkable, and actually anticipated by the Constitution. Recent studies by Hallin (1993) of the framing of the American wars in the media also make this point about the indirect influence of media on policy—although implying rather more manipulation by the political establishment when Vietnam coverage took its critical turn.

Let's welcome this book, then, as an up-to-date portrait of the state of the art, as well as a portend of where the next edition is likely to take us. Let's look forward to more empirical testing of the interrelations among the components of the systemic model of communication-conversation-opinion-organization-action implicit here. The system must be expanded, moreover, to include *within it* patterns of interaction between public opinion and policy making—as it is, and as it perhaps ought to be. It is not enough to ascribe "action" to those individuals or groups who have opinions; we want to see what forms these actions take—and the ways in which they are or are not noticed. In the meantime, there's plenty here to keep us busy.

ELIHU KATZ

REFERENCES

Abramson, J.B. (1992, October). *Democratic designs for electronic town meetings*. Paper presented at a conference on electronic town meetings, The Aspen Institute Wye Center, Queenstown, Maryland.

Beniger, J. (1987). Toward an old new paradigm: The half-century flirtation with mass society. *Public Opinion Quarterly, 51*, S46–S66.

Carey, J. (1989). *Communication as culture: Essays on media and society*. Boston: Unwin Hyman.
Converse, P. (1964). The nature of belief systems in mass publics. In D. Apter (Eds.), *Ideology and discontent* (pp. 206–261). New York: The Free Press.
Coser, L. (1966). *Men of ideas: A sociologist's view*. New York: The Free Press.
Dayan, D., & Katz, E. (1992). *Media events: The live broadcasting of history*. Cambridge: Harvard University Press.
Delli Carpini, M., & Williams, B. (1994). Methods, metaphors and media messages: The uses of television in conversations about the environment. *Communication Research, 21*, pp. 782–812.
Edelman, M. (1988). *Constructing the political spectacle*. Chicago: The University of Chicago Press.
Eliasoph, N. (1993). *Producing apathy: Politeness, power, and political silence*. Unpublished doctoral dissertation, University of California at Berkeley.
Ezrahi, Y. (1990). *The descent of Icarus: Science and the transformation of contemporary democracy*. Cambridge: Harvard University Press.
Fraser, N. (1992). Sex, lies and the public sphere: Some reflections on the confirmation of Clarence Thomas. *Critical Inquiry, 18*, pp. 595–612.
Gamson, W. (1992). *Talking politics*. Cambridge: Cambridge University Press.
Gerbner, G. (1993). Instant history: The case of the Moscow coup. *Political Communication, 10*, 193–203.
Habermas, J. (1989). *The structural transformation of the public sphere: An inquiry into a category of bourgeois society*. Cambridge: MIT Press. (Original work published 1962)
Hallin, D. (1993). *We keep America on top of the world: Journalism and the public sphere*. New York: Routledge.
Herbst, S. (1993). *Numbered voices: How opinion polling has shaped American politics*. Chicago: University of Chicago Press.
Iyengar, S. (199l). *Is anyone responsible? How television frames political issues*. Chicago: University of Chicago Press.
Iyengar, S., & Simon, A. (1993). News coverage of the Gulf crisis and public opinion: A study of agenda-setting, priming, and framing. *Communication Research, 20*, 365–383.
Jamieson, K.H. (1988). *Presidential debates: The challenge of creating an informed electorate*. New York: Oxford University Press.
Katz, E. (1992a). The end of journalism. *Journal of Communication, 42*, 5–12.
Katz, E. (1992b). On parenting a paradigm: Gabriel Tarde's agenda for opinion and communication research. *International Journal of Public Opinion Research, 4*, 80–85.
Katz, E., Dayan, D., & Motyl, P. (1981). In defense of media events. In R. W. Haigh, G. Gerbner, B. R. Byrne (Eds.), *Communication in the twenty-first century*. New York: Wiley.
Kim, J. (1994). *Communicative actions in the public sphere: Reconceptualizing mass media effects through the relations of media use, conversation, opinion formation, and participation*. Unpublished master's thesis, University of Pennsylvania, Philadelphia.

Kraus, S. (Ed.). (1962). *The great debate: Background, perspectives, effects*. Bloomington: Indiana University Press.

Lang, K., & Lang, G.E. (1983). *The battle for public opinion*. New York: Columbia University Press.

Lazarsfeld, P., & Merton, R. (1948). Mass communication, popular taste, and organized social action. In L. Bryson (Ed.), *The communication of ideas* (pp. 95–118). New York: Institute for Religious and Social Studies.

Liebes, T., & Bar-Nachum, Y. (1994). "What a relief": When the press prefers celebration to scandal. *Political Communication, 11*(1), 35–48.

Liebes, T., & Katz, E. (1990). *The export of meaning: Cross-cultural readings of Dallas*. New York: Oxford University Press.

Livingstone, S., & Lunt, P. (1993). *Talk on television: Audience participation and public debate*. London: Routledge.

Loshitzky, Y. (1993). *History in the making and history as a remake: The fall of the Berlin Wall and global television*. Paper presented at the annual meeting of SCS Conference, New Orleans, LA.

Meyrowitz, J. (1985). *No sense of place: The impact of electronic media on social behavior*. New York: Oxford University Press.

Molotch, H., Protess, D., & Gordon, M. (1987). The media connection: Ecologies and news. In D. Paletz (Ed.), *Political communication research: Approaches, studies, assessments*. Norwood, NJ: Ablex.

Morrison, T. (Ed.). (1992). *Race-ing justice, en-gendering power: Essays on Anita Hill, Clarence Thomas, and the construction of social reality*. New York: Pantheon Books.

Neuman, R. (1986). *The paradox of mass politics: Knowledge and opinion in the American electorate*. Cambridge: Harvard University Press.

Schudson, M. (1978). The ideal of conversation in the study of mass media. *Communication Research, 5*, 320–329.

Speier, H. (1950). Historical development of public opinion. *American Journal of Sociology, 55*, 376–388.

Tarde, G. (1898/1969). Opinion and conversation. In T. Clark (Ed.), *Gabriel Tarde: On communication and social influence*. Chicago: University of Chicago Press. (Original work published 1898)

Taylor, D. (1986). *Public opinion and collective action: The Boston school desegregation conflict*. Chicago: University of Chicago Press.

Wolfsfeld, G. (1988). *The politics of provocation: Participation and protest in Israel*. Albany, NY: State University of New York Press.

I

THE NATURE OF PUBLIC OPINION

1

Historical Tensions in the Concept of Public Opinion

John Durham Peters

There is a tension at the core of public opinion. Public opinion claims to be the voice of the people, a clear and direct utterance from the citizenry. It is indispensable to the legitimacy of all governments which claim to draw their power from "the consent of the governed." The very idea of democracy ("rule of the people") requires "the people" to take part in political discussion and decision-making. The question is how, through what institutional means or forums, can the people do so? For the ancients up to the 18th century—that is, until the modern "public" appeared—the answer was straightforward: assembly. Still today the Pnyx (the hill in Athens where the *ekklêsia* or assembly of citizens convened), the Roman forum, and the New England town meeting captivate the imagination of democratic thinkers. The tension is that the forms of communication that are normative for democratic ideas of public opinion—dialogue, interaction, critical consensus, and informed participation—are mismatched with the forms of communication that prevail in a vast modern nation-state. The mass media, above all, can offer a vast population a vision of the public sphere without giving them means for acting in it. *Public*, as outlined below, can mean both spectacle and participation: it has both theatrical and political senses.

In this chapter, I first offer a sketch of the history of this and related tensions in the concept of public opinion. Then I explore the public as an imagined fiction. I conclude that regarding the public in this manner offers a theoretically useful but still politically problematic way to understand current theories and debates about public opinion.

PUBLIC OPINION: NOTES TOWARD THE HISTORY OF A CONCEPT

Opinion

Although "public opinion" did not emerge as a political concept until late 18th-century Europe, both of its components have ancient roots. The relevant intellectual history of opinion starts with Plato's contrast of *doxa* (opinion) from *epistêmê* (knowledge). Against the sophists, who claimed that *doxa* was all that was available to human cognition, Plato made a fundamental contrast between the transient and the eternal: *doxa* was popular belief, unshaped by the rigors of philosophy, and was fickle and fleeting; *epistêmê* was sure knowledge of the unchanging "Ideas" underlying the visible world. *Doxa* was the stuff of the untutored many; *epistêmê* of the few. Plato believed that politics was a *technê* or skill that should be conducted according to scientific principles. Hence the task of ruling could be delegated to philosopher-kings or experts (who saw the universe according to *epistêmê)* ; Plato was no democrat.

Aristotle gave opinion a more favorable reading, partly due to his different understanding of politics, which he took to be a kind of *praxis* or human activity. As much as he admired *epistêmê*, exemplified by the beauty of mathematics and other sciences whose results could be demonstrated from sure premises, Aristotle believed that the sciences of action, namely politics and ethics, required grounding in a different kind of knowledge than *epistêmê*. Because all human action is historical, practical, and contingent (chiefly on other people's actions, but also on luck), there can be no principles for action that are fixed once and for all. Instead, Aristotle argued for practical wisdom (*phronêsis*) as the art of acting under conditions of uncertainty. To act wisely in his view one needed less a glimpse of eternity than the wisdom that comes from the accumulated experience of human affairs.

Aristotle bequeathed to subsequent intellectual history the idea of a kind of knowing that rests on judgment and informed guesswork rather than unfailing principles and that is uniquely suited to political deliberation and decision-making. As Hans-Georg Gadamer notes (1965, p. 348), the Greeks also used *doxa* for the decisions reached in political assemblies: *doxa* thus also has the sense of consensus or views held in common. The Romans translated *doxa* by *opinio* and *epistêmê* by *scientia*, and it is from them that English and other European languages inherit the sense of opinion as "judgment resting on grounds insufficient for complete demonstration" (*Oxford English Dictionary*). As Ian Hacking (1975, p. 20) points out, "Opinion" long had the sense of being the realm of prejudice, probability, and authority, as opposed to "science." The sense of opinion as informed judgment persisted well into the 18th century. Even today judges and physicians render legal or medical opinions: we are to understand that deciding a case or diagnosing an illness are acts of expert judgment, not of guaranteed truth. To give an opinion, one must be an authority. Something like this underlies the view that it is "the public" that best can determine public policy. The wearer knows best where the shoe pinches; the public knows best what it needs and wants (Dewey, 1927, p. 207).

Along with the sense of being the junior partner in knowledge, opinion long had the sense of esteem or reputation. As Jürgen Habermas observes (1962/1989, p. 89), "'Opinion' in the sense of a judgment that lacks certainty, whose truth would still have to be proven, is associated with 'opinion' in the sense of a basically suspicious repute among the multitude." The term has a strong collective sense: opinion has long referred to what passes among "the many" for truth. Thus when Blaise Pascal wrote in the 17th century that "opinion is the queen of the world" he probably had nothing like our "public opinion" in mind; rather, he noted how the informal fabric of customs and mores govern human affairs in general (Gunn, 1983, pp. 264–265). Similarly, the oft repeated 18th-century slogan, used by David Hume and James Madison among others, that "government is founded on opinion" was originally less an expression of the Jeffersonian notion that government rests on "the consent of the governed" than of the ancient idea, derived from Tacitus, that "names, titles, forms, and ceremonies" were crucial to sustaining a government's authority (Gunn, 1983, p. 20). As one political writer in 18th-century Britain noted, "Opinion is the principal support of power . . . century for all things subsist more by fame than any real strength" (Gunn, 1983, p. 27). "Opinion" in such slogans comes from the government to the people, not vice versa, and is achieved more through show and ceremony than reasoned debate, however much these usages anticipate later ideas of public opinion.

The most radical conceptual transformations of opinion take place in France and England in the second half of the 18th century, though scholars differ about the details (e.g., Gunn, 1983; Baker, 1990; Speier, 1950/1980; Habermas, 1962/1989; Ozouf, 1988b). Changes in the meaning of "opinion" clearly parallel the revolutionary changes in political institutions and ideas in this period. Baker (1990, pp. 167–168) clearly portrays the sharp shift by comparing entries on "opinion" in the *Encyclopédie* (1765) and the *Encyclopédie méthodique* (1784–1787). The first treats "opinion" solely as a philosophical matter and repeats the age-old contrast of opinion and science; the second has no article on "opinion" under philosophy at all yet gives "opinion publique" a grand *political* role. Baker explains, "Whereas before its principal characteristics were flux, subjectivity, and uncertainty, now they are universality, objectivity, and rationality. Within the space of a generation, the flickering lamp of 'opinion' has been transformed into the unremitting light of 'public opinion,' the light of the universal tribunal before which citizens and governments alike must appear" (1990, pp. 167–168). Opinion went from being a chief source of "prejudice" (the target of many thinkers of the Enlightenment) to being its banisher. Opinion, villain of philosophy, became public opinion, hero of politics.

Public

This dramatic shift could not have happened without the assistance of a modifier, "public." Like opinion, the contrast between public and private was of Greek origin but passed on by the Romans. Though Greek political institutions have not lasted, Greek political ideas have. On the one hand there was the *polis* or city-state in whose variegated and all-consuming public life—on the battlefield, in the courts, assemblies, theaters, and public places—citizens alone could participate.[1] On the other there was the *oikos* or household, the place of work (slaves) and family (women), whose labors gave the citizen freedom and leisure to engage in his (and only *his*) public activities. The conceptual contrast between *to koinon* (the public or common) and *to idion* (the private) mirrored this larger institutional division (Saxonhouse, 1983). We gain a sense of the value that Athenian elites (i.e., the ones whose texts we read today) accorded to private life when we reflect that our word "idiot" descends from the Greek word for private, just as "private" is related to "deprived." Women, slaves, and foreigners—none of whom had any public status—were thought to be literally deprived of the glory (and shame) that comes from the public life of the *polis*. Aristotle's remark that only "a beast or a god" could live without a *polis* emphasizes the dehumanization of those whose functions were restricted to the private sphere (1952, p. 446). To say, as he did, that humans are *political* animals meant simply that it is their nature to live in a *polis*. The maintenance of life in Aristotle's view is a necessary prerequisite to but insufficient for full humanity: in private one can have life, but not the *good life* (Taylor, 1989, p. 211).

The quest for fame or public renown colors Greek ideas about public life. Homer, whom elites in the classical period treated as the primary authority figure in Greek culture, portrayed self-sacrifice on the battlefield for the greater good of the city as the highest human good. The excellent warrior was in turn rewarded by fame, honor, and an undying reputation (*Kleos*). Excellence, then, is a public affair; it is openly visible to all. Homeric notions of excellence form the background for Athenian debates about both the good life for humans (MacIntyre, 1988) and politics. From the Greeks on down, public life has been conceived in overwhelmingly male terms, with ideas of citizenship connected to military prowess; the legacy for women has been troubled, to say the least (see Pateman, 1983, 1988). Though the honor ethic of public service has subsided, we can find a remnant of the ancient link of warrior and citizen in the right to bear arms which the U.S. Constitution (disastrously) guarantees to all citizens. In any case, to act in public, as Hannah Arendt (1958) vividly argues for the ancient Athenians, was to expose oneself to the highest praise and the strictest censure.

The Roman terms have a similar cluster of senses. *Public* comes from the Latin *poplicus*, an early form of *populus* (people), and was influenced by the related word *pubes*, that is, the adult male population (Hölscher, 1979, p. 41). "Public is what matters to the whole society, or belongs to this whole society, or pertains to the instruments, or institutions or loci by which the society comes together as a body and acts" (Taylor, 1990, p. 108). Things that concern the people as a body are public, and such concerns require public exhibition. In Greek and Latin, the concept of public has two main branches of meaning: *social–political* (the *polis* or the whole body of the people) and *visual–intellectual* (fame or open exhibition) (Hölscher, 1979, p. 37). The various senses of the verb *publicare* show a shading of the political into the visual register: "a. To make public property, place at the disposal of the community. b. to exhibit publicly. c. to prostitute" (Glare, 1982, p. 1512). Indeed, the term *prostitute* comes from the Latin meaning "to stand in public" (i.e., before the temple). Things exhibited before the public eye carry shame and glory: only highly valenced objects are paraded before the body of the people. Already in classical antiquity, then, public is an extremely polarized concept that combines senses both of honor and its violation.

Public persists as an important concept, especially in the legal and religious spheres, in the Middle Ages: trials were to be held, in Germanic law, only in open spots and in daylight; certain sins needed to be confessed "openly before the world" in the Biblical phrase (John 18:20); and marriages had to be publicly announced and witnessed to be legitimate (Hölscher, 1979, pp. 14–30). The idea of a public realm of citizens, however, was entirely lacking, and it is not until the 18th century that we can speak of a "public" as a sociological aggregate.

In medieval political thought, only one person was public: the feudal lord. The feudal lord stood for—represented, in fact—the body politic as a whole (Kantorowicz, 1957). Habermas (1962/1989, pp. 7–12) sees what he calls the "representative public sphere" in the High Middle Ages as the forerunner of the modern public. But *representation* here does not mean representing the people as individual citizens, but being the public symbol of the glory and honor of the social whole. The feudal lord had "publicness" in the sense that his dignity (and that of the knightly class) was publicly staged before the common people, both in personal accoutrements—badges, arms, dress, hair style, decorum, and rhetoric—and in festivals such as jousts (Habermas, 1989, p. 8). The public realm in this period of European history took form through the public display of the splendor of lords and ladies, not through civic debate or discussion—the modern notion of "citizen" did not yet exist. In "representation" Habermas sees the epitome of public life modeled on the theater: the elite few have speaking parts while the many groundlings can only hiss or cheer. (More recently Habermas has come to give the medieval "audience" of lordly bombast a more active role as a creative reader, but he is still critical of public life modeled on spectacle and spectatorship; 1990, pp. 17–18.)

The medieval sense of public—in which its visual–intellectual sense enveloped its social-political sense—continues in the early modern period. Baroque festivals put on by Absolutist states in the 17th and 18th centuries ritualistically enacted the cosmic and political order thought to be sustained by the king: court festivals made publicly visible the glory and honor of the monarch (Strong, 1984, p. 41). Raeff (1983, p. 82), drawing on legal regulations in early modern Germany, suggests,

> Conspicuous display and consumption were deemed an essential aspect of authority and power. . . . It behooved the rulers, the highest functionaries, and in general the members of the elites (including the academic) to 'show off.' . . . Public display was given legitimacy as an expression of prestige, authority, and ultimately of power, and for this reason it became the monopoly of the official establishment—the monarch and his officers.

The most famous example of such a monopoly of public pomp is the court of Louis XIV at Versailles, although even revolutionary France had its public festivals, of course of a very different sort (Ozouf, 1976/1988a). In the context of court festivals in Absolutist states, *public* affairs were those connected with the king and enacted so as to be visible to the eyes of others. Today, the publicity of pomp persists mainly in the Church, in academic regalia—and in the mass media.

The Public Sphere

The Enlightenment introduces a new meaning of public: a body of reasoning citizens. Richelet's *Dictionnaire française* of 1693 (Hölscher,

1979, p. 89) anticipates this new sense: "There is no judge more incorruptible [than the public], and sooner or later it renders justice." "The public" as the educated bourgeoisie was increasingly thought of as a contrapuntal voice of critique against an arbitrary state. Habermas (1962/1989) treats the rise of the middle-class public in 18th-century England, France, and Germany at length, as does Gouldner (1976, pp. 91–117); I rely here on both. The key thing for our purposes is that the social changes in this period allowed *public opinion* to become thinkable in its modern sense as the collective voice of the popular will.

Habermas's basic story is that the feudal order, which fused governance and production in one, started to crumble with the rise of an urban bourgeoisie. As the new capitalist class gained more control over finance and production, it also gained independence from the state. What was regarded from antiquity on as the private realm (property, family, market) provided the middle classes with a launching pad for assaults on the state and its policies. The tensions between the state and society, between public authority and private property, then, made space for the "bourgeois public sphere." (See Nathans, 1990, for a historian's critique of some details in Habermas's account.) Since the bourgeois public sphere was based on open admission and debate, it was public, but yet not sponsored by the state. Hence the modern *public* sphere, like the ancient, was based in *private* property (Gouldner, 1976, p. 99). The bourgeois public sphere takes form for Habermas in "the public reasoning of private people," a formulation that accentuates its amphibious status between state and society. The bourgeois public sphere was not the family, the market, nor the state—yet it could be intimate, mutualistic, and authoritative. Capitalism, then, incubates a new form of social life in which citizens as such have power—and this power is to be expressed through reasonable argument.

In the 18th-century public spheres in England, France, and especially Germany there was no single locus of assembly: the forum was created by discussion itself, wherever it happened to take place. Unlike ancient gatherings at the Pnyx in Athens or the Forum in Rome, the modern public exists in a physically dispersed *process* of communication (one that was already transnational in the 18th century). Coffeehouses, salons, debating societies, secret societies, and so forth all formed miniature public spheres in which people could debate issues in institutional locales that were outside the reach of the authority of church and state. "The public," because it bases social solidarity on participation in discourse rather than on locality or personal acquaintance, is a historically novel kind of social collectivity, "identical with neither the political concepts of 'state' and 'commonwealth' nor with the traditional designations for the multitude such as 'community' or 'people'" (Hölscher,

1979, p. 83). Gabriel de Tarde (1901) defined the public as a noncontiguous social collectivity dispersed in space but united by common symbols; it is a social form whose size rules out full face-to-face acquaintance. Indeed, in French and English all kinds of new terms pop up in the 18th century for new cultural forms based on the congregation of strangers: public libraries, concerts, theaters, and *opinion*. In such new terms, open access to all is the key.

The preeminent institution in all of this, of course, is the press, which enables a wide-scale conversation to take place, and which succeeds the court as the main site of publicity (Habermas, 1962/1989, pp. 15–26, 181). If the king represented the body politic through spectacular display, the newspaper portrays society through realistic description. Each performs a very different kind of representation. Public spectacle, whether feudal or baroque, presupposes a stupefied audience, one content to watch but not to speak. News on the other hand presupposes activity and discussion on the part of its audience. Its premise is to be grist for commerce and conversation. The founding ideology of the political press is something like Katz and Lazarsfeld's "two-step flow" (1955): it sees itself as the orchestrator of large-scale conversations among citizens; it offers the first step, and knows itself to be incomplete without further discussion from citizens. *Circulation* is not only the lifeblood of the newspaper business; it is also the social precondition of news as such.

The special mission of the newspaper, as a public-izer (or maker of publics), was funded by the Enlightenment doctrine of "publicity," which gave yet a new twist to the meanings of public. Though we are accustomed to contrast public and private, prior to the 18th century the chief contrast was public and secret (Hölscher, 1979). "Publicity" was a battle cry against the Absolutist state. Its aim was to expose secrecy, to make the deliberations within the state visible to all citizens, and hence subject them to public criticism. Outward pomp, inward secrecy: the Absolutist state could act without accountability or disclosure. The aim of the philosophes and their fellow travelers was to make the inside workings of the state publicly visible as well. The publishing of an encyclopedia alone, whatever its opinions, was a radical act in an age of absolutist censorship. By making its actions public to the public, the state would have to behave more reasonably, or so it was thought; here again we see the pairing of the visual-intellectual and the social-political sense of *public*. Gorbachev's term *glasnost* is in fact the precise Russian equivalent for this notion of publicity, in both its call for openness and its polemically implied departure from a history of censorship and oppression. Hence, to have public opinion was to (1) have a public or body of citizens (2) be enabled (by class, gender, race, education, political enfranchisement, or civil liberties) (3) engage in public discussion (4) be in public settings free from state sanctions (5) talk about public affairs or issues affecting the society as a whole (6) use arguments that appealed not to force, rank, or privilege but only to what Habermas calls "the power of the better argument." "Publicity" provided the openness to do so. An opinion was "public" if it could be openly known and discussed, even if "the public" that in fact did so was small. As Taylor (1990, p. 109) writes, "Public opinion, as originally conceived, is not just the sum of our private individual opinions, even where we spontaneously agree. It is something which has been elaborated in a debate and discussion, and is recognized by us all as something we hold in common."

Public Opinion

Public opinion is, first of all, an 18th-century invention, not an eternal given of human life. It emerged at a specific historical moment within a delicate balance of social and institutional conditions. Failure to recognize this can lead to imprecision. Elisabeth Noelle-Neumann (1984), for instance, treats John Locke's notion of the "law of opinion" or "law of private censure" (Locke, 1690/1975, pp. 353–357) as anticipating her own theory of the social control of opinion by perceived opinion ("the spiral of silence"). While Locke may well have spotted a tendency for all humans to adjust public loyalties in deference to perceived pressures from others, he is clearly, in historical context, engaged in clearing a new zone of social life—making "society" off limits to the intervention of other powers. His law of opinion is central to his larger project of creating a social order outside the control of church or state where ideas can be openly discussed.

Koselleck (1959/1988) has a very helpful chapter on "Locke's Law of Private Censure and its Significance for the Emergence of the Bourgeoisie." In positing a third realm of law governed only by people acting upon each other (the law of opinion), Locke attacked the traditional twofold division of divine and civil law, thereby challenging the claim of Church and State to possess sole authority in moral and legal matters. The notion that censure could be administered solely by one's fellows in "society" was scandalous to many. Locke imagined a private, social morality: "The carrier of this secret morality is no longer the individual [as in Hobbes]; it is 'society,' a structure taking shape in the 'clubs' in which philosophers, for instance, devote themselves especially to the investigation of moral laws" (Koselleck, 1959/1988, p. 55). The idea of public discussion in which nothing regulated the shock of opinion against opinion except the reasoned sanction of one's peers proposed a moral authority opposed to the arbitrariness of state edicts or the mystery of churchly rites. As Habermas (1981/1987, p. 328) says: "Since the 18th century, the features of a form of life in which the rational potential of action oriented to mutual understanding is set free have been reflected in the self-understanding of the humanistically imbued European middle classes—in their political theories and educational ideals, in their art and literature." "Action oriented to mutual understanding" in politics is "public opinion" by another name.

Thus Locke's law of opinion was not just a description of general opinion processes: it was the midwife of public opinion as a new social force in a particular historical moment. To think of private censure or public opinion as a social force in all times and places, as does Noelle-Neumann, is to miss the particular political senses that private and public have throughout the Enlightenment. For Locke private discussion has a strong public function: when state organs are rife with bombast and arbitrary power, rational talk in private can become a potent challenge. As the middle classes split open the old order, public discussion gained more and more political force. Speier (1950/1980, p. 152) puts it bluntly: "Public opinion is a phenomenon of middle-class civilization." Public opinion is precisely the novel political force Locke was seeking to safeguard.

The supposed power of public opinion sometimes reached great heights of fancy and bluster in Enlightenment talk. Consider a passage from Tunis Wortman's classic *Treatise Concerning Political Enquiry, and the Liberty of the Press* (1800/1970), which Leonard Levy (1985, p. 328) regards as "the book that Jefferson did not write but should have." Wortman begins by painting a picture of a tyrant "seated on the throne of Eastern pageantry and splendor"—the "Oriental despot," a stock villain dear to Enlightenment thought.

> But lo! a whisper is heard among the multitude . . . the tyrant trembles on his throne. Behold the eventful crisis has arrived!—the sovereign voice of public opinion has declared that Liberty should be established. In an instant the fairy spell of delusion is dissipated—the tremendous authority of this august and magnanimous despot, like the enchanted castle of the magician, vanishes forever.

Just so, arbitrary authority was expected to crumble before the decrees of public reason. As Schmitt (1985, p. 38) argues, "The light of the public is the light of the Enlightenment, a liberation from superstition, fanaticism, and ambitious intrigue. In every system of Enlightened despotism, public opinion plays the role of an absolute corrective."

Clearly, as Wortman's purple prose suggests, public opinion was often not a carefully worked out concept but a rhetorical invention. Baker (1990, p. 172) argues this thesis for late 18th-century France: "'Public opinion' took form as a political or ideological construct, rather than as a discrete sociological referent." Similarly in England, "public opinion" was used more to gesture to a real or imagined source of power outside of Parliament: "the people," a term which meant only a fraction of the populace in the late 18th century (Gunn, 1983). It is clear from recent studies that the power of "public opinion" in late 18th-century European politics owed as much to its strength as a persuasive symbol as an actual social force. Of course "public opinion" as a figure of speech cannot be easily separated from the real social and historical convulsions shaking Europe in the late 18th and throughout the 19th centuries: the rhetorical appeals were crucial in the century-long struggle to open the state to more and more popular control, from the French Revolution onwards.

The reign of the public generally seemed better as an imagined prospect than as an established fact. This is the gist of 19th-century reflections on public opinion. Disillusionment with the public and its competence is often thought to be a phenomenon of the 1920s (e.g., Lippmann, 1922, 1925; Lasswell, 1927, p. 4ff.), but doubts were already being expressed in the 1790s, in the wake of the French Revolution. A belief in the infallibility of public opinion "was too vulnerable to the rude shocks administered by day-to-day contact with ignorance, prejudice, and a servile loyalty to powerful ministers and traditional institutions" (Gunn, 1983, p. 306). The distance between the revolutionary hopes and empirical disappointments of public opinion gives 19th-century deliberations a decidedly mixed tone. In a letter of 1820 Sir Robert Peel, later Prime Minister of England, worried about "that great compound of folly, weakness, prejudice, wrong feeling, right feeling, obstinacy and newspaper paragraphs, which is called public opinion" (Gunn, p. 298). A year later G. W. F. Hegel wrote in a similar vein: "Public opinion deserves to be both respected and despised" (Hegel, 1821/1970, p. 485). Alexis de Tocqueville's *Democracy in America* (1835, 1840/1969) is centrally concerned about the potential and peril of the democratic public in the United States: public opinion, praised in the Enlightenment as a liberator from the bonds of ignorance, comes now in Tocqueville to be seen as a potential tyrant. John Stuart Mill in *On Liberty* (1859/1952, p. 302) is even less ambiguous than Tocqueville in seeing public opinion as a suffocating force of conformity; he even calls the public "a collective mediocrity" in a gloomier moment.

What Habermas calls liberal ambivalence toward public opinion (1962/1989, p. 129ff.) continues to be part of our way of talking, both as scholars and citizens, about the public. It informs the historical oscillation in debates in mass communication research: Are the mass media agents of mass leveling or organs of democratic participation? Is the media audience composed of somnolent tubers or critical citizens? These questions are the legacy of a much longer debate about public life that has been carried on since the French Revolution.

Vincent Price (1992) usefully traces competing conceptions of public opinion in scholarly research from the late 19th century to the present. The most important points for our purposes are that public opinion became an object of sustained social inquiry, rather than political speculation. First, public opinion was conceived of as an organic sociological process, a view found to an extent in a variety of earlier social thinkers but best associated with James Bryce, Charles Horton Cooley, Robert Park, Herbert Blumer, and others. By the 1920s and 1930s, public opinion was reconceived as a measurable quantity that could be tapped by survey research. Since then the polling of "public opinion" has been installed as both a symbol of democratic life and a cog in the machinery of the market and the state. "Public opinion" in this sense was "public" only in that it was about current public affairs, not in being created through a public process of deliberation and discussion. It was "opinion" because surveys tapped unstable belief, not because it was linked to a collective life of political participation or wisdom. (On the development of the social-scientific concept of opinion, see Fleming, 1967, p. 347ff.)

In sum, I argue that the concept of public opinion has roots in ancient political theory and that those roots continue to affect its senses today; in particular, the tension between *public* as something that all the people are involved in (the social–political sense) and *public* as something openly visible or known to all the people (the visual–intellectual sense) is still a dynamic central to our conception of the term. Recent debates about public opinion and democratic theory turn precisely on this issue: should the public participate in civic life actively, or is it enough that they have access to news and information in the media? How can the "public" participate when the media seem the sole providers of public space? As I pursue such questions in the next section, though without resolving them once and for all, I also extend the historical account of public opinion into the 20th century.

THE IMAGINED PUBLIC

Scale and the Necessity of Corporate Fictions

The thorn in the flesh of modern democratic thinkers is that there are natural limits to the size of a gathering of citizens. That polities had to be small was axiomatic for the Greeks (e.g., Plato, 1963, p. 1323; Aristotle, 1952, p. 530). Jean-Jacques Rousseau, one of the first to use the term "public opinion" and one of the last to insist on small scale in politics, wrote in *The Social Contract* (1762/1968, p. 90): "Just as nature has set bounds to the stature of a well-formed man, outside which he is either a giant or a dwarf, so, in what concerns the best constitution for a state, there are limits to the size it can have it if is to be neither too large to be well-governed nor too small to maintain itself. In the body politic there is a maximum of strength which must not be exceeded."

Since the 18th century, modern democrats have answered this claim with the concept of representation, most famously in *The Federalist Papers*. John Stuart Mill (1861/1952, p. 330), writing a century after Rousseau, captured both the political and the symbolic senses of the concept:

> In the ancient world, though there might be, and often was, great individual or local independence, there could be nothing like a regulated popular government beyond the bounds of a single city-community; because there did not exist the physical conditions for the formation and propagation of a public opinion, except among those who could be brought together to discuss public matters in the same agora. This obstacle is generally thought to have ceased by the adoption of a representative system. But to surmount it completely, required the press, and even the newspaper press, the real equivalent, though not in all respects an adequate one, of the Pnyx and the Forum.

Mill's description of how democracy is possible in a geographically extended society turns on two kinds of representation: *political* (elected officials, who represent the people in national assemblies) and *symbolic* (the newspaper press, which represents public affairs to the people).[2]

What Lewis Mumford (1934, p. 241) said about radio has been said about every other new form of long-distance communication: "Plato defined the limits of a city as the number of people who could hear the voice of a single orator: today those limits do not define a city but a civilization." Like Mill, Mumford recognizes the power of public media to constitute dispersed public spaces; like Mill, Mumford has his reservations. For we must admit that modern publics differ importantly from ancient assemblies—above all, in the power of the hearers to shape the flow of public discourse. Although few of the 6,000 citizens gathered at a 4th-century Athenian assembly would in fact speak, each nonetheless had the right to do so, the right, that is, to be heard by all in attendance (Hansen, 1991). A political assembly could never be experienced as a spectacle that passed indifferently before the audience's eyes, since every Athenian citizen had the theoretical option of contributing to the collective discourse, of being a coauthor of the public drama. This kind of civic cocreation of public discourse seems impossible for the modern "public." In modern times it is easier to form a visual–intellectual than a social–political public, to make something openly visible before the people (through the media) rather than involving them as active participants in self-governance. Institutions of public representation are far more developed than those of public participation (Peters & Cmiel, 1991). Active textual interpretation—celebrated of late by some students of media audiences—may sometimes have political consequences, but it is not the same thing as belonging to a common forum with the producers of those texts. An ingenious audience alone does not make for institutional transformation.

Public opinion, then, claims to be public in the first sense, as an expression of the popular will, but it is often in fact public as a visible fiction before the eyes of the people. Some have argued, like Mill, that the second (publicizing) sense makes the first (participatory) sense possible. In this view, the press is not only needed to provide "the public" with information, as all the civic and journalistic clichés suggest: it constitutes the very ground of participation in the first place. On this account political communication not only happens within the public sphere; it also constitutes the public sphere—a view with similarities to that found in "media events" studies, as is discussed below.

Tocqueville likewise viewed the newspaper as substitute sociability that compensated for the weakness of local ties in an extended republic. He saw the press as a means for coordinating the actions of a diversity of citizens who otherwise never would have been able to act in concert. "A newspaper is not only able to suggest a common plan to many men; it provides them with the means of carrying out in common the plans that they have thought of for themselves" (Tocqueville, 1840/1969, p. 518). Further, the newspaper brings people together and keeps them together, but this togetherness is not necessarily one of physical contiguity, as in some very big town square, for example. The public in this view is real, but it is formed by symbols. In reading the newspapers, the public reads about itself, and thus finds ways to come into existence. Following Anderson's suggestive notion (1983) of imagined communities, we can speak of the modern need to *imagine* the public. When we cannot see the assembled public at once—no Pnyx, no Forum—we look to its symbolic substitute in the media. The imagined public is not, however, *imaginary*: in acting upon symbolic representations of "the public" the public can come to exist as a real actor.

Techniques for representing the social whole have always gone together with public life. Michael Calvin McGee's work on the ways that social collectivities are called into being through rhetoric is of great relevance for showing the material ways that publics are formed. McGee's concern (1975) is the analogous concept, "the people." Where does this apparently unitary entity live and how does it come into being? "The people" is problematic, since it cannot appear to itself "in person" as it were. The scale of modern social orders prevents assembly of the whole populace: no stadium could contain them all. Symbolic representations of the social whole must therefore be circulated before the dispersed people. If persuasive, these representations can then invite them to act as a unified body. This is where rhetoric comes in: it is the means of articulating common identity and belief. Collective identity must first be made, often by a rhetor or leader, who, as a "flag-bearer for old longings" (McGee, 1975, p. 241), uses the fictions of rhetoric to evoke inarticulate predispositions on the part of "the people." Once that fiction is "bought" by a group of empirical individuals, it can become the most powerful of facts, as "the people" wage war, vote, buy, and so on. "The people," McGee argues, exist in both social fantasy and objective fact. Fictions, if persuasive, become material, political reality. In the region of politics, fact and fictions intermingle, often begetting one another.

The *rhetorical* transformation and constitution of the public sphere is also treated in Robert Hariman's (1992) analysis of "the courtly style." In his account, there are several political styles available to political actors. In the United States we are most familiar with a republican style, which emphasizes public debate, status leveling (or the pretense thereof), and informal modes of interaction. Reagan's presidency, in contrast, was largely characterized by a courtly style, in which the charismatic presence of the monarch's body, pomp and circumstance, and an immobilized spectatorship are the norm (cf. Habermas's representative publicity). The failed attempt by John Hinckley to assassinate Reagan probably activated this rhetoric, latent within our political culture: a normally garrulous collection of republican chatterers became a hushed nation reverentially attending the king's body. Hariman concludes that the power of the mass media lies less in their ability to propagate ideologies than to subtly transform "the basic context within which our civic activities occur" (Hariman, 1992, p. 166). While Habermas sees the structural transformation of the public sphere as a glacially historic change, Hariman notes the ability of charged symbols or events to rapidly reconstitute the public sphere, to suddenly endow all political actors with new roles and offices.

Since modern assembly exists in no physical place save in the media (understood in the broad sense as agencies of social self-representation), the modern public can exist only as a *fiction* in the robust sense—something fashioned and formed. My argument is therefore quite distinct from the long tradition of debunkers who treat public opinion as a mere figment in the overheated heads of democratic thinkers, Lippmann's *Public Opinion* (1922) and *The Phantom Public* (1925) being the most distinguished exhibits. Unlike Lippmann and many other thinkers of his era who viewed social fictions with alarm, I argue that "public opinion" since its 18th-century origins has never existed apart from mediated representations, and thus has always had an important "textual" or symbolically constructed component. "Public opinion" is the child of a form of social life in which the face-to-face concourse of citizens can no longer count as the sole basis of political order. Since the empirical body of the citizenry cannot act directly on itself, it requires corporate fictions, such as "the public," "the people's will," and so on, to represent it. Ironically, social-scientific public opinion research set out to abolish corporatist and symbolic understandings of the public, only to introduce them in a new form.

Public Opinion Research and the Critique of the Public

Public opinion research in its founding moments was an explicit and programmatic attack on nearly everything I detail above: the tradition of political philosophy and the necessity of corporate fictions. Trailblazing scientistic theorists of public opinion such as Lippmann (1922) and Allport (1937) attacked the earlier generation's view of public opinion as an organic product arising in community discourse, in the name of a leaner and more scientific concept. But their real hostility is reserved for the power of fictions in social life, a hostility that has both political and scientific motives. Allport assails metaphors of corporate social life—the spirit of the people, the will of the nation, the consensus of the group, and so forth. Society in his view is nothing but the concerted behavior of individuals, a point made explicitly in the title of his book *Institutional Behavior* (1933). "Society," "the public," and so on are in his view so many word-games. Allport's attack on corporate fictions stemmed not only from the scientific desire to reduce phenomena to their elementary constituents but from his humanistic commitment to the primacy of the individual. Lippmann is also possessed of a positivist spirit: he wants to purify the social vocabulary in order to make room for a more scientific study of the public, and with it, a more efficient management of public affairs. Both thinkers often treated the history of thought about public life and opinion as only so much fancy talk: it was time to find out what really went on. They wanted science, not opinion about society; public opinion, due to its inherently wavering nature, got short shrift from both.

In historical context, such thinkers had good reasons to engage in a campaign against social fictions, a campaign still waged in most introductory textbooks on methods of social research. The entire generation of social researchers in this period was busy restating the Platonic distinction between opinion and science. The quest for a language (that of scientific method) through which scientists and citizens could reason about social policy without the admixture of the other stuff that goes with it—dispute, passion, interest, symbol, rhetoric—was not an ignoble dream. Public opinion polling, it was thought, could cut through the jungle of corporate fictions such as "the public" and allow "the people" to speak in all their empirical truth.

Immediate history furnished examples of the perils that awaited those who took another path. The *Literary Digest*'s straw poll of 1936 has become the canonical example of the disastrous results of unrigorous method; Hitler is still the instance to which wagging fingers will point if one speaks of symbols as constitutive in some way of political life. Unrepresentative samples and unrepresentative politics, then, are the respective fears that keep scholars treating the public as an aggregate of dispersed individuals; to do otherwise has long seemed either unscientific or undemocratic. (There are obvious political–economic reasons for treating the public in this way as well.) Both objections to the imagined public stem from the same source—the alliance made between public opinion polling and a particular vision of popular democracy in the late 1930s: polls were thought to give "the people" a direct voice in government, unmediated by power, status, or institutions (see Gallup & Rae, 1940). The political stakes of public opinion research lie in the project of *representing* the public fairly, in both the political and scientific senses—senses that are indeed hard to distinguish (see Carey, 1989, p. 99ff.).

As Habermas points out, however, "representation" can also mean unfurling a spectacle, condensing a mess of empirical facts into a visible symbol. Once the king's natural body "represented" the body politic. His presence was a potent synecdoche, a physical part that stood for the political whole (Kantorowicz, 1957). What the king's body did in the Middle Ages is not so different from what pollsters do in modern societies: both offer punctuated statements of otherwise invisible realities. The results of public opinion polls are paraded before the people in the media: today information, not the royal purple, is what makes publicness. What originates as fact can be presented only as fiction—in the sense of a constructed and condensed symbol. However pure the science that taps "public opinion" on any topic, "public opinion" when published becomes a symbol of the whole. The Romans would have instantly understood the move from "the people" to "public exhibition"; for most 20th-century people, raised to believe that science gives a transparent window on the facts, it is hard to see that "the public" must always be represented in one way or another. Public opinion polls serve as symbolic mediators in representing the public to itself and hence can function as a modern version of the crown and scepter. Rather than simply democratizing, they can also *refeudalize* the public sphere, in Habermas's suggestive phrase (1962/1989).

The chief victim of the assault on corporate fictions was the concept of "the public," but it was a programmatic decision. Allport (1937), for example, in the founding article of *Public Opinion Quarterly*, expressly takes the public out of public opinion, such that the context of the formation and expression of public opinion is systematically removed from consideration.[3] Allport defines "public opinion" in a way that makes "public" circular: a public is defined as "the number of people holding a certain opinion, and the people holding that opinion would be identified as those belonging to the public" (Allport, 1937, p. 9). The term "public," as he notes, is thus rendered "superfluous for purposes of research." Scientific attention could thus shift from social sites of civic discussion to abstract clusterings of opinion in the population. What we call public opinion today is thus actually nonpublic opinion, as a number of critics have pointed out (Blumer, 1948; Habermas, 1962/1989, p. 211ff.; Bourdieu, 1979; Bellah, Madsen, Sullivan, Swindler, & Tipton, 1985, p. 305). Public opinion research makes the public a demographic segment or data set rather than a realm of action. Citizens do not themselves produce public opinion today; it must be generated through the machinery of polling. The power to constitute the public space, then, falls into the hands of the experts, not of the citizens.

Until the 20th century, concepts of *public* highlighted the conditions within which deeds and words are performed. To act in public was to be on a stage of sorts before one's peers; nothing less than one's honor was on the line. That very different opinions get expressed in public and private is an elementary fact of social life; even children quickly learn how to talk behind people's backs. Context and audience are fundamental shapers of all human speech. The querying of people in private contexts where anonymity is guaranteed, the typical practice in survey research, completely fails to capture a public element. Much is at stake in a public utterance, little where the speaker has no identity or voice. Ironically, Allport at least was very sensitive to the difference between public and private (see, e.g., Allport, 1937, p. 15); and his notion of "pluralistic ignorance" addresses how attitudes take different expressions in public and private realms (Katz, 1983). By assuming that private interviews in a setting without a public forum could tap public opinion, however, the technique and ideology of polling fundamentally reshaped the meaning of "public opinion." This aided what Habermas

(1962/1989, p. 244) calls "the social–psychological decomposition of the concept" of public opinion.

In removing the public, survey research combined with many social and economic forces that were making participatory conceptions of citizenship increasingly irrelevant to life in the modern capitalist state (Westbrook, 1983). Public opinion, as we now understand it, sees no need for the process of public discussion. The noble idea of using public opinion polls to enhance democratic participation not only backfired in practice, it confused the meanings of public and opinion. "Public opinion" in its common usage is a positively Orwellian expression.

Public opinion research was a modernist enterprise in spirit: to my complaint that it had lost critical ancient meanings in its central concepts, a Lippmann or Allport might respond, "Good riddance." The resistance of public opinion research to classic philosophical ideas of democracy reached an apex in an influential article by Bernard Berelson (1952, rev. in Berelson, Lazarsfeld, & McPhee, 1954, ch. 14). Berelson argued that public opinion research had shown the inadequacy of most classical ideas about democracy, such as involvement, interest, and discussion on the part of all citizens. He suggested that democratic theory should give place to empirical research, that old ideals that lacked an empirical correlate should be abandoned. (Interestingly, he thought that traditional democratic theory did empirically apply to a select group of citizens, the opinion leaders.) Berelson spoke for his age in dismissing democratic ideas held to be unrealistic. But in historical context, his supposedly purely scientific notions had a clear political agenda: to justify American "consensus" politics (Lukes, 1977). Old democratic ideas of popular participation got in the way and had to be pushed to the side (Lazarsfeld, 1957, called for a more conciliatory approach to political philosophy, but Berelson's views predominated).

Such a stance will no longer do today: public opinion research can no longer claim to be free of the influence of political thought or practice. Indeed, old debates help explain what happened in the 20th century. I began this chapter with the argument between Plato and Aristotle about the nature of politics: specialized skill (*technê*) or common human activity (*praxis*)? the "scientific knowledge" (*epistêmê*) of the experts or the shaky wisdom (*doxa*) of all human beings? This debate was carried on in the critical decade of the 1920s between the Platonist Lippmann and the Aristotelian John Dewey; as I have described elsewhere, Plato's forces won (Peters, 1989; Carey, 1989, pp. 69–88). Public opinion became a *technê*, a skill for specialists. Though the pollsters collect data from "the people," the task of constituting the public realm remains in technical, not civic hands. The ancient tensions in the concept of public opinion are important and useful, both intellectually and politically. Recovering lost meanings helps us discover more humane ideas and practices of citizenship: it helps us analyze and critique the current dominance of a spectacular over a participatory public.

Implicit Recognition of the Public as Symbolic in Recent Research

The 1988 Presidential campaign made clear to citizens, journalists, and political elites the ways that representations of public opinion can rebound back on public opinion itself (to speak for a moment as if it existed unproblematically). The older concern about the possible bandwagon effects of publicized exit polls became a more general and often dizzying discussion about mediated politics, spin control, and sound bites (e.g., Adatto, 1990). Many of the most fertile research programs about public opinion today are driven by a more or less frank acceptance of the fictive or symbolically constructed character of public opinion. Perhaps this dawning insight is a sign of the postmodern times, a reflection of late 20th-century transformations in the structure of political discourse. More likely, it is a deeper phenomenon inherent in the modern public that has been with us since the 18th century, since social scale demands corporate fictions. In any event, describing whether our recent political life is modern or postmodern requires a richer and more precise language of historical periodization than we have at present.

Noelle-Neumann's (1984) theory of the spiral of silence posits that media representations of public opinion can drive people to silence due to their fear of being out of step with the majority. The subtlety to her theory is that the pivot point is not the traditional one of how the mass media influence public opinion directly, but how media *representations* of public opinion influence public opinion. The key mechanism of her theory is public opinion as a staged image before the eyes of the people, not as a latent sociological or psychological entity. She does not, admittedly, abandon the idea of public opinion as ultimately located in people's attitudes, but the logic of her theory makes public opinion as a symbolic portrait the lever in opinion change.

Converse (1987), to take another example, notes "two faces of public opinion": political discourse and polls. In the 1964 presidential campaign, he notes, probably the biggest story was the rise of the John Birch Society as part of a growing conservative bloc critical of the New Deal hegemony. The Birchers had a vast influence on the shape of the public sphere that year and on the conduct of the election—yet representative samples contained barely one or two members. The symbolic-political influence of the John Birch Society was tremendous, yet it utterly escaped the polling technology. How to explain the discrepancy? What counts as public opinion: the actual stuff of politics, which has always involved the slinging of symbols, or the amassed opinions of the populace? Converse cites the 1964 campaign as an instance of the validity of Blumer's (1948) attack on polling: Blumer thought representative sampling missed the organic, sociological character of public opinion as a process. My argument has some sympathy with Blumer's, although I would emphasize that the Birchers were not just an organic outgrowth of a political reality but a planned and mediated phenomenon that sought representation in the public eye.

The implications of these "two faces" are pursued in studies by scholars at Northwestern University on investigative reporting and its influence on policymakers and the public (e.g., Ettema et al., 1991; Protess et al., 1991; Cook et al., 1983). Although investigative journalism, they argue, is premised on a "mobilization model" in which "the public" is supposed to be directly activated by exposés of wrongdoing, these scholars show that in most cases "the public" (in the sense of the collected citizenry) has little voice in policy-making. And yet critical reporting can indeed have large effects: what is the mechanism here? It is the *image* of an outraged public activated in investigative reporting that moves policy elites to action. The Northwestern scholars do a little muckraking of their own, exposing the standard journalistic faith that "the public" rises up to take a direct part in governing. For the "mobilization model" they substitute "The Coalition Model of Investigative Reporting" (Protess et al., 1991, pp. 250ff.), which is implicitly built on the model of a theater. The public is a spectator or bystander of the drama between policy elites, journalists, and others, but it does play an indirect role, since the drama cannot play long to an empty house. The public is the condition of elite action, but it is not usually an actor itself.

The notion that the fictionalization of the public is somehow "postmodern" is raised by Ettema et al. (1991). Perhaps this is so, in the sense that symbols (newspaper accounts) seem to motivate other symbols (outraged publics) without ever taking a dip in the cold waters of real social practice, and in the sense that the total image that the bystander public sees is fragmentary and chaotic. But in another sense, an immobilized public that watches elites perform is quintessentially premodern. As these scholars describe the social workings of investigative journalism today, it is a classic example of a representative public sphere.

Studies of the "third-person effect" (e.g., Davison, 1983; Rucinski & Salmon, 1990; Gunther, 1991) also turn on the insight that the perception or portrayal of effects may be the key in public opinion formation. Such studies demonstrate a systematic discrepancy between people's estimates of media influence on themselves and others (often phrased as "the public"), revealing some belief that others are more susceptible to influence than the self. Most students of the third-person effect seek opinions about the cognitive capabilities of actual sets of others from their informants. We can also, however, interpret the discrepant ratings symbolically and rhetorically, by recognizing that people are offering their views of corporate symbols (such as "other voters," "other Minnesotans," "the public" in general).[4]

The personified "public," which is a third person par excellence, is a descendent of the corporate social fictions of the Middle Ages: the body politic, the state, the voice of the people, and so on. (Kantorowicz, 1957). Almost all premodern states claimed a divine origin, a mandate of heaven or a descent from the sun; modern democracies take legitimacy from the secularized divinity of public opinion, a point implicit in the phrase *vox populi, vox dei* ("the voice of the people is the voice of God"). The idea that a corporate personality gives benediction to the state is not just an outlandish remnant left from earlier times; it is built into our political culture. Baker (1990, p. 172) argues that the modern notion of the public originates in "the transfer of ultimate authority from the public person of the sovereign to the sovereign person of the public" in late 18th-century France. However much social scientists of public opinion have sought to banish the legacy of corporatist social thought from their methods, as soon as their findings are transferred back into political discourse, such findings cannot help but assume older meanings. The legitimacy of constitutional government lies in its ability to gain a "mandate" from the electorate or an approval from "the people's will."

Judgments made about the capacities of the public thus might reflect the symbolic status of the corporate person at a given moment; perhaps in certain moments in late 18th-century Europe informants might have thought "the public" *wiser* than themselves. In other words, exaggerated estimates of the influence of a given item on "the public" or "other people" may be due more to people's sense of how that message will alter those constructs as central *symbols* of public life, rather than to any intuitively snobbish theory about the psyches of others. Like the concept of "public opinion" in the 18th century, we should perhaps see "the public" as a sign whose interpretation is to be fought over. To imagine that people in general will be more affected than the self is to imagine the general shape of public life: as an individual, I am not likely to be changed radically by receiving a new piece of information, but the space of public discussion certainly is. In inviting people to conjecture effects on various collectives, again, social scientists invite corporate and symbolic thinking.

For example, the Willie Horton advertisement in George Bush's 1988 campaign (Rucinski & Salmon, 1990) may not have in fact swayed much of the ABCs (affect, behavior, cognition) in the American public, but it did radically alter the character of "the public" as a realm, introducing new codes of decorum (or rather the lack thereof). Suddenly the rules of the game changed: hardball and racial politics were put into play. Michael Dukakis' inability to play ball in the newly constituted public space, to make a fitting counterattack, was itself an indication of his qualifications. The consistent overestimation of effects on the third person may thus arise from people's well-developed sense of how radically the public sphere can be affected by the appearance of a new symbol or message. As Hariman (1992) shows, minute fragments of discourse can have a gigantic influence on the constitution of the public realm by altering prevailing codes of behavior and styles of communication. As a vastly complex collage of symbols provided by journalists, pollsters, political actors, footage, and popular culture generally, "the public" is more susceptible to drastic Gestalt shifts than are aggregated individual psyches.

Conceiving of the public as a robust fiction helps clarify some of the classic debates about the effects of the mass media. Taken as a "text" studied by interpretive analysis, the "media audience" will necessarily be subject to all kinds of rapid changes. Taken as an aggregate of real individuals studied via the tools of empirical social science, it will be stubbornly immune to wild swings. Of course, in popular and policy discourse, media audiences are far more frequently (pre)texts for larger social concerns. The term "effects" even has a double sense: "impact" (as in "effects research") and "dazzling spectacle" (as in "special effects" in film). A sign or message broadcast by the media to the populace could have negligible short-term influence on "public opinion" as the ABCs of the adult members of the nation and still have a drastic effect on public life as a visible symbol. The structure of my attitudes and so on may change little when I watch the Shuttle disaster, but I know I live, act, and breathe in a radically different public space than the one before the disaster—knowledge that may in fact have a major impact on my behavior. Nevertheless, what drives this "impact" is not any "direct effect" of viewing the Shuttle disaster on my behavior but my reading of the symbolically changed public space. My evaluation of the disaster's public effect is what motivates its effect on me. Effects may be perceived effects.

The most developed account of the public as a fundamentally symbolic space that is capable of radical reframing is found in studies by Elihu Katz, Daniel Dayan, and their associates on "media events": "On these extraordinary occasions, television can define and unite a community, declare a holiday, reinforce values, change opinions, and sometimes change the world" (Katz, 1987, p. S39). Hence, Katz argues, the mass media can have massive impacts by rearranging the symbolic order of social life, not just by influencing individuals. Media events

> fulfill the technological potential of the electronic media. Television is capable of reaching everybody, everywhere, simultaneously, and directly—total, immediate, unmediated—although it does so only very rarely. And soon, even a certain amount of interactivity will prove possible. On these occasions, the public space is reinvigorated, and, ironically, its locus is the home. (Katz, 1991, p. 15)

Media events studies, of all new directions in public opinion and communication research, most explicitly view the public realm as capable of alteration and replenishment through rhetoric and symbols: my point is that this insight should be generalized to all studies of public opinion.

CONCLUSION

Media events studies are also deeply attuned to questions about political implications, as is indicated by Katz's modifier "ironically" above. Can a public space have as its locus the living room? Yes—but only in some cases. Rothenbuhler (1988), for instance, convincingly argues that national celebrations can take place in the living rooms of TV viewers. Audiences can and do *participate* in media events such as Royal weddings, moon landings, presidential funerals, Olympic contests, and so on: in viewing they reenact their membership in the larger social whole. These studies thus refute the thesis that the mass media have solely a stupefying effect, showing how they can lead to popular participation. But such participation is purely expressive. In none of these contexts can the audience determine the flow of public events: however actively viewers cheer or weep, the actors have no need to register the views of the audience. After a theatrical performance, going backstage to congratulate or query the actors is optional. Media events are *stately* affairs in which little information needs to be sent or received. They are solemn or joyous ritual dramas, not appropriate for political chatter; what could seem in worse taste than to try to talk politics at such an event? But *political* participation is another story: some registry of audience—or rather citizen—input is required. Media events studies address those occasions in which the public space is constituted as a participatory spectacle.

For Katz, Dayan, Rothenbuhler, and others, "participatory spectacle" is no oxymoron. They assume, with John Stuart Mill (1861/1952), that private political conversation—apart from any institutional structure of public follow-through—is a key kind of political participation. Certainly it is far easier with current technical and institutional arrangements to constitute a society as a collective of spectators than of actors. Given the scale of our social life, perhaps participatory spectacle is no mean political achievement. The question remains whether this exhausts what we mean by and want from a democratically participatory citizenry; I am not persuaded that it does. But we need a fuller account of the democracy and the role of the media in it in order to be more specific. We cannot hope to return to small scale social order in which assembly directly governs policy, however much it remains a normative ideal for democratic thought. What assembly was to the ancients mass communication is to the moderns: that which allows a collective vision of the collective. But the ancients could take part in the direct crafting of that vision in a way that is elusive for moderns. The problem theorists of the democratic role of the media must face is how to find a social–political or participatory public that is not overwhelmed by the visual–intellectual public of spectacle. The problem is central to a modern understanding of democratic practice and should be at the core of future debates about democracy and communication—debates, that is, about public opinion.[5]

NOTES

1. Recent research shows that women and foreigners could attend the theater, and women did play a key role in cultic rituals, which were central to Greek public life. And yet a noncitizen could be arrested and executed for participating in a political assembly; see Hansen (1991).

2. Even though Mill anachronistically speaks of "public opinion" in antiquity, he treats its formation through face-to-face discussion as the *exception*. He assumes a modern understanding of "the public" as spatially dispersed.

3. Allport's article, of course, is no aberration; as Davison (1987, p. S180) says, it is still "one of the best theoretical statements."

4. We should take seriously the linguistic sense of the "third person." As the great French linguist Émile Benveniste notes (1971, p. 198): "the 'third person' is not a 'person'; it is really the verbal form whose function is to express the non-person." As Benveniste shows, the third person lacks qualities of personhood that first and second person possess. (Studies should be done to measure predicted effects on the "second person," on "you"; Benveniste's theory would predict that such estimates, like first-person estimates, would be lower than for the third-person.)

5. I am grateful to Ken Cmiel, Al Gunther, Bob Hariman, Vince Price, Eric Rothenbuhler, and Dianne Rucinski for sharing ideas, manuscripts, references, and critiques of an earlier draft, and to Lorna Olson and Jay Semel

at The Center for Advanced Studies at The University of Iowa for offering a splendid place to do this work. A presentation of a draft of this chapter at the Annenberg School for Communication and discussion with Elihu Katz, Daniel Dayan, and students there was very helpful. Naturally, the ideas and errors in this chapter are my responsibility alone. This essay is a companion piece to another essay that explains Habermas's theory of the public sphere at length (Peters, 1993).

REFERENCES

Adatto, K. (1990, 28 May). The incredible shrinking sound bite. *New Republic*, pp. 20–23.

Allport, F. H. (1933). *Institutional behavior: Essays toward a re-interpretation of contemporary social organization*. Chapel Hill: University of North Carolina Press.

Allport, F. H. (1937). Toward a science of public opinion. *Public Opinion Quarterly*, *1*(1), 7–23.

Anderson, B. (1983). *Imagined communities: Reflections on the origin and spread of nationalism*. London: Verso.

Arendt, H. (1958). *The human condition*. Chicago: University of Chicago Press.

Aristotle. (1952). *Politics*. In R. M. Hutchins (Ed.), *Great books of the Western world* (vol. 9, pp. 437–548). Chicago: Encyclopedia Britannica.

Baker, K. M. (1990). *Inventing the French Revolution: Essays on French political culture in the eighteenth century*. Cambridge, England: Cambridge University Press.

Bellah, R., Madsen, R., Sullivan, W. M., Swidler, A., & Tipton, S. (1985). *Habits of the heart: Individualism and commitment in American life*. Berkeley: University of California Press.

Benveniste, É. (1971). Relationships of person in the verb (M. E. Meek, Trans.). In É. Benveniste, *Problems in general linguistics* (pp. 195–204). Coral Gables, FL: University of Miami Press.

Berelson, B. (1952). Democratic theory and public opinion. *Public Opinion Quarterly, 16*(3), 313–330.

Berelson, B., Lazarsfeld, P. F., & McPhee, W. N. (1954). *Voting: A study of opinion formation in a presidential campaign*. Chicago: University of Chicago Press.

Blumer, H. (1948). Public opinion and public opinion polling. *American Sociological Review, 13*, 542–549, 554.

Bourdieu, P. (1979). Public opinion does not exist. In A. Mattelart & S. Siegelaub (Eds.), *Communication and class struggle* (vol. 1, pp. 124–130). New York: International General.

Carey, J. W. (1989). *Communication as culture: Essays on media and society*. Boston: Unwin Hyman.

Converse, P. E. (1987). Changing conceptions of public opinion in the political process. *Public Opinion Quarterly, 51*(4), part 2, S12–S24.

Cook, F. L., Tyler, T. R., Goetz, E. G., Gordon, M. T., Protess, D., Leff, D. R., & Molotch, H. L. (1983). Media and agenda-setting: Effects on the public, interest group leaders, policy makers, and policy. *Public Opinion Quarterly, 47*(1), 16–35.

Davison, W. P. (1983). The third-person effect in communication. *Public Opinion Quarterly, 47*(1), 1–15.

Davison, W. P. (1987). [Comments]. *Public Opinion Quarterly, 51*(4), part 2, S179–S180.

Dewey, J. (1927). *The public and its problems*. New York: Henry Holt.

Ettema, J. S., Protess, D. L., Leff, D. R., Miller, P. V., Doppelt, J., & Cook, F. L. (1991). Agenda-setting as politics: A case study of the press–public–policy connection. *Communication, 12*(2), 75–98.

Fleming, D. (1967). Attitude: History of a concept. *Perspectives in American history, 1*, 287–365.

Gadamer, H-G. (1965). *Wahrheit und Methode: Grundzüge einer philosophischen Hermeneutik* [Truth and method: Fundamentals of a philosophic hermeneutic] (2nd ed.). Tübingen: Siebeck-Mohr.

Gallup, G., & Rae, S. R. (1940). *The pulse of democracy: The public-opinion poll and how it works*. New York: Simon and Schuster.

Glare, P. G. W. (Ed.) (1982). *Oxford Latin dictionary*. Oxford: Clarendon Press.

Gouldner, A. W. (1976). *The dialectic of ideology and technology: The origins, grammar, and future of ideology*. New York: Seabury.

Gunn, J. A. W. (1983). *Beyond liberty and property: The process of self-recognition in eighteenth-century political thought*. Kingston & Montreal: McGill-Queen's University Press.

Gunther, A. C. (1991). What we think others think: Cause and consequence of the third-person effect. *Communication Research 18*(3), 355–372.

Habermas, J. (1987). *The theory of communicative action: Vol. 2. Lifeworld and system: A critique of functionalist reason* (T. McCarthy, Trans.). Boston: Beacon Press. (Original work published in 1981)

Habermas, J. (1989). *The structural transformation of the public sphere: An inquiry into a category of bourgeois society* (T. Burger & F. Lawrence, Trans.). Cambridge: MIT Press. (Original work published in 1962)

Habermas, J. (1990). Vorwort zur Neuauflage 1990 [Foreword to the 1990 republication]. In J. Habermas, *Strukturwandel der Œffentlichkeit* [Structural transformation of the public sphere] (pp. 11–50). Frankfurt: Suhrkamp.

Hacking, I. (1975). *The emergence of probability: A philosophical study of early ideas about probability, induction, and statistical inference*. Cambridge, England: Cambridge University Press.

Hansen, H. M. (1991). *The Athenian democracy in the age of Demosthenes: Structure, principle and ideology* (J. A. Crook, Trans.). Oxford: Basil Blackwell.

Hariman, R. (1992). Decorum, power, and the courtly style. *Quarterly Journal of Speech, 78*, 149–172.

Hegel, G.W.F. (1970). *Grundlinien der Philosophie des Rechts* [Elements of the philosophy of law]. Frankfurt: Suhrkamp. (Original work published in 1821)

Hölscher, L. (1979). *Öffentlichkeit und Geheimnis: Eine begriffsgeschichtliche Untersuchung zur Entstehung der Öffentlichkeit in der frühen Neuzeit* [Publicity and secrecy: A conceptual-historical study of the genesis of the public sphere in the early modern period]. Stuttgart: Klett-Cotta.

Kantorowicz, E. H. (1957). *The king's two bodies: A study in mediaeval political theology*. Princeton: Princeton University Press.

Katz, E. (1983). Publicity and pluralistic ignorance: Notes on the "spiral of silence." In E. Wartella, D. C. Whitney, S. Windahl (Eds.), *Mass communication review yearbook 4* (pp. 89–99). Beverly Hills: Sage.

Katz, E. (1987). Communications research since Lazarsfeld. *Public Opinion Quarterly, 51* (4), part 2, S25–S45.

Katz, E. (1991). *Viewers work: The Wilbur Schramm memorial lecture*. Lecture given at the University of Illinois, Urbana–Champaign, 6 September 1990. (Rev. 1991)

Katz, E., & Lazarsfeld, P. F. (1955). *Personal influence: The part played by people in the flow of mass communications*. Glencoe, IL: Free Press.

Koselleck, R. (1988). *Critique and crisis: Enlightenment and the pathogenesis of modern society*. Oxford: Berg. (Original work published in 1959)

Lasswell, H. D. (1927). *Propaganda technique in the world war*. New York: Peter Smith.

Lazarsfeld, P. F. (1957). Public opinion and the classical tradition. *Public Opinion Quarterly, 21*(1), 39–53.

Levy, L. W. (1985). *Emergence of a free press*. New York: Oxford University Press.

Lippmann, W. (1922). *Public opinion*. New York: Macmillan.

Lippmann, W. (1925). *The phantom public*. New York: Macmillan.

Locke, J. (1975). *An essay concerning human understanding* (P. H. Nidditch, Ed.). Oxford: Clarendon Press. (Original work published in 1690)

Lukes, S. (1977). The new democracy. In S. Lukes, *Essays in Social Theory* (pp. 30–51). New York: Columbia University Press.

MacIntyre, A. (1988). *Whose justice? Which rationality?* Notre Dame: University of Notre Dame Press.

McGee, M. C. (1975). In search of 'the people': A rhetorical alternative. *Quarterly Journal of Speech, 61*(3), 235–249.

Mill, J. S. (1952). *On liberty*. In R. M. Hutchins (Ed.), *Great books of the western world* (vol. 43, pp. 267–323). Chicago: Encyclopedia Britannica. (Original work published in 1859)

Mill, J. S. (1952). *Considerations on representative government*. In R. M. Hutchins (Ed.), *Great books of the western world* (vol. 43, pp. 325–442). Chicago: Encyclopedia Britannica. (Original work published in 1861)

Mumford, L. (1934). *Technics and civilization*. New York: Harcourt Brace Jovanovich.

Nathans, B. (1990). Habermas's 'public sphere' in the era of the French revolution. *French Historical Studies, 16*(3), 620–644.

Noelle-Neumann, E. (1984). *The spiral of silence: Public opinion—Our social skin*. Chicago: University of Chicago Press.

Ozouf, M. (1988a). *Festivals and the French revolution* (A. Sheridan, Trans.). Cambridge, MA: Harvard University Press. (Original work published in 1976)

Ozouf, M. (1988b). "Public opinion" at the end of the Old Regime. *Journal of Modern History, 60* (supplement), S1–S21.

Pateman, C. (1983). Feminist critiques of the public/private dichotomy. In S. I.

Benn & G. F. Gaus (Eds.), *Public and private in social life* (pp. 281–303). New York: St. Martin's Press.

Pateman, C. (1988). The fraternal social contract. In J. Keane (Ed.), *Civil society and the state: New European perspectives* (pp. 101–127). London: Verso.

Peters, J. D. (1989). Democracy and American mass communication theory: Dewey, Lippmann, Lazarsfeld. *Communication, 11*(3), 199–220.

Peters, J. D. (1993). Distrust of representation: Habermas on the public sphere. *Media, Culture and Society, 15*(4), 541–571.

Peters, J.D., & Cmiel, K. (1991). Media ethics and the public sphere. *Communication, 12*, 197–215.

Plato. (1963). *The laws* (A. E. Taylor, Trans). In E. Hamilton & H. Cairns (Eds.), *The collected dialogues of Plato* (pp. 1226–1513). Princeton: Princeton University Press.

Price, V. (1992). *Public opinion*. In S. H. Chaffee & E. Wartella (Eds.), *Communication concepts: No. 5*. Newbury Park, CA: Sage.

Protess, D. L., Cook, F. L., Doppelt, J. C., Ettema, J. S., Gordon, M. T., Leff, D. R., & Miller, P. (1991). *The journalism of outrage: Investigative reporting and agenda building in America*. New York: Guilford Press.

Raeff, M. (1983). *The well-ordered police state: Social and institutional change through law in the Germanies and Russia, 1600–1800*. New Haven: Yale University Press.

Rothenbuhler, E. W. (1988). The living-room celebration of the Olympic games. *Journal of Communication, 38* (Autumn), 61–81.

Rousseau, J-J. (1968). *The social contract* (M. Cranston, Trans.). London: Penguin. (Original work published in 1762)

Rucinski, D., & Salmon, C. T. (1990). The 'other' as the vulnerable voter: A study of the third-person effect in the 1988 U.S. Presidential Campaign. *International Journal of Public Opinion Research* 2(4), 345–368.

Saxonhouse, A. W. (1983). Classical Greek conceptions of public and private. In S. I. Benn & G.F. Gaus (Eds.), *Public and private in social life* (pp. 363–384). New York: St. Martin's Press.

Schmitt, C. (1985). *The crisis of parliamentary democracy* (E. Kennedy, Trans.). Cambridge, MA: MIT Press. (Original work published in 1926)

Speier, H. (1980). The rise of public opinion. In H. D. Lasswell, D. Lerner, & H. Speier (Eds.), *Propaganda and communication in world history: Vol. 2. Emergence of public opinion in the west* (pp. 147–167). Honolulu: University of Hawaii Press. (Revised and enlarged version of work originally published in 1950)

Strong, R. (1984). *Art and power: Renaissance festivals, 1450–1650*. London: Roydell Press.

Tarde, G. de. (1901). *L'opinion et la foule* [Opinion and the crowd]. Paris: Alcan.

Taylor, C. (1989). *Sources of the self: The making of the modern identity*. Cambridge, MA: Harvard University Press.

Taylor, C. (1990). Modes of civil society. *Public Culture 3*(1), 95–118.

Tocqueville, A. de. (1969). *Democracy in America* (G. Lawrence, Trans., J. P. Mayer, Ed.). Garden City: Anchor Books. (Original work published in 1835, 1840).

Westbrook, R. B. (1983). Politics as consumption: Managing the modern American election. In R. W. Fox & T. J. J. Lears (Eds.), *The culture of consumption: Critical essays in American history, 1880–1980* (pp. 145–173). New York: Pantheon.

Wortman, T. (1970). *A treatise concerning political enquiry, and the liberty of the press* (L. W. Levy, Ed.). New York: Da Capo Press. (Original work published in 1800)

2

Public Opinion and Rationality[1]

Elisabeth Noelle-Neumann

This chapter is dedicated to clarifying the concept of public opinion.[2] Even as this century draws to a close, the discussion is still where it was when it began: The term "public opinion" is current; it is widely used in both scientific and everyday speech. But it has yet to be clarified. At the start of this century, the German historian Hermann Oncken commented on "public opinion" as follows:

> Anyone who tries to grasp it [the term public opinion] and pin it down recognizes immediately that he is dealing with a Proteus, a creature that is both visible in a thousand ways and yet shadowy, that is powerless and at the same time surprisingly effective, that manifests itself in countless different ways, that always manages to escape our grasp just when we think we have a hold on it. . . . It is not possible to comprehend something that is in a state of fluctuation and flow by forcing it to fit into a set formula. . . . After all, anyone who is asked knows exactly what public opinion means. (1914, pp. 224ff., 236)

Now, toward the end of the century, the following comments appeared in the *American Political Science Review*, in Bruce Altschuler's review of Arthur Asa Berger's book, *Political Culture and Public Opinion* (1989): "Instead of precisely defining . . . public opinion . . . , he tells the reader that the meaning . . . is 'rather obvious' . . ." (Altschuler, 1990, p. 1369).

Consider the famed second chapter of Harwood Childs' book, *Public Opinion: Nature, Formation, and Role*, with its 50 definitions of public opinion (Childs, 1965). Or the first sentence of W. Phillips Davison's article on public opinion in the *International Encyclopedia of the Social Sciences*, by D.L. Sills:

> There is no generally accepted definition of "public opinion." Nevertheless, the term has been employed with increasing frequency. . . . Later efforts to define the term precisely have led to such expressions of frustration as: "Public opinion is not the name of a something but a classification of a number of somethings." (1968, p. 188)

This paper posits that the 50 definitions cited by Childs all stem from just two different concepts of public opinion. In addition, there are a few definitions that are technical–instrumental in nature, in that public opinion is equated with the results of public opinion polls, defined as "the aggregation of individual attitudes by pollsters" (Beniger, 1987, p. S54; cf. Gollin, 1980, p. 448).

Practically all of the definitions compiled by Childs are related to the following two concepts:

1. Public opinion as rationality: it is instrumental in the process of opinion formation and decision making in a democracy.
2. Public opinion as social control: its role is to promote social integration and to insure that there is a sufficient level of consensus on which actions and decisions may be based.

As defined by Robert Merton (1949/1957) in Chapter 1 of *Social Theory and Social Structure* , the concept of public opinion as rationality implies a manifest function, whereas the concept of public opinion as social control involves a latent function.

Given the vast differences between the various concepts of public opinion, scholars from the 1920s (Palmer, 1936/1950, p. 12; see Habermas, 1962, p. 13) until today (Moscovici, 1991, p. 299) have urged that the term "public opinion" be abandoned, at least in scientific usage.[3] The present paper, however, contends that a concept that has been shown to exist since antiquity, and that has been used throughout the centuries ever since, cannot be discarded as long as no other equally comprehensive term has been found that is obviously more capable of conveying the meaning of this concept as it has been used since antiquity[4]—that is, in the sense of a certain form of social control. Were we to abandon the term "public opinion," we would lose our age-old knowledge of the latent function of public opinion, with which a sufficient consensus is maintained within a society—and perhaps throughout the world (B. Niedermann, 1991; Rusciano & Fiske-Rusciano, 1990). We would no longer be able to recognize the connections between such different phenomena as the climate of opinion, the *zeitgeist*, reputation, fashion, and taboos, and would thus revert to a level of knowledge prior to John Locke's "law of opinion, reputation and fashion."

The following discussion focuses first on the concept of public opinion as rationality, before turning to the concept of public opinion as social control. The latter part of this discussion includes a summary of arguments that support the contention that the concept of public opinion is more effective when viewed in terms of its latent function of social control.

PUBLIC OPINION AS A MANIFEST FUNCTION: THE FORMATION OF OPINION IN A DEMOCRACY

In scholarly terms, we are still in a phase dominated by the concept of public opinion as it began to take hold in the late 18th century. According to this concept, public opinion is characterized by rationality. Rationality in this context is taken to mean the conscious acquisition of knowledge by means of reason, the advancement of rationally sound judgments based on the thought process, as evidenced by the use of clear language and clear terms. The relationship of these terms to one another should be clearcut with regard to identity, overlapping aspects, and differences, as well as to superordination, ordering, and subordination; they are bound by the rules of logic, such as consistency and causality. Provided that these requirements are met, the knowledge acquired and judgments made are intersubjectively comprehensible, rationally clear, convincing, and sensible, resulting from the critical evaluation of arguments and counterarguments.

The concept of public opinion based on rationality is succinctly outlined in Hans Speier's classic definition, published in the *American Journal of Sociology* in an article entitled, "Historical Development of Public Opinion" (1950): "Let us understand by public opinion, for the purposes of this historical review, opinions on matters of concern to the nation freely and publicly expressed by men outside the government who claim a right that their opinions should influence or determine the actions, personnel, or structure of their government" (p. 376). Here, the relationship between public opinion and rationality is quite straightforward: They are identical. In practice—provided that there is freedom of the press—there is a high degree of agreement between public opinion and the prevailing published opinion in the media. The manifest function of public opinion is also incorporated in Speier's definition. Public opinion is related to politics; it supports the government in the formation of opinions and decisions in political matters.

This notion of public opinion as a sort of political *raisonnement* in the public sphere, as a correlate to the government (Habermas, 1962), appeared especially convincing because of the widespread belief that the concept of public opinion first emerged at the time of the Enlightenment in the 18th century. Even today, this claim is still found in encyclopedias and lexicons throughout the world. Frequently, the term is attributed to Jacques Necker, the French Minister of Finance, who had tried to keep the government's finances stable despite growing public turmoil shortly before the French Revolution.[5]

The first attempts to explain the term "public opinion" were made in the 19th century. Bryce, who deals with the different roles of public opinion in England and the United States in the fourth section of his book, *The American Commonwealth* (1888–1889), limits the concept of public opinion to the rational discussion of controversial political issues in a democracy. During his studies in Germany at the start of the century, Robert Ezra Park found himself torn between Toennies, his professor at the University of Berlin, who was trying to clarify the concept of public opinion theoretically, and Oswald Spengler, the author of *Decline of the West* (1918–1922) and also his teacher at the University of Berlin, who introduced him to the field of mass psychology. Mass psychology was then a relatively new field; it had been founded in the last few decades of the 19th century by the Italian criminologist Scipio Sighele, and by Gustave Le Bon and Gabriel Tarde. In his dissertation, *Masse und Publikum* (1904), published in English in 1972 as *The Crowd and the Public*, Park attempts to find a way out by attributing feelings to the crowd and reason to public opinion. Public opinion is the product of *raisonnement*, of debates in which various viewpoints are put forth, until one viewpoint finally emerges victorious and the opponents are merely subdued rather than convinced.

The method normally used to examine the concept of public opinion is exemplified by Francis G. Wilson's article in the *American Political Science Review* of 1933, "Concepts of Public Opinion" (pp. 371–391). The term is divided into the components "public" and "opinion," and then "the relation of opinion and the public, the relation of the public and government, and the relation of opinion and government" are analyzed (p. 382). These relations are characterized by the idea of *participation*. The meaning of "public" is restricted to "the body of persons having the right of participation in government" (p. 390). The pressure of this public opinion is seen as a burden upon government.

A similar approach was pursued about 30 years later by Harwood

Childs in Chapter 2 of *Public Opinion: Nature, Formation and Role*. Childs subdivides the chapter into a study of "Publics," "Opinions," and "Degree of Uniformity"; this is followed by "Process of Opinion Formation," "Quality of Opinions," "Who Holds the Opinions?" and "The Subject Matter of Opinions." He then proceeds to sketch the historical background and to characterize each decade of the 20th century with regard to topics of public opinion and techniques of influencing it. Finally, he describes how, since the 1930s, it has become more and more feasible and common to measure public opinion at regular intervals by means of public opinion polls. At this point, the chapter ends.

The great esteem in which rationality is held by Western civilization certainly explains why the concept of public opinion as the embodiment of rationality has survived. It also explains why some feel that taking apart the concept like a machine and defining the parts and their relationship to one another will enable them to grasp the nature of public opinion.

About half of the 50 definitions of public opinion compiled by Childs are rooted in the rational concept of its manifest functions in a democracy, as evidenced by the following examples: "The social judgment of a self-conscious community on a question of general import after rational, public discussion" (Young, 1923, pp. 577–578); "a substantial part of the facts required for a rational decision" (Holcombe, 1923, p. 36). At the same time, however, an underlying note of resignation can be heard: "Perhaps it sounds a bit harsh, but there is no such thing as a public opinion, and it requires only a moderate understanding of human nature to show that such a thing as an intelligent public opinion is not possible" (Jordan, 1930, p. 339).

The concept of public opinion has been, and still is, subjected to rather high-handed treatment, as if an arbitrary decision could be made on whether to retain or discard the concept or on the role it should be alloted in a democracy in the future. This tendency was apparent even in the first systematic paper on the subject, A. Lawrence Lowell's "Public Opinion and Popular Government" (1913), which is cited in Lazarsfeld's "Public Opinion and the Classical Tradition" (1957). In his article, Lowell establishes what he feels is "true" public opinion and thus ought to be heeded by the government: opinions that have been formed following thorough discussion. In addition, under his definition, only the opinions of individuals who have given thought to the matter carry any weight. And he further limits his definition by applying it only to those issues that fall under the jurisdiction of the government—not, for example, to religion.

The situation might not have changed had it not been for the dispute sparked by the emergence of the representative survey method in the early 1930s. People had no qualms speaking about "public opinion polls," about "public opinion research," or about giving the journal founded in 1937 the title, "Public Opinion Quarterly." But did the findings obtained from surveys really constitute what is called "public opinion"?

In part, researchers attempted—and are still attempting—to solve the problem by simply equating public opinion with the results of opinion polls. The strategy was to create a technical definition of public opinion, based on the tools and raw products of survey research. The following definitions are also included in Childs' chapter: "Public opinion consists of people's reactions to definitely worded statements and questions under interview conditions" (Warner, 1939, p. 377); "Public opinion is not the name of a something, but a classification of a number of somethings, which, on statistical arrangement in a frequency distribution, present modes or frequencies that command attention and interest" (Beyle, 1931, p. 183).

In his essay, "Public Opinion and the Classical Tradition," Lazarsfeld states: "Now that we have the reality of public opinion polls we will undoubtedly keep on calling public opinion a well analyzed distribution of attitudes" (1957, p. 43). In an article written on the occasion of the 50th anniversary of the *Public Opinion Quarterly*, James Beniger refers to Albert Gollin's "now ubiquitous definition of public opinion as the aggregation of individual attitudes by pollsters" (Beniger, 1987, p. 54; Gollin, 1980, p. 448).

The first researcher to take a critical view of this situation was Herbert Blumer. In his article, "Public Opinion and Public Opinion Polling," published in 1948, he sharply criticized "a paucity, if not a complete absence, of generalizations about public opinion despite the voluminous amount of polling studies of public opinion." Blumer continues,

> What impresses me is the apparent absence of effort or sincere interest on the part of students of public opinion polling to move in the direction of identifying the object which they are supposedly seeking to study, to record, and to measure. . . . They are not concerned with independent analysis of the nature of public opinion in order to judge whether the application of their technique fits that nature.
>
> A few words are in order here on an approach that consciously excuses itself from any consideration of such a problem. I refer to the narrow operationalist position that public opinion consists of what public opinion polls poll. Here, curiously, the findings resulting from an operation, or use of an instrument, are regarded as constituting the object of study instead of being some contributory addition to knowledge of the object of study. The operation ceases to be a guided procedure on behalf of an

> object of inquiry; instead, the operation determines intrinsically its own objective. . . . All that I wish to note is that the results of narrow operationalism, as above specified, merely leave or raise the question of what the results mean. (Blumer, 1953, p. 595)

Following this strong rebuff, Blumer turns to the investigation of the contents, formation and function of public opinion within a democracy, masterfully outlining the concept of a rational public opinion with its manifest function of informing politicians in a democracy about the attitudes of the functional groups that constitute a society's organizations. His primary focus is on interest groups—unions, business associations, chambers of agriculture, and ethnic groups.

Blumer does not say why these interest groups, and the pressure they exert on the politicians, may be termed "public opinion." However, he does convincingly portray the part these groups play in the formation of politicians' opinions; at the same time, he demonstrates how the politicians must take heed of the pressure exerted by these groups. Naturally, not all individuals in a society exert the same level of influence in the opinion-formation process. Many individuals enjoy high status, prestige, a high level of expertise; they are very interested and involved, they have considerable influence on a number of other persons. On the other hand, there are also individuals who show none of these qualities: they are uninterested, uninformed, and not influential. In representative surveys, however, all of these different people, whose judgment and influence do not carry the same weight, are treated equally. From the arguments presented, it is clear that Blumer does not consider surveys to be a suitable method for ascertaining public opinion.

Pierre Bourdieu advanced what were essentially the same arguments 30 years later, in his essay, "Public Opinion Does Not Exist" (Bourdieu, 1979; Herbst, 1992). At the 1991 conference of the Midwest Association of Public Opinion Research (MAPOR) in Chicago, a session was held on the topic of European concepts of public opinion, as described in a series of articles published subsequently in the *International Journal of Public Opinion Research* (see n. 2). At the session, the theories of public opinion developed by Foucault, Habermas, and Bourdieu were presented. All three of these positions are based on the assumption that opinion formation is a rational process.

Along with the growing interest in rational choice theories in the field of political science and the increasing fascination with cognitive processes among psychologists, the conception of public opinion as rationality seems to be becoming even more entrenched toward the end of this century. James Beniger, for example, expects a new paradigm to emerge along these lines. He remarked in 1987:

> If attitudes can be allowed to depend on cognition (knowledge and schemata) as well as affect . . . and possibly also on behavioral predispositions, then communication that changes "only" cognitions may be just as important to attitudinal change as communication with affective components. Indeed, public opinion research has a venerable literature suggesting that credible information can have a more lasting impact on public opinion than mere persuasive appeals. Further elaboration of the process paradigm toward the better understanding of this type of public opinion formation and change might be expected to play a central role in the pages of POQ during its second half-century. (pp. S58–S59)

PUBLIC OPINION AS A LATENT FUNCTION: SOCIAL CONTROL

At the 25th Annual Conference of the American Association for Public Opinion Research in 1970, in a session entitled "Toward a Theory of Public Opinion," Brewster Smith, a psychologist at the University of Chicago, stated that research had "not yet faced the problem of how opinions of individuals articulate to produce social and political consequences" (p. 454). In other words, there was still no answer to the question of how the sum of individual opinions, as determined by public opinion research, translates into the awesome political power known as "public opinion," with its political and social consequences.

Have we come very far since 1970, when Brewster Smith posed his impatient question? The answer to Smith's question was not forthcoming because nobody was regarding public opinion as a force capable of exerting pressure. The rational concept of public opinion does not account for the authority that public opinion must be able to wield if it is to have any influence on the government and the citizens. *Raisonnement* is enlightening, stimulating, and interesting, but it is not able to exert the kind of pressure to which—as John Locke said—not one in 10,000 remains invulnerable. Aristotle remarked, "He who loses the support of the people is a king no longer," (Aristotle, 1986, p. 1313a) while David Hume wrote, "It is . . . on opinion only that government is founded; and this maxim extends to the most despotic and most military governments, as well as to the most free and most popular" (Hume, 1741/1963, p. 29). The concept of public opinion as rationality does nothing to explain the power of public opinion. The earliest usage of the term public opinion discovered thus far is in a letter by Cicero dated 50 B.C., in which Cicero tells his friend Atticus that he had not taken on a clever opinion, but rather a false opinion due to the influence of public opinion.

The fact that "public opinion" is not to be taken lightly is indicated by John Locke, who uses the expression "Law of Opinion," explaining that the word "Law" was deliberately chosen in order to convey clearly the fact that pressure is being exerted here, that something malignant is in the offing, something that does not result directly from behavior itself—as, for example, in the case of an illness resulting from unhealthy behavior—but that is imposed *from without*. Rousseau alternates between the expressions "public opinion" and "unwritten laws." Although he also uses the word "law," this is not taken from Locke, but rather goes back to antiquity, where there was also mention of "unwritten laws" that were more carefully observed than written laws (see, e.g., Pericles' speech honoring the casualties of the Pelopponesian War: A. Niedermann, 1991). At the time of Richelieu (1585–1642), these laws were expressed in French as *Lois parlantes* (B. Niedermann, 1991). This age-old concept of public opinion was never forgotten completely, not even when the concept of public opinion as rationality began to take hold in the 19th century. In the literature on public opinion, however, the concept was not the subject of any coherent, systematic, and scholarly treatment.

In my inaugural lecture at the University of Mainz in 1965, I presented a systematic collection of empirical data and historical and literary documents that could be used to examine the concept of public opinion as social control in terms of its origin and validity (Noelle, 1966). Based on this, further empirical studies were described in 1973, ultimately leading to the development of the concept of the "spiral of silence" (Noelle-Neumann, 1973, 1984/1993).

This concept was developed to explain certain empirical findings—for example, the data obtained from our observations during the German federal elections of 1965. For more than eight months during the campaign, figures obtained on respondents' voting intentions indicated that the two major German parties were practically equal as far as voting intentions were concerned. But at the same time, the expectations as to who would win the election began to change. In our initial surveys early on in the campaign, both parties obtained equally strong results for this question, but two months before Election day, more than 50% of the population thought that one of the two parties would win, while only 16% were convinced that the other party would win. It was not voting intentions, but rather the climate of opinion that had changed completely. The theory posited that both parties were equally strong with regard to the number of supporters until only a few weeks prior to the election, but that the supporters of one party loudly voiced and publicly displayed their political convictions, while the others increasingly fell silent, and that it was this self-confident behavior in public that created the impression of one party's strength and the other's weakness.

Ultimately, the number of undecided voters who switched to the party that appeared strong in public was high enough that this party managed to win the election with a 9% lead, even though voting intentions had been neck-and-neck for such a long time. This may have appeared to be the result of the bandwagon effect, but the theory of the spiral of silence offers a different explanation.

The central assumption of this theory is that all societies threaten with isolation individuals who deviate from the consensus, and that individuals, in turn, experience fear of isolation. It is the combination of these two aspects that ensures integration and cohesion in a society, thus guaranteeing a society's ability to make decisions and take action. According to this hypothesis, the individual members of a society constantly observe their environment, in order to see which opinions and modes of behavior will win the approval of society and which will lead to their isolation. When one side in a political or social controversy is highly visible in public, other individuals adopt that position as well, displaying their convictions in public and thus reinforcing the impression that everyone else thinks that way too. When there is only low public visibility, there is a tendency for people to conceal their position in public, making this position appear even weaker than it really is and prompting others to fall silent as well.

Both the bandwagon mechanism and the spiral of silence rest on the common assumption that individuals carefully monitor the signals in their environment with regard to the strength and weakness of the various camps. But the difference lies in the motives for these observations. The bandwagon effect assumes that individuals want to be on the winning side; according to the theory of the spiral of silence, however, their motive is the desire to avoid isolation and negative sanctions.

Seven years after the theory of the spiral of silence was first formulated the same phenomenon was observed in the 1972 federal election, this time in favor of the other major political party. What are the reasons for a spiral of silence? Of course, there are differences between individuals with regard to their willingness to display their convictions in public, as well as differences in age, sex, education, articulateness, and temperament. These factors may play a role in the process of public opinion, but they cannot set a spiral of silence in motion.

In part, the notion of the spiral of silence has been grossly oversimplified, cast as a situation in which the supporters of the camp that is larger in numerical terms speak loudly and without fear of isolation in public and the supporters of the smaller camp fall silent. This oversimplified view is contradicted by the existence of the "silent majority," a phenomenon that has been empirically proven. The tenor of the media also plays an important role in the willingness to speak out, but this is also not enough to set a spiral of silence in motion. The social-psychological dynamics of approval and disapproval must come into play before the fear of isolation ultimately results in a spiral of silence. These relationships have been discussed in detail elsewhere (Noelle-Neumann, 1984/1993, 1991).

Historical studies have shown that as far back as Homer (Zimmermann, 1988) and the Old Testament (Lamp, 1988), one can find a sort of publicly displayed and publicly approved opinion, which appears under a number of different designations: "unwritten laws," "*vox populi*," "general opinion," "popular opinion," "*opinion generale*," "*pubblica voce*," and "consensus." At the time of Montesquieu, two different expressions were vying for acceptance in French, "*esprit publique*" and "*opinion publique*," with "*opinion publique*" winning in the end (Moores, 1990). The ultimate victor at that time was the expression that had persisted in many languages throughout the centuries. The two characters representing "public" and "opinion" have even been found in Chinese writings of the 4th century. From this, it seems reasonable to conclude that the term "public opinion" must be an especially effective expression of this social power. When Edward A. Ross used the term "social control," which was initially coined by Spencer (1879), for a series of articles and then in the title of a book, he was unabashedly dealing with public opinion as a form of social control (Ross, 1901/1969).

This is a far cry from the notion of public opinion as rationality, as *raisonnement*, where the best argument always wins. The concept of public opinion shaped by rationality is based on the notion of the rational, well-informed citizen capable of advancing sensible arguments and making sound judgments; it focuses on *political* life and *political* controversies. Realistically, most authors who use this concept do admit that although all citizens may potentially participate in the discussion, there is in fact only a small group of informed and interested citizens who actually do participate.

The concept of "public opinion as social control" affects *all* members of society. One must say "affects," since participation in this process of the threat of isolation and the fear of isolation is not voluntary: Rather, social control is powerful, it exerts pressure on the individual, who fears isolation, and on the government as well, which will also be isolated and eventually toppled without the support of public opinion. Considering the example of South Africa, it may even be assumed that nowadays an entire country can be isolated by universal censure until it is compelled to give in to the pressure of opinion.

The concept of public opinion as social control is not concerned with the quality of the arguments. The decisive factor is which of the two camps in a certain controversy is strong enough to threaten the opposing camp with isolation, rejection, and ostracism. Many writers have intuitively recognized that victory or defeat in the process of public opinion does not depend on what is right or wrong. Thus, as the German scholar of jurisprudence, Ihering, noted in 1883, the disapproval with which deviant behavior is punished does not have a rational character like the disapproval of "an incorrect logical conclusion, a mistake in solving an arithmetic problem, or an unsuccessful work of art," rather, it is expressed as the "conscious or unconscious practical reaction of the community to injury of its interests, a defense for the purposes of common security" (Ihering, 1883, p. 242, cf. p. 325).

In other words, this concept of public opinion is a matter of cohesion and a consensus on values in a society. This can only involve moral issues—notions of good and bad—or aesthetic issues—notions of beauty and ugliness—since only these have the emotional component capable of triggering the threat of isolation and the fear of isolation.

The concept of public opinion as social control is not as strange as it might seem to those who have grown used to the rational concept of public opinion. And this not only because the concept has been used by many authors since the Renaissance—Erasmus and Machiavelli, Sir William Temple and John Locke, David Hume and Madison, the Federalists in general, Rousseau and Tocqueville—although the concept is admittedly mentioned by these authors only in passing and is not their main focus.

Public opinion appears as the principal theme in a study by Carl von Gersdorff, "Ueber den Begriff und das Wesen der oeffentlichen Meinung" (1846). This forgotten work was rediscovered by Harwood Childs, who commented in 1965 that it was "the most detailed analysis of the subject of public opinion during the first part of the 19th century" (Childs, 1965, p. 28ff.).

Von Gersdorff did not limit public opinion to any certain historical period or to any specific area in politics, writing instead: "Public opinion, as I see it, must always exist in intellectual life . . . as long as people lead a social life." It can, he continues, "best be termed: the commonality of values a people assigns to the social subjects of its times, which is based in customs and history and is created, maintained and transformed by life's conflicts. . . . In this way, all aspects of social life are the object of public opinion" (pp. 10, 12, 5; Braatz, 1988, p. 76ff). Gersdorff suspects that a great deal of the power of public opinion is derived from the fearful silence of many individuals. He suggests "investigating the reasons for the silent abstention from making value judgments" (p. 50). Von Gersdorff also explicitly states that opinion formation processes are hardly the result of rational considerations, but are rather of psycho-anthropological origin. He writes of "galvanic currents." For a modern public opinion researcher, this immediately calls to mind the peculiar observations of how a change in a population's attitudes takes place in all groups of the population within only a few weeks' time: in the north and the south, in all age groups, in all social classes. This phenomenon must appear completely inexplicable to rationalists like Herbert Blumer or Bourdieu. But at the same time, these observations explain why the expression "climate of opinion," which was first used by Glanvill (Merton, 1949/1957), has endured throughout the centuries and why it still seems modern to us today: The way in which public opinion spreads throughout the population is strikingly similar to the climate, from which no one in a particular place and at a particular time is immune. The concept of public opinion as social control is limited only by time and place; otherwise, no topics are excluded, every topic is potentially value-laden, and every group of the population is affected. Gersdorff compares public opinion with a string instrument capable of playing all notes in the musical spectrum, yet only those strings that are actually played are heard.

Nietzsche apparently acquired his ideas on public opinion from von Gersdorff's son, who was his secretary in the 1870s, as is especially evident in Nietzsche's *Unzeitgemaessen Betrachtungen* ("Untimely Meditations," 1872/1873; cf. Braatz, 1988, p. 73). There was, in any event, never a break in the tradition of public opinion as social control. It was continued by scholars such as Edward Ross and Walter Lippmann, and Roscoe Pound, the dean of Harvard Law School, gave a lecture in 1930 titled, "Public Opinion and Social Control." In the opening article of the newly founded *Public Opinion Quarterly* (1937), Floyd Allport listed shovelling snow on the street in front of one's house as a manifestation of public opinion.

THE TWO CONCEPTS OF PUBLIC OPINION IN COMPARISON

In comparing the two different concepts of public opinion systematically, it must be emphasized that they are based on completely different assumptions about the function of public opinion. Public opinion as a rational process focuses on democratic participation and the exchange of different viewpoints in public matters, along with the demand that these ideas be heeded by the government and the concern that the opinion formation process may be manipulated by the powers of the state and capital, by the mass media and modern technology (Habermas, 1962).

Public opinion as social control is centered on insuring a sufficient level of consensus within society on the community's values and goals. According to this concept, the power of public opinion is so great that it cannot be ignored by either the government or the individual members of society. This power stems from the threat of isolation that society directs at deviant individuals and governments and from the fear of isolation, which results from the social nature of humans.

Brewster Smith was essentially asking in 1970, "How does the sum of individual opinions as determined by survey research translate into such an awesome political power, which has both political and social consequences?" Constantly monitoring the environment *and* observing the reactions of others, as expressed by the willingness to speak up or the tendency to remain silent, creates a link between the individual and society: It is this interaction that lends power to the common consciousness, common values, and common goals, along with the accompanying threats directed at those who deviate from these values and goals. The fear of isolation experienced in cases of deviation corresponds to the exhilaration felt during commonly shared group experiences. Researchers assume that these reactions evolved in the course of human development in order to ensure sufficient cohesion of human societies. Empirical evidence in support of this assumption is provided by the "experience sampling method," or EMS, which shows that being alone is connected with depression and low spirits for most people (Csikszentmihalyi, 1992).

Based on this concept, the following operational definition of public opinion may be put forth: Public opinion consists of opinions that *may* be expressed in public without risk of isolation, or opinions that *must* be expressed if one wishes to avoid isolation.

One of the major differences between the rational concept of public opinion and the concept of public opinion as social control, also called the "social–psychological dynamic concept," lies in the interpretation of the word "public." According to the democratic–theoretical concept of public opinion as the product of *raisonnement*, "public" is viewed in terms of the content of the themes of public opinion, which are political contents. The concept of public opinion as social control interprets "public" in the sense of the "public eye" (Burke, 1791/1826): "for all eyes to see," "visible to all," "*coram publico*." The public eye is the tribunal at which judgment is passed on the government and each individual.

The two concepts also diverge when it comes to the interpretation of the word "opinion." Opinion, according to the democratic–theoretical concept, is primarily a matter of opinions and arguments, whereas the concept of public opinion as social control applies it to a much greater area, in fact to everything that visibly expresses a value-related opinion in public, which may be directly in the form of opinions, but also indirectly in the form of buttons and badges, flags, gestures, hairstyles and beards, publicly visible symbols, and publicly visible, morally loaded behavior. This concept is thus able to explain phenomena above and beyond the political sphere—for example, in the area of fashion, as was already recognized not only by John Locke, but also by Socrates, who included the way sandals are tied among the unwritten laws (Plato, 1971).

This concept of public opinion may even by applied to the area of embarrassment (Goffman, 1956; Hallemann, 1989). Its relevance extends from all rules of a moral nature ("political correctness") to taboos—areas of severe, unresolved conflict that may not be addressed in public, lest social cohesion be threatened.

From the perspective of the democratic–theoretical concept of public opinion, one must take a critical stance on using the term "public opinion research" as a designation for representative surveys, as have Herbert Blumer, Bourdieu, and many other supporters of this concept. In surveys, the opinions of informed, committed, and influential persons and the opinions of uninformed, uninterested, and isolated persons are treated equally. That cannot reflect reality. According to this concept, the claim that public opinion is ascertained by means of surveys conducted among representative samples of the population must be rejected.

The situation is completely different when viewed from the perspective of public opinion as social control. This concept includes all members of society, regardless of the level of information, interest, and influence. All persons participate in the process of public opinion, in the conflict over values and goals aimed in part at reinforcing traditional values and in part at doing away with old values and replacing them with new values and goals. It is possible to observe this process with the tools of representative surveys. For the most part, however, the questions needed are much different from those included in conventional public opinion polls.

Along with questions designed to ascertain the respondent's opinion, questions on the climate of opinion are required. Respondents are asked about how they perceive their environment—What do most people think? What is increasing or decreasing?—without differentiating between opinions, symbols, fashion, and publicly visible, value-related consumer behavior. There are questions about the threat of isolation: Which supporters of which views and modes of behavior are booed? And questions are asked about the willingness to speak out and the tendency to remain silent.

According to this concept of public opinion, however, many questions included in polls today do not ascertain "public opinion." Rather, public opinion is ascertained only by questions that have something to do with value-laden opinions and modes of behavior with which the individual isolates or may isolate him- or herself in public.

Since the mid-1960s, there have been attempts to revive the concept of public opinion as social control (Noelle, 1966), but with astonishingly little success. One possible explanation for this is found in an analysis by Mary Douglas in her book, *How Institutions Think* (1986). Douglas writes, "First, on the principle of cognitive coherence, a theory that is going to gain a permanent place in the public repertoire of what is known will need to interlock with the procedures that guarantee other kinds of theories" (p. 76). Scientific theorists have developed a number of criteria that are used to test the quality of competing concepts. For example[6]:

1. Empirical applicability;
2. Determination of which findings are explained by the concept and how great the potential is for clarification;
3. Degree of complexity, that is, the magnitude of the areas included, or the number of variables included;
4. Compatibility with other theories.

The social–psychological dynamic concept of public opinion appears superior when judged by these criteria. First, it can be empirically tested. Provided that certain requirements of the theory are fulfilled,[7] it is possible to make valid forecasts on individual behavior (e.g., the tendency to speak out or remain silent) and on the distribution of opinions in society—the increase and decrease of groups holding a specific opinion (Noelle-Neumann, 1991).

It is also an explicative concept. The theory of the spiral of silence results in if–then statements—that is, it connects observable phenomena to other phenomena, by asserting and proving that there are certain social rules.

Using the rational concept of public opinion, it would be very difficult to explain the phenomenon first observed in 1965, when the stable distribution of individual opinions was accompanied by a completely independent development of the climate of opinion and a last-minute change in voting intentions. It would also be difficult to explain why the differences in the distribution of opinions among the various population segments (divided according to age, social class, etc.) are so much greater than the estimates made by the various groups about the perceived climate of opinion. And finally, it would be especially difficult to explain why those individuals who are the most informed about a certain topic—in other words, the experts—often find themselves alone in their opinion, confronted by the representatives of public opinion, journalists and individuals, who together take a position that is diametrically opposed to that of the experts. Empirical evidence on this situation has been presented by Stanley Rothman and other researchers (e.g., Snyderman & Rothman, 1988).

Third, the social–psychological dynamic concept of public opinion has a higher degree of complexity. It links the individual level with the social level, and pertains to many more areas than just politics.

The social–psychological dynamic concept of public opinion encounters the greatest difficulties when it comes to compatibility with other theories, as previously indicated. But it can be connected with social–psychological findings on group dynamics (Sherif, 1936/1965; Asch, 1951/1953, 1952) and also with Erving Goffman's social–psychological theories about embarrassment and stigmatization.

Although the capabilities of the two concepts of public opinion have been compared in this paper, this does not mean that one must choose between the two concepts as if choosing between two alternatives. The rational exchange of arguments, or *raisonnement*, does play a role in the process of public opinion, although there has been too little empirical research on this subject until now. Even morally loaded issues need cognitive support in order to assert themselves in public opinion.

The relationship between the rational concept of public opinion and the concept of public opinion as social control is perhaps best illustrated by returning to Robert Merton's differentiation between manifest and latent functions:

- *Manifest functions* are those objective consequences contributing to the adjustment or adaptation of the system which are intended and recognized by participants in the system;
- *Latent functions*, correlatively, [are] those which are neither intended nor recognized. (Merton, 1949/1957, p. 51)

It is easy to identify the manifest function of public opinion as rational discourse in the public sphere. On the other hand, the latent function of public opinion as social control, with its aim of integrating society and insuring a sufficient level of consensus, is neither intentional nor consciously recognized. This is why there are often such misapprehensions about the concept.

At the same time, this function is vital to the cohesion of society and is thus immensely powerful as a social force. Perhaps it will be possible someday, when social research has evolved further, to reconcile the intellectuals with the pressure exerted by public opinion on the individual to conform. This would turn the latent function of public opinion into a manifest function, which would thus be comprehended as a necessary force in society.

NOTES

1. Some of the present material has been included in the revised edition of *The Spiral of Silence: Public Opinion—Our Social Skin*, University of Chicago Press, 1993.

2. I am grateful to Wolfgang Donsbach for his comments on an earlier version of this chapter.

3. A forum section of the *International Journal of Public Opinion Research,* 1992, *4*(3), is devoted to the "MAPOR Session on Public Opinion Theory and Research: Critical Perspectives," held on November 22, 1991, with articles by Susan Herbst and James Beniger.

4. Cicero, *Cic. AH.* 6, 1, 18.

5. See, for example, *International Encyclopedia of the Social Sciences*, 1968, vol. 13, p. 192; *International Encyclopedia of Communications,* 1989, vol. 3, p. 387; *Staatslexikon: Recht–Wirtschaft–Gesellschaft,* 1988, vol. 4, p. 98; cf. Bucher (1887, p. 77), Bauer (1930, p. 234ff.).

6. Cited in accordance with Wolfgang Donsbach's letter of January 20, 1992, in which he discusses these criteria and their applicability to the theory of the spiral of silence.

7. For example, topicality, the moral or aesthetic component, and the position of the mass media.

REFERENCES

Allport, F. H. (1937). Toward a science of public opinion. *Public Opinion Quarterly, 1,* 7–23.

Altschuler, B. E. (1990). Review of *Political culture and public opinion. American Political Science Review, 84,* 1369–1370.

Aristotle. (1986). *Politik.* (O. Gigon, Ed. and Trans.). Munich: Deutscher Taschenbuch Verlag. [English edition: (1959): *Politics*. (H. Rackham, Trans.). London: Heinemann.]

Asch, S. E. (1951). Effects of group pressure upon the modification and distortion of judgments. In H. Guetzkow (Ed.), *Groups, leadership, and men.* Pittsburgh: Carnegie. Reprinted in: D. Cartwright and A. Zander (Eds.), (1953). *Group dynamics: Research and theory* (pp. 151–162). Evanston, IL: Row, Peterson and Co.

Asch, S. E. (1952). Group forces in the modification and distortion of judgments. In *Social psychology* (pp. 450–473). New York: Prentice Hall.

Bauer, W. (1930). *Die Oeffentliche Meinung in der Weltgeschichte*. Wildpark-Potsdam: Akademische Verlagsgesellschaft Athenaion.

Beniger, J. R. (1987). Toward an old new paradigm. The half-century flirtation with mass society. *Public Opinion Quarterly, 51*, S46–S66.

Beniger, J. R. (1992). The impact of polling on public opinion: Reconciling Foucault, Habermas and Bourdieu. *International Journal of Public Opinion Research, 4*(3), 204–219.

Berger, A. A. (1989). *Political culture and public opinion*. New Brunswick, NJ: Transaction Publishers.

Beyle, H. C. (1931). *Identification and analysis of attribute-cluster-blocs*. Chicago: University of Chicago Press.

Blumer, H. (1953). Public opinion and public opinion polling. In B. Berelson & M. Janowitz (Eds.), *Reader in public opinion and communication* (pp. 594–602). Glencoe, IL: The Free Press.

Bourdieu, P. (1979). Public opinion does not exist. In A. Mattelart & S. Siegelaub (Eds.), *Communication and class struggle* (Vol. 1, pp. 124–130). New York: International General.

Braatz, K. (1988). *Friedrich Nietzsche—Eine Studie zur Theorie der Oeffentlichen Meinung*. Monographien und Texte zur Nietzsche Forschung, no. 18. Berlin: de Gruyter.

Bryce, J. (1888–1889). *The American commonwealth* (2 Vols). London: Macmillan.

Bucher, L. (1887). Ueber politische Kunstausdruecke. *Deutsche Revue*, no. 12, pp. 67–80.

Burke, E. (1826). An appeal from the new to the old Whigs. In *The works of the Right Honourable Edmund Burke* (Vol. VI, pp. 73–267). London: C. and J. Rivington. (Original work published in 1791)

Childs, H. L. (1965). *Public opinion: Nature, formation and role*. New York: D. van Nostrand.

Cicero, M. T. (1990). *Atticus-Briefe, Lat.-dt.* (H. Kasten, Ed.). Darmstadt: Wissenschaftliche Buchgesellschaft.

Csikszentmihalyi, M. (1992, January 22). *Public opinion and the psychology of solitude*. Paper presented at the Johannes Gutenberg University of Mainz.

Davison, W. P. (1968). Public opinion: Introduction. In D. L. Sills (Ed.), *International encyclopedia of the social sciences* (Vol. 13, pp. 188–197). New York: Macmillan Co. and The Free Press.

Douglas, M. (1986). *How institutions think*. Syracuse, NY: Syracuse University Press.

Gersdorff, C. E. A. von (1846). *Ueber den Begriff und das Wesen der oeffentlichen Meinung. Ein Versuch*. Jena: J. G. Schreiber.

Glanvill, J. (1661). *The vanity of dogmatizing: Or confidence in opinions: Manifested in a discourse of the shortness and uncertainty of our knowledge, and its causes: With some reflexions on peripateticism: And an apology for philosophy*. London: E. C. for Henry Eversden at the Grey-Hound in St. Pauls-Church-Yard.

Goffman, E. (1956). Embarrassment and social organization. *The American Journal of Sociology, 62*, 264–271.

Gollin, A. E. (1980). Exploring the liaison between polling and the press. *Public Opinion Quarterly, 44*, 445–61.

Goodnight, T. (1992). Habermas, the public sphere and controversy. *International Journal of Public Opinion Research, 4*(3), 243–255.

Habermas, J. (1962). *Strukturwandel der Oeffentlichkeit. Untersuchungen zu einer Kategorie der buergerlichen Gesellschaft*. Neuwied: Luchterhand.

Hallemann, M. (1989). *Peinlichkeit. Ein Ansatz zur Operationalisierung von Isolationsfurcht im sozialpsychologischen Konzept oeffentlicher Meinung*. Dissertation, Johannes Gutenberg-Universitaet, Mainz.

Herbst, S. (1992). Surveys in the public sphere: Applying Bourdieu's critique of opinion polls. *International Journal of Public Opinion Research, 4*(3), 220–229.

Holcombe, A. W. (1923). *The foundations of the modern commonwealth*. New York: Harper & Row.

Hume, D. (1963). *Essays moral, political and literary*. London: Oxford University Press. (Original work published in 1741)

Ihering, R. von (1883). *Der Zweck im Recht* (Vol. 2). Leipzig: Breitkopf & Hartel.

International encyclopedia of communications. (1989). New York: Oxford University Press.

Jordan, E. (1930). *Theory of legislation*. Indianapolis: Progress Publishing Company.

Lamp, E. (1988). *Oeffentliche Meinung im Alten Testament. Eine Untersuchung der sozialpsychologischen Wirkungsmechanismen oeffentlicher Meinung in Texten alttestamentlicher Ueberlieferung von den Anfaengen bis in babylonische Zeit*. Dissertation, Johannes Gutenberg-Universitaet, Mainz.

Lazarsfeld, P. F. (1957). Public opinion and the classical tradition. *Public Opinion Quarterly, 21*, 39–53.

Lowell, A. L. (1913). *Public opinion and popular government*. New York: Longmans, Green, & Co.

Merton, R. K. (1957). *Social theory and social structure*. Glencoe, IL: The Free Press. (Original work published in 1949)

Moores, K. M. (1990). *Die oeffentliche Meinung im Werk Montesquieus*. Master's thesis, Johannes Gutenberg-Universitaet, Mainz.

Moscovici, S. (1991). Silent majorities and loud minorities. Commentary on Noelle-Neumann. In J. A. Anderson (Ed.), *Communication yearbook, 14* (pp. 298–308). Newbury Park, CA: Sage.

Niedermann, A. (1991). *Ungeschriebene Gesetze. Ein sozialpsychologischer Ansatz zur Beschreibung des Spannungsfeldes zwischen oeffentlicher Meinung und Recht*. Dissertation, Johannes Gutenberg-Universitaet, Mainz.

Niedermann, B. (1991). *Oeffentliche Meinung and Herrschaft am Beispiel des erfolgreichen Politikers Kardinal Richelieu*. Master's thesis. Johannes Gutenberg-Universitaet, Mainz.

Noelle, E. (1966). *Oeffentliche Meinung und soziale Kontrolle*. Tuebingen: J.C.B. Mohr (Paul Siebeck).

Noelle-Neumann, E. (1973). Return to the concept of powerful mass media. *Studies of Broadcasting, 9*, 67–112.

Noelle-Neumann, E. (1993). *The spiral of silence: Public opinion—Our social skin*. Chicago/London: University of Chicago Press. (Original English edition published in 1984) [German edition (1980): *Die Schweigespirale: Oeffentliche Meinung—unsere soziale Haut*. Munich/Zurich: Piper. Revised and enlarged German edition (1989): *Oeffentliche Meinung: Die Entdeckung der Schweigespirale*. Frankfurt and Berlin: Ullstein.]

Noelle-Neumann, E. (1991). The theory of public opinion: The concept of the spiral of silence. In: J. A. Anderson (Ed.), *Communication Yearbook, 14*, (pp. 256–287). Newbury Park, CA: Sage.

Oncken, H. (1914). Politik, Geschichtsschreibung und oeffentliche Meinung. In *Historisch-politische Aufsaetze und Reden* (Vol. 1, 203–243). Munich: R. Oldenbourg.

Palmer, P. A. (1950). The concept of public opinion in political theory. In B. Berelson & M. Janowitz (Eds.), *Reader in public opinion and communication* (pp. 3–13). Glencoe: The Free Press. (Original work published in 1936)

Park, R. E. (1975). *The crowd and the public and other essays* (H. Elsner, Jr., Ed.; C. Elsner, Trans.). Heritage of Sociology Series. Chicago: University of Chicago Press. (Original work published in 1972)

Peer, L. (1992). The Practice of opinion polling as a disciplinary mechanism: A Foucauldian perspective. *International Journal of Public Opinion Research, 4*(3), 230–242.

Plato. (1971). *Werke in acht Bänden. Griech.-dt.* (G. Eigler, Ed.). Darmstadt: Wissenschaftliche Buchgesellschaft.

Pound, R. (1930). Public opinion and social control. *Proceedings of the National Conference of Social Work*. 57th annual session held in Boston, MA, June 8–14. Chicago, IL: University of Chicago Press.

Ross, E. A. (1969). *Social control: A survey of the foundations of order*. Cleveland and London: The Press of Case Western Reserve University. (Original work published in 1901)

Rusciano, F. L., & Fiske-Rusciano, R. (1990). Toward a notion of "world opinion." *International Journal of Public Opinion Research, 2*(4), 305–322.

Sherif, M. (1965). *The psychology of social norms*. New York: Octagon Books. (Original work published in 1936)

Sills, D. L. (Ed.) (1968). *International encyclopedia of the social sciences*. New York: Macmillan.

Smith, B. (1970). Some psychological perspectives on the theory of public opinion. *Public Opinion Quarterly, 34*, 454–455.

Snyderman, M., & Rothman S. (1988). *The IQ controversy. The media and public policy*. New Brunswick, NJ: Transaction Books.

Speier, H. (1950). Historical development of public opinion. *American Journal of Sociology, 55*, 376–388.

Spencer, H. (1966). The data of ethics. In *The works of Herbert Spencer* (Vol. 9). *The principles of ethics* (Part 1, pp. 1–303). Osnabrück: Otto Zeller. (Original work published in 1879)

Staatslexikon. Recht–Wirtschaft–Gesellschaft. (1988). Freiburg, Basel, and Vienna: Verlag Herder.

Warner, L. (1939). The reliability of public opinion surveys. *Public Opinion Quarterly, 3*, 376–390.

Wilson, F. G. (1933). Concepts of public opinion. *American Political Science Review, 27*, 371–391.

Young, J. T. (1923). *The new American government and its work*. New York: Macmillan & Co.

Zimmerman, T. (1988). *Das Bewusstsein von Oeffentlichkeit bei Homer*. Master's thesis, Johannes Gutenberg-Universitaet, Mainz.

3

Levels of Analysis in Public Opinion Research

Jack McLeod
Zhongdang Pan
Dianne Rucinski

Public opinion has been regarded as the embodiment of the "consent of the governed" in democratic systems. The basis of American government, Jefferson claimed, was the opinion of the people (Jefferson, 1787/1903–1904). In his view, public opinion, though sometimes momentarily led astray, was self-correcting and the only legitimate censor of government. We can find this Jeffersonian view of public opinion in various theories of democracy (see Sartori, 1987) and in various working models of American politics (see Bennett, 1980; Corbett, 1991).

Due to its theoretical and practical importance, the concept of public opinion has attracted much attention from scholars in diverse fields of social and behavioral science. But the treatment of the concept has not yet gone much beyond elusive descriptions of "public sentiment" and numerical reports of opinion poll results. The failure to come to grips with the perplexing problems of its definition has frustrated the development of empirically grounded theories of public opinion. One consequence of the lack of conceptual analysis has been the disconnection of two fundamental ways in which the phrase "public opinion" has been used. First, public opinion is used to refer to opinions affecting and being influenced in the *public* arena by major social and political institutions, such as government, the media, schools, industries, and so on. Second, public opinion refers to individual persons making judgments that are sometimes expressed *publicly* about *public* issues.

Normative and other nonempirical theories of democracy (see Sartori, 1987) conceive of public opinion in its first implied meaning, as a societal phenomenon closely tied to political institutions in democratic processes. Such theories give little consideration to how individuals form, maintain, and change their opinions. Critics have charged that such abstract conceptions have at times presented public opinion as a reified entity imbued with properties, purposes, and dynamics of individuals, yet independent of individuals (Allport, 1937; Bourdieu, 1972).

In contrast, theories of opinions and attitudes are formulated to address the individual cognitive level. In these theories, opinions and their formation and change are described as individuals' cognitive and affective activities. Individual opinions are social at most in that individual sentiments are affected by interactions with others in diverse settings. Largely overlooked in this second meaning of public opinion is how societal institutions affect individual opinions and how it is that individual opinions get transformed into collective actions and social structural processes (Rusciano, 1989).

For most people, however, contact with public opinion comes not directly from either type of meaning but rather through reports of surveys or polls conducted with cross-sectional samples of individuals. Opinions reported in polls are "public" in two senses: first, they often deal with public policies and societal issues (i.e., opinions about public issues), and second, they are thought to represent opinions of publics in America or in other societal units (i.e., opinions of publics) through the process of aggregation (Sartori, 1987). Aggregation, either across all respondents (e.g., x% of Americans favor capital punishment) or of a sub-group (e.g., x% of women agree with a pro-choice statement), is used to infer public opinion at the societal level. But throughout the history of public opinion research, this aggregation procedure has been the subject of criticism (see Lowell, 1913; Blumer, 1948; Bourdieu, 1972; Lemert, 1981; Price & Roberts, 1987). An important tenet common to these critiques is that reducing public opinion to aggregations of individual responses fails to make conceptual correspondences and theoretical connections between individual opinions and macro-level public opinion (Lemert, 1981, p. 9).

These critiques of public opinion make it clear that the concept of public opinion must be viewed as representing complex social and political processes that involve individuals, groups, and organizations, as well as institutions. A multilevel perspective is needed to examine the linkages and mechanisms both within and across the micro and macro levels of analysis. Such a perspective may help to avoid segmenting the components of complex processes into isolated bits and pieces. This chapter presents such a multilevel perspective, and discusses strategies for linking micro and macro levels.

PUBLIC OPINION AS PROCESSES

The key problem underlying the various conceptions of public opinion is how to link the "unenlightened" and "diffused" individual sentiments with the opinion process as they interact with public policies (Neuman, 1986; Ferejohn, 1990). Although it has been recognized that public opinion is most appropriately viewed as a complex process (e.g., Price & Roberts, 1987), little progress has been made toward the difficult task of developing empirically testable propositions linking the components of the process across different levels of abstraction. Bryce (1900) anticipated this task in his description of public opinion processes at the turn of this century. We are following Bryce's lead in presenting a graphic depiction of public opinion processes (see Figure 3.1).

In this model, we assume that the initiation of the process is some kind of occurrence—event, policy move, social change, and so on. If sufficiently strong, this occurrence may initiate processes at both the individuals and social system levels. At the individual level, this occur-

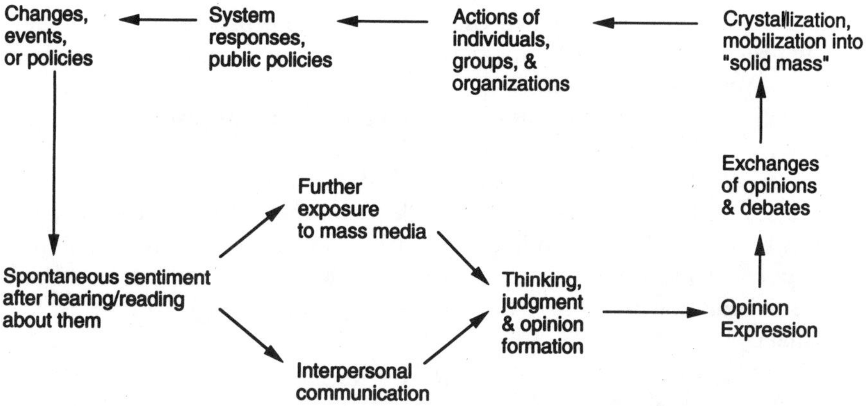

FIGURE 3.1. A schematic representation of Bryce's description of public opinion process.

rence may activate minimally some diffuse, unfocused, nonarticulated sentiment in certain individuals. Maximally, it might in some other individuals connect with well-developed opinions or attitudes through available sociocognitive interpretive frameworks.

At the social systems level, the occurrence may capture the attention of system surveillance processes—for example, people start talking about it and media begin covering it. The activated mass and interpersonal communications function as important processes for people to develop their previously unfocused sentiments into more specific opinions. The communication activities accelerate as people begin expressing their opinions at varied levels of articulation with individual opinions becoming crystallized into the opinions of a *public*—that is, a group of individuals with shared interests or concerns over a particular policy issue. Such a transformation of individual opinions into "public opinions" involves the processes characterized by (1) public policy debates and deliberations, in which political leaders or elites representing different constituents articulate their opinions and influence the course of opinion development, and (2) opinion alignment and representations, in which coherent group opinions are formed through negotiations and promotion by social organizations.

Mass media have dual functions in these processes: as a conduit of debates and negotiations as well as a source of influence. Media possess the resources to gather and disseminate information about a news event or an issue. They also may choose various options: to portray the distribution of public sentiments concerning the event or issue; to represent the conceptions and opinions of different groups concerning the event or issue; and to specify the language and symbols used as tools for debates and negotiations over the event and issue. Mass media, therefore, are uniquely placed in the system and the process to exert influences on the relationships both within the micro and macro levels and across the two levels.

Finally, political debates and opinion alignment lead to calls for actions by different interest groups. These actions may in turn lead to responses at the system level: modification or innovations in public policies and/or changes of political leaders, and so on. An excellent illustration of this dynamic process from an occurrence to a system response is presented in a case study describing the campaign against the nomination of Robert Bork to the Supreme Court (Pertschuk & Schaetzel, 1989).

This process model presents public opinion as crucial to important aspects of social change. We must make it clear, however, that of the many occurrences in the social environment few reach the final stage of inducing policy or social change. Many are not strong enough to initiate the process and others are absorbed or atrophy in one of the intermediate stages.

Two additional qualifications to the descriptive model need to be made. One is that some issues become prolonged public concerns because consensus formation is prevented by a special balance of power among the publics holding different positions. Examples of these issues include stricter gun controls and environmental conservation. Another qualification is that the notion of a sequential process does not preclude the possibility of simultaneous activation of various components of the public opinion process. In fact, with increasing frequency the formation of individual opinions and public policy decisions occur almost simultaneously. Two factors have contributed to this trend: the instantaneous reporting of public sentiment and public policies by electronic media and the tendency for policy makers to consider policy issues based on anticipated public reactions (Protess et al., 1987; Cook, 1989).

A FRAMEWORK OF FOUR TYPES OF RELATIONSHIPS

The public opinion process depicted in Figure 3.1 is highly complex. Neither micro theories of individual attitude change nor macro theories of society alone can provide sufficient theoretical accounts of this process. A clear understanding of the public opinion process, therefore, requires an integrated multilevel perspective.

A multilevel perspective needs clear distinctions between micro-level individual and macro-level social concepts, as well as specification of linkages between the two sets of concepts. Concepts such as individuals' opinions and policy makers' perceptions are clearly appropriate to the micro level, while concepts such as public opinion and public policies and their implementation are clearly appropriate to macro-level analysis. Linkages between these two sets of concepts are called cross-level linkages.

For most practical and theoretical purposes, it is useful to consider a modified Coleman model of four types of relationships: macro–macro, micro–micro, macro–micro, and micro–macro (Coleman, 1986, 1987; Pan & McLeod, 1991). We can use a diagram to represent the four types of relationships:

At the micro–micro level, researchers examine individual cognitive and affective processes of opinion formation, change, and expression (e.g., Sniderman, Brody, & Tetlock, 1991; Iyengar, 1990). Such micro–micro relationships are represented in Figure 3.1 by the psychological processes of individuals following exposure to occurrences and events:

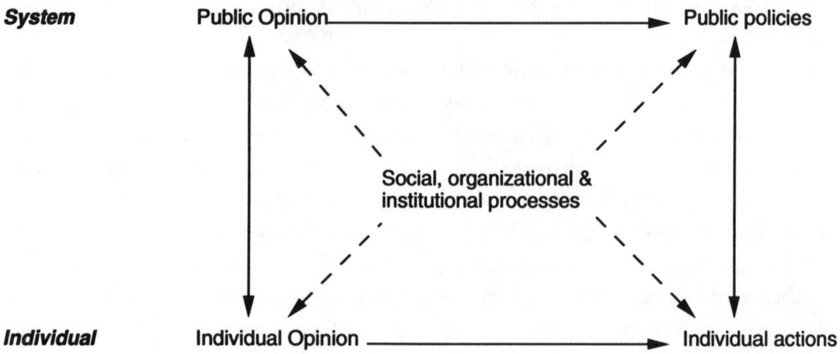

FIGURE 3.2. Four types of relationships. Adapted from Pan and McLeod (1991).

developing diffused sentiments, thinking about the issues, and forming their opinions. At the macro–macro level, questions related to public opinion, public policies, and the roles of mass media in linking the two, are dealt with (e.g., Best, 1973; Caldeira, 1987; Herman & Chomsky, 1988; Linsky, 1986; Page & Shapiro, 1992). For example, we can consider the relationships in Figure 3.1 of political actions taken by political groups and responses in public policies as macro–macro relationships.

The two within-level relationships are connected by cross-level linkages. Two types of such linkages are distinguished: macro–micro and micro–macro. This distinction is based on the enactment of different sources of influence and implied directional flow of these influences. For example, a candidate's campaign spending, strategies, and messages are designed to influence individual voters' perceptions of the candidate or his or her opponents. This part may be described as a macro–micro process because of a top-down flow of influences. But effects on a single individual are virtually meaningless to the macro electoral process because one person's vote almost never determines an election outcome. When functioning in an institutionalized system, individuals' actions under certain conditions may be consolidated as system level effects (Ferejohn, 1990; Carmines & Kuklinski, 1990). This latter part represents a micro–macro process due to an opposite flow of influence.

Various concepts in the literature are useful to describing the two types of cross-level linkages. The concept of *social control* refers to a "top-down" process from macro-level social institutions to micro-level individuals. The notion of *aggregating* individual opinions into "public opinion" refers to a "bottom-up" process of transactions of power and influence resulting in their accumulation as systemic level factors. But not all cross-level linkages are unidirectional. Many cross-level concepts describe bidirectional processes between two persons, between individuals and groups, organizations, or institutions. For example, the concept of reference group comparison refers not only to the influence of the group's norms, codes, and behavioral patterns, but also to the individual's perception of these norms, codes, and patterns (Festinger, 1954; Newcomb, 1958; Kelley, 1968). The distinction between the two types of cross-level linkages often can be clarified by examining the specific research question. For example, if a research question asks how public communication helps organize individual opinions into effective public opinion, then one needs to examine the cross-level linkage from micro to macro. If one tries to examine effects of mass media coverage of an issue on individuals' opinions about the issue, it would be necessary to look at the macro–micro cross-level linkage.

We must point out here that the designation of the concepts at a given level as macro or micro is relative to what other set of concepts is being used for comparison. In other words, there is a continuum from micro to macro (Eulau, 1986, 1977), and the terms "micro level" and "macro level" are meaningful only in specified theoretical domains. As Eulau (1986) says, "What in this continuum is micro and what is macro depends on the point on the micro–macro scale where the observer 'dips in,' where he fixes the object unit of analysis." Further, "what is micro and what is macro . . . changes with changing theoretical standpoints" (Eulau, 1986, p. 90). In public opinion research, there are no "natural units" that can be readily utilized to distinguish micro and macro levels. Rather, distinguishing and linking various levels can only be made via careful specification of concepts and their variations.

As Figure 3.2 implies, the cross-level view of public opinion processes takes the two cross-level linkages as equal in importance to the within-level linkages. Cross-level connections are not simply matters of statistical data manipulation such as data reduction or aggregation, even though these are among the necessary operational procedures. Rather, the procedure here is first to specify "cross-level auxiliary theories" that "connect micro and macro processes" (Hannan, 1971, pp. 4–5), and then to test the hypotheses derived from these "auxiliary theories." Auxiliary theories refer to functional relationships between micro and macro variables (Hannan, 1971). But very often in public opinion research, the cross-level linkages are the central focus of research (e.g., Price, 1988). In this case, cross-level linkages become an integral part of theory construction rather than being relegated to an "auxiliary" position. Figure 3.2 implies equal importance of all four types of relationships. Further, in this multilevel framework, cross-level linkages can be explicated using diverse theoretical perspectives of social, organizational, and institutional processes. This point will be elaborated further in a later section.

CONCEPTUALIZING TWO WITHIN-LEVEL RELATIONSHIPS FOR CROSS-LEVEL EXPANSION

This multilevel framework may help to shed new light on some of the concepts traditionally used to describe and explain the two within-level relationships. While recognizing the need to avoid the logical fallacies that may result from casual crossing of the levels of analysis by clearly specifying within-level concepts (Reeves, 1989), our framework also argues for theoretical explication of the two cross-level linkages to more fully appreciate the theoretical richness of within-level theories. What this means is that we should use as criteria for evaluation of various within-level concepts, not only the usual scientific criteria, but also their standing on the dimension of "level-friendliness," that is, their potential to be connected to levels above or below their usual levels of conceptualization. Such a conceptual exercise helps to accumulate those concepts within each level that are expandable beyond their original level of residence. Indeed, even a nonsystematic review of the existing literature reveals a rich repertoire of "level-friendly" concepts.

Micro-Level Individual Relationships

According to our multilevel framework, micro individual relationships describe the cognitive, affective, motivational, and personality bases of individuals' attitude development and change, as well as opinion formation and expression. The processes at this level, as they are depicted in Figure 3.3, may be categorized by three types of related activities: media exposure and processing behavior, cognitive processing and inference making, and opinion expression.

In this descriptive model, individuals are represented as actors who make decisions at every step of opinion formation. Decision making may operate either through conscious efforts or in a more habitual fashion involving very low levels of cognitive resources. Further, this model assumes that most individuals first encounter occurrences that initiate the public opinion process through mass media news coverage. The news input has two functions for individuals: as one source of informational input into their cognitive systems and as a framework

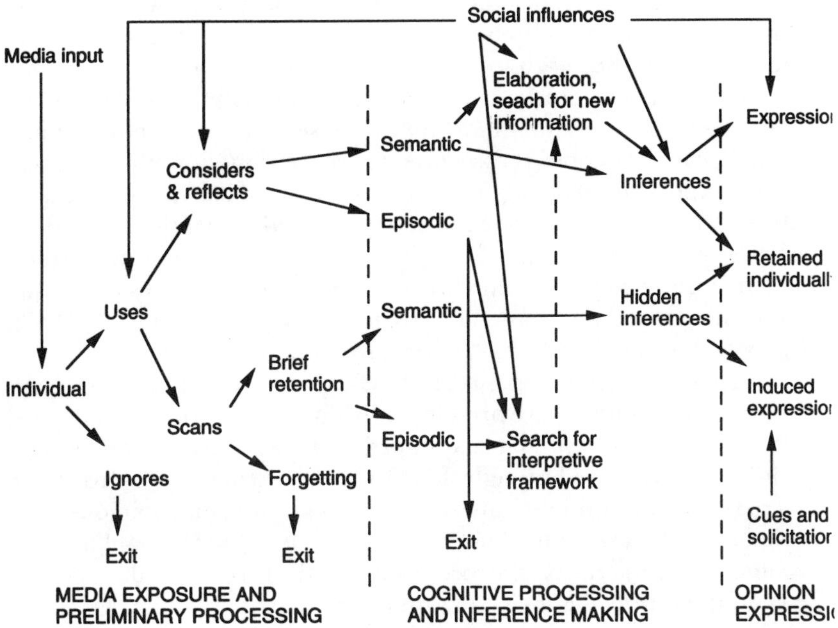

FIGURE 3.3. A schematic representation of micro-level opion formation processes.

structuring their cognitive understanding of various public policy issues and events.

News input does not automatically have an impact on audience members. Rather, individual actors may choose either to attend to media messages or to ignore them. More generally, audience members develop relatively stable and distinctive patterns of media use and media orientations (McLeod & McDonald, 1985; Blumler & Katz, 1974). They also adopt various molar strategies: for example, selective scanning rather than more completely auditing news, active processing rather than passively accepting content, thinking and reflecting about it later rather than merely consuming it at the moment of exposure (Kosicki, McLeod, & Amor, 1986; Kosicki & McLeod, 1990; Graber, 1988).

The choice among the strategies will have consequences as to how information is to be stored in memory: forgotten, fragmented, or organized (see Gunter, 1987; Robinson & Levy, 1986). For those who choose to think and reflect on the news stories actively, the stories may be retained in a better-organized fashion for a longer period of time. For those people who lack interpretive frameworks, memory of news items will be episodic, while for others who possess such frameworks, it may be semantic in nature (Shoben, 1984; Graber, 1988; McLeod, Pan, & Rucinski, 1989). But even for the latter, certain details are likely to be lost (Gunter, 1987). Stories that have been stored episodically will become meaningful only after individuals find suitable interpretive frameworks. For many people, these stories are simply lost. For others, search for more information through either mass media or interpersonal channels will continue. When a news story is stored semantically, further elaboration may take place. This process involves fitting a news story into an existing cognitive framework and making inferences about the causal antecedents and consequences of the story (McLeod et al., 1989; Neuman, Just, & Crigler, 1992; Iyengar, 1991).

Individual opinions arise from these cognitive activities. When conducive social conditions are present, individuals may express their opinions in particular ways that may function as input triggering certain cross-level processes. Through these processes, activities may move to macro levels. But, under many circumstances, individual opinions may be kept within the individual rather than being made "public," or become lost in micro-social processes ineffectively connected by power or communication channels to more macro units.

Many theories and models have been developed to account for individual opinion formation and change. Two of them appear to hold a greater promise for cross-level applications: cognitive consistency theories and information processing perspectives.

Cognitive consistency theories focus on the elements of individuals' cognitive structures (Markus & Zajonc, 1985). The common premise shared by the most influential consistency theories (Heider, 1958; Festinger, 1957; Osgood & Tannenbaum, 1955) concerns the structural dynamics of individuals' cognitions: an inconsistent cognitive configuration is in a state of tension, and the tension calls for resolution directed toward restoring consistency (balance, consonance, or congruency). Among the possible resolutions is the modification of certain cognitive elements: attitudes, opinions, perceptions, and so on.

Although cognitive consistency theories have been widely applied to provide intraindividual motivational explanations of attitude and opinion changes, they also provide a rich repertoire of concepts that are potentially level-friendly. For example, conflict among cognitive elements may be connected to conflict among social groups and interests through applications of theories of social perception, categorization, and judgment procedures (e.g., social stereotyping and its role in attitude change). Research in this area would focus on relationships between social and cultural climate and individual cognitive elements of different social groups, interpersonal relationships, intergroup relationships, as well as of relationships between individuals and groups or organizations. Most important to cross-level theorizing in public opinion research is that cognitive consistency theories articulate mechanisms of social influence on individual cognitions and attitudes. A research example of such cross-level expansion might be that of balance theory (Heider, 1958) being applied in the analysis of interpersonal communication process (e.g., Newcomb, 1958; McLeod & Chaffee, 1972). In mass communication research, tensions among internal cognitive elements have been considered an important factor conditioning media influences, mainly through selective exposure behavior (e.g., Frey, 1986).

If earlier cognitive consistency theories focused on "hot cognitions"—that is, structural tensions of cognitive elements and the resulting motivational forces—the recent information processing approach focuses on "cold cognitive structure" (Markus & Zajonc, 1985). Cognitive representations of events, issues, objects, and persons are the major concerns. Individuals' cognitive representations are assumed to consist of relatively abstract units, such as, schemata, scripts, categories, and frames (Hastie, 1981; Wyer & Srull, 1981; Cantor & Mischel, 1979; Schank & Abelson, 1977; Rumelhart, 1984). These units form structural configurations (Collins & Loftus, 1975; Anderson, 1983) according to their semantic proximity and degrees of accessibility (Wyer & Srull, 1989). Cognitive representations have inferential properties—that is—generating schematically consistent information and inferences—as well as behavioral implications such as aiding cognitive tactics to economize information processing tasks (Iyengar, 1990; Graber, 1988).

Concepts developed in this approach may be expanded for cross-level theorizing. For example, the notion of *concept accessibility* (Higgins & King, 1981; Wyer & Srull, 1981) may be conceptually expanded to become a link in macro–micro influences: the frequencies and emphasis of media coverage of issues as macro-level variables are translated into micro-level conditions influencing individuals' perceptions of issue salience and causal attributions of public policy issues (Iyengar & Kinder, 1987; Iyengar, 1991). Another research example comes from the application of the schema concept to account for the development of "frames of reference" shared by collections of individuals (Schramm, 1972; Snow, Rochford, Worden, & Benford, 1986). In the macro–micro process, individual schemata are developed through sharing common symbolic resources and packaged information supplied by the media (Gamson & Modigliani, 1989; Edelman, 1988). A third example is how media news content may affect individuals' causal attribution concerning responsibility and consequences of government policies (Kinder & Mebane, 1983; Iyengar, 1991). News coverage may place stories in explicit causal contexts or imply who or what is responsible through devices such as personalization and metaphors. Micro-level individual attributions, when articulated, may be consolidated into macro-level public opinions concerning public policies and political candidates. Although further development of "level-connecting" concepts is needed to make full use of their potential, these examples do illustrate how micro-level concepts may be expanded to connect with macro-level processes.

Mass media play a key role in cross-level processes through their influences on individuals. Studies of media effects on individuals may benefit greatly from cross-level expansion of the micro-level concepts. One promising application of the microlevel concepts is the examination of mass media influences on people's reasoning process in addition to knowledge and opinion outcomes media content might induce (Pan & Kosicki, 1994). Mass media initiate cognitive and affective activities within individuals through messages attributes, including: (1) content, that is, main themes, concepts, ideas; (2) appeals to fear, joy, reasoning, and so on, and (3) textual and visual structures (Reeves, Thorson, & Schleuder, 1986; van Dijk, 1988). Researchers have related these dimensions of message attributes to activation of certain concepts and causal contexts and short cuts in processing new information (Iyengar, 1990, 1991; McLeod et al., 1989) and to the usage of certain symbolic devices in public policy reasoning (Gamson & Modigliani, 1989; Lakoff, 1991). More traditional studies may also benefit from applying these micro-level concepts. For example, cognitive concepts may be used to study media influences on perceived opinion distributions in a population (Noelle-Neumann, 1984) and perceptions of media effects on others (Davison, 1983).

Macro-Level System Relationships

The theoretical significance of public opinion as a concept requires consideration of its macro-level characteristics. That is, public opinion is assumed to represent certain collective properties of a general public. It is thought to play a vital role in connecting system changes and public policy initiatives (Best, 1973; Sartori, 1987). Further, it is presumed to be the standard for measuring public consent to government, including giving legitimacy to those who are selected and placed in decision making roles and the processes of public policy deliberation and implementation. The macro–macro processes are represented in descriptive terms in Figure 3.4.

Parallel with Figure 3.1, the initiation of the macro processes of public opinion are occurrences: for example, events, policy changes,

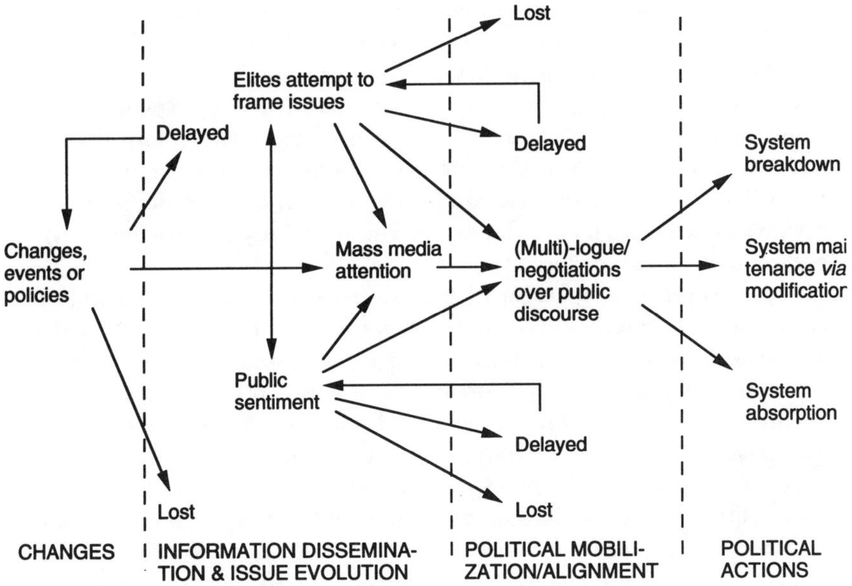

FIGURE 3.4. A schematic representation of macro-level processes of public opinion.

and activities of interest groups or individuals. Those events that do reach the threshold of media surveillance will get mass media coverage (Carmines & Stimson, 1989). Several factors may influence the entry of certain issues or events into public discourse, as it is shown in some macro-level oriented "agenda-setting" and "gatekeeping" research (e.g., Donohue, Tichenor, & Olien, 1972; Brosius & Kepplinger, 1990; Neuman, 1990). Mass media may play a significant role at this early stage: reflecting or even determining the threshold levels, reflecting public sentiment and elites' reactions, with the officials and political elites providing the initial frames or definitions of issues, and supplying symbolic tools such as metaphors, images, and catch phrases that become important parts of an issue culture (Carmines & Stimson, 1989; Cobb & Elder, 1983; Gamson & Modigliani, 1989).

Issues that have caught the attention of both elites and the general public with sufficiently strong forces may continue to evolve into policy and political controversies. Different political forces, interest groups as well as individuals, might join the political debates, engage in negotiations and in the development of political discourses. Political alignment and mobilization may follow. Mass media continue to play important roles in this process through their coverage of the debates and by the distribution of simple pro and con measures of "public opinion."

As a result of these activities, a system is ready to respond. System responses could range from system breakdown (e.g., revolutionary transitions of East European nations), to system absorption—that is, when a system digests the changes or disguises and/or marginalizes them. Under certain specific conditions, a system may modify itself in certain ways through changes in legislation, in bureaucratic hierarchy, and/or in political leadership.

The central component of this macro process is the dynamic of issue management and evolution (Carmines & Stimson, 1989; Margolis & Mauser, 1989). An issue may be defined as a specific social, political, economic, or public policy concern that involves different perceptions of causal attribution, consequences, and solutions. There are three major active forces in issue evolution: political elites, the general public, and mass media (see Blumler & Gurevitch, 1981).

Political elites are defined as those who have direct access to political power, organizational resources, knowledge and expertise, as well as to communication channels. They include politicians, spokespersons of interest groups or government agencies, and leading journalists and commentators. Issues are often sponsored, defined, and promoted by these elites for the purpose of advancing their own policy agenda and/or maximizing their group's interests (Gamson, 1988).

Political elites' efforts in issue definition and promotion have direct consequences for determining the agenda of political discussion. For example, since Franklin Roosevelt, the executive branch of the U.S. government has increasingly intensified its efforts to shape public opinion or, at least, to "prepare" the public for new and unproven federal policies (Steele, 1985; Page & Shapiro, 1989). Increasingly, political leaders rely on public relations specialists and image makers to cultivate their own images, to ridicule those of the opposition, and to frame issues (e.g., Bloom, 1973; Ansolabehere, Behr, & Iyengar, 1991). We may recall how Ronald Reagan used an "evil empire" label to describe the Soviet Union in order to justify his program of expanding defense spending and how George Bush used the "pledge of allegiance" and prisoner furlough to define his opponent's image.

Other political elites also appear to have significant impact on public opinion. For example, there is at least some empirical evidence showing the Supreme Court leading public opinion (Marshall, 1987; Caldeira, 1987; Franklin & Kosaki, 1989). Page, Shapiro, and Dempsey (1987) found that news commentators, experts, and popular presidents all were able to push public opinion in the directions that they advocated. Erikson and his colleagues (Erikson, McIver, & Wright, 1987; Erikson,

Wright, & McIver, 1989) found that political parties in each state appeared to function as forces intervening between state policies and aggregate public opinion at the state level. Stimson (1991) showed swings and cycles of greater scopes and time lapses that aggregate American public opinions on domestic policies seemed to reveal historically.

Clearly, all these macro-level efforts are directed toward cultivating individuals' perceptions of issues and candidates. Therefore, concepts employed at this level in analyzing issue evolution can be fruitfully connected to such micro-level concepts as schema, category accessibility, affect toward a candidate, and so on. Moreover, studies at the macro level also require micro-level analysis of individuals in each of the macro categories: political elites, media professionals, and general public.

At the macro level, the media industry is located at a pivotal position in public opinion processes (Blumler & Gurevitch, 1981; Turow, 1984; Gandy, 1982; Herman & Chomsky, 1988). With some gross simplification, we may summarize the roles of mass media at the macro level in terms of four theoretical relationships: (1) the relationship between concentration of ownership and diversity of perspectives represented in media content; (2) the relationships between legal stipulations on freedom of press, prior restraint, libel and slander, and the coverage of political issues and events; (3) the relationships between news departments and the profit-seeking organizations in which they belong, as well as the relationships between media organizations and other business organizations; and (4) the relationships between media organizations as fully legitimized organizations and other special interest groups and/or social movements that are attempting to gain legitimation. Serious efforts are needed in cross-level explication to trace these macro relationships across levels: from institution to industry, to organization, to departments and roles within organizations. A variety of mechanisms and constraints constitute the operating principles of relationships across levels: legal restraints and sanctions; allocation of resources; constraints resulting from the nature of the medium; bureaucratic structures and rules; professional working principles and rewards; and role relationships between journalists, sources, and the public. These operating principles, deriving in large measure from the macro relationships, constitute the framework within which individual journalists define and carry out their work.

EXPLICATING CROSS-LEVEL PROCESSES

The potential of many within-level concepts to be extended or connected to another level of analysis has been noted earlier. From these "level-friendly" concepts, the development of a multilevel perspective of public opinion requires two critical steps: the explication of "level-connecting" concepts and the specification of cross-level theoretical propositions that are testable and/or consistent with the two within-level theoretical formulations (Hannan, 1971).

The specification of the two types of cross-level linkages represents two prototypical cross-level concerns. First, how are individuals influenced by forces beyond their own physical, cognitive, and affective states? Second, how are individual opinions and actions consolidated into social and political forces that lead to systemic responses? Perhaps the best place to "dip in" to seek theoretical answers to these questions may be the individual's behavior in specific social situations.

On the macro–micro crossing, researchers need to explicate structural constraints and incentives that members of organizations or groups experience and to which they react and to conceptualize the mechanisms of social influences. Structural constraints and incentives were examined in the previous section on macro–macro relationships. The mechanisms of social influence need some elaboration.

Social influences operating on those individuals who use various sources for information emanate from those who construct and transmit such information. These influences are multi-faceted: acquisition of information, arrangement of perceived issue priorities; framing of issues in cognitive configurations; formation and change in opinions; motivation to express opinions; and modes of expression as shaped by political resources. Familiar concepts are used to describe such influence processes: for example, persuasion, conformity, cultivation, social learning.

Channels of influence pervade modern society (Pratkanis & Aronson, 1991). Intentional individual choice in exposure to information may play an increasingly minor role in the influence process as paid advertising and "free" media persuasive attempts have become more ubiquitous and sophisticated. Going to party rallies and meeting candidates, however, characterize only a small portion of the American electorate (Verba & Nie, 1972; Neuman, 1986). Resistance to mediated "conversion" attempts continue to be fostered by socioeconomic location and by partisan political attachments (Berelson, Lazarsfeld, & McPhee, 1954; Erikson et al., 1987; Huckfeldt & Sprauge, 1990). The individual may be influenced, nonetheless, without active information seeking. Such influence may come from two different sources: from involuntary contact with media messages and from the person's social environment.

The micro–macro crossing raises issues such as whether individuals can make any difference at the system level and, if so, how this takes place. The theoretical concern is to describe and explicate the process of integration and consolidation of individuals up into publics and systems. This process develops in parallel with the one that runs in the opposite direction—that is the process of macro–micro influences. Arithmetic aggregation of individual opinions is not a theoretically satisfactory cross-level mechanism partly because it is based upon some false and unworkable assumptions. One such assumption is that a democratic system is based upon equal representation and equal participation on the basis of equal interest and information. It has been argued that this assumption is not only an unrealistic ideal but that perhaps it is also an undesirable objective (Ferejohn, 1990; Carmines & Kuklinski, 1990). Participation through individual actions, according to this argument, becomes meaningful at the system level only if it takes place through transactions of power in an institutional context, which means the interplay of micro–macro and macro–micro processes.

Various reasons are offered for asserting that the equal participation assumption is problematic. First, attempts by individuals to affect change in the system are rarely successful unless they are part of joint efforts. Joint efforts require that individuals recognize which others have common interests, and that they are able to organize themselves in ways that can accumulate and effectively use power. However, media access needed for information dissemination and mobilization is always limited and unequally distributed. Inequality is thus a chronic condition of the social system.

Second, political participation occurs in various modes, with differing degrees of potential for particular kinds of influences on system level responses (Verba & Nie, 1972). The common modes of participation include voting to elect officials to public office, expressing opinions to legislators by lobbying or petitions, presenting legal cases directly to courts, attending meetings or rallies for a candidate or cause, and promoting certain opinions to influence opinion climates as well as public discourse. Not all these modes of participation can be employed with equal effectiveness by people with differing political resources.

Third, a modern democratic system has built-in incentives for individuals with political resources, talent, and ambition to champion and articulate issue positions of interest groups. These visible champions of various groups, in turn, serve to anchor opinions and voting decisions of the general public (Carmines & Kuklinski, 1990).

The interplay of macro–micro and micro–macro influences can be seen in the nomination of Supreme Court justices. In the Robert Bork case, a temporary coalition among various interest groups and forces in Congress was among the decisive factors leading to the defeat of the nomination (Pertschuk & Schaetzel, 1989). The coalition largely succeeded in framing the issue in the terms that had a broad appeal and in motivating people with diverse interests and opinions to work for the common goal: defeating the nomination. In this process, opinions were constantly negotiated and modified so as to produce a coherent presentation with a single goal. This is the micro–macro part of the dynamic. At the same time, various structural factors might have contributed to the meanings of individual actions to the system responses and the success of the coalition: sending a conservative to the high court in this case would decisively shift the court to a new ideological balance feared by people from a wide spectrum of the society; Bork had left a clear paper trail pointing to his strongly conservative stance; and his testy demeanor before the Congressional committee was consistent with the public image of an ideologue. Oppositional forces were unable to mount a unified campaign in the subsequent Supreme Court nominations of David Souter, who left few traces of his views, nor of Clarence Thomas, who was both humble and infinitely willing to retract any clear views previously stated.

Many theoretically interesting formulations may be developed to describe and account for the two cross-level linkages. Our model distinguishes three types of mechanisms: social, organizational, and institutional. *Social processes* refer to the mechanisms of interpersonal interaction and group dynamics and exchanges through culturally shared symbols. Examples of social processes that can be borrowed for public opinion research include reference group influences (Festinger, 1954; Shibutani, 1955), minority and majority influences (Moscovici & Lage, 1976), coorientation (McLeod & Chaffee, 1972), conformity (Asch, 1956), and bargaining and coalition formation (Komorita & Kravitz, 1983). *Organizational processes* refer to the mechanisms and procedures that are directly related to the hierarchy of organizational composition and role structure (Whitney, 1982; Gurevitch & Blumler, 1982; Dimmick, 1979), while *institutional processes* refer to the constraints resulting from formally established regulations and legitimacy, as well as shared norms, values, and standard practices (Hughes, 1969; Tuchman, 1978; Gandy, 1982; Turow, 1984; Herman & Chomsky, 1988).

We believe that a clear distinction among social, organizational, and institutional processes serves the purpose of theoretical integration. Too often, researchers cultivate their research territories in one or another domain without specifying the points and mechanisms of connections with others. For example, researchers interested in minority and majority influences most often examine anonymous individuals in experimentally formed groups without connecting them to the development of more stable social groups or organizations. In many organizational studies, organizational structure is very often taken as an exogenous entity, without its being connected to the social process of transforming informal social interactions into structural patterns (cf. Turner, 1988).

The roles of mass media in the cross-level processes may be constructed in terms of their functions as (1) channels or connectors, (2) change agents, and (3) epistemological devices.

As channels or connectors, mass media make it possible for the communications essential for public opinion processes to occur among three categories of actors: political elites, journalists, and the general public. Individuals in each of the three categories have different levels of control over media channels for information gathering and dissemination and also for receiving and comprehending messages.

Mass media also function as a major source of influence. Mass media have been utilized as key channels in communication campaigns designed for behavioral changes and changes in public perceptions of certain issues (Rogers & Storey, 1987). Mass media also take initiatives to exert influence on the salience of various issues through, for example, relatively in-depth theme or issue reporting in network evening news programs (e.g., The American Agenda on ABC). Mass media's change agent role in the public opinion processes is reflected in several other ways: in the increasing frequency of their carrying packaged public relations materials (Cook, 1989); in their reluctance to present dissent (Herman & Chomsky, 1988); in their ability to frame news events or issues in particular ways (Gamson, 1988; Pan & Kosicki, 1993); and in the scarcity of mobilizing information (Lemert, 1981)—for example, instructions about how and when meetings will take place, where to register to vote, and public service ads instructing people to seek help or to provide help.

The concept of mass media functioning as epistemological devices shows a direct linkage from macro-level operations of media and collective culture to individual cognitive processes. Mass media not only provide information to audiences in general, but also influence what we know and how we know (Kosicki & McLeod, 1990; Kosicki et al., 1986). Pertinent to cross-level linkages is the roles that mass media play in connecting each individual's quest to know to the collective efforts to know. Transformation of individual attention regarding an issue to aggregate level salience of the issue is one example (McCombs & Shaw, 1972; Funkhouser, 1974; Iyengar & Kinder, 1987). Providing the statistics or impressions for us to develop rather accurate perceptions of opinion climate and trends is another example (Noelle-Neumann, 1984). In addition, mass media also stimulate and provide the language for interpersonal discussions (Katz & Lazarsfeld, 1955; Chaffee, 1972; Gamson, 1988) and establish the behavioral premises for such interactions by "informing" us how other people may have been influenced by mass media (Perloff, 1989; Mutz, 1989).

Despite the temptation and need to do so, we must acknowledge that it is much beyond the scope of this chapter to develop substantive theories of the cross-level linkages in public opinion processes. The best we can do here is to discuss five dimensions that locate the diverse theoretical formulations in the existing literature. Together, these dimensions may help to outline a broad territory where scholars might search for theoretical insights from existing literature and develop new "level-connecting" concepts.

1. *Unidirectional versus bidirectional formulations*. Certain cross-level formulations assume unidirectional causal flow while others allow for reciprocal influences. Concepts such as institutionalization, control, allocation of resources and opportunities, acculturation, aggregation, and "mainstreaming" represent unidirectional conceptions of cross-level linkages. They assume that societal level properties do not involve interactions and structural constraints among members of the society (Eulau, 1986; Bunge, 1977–1979). In contrast, concepts such as socialization (when conceived as reciprocal influences between agent and socializee), conformity, and coorientation involve bidirectional processes between individuals and society.

2. *Direct effects versus internalization formulations*. Cross-level linkages can be differentiated according to whether they are assumed to have direct cause-and-effect impact or to have indirect relationships mediated by individuals' internalization of societal influences. For example, those forms of using power associated with coercion are not concerned with the internalization process that involves opinion or belief change along with behavioral change. But institutionalization may involve recognizing and accepting institutional rules, norms, and values. Not all the cross-level concepts can be clearly distinguished as representing either direct effects or internalization formulations. For example, conformity may or may not involve internalization (Asch, 1956). It is not at all clear in the "spiral of silence" theory (Noelle-Neumann, 1984) whether individuals who remain silent when on the minority side of opinion trends will internalize the majority opinion or merely retain their original opinions in silence.

3. *Individual-centered versus society-centered formulations*. Differences also exist among various theoretical formulations as to whether individuals or social systems are conceived of as being the locus of enactment. Notions such as coercion and social control clearly attribute the primary role to society. In contrast, concepts such as those of social interaction and coorientation allow individuals more freedom of action.

In the "spiral of silence" theory, fear of isolation is the primary intraindividual motivational force behind unwillingness to express opinions when on the minority side. Although opinion expression certainly involves action initiated by individuals, the true force comes from social pressures of "public opinion" (Noelle-Neumann, 1984). At this level, the theoretical formulation is "society-centered."

4. *Conflict versus constraint formulations*. In constructing cross-level linkages, social processes can be conceptualized as either being dominated by conflicting groups of individuals who act to maximize their own interests or as individuals being constrained by socioeconomic status, norms, organizational hierarchies, and other sources of structural constraints. Conflict theories (e.g., Marxist theories) tend to focus on inevitable conflict of interests and are oriented toward large-scale or revolutionary change. Structural constraint theories (e.g., functionalist theory) tend to be oriented toward social order and structure or to focus on the conflicts inherent in certain structural formulations that provide the vitality and energy for dynamic changes (e.g., Tichenor, Donohue, & Olien, 1980). Concepts such as those describing control strategies and motivation to maximize group interests are consistent with conflict theories. But concepts such as "fear of isolation" and conformity tend to be constraint theories.

5. *Static versus dynamic formulations*. Another important distinction among various cross-level linkages is whether the focus is on social change or maintenance of the system equilibrium. All theories of social change involve cross-level mechanisms. For example, in theories of political movements and revolution, political mobilization is conceived as mechanisms leading to social change (Cameron, 1974). Concepts such as social control and conformity are major mechanisms for system stability.

SUMMARY AND REFLECTIONS

In this chapter, we presented a multilevel framework to conceptualize public opinion processes. The key components of this framework are: (1) the two within-level and two cross-level relationships and (2) the dynamics of the probabilistic sequences as processes at each of the levels connected by cross-level linkages.

Over the years, scholars have made serious efforts to deal with some persistent conceptual difficulties in public opinion research. These difficulties are exemplified in the sharp contrast between the complexities of structure and dynamic processes that we would like to capture in our conceptual definitions, and the simplistic measurement of public opinion as aggregates of static observations of individual opinions recorded in public opinion polls. In the multilevel framework, two processes are seen as developing in close connection: individual opinion formation and expression on the one hand, and the linking of public opinion and public policy on the other. The mechanisms that connect the two include social interactions and organizational dynamics, as well as the institutional norms and values that account for the formation, articulation, and negotiation of collective opinions and decision making.

It is essential to develop cross-level theories if we are to understand such multilevel dynamics. Through the multilevel framework, public opinion is no longer a reified macro-level entity nor is it a simple aggregate of individual reports in opinion polls. Rather, it is an important theoretical construct needed to understand the social and political dynamics of modern democracy. Public opinion as generally conceived and measured may have some pragmatic validity in describing and even predicting aggregate reactions to specific policy statements, but it may lead to a dangerously simplistic view of democracy as "majority rule" (Sartori, 1987; Laufer & Paradeise, 1990).

It also becomes problematic when we attempt to apply simplistic notions of public opinion to our understanding of the issues such as policy making, social movements, public consent *versus* individual opinions, and so on. For example, the dispute over the "causal" relationship between public policies and the state of public opinion cannot be resolved without a clear theoretical formulation of the processes linking individual members first to integrated publics and then to individual decision makers. At a more pragmatic level, a multilevel conception of public opinion is also very important. Without such a theoretical development, it will continue to be difficult for public opinion researchers to predict the future state and direction of public opinion or to assess the antecedents that are responsible for the formation and change of public opinion.

The multilevel framework discussed in this chapter represents a start toward developing multilevel models of the public opinion process. Despite the complexity of this multilevel framework, it is only a simplified approximation of the actual public opinion process. It is simplified in several respects, which can be delineated as follows.

First, for ease of presentation, the continuum of micro and macro is reduced to two discrete levels: micro and macro. In addition, we also simplified each level by discussing only micro-individual and macro-societal levels. Between these two levels, many possible levels of analysis may be interjected. Levels are also possible outside of the macro and micro terms as we use them. For example, studies on persuasion may be conducted at the psychophysiological level below the cognitive domain of our micro individual level (e.g., Reeves et al., 1986; Cacioppo & Petty, 1989). In a specific research project, the macro level could be at the level as low as a (micro social) dyad or family (McLeod & Chaffee, 1972; Chaffee, McLeod, & Wackman, 1973) or as high as communities and neighborhoods (see Glynn, Ostman, & McDonald, Chapter 10 in this volume), social institutions (e.g., Blumler & Gurevitch, 1981; Blumler, 1983), or societies (e.g., Ingelhart, 1990; Almond & Verba, 1963). The micro and macro levels and the labels representing the variables at each of the levels (see Figure 3.2) are only used as generic terms to encompass the broad range of possible theoretical formulations along the micro and macro continuum (Eulau, 1986; Pan & McLeod, 1991). A researcher operating within this multilevel metatheoretical framework may choose more empirically fine-tuned concepts to develop his or her unique theoretical perspective.

Second, the two figures (Figures 3.3 and 3.4) depicting the dynamic nature of the micro and macro processes also oversimplify the range of responses at each successive stage. In addition, each depicts only a linear sequential process, while our conceptual framework calls for an endogenous feedback process at each level. Although representation as a series of dichotomous choices may improve understanding, we may come closer to reality by conceiving responses at each stage as falling on a continuous scale and each choice on that scale as carrying with it certain probability contingent upon a host of factors. One of the response categories with a non-zero probability is the feedback loop. For example, it is conceivable that individuals may choose to replay the act of exposure to the messages that they have already processed at conscious level. At this stage, the model presented in this chapter only serves a descriptive function because it does not contain the conceptual and empirical bases for specifying the possible range of responses at each stage and the factors that affect the probability of each.

Third, the multilevel model presented in this chapter lacks a clear theoretical specification of individual occurrences. This omission reflects our lack of conceptual understanding of issue evolution as a joint process of individual cognition and social interactions. We argued in this chapter that not all occurrences will stimulate the necessary responses to complete the multistage process at each level. In other words, not all occurrences will become public issues that will stir strong enough public concern to initiate complete multilevel processes. In such cases, the question becomes what types of variations in occurrences are responsible for the variations in subsequent responses. In other words, what conceptual attributes of occurrences will allow us to predict the various responses at each stage? Empirical success of this multilevel perspective of public opinion seems to depend fundamentally on the development an empirical theory of issue evolution, which in turn depends on the successful conceptual classification of issues on the basis of a few manageable attributes.

Clearly, the multilevel perspective is not meant to be equivalent to an empirical model to be tested in a single study. It is entirely possible and even desirable to isolate one set of relationships and test it thoroughly in a specific study. But the theoretical significance of one's formulation of an empirical hypothesis may very well depend on whether the hypothesis is consistent with other relationships in a multilevel theory. A hypothesis isolated from such a theoretical context is likely to contribute little to the much needed theoretical development on public opinion. In addition, specific methodological approaches to empirical public opinion research also may be assessed in the context of this multilevel perspective. Public opinion polling practices may continue to be an important part of the repertoire of tools for public opinion research. The difference now is that, with the multilevel framework, we may be on a more solid theoretical ground to assess the validity of poll data and the utility of polling practices instead of equating polls with states of public opinion, as it is commonly done.

The multilevel perspective by its nature calls for diversity in research methodology (Pan & McLeod, 1991). First, studies designed to test different types of relationships ask very different research questions about diverse units of analysis. They are likely to require different types of data. The diversity in research questions and units of analysis imply methodological pluralism: varied combinations of methods, types of evidence, and analytical strategies. Also implied is the desirability of adopting comparative frameworks across time and space (Blumler, McLeod, & Rosengren, 1992; Przeworski & Teune, 1970). To identify contextual effects in the public opinion process, systematic differences in culture and social units need to be identified and analyzed while study of social units over longer and shorter time periods provides the dynamic changes necessary to study public opinion as a process.

Second, not all relationships in a multilevel model are empirically testable with quantitative data. Statistical analysis of multilevel data has been a major challenge to social and behavioral scientists (e.g., Goldstein, 1987). In multilevel research, then, logical coherence as a criterion in assessing theories becomes even more significant. It is possible that one may test a within-level relationship that is logically derived from a coherent cross-level theory, or vice versa. In the conduct of multilevel public opinion research, a researcher's imagination and creativity are the only real limitations on developing theoretical propositions to be tested and combining research methods to be employed.

REFERENCES

Allport, F. H. (1937). Toward a science of public opinion. *Public Opinion Quarterly 1*, 7–23.

Almond, G. A., & Verba, S. (1963). *The civic culture: Political attitudes and democracy in five nations*. Princeton: Princeton University Press.

Anderson, J. R. (1983). *The architecture of cognition*. Cambridge, MA: Harvard University Press.

Ansolabehere, S., Behr, R., & Iyengar, S. (1991). Mass media and elections: An overview. *American Politics Quarterly 19*, 109–139.

Asch, S. E. (1956). Studies of independence and conformity: A minority of one against a unanimous majority. *Psychology Monograph 70* (9, Whole No. 416).

Bennett, W. L. (1980). *Public opinion in American politics*. New York: Harcourt Brace & Jovanovich.

Berelson, B., Lazarsfeld, P. F., & McPhee, W. N. (1954). *Voting: A study of opinion formation in a presidential campaign*. Chicago: University of Chicago Press.

Best, J. J. (1973). *Public opinion: Micro and macro*. Homewood, IL: Dorsey Press.

Bloom, M. H. (1973). *Public relations and presidential campaigns: A crisis in democracy*. New York: Crowell.

Blumer, H. (1948). Public opinion and public opinion polling. *American Sociological Review 13*, 542–554.

Blumler, J. G. (Ed.) (1983). *Communicating to voters: Television in the first European parliamentary elections*. Newbury Park, CA: Sage.

Blumler, J. G., & Gurevitch, M. (1981). Politicians and the press: An essay in role relationships. In D. Nimmo & K. Sanders (Eds.), *Handbook of political communication* (pp. 467–493). Beverly Hills, CA: Sage.

Blumler, J. G., & Katz, E. (Eds.) (1974). *The uses of mass communications: Current perspectives on gratifications research*. Beverly Hills, CA: Sage.

Blumler, J. G., McLeod, J. M., & Rosengren, K. E. (Eds.) (1992). *Comparatively speaking: Communication and culture across space and time*. Newbury Park, CA: Sage.

Bourdieu, P. (1972). Public opinion does not exist. In A. Mattelart & S. Siegetaub (Eds.), *Communication and class struggle: Part I. Capitalism and imperialism* (pp. 124–130). New York: International General.

Brosius, H. B., & Kepplinger, H. M. (1990). The agenda-setting function of television news. *Communication Research 17*, 183–211.

Bryce, J. (1900). *The American commonwealth II*. New York: Macmillan.

Bunge, M. A. (1977–1979). *Treatise on basic philosophy* (Vols. 3–4). Dordecht, Holland: D. Reidel.

Cacioppo, J. T., & Petty, R. E. (1989). Social psychophysiology: A new look. In L. Berkowitz (Ed.), *Advances in experimental social psychology 22* (pp. 39–91). New York: Academic Press.

Caldeira, G. A. (1987). Public opinion and the U.S. Supreme Court: FDR's court-packing plan. *American Political Science Review 81*, 1139–1153.

Cameron, D. R. (1974). Toward a theory of political mobilization. *Journal of Politics 36*, 138–171.

Cantor, N., & Mischel, W. (1979). Prototypes in person perception. In L. Berkowitz (Ed.), *Advances in experimental social psychology 12* (pp. 4–54). New York: Academic Press.

Carmines, E. G., & Stimson, J. A. (1989). *Issue evolution: Race and the transformation of American politics*. Princeton: Princeton University Press.

Carmines, E. G., & Kuklinski, J. H. (1990). Incentives, opportunities, and the logic of public opinion in American political representation. In J. Ferejohn & J. Kuklinski (Eds.), *Information and democratic processes* (pp. 240–268). Urbana: University of Illinois Press.

Chaffee, S. H. (1972). The interpersonal context of mass communication. In F. Kline & P. Tichenor (Eds.), *Current perspectives in mass communication research* (pp. 95–120). Beverly Hills, CA: Sage.

Chaffee, S. H., McLeod, J. M., & Wackman, D. B. (1973). Family communication patterns and adolescent political participation. In J. Dennis (Ed.), *Socialization to politics* (pp. 349–364). New York: Wiley and Sons.

Cobb, R. W., & Elder, C. D. (1983). *Participation in American politics: The dynamics of agenda-building* (2nd ed.). Baltimore: The Johns Hopkins University Press.

Coleman, J. S. (1986). Social theory, social research, and a theory of action. *American Journal of Sociology 91*, 1309–1335.

Coleman, J. S. (1987). Microfoundations and macrosocial behavior. In J. Alexander, B. Giesen, R. Munch, & N. Smelser (Eds.), *The micro–macro link* (pp. 153–176). Berkeley: University of California Press.

Collins, A. M., & Loftus, E. F. (1975). A spreading-activation theory of semantic processing. *Psychological Review 82*, 407–428.

Cook, T. E. (1989). *Making laws and making news: Media strategies in the U.S. House of Representatives*. Washington, DC: The Brookings Institution.

Corbett, M. (1991). *American public opinion: Trends, processes, and patterns*. New York: Longman.

Davison, W. P. (1983). The third-person effect in communication. *Public Opinion Quarterly 47*, 1–15.

Dimmick, J. (1979). The gatekeeper: Media organizations as political coalitions. *Communication Research 6*, 203–222.

Donohue, G. A., Tichenor, P. J., & Olien, C. N. (1972). Gatekeeping: Mass media systems and information control. In F. Kline & P. Tichenor (Eds.), *Current perspectives in mass communication research* (pp. 41–69). Beverly Hills, CA: Sage.

Edelman, M. J. (1988). *Constructing the political spectacle*. Chicago: University of Chicago Press.

Erikson, R. S., McIver, J. P., & Wright, G. C., Jr. (1987). State political culture and public opinion. *American Political Science Review 81*, 797–813.

Erikson, R. S., Wright, G. C., Jr., & McIver, J. P. (1989). Political parties, public opinion, and state policy in the United States. *American Political Science Review 83*, 729–749.

Eulau, H. (1977). Multilevel methods in comparative politics. *American Behavioral Scientist 21*, 39–62.

Eulau, H. (1986). *Politics, self, and society: A theme and variation*. Cambridge, MA: Harvard University Press.

Ferejohn, J. A. (1990). Information and electoral process. In J. Ferejohn & J. Kuklinski (Eds.), *Information and democratic processes* (pp. 3–17). Urbana: University of Illinois Press.

Festinger, L. (1954). A theory of social comparison processes. *Human Relations* 7, 117–140.

Festinger, L. (1957). *A theory of cognitive dissonance*. Stanford, CA: Stanford University Press.

Franklin, C. H., & Kosaki, L. C. (1989). Republican schoolmaster: The U.S. Supreme Court, public opinion, and abortion. *American Political Science Review 83*, 751–771.

Frey, D. (1986). Recent research on selective exposure to information. In L. Berkowitz (Ed.), *Advances in experimental social psychology 19* (pp. 41–80). New York: Academic.

Funkhouser, G. R. (1974). The issues in the sixties: An exploratory study in the dynamics of public opinion. *Public Opinion Quarterly 37*, 62–75.

Gamson, W. A. (1988). A constructionist approach to mass media and public opinion. *Symbolic Interaction 11*, 161–174.

Gamson, W. A., & Modigliani, A. (1989). Media discourse and public opinion on nuclear power: A constructionist approach. *American Journal of Sociology 95*, 1–37.

Gandy, O. H., Jr. (1982). *Beyond agenda setting: Information subsidies and public policy*. Norwood, NJ: Ablex.

Goldstein, H. (1987). *Multilevel models in educational and social research*. London: Charles Griffin and Company, Ltd.

Graber, D. A. (1988). *Processing the news: How people tame the information tide* (2nd ed.). New York: Longman.

Gunter, B. (1987). *Poor reception: Misunderstanding and forgetting broadcast news*. Hillsdale, NJ: Lawrence Erlbaum.

Gurevitch, M., & Blumler, J. G. (1982). The construction of election news at the BBC: An observational study. In J. Ettema & D. Whitney (Eds.), *Individuals in mass media organizations: Creativity and constraint* (pp. 179–204). Beverly Hills, CA: Sage.

Hannan, M. T. (1971). *Aggregation and disaggregation in sociology*. Lexington, MA: Lexington Books.

Hastie, R. (1981). Schematic principles in human memory. In E. Higgins, C. Herman, & M. Zanna (Eds.), *Social cognition: The Ontario Symposium 1* (pp. 39–88). Hillsdale, NJ: Lawrence Erlbaum.

Heider, F. (1958). *The psychology of interpersonal relations*. New York: Wiley and Sons.

Herman, E. S., & Chomsky, N. (1988). *Manufacturing consent: The political economy of the mass media*. New York: Pantheon Books.

Higgins, E. T., & King, G. (1981). Accessibility of social constructs: Information-processing consequences of individual and contextual variability. In N. Cantor & J. Kihlstrom (Eds.), *Personality, cognition, and social interaction* (pp. 69–121). Hillsdale, NJ: Lawrence Erlbaum.

Huckfeldt, R., & Sprague, J. (1990). Social order and political chaos: The structural setting of political information. In J. Ferejohn & J. Kuklinski (Eds.), *Information and democratic processes* (pp. 23–58). Urbana: University of Illinois Press.

Hughes, E. C. (1969). Institutions. In A. Lee (Ed.), *Principles of sociology* (pp. 125–185). New York: Barnes and Noble Books.

Inglehart, R. (1990). *Culture shift in advanced industrial society*. Princeton: Princeton University Press.

Iyengar, S. (1990). Shortcuts to political knowledge: The role of selective attention and accessibility. In J. Ferejohn & J. Kuklinski (Eds.), *Information and democratic processes* (pp. 160–185). Urbana: University of Illinois Press.

Iyengar, S. (1991). *Is anyone responsible? How television frames political issues*. Chicago: University of Chicago Press.

Iyengar, S., & Kinder, D. R. (1987). *News that matters*. Chicago: University of Chicago Press.

Jefferson, T. (1903–1904). *The writings of Thomas Jefferson* (20 Vols.) (A. Lipscomb, Ed.). Washington, DC. (Original work written in 1787)

Katz, E., & Lazarsfeld, P. F. (1955). *Personal influence*. New York: Free Press.

Kelley, H. H. (1968). Two functions of reference groups. In H. Hyman & E. Singer (Eds.), *Readings in reference group theory and research* (pp. 77–93). New York: Free Press.

Kinder, D. R., & Mebane, W. R., Jr. (1983). Politics and economics in everyday life. In K. Monroe (Ed.), *The political process and economic change* (pp. 389–425). New York: Agathon Press.

Komorita, S. S., & Kravitz, D. A. (1983). Coalition formation: A social psychology approach. In P. B. Paulus (Ed.), *Basic group process* (pp. 179–204). New York: Springer-Verlag.

Kosicki, G. M., & McLeod, J. M. (1990). Learning from political news: Effects of media images and information processing strategies. In S. Kraus (Ed.), *Mass communication and political information processing* (pp. 69–83). Hillsdale, NJ: Lawrence Erlbaum.

Kosicki, G. M., McLeod, J. M., & Amor, D. L. (1986). *Processing the news: Some individual strategies in selecting, sense-making, and integrating*. Paper presented at the International Communication Association Convention, Chicago, IL.

Lakoff, G. (1991). The metaphors of war. *Propaganda Review 8*, 18–21, 54–59.

Laufer, R., & Paradeise, C. (1990). *Marketing democracy: Public opinion and media formation in democratic societies*. New Brunswick, NJ: Transaction Publishers.

Lemert, J. B. (1981). *Does mass communication change public opinion after all?* Chicago: Nelson-Hall.

Linsky, M. (1986). *Impact: How the press affects federal policymaking*. New York: W. W. Norton.

Lowell, A. L. (1913). *Public opinion and popular government*. New York: Longman, Green and Co.

Margolis, M., & Mauser, G. A. (Eds.) (1989). *Manipulating public opinion: Essays on public opinion as dependent variable*. Pacific Grove, CA: Brooks/Cole Publishing Company.

Markus, H., & Zajonc, R. B. (1985). The cognitive perspective in social psychology. In G. Lindzey & E. Aronson (Eds.), *The handbook of social psychology I* (3rd ed., pp. 137–230). New York: Random House.

Marshall, T. R. (1987). The Supreme Court as an opinion leader. *American Politics Quarterly 15*, 147–168.

McCombs, M. E., & Shaw, D. L. (1972). The agenda-setting function of mass media. *Public Opinion Quarterly 36*, 176–187.

McLeod, J. M., & Chaffee, S. H. (1972). The construction of social reality. In J. Tedeschi (Ed.), *The social influence processes* (pp. 50–99). Chicago: Aldine.

McLeod, J. M., & McDonald, D. (1985). Beyond simple exposure: Media orientations and their impact on political processes. *Communication Research 12*, 3–33.

McLeod, J. M., Pan, Z., & Rucinski, D. M. (1989). *Framing a complex issue: A case of social construction of meaning*. Paper presented at the International Communication Association Convention, San Francisco, CA.

Moscovici, S., & Lage, E. (1976). Studies in social influence: III. Majority versus minority influence in a group. *European Journal of Social Psychology 6*, 149–174.

Mutz, D. (1989). The influence of perceptions of media influence: Third person effects and the public expression of opinion. *International Journal of Public Opinion Research 1*, 3–23.

Neuman, W. R. (1986). *The paradox of mass politics: Knowledge and opinion in the American electorate*. Cambridge, MA: Harvard University Press.

Neuman, W. R. (1990). The threshold of public attention. *Public Opinion Quarterly 54*, 159–176.

Neuman, W. R., Just, M. R., & Crigler, A. N. (1992). *Common knowledge: News and the construction of political meaning*. Chicago: University of Chicago Press.

Newcomb, T. M. (1958). Attitude development as a function of reference groups: The Bennington study. In E. Maccoby, T. Newcomb, & E. Hartley (Eds.), *Readings in social psychology* (3rd ed., pp. 265–275). New York: Holt, Rinehart and Winston.

Noelle-Neumann, E. (1984). *The spiral of silence: Public opinion—Our social skin*. Chicago: University of Chicago Press.

Osgood, C. E., & Tannenbaum, P. H. (1955). The principle of congruity in the prediction of attitude change. *Journal of Personality and Social Psychology 3*, 235–244.

Page, B. I., & Shapiro, R. Y. (1989). Educating and manipulating the public. In M. Margolis & G. A. Mauser (Eds.), *Manipulating public opinion: Essays on public opinion as a dependent variable* (pp. 294–320). Pacific Grove, CA: Brooks/Cole.

Page, B. I., & Shapiro, R. Y. (1992). *The rational public: Fifty years of trends in Americans' policy preferences*. Chicago: University of Chicago Press.

Page, B. I., Shapiro, R. Y., & Dempsey, G. R. (1987). What moves public opinion? *American Political Science Review 81*, 23–43.

Pan, Z., & Kosicki, G. M. (1994). Voters' reasoning processes and media influences during the Persian Gulf War. *Political Behavior 16*(1), 117–156.

Pan, Z., & McLeod, J. M. (1991). Multi-level analysis in mass communication research. *Communication Research 18*, 138–171.

Pan, Z., & Kosicki, G. M. (1993). Framing analysis: An approach to news discourse. *Political Communication 10*, 55–75.

Perloff, R. M. (1989). Ego-involvement and the third-person effect of television news coverage. *Communication Research 16*, 236–262.

Pertschuk, M., & Schaetzel, W. (1989). *The people rising: The campaign against the Bork nomination*. New York: Thunder's Mouth Press.

Pratkanis, A., & Aronson, E. (1991). *Age of propaganda: The everyday use and abuse of persuasion*. New York: W. H. Freeman and Company.

Price, V. (1988). On the public aspects of opinion: Linking levels of analysis in public opinion research. *Communication Research 15*, 659–679.

Price, V., & Roberts, D. F. (1987). Public opinion processes. In C. Berger & S. Chaffee (Eds.), *Handbook of communication science* (pp. 781–816). Newbury Park, CA: Sage.

Protess, D. L., Cook, F. L., Curtin, T. R., Gordon, M. T., Leff, D. R., McCombs, M. E., & Miller, P. V. (1987). The impact of investigative reporting on public opinion and policy making. *Public Opinion Quarterly 51*, 166–185.

Przeworski, A., & Teune, H. (1970). *The logic of comparative social inquiry*. New York: Wiley.

Reeves, B. (1989). Theories about news and theories about cognition: Arguments for a more radical separation. *American Behavioral Scientist 33*, 191–198.

Reeves, B., Thorson, E., & Schleuder, J. (1986). Attention to television: Psychological theories and chronometric measures. In J. Bryant & D. Zillmann (Eds.), *Perspectives on media effects* (pp. 251–279). Hillsdale, NJ: Lawrence Erlbaum.

Robinson, J. P., & Levy, M. R. (1986). *The main source: Learning from television news*. Beverly Hills, CA: Sage.

Rogers, E. M., & Storey, J. D. (1987). Communication campaigns. In C. Berger & S. Chaffee (Eds.), *Handbook of communication science* (pp. 817–846). Newbury Park, CA: Sage.

Rumelhart, D. E. (1984). Schemata and the cognitive system. In S. Wyer & T. Srull (Eds.), *Handbook of social cognition 1* (pp. 161–188). Hillsdale, NJ: Lawrence Erlbaum.

Rusciano, F. L. (1989). *Isolation and paradox: Defining "the public" in modern political analysis*. New York: Greenwood Press.

Sartori, G. (1987). *The theory of democracy revisited*. Chatham, NJ: Chatham House Publishers.

Schank, R. C., & Abelson, R. P. (1977). *Scripts, plans, goals and understanding: An inquiry into human knowledge structure*. Hillsdale, NJ: Lawrence Erlbaum.

Schramm, W. (1972). The nature of communication between humans. In W. Schramm & D. Roberts (Eds.), *The process and effects of mass communication* (rev. ed., pp. 3–53). Urbana: University of Illinois Press.

Shibutani, T. (1955). Reference groups as perspectives. *American Journal of Sociology 60*, 562–569.

Shoben, E. J. (1984). Semantic and episodic memory. In R. Wyer & T. Srull (Eds.), *Handbook of social cognition 2* (pp. 213–232). Hillsdale, NJ: Lawrence Erlbaum.

Sniderman, P. M., Brody, R. A., & Tetlock, P. E. (1991). *Reasoning and choice: Explorations in political psychology*. Cambridge, England: Cambridge University Press.

Snow, D. A., Rochford, E. B., Jr., Worden, S. K., & Benford, R. D. (1986). Frame alignment process, micromobilization, and movement participation. *American Sociological Review 51*, 464–481.

Steele, R. W. (1985). *Propaganda in an open society: The Roosevelt Administration and the media, 1933–1941*. Westport, CI: Greenwood Press.

Stimson, J. A. (1991). *Public opinion in America: Moods, cycles, and swings*. Boulder, CO: Westview.

Tichenor, P. J., Donohue, G. A., & Olien, C. N. (1980). *Community conflict and the press*. Beverly Hills, CA: Sage.

Tuchman, G. (1978). *Making news: A study in the construction of reality*. New York: Free Press.

Turner, J. H. (1988). *A theory of social interaction*. Stanford, CA: Stanford University Press.

Turow, J. (1984). *Media industries: The production of news and entertainment*. New York: Longman.

van Dijk, T. A. (1988). *News as discourse*. Hillsdale, NJ: Lawrence Erlbaum.

Verba, S., & Nie, N. H. (1972). *Participation in America: Political democracy and social equality*. New York: Harper & Row.

Whitney, D. C. (1982). Mass communicator studies: similarity, difference, and level of analysis. In J. Ettema & D. Whitney (Eds.), *Individuals in mass media organizations: Creativity and constraint* (pp. 241–254). Beverly Hills, CA: Sage.

Wyer, R. S., & Srull, T. K. (1981). Category accessibility: Some theoretical and empirical issues concerning the processing of social stimulus information. In E. Higgins, C. Herman, & M. Zanna (Eds.), *Social cognition: The Ontario Symposium 1* (pp. 161–197). Hillsdale, NJ: Lawrence Erlbaum.

Wyer, R. W., & Srull, T. K. (1989). *Memory and cognition in social context*. Hillsdale, NJ: Lawrence Erlbaum.

II

THE INSTITUTION OF PUBLIC OPINION

4

On the Disappearance of Groups: 19th- and Early 20th-Century Conceptions of Public Opinion

Susan Herbst

Questions about the nature of public opinion, and how best to gauge the popular sentiment, are as old as democratic theory itself. As Peters (Chapter 1 in this volume) and other scholars have pointed out, Plato, Aristotle, and a variety of pre-Enlightenment thinkers struggled to conceptualize the essence of public opinion, usually within the context of debates about human nature. Several of these theorists, like Machiavelli, wrote eloquently about the importance of "sensing" the public sentiment, by monitoring peoples' behavior, listening to their grievances, and sustaining a dialogue among elites about the public. Despite a keen interest in public opinion among theorists and statesmen, however, an obsession with the systematic measurement of public opinion emerged much later, in the highly charged partisan atmosphere of mid-19th-century America.

In this chapter, I explore how public opinion was expressed and measured in the days before the diffusion of the "sample" or "scientific" survey. While the history of opinion measurement is an extraordinarily long one, there are some discernable trends in that lengthy narrative. After a brief discussion of definitional problems surrounding the phrase "public opinion," and a sketch of some historical trends, I focus on the expression and assessment of the popular mood in the mid-19th century—a particularly interesting period for historians of public opinion. During that era, a growing number of citizens, party leaders, statesmen, and scholars became interested in polling. Ironically, however, there was a fundamental contradiction between the aggregation-oriented assumptions of polling and the arrangement of political institutions at the time. Although "public opinion" connoted the activities of *groups* (parties, in particular) in the years just before and after the Civil War, methodologies for assessing public opinion increasingly focused on *individuals*. Evaluating polling in the 19th and early 20th centuries not only sheds light on the roots of contemporary survey research; it also forces us to ask a variety of important questions about the changing assumptions and definitions behind opinion assessment methodologies.

As a preface, I should note that this chapter is not an argument for a new definition of public opinion, although that is how many essays on this topic begin or conclude (e.g., Key, 1961). I do, however, ask the reader to shed his or her preconceptions about the meaning of public opinion, in order to imagine how the phrase might have been used and understood at a time when our political culture was very different. Although 20th-century political operatives, scholars, and practitioners began to reach a general agreement about the meaning of public opinion in the 1920s (e.g., Holcombe, 1925), the definition of the phrase was rarely discussed before that time by anyone at all. These days we tend to believe that public opinion is the aggregation of individual opinions as measured by the sample survey. Despite resistance from a few social theorists (e.g., Blumer, 1948; Bourdieu, 1979), this definition is now hegemonic: when most of us consider the meaning of public opinion, we can't help but think about polls or surveys. Yet since it wasn't always this way, historians of public opinion must try to piece together past connotations of "public opinion" by evaluating memoirs, newspapers, civics texts, and other cultural artifacts.

THE EARLY HISTORY OF PUBLIC OPINION: MEANING AND MEASUREMENT

Before we can speak about measuring public opinion (or any other construct), we have to define it. Unfortunately, tracking the origins of "public opinion," and sketching changes in the meaning of the phrase, has been one of the most frustrating of all projects in intellectual history. Uncovering the history of events, or tracing the development of a social group over time is always difficult: archival sources may be hard to find, and records, once discovered, are often incomplete or of dubious veracity. Yet trying to understand the development of a *concept* is among the most baffling tasks for the historian, who typically wants to link that concept to changes in social structure, economic trends, or political upheaval. A few scholars have been somewhat successful in tracing the connotations of important words or phrases over time (e.g., Condit & Lucaites, 1993; Rodgers, 1987), but there are inevitable gaps in the narratives they present.

A variety of researchers, from a variety of fields, have attempted to map the evolving meaning of "public opinion," but at this point, the history of the phrase is largely incoherent. Some scholars collect and analyze as many definitions as they can find (e.g., Childs, 1965). Others bring a theoretical agenda to the history, in order to demonstrate definitional consistency over time (e.g., Noelle-Neumann, 1984), while still others try to link definitions with great theorists, statesmen, or social movements (e.g., Bauer, 1930; Minar, 1960; Palmer, 1934, 1964; Speier, 1950; Tonnies, 1957; See also Gollin & Gollin, 1973).

There are several reasons why defining public opinion is so complex and frustrating. First, there is the problem of intellectual history versus social history. Philosophers have written about public opinion or synonymous phrases (e.g., Rousseau described the "general will"), but those without education or high social status probably thought about public opinion and persuasion as well, even if they didn't produce philsophical tracts on the subject (see Bauer, 1930). In writing about the history of public opinion, then, one is constantly torn between the words used by great men and the actions of (and implicit meanings of public opinion among) common folk. Choosing between these two approaches is troubling, and there are tremendous analytical problems associated with each. With the formal philosophical tracts, it is often unclear whether the theorist is making normative arguments about the way public opinion *should* be defined, or descriptive arguments about the way it was defined at the time of his writing. In terms of the social (or "low") history of public opinion, one is forced to look for connotations of the phrase in the actions of the masses—bread riots, petitioning, fragments of public speeches, and so on—for which archives are scanty.

In addition, public opinion has been defined differently by different parties because they had idiosyncratic agendas: Marx wrote about the public sentiment in order to demonstrate how it was shaped by historical circumstance, and by economic arrangements in particular. Rousseau wrote about public opinion because he was interested in the essence of human nature, and the ingredients of the social contract. Gallup wrote about public opinion in the context of measurement through aggregation, and his efforts were animated by entrepreneurial goals as well as intellectual ones. While some of these writers were more eloquent or rigorous than others, it is futile (and unfair) to characterize these tracts as right or wrong.

One way to approach the history of public opinion is to avoid discovering the true meaning of the phase, and simply grant that the definition is fluid. It changes with transformations in social structure, economic and political reform, and technological advances (see Habermas, 1974; Herbst, 1993). I believe that in order to trace the changing definition of public opinion we must evaluate what *Annales* historian Ferdinand Braudel has called the *longue durée* (Braudel, 1980)—the long, extended history that reaches across periods and across regions. Focusing on the *longue durée* demands that one look for broad structural trends in history, studying "whole centuries at a time" (p. 74), as Braudel himself does so well in his work on the Mediterranean (1973). Perhaps the most successful student of the *longue durée* in the area of public opinion is Jürgen Habermas, whose early work on the subject considered the popular sentiment over several centuries in several nations (Habermas, 1989).

TRENDS IN THE HISTORY OF PUBLIC OPINION

If we take Braudel's advice seriously, and concentrate on the *longue durée*, we can discern several interesting trends in the history of public opinion—its meaning *and* its measurement. No matter how hard we try to separate the two, they are so often conflated that it is best to recognize and highlight their connections, and try to learn something from these connections. Three trends in the social history of public opinion are: (1) a shift from the "bottom-up" to the "top-down" communication of popular sentiment; (2) the increasing rationalization of opinion expression and measurement; and (3) growing anonymity in the articulation of opinions.

Benjamin Ginsberg (1986) noted the first trend in the history of public opinion, arguing that voting and opinion polling were techniques introduced *by the state* in the early 18th century in order to manipulate or "domesticate" public opinion. While election results and survey responses are evidence of public opinion, the format and intensity of these opinions is dictated by the state. In contrast, he attempts to show (albeit with limited evidence), that early expressions of public opinion—food riots, destruction of property, petitioning, and so on—came directly *from the people* and were therefore more honest and more reliable. While his argument may be difficult for us to swallow, since most nations seem to have become more and not less democratic over time, Ginsberg's analysis is quite compelling. There are still riots and demonstrations in the 20th century, yet polling and voting have probably obviated, to some extent, the need for these sorts of protest. Conducting surveys and polls is a way that elites can structure public opinion, and control it.

Along these lines, I have argued that opinion polling is an important means of surveillance. In the days before the diffusion of the sample survey, public opinion would erupt with very little warning. In the 17th century local elites might have known that the peasants were unhappy, but it was hard to predict when they might engage in rioting. In the 20th century, on the other hand, private polling by leaders, in combination with published polls, enable elites to monitor opinions more closely and steadily. This form of opinion surveillance mimics, in some ways, forms of panoptic observation described by Michel Foucault (see Foucault, 1979; Herbst, 1993, pp. 23–27; Peer, 1992).

A second trend in the history of public opinion is that of escalating rationalization. Max Weber (1946, 1958, 1978) has argued that all aspects of social life, from the laws we live by to the emotions we express in private, have become increasingly more systematized and formalized over time. While Weber concentrated on the growth of bureaucracy, which provides evidence for the increasing structuration of our lives, even our most intimate activities have become more organized and "arranged." For example, the appearance of computer dating services, support groups, 800 help "hotlines," and other such phenomena all underscore the increasing formalization of our social practices. As I have argued elsewhere, public opinion has not escaped the trend toward increasing rationalization: our means of communicating to our leaders, and their attempts to monitor our feelings, have become more and more systematized over time (Herbst, 1993, pp. 43–68). On the one hand, growing rationalization is a good thing, since organizing practices leads to efficiency in reaching goals (in this case, understanding the public mood). Yet the rationalization of public opinion has also meant that our feelings and beliefs are channeled and labeled. Closed-ended survey questions and referenda "tap into" our belief systems, but they limit the character, and intensity of our political expressions.

With regard to the third trend, public opinion expression was usually *attributed* before the diffusion of the general election and the sample survey. It was difficult to make one's feelings known, about a political, economic, or social issue, without somehow taking responsibility for those opinions. In the 20th century, however, with the growing popularity of survey research, anonymity characterizes opinion expression. When one is polled, usually over the telephone, he or she is assured that all opinions expressed are confidential: the pollster will never link a respondent's name to his or her opinions. Like rationalization, growing anonymity in opinion expression has positive and negative aspects. People may feel more freedom to express their ideas when they know that their name will never be published in connection with their beliefs. Yet without attribution, people are never responsible for their opinions and may take the entire expression process less seriously than they would otherwise.

This brief sketch of trends in opinion expression and measurement provides a background for a discussion of public opinion in the mid-19th century. In many ways, the 19th century is a transition period. We can find traces of all the trends outlined above, although top-down measurement approaches, rationalization, and anonymity were not nearly as evident as they are today. Most interesting, however, is the way that a new technique of opinion measurement—the straw poll—collided with the highly partisan political structure of the period.

COMMUNICATION OF PUBLIC OPINION IN THE 19TH CENTURY

Popular politics in the mid-19th century revolved around elections, as it does today. Local, state, and national campaigns structured political life in the young republic, and elections served as powerful symbols of freedom and sovereignty. Without a doubt, the most important force in mid-19th-century politics was partisanship. Parties performed a variety of functions: They mobilized the public, served as channels for opinion expression, educated the people about issues, organized debate about those issues, and disbursed resources and patronage jobs to their loyalists, among other things. Michael McGerr, in his fascinating book about northern politics after the Civil War, describes the role of partisanship in American life this way:

> Party was an essentially simple creed, but one woven deeply and intricately into the pattern of Northern society. Partisanship entailed more than attachment to a particular political organization. For mid-19th-century Northerners, party became a natural lens through which to view the world. Most men found it second nature to perceive events from a partisan perspective and to imagine a black-and-white world of absolutes, of political friends and enemies. . . . Mid-19th-century partisanship was aggressive, demonstrative, contentious, and often vicious. Party membership was part of men's identity; as such, their partisanship had to be paraded and asserted in public. (1986, p. 14)

And asserted it was. Politics was serious business in the mid-19th century, but it was also one of the major forms of entertainment during the period. While women played only symbolic roles in politics, and were, along with blacks and other marginalized groups, relegated to the sidelines (Ryan, 1990), men found considerable satisfaction in public displays of partisanship. Membership in parties was extremely high, as was straight-ticket voting, but even more interesting was the way that people expressed their feelings for their parties in the streets. Torchlight parades, pole-raising, and rallies of various sorts always attracted large numbers of men, and the excitement associated with politics was contagious. Turnout among eligible voters was often as high as 80% in national elections, and historians estimate that from 20 to 25% of electors were immersed in campaigning—attending rallies, organizing events, distributing campaign materials, and marching in parades (Dinkin, 1989).

Parties depended upon their loyalists to help shape public opinion during and between campaigns, but the newspaper was one of the more effective means of spreading party ideology. The parties supported many newspapers by awarding them large printing contracts, and often simply subsidized them directly (see Baldasty, 1992). As a result, the typical 19th-century newspaper had a very obvious political slant, which ran throughout the text. The distinction made today between editorial and news reporting was not conventional. As late as 1891, James Bryce, British statesman and visitor to the United States, could still write:

> As the advocates of political doctrines, newspapers are of course powerful, because they are universally read and often ably written. . . . What struck me was that in America a leading article carries less weight of itself, being discounted by the shrewd reader as the sort of thing which the paper must of course be expected to say, and is effective only when it takes hold of some fact (real or supposed), and hammers it into the public mind. (p. 264)

Newspapers, Bryce argues, were indispensable to parties who needed to influence as well as monitor public opinion.

Parties and public opinion were intertwined in the mid-19th century far more than they are today. In the 20th century, with the decline of partisanship, public opinion seems an independent force that is expressed through news reports and survey data. In the 19th century, however, parties were integral to the very infrastructure of public opinion—its meaning, its forms of expression, and its measurement (see Herbst & Beniger, 1994). To think of public opinion apart from the parties would have been odd, since parties held such a tight grip on the nature of political debate. Indeed, party activity *defined* public opinion in the 19th century. Party strength was such that de Tocqueville noted of the American political scene:

> Lacking in great parties, the United States is creeping with small ones and public opinion is broken up ad infinitum about questions of detail. It is impossible to imagine the trouble they take to create parties; it is not an easy matter now. . . . The ambitious are bound to create parties, for it is difficult to turn the man in power out simply for the reason that one would like to take his place. Hence all the skill of politicians consists in forming parties. (1969, p. 177)

Both Bryce and de Tocqueville, in their travels, noted repeatedly how public opinion was cultivated and expressed by parties. And contemporary historians of American politics have even found jokes, humorous slogans, and songs that attest to the relationship between popular sentiment and the parties:

> Now, to keep all these glorious feeturs
> Thet characterize morril an' reasonin' creeturs,
> Thet give every paytriot all he can cram,
> Thet oust the untrustworthy Presidunt Flam,
> An' stick honest Presidunt Sham in his place,
> To the manifest gain o' the holl human race,
> An' to some indervidgewals on't in partickler,
> Who love Public Opinion an' know how to tickle her,-
> I say thet a party with gret aims like these
> Must stick jest ez close ez a hive full o' bees.
> (quoted in Baker, 1985, p. 178; see also Baker, 1983)

Parties were not the only group that channeled public opinion in the 19th century, of course. There were a variety of smaller, less influential associations and clubs. James Q. Wilson (1973), for example, has noted that a tremendous number of interest groups first appeared in the mid-19th century: the National Grange, Elks, Knights of Pythias, college fraternities, and craft unions, among others. Yet when it came to popular, electoral politics, parties were crucial.

While the parties enjoyed their "golden age" of influence in the mid-19th century, there was a parallel development in the communication of public opinion. Journalists and party activists themselves became increasingly infatuated with the "straw poll" or "straws" as they were often called. Straw polls are unscientific surveys, conducted orally or with pen and paper, usually before an election. It isn't quite clear why the polls were called "straws," but labeling the polls this way implied that they were mock (or false) votes in the same way that a "straw man" is an artificial argument. Although straw polls are still conducted, through radio and television call-in programs or by roving photographers working for *USA Today*, policy makers, candidates, journalists, and political activists pay much more attention to data derived from sample surveys.

Most students of public opinion are familiar with the famous *Literary Digest* polls of the early 20th century. The *Digest* polled thousands of individuals through the mail, and despite its unscientific methodology, was successful in predicting U.S. presidential election outcomes until 1936. The *Digest*'s editors were humiliated by their failure to predict a Roosevelt victory, and the *Digest* ceased publication shortly thereafter.

Although the story of the *Digest* provides a good cautionary lesson to today's pollsters, the straw polls of the 19th century are far more interesting than the huge *Digest* polls. Unlike the *Digest* polls, early straw votes were conducted with the unique brand of creativity and flair that characterized partisan politics of the period. Since newspapers were extremely partisan in the mid-19th century, editors used straw polls constantly before elections, to boost the image of their favored candidates. Results of straw polls were woven into the texture of partisan periodicals in ways that seems quite foreign to us today: the polls were clearly thought to be scientific or predictive, yet they were employed primarily as rhetorical weapons in the fierce, ideological war of words that preceded most elections.[1] During the weeks just before an election, major newspapers like the *Chicago Tribune* or *The New York Times* would often print several polls a week. There were three types of straw polls commonly published in the typical 19th-century daily: those conducted by reporters for the newspaper, those conducted by party activists or a like-minded paper in another city, or those sent to a newspaper by voters themselves.

Often, journalists would travel great distances to cover a campaign, and conducted straw polls on trains or steamers on the way to a rally or demonstration. Reporters asked for a show of hands, or approached people as they headed toward hotels, taverns, or fairgrounds. Vote tallies were then reported in their articles, and used to buttress their analyses of the campaign. Often, journalists would obtain straw vote results from factory managers who polled their employees, or from party workers. In this example, from the 1896 race between McKinley and Bryan, a *Chicago Tribune* journalist wrote:

> Estimates received at Republican National headquarters indicate that 90 per cent of the railway employees favor the St. Louis platform and nomi-

> nees. The activity shown by them in organizing sound money clubs throughout the country is given as evidence in proof of these estimates. . . . A visitor from Nebraska said he knew of thirty sound money Populists in one neighborhood out there who would cast their ballots this year for the Republican candidate. (8/27, p. 12)

The same sorts of polls were often shared among like-minded partisan papers in particular regions, while straws and election estimates from opposing papers were criticized. Despite their own fascination with quantitative prediction, the staunchly Republican editors of the *Tribune* often mocked the political arithmetic of other opposing dailies, as in this 1876 piece:

> The Madison *Democrat* ciphers out the result of the Presidential election by logarithms, or the integral calculus, and gives TILDEN 206 votes to 168 for HAYES. In order to secure these estimates it grabs Wisconsin's 10 votes for TILDEN. It very coolly walks off with the electoral votes of New York, California, Colorado, Florida, Nevada, New Jersey, North Carolina, and Oregon, which shows the foolishness, if not idiocy, of such figuring. (9/30, p. 4)

In general, the partisan papers of the 19th century approved of straw votes, and predictions derived from those polls, when they needed them for rhetorical purposes. Yet these same papers argued against such methods when straws were employed by other papers.

Perhaps the most intriguing types of straws were those sent in by ordinary readers, who paid close attention to politics. Since men looked to party politics as a form of entertainment, conducting straw polls among friends, neighbors, and coworkers was great fun. It enabled social comparison, and was most probably a starting point for dialogue about the upcoming election. A *Tribune* reader with the initials "J. B. C." sent in this letter, the summer before the 1856 presidential campaign between Buchanan, Fremont, and Fillmore:

> Below you will find a statement of a vote taken on the train of the Chicago, Burlington, and Quincy railroad, to-day, August 25th: Fremont, 88; Buchanan, 30; Fillmore, 10.
>
> Yours truly,
>
> J. B. C.
>
> P.S. Several of those tallied for Buchanan were unnaturalized Irish catholics. (8/26, p. 3)

On the same day, the *Tribune* printed this letter from another reader:

CAR VOTING.—Editors Tribune: Gents—The following is the result of a canvass I made on the Saturday evening train to Milwaukee. Among the gentlemen, Fillmore 5, Buchanan 13, Fremont 41.—Among the ladies, of whom about one half only voted, the vote was, Fremont 9, Fillmore 2, Buchanan ("purely out of sympathy for his lonesome condition ") one. (8/26, p. 3).

Yours, SC,

E. F. B.

The straws sent in by readers are indicative of just how well the parties had mobilized its loyalists. Men not only turned out for rallies and torchlight parades in great numbers; they also canvassed for the party, making quantitative estimates of public opinion wherever possible—while traveling by train or in their own communities.

That straw votes were popular is obvious to scholars who immerse themselves in the discourse of mid- and late 19th-century newspapers. What is not so obvious is the way that the assumptions of straw polling contradicted the structure of party politics. Public opinion was thought to be formed, expressed, and monitored by parties—by *groups* whose livelihood depended on understanding and shaping public opinion. Yet the straw poll was a technique for opinion assessment that assumed public opinion to be an aggregation of atomized, anonymous *individuals*. In other words, during the mid-19th century we begin to see a clash between commonly understood conceptions of public opinion as *party* opinion, and new methodologies that in many ways ignored groups altogether. For Bryce, de Tocqueville, and other observers of American politics of the period, groups were the key to understanding collective opinion. But the straw poll—based upon the notion of aggregating individuals to assess the popular sentiment—was also becoming a central means for understanding collective opinion.

PARTIES AND OPINION IN THE 20TH CENTURY

By the early 20th century, parties had lost considerable ground. While a decline in voter turnout after the turn of the century probably had many causes (e.g., shifting demographics of the electorate, and the rise of leisure activities), some historians attribute increasing alienation of voters to the inability of parties to motivate their constituencies. Even before the rise in split-ticket voting and the decline of partisan feeling in the mid-20th century, documented so well by Wattenberg (1986), citizens had already begun to lose interest in the sort of frantic participation that characterized the previous century. As McGerr (1986) puts it:

"Elections [of the early 20th century] lost their role as expressions of martial spirit, leisure, personal identity, communal life, and class theater" (p. 206). A shift to advertising and slick campaign management by the national parties obviated much of the local activity that drew men into politics. By the 1930s and 1940s, as I have argued elsewhere (Herbst, 1993), one no longer found citizens' straw polls in newspapers. Professional pollsters like *The Literary Digest*, Gallup, and Roper began to measure public sentiment before elections. Parties and the sorts of ritualized politics they promoted, had become superfluous in an increasingly professionalized and rationalized electoral sphere.

Although we are not accustomed to thinking about parties as "technologies" for public opinion expression and measurement, we certainly should, since they filled these critical functions up until the early decades of the 20th century. Yet after that period, polls "won out" over parties as the dominant means of expressing and assessing public opinion. Parties are still omnipresent in American electoral politics, as are interest groups. But we tend not to think of them as key purveyors of public opinion, since polling seems so much more reliable and scientific. In many ways, polls do seem to be the most appropriate means for public opinion expression and measurement in a mass society such as ours. Group-oriented meanings of public opinion seem almost naive in an environment where few people participate in local party activities, and many more are disgusted by the parties' lack of definition (see Miller & Traugott, 1989; on third parties and public opinion, see Herbst, 1994).

In his well-known critique of opinion polling, Herbert Blumer (1948) tried to revive the notion that one must study social groups in order to discern public opinion. He scolded survey researchers for ignoring social and political structure—the fact that some groups are more powerful than others, and will influence public policy regardless of what surveys indicate. Though it was never articulated in this fashion, Blumer's group-oriented definition of public opinion presided in the mid-19th century. By the time Blumer was able to launch his sociological analysis of public opinion, though, survey research was a thriving industry. Far too many people had far too much invested in the new business of polling to reconsider the meaning of public opinion. With parties on the decline, surveys seemed an excellent replacement: they conveyed public opinion in an efficient, seemingly objective manner—something the parties had not done, and might never be able to do.

Interestingly, poll results reported in today's major newspapers and popular magazines often focus on groups, despite the fact that the individual is the unit of analysis in survey research. Pollsters and journalists in the 20th century believe that statistical categories help readers to conceptualize opinion enclaves within the electorate. Often, pollsters break down their results, indicating how men versus women feel about a candidate, or whether approval of a particular policy is highest among blacks, whites, Hispanics, or Asians. One could argue that using such categories gives survey data the sort of texture Blumer asked for, since readers can note how class, race, ethnicity, gender, education, and other variables are correlated with public opinion.

I would argue that such categories, while potentially useful to policy makers and candidates, are problematic in several ways. For one, the practice implies that categories *are* social groups—that blacks, for example, are an organized, potentially active social and political entity. This is clearly not the case at all, however, since the African Americans polled in a typical national survey do not know each other and undoubtedly live in different neighborhoods or regions of the country. Second, and more importantly, the way pollsters categorize people does not necessary "map onto" the way members of the sample see themselves. For example, suppose a pollster supplies her client (a news organization) with a survey indicating popular attitudes toward law enforcement. The data are broken down into categories by race and income. Why those categories? Why not religion, gender, community-mindedness, political efficacy, alienation, or some other even more complex constellation of demographic or psychographic variables? This problem is especially troubling when pollsters collect opinion data about events that conflate several group affiliations at once. During the Clarence Thomas nomination hearings in 1991, for example, gender, race, class, education, and feminist ideology were all important factors in public discourse about the event. To break down poll data by race or gender seems a rather weak attempt at the sort of social group analysis Blumer argued for.[2]

All this is not to say that pollsters should not try to analyze their data more rigorously, or that they should abandon categorical analysis. I am simply using recent survey research practices to demonstrate how it is that the meaning of public opinion has changed over time, and that meanings of public opinion are always intertwined with measurement techniques. Behind every methodology is a philosophy of what public opinion actually is. During the 19th century, public opinion meant the activity of parties, although the acceleration of straw polling reflected gradual changes in that connotation. In contemporary American political discourse, the notion that the public is composed *not* of social groups but of atomized individuals, serves as the philosophy behind our dominant measurement technique. This philosophy may change, as it has so many times throughout the history of public opinion communication, and students of public expression should be attuned to these sorts of fundamental transformations in political culture.

NOTES

1. Polls are still used rhetorically during campaigns, of course. Yet the quality of 19th century polling rhetoric was far different than it is today. On polling rhetoric in 1992, see Sandra Bauman and Susan Herbst (1994).

2. Most pollsters would argue that they aren't attempting to engage in social group analysis, and that may be true. Yet, the way categorical data are discussed by journalists, policy makers, and others (after publication) does reify these groups, whether pollsters like it or not. Should polling professionals try to "correct" public discourse and rhetoric about groups, inspired by their categorical presentation of data? This is a question unaddressed by the industry, but important nonetheless.

REFERENCES

Baker, J. (1983). *Affairs of party: The political culture of northern Democrats in the mid-nineteenth century*. Ithaca: Cornell University Press.

Baker, J. (1985). The ceremonies of politics: Nineteenth-century rituals of national affirmation. In W. Cooper, M. Holt, & J. McCardell (Eds.), *A master's due: Essays in honor of David Herbert Donald* (pp. 161–178). Baton Rouge: Louisiana State University Press.

Baldasty, G. (1992). *The commercialization of news in the nineteenth century*. Madison: University of Wisconsin Press.

Bauer, W. (1930). Public opinion. In E. Seligman (Ed.), *Encyclopaedia of the social sciences* (pp. 669–674). New York: Macmillan.

Bauman, S., & Herbst, S. (1994). On managing perceptions of public opinion: Candidates' reactions to the 1992 polls. *Political Communication, 11*, 133–143.

Blumer, H. (1948). Public opinion and public opinion polling. *American Sociological Review 13*, 242–249.

Bourdieu, P. (1979). Public opinion does not exist. In A. Mattelart & S. Siegelaub (Eds.), *Communication and class struggle* (pp. 124–130). New York: International General.

Braudel, F. (1973). *The Mediterranean and the Mediterranean world in the age of Philip II*. London: Fontana.

Braudel, F. (1980). *On history*. London: Weidenfeld & Nicolson.

Bryce, J. (1891). *The American commonwealth*. New York: Macmillan.

Childs, H. (1965). *Public opinion: Nature formation, and role*. Princeton: D. Van Nostrand.

Condit, C., & Lucaites, J. (1993). *Crafting equality: America's Anglo-African word*. Chicago: University of Chicago Press.

Dinkin, R. (1989). *Campaigning in America: A history of election practices*. Westport, CT: Greenwood Press.

Foucault, M. (1979). *Discipline and punish: The birth of the prison* (A. Sheridan, Trans.). New York: Vintage.

Ginsberg, B. (1986). *The captive public: How mass opinion promotes state power*. New York: Basic Books.

Gollin, G., & Gollin, A. (1973). Tonnies on public opinion. In W. Cahnman (Ed.), *Ferdinand Tonnies: A new evaluation* (pp. 181–203). Leiden: E. J. Brill.

Habermas, J. (1974). The public sphere: An encyclopedia article. *New German Critique 1*, 49–55.

Habermas, J. (1989). *The structural transformation of the public sphere: An inquiry into a category of bourgeois society*. Cambridge, MA: M.I.T. Press.

Herbst, S. (1993). *Numbered voices: How opinion polling has shaped American politics*. Chicago: University of Chicago Press.

Herbst, S. (1994). *Politics at the margin: Historical studies of public expression outside the mainstream*. New York: Cambridge University Press.

Herbst, S., & Beniger, J. (1994). The changing infrastructure of public opinion. In C. Whitney & J. Ettema (Eds.), *Audiencemaking* (pp. 95–114). Newbury Park, CA: Sage.

Holcombe, A. (1925). Round table on political statistics: The measurement of public opinion. *American Political Science Review 19*, 123–126.

Key, V. O. (1961). *Public opinion and American democracy*. New York: Alfred A. Knopf.

McGerr, M. (1986). *The decline of popular politics: The American North, 1865–1928*. New York: Oxford University Press.

Miller, W., & Traugott, S. (1989). *American national election studies data sourcebook, 1952–1986*. Cambridge, MA: Harvard University Press.

Minar, D. (1960). Public opinion in the perspective of political theory. *Western Political Quarterly 13*, 31–44.

Noelle-Neumann, E. (1984). *The spiral of silence: Public opinion—Our social skin*. Chicago: University of Chicago Press.

Palmer, P. (1934). *The concept of public opinion in political theory*. Unpublished doctoral dissertation, Harvard University.

Palmer, P. (1964). The concept of public opinion in political theory. In C. Wittke (Ed.), *Essays in history and political theory in honor of Charles Howard McIlwain* (pp. 230–257). New York: Russell & Russell.

Peer, L. (1992). The practice of opinion polling as a disciplinary mechanism: A Foucauldian perspective. *International Journal of Public Opinion Research 4*, 230–242.

Rodgers, D. (1987). *Contested truths: Keywords in American politics since Independence*. New York: Basic Books.

Ryan, M. (1990). *Women in public: Between banners and ballots, 1825–1880*. Baltimore: Johns Hopkins University Press.

Speier, H. (1950). Historical development of public opinion. *American Journal of Sociology 55*, 376–388.

Tonnies, F. (1957). *Community and Society* (C. Loomis, Trans.). East Lansing: Michigan State Press.

Tocqueville, A. de (1969). *Democracy in America*, (J. P. Mayer, Ed. and Trans.). New York: Anchor.

Wattenberg, M. (1986). *The decline of American political parties, 1952–1984*. Cambridge, MA: Harvard University Press.

Weber, M. (1946). Science as a vocation. In H. Gerth & C. Wright Mills (Eds. and Trans.), *From Max Weber: Essays in sociology* (pp. 129–158). New York: Oxford.

Weber, M. (1958). *The Protestant ethic and the spirit of capitalism* (T. Parsons, Ed. and Trans.). New York: Charles Scribner's Sons.

Weber, M. (1978). *Economy and society: An outline of interpretive sociology* (G. Roth & C. Wittich, Eds.). Berkeley: University of California Press.

Wilson, J. Q. (1973). *Political organizations*. New York: Basic Books.

5

The Industry of Public Opinion

Peter V. Miller

Tools are usually employed automatically, without a second thought. So a description of tools and how they are used should strike practitioners as an "of course" and a "so what?"—as true to life but unremarkable. Methodology, how these tools are used as tools, is just what everyone knows.

—MARTIN KRIEGER, (1989)

Never mind telling your children where babies come from; instead, give them news they can use, like where Public Opinion comes from.

—WILLIAM SAFIRE, *The New York Times*

This chapter overviews the "public opinion industry"—commercial, governmental and academic organizations that produce knowledge of people's sentiment and behavior through polls or surveys. Previous literature on this subject is characterized by an odd duality. On the one hand, there is a voluminous body of knowledge on survey methodology, involving the minutiae of measurement theory, sampling, questionnaire design, data analysis and the like. This literature, in public opinion textbooks and in methodological texts and journals, speaks only indirectly about the industry; it is narrow, technical, and institutionally unreflective. The notion that public opinion information costs money and involves organizations that constitute an industry is only a subtext in these works.[1] In addressing questions about how the work of public opinion measurement should be done, however, these writings make up the major literature on the "industry" produced by those who work within it.

The other side of the duality is represented mainly by works of "outsiders" who describe and criticize the assumptions, practices, and products of the industry as a whole. These writings emphasize the political and economic underpinnings of public opinion measurement. A major theme underlying these critiques is that survey-based public opinion information is the result of a *manufacturing*, rather than a *measuring* process. Assertions that "public opinion does not exist" (Bourdieu, 1979), and that polls transform public opinion from a "voluntary to an externally subsidized matter" (Ginsberg, 1986) are exemplary of this theme.

The writings of "insiders" and "outsiders" exist independently, side by side. One speaks of tools, the other of the interests served by their use. One emphasizes components of a process while the other takes on the process as a whole. One asks how to do the work well, and the other asks whether the work should be done at all.

My aim in this chapter, speaking as an industry "insider," is to offer a more organized, focused, and contextualized view of the industry than might be gleaned from reading public opinion textbooks or the survey methodological literature, and, at the same time, to provide a more rich and variegated perspective than might be obtained from a review of survey critics' writings.

Following Krieger (1989), I suspect that other "insiders" will view much of what I say as "an 'of course' and a 'so what'" (although I hope to provide a different perspective on issues that practitioners normally take for granted). For "outsiders," I hope that my view of the industry will undermine a monolithic perception of it, and will point to matters of interest for all of us—of whatever background or research approach—who are interested in "public opinion." Fully conscious of the possible folly of the approach, I speak to two distinct audiences, and hope that I can give each culture a different and better picture of the public opinion industry than they now have.

ORGANISMS AND AGGREGATES

Matters of Definition

The work of those in the public opinion industry is to produce and interpret aggregates of individual opinions that are supposed to represent public opinion on the whole. The production process is the focus of this chapter. Before examining it, however, we need to understand the definition of "public opinion" that appears to underlie the opinion aggregates, and contrast it with the definition of public opinion used by industry outsiders. Much of the criticism of the industry can be traced to this definitional difference.

It is generally agreed that there is no agreement on just what public opinion is (see, e.g., Winkler, 1984). There are some dimensions of definition along which various constructions of the term may be classified, however. In broad strokes, the *public* for industry outsiders, (e.g., Albig, 1939; Blumer, 1948; and Habermas, 1989), means an interacting group, focused on matters of common interest. Though not necessarily a formally organized collective, the public in this construction has voluntary, indigenous, "organic" form, and is conscious of trying to have an impact on policy through rational discourse. The *opinions* expressed by this sort of public are characterized as reasoned, informed, and "genuine" (viz. Cantrell, 1989).

Measures of public opinion produced in surveys rely upon different, more inclusive, implicit definitions of "public" and "opinion." The public is a *population* of individuals (often citizens or residents of a geographic region) who *may* have an opinion about the subject matter of the survey. In operational terms, the public in a given survey is a *sample* of this larger population of eligible individuals. Some of the opinions in these opinion aggregates may be informed, intense, and policy directed, while others may be ignorant or ephemeral. Samples of individuals gathered in surveys do not include, typically, people who interact with one another about common interests. Rather, surveys try to capture individual opinions that may be the product of such interaction. The aggregates of individuals in public opinion surveys are not groups with a life of their own, but "cross-sections" of the kind of social life that others have called "publics."

The definition of public implied in surveys, then, emphasizes individuality and broad eligibility. Public opinion in surveys is the sum of individual opinions expressed to interviewers under guarantee of confidentiality. These privately expressed opinions may have been well formed and tested in discussion with others, may signify a plan to influence policy, or may not.[2] Surveys organize individual opinions as in a *plebescite*, urging maximum participation and candor in opinion expression without fear of reprisal or social sanction. Direct democracy, with referenda on issues structured in the form of survey questions, is the conceptual and philosophical model underlying the construction of opinion aggregates through public opinion surveys (see, e.g., Gallup & Rae, 1940; Crespi, 1989). As is true of much contemporary rhetoric on electoral participation, the normative ideal in surveys of public opinion is for everyone's views to be represented. Whereas for Habermas (1989) the expansion of the bourgeois public sphere to other social groups led to its degeneration, the inclusion of all sectors of society in surveys is viewed by survey practitioners as a primary goal. Those who conduct surveys spend a great deal of time, money, and ingenuity on the issues of individual participation in, and aggregate representativeness of, the quasi-electoral survey process.

Matters of Judgment

The value of the *aggregate* model of public opinion, for those who believe in it, is its appeal to the democratic ideal of popular sovereignty. As Cantrell (1989, p. 313) has noted, the "universe of the electorate" from which survey practitioners sample respondents is not a creation of the survey process, but is a "function of the legitimated political structure of the United States [or of other democratic regimes]." Periodic survey "referenda" on important matters of public policy can supplement whatever information is gleaned about the public will from electoral results. Since elected representatives and other policy makers often face issues about which the views of the public are unknown, surveys can play an important informative role by providing systematic evidence of public opinion. The legislator need not rely exclusively on the views of lobbyists in arriving at a decision; survey data can serve as a counterweight to the influence of elite "special interests" in the legislative process. Further, the potential effectiveness of various policy options can be gauged by carefully collected information on public beliefs and behavior, leading, in theory, to more enlightened decision-making. (See, e.g., Green, 1992, and Page & Shapiro, 1992, for comprehensive analyses of public preferences and their effects on policymaking over time.)

For those who do not give credence to public opinion surveys, the "direct democracy" definition that underlies the survey enterprise is inaccurate, naive, misguided, deleterious, or all of these. Blumer (1948), an often-cited exemplar of survey critics, characterized the plebiscitary idea as normatively laudable, but as empirically inaccurate. We do not know much about public opinion, he said, but we know that it is the influence of organized interests, and not the will expressed by aggregated preferences of individual citizens. To argue otherwise, he implied, is merely to wish for a kind of government we do not have.

More recent critics have added to Blumer's view the idea that public opinion as expressed in surveys is not only wrong, but pernicious. To cite one example, Ginsberg (1986) argues that polls domesticate protest, and are a mechanism used by elites to give the illusion of citizen participation. His critique follows in the footsteps of Pollock (1955) and Mills (1959), who pointed out that surveys structure public opinion expression within a particular set of political "givens." In surveys, it is argued, people are asked to *react* to issues framed by elites according to acceptable status quo assumptions. Added to this perspective is a kind of "Gresham's Law" argument: survey-type public opinion tends to delegitimate or drive out other forms of opinion expression because surveys are "cloaked in the guise of science." The contention is that real "grass roots" opinion expression has been supplanted over this century, as various types of collective action, *salon* discussion, reading societies and straw polls—common in the 18th and 19th centuries—have been replaced by the rationalized-elite sponsored survey (see Beniger, 1983; Cantrell, 1989; and Herbst, 1991). Opinion expression through surveys undoubtedly would be seen by some critics as an example of the "degeneration" of the "public sphere" (Habermas, 1989).

An Evaluation

How do we evaluate these conflicting ideas about public opinion? Is the inclusive, plebiscitary model underlying surveys actually a subterfuge through which public opinion is spuriously created? Are opinions expressed in surveys artificial and those expressed in town meetings genuine? Have surveys replaced modes of genuine opinion expression? This chapter cannot answer such questions thoroughly, but we need to address them sufficiently to be able to provide a context for subsequent description and analysis of the public opinion industry.

Let us take up the "manufacturing" charge first. It is clear that survey measurement is a rationalized, and, in some aspects, bureaucratized process. There are systematic procedures for selecting, contacting, and interviewing respondents, as well as for coding and aggregating responses, assessing relationships, and estimating errors of various kinds. The measurement process is often expensive, involving the combined efforts of teams of professionals, or teams of organizations. The rationalization of opinion research in surveys means that there is a carefully defined framework for gathering and interpreting observations; the framework is designed to capture and channel opinions so as to be able to make particular kinds of sense. Since the framework is designed to permit specific ways of looking at public opinion, to a greater or lesser degree it will not capture or will "misinterpret" people's views. The often expensive nature of the measurement process means that topics that are investigated through surveys are those that can garner sufficient financial support. Clients who provide the essential funds for survey research, therefore, exercise at least *de facto* control over what research gets done and how it is conducted.

Rationalization and dependence on financial support are buttresses in the argument that surveys "manufacture" public opinion. It is clear, however, that *any* product of a measurement process—whether it is well defined and systematically carried out or vague and haphazard—is shaped to some degree by the process. One cannot avoid framing issues and observations; it is impossible to study any phenomenon in a completely disinterested, all-encompassing and unobtrusive way. Participant observation, fieldwork, historiography, and surveys all involve defining the problematic issues, deciding what is notable, and making interpretations. A primary value of survey measurement is that it offers a more comprehensive and explicit way to understand the shaping influence of the measurement process itself than do other approaches that claim to be more "naturalistic." The corresponding handicap of surveys is that their funding requirements and design parameters sharply constrain the way public opinion is studied and the inferences that can reasonably be made.

Surveys do not inherently "manufacture" public opinion any more than any other method of study. The opinions expressed by survey respondents are intrinsically no less genuine. (The opinions may, depending on one's purpose for knowing, be *more* genuine than those expressed in a public meeting where the possibility of social sanction may profoundly shape the views declared.) It is fair to say, however, that survey evidence is often *used* to manufacture public opinion when the constraints of the measurement process are ignored or hidden, and when the sample public is reified and inferences go beyond the intended survey framework. As official counterweights to this practice, the methodological literature and public opinion industry standards that flow from it mandate that all publicized survey-based claims about the nature of public opinion contain information about how the survey evidence was produced, and for whom. The matter of survey standards is discussed further below.

No form of opinion expression is beyond critique, and there was no "golden age" of opinion expression. Schudson (1992) has noted that the American experience in the 18th and 19th centuries is not on the whole supportive of Habermas's (1989) claim about a rational "public sphere." At various points, he argues, participation was not very widespread, and when widespread was not necessarily "rational." Mansbridge (1980) has pointed out that attendance at New England town meetings was not very high on a regular basis, unless residents were fined for being absent. Political campaigning in the latter 19th century, long before polls were systematized, was imbued with a kind of "hoopla" perhaps worse than we decry today (Schudson, 1992). Surveys have not, in and of themselves, made the climate of opinion expression worse than it used to be. The inclusive, plebiscitary survey—with all of its limitations—supplements rather than supplants other modes of opinion expression, each with its own limitations.

Acceptance of one of the definitions of public opinion sketched out here, then, does not logically imply rejection of the other. It is perfectly possible to study public opinion expression in the manner advocated by Blumer—begin with a policy decision and work backward to identify the influence of public opinion—and *also* study the characteristics of "mass" opinion collected in a survey. Each perspective can teach us something about public opinion.

In a purely pragmatic sense, in fact, it is now necessary for scholarship to deal simultaneously with the "organic" and "aggregate" views of public opinion, since "discourse in the public sphere" is apt to include organized groups' claims based on purchased survey evidence, about "the public's" support for their positions. It may have been possible once to segregate organized, interested, active public opinion from constructed opinion aggregates, but now the aggregates play an important role in the arguments built by organized "publics" to further their causes (see, e.g., Clymer, 1991; Herbst, 1991). To paraphrase Blumer, it may be normatively laudable to think about public opinion as organic, informed, involved, interactive, and so forth, but it is *empirically* inaccurate and naive to restrict its meaning to this sense. If "the public" uses surveys to talk about itself, we must recognize that the plebiscitary concept of public opinion is not merely a self-interested commercial claim made by pollsters.

The important role played by survey-based public opinion aggregates in the "public sphere" mandates that we look closely at how they are produced. We turn now to that task, recognizing that insights into the public opinion industry are not merely grist for the mill of survey critics, but are essential to understanding a major aspect of discourse about the public.

THE INDUSTRY DESCRIBED

Pictures of public opinion from surveys are a function of two crucial relationships: that between the survey organization and the client, and that between the organization and the individuals whose opinions are collected. We will look at these relationships in some detail, starting at the individual organization level and then moving to consider the industry's place in society. Our first task, however, is to define and describe the public opinion industry.

Industry Demarcation

Any definition of the public opinion industry is somewhat arbitrary. There is a wide array of survey organizations specializing in different kinds of measurement; practitioners in one of these subcultures may not think of themselves as working in the same industry with those in another group. For example, researchers in the federal statistical establishment who produce major, ongoing surveys such as the Health Interview Survey and the National Crime Survey have research priorities that are quite different from those of researchers who work in organizations that specialize in ad hoc political polling. The former group tends to focus on behavioral and experiential measurement (illnesses, hospitalizations, crime victimization, employment) while the latter are more interested in "opinions," expressions of perception and preference, classically defined. To catalog such different organizations under the same "industry" label is to ignore these differences.

At the same time, however, the fundamental problems of producing survey-based information are the same for workers in these separate groups. All must be concerned with client support and expectations. All must recruit and collect information from more or less willing respondents. All must be attentive to the way the information they gather is used or misused, since the client's usage, even more than how well the survey work is done, may determine their reputations. In addition, while measuring experience seems different from measuring opinions, the difference is not as great as it might seem. Even survey practitioners who seek the cold, hard facts of behavior and experience often rely upon the subjective perceptions, recollections, and accounts of humans to measure them. That "hard" indicators like employment, ethnicity and housing have marked "opinion-like" characteristics has been noted by Bailar and Rothwell (1984), Smith (1984) and Newman (1984).

Governmental, academic, and commercial survey organizations appear, at least in a general sense, to constitute what DiMaggio and Powell (1983, p. 148) call an *organizational field*: "those organizations that, in the aggregate constitute a recognized area of institutional life." They exhibit "connectedness" among one another, and "structural equivalence" in their relationships to other types of organizations. Survey organizations are "connected" sometimes through formal contract, as when a survey design firm hires sampling and fieldwork services from other firms. Additionally, they are connected by virtue of the fact that personnel who work within individual organizations participate in the same professional associations and migrate among organizations in search of alternative employment. Survey organizations may be seen as "structurally equivalent" in that they have similar positions in a network of clients and respondents.

Because of such considerations, for our purposes here the "public opinion industry" will consist of governmental, academic, and commercial organizations. In broad strokes, considering all three types of organizations, it is fair to say that the industry in the United States is a multibillion-dollar enterprise, involving contacts with tens of millions of people each year.

Government and Academic Surveys

Surveys conducted or sponsored by the federal government account (conservatively) for well over 1,000,000 interviews each year, independent of the decennial census measurements (Turner & Martin, 1984; Bradburn & Sudman, 1988). The Current Population Survey sponsored by the Bureau of the Labor statistics alone involves upwards of 700,000 face-to-face interviews annually, with a cost in the tens of millions of dollars. Other federal agencies, such as the National Center for Health Statistics and the Bureau of Justice Statistics, sponsor surveys, usually in collaboration with the Bureau of the Census; their respondents number in the hundreds of thousands annually. Additionally, a considerable amount of federal government survey work is conducted by commercial research firms. In 1989, Westat, a policy research firm specializing in large-scale federal research contracts, had operating revenues of nearly $66,000,000 (including funds paid to subcontractors), a hefty percentage of which was the result of work on one federal contract—the National Medical Expenditures Survey.

Large, continuing federal surveys produce regular reports for numerous client groups in and out of government. Additionally, the databases are archived and made available to the public for secondary analyses. In these features, federal surveys like the National Crime Survey or the Health Interview Survey resemble commercial syndicated survey operations (discussed further elsewhere in this chapter). Many federal survey grants and contracts, however, have narrower foci and fewer interested constituencies, and do not support ongoing information-gathering efforts. These surveys are more like the "custom" commercial surveys discussed below.

Much of the work of academic survey organizations is sponsored, in one way or another, by federal, state, or local governments. Bradburn and Sudman (1988) counted some 60 academic survey organizations, ranging from small university service operations to NORC at the University of Chicago, and the Institute for Social Research at the University of Michigan, each of which have annual revenues in the $20–40 million range. No current total figures on revenues, number of studies, or number of interviews is available for the academic survey domain, and disentangling academic survey work from governmental efforts is very difficult. It is probably reasonable to speak of academic studies, independent of federally sponsored work, numbering in the hundreds each year, with respondents numbering in the tens of thousands.

Commercial Surveys

By any calculation, commercial public opinion work, independent of government-sponsored projects, dwarfs the efforts undertaken in the governmental and academic sphere. The number of "customer satisfaction" interviews done just for the regional Bell operating telephone companies in any year exceeds all of the interviews done in federally sponsored surveys, with the exception of the decennial census. Turner and Martin (1984), for example, reported that AT&T's Telephone Service Attitude Measurement (TELSAM) program involved more than 5,000,000 interviews annually in the early 1980s. By the latter half of the decade, the number of Pacific Telesis' customer satisfaction interviews alone rivaled the earlier AT&T figure.

Significantly, some TELSAM surveys fit in a category called "in house" studies—efforts undertaken by companies using their own internal personnel and other resources, rather than contracting with outside survey firms for measurement services. "In house" surveys are not normally included in estimates of the size and scope of the public opinion business, at least in part because of the difficulty in getting the information to count them. For this and other reasons, the more "official" estimates, which we review next, clearly understate the magnitude of the public opinion industry.

Honomichl, using data largely supplied by the Council of American Survey Research Organizations (CASRO), has published annual analyses of the commercial public opinion industry since 1974, all but the two most recent of which have appeared in *Advertising Age*, a weekly periodical devoted to the advertising industry. What follows is a distillation of major lessons from these reviews over the past decade.

First, as is the case with some major media and packaged goods companies that support the research industry, the survey business is dominated by a few major players that have grown rapidly, often through merger and acquisition. Honomichl's (1991) review of 1990 gross revenues for some 155 companies with business in the United States estimates that two firms—A. C. Nielsen and IMS International,

Inc., both subsidiaries of Dun and Bradstreet—account for roughly 48% of the total $3.1 billion revenues for all of the companies. The top four companies (combining Nielsen and IMS with The Arbitron Company, a subsidiary of Control Data Corporation, and Information Resources Incorporated [IRI]) collected some 60% of all revenues of all 155 companies reviewed.

The four giants are primarily known for their *syndicated database* products—specializing in collecting information over time about some form of behavior (e.g., television viewing, purchasing) from groups of responding units (individuals, households, stores) and producing standard reports for multiple clients on a regular basis.

In marked contrast to the syndicated database firms, the great majority of their industry fellows conduct one study for one client at a time. These "custom" research firms may do only survey design work, and rely on subcontractors for sampling, fieldwork, and analysis. The subcontractors are a major part of the business, though they do not appear in Honomichl's industry summaries. (The subcontractors do present a difficult accounting problem, since their revenues may be counted as part of the cash flow of companies that hire them.) Other firms—known as "full service"—handle all of the various components of the measurement job. Full service custom firms (which represent the majority among Honomichl's top 50 revenue companies) may have hundreds of employees, their own buildings, elaborate computer systems, many telephone interviewing stations, focus group facilities, and gross revenues in the tens of millions (viz. Maritz Marketing Research, Market Facts). Those companies that just do study and questionnaire design may be one-person operations, housed in dens of suburban residences.

As Wheeler (1976) pointed out, one doesn't need a large capital investment to get into the survey business, particularly if one opts for doing just the design, analysis, and report-writing. The significant choice for entrepreneurs is whether to take on the overhead expense of physical facilities, equipment, and personnel in order to control the entire measurement process and reap the potential benefits of added business. The picture of the public opinion industry we summon up if asked to imagine it probably consists of those entrepreneurs, from Gallup, Crossley, Roper, and Politz forward, who have taken the gamble and survived. There are, of course, many others for whom the overhead risk was too high, or who tried and failed. Honomichl's annual industry reviews, focused as they are on the more established firms, do not reveal the "boom or bust" nature of the business for most of the smaller companies engaged in it.

Polling Firms

The great majority of those who do *private* political polling for candidates belong in that category of small commercial companies that do not make Honomichl's list (nearly 300 such organizations are advertised in the February 1992 edition of *Campaigns and Elections*). If smoothing out the revenue stream (dealing with "boom or bust") is an issue for all custom survey firms, it is certainly the primary problem for political pollsters, regulated as they are by the periodicity of elections.[3] The revenues record for the largest and most successful of their number (two that *are* in Honomichl's "top fifty," though never higher than 27th, averaging combined revenues of about 2% of Nielsen's) is indicative of the fluctuations these firms must tolerate.

The Wirthlin Group (formerly Decision/Making/Information) and Market Opinion Research (MOR), both Republican polling firms, have worked for many Congressional and Senate candidates, and have traded off the major role in Presidential elections during the past decade—Richard Wirthlin serving as Ronald Reagan's pollster, and Robert Teeter, former president of MOR, working for George Bush. Teeter and a number of other senior personnel left MOR in 1989 and formed new companies. Teeter, who became Bush's chief campaign advisor in 1992, heads up a research design firm that subcontracted for sampling and fieldwork services for the Bush–Quayle reelection campaign from Market Strategies, the major company formed by ex-MOR executives. During the 1980s, Wirthlin and MOR were the most prominent among private political pollsters. Both firms were diversified to some degree, with commercial and governmental clients cushioning them against revenue losses in nonelection years. Even so, the average year-to-year difference in gross revenues for these two companies, reported by Honomichl from 1985 to 1989, was 28%. In other words, the gross revenues for these major political public opinion firms rose or fell each year by a quarter to a third on average, despite diversification and despite the benefits of being known as "the President's pollster." If this magnitude of variability is experienced by the most prominent firms, one can guess what things must be like for the smaller companies that focus exclusively on politics.

Public polling operations are a varied lot, including both profit and nonprofit, in-house, in-house with subcontractors, or full service organizations that just do political polling, or do it as part of their custom survey business. For example, *The New York Times* and CBS have full service, in-house, nonprofit political polling operations. *The Washington Post* and ABC do in-house design work, but subcontract for sampling and field services. Other media outlets subcontract all of their polling work to outside vendors. Finally, there are full-service, custom survey firms that do public political polling as one part of their business; among this group of firms is numbered the "household name" syndicated pollsters—Harris, Gallup, Roper.

Skipping the in-house operations and the regional businesses for which we have no data, a few comments can be made from Honomichl's reviews about the placement of some of the "household names" among others in the commercial industry. As far as revenues are concerned, the firms whose names are emblematic of the public opinion business are minor to middle-size players on Honomichl's list. Louis Harris and Associates is the largest grossing of this group during the 1985 to 1989 period (averaging approximately 18 million dollars), at least double that of Gallup. The differential between Harris and Gallup was largely the result of Harris' foreign revenues, which averaged about half of that company's total and grew substantially during the period. (Louis Harris recently left the company that he founded and that still bears his name to start up another research firm.) Starch-INRA-Hooper, parent of Roper Marketing Research (which does the polling), had about half the revenues of Harris in 1985, but grossed more than Harris in 1989, largely because of the acquisition of a shopping mall-based field service that added substantially to its revenue from media studies and custom marketing research. The Gallup Organization vanished from Honomichl's industry summary in 1988, after it was acquired by Selection Research Incorporated and the parent company did not report its revenues.

In summary, the "names" in public political polling, like the major private pollsters, are secondary figures in the commercial industry. Gallup, Harris, and Roper are subsidiaries of other firms. Compared to the largest custom firms that do no public political polling (Westat, Maritz, Elrick, and Lavidge, M/A/R/C), even Harris' gross revenues are only half the size; compared to Nielsen or Arbitron, the revenues for the polling firms are insignificant. And it is good to remember that the public polling portion of any of these businesses is not a significant money-maker (Bogart, 1972), although the exact contribution for any company is unknown. As far as revenues are concerned, then, public political polling, even conducted by well-known pollsters, is a relatively unimportant part of the commercial public opinion industry, though its cultural and political importance is undoubtedly much greater.

Recapitulation

As I have defined it, the public opinion industry in the United States is a multibillion dollar enterprise, involving tens of millions of contacts with the public annually. It is divided between organizations that emphasize large-scale, continuing syndicated measurement services and those that do custom survey work. The former organizations dominate the industry in terms of revenues. Of the latter type, private and public political polls account for a fairly small part of the business.

SURVEY ORGANIZATIONS AT WORK

The Nature of the Job

Stinchcombe (1959, 1987) provides a useful way to think about the organization of work activities. He argues that the purpose of much of the administrative apparatus in a company is to adjust objectives to variability in the environment. The survey process may be classified as one high in "social reconstruction," using his terminology. The work of a survey firm entails "shifting productive purpose" and "unsteadiness in the flow of projects," which requires rapid reorganization of specialized personnel (Stinchcombe, 1987). In short, running a survey business entails the configuration and reconfiguration of sets of skilled workers in order to complete projects and keep the organization alive.

Executing a survey requires study design, sampling, questionnaire writing and testing, interviewing, data entry, tabulation and cleaning, and analysis and reporting of results. As noted above, sometimes all of the skills implied by these tasks are housed under one roof (the "full service" firm). But throughout the history of survey research, there is ample precedent for some tasks being fulfilled on a contract basis, rather than being maintained within the firm designing the study. The most common contract arrangement involves field (interviewing) and sampling services.

Managing the flow of work in a full-service survey firm is a significant challenge. The variability in the number of studies contracted for is such that there will almost inevitably be times when the personnel who make contact with respondents are either idle or overworked. As a result, some firms have historically offered the services of their sampling and field operations to other survey designers on a contract basis. Alfred Politz, one of the most famous market researchers, developed an excellent national interviewer corps in the 1940s and early 1950s, but then found that he couldn't keep them busy, and decided to "spin off" the field operation as a separate company that sold interviewing services to a variety of survey designers (Hardy, 1990). This approach has been copied many times by other firms. In today's survey industry, there are numerous firms that provide fieldwork services alone.

The same historical pattern applies to sample design and execution, although to a lesser degree prior to the widespread adoption of the telephone for survey research. Now, because of almost universal telephone penetration and the development of efficient methods for sampling telephone numbers using random digit dialing (RDD), independent firms (e.g., Survey Sampling, Inc.) compete to offer RDD samples to those who plan to do a telephone survey. It is fair to say that the use of the telephone has heightened the tendency for survey work to be administered through contracting and subcontracting. High volume sample design and interviewing work provides economies of scale that are difficult to achieve in the full-service firm.

At the same time, however, the subcontracting arrangement lessens the extent to which any one actor or entity has control over the entire measurement process. Each subcontractor has its own procedures and mores, since there are no generalized craft certification mechanisms for interviewers or sampling clerks, such as those assuring competence in the building trades. Therefore, for clients, conducting a survey may entail paying a higher premium for the control offered by a full-service firm, or relinquishing some control to benefit from the economies of scale provided by independent sampling and field operations.

Recruiting Clients

The survey organization also faces uncertainty in the recruitment of those with resources to pay for public opinion research. Survey firms employ a variety of strategies, apart from keeping overhead low by subcontracting for sampling and field services, in order to decrease the uncertainty. As is discussed below in the section on practice and performance standards, buyers of survey services are often unable to discern which firms are competent and do good work, and which are incompetent. There are no minimum standards of quality that screen incompetents out of the industry. Therefore, it behooves the survey practitioner to find ways to gain name recognition and a positive reputation. The media have historically served this function for survey firms. If a survey organization can gain publicity by doing polling work for a media client, the exposure can pay dividends by recruiting clients who learn of the firm through the media work. Preelection polling work is particularly useful as a reputation builder, since there is a tangible "benchmark" against which the survey firm's work can be matched. Syndicated reports—provided to multiple media clients—increase the breadth and depth of exposure. Combining media, election and syndicated research was a business success key for George Gallup, Elmo Roper and Archibald Crossley. Media polling was the "loss leader" that attracted more lucrative business in other spheres.

In addition to reputation-building in this fashion, specialization in "lines of business" or in interviewing particular demographic groups (e.g., Hispanics, children, the affluent) is another strategy to attract clients. A syndicated survey product, such as a continuing study of purchasing or advertising awareness, or a report on the opinions of a demographic group that is of interest to multiple clients can serve not only to build a reputation, but also can provide a more stable revenue stream than do ad hoc projects. If a firm's survey product comes to take on the quality of quasi-official information (viz. Nielsen's television ratings or J. D. Powers' automobile quality ratings) the perception of expertise may extend to projects in which the firm has little or no experience.

Finally, clients may be attracted through the offer of a fast, efficient way to contact respondents. Survey firms advertise large capacity WATS telephone interviewing facilities, shopping mall research facilities, focus group rooms, or a door-to-door interviewer corps. Other techniques include maintaining a panel of respondents who are interviewed periodically when client demand dictates, or conducting a periodic "omnibus" survey, in which multiple clients buy a few questions and split the cost of the venture.

However clients are attracted, they are absolutely essential to the conduct of public opinion surveys. Without the financial support of clients public opinion aggregates would not be constructed through surveys. It is often a delicate task for the survey firm to recruit clients and then "train" them as to what is possible and appropriate to achieve in a survey. In addition to performing work for their clients, survey firms have an obligation to the profession and to the public at large to understand and convey the limitations of their work. This responsibility often brings firms into conflict with clients, who may want more out a research project than can or should be accomplished. Industry standards of ethical conduct and disclosure of methodology, discussed below, provide some benchmarks and ammunition in such disputes with clients.[4]

Recruiting Respondents

Finding, screening, and persuading people to respond to surveys constitute the major cost of doing surveys. As has been pointed out by various authors (e.g., Steeh, 1981), response rates have been declining in recent years, and this fact makes the task of recruiting respondents even more momentous. Constructing opinion aggregates according to the rules means strict adherence to probability sampling procedures so that the valued "margin of sampling error" (the only quantifiable error in a survey estimate that is typically mentioned in media accounts of surveys) can be calculated. Various shortcuts, including substitution for people originally sampled but impossible to interview, lower the cost of finding respondents at the price of leaving us in the dark about sampling error.

There are various techniques that survey practitioners use to reduce the uncertainty of getting people to be respondents. Among the procedures that may lower cost without automatically biasing survey estimates is the Mitofsky-Waksberg method, a two-stage telephone number sampling procedure in which the first stage is used to narrow down the search pattern to working household telephone numbers (Waksberg, 1978). Incentives to participate and increased persuasion attempts involve tradeoffs between costs and participation.

There are a number of commonly employed techniques for finding potential respondents, particularly common in the commercial portion of the industry, that threaten or invalidate the integrity of the opinion aggregates constructed in surveys. Shopping mall contacts are apt to produce unrepresentative, self-selected groups of respondents. Various forms of self-selection also invalidate the samples assembled in "call-in" polls and "warranty card" questionnaires. These aberrations and violations of research ethics are discussed in the section below on industry standards. Commercial efforts that distort the research process by disguising selling with research, or by linking individual's names and responses to commercial databases, exacerbate the problem of trust in the research process.

The major shaping of opinion aggregates in surveys comes in the administration of the questionnaire. We know that question wording and order can have major impacts on the opinions expressed (viz. Schuman & Presser, 1981; Belson, 1981). Interviewing techniques can also have a major effect on the responses obtained (Cannell, Miller, & Oksenberg, 1981). But these effects should not all be viewed as "artifacts"—errors that result from methodological factors. We can use what we know about how wording or interviewing affects responses to make the conditions of measurement more transparent (Schuman, 1982).

Further, we should be careful in making judgments such as the one commonly made by survey critics, that surveys push people to answer questions that they do not have answers to. Contrary to the claim that survey practitioners blithely assume that everyone has an opinion on every question, there has been considerable research and contrary comment on this issue. Alfred Politz pointed out that market research is not intended to find out what consumers want, since they often don't know what they want (Hardy, 1990). Survey practitioners have investigated the "no opinion" issue on numerous occasions, including Converse's

(1970) seminal paper on "non-attitudes," and Bishop, Oldendick, Tuchfarber, and Bennett's (1980) and Schuman and Presser's (1981) experiments on opinions on fictitious or little known issues. The evidence from these studies does not support the view that people in general will offer an opinion to a survey question if they do not have one. Bourdieu's (1984) discussion of political opinions observes strong class and gender differences in France in the expression of a political opinion. Whether the differences he observed would still be found today is an empirical matter. In any case, the data Bourdieu examines offer strong refutation of the general hypothesis that respondents offer opinions to survey questions on unfamiliar matters. Most recently, Yankelovich (1991) has proposed a set of indicators for measuring the "quality" of opinions measured in surveys. A key advantage of surveys, as Schuman (1982) points out, is that the method has the capacity to measure its own "artifacts," so that the nature of opinions as well as their frequency can be investigated.

The survey interviewer, who was sort of a free lance journalist in early survey ventures, has, by virtue of rapid and profound changes in the technology of data collection, become a much more standardized and monitored force for consistency in contacts with respondents. Centralized telephone interviewing facilities permit careful scrutiny of questionnaire administration, particularly when the questionnaire is controlled by a computer-assisted telephone interviewing (CATI) system. While the telephone has led to the growth of autonomous fieldwork research houses, it has meant a substantially more rationalized and bureaucratized environment in which interviewers do their work.

These sections on the relationships between survey firms, clients, and respondents have briefly touched on some of the key trends in the industry, and have identified some issues in these crucial relationships that speak to the place of the survey industry in society today. The next section takes up some of these matters on an institutional level, and reviews the industry's response to them.

THE INDUSTRY IN SOCIETY

The Industry's Image

The sociopolitical climate in which public opinion measurement is done is decidedly ambiguous. The multiple roles played by various segments of the industry—societal accounting mechanism, commercial intelligence service, popular culture and news generator, "voice of the people"—appear to insure it a prominent status in society. Public and private sector elite investment in survey measurements is a testament to the view that surveys can provide valuable scientific, policy-making and commercial information. The use of public opinion surveys in journalism (probably the best known application of the tool), furthermore, has imbued surveys with the quality of protected free expression.[5] As noted earlier, the use of survey information by organized "interest groups" to bolster their cases is a powerful statement of the perceived legitimacy of public opinion surveys. And, those studies that have directly asked people (admittedly, those who have agreed to be interviewed) about their experience as survey respondents find generally positive reactions (Bradburn & Sudman, 1988).

The industry's image as facilitator of public expression is balanced by the view that it is a nuisance and a threat. Starr (1983) points out in his history of official statistical systems that the original purposes of government censuses were surveillance and control. The modern census, by contrast, is conducted with an assumption of cooperation between government and citizens, facilitated by the rise of popular democracy, increasing rationalization of many aspects of life, and, at least in the United States, a popular affinity for quantification (Cohen, 1982). But the broadly cooperative arrangement between government and citizens in the census is continually tested, as is the more general cooperative arrangement between survey sponsors/organizations and respondents.

Critics of the survey enterprise, we noted above, emphasize the real or potential uses of survey data in surveillance and control. Developments in "direct marketing," largely outside of the survey industry but often confused with it, lend credence to the idea that surveys are nefarious invasions of privacy or ruses through which sales pitches and money requests are made. The barrage of "surveys" and "polls" one encounters in virtually every walk of life probably has led to a trivialization of survey data; additionally, data used to draw inappropriate inferences undermines survey credibility.[6] Finally, "respondent burden," created by time and effort requested by surveys (especially for select populations such as physicians) may be on the rise.

Industry Standards

How does the industry on the whole try to deal with its ambivalent relationship to society? The major institutional response has been for various industry organizations to promulgate an array of professional standards, involving procedures and performance, ethical conduct, and disclosure of methodological information. Additionally, "white papers" on undesirable practices—for example, "call-in" polls or selling under the guise of research—are sometimes sponsored by industry associations (e.g., Gollin, 1987; Advertising Research Foundation, 1987). Let us focus here on the various types of survey standards and their significance.

Standards of survey *practice and performance* address the issues of how surveys should be conducted, and what minimum level of data quality should be achieved. For example, standards of practice might address the methodological research underlying question strategies, or interviewer training and monitoring. Performance standards might set benchmarks for response rates or reliabilities of measures. Such desiderata are relevant to the essential issue of credibility: can survey results be relied upon? Standards of practice and performance also facilitate comparison among surveys and generalization across them.

Though these benefits are clear, and the economic literature on standardization points to advantages of industry-wide standards in other fields (see, e.g., Kindlesberger, 1983; Stoneman, 1987), standards of practice and performance have not been adopted widely in the public opinion industry, and where they have been adopted they are not adhered to very faithfully (Bailar & Lamphier, 1977). Dodd (1947) attempted to lay out a comprehensive set of standards for public opinion research, but, outside of some standards set for federal government surveys and broad hortatory language for others (viz. the American Association for Public Opinion Research's [1986] *Code of Professional Ethics and Practices*), his call has not been needed. Rather, the marketplace has been relied upon to determine practice and performance standards on a study-by-study basis. There is some logic to this, since data quality requirements do differ among studies, and since setting minimum quality standards can restrict economic competition and, therefore, raise the price of surveys generally.

But, as Leland (1979) notes, minimum standards are valuable to buyers of products and services in certain kinds of markets because of the "information asymmetry" between sellers and buyers. It is difficult or impossible for an inexperienced buyer of survey services or consumer of survey information to know, for example, whether a particular survey producer is competent or not (just as it is difficult to know if a physician is competent). Minimum standards of practice or performance would help to weed out the "quacks" and the "lemons." The marketplace, however, is not apt to provide a mechanism for setting minimum standards.

As is pointed out above, buyers may not be able to discern differences between sellers who offer "high quality" work and those turning out "low quality" products. If this is the case, the "high quality" firm alone will have to absorb the costs of its better service and, because of competitive pressure, will eventually have to match competitors' lower level of performance. Even if "high" and "low" quality service is distinguishable, the extent to which a firm's offering a higher quality service is able to raise the *average* quality in the industry (setting *de facto* a new minimum standard of work) declines as the number of competing firms in the industry increases. This is because when a firm is part of a large industry, its solitary actions are bound to have less impact than if the number of competitors is small. Thus, outside the government sector of the survey business, the large number of competing organizations sets a major economic constraint on innovation that might lead to establishing minimum practice and performance standards.

These considerations help to explain why minimum quality standards are almost entirely lacking in the public opinion industry. Rather, quality is negotiated—sometimes informally—on an ad hoc basis. There can be "misunderstandings," as when Beecham, Inc., a packaged goods firm, sued Yankelovich, Skelly, White/Clancy, Schulman, a marketing research firm, because of what it viewed as a faulty sales forecast for a new product. When this suit shook the market research community, one response by CASRO was to educate members on how to draw up service contracts to lessen legal exposure. As a result of the lack of minimum quality standards, the comparability of studies, the ability to generalize findings over studies, and the credibility of the industry, are not what they could be.

Standards of *ethical conduct* toward clients and respondents, by contrast, have been widely adopted in the industry and have been codified in federal regulations on the research use of human subjects. With respect to respondents, these standards address the areas of recruitment, description of the research and its purposes, and the handling of information received in answer to questions. In brief, standards of ethical conduct toward respondents state that the voluntary nature of the research should be emphasized, that the purpose and nature of the research should be made clear, and that information provided by respondents should be held in confidence (see AAPOR, 1986; CASRO, 1986). With respect to conduct toward clients, standards enjoin research organizations to maintain privileged communication with clients, recognize the limitations of research and not advertise more than can be achieved, and correct misinterpretations or misuses of research findings by clients or others.

The issues of informed consent and confidentiality in social research reflect a good deal of philosophical and methodological soul-searching, especially since the late 1960s and early 1970s (viz. Brodhead & Rist, 1978; Goldfield, Turner, Cowan, & Scott, 1978; Singer, 1978; Beauchamp, Faden, Wallace, & Walters, 1982). These standards seek to address the possibility of manipulation or harm through research protocols, deception in research objectives or, worse, deception in using research as a cover for other activities. The standards also address the need to protect the privacy of those who reveal their thoughts in answer to survey questions. In their aims and in their execution by governmental, academic, and commercial entities, these ethical standards are institutional mechanisms for seeing to it that surveys are not exploitative instruments, and that they do not use the good will of individuals to harm or control them.

Similarly, ethical standards concerning behavior of survey organizations toward clients are institutional responses to the claim of survey critics that polls are routinely "rigged" or shaped in such a way as to provide the "right answer" for the clients who pay for them. By telling survey researchers that they have the "right" (CASRO) or the "obligation" (AAPOR) to correct misuses of survey information by clients, these ethical standards serve to buttress researchers' claims to professional autonomy. They are institutional declarations of research limitations and integrity.

Industry standards of *disclosure* combine the concern for standards of practice and performance with ethical standards. In the absence of minimal standards of practice and performance, disclosure of information about how a survey was carried out, by whom it was sponsored, what benchmarks of quality it achieved, and so on provides a less than ideal but workable method of comparing survey findings and testing survey credibility. Additionally, the obligation to disclose methodological information in cases where survey findings become public separates the researcher's interest in a study's integrity from the client's potential interest in stretching the findings to suit his or her aims.

To summarize this discussion of industry standards and their implications for the industry's image and role in society, we can say that the most universal standards across all segments of the industry are those dealing with ethical conduct and disclosure of methodological information. The language in these standards and the enforcement mechanisms set up by the industry associations that promulgate them attempt to address some of the prominent charges of survey critics—for example, that people are duped or manipulated to give their opinions, that research is used as a guise for other activities, that the public opinion pictures put together in surveys are fixed to represent client interests.

One can argue that, whatever the standards' intentions, they are not effective in halting inappropriate actions in the survey business.[7] But more important, perhaps, is the fact that industry standards are straightforward *codified acknowledgments* of many of the points that survey critics raise against the method. In contrast to the naive view that those who conduct public opinion surveys are unaware, for example, of the potential for respondent manipulation, for client influence, or for inappropriate inferences from surveys, industry standards anticipate such issues and give recommendations for dealing with them. Rather than uncritically reifying the "direct democracy" model of public opinion, industry standards point to numerous ways in which the "voice of the people" is shaped and controlled in the survey process. Industry standards and the entire body of methodological research that underlies them constitute the definition of the frame within which public opinion measurements are made in surveys. That carefully constructed frame delimits the kinds of inferences that should be drawn from surveys, and explicitly points out the method's limitations.

CONCLUSION

The "public opinion industry" is a complex phenomenon, far more complex than could be covered completely in this space. I have tried to highlight some important aspects of how the industry functions and how it operates in society. My view has been that industry "insiders" are more diverse and more reflective than is apparent from reading the works of industry critics. Thoughtful practitioners grant that surveys are only one way to learn about public opinion, and that the survey method is limited in the kind of pictures of public opinion it can provide. This inside look at some of the factors that shape how knowledge of public opinion as produced in surveys is intended to give both practitioners and critics a more basic understanding of a major political, economic, and social force in our society.

NOTES

1. Treatments of sample design typically deal with costs in construction of optimal sample designs (e.g., Kish, 1965). Groves (1989) has expanded this approach to consider other cost-error tradeoffs in surveys. Converse's (1987) historical overview of the development of survey research in the United States provides considerable information on the growth of the public opinion industry, and Turner and Martin (1984) and Honomichl (1984) directly treat characteristics of the industry in addition to methodological discussions.

2. This is not to say that surveys have *no* eligibility criteria. Each survey must specify the kinds of people who are eligible, and screening criteria are set up to locate them and avoid ineligibles. Common eligibility criteria in preelection polls include adult status and voter registration. Surveys may seek to

interview only those who are deeply involved in an issue. The purpose for which a survey is conducted (and the budget) shape the nature and scope of the eligibility criteria, and the resources devoted to finding individuals who meet them.

3. Lang and Lang (1991) attempted to study the "political polling industry," including both private and public pollsters. They report considerable difficulty establishing a sampling frame and, then, a notable incidence of firms no longer in existence when contact attempts were made.

4. Survey firms, of course, are not alone in their need for financial support to do public opinion research. The requirements of technical expertise and the coordination of a complex set of activities conducted by trained professionals, however, increases the need for financial support, in contrast to the needs of organizations such as the "mass observation" group in England earlier in this century. Mass Observation's corps of untrained, volunteer diarists and observers made it possible to collect observations of public opinion more cheaply, if also less systematically. See Harrisson and Madge (1986) and Calder and Sheridan (1984).

5. For example, during the Senate hearings on the (unsuccessful) confirmation of Robert Bork as a Justice of the U.S. Supreme Court, Senator Oren Hatch, while criticizing a Louis Harris poll on the Bork confirmation, said that while "everyone has a right to do a poll," there is no right to perform "character assassination."

6. The most prominent mismatches between survey data and "reality" probably result from preelection polling exercises. Because of the particular difficulties of estimating voter registration, turnout and preference, because of sometimes shoddy work, and because of media sponsors' abiding ignorance about and misuse of poll data, preelection polls sometimes hold the survey profession up to ridicule. See Crespi (1988) for a review of factors in preelection poll accuracy. For a cross-cultural comparison, see Miller (1991).

7. As a former chair of the Standards Committee of the American Association for Public Opinion Research (AAPOR), I am well aware of the limitations of the ability of such a voluntary association to police the industry. Standards cases sometimes bring the threat of lawsuits, or the withdrawal of the offending party from the association. Still, the fact that there is a body of standards with an enforcement mechanism, however weak, is a public recognition of problems in the survey enterprise and a commitment to reduce them.

REFERENCES

Advertising Research Foundation. (1987). *ARF position paper: Phony or misleading polls.*

Albig, W. (1939). *Public opinion.* New York: McGraw-Hill.

American Association for Public Opinion Research. (1986). *Code of professional ethics and practices.* Ann Arbor, MI: Author.

Bailar, B., & Lamphier, C., (1977). *Development of survey methods to assess survey practices.* Washington: American Statistical Association.

Bailar, B., & Rothwell, N.D. (1984). "Measuring employment and unemployment." In C. Turner & E. Martin (Eds.), *Surveying subjective phenomena* (Vol. 2, pp. 129–142). New York: Russell Sage Foundation.

Beauchamp, T., Faden, R., Wallace, R. J., Jr., & Walters, L. (1982). *Ethical issues in social science research.* Baltimore: The Johns Hopkins University Press.

Belson, W. (1981). *The design and understanding of survey questions.* Aldershot: Gower.

Beniger, J. R. (1983). "The popular symbolic repertoire and mass communication." *Public Opinion Quarterly 47*, 479–484.

Bishop, G., Oldendick, R., Tuchfarber, A., & Bennett, S. (1980). "Pseudo-opinions on public affairs." *Public Opinion Quarterly 44*, 2.

Blumer, H. (1948). "Public opinion and public opinion polling." *American Sociological Review 13*, 542–544.

Bogart, L. (1972). *Silent politics: Polls and the awareness of public opinion.* New York: Wiley-Interscience.

Bourdieu, P. (1979). "Public opinion does not exist." In A. Mattelart & S. Siegetaub (Eds.), *Communication and class struggle: Part I. capitalism and imperialism* (pp. 124–130). New York: International General.

Bourdieu, P. (1984). *Distinction: A social critique of the judgment of taste* (R. Nice, Trans.). Cambridge, MA: Harvard University Press.

Bradburn, N., & Sudman, S. (1988). *Polls and surveys: Understanding what they tell us.* San Francisco: Jossey-Bass.

Brodhead, R. S., & Rist, R. C. (1978). "Why social science discovered morality." *Social Policy 9*, 36–40.

Calder, A., & Sheridan, D. (Eds.). (1984). *Speak for yourself.* London: Jonathan Cape, Ltd.

Cannell, C., Miller, P., & Oksenberg, L. (1981). "Research on interviewing techniques." In S. Leinhardt (Ed.), *Sociological methodology, 1981.* San Francisco: Jossey-Bass.

Cantrell, P. (1989). *Political polling in America: A study of institutional structures and processes.* Unpublished Ph.D. Dissertation, New School for Social Research.

Clymer, A. (1991, June 25). "Abortion foes say poll backs curb on advice." *The New York Times,* Section A, p. 23.

Cohen, P. (1982). *A calculating people: The spread of numeracy in early America.* Chicago: University of Chicago Press.

Converse, J. M. (1987). *Survey research in the United States: Roots and emergence 1890–1960.* Berkeley: University of California Press.

Converse, P. (1970). "Attitudes and non-attitudes: Continuation of a dialogue." In E. Tufte (Ed.), *The quantitative analysis of social problems* (pp. 168–190). Boston: Addison-Wesley.

Council of American Survey Research Organizations. (1986). *Code of standards.* Port Jefferson, NY: Author.

Crespi, I. (1988). *Pre-election polling: Sources of accuracy and error.* New York: Russell Sage Foundation.

Crespi, I. (1989). *Public opinion, polls and democracy.* Boulder, CO: Westview Press.

DiMaggio, P., & Powell, W. (1983). "The iron cage revisited: Institutional isomorphism and collective rationality in organizational fields." *American Sociological Review 48*, 147–160.

Dodd, S. (1947). "Standards for surveying agencies." *Public Opinion Quarterly 11*, 115–130.

Gallup, G., & Rae, S. (1940). *The pulse of democracy: The public opinion poll and how it works*. New York: Greenwood.

Ginsberg, B. (1986). *The captive public: How mass opinion promotes state power*. New York: Basic Books.

Goldfield, E., Turner, A., Cowan, C., & Scott, J. (1978). "Privacy and confidentiality as factors in survey response." *Public Data Use 6*, 3–17.

Gollin, A. (1987). *Phony polls, the profession and the public interest.* Paper presented to the 33rd Annual Conference of the Advertising Research Foundation, New York, NY.

Green, D. P. (1992). "The price elasticity of mass preferences." *American Political Science Review 86*(1), 128–148.

Groves, R. M. (1989). *Survey errors and survey costs*. New York: Wiley.

Habermas, J. (1989). *The structural transformation of the public sphere: An inquiry into a category of bourgeois society* (T. Burger, Trans.). Cambridge, MA: MIT Press.

Hardy, H. S. (1990). *The Politz papers: Science and truth in marketing research.* Chicago: American Marketing Association.

Harrisson, T., & Madge, C. (1986). *Britain by mass observation*. London: The Cresset Library.

Herbst, S. (1991). "Classical democracy, polls and public opinion: Theoretical frameworks for studying the development of public sentiment." *Communication Theory 1*, 225–238.

Honomichl, J. (1984). *Marketing/research people*. Chicago: Crain Books.

Honomichl, J. (1991, May 27). "The Honomichl 50: Spending for research shows 3.5% growth." *Marketing News,* p. 1.

Kindlesberger, C. P. (1983). "Standards as public, collective and private goods." *Kyklos 36*, 377–396.

Kish, L. (1965). *Survey sampling*. New York: Wiley.

Krieger, M. (1989). *Marginalism and discontinuity*. New York: Russell Sage Foundation.

Lang, K., & Lang, G. (1991). "The changing professional ethos: A poll of pollsters." *International Journal of Public Opinion Research 3*(4), 323–339.

Leland, H. E. (1979). "Quacks, lemons and licensing: A theory of minimum quality standards." *Journal of Political Economy 87*, 1328–1335.

Mansbridge, J. (1980). *Beyond adversary democracy*. New York: Basic Books.

Miller, P. V. (1991). "Which side are you on? The 1990 Nicaraguan poll debacle." *Public Opinion Quarterly 55*, 281–302.

Mills, C. W. (1959). *The sociological imagination*. New York: Oxford University Press.

Newman, S. (1984). "Housing research: Conceptual and measurement issues." In C. Turner & E. Martin (Eds.), *Surveying subjective phenomena* (Vol. 2, pp. 143–158). New York: Russell Sage Foundation.

Page, B. I., & Shapiro, R. Y. (1992). *The rational public*. Chicago: University of Chicago Press.

Pollock, F. (1955). "Gruppen experiment—Ein Studienbericht." In T. Adomo & W. Dirks (Eds.), *Frankfurter Beitrage zur Sociologie*, Bd. 2. Frankfurt: Europaische Verlagsanstalt.

Schudson, M. (1992). "Was there ever a public sphere? If so, when? Reflections on the American Case." In C. Calhoun (Ed.), *Habermas and the public sphere*. Cambridge, MA: MIT Press.

Schuman, H. (1982). "Artifacts are in the mind of the beholder." *The American Sociologist 17*, 21–28.

Schuman, H., & Presser, S. (1981). *Questions and answers in attitude surveys*. New York: Academic Press.

Singer, E. (1978). "Informed consent: Consequences for response rate and response quality in social surveys." *American Sociological Review 43*, 144–162.

Smith, T. (1984). "The subjectivity of ethnicity." In C. Turner & E. Martin (Eds.), *Surveying subjective phenomena* (Vol. 2, pp. 117–128). New York: Russell Sage Foundation.

Starr, P. (1983). "The sociology of official statistics." In W. Alonso & P. Starr (Eds.), *The politics of numbers*. New York: Russell Sage Foundation.

Steeh, C. G. (1981). "Trends in nonresponse rates, 1952–1979." *Public Opinion Quarterly 45*, 40–57.

Stinchcombe, A. (1959). "Bureaucratic and craft administration of production: A comparative study." *Administrative Science Quarterly 4*, 168–187.

Stinchcombe, A. (1987). *Constructing social theories*. Chicago: University of Chicago Press.

Stoneman, P., (1987). *The economic analysis of technology policy*. Cambridge, England: Clarendon Press.

Turner, C. F., & Martin, E. (Eds.). (1984). *Surveying subjective phenomena* (2 Vols). New York: Russell Sage Foundation.

Waksberg, J. (1978). "Sampling methods for random digit dialing." *Journal of the American Statistical Association 73*(361), 40–46.

Wheeler, M., (1976). *Lies, damn lies and statistics: The manipulation of public opinion in America*. New York: Liveright.

Winkler, A. M. (1984). "Public opinion," In J. Greene (Ed.), *Encyclopedia of American political history* (Vol. 3). New York: Charles Scribner's Sons.

Yankelovich, D. (1991). *Coming to public judgment*. Syracuse: Syracuse University Press.

6

The Press and the Illusion of Public Opinion: The Strange Case of Ronald Reagan's "Popularity"

Elliot King
Michael Schudson

By the time Ronald Reagan was inaugurated as the 40th president of the United States, he was already widely acknowledged by the news media to have a unique ability to communicate with the American people. Reporting on Reagan's first inaugural address, George Skelton, a staff writer for the *Los Angeles Times*, wrote: "This speech was most striking for its skilled, faultless, delivery and straightforward message. . . . What Americans saw was a leader with exceptional skills at communicating with the public. Certainly not since John F. Kennedy, and before that Franklin D. Roosevelt, has the country had a President who could match Reagan's skills in front of the microphone or camera" (January 21, 1981, p. 1).

Skelton's observations were not new. Almost from the moment Reagan entered public life with his campaign for the governorship of California, reporters sensed that he had something special. *Time* reported that Reagan was "the most magnetic crowd puller" California had seen since John Kennedy. "He can hold an audience entranced through 30 to 40 minutes of statistics, gags, and homilies" (October 7, 1966, p. 31). Reviewing Reagan's first year as governor, Jules Duscha, a professor at Stanford University reported in the *New York Times Magazine*, "Reagan has enormous plausibility . . . and the glamour of Kennedy" (Duscha, 1967, p. 28). In reflecting on the 1976 primary battle Reagan waged against Gerald Ford, *Time* concluded that Reagan's surprisingly effective challenge was due to the fact that "Reagan had touched a public nerve" (August 2, 1976, p. 10).

The assertion that Reagan could touch a public nerve directly became increasingly common in the media, especially after his election in 1980 as president. In the first months of his administration, *U.S. News and World Report* wrote, "Many already are acclaiming him as the most adept communicator in the Oval Office since Franklin Roosevelt" (March 2, 1981, p. 14). On March 14 the *National Journal* wrote of him as a "skilled communicator" and observed that "no President since Lyndon Johnson has had the entire Washington political establishment under the magic of his charm as Reagan, at least at this stage of his Administration" (p. 456). Within 6 months, Ronald Reagan was routinely described as the "Great Communicator."[1] Reagan's mystique as a communicator peaked only in 1986, when *Time* wrote, "The Great Communicator has come to communicate with the American people on a tribal level, a fascinating feat considering the U.S. embraces so many different competing tribes" (July 7, p. 14).

When the Iran–Contra scandal broke, the news media suggested that it was the first event in Reagan's 6 years in office to threaten his general popularity. "For six years, President Reagan floated in a lofty cloud of public trust," according to a *New York Times* editorial (July 18, 1987). Because of the scandal, political analyst William Schneider wrote in the *Los Angeles Times*, "Reagan has lost the principal source of his political effectiveness, a special relationship with the American people" (January 4, 1987, p. V-1). Indeed, some observers speculated that it was, in part, that perceived special relationship to the American people that had allowed the scandal to go undetected. Liberal political activist Mark Green held that Reagan escaped press criticism for so long because "many journalists were mesmerized by the aura of the presidency in general and Reagan's stratospheric poll ratings in particular" (Green, 1987, p. 10).

While many observers speculated about how Reagan established his special rapport with the American people, a more important question is why the news media—and many others—believed that Ronald Reagan in fact had a special rapport with the American people. On what evidence did they base their conclusions?

It wasn't from the available polling data. All the polling data from the first 2 years of the Reagan administration indicate that far from being the most popular politician in America, as popular memory now has it, Ronald Reagan was, in actuality, the least popular president in the post-World War II period. Far from having "stratospheric" poll ratings as even his political enemies seemed to believe, his polls were lower for his first 2 years in office than those for any other newly elected first-term president since such numbers began to be tracked. Just 2 months into his administration, during what should have been his "honeymoon," Gallup reported that Reagan's job approval rating was lower than any other elected president 2 months into the first term (*The Gallup Poll 1981*, p. 59).

This has now been reported widely in popular and professional journals without, I think, having done much to dent the general popular memory.[2] At any rate, the data are so firmly established that we can report them briefly here. Compared to his elected predecessors, Reagan had the lowest average approval rating for the first 2 years of his administration—precisely the years his legend as the Great Communicator grew. After a month in office, his rating of 55% compared to Carter's 71%, Nixon's 61%, and Eisenhower's 68%. At the end of a year his rating of 47% compared to Carter's 52%, Nixon's 61%, Kennedy's 77%, and Eisenhower's 68%. At the end of 2 years, his 35% job approval rating trailed Carter's at 43%, Nixon's 56%, Kennedy's 76%, and Eisenhower's 69% (see Table 6.1). In his third year, Reagan still trailed Nixon and Eisenhower, though he had a higher approval rating than Jimmy Carter. In January of the fourth year of his administration, Reagan's approval rating once again trailed Carter as well.

Of course, the first 2 years of the Reagan administration were marked by a serious recession. So while his policies may have been unpopular, the press regularly reported that his *personal* popularity

TABLE 6.1. Reagan's Public Approval Compared to Other Presidents

	After one month	6 months	12 months	18 months	24 months	30 months
Reagan	55	60	47	41	35	42
Carter	71	67	52	39	43	29
Nixon	61	65	61	55	56	50
Kennedy	—	71	77	71	76	61
Eisenhower	68	71	68	61	69	72

Data from Gallup Organization. Adapted from "Reagan and His Predecessors," 1987, *Public Opinion, September/October*, 40. All figures indicate the percentage of those surveyed who said they "approve" of the way the President is handling his job as president.

remained high and that, as *Newsweek* put it, the president's tactical problem was "transferring his glow from his person to his policies" (May 4, 1981, p. 22).

But was there a personal glow? While public approval of Reagan's general job performance generally ran higher than that of his specific programs, Reagan did not fare any better than other presidents when the public was asked to rate his personality. In a poll reported by Gallup on May 20, 1982, which compared personality approval at equivalent moments in their administrations, Gallup observed that "contrary to a widely held belief, Reagan's personal popularity is not disproportionately greater than his predecessors." At that time, Reagan's job approval rating was 44%, while public approval of his personality was 69%. This is a perfectly ordinary disparity. Eisenhower's job approval was 52% when his personality approval was 84%; Johnson's job approval was 48% when 80% of the public liked Johnson personally. For Kennedy, comparable figures are 64% and 86%, for Nixon 55% and 78%, for Ford 44% and 69%, and for Jimmy Carter 48% and 72%. Curiously, no leading national publications ran a story on this Gallup report (*The Gallup Poll 1982*, p. 107)—or on a similar one released the following fall (*The Gallup Poll 1982*, p. 243).

It is not these well-established polling facts we seek to explain but the disparity between them and the image of Reagan as an extraordinarily popular president. Why should a sense of Reagan's enormous popularity grow at a time when the best available evidence of popularity—national opinion polls—showed consistently low ratings? How could the press speak so confidently of Reagan's high estimation in "public opinion" while ignoring the conflicting evidence of the polls? In institutions often criticized for following polls all too slavishly, why did the media consistently ignore or misread the polls on Reagan's popularity?

REAGAN'S LOW POLL RATINGS 1981–1983

Reporters should have been well aware of Reagan's performance in the polls. Leading papers dutifully reported the poll results. But these same papers then carried stories which read as if the polls were mistaken or the latest polls an aberration. Our review of coverage in the *New York Times*, *Washington Post*, *Los Angeles Times*, *Time*, and *Newsweek* demonstrates that journalists wrote as if they believed that Reagan's popularity was inviolate and transcendent.

As early as March 1, 1981, the *Washington Post* reported the NBC/AP poll showing Reagan slightly behind Carter at the same point in his term of office. On March 18, 1981, the *New York Times* ran a report of the latest Gallup poll in three inches at the bottom of page 22. The story was certainly clear enough: "President Reagan's handling of his job after 8 weeks in office wins less approval from the public than any newly elected President in 28 years, according to the Gallup poll." It was actually much worse than that for those who read the whole story—not only were Reagan's "approval" ratings the lowest, but his "disapproval" ratings were nearly 3 times higher than for any other newly elected president. The *Los Angeles Times* placed their Gallup story on page one below the fold, the *Washington Post* on page three.

On the same day's *New York Times* op-ed page, James Reston wrote a column in which he reported that even Democratic leaders in Congress "concede that the President has public opinion on his side" (March 18, 1981, p. A-27). Why did they concede that? What evidence supported this assumption? There seems to have been a great disjunction between what the polls said and what Washington insiders believed.

On April 25 in the *Washington Post*, Barry Sussman's assessment of the first 100 days of the Reagan administration attributed Reagan's high job approval rating (73% according to the ABC/*Washington Post* poll) to his "personal magnetism," and held that "in every personal measure Reagan stands about as high as anyone who espouses such controversial measures could" (p. A-1). The story noted the upward turn in the polls after the assassination attempt but did not mention the surprisingly low polls of the first 2 months in office. There is little doubt that the upward turn in Reagan's April polls was a sympathetic rally-round-the-president response to the assassination attempt on March 30. *Newsweek* made exactly that judgment on May 4, but one week later reported, without any mention of the low polls for Reagan's first months in office, that Reagan's presidency was suffused in "a blanket of personal goodwill unmatched since Dwight Eisenhower" (May 11, 1981, p. 22). In what may have been the low point in press coverage of Reagan's popularity, the magazine reported that Reagan's popularity ratings in some surveys "are the highest in polling history." That was simply false. The evidence *Newsweek* cites was a Robert Teeter poll in which 48% of the public held the country to be on the wrong track, compared to 82% in 1979. This is not a direct measure of Reagan's popularity at all (May 11, 1981, p. 22).

On May 18, *Newsweek* reported that Reagan was the most popular and best liked president since Eisenhower and that "a swell of personal sentiment and political support for Reagan in the outlands" settled the Congressional battle over the budget. *Newsweek* cites no source for its intimate knowledge of the outlands (May 18, 1981, p. 38).

In August, Hedrick Smith wrote of Reagan in the *New York Times*

Magazine, "As a newly elected public figure, he has enjoyed warm popularity and a successful honeymoon" (Smith, 1981, p. 14). Compared to other presidents, this was not true, if the polls are to be believed. The June Gallup polls, released seven weeks before Smith published his story, showed a 59% approval rating (28% disapproval, 13% undecided or no opinion), compared to Carter's at the same point in his administration of 63% (19% disapproval and 18% with no opinion). Comparable figures for Nixon were 63%, 16%, and 21%; for Kennedy, 71%, 14%, and 15%; for Eisenhower, 74%, 10%, and 16% (*Washington Post*, June 21, 1981, p. A4).

By the fall of 1981, Adam Clymer reported in the *New York Times* that "President Reagan's once solid grip on public support appears to be loosening somewhat because of concern about the economic situation, and his speech Thursday calling for more budget cuts did little or nothing to reverse the slippage, the latest *New York Times*/CBS News Poll shows" (September 29, 1981, p. A-22). All well and good—except that his opening phrase refers to Reagan's "once solid grip on public support." There is no polling evidence that Reagan ever had such a grip while in office. All newly elected Presidents get the benefit of the doubt from citizens—but Reagan got considerably less than his predecessors.

The new year began with a new Gallup poll and a report of it in the *New York Times*: "Public approval of President Reagan has slipped below 50% for the first time and he now stands lower than President Carter did four years ago, according to the latest Gallup Poll" (January 10, 1982). This is a bit misleading. It suggests (by the word "now") that slipping below Carter in the polls was a new development. In fact, for the first 11 monthly Gallup polls, Carter surpassed Reagan 8 times. In Reagan's 3 winning months, his margin of victory was 4, 4, and 5 points while Carter's margin averaged 8 points. The Roper polls showed Carter outdoing Reagan every time in the first 30 months in office, Reagan outpolling Carter for the first time only in the summer of 1983 (Roper, 1983).

On January 21 Lou Cannon, widely regarded as the most astute Reagan watcher in the Washington press corps, observed in the *Washington Post* Reagan's low poll ratings but then noted that Reagan is personally more popular than his policies (failing to note, of course, that this is typical for presidents). Ellen Goodman wrote 2 days later in her syndicated column of Reagan's "protective coating of likability." She stressed, as if it were a peculiarity of Reagan and not a normal feature of every presidency, that "it has been as if his personal popularity had a life of its own, beyond his policies" (*Washington Post*, January 23, 1982, p. A-15). In the *New York Times* some weeks later, Martin Tolchin reported that seven Republican senators running for reelection in November were seeking to distance themselves from the administration's unpopular policies. Tolchin adds, "Although the President remains personally popular in each of their states, he is coming under increasing criticism for the worsening economy, growing unemployment and continued high interest rates" (March 8, 1982, p. A-16). At that time, after 1 year in office, Reagan's approval ratings in the Gallup polls was 47%. At the same point in their administrations, Jimmy Carter's approval rating was 52%, Nixon's 63%, Eisenhower's 68%, and Kennedy's 79%.

David Broder understood this when he wrote on the front page of the *Washington Post* in early April that Ronald Reagan "is the least popular president at this point in his term of any White House occupant since Harry Truman," and followed this with a careful analysis of Reagan's popularity. But even here the headline suggests that Reagan had once been very popular—"2nd-Year Slump: Reagan's Popularity Nosedives In a Familiar Presidential Pattern." Broder himself gives some support to the headline writer in declaring that "now Reagan has found, as his predecessors did, that popularity is short-lived." But there was no evidence in the polls, apart from the weeks immediately after the assassination attempt, that Reagan ever enjoyed general popularity (April 4, 1982, p. A-1).

Reporters did not create their assumptions about Reagan's popularity out of thin air. But since the polls provided no evidence for Reagan's popularity, how did the press arrive at their judgment? How did it happen that the press was, as Elizabeth Drew said, cowed by Reagan's popularity, or as Lou Cannon said, sharing in a national euphoria of Reagan's popularity after a string of presidents perceived of as failures? How did it happen that, as David Broder said, the press decided "not to make pests of ourselves" even when not bemused by Reagan (Boot, 1987, p. 29)? Michael Kinsley wrote later that critics of Reagan felt him to be neither bright, nor thoughtful, nor very honest, nor really competent for the Presidency, "but a large majority of people seemed not to mind." Reagan seemed to have a special magic with the public and, Kinsley recalls, "even Reagan's critics became deeply superstitious about this alleged magic. They became afraid to say, or even forgot that they think, that he's just an old movie actor. They themselves came to believe that to criticize Reagan personally was to cut yourself off from the democratic life force" (*Los Angeles Times*, December 4, 1986, p. II-7). How did it happen, as Yale professor Edward Tufte put it, that the Reagan team convinced their Democratic opponents, the Washington establishment, and "the 50,000 people that really matter," that Reagan was "really tuned into America?" (cited in Griffith, 1983, p. 45). Why, when available statistical evidence indicated President Reagan to have modest public support, did Washington elites and the news media believe in his invincible popularity?

FACE-TO-FACE COMMUNICATION IN THE TELEVISION AGE

Reagan's image as the Great Communicator did not grow due to narrowly defined oratorical skills. Describing the speech outlining his economic program, the start of the Reagan Revolution, *Time* reported, "The master of the television homily and the after dinner pep talk appeared not only ill at ease, but even a bit defensive." *Time* noted that Reagan rushed his delivery and misjudged his applause lines in a grade B performance (March 2, 1981, p. 10). Several other speeches were similarly graded by the press. If the press gave Reagan's platform performances mixed reviews, his ability to handle himself in press conferences was savaged. In his first press conference, held in the "honeymoon period" as the Reagan juggernaut was just beginning to roll, *Time* offered the back-handed compliment that Reagan displayed "charm, aplomb and the indifference to some details in the briefing books that has distinguished his public performances from those of his fact happy predecessor Jimmy Carter" (Febuary 9, 1981, p. 22). *Newsweek* described his first press conference after the assassination attempt as "full of faux pas. He may have a foreign policy but he has plenty of trouble explaining it" (June 29, 1981, p. 20). On a February 1982 press conference, *Newsweek* wrote of Reagan's ragged sessions "reinforcing the impression that the president is uncomfortable off the cuff." In that particular press conference, *Newsweek* reported, Reagan ducked questions, suffered from slips of the tongue and made factual errors (March 1, 1982, p. 28).

In his first year, Reagan held only five press conferences, fewer than any president in 50 years. He held to that pace throughout most of his administration. And the reviews of his performance rarely improved. "The White House press conference," wrote William Boot in the *Columbia Journalism Review*, "has been converted by Ronald Reagan into a forum for inaccuracy, distortion, and falsehood" (Boot, 1987, p. 20). Reagan's embarrassing press conferences became an issue early in his first term; his handlers sought to preserve his image by keeping him secluded from situations of spontaneous communication.

The evidence suggests that at no time in Reagan's first years was the general public as charmed by Ronald Reagan as was the news media. The picture reporters presented of Reagan as a Great Communicator did not arise from Reagan's ability to communicate to the masses. It can be explained, however, by 5 other factors: (1) Reagan's skills and the skills of his staff in communicating personally to the press corps and the Congress; (2) a changed political balance of power in Washington after the election of 1980 and a concerted effort to take advantage of this; (3) Reagan's ability to mobilize a key right-wing constituency; (4) the tendency of the press to defer to legislative success and to read it as popularity; and (5) the exaggerated importance that the mass media and Washington insiders attribute to the role of television in shaping public opinion—and to "public opinion" itself.

First, then, it is important to examine the power of face-to-face communication in the television age. What may have been Ronald Reagan's greatest strength as a communicator was not the well-trained radio voice or professional actor's skills but his frequent roles in Hollywood as "best friend." He retained that "best friend" persona, the kind of guy you just can't stay mad at, with the press and the Congress.

People in Washington genuinely liked Ronald Reagan. *U.S. News* reported as early as March 2, 1981 that a large number of White House reporters liked Reagan even though they did not share his conservative outlook (p. 28). *Newsweek* reported a year later that "most journalists who cover the White House like him personally" (March 29, 1982, p. 77). Jody Powell said, a year thereafter, "Most reporters I talk to say they generally like the guy" (cited in Griffith, 1983, p. 63). Steven Weisman's account of Reagan's first 100 days describes him as being able to command the public's attention, court new friends, keep opponents off guard, and maintain a friendly posture. Official Washington, he reported, was captivated by Reagan's affability (Weisman, 1981, p. 80).

Reagan's likeability contrasted to outgoing President Jimmy Carter. The press did not like Carter. *Newsweek* reported that Carter hated the Washington establishment and the establishment reciprocated the feeling (November 17, 1980, p. 30). In contrast, Reagan's first postelection visit to Washington showed Reagan sweeping the city's "glitterati" off their feet. Carter, *Newsweek* said, had been too stubbornly the standoffish outsider. He was too unsocial, too—even billing Congressional leaders for White House breakfasts (December 1, 1980, p. 30). Reagan and his aides began meeting with Washington leaders immediately after the election—and, in sharp contrast to the Carter White House, attended Georgetown parties (Hertsgaard, 1989, p. 43). *Newsweek* happily noted that it had been years since Washington heard a president laugh at himself (December 1, 1980, pp. 30–32). Carter's "self-righteousness irritated many reporters" according to John Herbers (Herbers, 1982, p. 96). Thus, not only did they like Reagan, but they felt a great relief and great contrast to the Carter years. "Ronald Reagan," said his 1980 campaign press secretary Lyn Nofziger, "whether you like him or not, always comes across as a nice man. Carter does not come across as a nice man. And I think that has to have a subconscious effect over reporters" (Robinson & Sheehan, 1983, p. 137).

This was not a matter only of Reagan personally but of a public relations staff that received widespread approbation. John Herbers wrote in the *New York Times Magazine* that James Baker had put together a very professional and amiable staff—with Larry Speakes and David Gergen both singled out (Herbers, 1982, p. 96). Baker assembled "an extraordinarily capable staff," Hedrick Smith later wrote (Smith, 1988, p. 316). Morton Kondracke praised Gergen's abilities in *The New Republic* (December 31, 1983, p. 11).

Reagan's affability with Congress was as important as his likeability with the press. His personal appeal seemed especially important with the Democrats. House Speaker Thomas P. (Tip) O'Neill was quoted in the press on his personal liking for the President. The *Washington Post* (November 8, 1981) quoted his comments: "People like him as an individual, and he handles the media better than anybody since Franklin Roosevelt, even including Jack. There's just something about the guy that people like. They want him to be a success." *Time* (February 22, 1982) quoted O'Neill as saying, "Generally, I like the fella. He tells a good Irish story" (p. 12).

But Reagan's way with the Congress, too, was much more than his pleasing personal style; personally and through what was widely acknowledged as an unusually skillful and professional staff, Reagan courted Congressional support. Tip O'Neill recalled later that Reagan's staff work with the Congress was extraordinary—"the Reagan team in 1981 was probably the best- run political operating unit I've ever seen" (O'Neill, 1987, p. 345). Max Friedersdorf, Reagan's first Congressional liaison, was widely praised for the skill with which he guided the Reagan program through Congress in 1981. Friedersdorf arranged 69 meetings for key Congressmen in the Oval Office in Reagan's first 100 days. He brought 60 Democrats to the White House the week before the key budget vote in May, 1981, and himself accompanied undecided Congressmen to concerts and the opera the nights before the final vote. Within hours after the vote, thank-you notes signed by the President were delivered to all who voted with him (*Congressional Quarterly*, 1982, p. 19). James Reston reported early on that the President was solicitous of the Congress, calling leaders to private White House dinners and establishing an effective liaison. In his first months, he clearly had better relations with Congress than Carter ever did (*New York Times*, March 18, 1981, A27). Reagan may have delegated much of his work to others but he did not delegate the job of "Chief Salesperson," as *U.S. News* put it. He spent hours a day selling his policies to legislators. "We had to keep him off the Hill when we first arrived or he'd have been there every day," remarked Tom Korologos, the Congressional liaison officer during the transition from the Carter administration (*Newsweek*, May 18, 1981, p. 40). Reagan was lavish in his use of social invitations, his distribution of presidential cuff-links and signed photographs, and his timely phone calls to key Congressmen (Cannon, 1982, p. 333). By the fall of 1981, Haynes Johnson could conclude in the *Washington Post*, "For the first time in years Washington has a president it really likes, one who clearly relishes the role and is good at it to boot" (November 22, 1981, A3). The operative word here is "Washington." Whatever the general public was feeling was in large measure irrelevant; Reagan and his staff had won the applause of the local opinion-makers and politicians.

But Washington would not long have been impressed if the Reagan administration offered nothing more than bonhommie and good cheer. Washington admires success—and Reagan was quickly able to achieve it. Some of this may have been done with mirrors, of course. This is particularly true of the interpretation of Reagan's electoral victory as a great "mandate" for his policies. Before the election, it was reasonably clear that what candidate Reagan had going for him most of all was the public's distaste for an apparently ineffectual Carter administration held hostage by the Iran crisis. Just before the election, for instance, *Newsweek* described President Carter as "the least popular president to run for reelection since Hoover" (October 27, 1980, p. 15). But within weeks, the same magazine, while reporting that 4 out of 5 Reagan voters supported him because of Carter's poor performance (according to exit polls), also concluded that the election was a "rousing vote of confidence" in Ronald Reagan and his "politics of nostalgia" (*Newsweek*, November 17, 1980, 27–32). The 1980 election came quickly to be remembered as a Reagan landslide and a mandate for his policies. And it was true that Reagan's margin over Carter was substantial—but John Anderson picked up a significant share of votes, giving Reagan under 51% of the popular vote. Most observers now recognize the election as a referendum on Carter, but the Reagan administration worked hard to reshape perceptions of the November test as a validation of Reagan's new conservative agenda. All of this may have been accentuated because the results were a surprise. Days before the election some pollsters still judged the race too close to call.

In retrospect, most political scientists agree that one need not invoke anything at all about Reagan's personal appeal to explain his 1980 victory (or his 1984 landslide); a simple model of "economic voting" fits the evidence very nicely (Kiewiet & Rivers, 1985; Hibbs, 1987, pp.

186–187). But in what social psychologists refer to as the "fundamental attribution error" in lay judgments about causality, people seek actor-based rather than situation-based explanations of phenomena they want to understand. The media are far from immune to this error, particularly when it comes to understanding elections and Presidential popularity. In fact, it may be that making the "attribution error" is a *requirement* of story-telling journalism; identifiable human actors a reader can love or hate, not abstract social forces and social structures, are essential elements in the conventions of news writing.

Reagan followed his electoral victory with an aggressive and uncompromising legislative program. In his first 100 days, he proposed a budget that severely cut social programs and rapidly increased defense spending. With battle lines drawn by the press as the President on one side and the Congress on the other, the measure of Reagan's authority and political strength was taken with every legislative skirmish. Reagan did remarkably well at these tests. According to *Congressional Quarterly*'s study of presidential support in Congress, Congress followed Reagan's wishes 82.4% of the time in his first year, the best record for a president since Lyndon Johnson won Congressional approval for 95% of his programs in 1965 (*Congressional Quarterly*, 1982, p. 18). Perhaps more impressive, Reagan's bills passed relatively unsullied by compromise with the Congress. House Majority Leader Jim Wright complained, "There has never been an administration that has demanded to dictate so completely to the Congress. I don't know what it will take to satisfy them, I guess for Congress to resign and give them our voting proxy cards" (*Congressional Quarterly*, 1982, p. 15).

Within his first 2 months in office, Reagan found the Congress bowing to his legislative wishes. This required much more than a smiling television personality and good Congressional liaison. In the 1980 elections, Republicans captured control of the Senate, turning a 58–41 Democratic edge into a 53–47 Republican majority. In the House, Republicans gained 33 seats, giving them 192 to the Democrats' 243. With 30 avowed conservatives numbered among the Democrats, it was clear that the Congressional balance of power had swung to the Republicans. There was even a moment in November when 26 conservative Democrats thought of joining the Republicans to form a new majority (*National Journal*, November 8, p. 3295; November 15, p. 1943). The Democrats were in disarray.

From the moment the 1980 elections were tallied, then, and the Senate in Republican control for the first time in a generation, it was clear that the House would be the main battleground for Reagan's new programs. This made for a simple story line in the news—a new protagonist in the White House battling an entrenched Congressional establishment in the House. When Reagan's spartan budget made its way through the House in May by a vote of 218 to 214, *Newsweek* wrote, "The citadel fell to an irresistible force named Ronald Reagan and his cut and slash assault on big government" (May 18, 1981, p. 38).

A leading explanation for Reagan's stunning success—and it was indeed a stunning success—was Reagan's ability to take his case to the people to intimidate and overcome the Congress. Recent analysis casts serious doubt on this explanation. In a detailed examination of the politics of Reagan's 1981 tax and budget cuts, Marc Bodnick takes issue with Sam Kernell's influential account (1986) of the growing importance to presidential power of "going public" rather than "bargaining" directly with Congress. While Kernell is certainly correct in emphasizing that both access to television and to jet airplanes offers new flexibility to the Presidential arsenal, Bodnick argues that "bargaining" for Reagan in 1981, at least, remained the primary weapon of the Presidency. According to Bodnick, it was not public appeals that won the day but real compromises in the tax and budget packages to please a Congress already, without pushing or persuasion, notably conservative (Bodnick, 1990).

In fact, Congressmen were hearing from their constituents that they should support the president. Congressmen take their mail seriously as a measure of public opinion, but there is grave doubt about the wisdom of doing so, especially when the polls are telling a different story. Why did the Congress get so much pro-Reagan mail? We have to assume that, in fact, they did; Tip O'Neill reports that he did. He also recalls that some of the Democrats who supported Reagan's programs "came to me and explained that the people back home really wanted them to support the president—which was undoubtedly true" (O'Neill, 1987, pp. 344, 349). Certainly the *volume* of mail increased remarkably; Congressional mail before 1981 had never reached 30 million letters a year and suddenly, in 1981 it jumped to 40.1 million letters, more than 26% higher than in 1980 (Ornstein, Mann, & Malbin, p. 175). But the likeliest explanation for the burgeoning mail bags is that Reagan had successfully mobilized a new constituency, the "New Right," that had never before had one of their own in the White House.

The advent of the New Right not only led to a new slant in the Congressional mailbag but a new orientation in the newspapers, too. A whole set of newly legitimate sources arose and colored the political atmosphere in Washington. Between 1979 and 1981, the number of stories written about the conservative movement soared. In 1979, for example, in magazines indexed in the *Reader's Guide to Periodical Literature*, there were 22 articles about the conservative movement listed. In 1980, there were 57 articles: in 1981, there were 106 articles. Spokespeople for the leading elements of the conservative movement—Terry Dolan and Richard Viguerie for the New Right, Irving Kristol for neoconservatives, and Jerry Falwell, for the religious right, became extremely newsworthy. In 1979 Jerry Falwell had been the subject of one magazine story; in 1980, 22 stories; in 1981, 32 stories. Terry Dolan and the National Conservative Political Action Committee was covered once in the *Washington Post* in 1979, 3 times in 1980, 25 times in 1981. By 1982, it was clear the media had oversold the New Right (Rosenberg, 1982). But by then, in a sense, the damage was done, Reagan's momentum in Congress well established, and the self-fulfilling legend on a roll.

There was no question but that Reagan effectively mobilized this conservative constituency for political action. "From 15 years of criss-crossing America in the cause of conservatism," Hedrick Smith wrote in 1982, "Ronald Reagan has developed the most potent network of political activists in the nation." Smith's essay on "Taking Charge of Congress" in the *New York Times Magazine* details how, under Lyn Nofziger's direction, the Reagan administration pressured Congressmen, especially "boll weevil Democrats" and other wavering representatives, through mobilizing political activists in their own districts to urge their support for specific presidential policies (August 9, 1981, p. 17). The Reagan administration carefully nurtured its core supporters, with the President addressing groups in person, on closed circuit television, or on tape, arranging programs in Washington and in home districts—and making sure that political allies let members of Congress know they cared (Hertsgaard, 1989, p. 120). News commentators may have imagined that the huge response Reagan received to some of his early television addresses was altogether spontaneous, but the White House had not left this to chance or to charisma.[3] Before a television address Reagan provided previews to political allies, several hundred at a time, and instructed them to notify their compatriots to send a message to the Congress. The flow of phone calls, telegrams, and letters was primed by this activity (Wayne, 1982, p. 55). Congress was indeed hearing from its constituents, but far from a random sample, it was a carefully orchestrated chorus of conservative voices. It should scarcely be forgotten that 1980 saw the defeat of 6 prominent liberal Senators—Birch Bayh, Frank Church, George McGovern among them, and John Brademas and other prominent House liberals. This enhanced the idea of a general conservative mood, although it, too, probably owed more to a carefully orchestrated and effectively targeted political campaign.

One legislative success led to another, each success impelled by the reputation that prior success afforded. Routines of news coverage in the press amplified the power of prior success, too. The press is more willing to judge a president's skills as a politician and as a marketable image during a term of office than to evaluate the public worth of his policies. Reagan's persona fit remarkably well into the tendency of the news media to judge effective accomplishment stylistically rather than substantively. The political press corps is willing to make judgments about political effectiveness and style but believes judgments about political substance to be out of bounds and beyond its own expertise. The result, in covering Reagan, was to play down exactly those elements of the Reagan presidency—his policies—that were not, in fact, playing very well in Peoria, and to exaggerate those elements that—whatever their effect in Peoria—were taking Washington by storm.

The press believed, then, that Reagan won his legislative victories because he was a great communicator. To some extent, the reverse is true: his image as the Great Communicator was confirmed because he won the legislative victories. The aura of victory carried with it a kind of protective shield that made both Congressional opponents and the media shy of criticizing the President. As Anthony Lewis wrote early in 1982, "He won big in 1980. He won again last year in the Congressional tax and budget battle. He has a political legitimacy that may well make the press shy" (*New York Times*, February 22, 1982, p. A-17).

So the perception of Reagan's widespread success with the American people was in some measure a projection onto the American public of his popularity as a politician and a person in Washington, an extrapolation from his effectiveness with the Congress, and an outcome of his effectiveness in mobilizing the active opinion of a new right-wing constituency. The final factor in manufacturing the sense of Reagan's general popularity was the belief in Washington, by now an article of faith, that politics today is in the television age and that a man with Reagan's evident personal charm on the television screen has practically irresistible power to shape public opinion. One need not look too carefully at the polls; one need only to turn on the evening news and see what a winning way the president has on television.[4]

In subscribing to this view, the media may have proved too clever by half. Not wanting to mistake image for substance, the news media have grown more and more sophisticated in the past decade in looking behind the scenes at how a president or presidential candidate shapes his image. If television runs the well-crafted photo opportunity and the newspapers follow with the obligatory news photograph, at the same time the commentators in print and occasionally on television as well observe that this was a well-calculated photo opportunity. (That the term "photo opportunity" became common parlance in the Reagan years is not an accident.) All presidents attempt to manipulate the press and control their own image, but Reagan's advisers seemed particularly skillful at this task, and the press seemed particularly awed by their image-making machinery. By the fall of 1981 when Sid Blumenthal in the *New York Times Magazine* dubbed Reagan the nation's "Communicator in chief," there was plenty of news attention to Reagan's "marketing brain trust." James Baker, David Gergen, Larry Speakes and others were all given high marks for professionalism and inventiveness in selling the President's image (Blumenthal, 1981; Herbers, 1982, p. 96; Smith, 1988, pp. 316, 319). But the news media assumed too quickly that if a lot of time and money was being spent on something—image-making, for instance—that time and money surely would bring results in its direct impact on public opinion.

Laurence Barrett, senior White House correspondent for *Time*, argued in a 1982 book on Reagan that the skill of the Reagan White House in shaping the president's image came to be a "minor myth" in Washington. He found the close coverage of White House media policy in the *National Journal* to be a kind of "gee whiz" journalism. He attributed what he calls the "fairy tale" of White House media omnipotence to the contrast of the smoothly running Reagan White House to the ineffective Carter White House. He also noted that the skill of the president's lieutenants was overrated because the lieutenants themselves were the sources for the "behind-the-scenes in White House image-making" stories; far from being examples of aggressive, muckraking reporting, these pieces served the self-promotional ends of White House insiders (Barrett, 1984, p. 443).

Print journalists particularly tended to overrate the power of the television image. Thomas Griffith wrote in a *Time* "Newswatch" column that the "people in Peoria" are more receptive to Reagan's message than "those who follow public affairs more closely." "The Reagan administration, more than any before it, aims its message to the big television audience and wastes little time on those who want to follow the fine print." This was, he wrote disapprovingly, "a TV presidency and the skillful merchandising of personality" (*Time*, August 16, 1982, p. 44). Mark Crispin Miller wrote an angry and intermittently brilliant column in *The New Republic* (April 7, 1982, p. 28) that tore into television news reporters. "The press," he asserted "and TV in particular elected Ronald Reagan. . . . Reagan won because his image was a perfect television spectacle. . . . Television has reduced our political culture to a succession of gestures, postures, automatic faces." But there was no evidence to suggest that Reagan's television brilliance rather than Carter's Iran hostage problem and a faltering economy decided the election. What evidence is there that everything in American politics follows from the television image—in particular, that public opinion is pawn to televisual politics? Not, when it comes down to it, very much evidence at all. The news establishment has a delusion not only about the power of the media but about the power of the public. The media, convinced that the story of modern politics is the story of the capacity of candidates and officials to appeal directly to the public, attribute enormous power to "public opinion." However, that "public opinion" is expressly known only through polls or elections. Otherwise, it must be coaxed into existence by leadership of various kinds—articulated by parties and interest groups, mobilized by social movements, sounded by reporters and Congressional aides talking to cab drivers or irate constituents respectively. It is not something that exists bodily. It is not something that storms down doors or barricades streets. Rather, it is a set of beliefs in the heads of key decision-makers about what people who are rarely asked to express their opinions publicly believe.

A good illustration of this comes in the frequent assertion in Washington that "the public" or "the people" wanted the president to succeed because they were tired of failed presidencies. Lou Cannon claimed, "Everybody wants our president to be up on a pedestal a little" (cited in Griffith, 1983, p. 62); Meg Greenfield argued that, "People wanted to break the spell of a series of doomed presidencies" (*Newsweek* March 22, 1982, p. 92). Haynes Johnson similarly maintained, "Americans do not want to see another failed presidency" (*Washington Post*, January 24, 1982, p. A-3). John Herbers also reported that people wanted to see this President succeed after a string of failures (Herbers, 1982, p. 75).

While all of this could plausibly be true, never did the commentators offer any evidence of it, and it is at least reasonable to suspect that the Washington community, not "the public," wanted the President to succeed and projected its feeling onto the public. Whatever the general public might have felt, the media had a strong desire to "reverse the trend of failed presidencies," as *Time* correspondent Laurence Barrett observed (Barrett, 1984, p. 444). The public did not hesitate to give Reagan low marks for his policies even if the press and the Congressional elite did; and if they tended to rate his personality higher than his policies, they nonetheless rated it lower than the personalities of his predecessors. If the public was rooting for Reagan, they did not mention this to the pollsters. In August, 1982, Richard E. Meyer of the *Los Angeles Times* wrote a front-page story, "Third of Reagan Voters Wouldn't Back Him Again." This was a conservatively worded headline: less than half (49%) of voters who voted for Reagan in 1980 asserted they would like him renominated, 35% wanted him dumped, and 16% had no opinion (*Los Angeles Time*, August 8, 1982, p. I-1).

CONCLUSION

We believe the evidence indicates that Ronald Reagan came to be described as a Great Communicator in the press not because of special skills in communicating directly to the American people but because of significant skill in communicating with key elites, including the media itself. In their attempt to evaluate their own personal impressions of Reagan, his series of legislative victories, and the information they were receiving from a fresh set of legitimate conservative sources, the national media determined that Reagan could communicate with the public unusually effectively. There is no evidence from his first 2 years in office, the period in which the media drew this self-sustaining conclusion, that the public agreed with the assessment. Reagan's honeymoon in the polls was less intense than with previous presidents; his rating on personal likeability was high but no higher than for previous presidents; and the percentage of people disapproving his policies (rather than having no opinion) was much higher than for his predecessors.

Is it wise to rely on the polls on these matters? We do not want to argue that they are the only measure of public opinion or that they are a "true" measure. They are a construct, just as is the informed but informal judgment of Washington pundits. They give more credit to the silent and the apathetic than do other measures—and critics of the polls suggest, rightly in our judgment, that this makes them misleading as a measure of "opinion." They evoke "opinions" where people have no opinion or no strong opinion but feel obliged to say something. The polls, for this and other reasons, are far from perfect. Still, if they are not the last word on public opinion, they are certainly the first word. And many of the reports of Ronald Reagan's popularity implicitly or explicitly take the polls to be the benchmark of popularity, the measure of the effectiveness of Ronald Reagan as a "communicator" with the general public.[5]

In the past 50 years, the direct relationship between the President and the people has grown enormously. However, the press has overrated the extent to which this communication is, even in the age of television and photo opportunities, "unmediated." Thomas Griffith, writing in *Time* in 1982, noted that President Reagan gave more prime-time television speeches than any other president and only a third as many press conferences as Jimmy Carter, commenting, "As an actor, Reagan learned that the box office is more important than the critics" (*Time*, August 16, 1982, p. 44). This statement reveals what it pleased Washington to believe the president learned. But Reagan assiduously curried favor with the Congress and the media; the general public was by no means his only or even primary concern. We have argued that just as important in the assessment of a president's image is his ability to communicate directly with key elites, including the media. The White House press corps experiences the president bodily, personally, emotionally. Yet, since the canons of objective journalism prohibit the overt expression of personal impressions in most brands of news, the nature of the unmediated experience must either be held in check or attributed elsewhere. In this case, we believe, the feeling in the press corps that Ronald Reagan was a nice guy, a feeling confirmed by other Washington sources who also judged him from first-hand experience to be a nice guy, was attributed to the wider public.

Indeed, it appears the only community not enamored with the Reagan performance in his first years were the folks in South Succotash, the people with whom Reagan was purportedly communicating on a tribal level. But the press, instead of labeling this president The Great Conservative, a description driven by an analysis of his policies; or calling him one of the most controversial modern presidents, a description driven by his divided poll ratings, dubbed him the Great Communicator, a description based in large part on the experience of Congressmen and reporters with an "unmediated" president.

Washington journalism is an oral culture at the center of a national network of print and broadcast culture. Washington reporters use no documents at all in some 75% of their stories, apart from press releases. Where they do use documents, a third of the "documents" are other newspaper articles. The "interview" is the mainstay of the Washington reporter, face-to-face, person-to-person. The inhabitants of the world of Washington politics, naturally enough, talk more to one another than to other people, but there is the danger that this practice can become self-enclosed. "The echo chamber of this world," writes political analyst Stephen Hess, "gives a special resonance, like the corridors in a hospital or penal institution" (Hess, 1981, p. 118). "If you send a reporter to Washington," said Steve Isaacs, then editor of the *Minneapolis Star*, "that reporter tends to be co-opted by the elitist values and nincompoop news sense there" (cited in Griffith, 1981, p. 92). That may be too cruel a judgment, but it is one for which, in this specific instance, our own research provides support.

NOTES

1. On August 2, 1981, Lou Cannon wrote in the *Washington Post* that it is fashionable to call Reagan the Great Communicator. On August 20, 1981, Richard E. Vatz and Lee S. Weinberg in a *Baltimore Sun* op-ed column on "Reaganspeak and the New Imperial Presidency" also make it clear that the term "Great Communicator" was a common appellation for Reagan. On June 5, 1981, Stephen Rosenfeld's column in the *Washington Post* refers to Reagan as the "Great Non Communicator." See also Sidney Blumenthal, "Marketing the President," *New York Times Magazine* (September 13, 1981), 43, who refers to

Reagan as "Communicator in Chief" and the February 21, 1981, *New Republic* TRB column that refers to Reagan as "our first communicator-executive."

Other notable coinages came later. The "Teflon President" was coined by Patricia Schroeder (Democratic Representative from Colorado) who referred to Reagan as "Teflon-coated" in a House speech August 2, 1983 (see the *New York Times*, August 9, 1983, p. 18).

2. We are not the first to note this misperception. Within the political science profession, the phenomenon we point to now—and that appears to be startling news even today to many people—has been widely recognized. Fred Greenstein, for instance, observed it early on. In a 1983 book, he noted that members of Congress had apparently bought the Reagan administration claim that the 1980 election was a mandate for Reagan's policies. "Although experienced politicians discount such presidential claims, members of Congress, bolstered by near uniformity in mass media accounts and by partially engineered constituency pressure, clearly were persuaded at the time of the 1981 Reagan tax and expenditure cuts that the president was riding high." Greenstein adds that they found it hard to believe "that such an effective communicator had not won the public over." But he then cites the Gallup Poll evidence that, in fact, he had not (Greenstein, 1983, p. 174). William C. Adams reported in *Public Opinion* in 1984 that Reagan was not, contrary to widespread belief, more popular than his policies (Adams, 1984). Everett C. Ladd noted some of the evidence about Reagan's poll ratings in *Public Opinion* in 1985 (Ladd, 1985) as did George C. Edwards in the same journal, calling Reagan "the least well-liked" president in three decades (Edwards, 1985). Far from magnetically uniting the public, Edwards found the polls revealed that Reagan had polarized the polity "along partisan, racial, and sexual lines." Another political scientist, Martin Wattenberg, working from the National Election Studies data rather than the Gallup polls, convincingly arrived at the same conclusion a year later: "Overall, Reagan was the least popular candidate to win election to the presidency since the election studies began in 1952," he wrote. "Never before had a candidate come to office with such lukewarm backing from his followers." Far from being overwhelmingly popular, Reagan had proved an "extremely polarizing" chief executive (Wattenberg, 1986). Thomas Ferguson and Joel Rogers (1986) debunked both the myth of Ronald Reagan's popularity and the myth of a general "turn to the right" in American public opinion. Robert Entman and David Paletz (1980) had early on noted that the prevailing wisdom that America had turned to the right was not supported by public opinion polls. We first reported our own findings in *Columbia Journalism Review* (King & Schudson, 1987) and later in *Psychology Today* (King & Schudson, 1988) and the *Los Angeles Times* (Schudson & King, 1988). See also Michael Benhoff (1989, p. 11).

3. It is important to note that the big response Congress noticed to the Reagan television appearances did not normally translate into increased popularity judged by the polls. A recent analysis argues that, over his career in office, Reagan's popularity in the polls was affected most powerfully by the "environment," especially economic upturns and downturns. It was to a lesser extent affected by "political drama," but even here the most powerful political

drama was the sort the President was least able to control. That is, events like Reagan's colon surgery or prostate surgery, the bombing of Libya, and the summit with Gorbachev had notable positive results for Reagan in the polls, and events like the PATCO strike, the stock market crash, and Iran-Contra had notable negative consequences for Reagan's popularity. But "discretionary" political drama—television speeches and presidential travel—had very little impact (Ostrom & Simon, 1989).

4. Widespread as this view is today, there have been some convincing dissenters for some time: we note especially political scientists Thomas Patterson and Robert McClure (1976) and journalist Jeff Greenfield (1982).

5. For a critique of polling, see Benjamin Ginsberg (1986). We rely primarily on the Gallup polls here, but other polls arrived at similar results. The Roper poll was quite comparable to Gallup (see Roper, 1983). That article interestingly argues that Reagan's "personal" popularity as compared to his "job performance" rating had been misinterpreted—that it was likely that Reagan's job performance was regarded more highly than Reagan as a person in his first years in office.

The only poll results I know that give any credit to the myth of Reagan's popularity come from the University of Michigan National Election Studies of 1980 and 1982 as reported in Citrin and Green (1986). In the 1980 survey, voters were asked to compare Carter and Reagan on several different dimensions of personality and character. Carter had the edge on four of the seven categories. The category where Reagan had the biggest lead was "strong leader." It appears people judged Reagan to be a "strong leader." That certainly has some bearing on "popularity," although it is not the same thing.

REFERENCES

Adams, W. C. (1984). Recent fables about Ronald Reagan. *Public Opinion 7*, 6–9.

Barrett, L. (1984). *Gambling with history: Reagan in the White House.* Harmondsworth: Penguin.

Benhoff, M. (1989, March/April). More gloss for the Gipper: The myth of Reagan's "enormous popularity." *Extra!,* p. 11.

Blumenthal, S. (1981, September 13). Marketing the president. *New York Times Magazine*, p. 110–115, 118.

Bodnick, M. A. (1990). "Going public" reconsidered: Reagan's 1981 tax and budget cuts, and revisionist theories of presidential power. *Congress and the Presidency 17*, 13–28.

Boot, W. (1987, March/April). Iranscam: When the cheering stopped. *Columbia Journalism Review,* pp. 25–30.

Broder, D. (1982, April 4). 2nd year slump. *Washington Post*, p. A-1.

Cannon, L. (1982). *Reagan.* New York: Putnam.

Citrin, J., & Green, D. P. (1986). Presidential leadership and the resurgence of trust in government. *British Journal of Political Science 16*, 431–453.

Clymer, A. (1989, April 25). At day 100, the people like Reagan. *Washington Post*, p. A-1.
Congressional Quarterly. (1982). *Reagan's first year.* Washington, DC: Congressional Quarterly Press.
Duscha, J. (1967, December 10). Reagan: Not great, not brilliant, but a good show. *New York Times Magazine*, pp. 27–29, 122–132.
Edwards, G. C. (1985). Comparing chief executives. *Public Opinion 89*, 50–51, 54.
Entman, R., & Paletz, D. (1980). Media and the conservative myth. *Journal of Communication 30* (Autumn), 154–165.
Ferguson, T., & Rogers, J. (1986). *Right turn.* New York: Hill and Wang.
Gallup Organization. (1982). *The Gallup Poll 1981.* Wilmington, DE: Scholarly Resources.
Gallup Organization. (1983). *The Gallup Poll 1982.* Wilmington, DE: Scholarly Resources.
Goodman, E. (1982, January 23). Reagan's protective coating. *Washington Post*, A-15.
Ginsberg, B. (1986). *The captive public.* New York: Basic Books.
Green, M. (1987, June/July). Amiable dunce or chronic liar? *Mother Jones 12*, 9–17.
Greenfield, J. (1982). *The real campaign: How the media missed the story of the 1980 campaign.* New York: Summit Books.
Greenfield, M. (1982, March 22). The challenge to Reagan. *Newsweek*, p. 92.
Greenstein, F. I. (1983). *The Reagan presidency: An early assessment.* Baltimore: Johns Hopkins University Press.
Griffith, T. (1981, May 25). *Newsweek*, p. 92.
Griffith, T. (1983, July 11). Newswatch: Going too easy on Reagan? *Time*, pp. 62, 63.
Griffith, T. (1983, September 12). Newswatch: Hype and macho rhetoric. *Time*, p. 45.
Herbers, J. (1982, May 9). The president and the press corps. *New York Times Magazine*, 45–47, 74–75, 96–98.
Hertsgaard, M. (1989). *On bended knee.* New York: Schocken.
Hess, S. (1981). *The Washington reporters.* Washington, DC: The Brookings Institution.
Hibbs, D. A. (1987). *The American political economy.* Cambridge, MA: Harvard University Press.
Johnson, H. (1981, November 22). Time for Bonnie Ronnie to show esteem for his rank-and-file. *Washington Post*, p. A-1.
Johnson, H. (1982, January 24). Reagan's presidency: Make or break year for him and the nation. *Washington Post*, p. A-3.
Kernell, S. (1986). *Going public: New strategies of presidential leadership.* Washington, DC: Congressional Quarterly Press.
Kiewiet, D. R., & Rivers, D. (1985). The economic basis of Reagan's appeal. In J. E. Chubb & P. E. Peterson (Eds.), *The new direction in American politics* (pp. 69–90). Washington, DC: The Brookings Institution.

King, E., & Schudson, M. (1987). The myth of the great communicator. *Columbia Journalism Review* *26*, 37–39.

King, E., & Schudson, M. (1988). Reagan's mythical popularity. *Psychology Today* *22*, 32–33.

Kinsley, M. (1986, December 4). A case for glee at Reagan's comeuppance. *Los Angeles Times*, Pt. II, p. 7.

Kondrake, M. (1983, December 31). White House watch. *New Republic*, p. 11.

Ladd, E. C. (1985). Reagan ratings: The story the media missed." *Public Opinion* *89*, 20, 41.

Lewis, A. (1982, February 22). Why the kid gloves. *New York Times*, p. A-17.

Litwak, L. (1965). The Ronald Reagan story: or Tom Sawyer enters politics. *New York Times Magazine* pp. 23, 46–47, 174–185.

Miller, M. C. (1982, April 7). On television: Virtu, Inc. *New Republic*, p. 28.

Meyer, R. E. (1992, August 8). Third of Reagan voters wouldn't back him again. *Los Angeles Times*, p. A-1.

O'Neill, T. (with W. Novak). (1987). *Man of the House: The life and political memoirs of Speaker Tip O'Neill.* New York: Random House.

Ornstein, N., Mann, T., & Malbin, M. (1987). *Vital statistics on congress, 1987–1988*. Washington, DC: Congressional Quarterly Press.

Ostrum, C. W., Jr., & Simon, D. M. (1989). The man in the Teflon suit? The environmental connection, political drama, and popular support in the Reagan presidency. *Public Opinion Quarterly 53*, 353–387.

Patterson, T. E., & McClure, R. D. (1976). *The unseeing eye: The myth of television power in national elections.* New York: Putnam.

Reagan and his predecessors. (1987). *Public Opinion September/October,* p. 40.

Reston, J. (1981, March 18). Hard times for democrats. *New York Times*, p. A-27.

Robinson, M., & Sheehan, M. A. (1983). *Over the wire and on TV.* New York: Russell Sage Foundation.

Roper, B. (1983, October/November). Presidential popularity: Do people like the actor or the actions? *Public Opinion 6*, 42–44.

Rosenberg, T. (1982, May). How the media made the moral majority. *Washington Monthly,* 26–34.

Schneider, W. (1987, January 4). Lame ducks and horse races. *Los Angeles Times,* Pt. 5, p. 1.

Schudson, M., & King, E. (1988, September 14). By charming the Washington crowd, Reagan put a lock on his popularity. *Los Angeles Times.*

Skelton, G. (1981, January 21). Speech display's enthusiasm for nation's future. *Los Angeles Times,* Pt. 1, pg. 1.

Smith, H. (1981, August 9). Taking charge of Congress. *New York Times Magazine,* 12–20, 47–50.

Smith, H. (1988). *The power game: How Washington works.* New York: Random House.

Sussman, B. (1981, April 25). At day 100, the people like Reagan. *Washington Post,* p. A-1.

Tolchin, M. (1982, March 8). Campaign worry: Reagan's influence. *New York Times,* p. A-16.

Wattenberg, M. P. (1986, July). The Reagan polarization phenomenon and the continuing downward slide in presidential candidate popularity. *American Politics Quarterly 14*, 214–245.

Wayne, S. J. (1982). Congressional liaison in the Reagan White House: A preliminary assessment of the first year. In N. Ornstein (Ed.), *President and Congress: Assessing Reagan's first year* (pp. 44–65). Washington: American Enterprise Institute.

Weisman, S. (1981, April 26). A test of the man and the presidency. *New York Times Magazine*, pp. 51–52, 76–84.

7

Propaganda and the Technological System

Clifford G. Christians

How small of all that human hearts endure
that part which laws or kings can cause or cure.
—Samuel Johnson (1955)

The Latin roots of propaganda are pastoral, even idyllic: to sow, to propagate. Undoubtedly the Vatican traded on that innocence when it formed the Congregatio de Propaganda Fide (Missionaries for Propagating the Faith) in 1622. But today propaganda is a term of reproach. With only slight variations across many languages, it carries pejorative connotations. The Congregatio de Propaganda Fide served as an agent of the Counter-Reformation, wooing in a generally positive manner those disenchanted with the Roman Catholic Church. But it also discredited Galileo as an enemy when the Inquisition convicted him of heresy in 1633. Severin and Tankard (1979, p. 115) remark, "Perhaps the term propaganda picked up some of its negative associations or its connotations of untruth from this major incident in which the Church was left arguing for a position that was scientifically demonstrable as false."

The propaganda machine of World War I made inescapable this rhetorical form as a menace to the public good. The classic study by Harold Lasswell (1927, p. 129) used the war as its laboratory setting. He defined propaganda's objectives as mobilizing hatred against the enemy and preserving friendship among allies. And when the Institute for Propaganda Analysis was established in 1937 by Hadley Cantril, it was preoccupied with the rise of Nazi propaganda through Hitler and Joseph Goebbels.[1]

Mainstream definitions continue to reflect this legacy of propagandistic powerblocs controlling the popular mind—the church in the 17th century and especially governments in the 20th. The *Propaganda Review* (Darnovsky, Steiner, Rappleye, & Stout, 1989, p. 11), for example, isolates propaganda as "a conscious conspiracy that uses the mass media to facilitate or to influence the activities of the state through the manipulation of public opinion."

Unhinging propaganda from its political base is an important spinoff within this tradition. Already in 1930, George Viereck recommended that propaganda be expanded to include attempts "on the part of *any group* representing some specific interest to put over its point of view, irrespective of facts" (p. 38). By 1937 Lasswell wanted to include every persuasive technique that influences human activity by manipulation (pp. 521–522). And a famous book (Lee & Lee, 1939) from the Institute for Propaganda Analysis written simply enough for public school education, warned of deception and thought control wherever examples could be found in social communication. But throughout these efforts to extend propaganda beyond the political domain, the emphasis remained on evil intention, overt action, and behavioral effects.[2] The Nazi information machine was still the archetypal case, and calculating manipulation has remained intact as propaganda's essential property.

The intellectual benefits of this perspective are significant: recognizing this form of persuasive communication as coercive raises our social awareness. Expanding the repertoire of machinations increases our critical consciousness, while specifying audience impact strengthens our educational strategies in combatting it. The French social theorist, Jacques Ellul, endorses this research on *overt* propaganda and contributes to its details.

But Ellul concentrates his scholarship on a totalizing model of *covert* propaganda, largely overlooked and misunderstood in the conventional wisdom since Lasswell. In the process he thoroughly redefines the meaning of propaganda, identifying with this term a comprehensive paradigm of unusual power. As a radical framework for understanding how communication structures come to dominate public opinion, it sets the standard for ideology and propaganda studies.[3] Modern pervasive means of communication, for Ellul, are not informational devices through which citizens guide politics; they are not merely stimuli but agents of propagandization. They do not exchange neutral messages, but subtly stitch humans into the warp and woof of an efficiency-dominated culture. Ellul's analogies here are bread—changed to fit the machine—and California tomatoes, the skins of which were thickened and the size standardized to allow for machine picking. In the same manner, he worries throughout his 50 books that humans are being gradually molded to fit the technological imperative (cf. Hanks, 1984). Ellul's sophisticated formulation centers the problem on *la technique* and thereby offers a more sure-handed direction for social change than one based on the received view.

TECHNOCRATIC CULTURE

Jacques Ellul was born into the Serbian aristocracy and was a member of a wealthy shipbuilding dynasty until the worldwide depression in 1929 plunged his family into poverty. As he roamed the ocean wharves of Bordeaux during his teenage years, he confronted first-hand the death and stark exploitation of this port city's longshoremen and sailors. While studying at the University of Bordeaux, Marx's *Das Capital* dramatically explained for him the economic upheaval in his home and cruel injustice along the docks. "When I was nineteen," Ellul (1970a, p. 5) writes, "I became 'Marxist' and devoted a great deal of my time to the study of his writings. . . . What Marx brought to me was a certain way of 'seeing' political, economic, and social problems—a method of interpretation, a sociology." He disdained Communist Party membership for its trivial agenda, although his conversion to Marxism continued to inspire him until his death on May 19, 1994.

Ellul's political activism is legendary (e.g., Ellul, 1981b, pp. 18–28). He participated briefly in the Spanish Civil War, joined the Paris riots against the Fascists, and openly opposed the Vichy government in 1940 until he was dismissed from his professoriate at the University of Strasbourg. During World War II, along with Camus, Malraux, and Sartre, he was a leader in the French Resistance, operating from a small farm outside Paris. After liberation, Ellul worked for three years as the deputy mayor of Bordeaux, concentrating on commerce and public works. On the national scene, he spearheaded the successful campaign of a group of intellectuals to force the French government to withdraw from Algeria.

While refusing to relinquish his crusades entirely, Ellul spent the bulk of his career (1947–1980) as a professor in the Institute of Political Studies at the University of Bordeaux, specializing in the history and sociology of institutions, Marxism, Roman law, technology, and propaganda. Ellul's assessment of political involvement becomes integrated with his historical and theoretical analysis of social institutions, leading him to a distinctive conclusion about the media and public opinion in 20th century industrial societies.

For Ellul, the technological phenomenon decisively defines contemporary life. As an explanatory element, he argues, it plays the part of capital in Marx's interpretation of the 19th century. Ellul does not mean that technology has the same function as capital, nor that the capitalist system is a thing of the past. It still exists, but capital no longer fulfills the role Marx claimed for it. Whereas work creates value for Marx, in extremely technological societies the determining factor is *la technique*. This is the force that now creates value and it is not peculiar to capitalism. The characters in the struggle for political and economic power have changed. In his earliest days as a Marxist, Ellul divided society into capitalists and workers, but he recognizes that the situation at present is completely different and operates on a more abstract level. We now have technological organizations on one side and all humanity on the other—the former driven by necessity and the latter demanding freedom. Ellul (1982, pp. 175–177) concludes that we must read the world in which we live in terms of technology, rather than capitalist structures. While this analysis privileges industrial nations, even that part of the globe that is non-technological as yet actually defines itself in terms of technological parameters, that is, as "primitive" or "undeveloped."

From Ellul's perspective, we have now entered a technological civilization. "Technology constitutes an engulfing universe for man, who finds himself in it as in a cocoon" (Ellul, 1965, p. xvii). The technical artifice is not merely one more arena for philosophers and sociologists to investigate, but a new foundation for understanding the self, human institutions, and ultimate reality. A society is technological, Ellul argues, not because of its machines, but from the pursuit of efficient techniques in every kind of human endeavor. Unlike previous eras where techniques are constrained within a larger complex of social values, the pervasiveness and sophistication of modern techniques reorganizes society to conform to their demand for efficiency. Scientific techniques are applied not just to nature, but to social organizations and our understanding of personhood. Ellul realizes that civilizations across history have engaged in technical activities and produced technological products, but a qualitative change has occurred in the 20th century. Modern society has sacralized the genius behind machines and uncritically allowed its rampaging power to infect not just industry, engineering, and business but also politics, education, the church, labor unions, and international relations.

Ellul's concern is not primarily with machines and tools but rather with the spirit of machineness that underlies them. In his view, modern society is so beguiled by technical productivity that it unconsciously reconstructs all social institutions on this model. Technical efficiency becomes a force so powerful that is casts aside all other imperatives. Ellul (1967a, p. 75) notes that "in ancient days men put out the eyes of nightingales to make them sing better," and laments that in today's technocratic culture, all other values are sacrificed to maximum efficiency. Unable to establish a meaningful life outside the artificial ambience of a technological culture, human beings place their ultimate hope in it. Seeing no other source of security, and failing to recognize the illusoriness of their technical freedom, they become slaves to the exacting determinations of efficiency.

The transition to a technological society is for Ellul (1989, pp. 134–135; cf. 1980) more fundamental than anything the human race has experienced over the last 5,000 years:

> The creation of the technological environment . . . is progressively effacing the two previous ones. Of course, nature and society still exist. But they are without power—they no longer decide our future. There are still earthquakes, volcanic eruptions, and hurricanes. But humanity is no longer helpless when faced with such disasters. It has the technical means to respond; . . . and this is why nature is always menacingly present as an environment that is subordinate and no longer basic. The same applies to society. It remains a secondary environment. . . . Technology imposes its own law on the different social organizations, disturbing fundamentally what is thought to be permanent (e.g., the family), and making politics totally futile. Politicians can decide only what is technologically feasible. All decisions are dictated by the necessity of technological growth.

Cultures are symbolic worlds of mediated meaning; in a technicistic epoch, our symbolic formations are dominated by technological structures. Thus, to define the contemporary era, we use labels such as the information age, the telematic society, the communications revolution, and the television generation. In Ellul's framework, communications media represent the meaning edge of the technological system, the arena where the latter's soul is clearly exposed. While exhibiting the structural elements of all technical artifacts, their particular identity as a technology inheres in their function as bearers of symbols. Information systems thus incarnate the properties of technology while serving as the agents for interpreting the meaning of the very phenomenon they embody. Ellul (1978, p. 216) calls our communication systems the "innermost and most elusive manifestation" of human technological activity. All artifacts communicate meaning in an important sense, but media instruments carry that role exclusively. As the mass media sketch out our world for us, organize our conversations, determine our decisions, and influence our self-identities, they do so with a technological cadence, massaging into our souls a technological rhythm and predisposition.

In Jean Baudrillard's terms, industrial society has become a world of simulated images. The proliferation of information technologies has shifted modern civilization from production to reproduction, from economic and political institutions to hyper-reality, where "everything becomes immediately transparent, visible, exposed in the raw and inexorable light of communication" (Baudrillard, 1983, pp. 21–22). All aspects of life, even the most private and sacred, become realms of terror in which humans exist as "terminals of multiple networks" (p. 16). In what Baudrillard (1983, p. 32) calls "the precession of the simulacra," we create cybernetic models to organize reality, but in actuality a reversal occurs and reality arises from them instead. "The real is produced from miniaturized units, from matrices, memory banks and command modules" (p. 3). We float anchorless in a sea of electronic images.[4]

COMMUNICATIONS TECHNOLOGY

This theoretical framework enables Ellul to identify the modern mass media as covert sociological propaganda. Propaganda is Ellul's term for the dominance of technical means over a society's goals. Rather than biased acts of persuasion, he redefines it as a composite of omnipresent methods that coordinate life in nations that are industrially advanced. In his scheme, the principle of efficiency that characterizes the technological enterprise as a whole also dominates the communications apparatus; the media do not transmit neutral stimuli, but integrate us into the overall system. Like the fish's perfect adaptation to its water environment, we are enveloped in data, absorbed in a monodimensional world of stereotypes and slogans, and integrated into a homogeneous whole by the machinery of conformity. The mass media provide heroes for the impotent, friends for the alienated, and simplified attitudes for the uncertain: "They codify social, political, and moral standards" (Ellul, 1965, p. 163). In the process they have become so powerful, Ellul contends, that congruity with the social system is considered normal—even desirable—and we ironically declare that new ideas or alternative worldviews are ideologies or "just propaganda." Our own voice and identity are replaced by a technicized worldview, consigning us, in Paulo Freire's terms (1970, pp. 134–150), to an oppressive culture of silence.

Ellul's distinctive approach eliminates intentional and personal manipulation as a necessary component of propaganda, but retains the negative connotations associated with the word. He is not concerned with counteracting specific biases in reporting or raging against questionable entertainment; he concentrates on the totality of the propagandistic system in which media participate. Particular deviations from prevailing media patterns are of secondary importance and actually divert attention from the human and social values of the controlling culture. His undying concern is over the mass media's in-depth molding until technicized conceptions of life determine how we act and think.

Because it is most recognizable, the least important expression of propaganda is demagoguery—the political leader agitating vertically downward to the masses with irrational appeals for change. As Jay Black (1991, p. 57) complains in jest: "Ellul took the fun out of the old-fashioned and sometimes simplistic search for bad guys who tell the Big Lie." The bulk of current propaganda is not targeted at social unrest by deceitful politicians, but aims at conforming individuals to the established order. As its primary network, propaganda uses a horizontal interaction between individuals through which to establish collective standards, peer pressure, and group norms. To Ellul, using irrational lies is an ineffective strategy; propaganda that appears outwardly rational overwhelms individual and group life with true but selectively edited new information, statistics, figures, and facts.

Ellul's organizing idea, *la technique*, not only redefines propaganda but also prompts us to reexamine our common democratic commitment to unlimited information. Democracy will not function, we are told, without everyone's full access to the day's events (cf. Westin, 1971). His *Propaganda*, *Political Illusion*, and *Humiliation of the Word* force us to question the informational lifeline per se. If *la technique* saturates our contemporary climate of opinion as Ellul contends, the public media cannot possibly fulfill their role of enhancing social life and citizenship.

Information, from Ellul's perspective, does not exist in industrial democratic societies. We delude ourselves into assuming, he argues, that open political processes can restrain our relentless march toward a unitary culture. Instead, in Ellul's judgment (1967b, pp. 160–161), "democratic control is impotent with respect to the administrative motif." The cultural uniformity imposed on democracies by mass media technologies is a subtle form of propaganda "as totalitarian, authoritarian, and exclusive" as that used in a dictatorship (Ellul, 1965, p. 249).

In a spirit akin to the monotechnics of Lewis Mumford, Ellul outlines an adjustment–conformity emphasis fundamentally destructive of democracy's very point of departure: its pluralism. All our various forms of communication may appear diffuse on the surface, but our many media messages are really "in basic accord with each other and lead spontaneously in the same direction, . . . and produce a general conception of society, a particular way of life" (Ellul, 1965, p. 65). Ellul worries that the media work upon our unconscious habits from all sides, molding our root identities and motivations. Thus we experience an imperceptible "persuasion from within" that we often undergo unwittingly:

> For example, when an American producer makes a film, he has certain definite ideas he wants to express, which are not intended to be propaganda. Rather, the propaganda element is in the American way of life with which he is permeated and which he expresses in his film without realizing it. (Ellul, 1965, p. 64)

The information explosion produces not informed citizens but those whose self-perceptions and basic attitudes have become crystallized. Ellul (1967b, pp. 57–58) compares such citizens with frogs incessantly stimulated: "We know what finally happens to a frog's muscles: they become rigid. This is not very conducive to political maturity." Abundant media actually short-circuit exacting thought and the exercise of conscience. We find ourselves caught in a "ceaseless kaleidoscope consisting of thousands of pictures, each following the other at an extraordinary pace" (Ellul, 1957, p. 75). As a consequence, the world "looks like a pointilliste canvas—a thousand details make a thousand points" (Ellul, 1965, p. 145). Today's monumental stream of current events drowns the citizenry rather than enabling it, inebriates rather than informs. We become, in Michael Shamberg's phrase, "information junkies" without bedrock. Forms of representation flash through our experience like the remote-control grazing of cable television.

Ellul's description of people obsessed with current events directly contradicts democracy's image of a public attentive and vitally involved. Viewers and readers riveted to the latest image reject "the truly fundamental problems," and "lacking landmarks" draw no accurate relationship between events and truth (Ellul, 1967b, p. 60). Media systems do not necessarily produce rapid and spectacular results, but gradually mold us in-depth as though "inducing a sort of hypnosis" (Ellul, 1965, p. 87). Overpowered by *la technique*, human beings are imperceptibly "tailored to enter the artificial paradise" (Ellul, 1964, p. 227).

Experts in public opinion and advocates of the first amendment rail at any suppression of material; they insist on unshackled information. Ironically, the net impact can be a withering of the critical intelligence as a political force—the very opposite of the intended result. The question so cavalierly ignored, according to Ellul, is not whether we receive every scrap of information, but how persons can be freed from the symbolic universe of mass-mediated societies where the human environment very obviously has a uniform color. The issue is not finally state coercion, as in the traditional worry over political propaganda, but a sophisticated media technology burying us in ephemeralities.

In this context, Ellul dismisses democracy's vital information premise as illusory. Public opinion is for him more a fad than the product of serious judgment based on a conscious discussion of facts. Contemporary media are not information channels, but purveyors of homogeneity. Democracy as a political philosophy finds sociological propaganda offensive. Yet large democratic states cannot govern without a web of standardized integration. The conflict between democracy and efficiency is irreducible and the choices are enormously unpleasant. Democracy must either utilize mass communications networks—which in Ellul's definition are by nature antidemocratic—or it will perish. Hans Magnus Enzensberger (1974, pp. 95–128) insists that the media's usual authoritarian, centralized, and repressive structures can be replaced by emancipatory, equitable organizations, but Ellul refuses to entertain such utopian visions. With maddening thoroughness he makes inescapable the dilemma of modern democracies dependent on the mass media.

In the very complex issues now surrounding democratic politics, *la technique* adds a crucial component by demonstrating why modern communications are fundamentally impervious to all moral considerations. From Ellul's perspective (1981a, pp. 160–165), we have taken on a new amoral posture that brings human behavior into harmony with the technicized world and in the process precludes all normative appeals. In Ellul's framework, technologically advanced societies are devoid of any concern with rightness or wrongness, their moral purpose sacrificed to organizational excellence.

Ellul recognizes the increasing concern among professional communicators for more responsible practice; yet, he argues, stronger codes and greater accuracy are ephemeral—despite all the rhetoric. Ultimately, underneath the externals, the media are predisposed toward efficiency, the evidence of which Ellul uncovers everywhere. This is precisely the framework in which technocratic societies place new media inventions; they trumpet each faster and more complicated device as a "revolutionary development" *ipso facto*. Ultimate triumph is almost invariably sought in streamlined methods, faster computer banks, and increasingly sophisticated multivariate scales. Empiricism and specialization extend *la technique* into our assumptions of what constitutes legitimate academic research. In product development, the supreme goal becomes cheap and accessible electonic centers that can call up unlimited quantities of news and entertainment.

La technique fosters a self-augmenting process that follows its own imperatives rather than human ends. Thus, once the printing press was established as a crucial technical apparatus, a kinetics was set in motion for constantly increasing its capacity, speeding its production, and refining it organizationally. Obeying the same autonomous development according to its own inherent patterns, electronic technology expands from the Atlantic cable to communication satellites, from seven TV channels to forty, from specialized companies to multinational conglomerates. Ellul (1964, p. 86) observes: "The accretion of manifold minute details all tending toward the perfect ensemble, is much more decisive than the intervention of the individual who assembles the data, or adds some element . . . that will bear his name." Thus the ethical issues in the media cannot be reduced to professional lapses by individual decision makers. Moral guideposts have been eliminated; the media constitute a self-augmenting system, operating only by administrative methods (a climate totally foreign to moral imperatives). The principle of efficiency—a technicized amorality—dominates today's communication apparatus as supremely as it does modern governments and industry.

Global realities demand global communications. The human race cannot be woven together effectively by politics or transnational economics. Information is a social necessity for the modern planetary system; but as the system is expanded, its content thickened, and its transmission speeded up, a normative base is being undermined that is needed now more than ever, given the complexities of a global technological civilization. Whatever is gained in transmission is lost in ethics. In the process of fabricating expert mechanical systems, the world is sanitized of moral imperatives. Society is increasingly trapped in Kurt Vonnegut's (1952) conundrum: When he reaches into his repertoire of commitments, wisdom, and intelligence, he comes up empty-handed, precisely at the momemt he needs them most.

CRITICAL CONSCIOUSNESS

Ellul's social theory upsets our intellectual applecarts. He blurs the distinction between information and propaganda, between democratic and totalitarian politics. For Ellul, our typical conclusion—that "propaganda is to democracies what a bludgeon is to a totalitarian state" (Chomsky, 1991, p. 8)—is only a half-truth in technologically sophisticated societies. Domination and mutual consent are not radical opposites. He calls into question our commonplaces that information emancipates and that abundant media fare makes democratic progress possible.

We could quarrel with his claims and presuppositions. However, despite its excesses and inadequacies, Ellul's sociological propaganda stimulates our moral awareness and increases our critical consciousness. He challenges us to identify the appropriate enemy. From his perspective, our task is more complicated than condemning the political spin doctors, zeroing in on totalitarian propagandists around the world, and ridiculing the public relations apparatus of modern governments. While laudatory in itself, resisting political coercion is insufficient.

Ellul centers his protest on the technological imperative. He is calling for opposition not to technological products, but to technicism. He is not a medievalist or a Luddite. The issue is the psychopolitical imaginary universe which humans constitute and reinforce. The mass media as the cutting edge of the technical artifice must be understood as only the tip of the iceberg.

A critical consciousness entails that we desacralize the technological system as a whole. We must free both our public and personal language from technological metaphors, and emancipate ourselves from what Manfred Stanley (1978) calls the technological conscience. Revolution means being released from the grip of a superstitious acquiescence in our enthralling discourse about the technological fairy (Ellul, 1990). Even if military dictatorships were replaced by progressive democracy, Ellul (1971) would argue, or Stalinism became enlightened socialism, without a radical reversal of the technicism in these political orders, the subversion is illusory.

Those empowered with a critical consciousness condemn technicism. Where technical activity has been turned into the Myth of Technique, "a pseudo-messianic pretension" reigns that technology possesses "the ultimate key to all problems" (VanLeeuwen, 1968, p. 19). The human will to power uncritically presumes that technology has a sacred character, that it merits our unshakeable allegiance. In Dietrich Bonhoeffer's terms, something of penultimate value—human technical effort—becomes deified with ultimate status.

One essential condition for social transformation, therefore, is destroying technicism as the unacceptable worship of a modern god. The empowered resist the idolatrous attitudes, intentions, desires, and aims that drive technology forward. They condemn unqualified worship of the technological enterprise for its own sake. Against an overweening technocratic mystique, they articulate a view of culture in which questions of meaning, life's purpose, and moral values predomiate. To demythologize technology effectively means to sever at its root the blind faith that technological prowess will lead to one achievement after another. It drives home the contrast between a technology touted as humanity's best hope for the future and one of limited means to achieve socially important goals.

David Gill (1984) correctly criticizes those of Ellul's detractors who conclude that he opposes technology rather than confronting the "sacralized phenomenon, the ensemble of means, the way of thinking" that our frenzied technological efforts represent.[5] Ellul exposes the powerful phenomenon of machineness as a dehumanizing force. He (1964, p. vi) castigates the mind-set that is "committed to the quest for continually improved means to carelessly examined ends."

Technicism in politics insists on direct participation as the catchword for effective government. Through sophisticated communications technology, everyone can share in the decision-making process and finally achieve in practice the popular democracy long heralded in theory. Electronic hardware, we are assured, can provide accounts so detailed, swift, rich, and accurate that at last people will bring their "intelligence to bear on resolving the central problems of society" (Westin, 1971, p. 1). In that spirit, technicists anticipate a vast decentralization of political authority made possible by mechanized information networks. The golden moment will be realized especially when opinion polling becomes thoroughly streamlined to the issues at hand. R. Buckminster Fuller (1963, pp. 4, 18) reaches the epitome of technological saviorhood:

> I see god in the instruments and mechanisms that work reliably, more reliably than the limited sensory departments of the human mechanism. . . . Devise a mechanical means for voting daily and secretly by each adult citizen of Uncle Sam's family: then—I assure you—will democracy be saved, indeed exist, for the first time in history. This is a simple mechanical problem.

Ellul regards direct democracy—in all its variations—as a dangerous delusion that actually resolves nothing since the fundamental issue lies elsewhere, embedded in the nature of technology itself.

Being liberated from technicism is not only a question of message, but of the medium as well. There can be no isolated, neutral understandings of technology as though it exists in a vacuum, unframed by presuppositions. Instead, technology proceeds out of our entire human experience and is directed by our ultimate commitments. Technology is value-laden, the product of our primordial valuing as human beings. Values are not only pertinent when technology confronts the social and political; every technological instrument embodies particular values that by definition give to this tool properties that other artifacts do not possess. Harold Innis and Marshall McLuhan recognize this fact regarding communication technologies, for example. Innis argues that each medium is "biased" in a particular way—print having proclivities toward space, oral communication toward time, television toward immediacy, and cinema toward visual realism. Thus, reordering the size and shape of technological products is imperative for enabling a critical consciousness to prosper.

One element in our task is developing an alternative media system characterized by what Ivan Illich calls convivial tools. "Convivial" is Illich's (1973, pp. xii–xiii) technical term for designating "a modern society of responsibly limited tools . . . [in which they] serve politically interrelated individuals rather than managers. I choose the term 'conviviality,'" he writes,

> to designate the opposite of industrial productivity. I intend it to mean autonomous and creative intercourse among persons . . . and with their environment; this is in contrast with the conditioned response of persons to the demands made upon them . . . by a man-made environment. I consider conviviality to be individual freedom realized in personal independence and, as such, an intrinsic ethical value. (Illich, 1973, p. 11)

Convivial technology arises from a critical consciousness; it respects the dignity of human work, needs little specialized training to operate, is generally accessible to the public, and emphasizes personal satisfaction and creative ingenuity. Such convivial tools would be feasible, Illich says, if we simply placed limits on the extent, scale, and power of industrial tools—on the speed of vehicles, the size of engines, the right to extraordinary amounts of packaged medical care or education, and the requirements for professional certification.

Convivial tools are dialogical; they maintain a kind of open-ended conversation with their consumers. Because convivial technologies conform to the purposes of their users rather than transforming human desires to fit the tools' shape, they can truly extend human subjects. Because of their simplicity and openness, they cannot be mystified and do not give rise to professional monopolies of knowledge. Women and men can use convivial tools to act directly in the world, rather than letting a technocratic culture dictate their way of life (Pauly, 1983).

Democratized media are a current trend worldwide. The Shah of Iran, though controlling a comprehensive mass media fortress, was brought down by oppositional forms—audio cassettes, photocopiers, and local small-group assemblies. Since that historic occasion we recognize that independent film companies, underground presses, people's radio, and popular theater can go for efficiency's jugular and provide an alternative media system from below. These are rivers of hope in the vast arid plain we call technocratic culture. In the vernacular tongue they nurture communities of resistance against sociological propaganda. These local settings, emancipated from insidious adaptation to the status quo, are the incubators of civic transformation. TV Globo has a virtual monopoly in Brazil, for example. But video cassettes have provided a convivial communication system; backyard groups use them as a tool for social change. The Metalworkers Union of Sao Bernardo has initiated a training project called Workers' TV. Since political repression has closed the door to democratic opposition, the diffusion of video among union locals gives a voice to audiences outside government control. These radical shifts in the size and shape of the technologies themselves are vital links in a technological infrastructure built to desacralize a streamlined technicistic media system (Festa & Santoro, 1987).

One label for Ellul's (1969) strategy is radical nonviolence, a careful decision to withhold some vital part of the self, a conscientious exclusion of all physical and psychological violence. The critical matter for Ellul, as it was for Max Weber (Mayer, 1943, p. 128), is withstanding a preemption, protecting ourselves from "parcelling out our soul, from the supreme mastery of the bureaucratic way of life." Ellul does not advocate ideological or pietistic pacifism, but our taking deliberate exception to today's monolithic apparatus. He (1967b, p. 221) does not recommend that we abandon all interest in the *res publica*, "but on the contrary . . . [that we] achieve it by another route, come to grips with it again in a different way, on a more real level, and in a decisive contest." Preemption is the initial phase, not the conclusion.

Ellul places himself in that powerful tradition of moral philosophy, self-realization ethics, where effectiveness emerges only from opinions fundamentally altered, lives nourished deeply at a fresh source, not under *la technique's* tutelage. However, Ellul is very careful here. Our choices are always existential ones, their precise content freely determined at each new moment of decision. Any prefabricated programs may simply constitute another realm of necessity that prevents our liberation. Thus Ellul will not construct a fixed model, insisting instead that we work out for ourselves effective involvement in the modern world covertly integrated by propaganda.

Certainly we should be concerned about obvious forms of oppressive power—sexual, economic, psychological, and political. However, Ellul continually asks how we can empower people instead. He understands how easily we make people cannon fodder for our own self-styled revolutions. He deals with personal issues, but not at the expense of structural ones. He merely insists that we must first fill our own political space before our revolutionary action can mean anything. Ellul presents a theory of nonoppressive praxis, but it is systemic, too. The question is how we develop a process of social transformation that is totally opposite in character from *la technique*.

The revolutionary axis is at the interstices of institutions. While most organizations are oppressive, Ellul believes that for any groundswell to continue we must go beyond confrontation to build a new culture. The revolution can only be nurtured in the open spaces, that is, within voluntary associations, among families and neighborhoods and tribes not completely bureaucratized by the political and economic elite. It is futile to presume an entire restructuring of the political–industrial system in the absence of vital insurgency at the interstices. Ellul is concerned that subgroups be agents of activism and not just centers of contemplation or protest. To argue against action at the interstices rather than at the institutional center, Ellul believes, entails full-scale destruction and bloodshed, and may even be a misguided primitivism.[6]

CONCLUSION

> Day after day the wind blows away the pages of our calendars, our newspapers, and our political regimes, and we glide along the stream of time without any spiritual framework, without a memory, without a judgment, carried about by "all winds of doctrine" on the current of history. Now we ought to react vigorously against this slackness—this tendency to drift. If we are to live in this world we need to know it far more profoundly; we need to rediscover the meaning of events, and the spiritual framework which our contempories have lost. (Ellul, 1967a, p. 138)

Ellul's critique of sociological propaganda challenges us to know the world more profoundly. In his view, the traditional mode for considering propaganda is premised on fundamentally incorrect notions. His theory contradicts our easy distinctions and our commonplaces. His perspective, at a minimum, prevents us from pursuing supercilious options, chasing organizational rainbows, and peddling panaceas. In the process, he introduces concepts that avoid ideological confrontation while facilitating a discussion of fundamentals.

Ellul's work is not immune to criticism.[7] His analysis of mass communication tends to be reductionist, tracing all issues to the fundamental problem of totalitarian domination through technique. He is a devil's advocate, questioning our unexamined assumptions and making us admit to undesirable outcomes. But he is also a major systematic thinker whose work touches on communications at all levels. Precisely because Ellul seems so foreign to the dominant approaches to propaganda research, he may be a most significant contributor to furthering the work of the field—expanding, deepening, and strengthening it.

In the course of elaborating on the technical artifice, Ellul stoutly contradicts the democratic assumption that citizens can have sufficient information to participate constructively in the governing process. *La technique* converts message systems into propagandizing networks and erects an inflexible boundary that democracy cannot cross. Contemporary media are not information channels, but purveyors of sociological propaganda. Public opinion does not result from knowledgeable use of information but is simply a crowd's unpredictable arousal through the propagandizing media.

Ellul brings the media technology literature into our calculus, within the context of a technical artifice that is decisively new. The realities of modern communication technology create a firestorm of complicated issues at present. Global information systems are redefining national boundaries and economic structures. Ellul's penetrating discourse strikes at the heart of today's conundrums and paradoxes. While we never encounter truth pure, Ellul orders the territory around theoretical insights of the highest magnitude.

NOTES

1. Ellul (1965, pp. xi–xii, 71, 118) recognizes the dramatic results from this stream of research on the Fascists, Mussolini's Italy, the Nazis, and Communists. But he concludes that defining propaganda as a "tissue of lies" overgeneralizes this research.

2. A recent issue of *Propaganda Review* (*8*, Fall 1991) for example, is dominated by political chicanery: military "myths and lies" in the Gulf War, the CIA, a history of U.S. government propaganda operations since Woodrow Wilson, and so forth. But it also includes in its broad scope many illustrations of nonpolitical propaganda, such as Exxon's public relations SWAT Team after Valdez, the educational right-wing's agenda in generating a furor over political correctness, the mainstream media's cooptation of radical environmentalists and the Catholic Church's involvement during the 1960s in persuading Cuban families to send their children to camps in the Florida Everglades. Ted J. Smith (1989, p. 80) offers a mainstream definition of propaganda: "Any conscious and open attempt to influence the beliefs of an individual or group, guided by a predetermined end and characterized by the systematic use of irrational and often unethical techniques of persuasion." (See also Jowett & O'Donnell, 1986, for a description of the standard view.)

3. There are three other major treatises from a totalizing perspective. Antonio Gramsci's ideological hegemony (1971; cf. 1977–1978, 1985) is likewise critical and all-encompassing; the dominant ideology that permeates all social institutions is characterized by consent, but the state's power sustains it by coercion. However, for all of Gramsci's sophistication, he is not rigorous in his assessment of the role of technology. Whereas the problem for him is political transformation within monopoly capitalism, Ellul forces advanced industrialism to the forefront. Two other authors both add nuances rather than compelling alternatives: Herbert Marcuse (1964) and Hans Enzenberger (1974).

4. While Baudrillard's simulacra and Ellul's sociological propaganda are basically similar in their orientation, Ellul more systematically integrates the mass media into the technological order; he considers them the semantic edge of the technical artifice.

5. Much of the misunderstanding has been perpetuated by the substitution of technology for *la technique* in a number of the English translations of Ellul's works—a substitution that Ellul claims he never approved. Harper and Row (e.g., Ellul, 1982) now uses "technique" (lower-case t) when referring to individual technical acts and "Technique" (upper-case T) to designate the sacralized totality of means, the spirit of efficiency.

6. See Ellul's *Ethics of Freedom*, for example, pp. 395–398. Fasching (1990) concludes: "Ellul . . . favors anarchism as a political strategy of revolt against the authority of all political institutions. He does not think anarchists can be successful in destroying the state. But in a world where all nation-states tend to abuse their power, only a strategy of anarchism (non-violent in his case) can make a dent in the bureaucratic social order so as to make some modicum of freedom possible."

7. His weaknesses in detail and with subunits are obvious, and I have shared in articulating such criticisms (e.g., Christians & Van Hook, 1981). Ellul also invites attack because, as a generalist, he refuses to stay within the confines of the usual literature, authorities, topics, methods, and vocabulary of a single field. His work on the mass media overflows into education, political science, religion, law, economics, and history (cf. Christians & Real, 1979).

REFERENCES

Baudrillard, J. (1983). *Simulations* (P. Foss, P. Patton, & P. Beichtman, Trans.). New York: Semiotext[e].

Black, J. (1991). Review of *Propaganda: A pluralistic perspective* (T. J. Smith). *Journal of Mass Media Ethics 6*(1), 57–60.

Chomsky, N. (1991). Twentieth century American propaganda. *Propaganda Review 8* (Fall), 8–11, 37–44.

Christians, C., & Real, M. R. (1979). Jacques Ellul's contributions to critical media theory. *Journal of Communication 29*(1), 83–93.

Christians, C., & Van Hook, J. (Eds.) (1981). *Jacques Ellul: Interpretive essays* (pp. 147–173). Urbana: University of Illinois Press.

Darnovsky, M., Steiner, C. S., Rappleye, C., & Stout, F. (1989). What is propaganda, anyway?—Dialogue. *Propaganda Review 5* (Summer), 6–13.

Ellul, J. (1957). Information and propaganda. *Diogenes: International Review of Philosophy and Humanistic Studies* (June), 61–77.

Ellul, J. (1964). *The technological society* (J. Wilkinson, Trans.). New York: Vintage.

Ellul, J. (1965). *Propaganda: The formation of men's attitudes* (K. Kellen, Trans.). New York: Alfred A. Knopf.

Ellul, J. (1967a). *Presence of the kingdom* (O. Wyon, Trans.). New York: Seabury Press.

Ellul, J. (1967b). *The political illusion* (K. Kellen, Trans.). New York: Alfred A. Knopf.

Ellul, J. (1970a). From Jacques Ellul. In J. Holloway (Ed.), *Introducing Jacques Ellul* (p. 5). Grand Rapids, MI: Eerdmans.

Ellul, J. (1970b). *The ethics of freedom* (G. Bromiley, Trans.). Grand Rapids, MI: Eerdmans.

Ellul, J. (1971). *Autopsy of revolution* (P. Wolf, Trans.). New York: Alfred A. Knopf.

Ellul, J. (1978). Symbolic function, technology and society. *Journal of Social and Biological Structure* (October), 207–218.

Ellul, J. (1980). Nature, technique and artificiality. *Research in Philosophy and Technology 3*, 263–283.

Ellul, J. (1981a). The ethics of propaganda: Propaganda, innocence, and amorality. *Communication 6*, 159–175.

Ellul, J. (1981b). *Perspectives on our age* (J. Neugroschel, Trans.). New York: Seabury Press.

Ellul, J. (1982). *In season out of season: An introduction to the thought of Jacques Ellul* (L. K. Niles, Trans.). New York: Harper and Row.

Ellul, J. (1985). *The humiliation of the word* (J. M. Hanks, Trans.). Grand Rapids, MI: Eerdmans.

Ellul, J. (1989). *What I believe* (G. Bromiley, Trans.). Grand Rapids, MI: Eerdmans.

Ellul, J. (1990). *The technological bluff* (G. Bromiley, Trans.). Grand Rapids, MI: Eerdmans.

Enzensberger, H. M. (1974). *The consciousness industry: On literature, politics and the media*. New York: Seabury Press.

Fasching, D. (1990). The dialectic of apocalypse and utopia in the theological ethics of Jacques Ellul. *Research in Philosophy and Technology 10,* 149–165.

Festa, R., & Santoro, L. (1987). Policies from below—Alternative media in Brazil. *Media Development 1*, 27–30.

Freire, P. (1970). *Pedagogy of the oppressed*. New York: Seabury Press.

Fuller, R. B. (1963). *No more second hand god.* Carbondale: Southern Illinois University Press.

Gill, D. W. (1984, January–February). Interview with Jacques Ellul. *Radix,* pp. 7, 28.

Gramsci, A. (1971). *Selections from the prison notebooks* (Q. Hoare & N. G. Smith, Trans.). London: Lawrence and Wishart.

Gramsci, A. (1977–1978). *Political writings* (Vols. 1–2) (J. Mathews & Q. Hoare, Trans.). New York: International Publishers.

Gramsci, A. (1985). *Selections from cultural writings* (D. Forgacs & G. Nowell Smith, Trans.). Cambridge, MA: Harvard University Press.

Hanks, J. M. (1984). *Jacques Ellul: A comprehensive bibliography*. Greenwich, CT: JAI Press.

Illich, I. (1973). *Tools for conviviality*. New York: Harper and Row.

Johnson, S. (1955). Goldsmith's *The Traveller*. In R. W. Chapman (Ed.), *Selections from Samuel Johnson, 1709–1784* (pp. 243–244). London: Oxford University Press.

Jowett, G., & O'Donnell, V. (1986). *Propaganda and persuasion*. Beverly Hills, CA: Sage.

Lasswell, H. D. (1927). *Propaganda technique in the World War*. New York: Peter Smith.

Lasswell, H. D. (1934). Propaganda. In E. R. A. Seligman & A. Johnson (Eds.), *Encyclopedia of the social sciences* (Vol. 12, pp. 521–528). New York: Macmillan.

Lee, A. M., & Lee, E. B. (Eds.). (1939). *The fine art of propaganda*. New York: Harcourt Brace.

Marcuse, H. (1964). *One-dimensional man*. Boston: Beacon Press.

Mayer, J. P. (1943). *Max Weber and German politics*. London: Faber and Faber.

Pauly, J. (1983). Ivan Illich and mass communication studies. *Communication Research 10*(2), 259–280.

Severin W. J., & Tankard, J. W. (1979). *Communication theories: Origins, methods, uses*. New York: Hastings House.

Smith, T. J. (Ed.). (1989). *Propaganda: A pluralisitc perspective*. New York: Praeger.

Stanley, M. (1978). *The technological conscience: Survival and dignity in an age of expertise*. Chicago: University of Chicago Press.

VanLeeuwen, A. T. (1968). *Prophecy in a technocratic era*. New York: Scribner's.

Viereck, G. S. (1930). *Spreading germs of hate*. New York: Liveright.

Vonnegut, K. (1952). *Player piano*. New York: Bantam Doubleday.

Westin, A. (1971). *Information technology in a democracy*. Cambridge, MA: Harvard University Press.

III

SOCIAL AND PSYCHOLOGICAL CONTEXTS FOR PUBLIC OPINION

8

Social–Psychological Perspectives on Public Opinion

Vincent Price
Hayg Oshagan

A defining feature of social psychology is an interest in explaining the discontinuity between individual and collective behavior, or as Moscovici (1985, p. 347) put it, the "transformation of the individual's psychic state when in a social setting." According to Allport (1968, p. 1), social psychology is an effort "to understand and explain how the thought, feeling, and behavior of individuals are influenced by the actual, imagined, or implied presence of others." These are no doubt time-honored research concerns. The roots of modern social psychology reach at least as far back as LeBon's (1895) delineation of the "contagious" effects of crowds and Tarde's (1890) attempts to explain the regularity of human behavior through "laws of imitation." In American social science, seminal thinkers such as James (1890), Baldwin (1893), and Mead (1934) were just as deeply interested in understanding the social nature of the individual, and each in his own terms postulated that a person's very identity is a product of social interaction, formed out of a personal history of self-appraisals based upon others' actions. Following upon these early concerns and theoretical formulations, social psychology has investigated myriad forms of social influence on diverse phenomena including perception, cognition, emotion, and behavior. But the common tie that binds together social–psychological research—what we mean here by a "social–psychological perspective"—is that it takes as a primary concern the effects of social interaction upon individuals.

This definition of social psychology, which essentially equates it with the study of social influence, is a very traditional one; but we hasten to add that it is clearly not representative of *all* lines of research feeding into the contemporary academic discipline of social psychology. The field has become increasingly broad in scope, moving well beyond social influence and now encompassing research on almost limitless forms of human behavior. Current textbooks and overviews in social psychology, for example, will generally include studies of such disparate concerns as the causal attributions people make in explaining their environments, person and object perception, the experience and recognition of emotions, the development of personality, as well as an array of research in specialized domains such as health behavior or the giving and receiving of social support. Here we concern ourselves with a clearly more limited view of social psychology—that is, with only those lines of inquiry that deal primarily with the influence of groups on individuals.

We are also concerned at present, not so much with social psychology *qua* the study of social influence, but with its application to explaining public opinion. Given the view outlined above, we can state the matter simply: When applied to public opinion, *a social–psychological perspective is one driven by a interest in understanding the various social forces that impinge upon individuals as they think about, understand, and express their opinions*. The social psychologist interested in public opinion seeks fundamentally to explain how "opinion" is modified by the fact that it is "public"—to explain, in other words, the various ways in which ideas and opinions are shaped and altered through interaction among people and the social groups they constitute.

In an effort to elaborate social–psychological perspectives on public opinion, this chapter pursues two related goals. First, we provide an outline of some basic lines of research in social influence, in order to illustrate the fundamental ways in which peoples' judgments can be affected by their social surroundings. Rather than attempt any comprehensive account of available theories or a detailed review of the research literature (which is clearly beyond the scope of this chapter), we aim instead at identifying and organizing for our readers some basic theoretical approaches in social psychology that are potentially useful to the student of public opinion. In the second part of our essay, we will place the set of approaches we have identified within the larger context of public communication and public opinion formation. Because various lines of social–psychological research often remain theoretically disconnected and compartmentalized, their systematic contribution to public opinion research can be easily obscured. To better illuminate the potential contributions, then, we will organize social–psychological research within a broader model of the way public opinion is formed and shaped, focusing not only on the different *forms* of social influence that are operative but also on the way these influences are *mediated* through different channels of communication. By way of summary, we will propose a simple but general typology that illustrates the wide range of social influences that enter into the processes of public opinion formation and change.

THEORETICAL PERSPECTIVES ON SOCIAL INFLUENCE

A great deal is known today about various processes and conditions relevant to social influence, which has been the object of systematic empirical analysis for over half a century. In spite of an expansive catalogue of experimental and survey research findings, however, a single complete theoretical explanation of social influence is not available. Some of the most ambitious theories advanced in this area of research (e.g., Festinger's 1954 theory of social comparison processes) have attempted very general, parsimonious explanations designed to account for a wide range of social influence phenomena. However, such broad theories are clearly more the exception than the rule. The most intense bursts of theoretical interest occurred during the 1940s and 1950s, when research on conformity in group settings (in psychology) and on the influence of reference groups (in sociology) held sway. The flood of research in both areas receded somewhat in the 1960s and 1970s, as the initial excitement for an integrated and cumulative body of theory about social influence waned (see, e.g., Singer, 1981; Eagly, 1987). Nonetheless, research on social influence processes has remained a steady and vital line of social–scientific research over the past quarter century. And the dimming of hope for unified or general theory seems to have given way in the 1980s to a new enthusiasm for diversity in research themes and for smaller-scale theories offered to account for multiple aspects of what is acknowledged to be an extremely complex process (Eagly, 1987).

In spite of the fact that no single theoretical framework is available for explaining how social influence operates, there are some important organizing principles and key conceptual models that have emerged from the decades of research. One organizational framework that continues to be a useful heuristic for outlining the nature of social influence was proposed by Deutsch and Gerard in 1955. They distinguished two broad forms of social influence. *Normative* social influence occurs when someone is motivated by a desire to meet (i.e., conform to) the positive expectations of another person or group. The motivations for meeting such expectations rest in the various rewards that accompany social conformity (such as feelings of social approval and heightened self-esteem) or in the possible negative sanctions that attend nonconformity (such as social isolation and alienation). *Informational* social influence, on the other hand, occurs when someone accepts information from another person or group as valid evidence about reality. It is clearly possible, Deutsch and Gerard (1955, p. 629) note, "to accept an opponent's beliefs as evidence about reality even though one has no motive to agree with him, per se." When it was originally proposed, the distinction between normative and informational forms of social influence help to integrate a diverse collection of findings from the previous two decades of research, and it remains even to this day a conceptual framework central to the area.

In proposing their distinction, Deutsch and Gerard were concerned primarily with organizing earlier experimental studies of communication and conformity in small groups. Interestingly, just a few years before, Kelley (1952) had proposed a very similar distinction to help organize reference group theory and research—a more sociologically oriented tradition that studied the ways people orient themselves to particular social groups for direction in adopting attitudes and behaviors, or as points of comparison for evaluating their social position. For his part, Kelley distinguished the *normative* function of reference groups, in which groups serve as the source of attitudes, behaviors, or values for individuals, from their *comparative* function, in which reference groups serve as standards of comparison for social or self-evaluations.

Kelley's concept of normative group reference is essentially identical to the notion of normative social influence proposed by Deutsch and Gerard, and the concepts have been subsequently employed in very similar ways in small-group studies and in reference group research. Although there is no direct correspondence between informational social influence (from Deutsch & Gerard, 1955) and comparative reference group processes (from Kelley, 1952), these concepts also bear very strong similarities. Informational social influence appears to be somewhat broader in its meaning: as used in small group research, it encompasses both instances where people are affected by arguments themselves (e.g., Burnstein & Vinokur, 1977) and also those instances where people take others' opinions, or those of groups as a whole, as points of reference (see Deutsch & Gerard, 1955). As applied in reference group research, on the other hand, the concept of comparative group reference is used to refer only to those situations in which people take other opinions as a point of comparison (see Hyman & Singer, 1968; Singer, 1981).

Both Deutsch and Gerard (1955) and Kelley (1952) noted that their distinctions were solely conceptual and analytical, and that the same person or group could, and often does, exert both types of influence simultaneously. But the "normative versus informational/comparative" framework identified two important if not wholly independent dimensions of social influence, and it thus allowed subsequent research to proceed more systematically in pursuit of explaining each set of processes. In keeping with this tradition of conceptualizing social influence, our discussion of theoretical perspectives proceeds in two steps. First, we discuss the *normative* influence of groups, considering how and why social norms are created and the ways in which they are maintained through conformity processes. Then we turn to the *informational* influence of groups, identifying several lines of research that investigate the ways in which groups enter into individual thinking, feeling, and acting, not so much as normative forces, but as points of reference or comparison having informational value to individuals.

Normative Social Influence

Contemporary research on normative influence and conformity had its beginnings in the innovative research of Muzafer Sherif in the 1930s. In a series of studies, Sherif investigated the creation of social norms in experimental groups and their consequent influence on individual group members (Sherif, 1935, 1936; Sherif, White, & Harvey, 1955). Presented with a point of light in a darkened room, subjects in groups were asked to estimate the distance that the light (which was in fact stationary) appeared to move. Random fluctuations of the light due to the "autokinetic" effect, combined with the darkened room, deprived the subjects of any readily applicable frame of reference for interpreting the stimulus. Sherif found that in this situation people interacted socially to resolve the ambiguity and eventually converged upon a consensual group decision concerning the supposed movement of the light. In this way, he was able to investigate the ways in which group norms are formed in response to uncertainty. Moreover, he discovered, once these norms had been created they persisted well after the groups disbanded, giving stability to his subjects' individual judgments about the autokinetic effect for a lengthy period of time.

As we will discuss in greater detail below, Sherif's experimental situation probably involved, at least in its initial phases, informational as well as normative processes. Because the subjects were rather unsure of objective reality, they were in all likelihood willing to accept other people's views of what was occurring as valid judgments. But importantly, Sherif's investigations also clearly established the normative influence of groups, in his discovery that the consensual group norms, once they were determined, provided stability and uniformity for individual behavior. His work thus paved the way for future research and theory concerning the normative impact of groups. Here we briefly discuss two important lines of subsequent research: studies of majority pressure and group conformity (e.g., Asch, 1952, 1956; Allen, 1965) and investigations of the influence exerted in naturally occurring situations by normative reference groups (e.g., Newcomb, 1946, 1948, 1962).

Majority Pressure and Group Conformity

Although Sherif's work was the genesis of experimental study of normative influence, the primary galvanizing agent for most contemporary research in this area was the work of Solomon Asch (1952, 1956). Asch created stark conformity situations by presenting subjects with group pressure concerning a completely *un*ambiguous objective reality. Lone subjects grouped with experimental confederates were shown lines of clearly varying lengths, and were asked to determine which were the longest or shortest lines. When confronted by a group of confederates who were unanimous in their *in*correct response, about one third of the time Asch's subjects were willing to discard their personal judgments and accept the obviously incorrect group position. As reality was unambiguous in this setting, it seemed to be primarily the normative influence of the majority that contributed to this outcome. The studies by Asch forged one of the core areas of interest in social psychology (group conformity), and defined for some time to come the nature of the problem in terms of majority influence in small group settings. As we discuss below, not until the early 1970s did interest in minority influence begin to gain critical attention.[1]

Why did some of Asch's subjects conform so readily to a clearly incorrect majority position? For his part, Asch (1952) suggested that they wished to avoid social isolation, citing as evidence the fact that his subjects reported experiencing considerable anxiety when placed alone against unanimous opposition. He further noted that when provided with just a single "true partner," who would break with the majority and state the correct response, subjects' tended to hold their own course against the group. Rates of conformity in this situation declined substantially from the usual 33% or so to around 5%. By Asch's reasoning, the partner helped to deflect potential embarrassment or other possible negative sanctions that invariably accompany deviance from the group. In support of this hypothesis, he pointed out that subjects did in fact report significantly less emotional distress over group opposition when they had a partner who would take their side. Later research brought more evidence to bear on this matter, finding rather consistently that anything less than a unanimous majority tends to produce dramatically lower rates of conformity and bolsters subjects' willingness to dissent (Allen, 1965, 1975).

Findings from many subsequent majority pressure experiments have allowed researchers to identify a large number of additional factors that are important in affecting rates of social conformity. Deutsch and Gerrard (1955) found that the effects of normative social influence are magnified when the individuals being pressured are part of a social group (as opposed to socially detached individuals), and also when their personal judgments are publicly identified. Generally, the more difficult the task undertaken by a group, the more ambiguous the correct response to a situation, the greater the observed rate of conformity under group pressure (Luchins & Luchins, 1955). Similarly, the more information a person has about a topic, (and thus the more confident he or she is about the matter) the less susceptible to group pressure he or she will be (Snyder, Mischel, & Lott, 1960). Other studies have found increased levels of conformity if future interaction with group members is expected (Lewis, Langan, & Hollander, 1972), when group pressure is more intense, and when extreme group norms exist (Campbell, Tesser, & Fairey, 1986). More recently, research by Eagly (1983) has uncovered a pattern of gender-related differences in conformity rates, pointing to the role played by status differences and social role expectancies in determining the extent of normative influence.

Personality factors have also been studied extensively, largely in an effort to determine what kinds of people are most likely to conform to social expectations. A number of scales and traits have been defined, including, among others, authoritarianism (Adorno, Frenkel-Brunswick, Levinson, & Sanford, 1950), persuasibility (Hovland & Janis, 1959), social self-esteem (e.g., Janis & Field, 1959; Rosenberg, 1965), susceptibility to social desirability (Marlowe & Crowne, 1961), desire for control (Berger, 1987), and self-monitoring (which assesses the degree to which a person tends to monitor other people's reactions to him- or herself; Snyder, 1974). Investigations using personality constructs have uncovered interesting results, such as the finding that people who are low in private self-consciousness or high in self-monitoring exhibit more normative behavior (Miller & Grush, 1986). However, the research has tended to apply personality attributes to normative influence situations in a piecemeal fashion, and the connection between personality theory and social influence remains as a whole relatively underdeveloped and poorly integrated.

The Normative Influence of Reference Groups

While small-group experiments on majority pressure and group conformity have enumerated many important aspects of normative influence, they generally investigate these processes in highly controlled and artificial settings where groups of subjects interact on a limited basis with nonacquaintances. In real-world settings, normative forces are myriad and complex and may originate from a variety of group affiliations. A realistic treatment of group influence on personal judgments eventually needs to consider the role of multiple reference groups—some directly experienced by the individual, which we may call *primary* groups, and many others more distal—in structuring one's psychological and physical environment. Majority influence, as typically created in an experimental setting, is encountered by subjects in a straightforward manner. But the force of a diffuse majority (as in a nation-wide majority) will have to compete with, or filter through, a person's other points of social reference; and as often as not, the normative force of such majority may not transcend the more proximate social reality constituted by an individual's close network of friends.

The sociological tradition of research on reference groups, which originated with the work of Hyman (1942), Newcomb (1943), and Stouffer (1949), provides an important counterpart to the experimental study of normative influence. In his seminal study of women enrolled at Bennington College, for example, Newcomb (1943) examined the way in which the students related to their college community as a reference group, leading to the adoption and maintenance of certain attitudes. The Bennington community created an influential "climate of opinion" that helped determine, among other things, the nature of issues discussed by students and the choice of perspectives taken. Moreover, a follow-up study 25 years later indicated that the Bennington experience produced a lasting effect on the students' attitudes and political outlook (Newcomb, 1943, 1948; Newcomb, Koenig, Flacks, & Warwick, 1967).

Newcomb (1950) distinguished two broad types of normative reference groups: positive and negative. The former groups are those (like the Bennington community) that are valued by an individual, serving as a source of norms to be adopted; conversely, the latter are those groups that are *dis*liked and that serve as sources of norms to be rejected. Rather little has been made of negative reference groups in research until recently, in the form of studies on "ingroup/outgroup" processes (discussed below); positive reference group influence, on the other hand, was studied extensively beginning in the 1940s and 1950s. It became clear early on that individuals shared allegiances with many such reference groups, which could result in normative cross-pressures (Sherif, 1953, 1964). Research also established that reference groups could include both membership groups, through which a person actually interacted with other members, as well as nonmembership groups, which serve as important points of reference even though they are not a medium for direct social interaction (Stern & Keller, 1953; Shibutani, 1955; Turner, 1956). Findings generally indicated, however, that the strongest normative influences resulted from membership reference groups (Siegel & Siegel, 1957), and from primary groups of close friends (Kaplan, 1968; Walsh, Ferrell, & Tolone, 1976). Available evidence also suggests that people attach different reference groups to different kinds of public issues (e.g., Walsh et al., 1976), and that, in the absence of any particular reference group norms, diffuse social majority norms can be influential as well (Charters & Newcomb, 1958).

As with research on group pressure and social conformity, studies of normative reference groups uncovered a number of conditional variables. For example, normative influence was found to be greater when group norms are clear (Hyman, Wright, & Hopkins, 1962), or when group attachments are stronger and greater personal importance is assigned to the group (Suchman & Menzel, 1955; Braungart & Braungart, 1979). At the same time, stronger perceptions of the validity of one's personal opinions resulted in diminished reference group influence (Geller, Endler, & Wiesenthal, 1973). Some of the more intriguing studies in the reference group tradition demonstrated that merely increasing the *salience* of a particular reference group (i.e., reminding people of certain social group affiliations) is often sufficient to induce more normative group behavior (Sherif, 1953; Kelley, 1955; Charters & Newcomb, 1958).

Informational Social Influence

These two lines of research illustrate the variety of ways in which normative influence can be conceptualized and researched. We would be severely limiting our understanding of social influence, however, if we were to confine our analysis solely to the processes of social norm enforcement and group pressure. As Moscovici (1976) has observed, if normative pressure were the only operative mechanism of group influence, social norms would remain static and groups would be unable to adapt and respond to changing circumstances. Just as it is clear that social norms *can* be influential, it is apparent that normative processes are not the whole story. When we are faced with the need to act, we look to the actions of other people not only because they can tell us what is normative, or what "ought" to be done, but also because they can provide us with much useful information about the problem at hand, give us a basis for evaluating the accuracy of our own ideas, or offer a degree of validation for our opinions.

In many cases, both normative and informational influence processes operate together to amplify or attenuate one another. Even in the stark group pressure situations created by Asch, subjects appeared to be responding not only to normative group pressure, but also to the actions of the majority as valid informational cues. From his postexperimental interviews with subjects, Asch (1952, 1956) discovered that those who submitted to the majority (by altering their judgments of unambiguous matching line lengths) often began to doubt the accuracy of their own senses, taking the fact of unanimous opposition as evidence that they were somehow simply misperceiving the situation altogether.

The extent to which influence will be normative or informational in nature depends heavily upon the ambiguity of the situation faced by a group. If a consensually validated or "proper" response to the situation is not clear, there exists a great likelihood that the actions of other people will be interpreted not simply as instantiations of group pressure, but as valid data to be considered in the formulation of a response. The experiments of Sherif (1935, 1936) were just these kinds of situations. Initially at least, the subjects in these studies lacked any established frame of reference for interpreting the ambiguous visual stimulus under discussion and had no objective point of reference for confirming the accuracy of their interpretation. Both the Sherif and Asch experimental settings presented some ambiguity to subjects, but they differed in one very important regard. In the Sherif studies, the stimulus (a beam of light on the wall that appeared to move) was itself objectively ambiguous; in the Asch studies, the stimulus (lines of clearly differing lengths, to be matched with another line) was objectively simple and *un*ambiguous, but the unanimous and incorrect response of the confederate majority was apparently sufficient to induce uncertainty and doubt in the minds of naive subjects. As Moscovici (1985) points out, uncertainty is not merely "objective" as a function of reality. It is, in an important sense, the product of social disagreement. When people committed to different interpretations of reality clash in a group setting, as they did in the Asch studies, the state of disagreement has the potential to *create* uncertainty in people's minds, thus rendering the object under debate ambiguous. Ambiguity (as a quality of the situation) and uncertainty (as a state of the individual) are in this way critically related to one another.

Regardless of whether its causes are objective or subjective, the principal consequence of uncertainty within a group appears to be increased communication (Sherif, 1935; Festinger, 1950). Above we considered the ways in which, when a functioning group norm is well established, this communication will often be aimed at pressuring those within the group who hold a counter-normative opinion to conform to the group. Let us now turn to the informational side of social influence and take a closer look at the ways in which communication, driven by desires for accuracy or for self-validation, can also be aimed at gathering information for comparative purposes. The literature bearing on these processes is currently expanding quite rapidly, having eclipsed research framed in normative terms (which seems to have peaked in the 1950s and early 1960s). In this section, we will look at four broad areas of research: social comparison theory (e.g., Festinger, 1950, 1954), studies of comparative reference group processes (e.g., Hyman, 1942; Merton & Rossi, 1957; Runciman, 1966), research on minority innovation (e.g., Moscovici & Faucheux, 1972; Moscovici, 1976, 1980) and studies of social categorization and its effects (e.g., Tajfel, 1969; Tajfel & Turner, 1979; Turner, 1982, 1985; Wilder, 1981).

Social Comparison Theory

Festinger's (1950, 1954) social comparison theory is a useful starting point, because it provides a very broad analytical framework for understanding both the antecedents and consequences of social communication. Festinger (1950) outlined several reasons why communication occurs: it stems from a pressure toward uniformity in groups, from drives among individuals to change their position (or status) in a social structure, and also from needs for emotional expression. Pressures toward group uniformity, in Festinger's view, arise out of a group's need for consensus to achieve certain collective goals, and also out of a basic drive shared by all human beings to evaluate their ideas, opinions and abilities. Social comparison theory proposes, essentially, that when an objective, nonsocial basis for evaluation exists, people will rely upon it; but when objective reality is not so easily appraised, people naturally turn instead to others (to their "social reality") for comparison and validation.

Festinger (1950, 1954) proposed a large number of specific hypotheses flowing from his general postulates. Among these, for example, is the proposition that pressures to communicate will increase with (1) greater perceived discrepancies in opinion within a group, (2) greater relevance of the issue to the group, and (3) greater cohesiveness (mutual attraction among members) within the group. The likelihood that a particular person within a group will receive communication, according to Festinger, will increase with (1) greater perceived discrepancy of opinion between that person and the rest of the group, (2) stronger perception that the person is an member integral to the group, and (3) greater perceived ability to change the person's opinion.

The consequences of communication, by the reckoning of social comparison theory, are primarily two: either members of the group change their *opinions* to achieve the requisite uniformity, or *relationships* within the group must change (through the subtraction or addition of members). Thus Festinger's theory offers an account of the sources of group communication, its likely volume and pattern, as well as its probable consequences. At the core of social comparison theory is the idea that "an opinion, a belief, an attitude is 'correct,' 'valid,' and 'proper' to the extent that it is anchored in group of people with similar beliefs, opinions and attitudes" (Festinger, 1954). It is a need for social validation that drives people to compare themselves spontaneously with others, to check the accuracy of their own individual appraisals. Influence occurs, then, not just because people respond to a particular social norm, but because they seek out and are informed by comparative social appraisals.

In the years since Festinger originally proposed his theory, its basic propositions have been modified and expanded (see Wheeler, 1991). Festinger hypothesized, for example, that people would only compare themselves with those who hold reasonably *similar*, and not extremely divergent, opinions. This proposition was based on the idea that accurate self-appraisal could only be gained through comparison with others who are roughly similar. But accuracy is only one possible motive for comparison. Another motive that seems well established in the research literature is self-*validation*, or the maintenance of self-esteem (Singer, 1966; Goethals & Darley, 1977). Kruglanski and Mayseless (1987) recently outlined three different motives for social comparison: avoiding invalid opinions (which is much like Festinger's proposed drive for accuracy), maintaining a cognitive structure (a need for cognitive clarity), and maintaining certain conclusions that are pleasing, even if not entirely accurate (which is, essentially, a drive for self-validation and esteem enhancement). Their research illustrates that the selection of people for opinion comparison depends heavily upon the primary motive for the comparison. When in search of accurate opinions, people may actually seek out opposing views, or opinions from very different people, or expert opinions, deliberately in order to test their ideas. Those who need cognitive structure or who are motivated to confirm and validate their own ideas, on the other hand, may seek out agreeable opinions from people perceived to be similar in relevant attributes to themselves.

Comparative Processes in Reference Group Research

The multiplicity of motives for selecting comparison groups was recognized early on by researchers in a second line of work, the more sociologically oriented tradition of research on comparative reference groups. Hyman (1942), for example, studied the ways in which people spontaneously compared themselves to others for the purposes of status enhancement or deprecation. As Singer (1981) points out, small-group researchers in psychology tended to focus on individual motives (especially the need for accurate self-appraisal), while sociologists studying naturally occurring situations have instead focused on the ways in which the structure of the *situation* (e.g., the prominence and salience of others in the social setting) can force particular comparisons to be made, implicating a wide variety of evaluative processes.

Perhaps the most dramatic example of such social constraints can still be found in the work of Stouffer, who in 1949 identified a phenomenon labeled *relative deprivation*. Even though men in the United States Army military police during World War II had lower rates of promotion than men in the air corps, the former group evaluated military promotion policies more favorably than the latter. Why should this be so? Stouffer determined that soldiers in the group that was objectively better off (the air corps) were nonetheless more dissatisfied with their lot because they could easily compare themselves to others who were promoted, thus generating higher expectations for promotion (Stouffer, 1949). Subsequent studies in the comparative reference group tradition (e.g., Pettigrew, 1964; Runciman, 1966; Rosenberg & Simmons, 1972) went on to establish that social–structural variables can lead to forced comparisons with people and groups who are proximate or salient in the environment, leading to distinctive patterns of group and self-evaluations—such as the finding that black children attending integrated schools have lower levels of self-esteem than their counterparts in segregated schools (Rosenberg & Simmons, 1972). Social comparisons, then, stem from qualities of the situation as well as from individual motivations.

Festinger's original theory focused primarily upon the consequences of social comparison for opinion change, but subsequent studies both in experimental small-group settings and in naturally occurring settings have extended the theoretical framework, to include as important consequences several kinds of self- and social evaluations, such as status enhancement, personal validation, and group or individual dissatisfaction (see Hyman & Singer, 1968; Singer, 1981; Goethals & Darley, 1977). The literature exploring social comparison processes is extensive, and it has experienced a resurgence in the past few years.

Here we should simply point out that this line of research—both in sociology and in experimental psychology—continues to grapple with the ways in which social groups can have informational as well as normative value.

Research on Social Innovation and the Role of Minorities

A third, rather different approach to social influence shares with social comparison theory a fundamental interest in the communication and social information processing that ensues when group consensus is absent or disrupted. In 1976, Moscovici argued against what he termed the predominant "functionalist" model of society, in which social systems are viewed as immutable and self-regulating, and in which social influence is almost entirely associated with the exercise of social control, norm enforcement, and the maintenance of social–structural stability. Such a view, Moscovici contended, overemphasized the acceptance of social norms and relegated antinormative behavior or deviance as dysfunctional for the social system. He proposed, alternatively, that social systems are best conceptualized as dynamic and that social norms are transitory and momentary—simply the current product, at any given moment in time, of reciprocal actions and reactions among contesting people and groups within the system. Norms do indeed provide for social uniformity and stability, but they are in a continual state of flux as groups respond to internal and external changes and events. What minorities contribute is *innovation*, through their active questioning of existing social norms. And it is this innovation, suggested Moscovici, that keeps a social system moving forward.

Moscovici's initial experimental studies of minority influence (Moscovici, Lage, & Naffrechoux, 1969; Moscovici & Faucheux, 1972; Moscovici & Neve, 1972; Moscovici & Lage, 1976) established that minorities *can*, at least in laboratory settings, influence majorities to a significant degree. Many of these studies employed a perceptual task, where a majority of several (e.g., four) naive subjects and a minority of two experimental confederates looked at a trial series of unambiguously blue slides. What Moscovici and his colleagues found is that when the two confederates claimed to see green, the majority was influenced (with about a third giving *in*correct green responses). Thus the Asch experimental conformity situation was, in a sense, turned on its head. Importantly, this minority influence effect was only found when the minority was consistent in its judgment, both among themselves and across every repeated trial.

The fact that only united and consistent minorities proved influential formed the basis of Moscovici's theoretical explanation of minority innovation (recently refined and elaborated by Mugny & Pérez, 1991). The process unfolds, he posited, when a group sharing a consensual opinion is disrupted by one or more members who adopt and steadfastly promote a new, alternative opinion. The conflict produces, just as Festinger hypothesized, attempts on the part of the majority to restore uniformity through influence attempts aimed at the deviant minority. But if the minority refuses to yield and cannot be successfully disregarded, the conflict may eventually succeed in introducing some doubt concerning the validity of the existing norm. If a minority expresses sufficient autonomy and commitment, they can generate enough uncertainty in the minds of other group members to call the reality of the situation into question. This uncertainty thus opens the door for internal conversions of majority members to the new alternative view. Following Kelley (1967), Moscovici proposed that people are likely to attribute validity to a minority claim when it is distinctive, when it enjoys some consensus among people, and when those people voice the claim consistently across different situations (Moscovici & Nemeth, 1974).

Moscovici (1980, 1985) further argues that whereas those who conform to a majority position often persist privately in maintaining their own independent ideas, minority influence is more likely to result in true, internal *conversions*. Because the basis for influence in conformity rests in the authority of the majority and the threat of negative social sanctions, the behavior of the submissive minority will often amount to compliance rather than true conversion or internalization of an opinion (Kelman, 1961). When authority demands a particular response, people simply obey (Milgram, 1974) or else express the conforming opinion to derive positive feelings of group affiliation (Kelman, 1961). But these responses do not necessarily involve private acceptance of an opinion, nor the incorporation of an idea into one's system of beliefs, attitudes, or values. On the other hand, according to Moscovici, the influence of minorities is primarily informational and operates through a disruption of people's confidence in their views. Lacking any ability to pressure obedience (because they lack social power) and devoid of any positive attraction to majority members (because deviants are generally disliked), minorities have an effect by causing others to reappraise the issue in question.

Experimental studies have supported the hypothesis that minority influence can lead not just to overt expressions of the alternative viewpoint, but to the internalization of the new minority position as well (e.g., Kimball & Hollander, 1974). Minority pressure can also produce entirely novel ideas and associations among members of the majority, leading indirectly to opinion change (Nemeth & Shaw, 1989; Mugny &

Pérez, 1991). Some of Moscovici's original formulations have undergone significant revision and expansion. Subsequent research has suggested, for example, that consistent minority behavior is not itself sufficient to produce influence effects. Mugny (1984; Mugny & Pérez, 1991) has argued that the social context within which majority–minority interaction is carried out must be understood, for it can alter fundamentally the relative success of minorities in pressing their views. He notes that minorities always exist in a triangular relationship with social authority and the population at large, and if they are to be successful, they must be seen as firm, self-confident, and autonomous in this relationship. In other words, a minority has to be successful in separating itself from those who represent power, even while being sufficiently flexible in their negotiations to attract some support from the general population. Thus, Mugny points out, one must be careful to distinguish liberal from reactionary minorities, because the larger system of social relationships surrounding each differs markedly, and thus their behavior is likely to be interpreted differently by the population.

Our discussion of social influence situations brings us naturally to another important point, namely, that such processes (except in minimal, dyadic social systems) nearly always involve the organization of a social system, through debate and negotiation surrounding issues, into majority and minority factions and subgroups. The ways in which these subgroups are perceived by interacting parties becomes a matter of critical importance for understanding negotiation and influence processes. Mugny and Pérez (1991) note in this connection that once a minority is categorized by the population as dogmatic (as an outgroup whose attributes justify discrimination), there is little hope that this minority can still exert influence. For this reason, members of a majority may purposefully attempt to identify members of a challenging minority as a peculiar group having its own special attributes distinguishing it from the rest of the population (i.e., as an outgroup). The difficult twin tasks of a minority, then, are the maintaining of a group awareness sufficient for its own members to function with a shared sense of social identity, while at the same time establishing enough "sameness" with members of the general population to break down any discriminatory reactions that accompany their classification as an exclusive outgroup.

Social Categorization and Social Identification

There is in fact a large and growing body of research on social group perception that has a theoretical bearing on most of the informational and comparative processes discussed above. Although there have been some recent efforts to incorporate research on social categorization and social identification with studies of minority–majority relations (e.g., Simon & Brown, 1987; Mugny & Pérez, 1991) and with social comparison theory (e.g., Goethals & Darley, 1977), research on group perception as a whole has not been well integrated with the three informational approaches previously discussed.

The basic concerns of research on social categorization, following the pioneering work of Tajfel (1969, 1982; Tajfel & Wilkes, 1963) center on the ways people classify themselves and others in a behavioral setting as members of distinct social categories (i.e., as groups). Tajfel's social categorization hypothesis proposed that the classification of people into categorical groups has two primary perceptual effects: it increases perceived differences between groups and decreases the differences perceived within groups. Subsequent studies have by and large supported Tajfel's hypothesis, and established that social categorization is in essence a stereotyping process, producing accentuated perceptions of homogeneous group characteristics (Allen & Wilder, 1979; Doise, Deschamps, & Meyer, 1978; Wilder, 1981, 1984) and exaggerated perceptions of differences between groups (e.g., Doise et al., 1978; Allen & Wilder, 1979; Wilder, 1984). Groups of people seem to be perceived as single units, the characteristics of which are perceptually exaggerated or, as Mackie (1986) put it, "extremetized." Social categorization, then, is marked by two perceptual tendencies: *homogenization* (the perception of similarity across persons within groups) and *polarization* (the perception of accentuated or exaggerated group characteristics).

The process of categorizing oneself as a member of a social group has behavioral as well as perceptual implications. As we noted above, when people are simply reminded of their group memberships, they tend to conform behaviorally to the norms of their group (e.g., Charters & Newcomb, 1958; Kelley, 1955). These effects have traditionally been interpreted in terms of normative group influence, but recently Turner (1982) has proposed a theory of social identification (which he classifies as "referent informational influence") that recasts such effects in a different light, treating them as the product of the basic cognitive and perceptual processes associated with social categorization. Turner (1985) argues that many of the features of groups that have been cast in social psychology as determinants of normative group behavior—such as cohesiveness and mutual attraction—are actually *consequences* of mutually perceived similarity between the self and others in terms of the defining characteristics of the group category; that is, as outcomes of people's basic tendency to "self-stereotype" themselves as group members. This is so, he posits, because social self-categories tend to be evaluated favorably in the service of maintaining a positive social identity.

In essence, argues Turner, when we categorize ourselves as members of a particular group, we consequently tend to like the group and its members and also to exhibit prototypical group behaviors.

Social uniformities occur, according to this line of thinking, not because of normative pressure from the group but because the field of social behavior is structured perceptually along social–categorical lines. Since people are motivated to maintain a positive social identity, the comparisons they draw between their own group (the ingroup) to salient outgroups are biased, distinguishing the ingroup favorably against others. Moreover, people maintain the positive distinctiveness of the ingroup by taking on relevant stereotypical group characteristics. In other words, when people organize their social field categorically in terms of ingroups and outgroups, they tend to perceive, think, and behave *as members of those groups* rather than as individuated persons. Turner frames the influence of social groups as a fundamental cognitive process, in which people "assign themselves" perceived group attributes following the social categorization of their environment. It is not attraction to a group that leads to behavioral influence, but instead the critical process of self-categorization. This is why, Turner suggests, that not only functionally interdependent groups but also broad social categories (e.g., "housewives," "career women," "punks," "professors") can have behavioral impact.

As we noted earlier, studies of ingroup/outgroup perception and social identification have not been well integrated to date with other areas of research on social influence. But a few interesting efforts along these lines have been made. For example, Simon and Brown (1987) recently proposed, on the basis of Tajfel's social categorization hypothesis and Turner's theory of social identity, that members of minority and majority groups would perceive differing degrees of homogeneity within their respective ingroups and outgroups. Because membership in a minority may threaten self-esteem, Simon and Brown reason, members of a minority group will compensate by perceiving greater group solidarity (that is, greater homogeneity within their group, relative to the majority outgroup). At the same time, members of the majority, who do not experience a similar threat, will perceive greater homogeneity in the outgroup (the minority) than in the ingroup. Experimental work by Simon and Brown (1987) confirmed these hypotheses, and also suggested that members of minority groups may identify more strongly with their group than do members of the majority. These findings have an interesting parallel in recent survey research by Scott and Schuman (1988), which has found more intense attitudes and higher levels of political activity among citizens opposed to abortion rights (the minority) than among their "pro-choice" counterparts in the majority. Precisely how the perceptual processes studied by Simon and Brown might play a role in affecting minority group solidarity or the course of majority/minority relations, however, has not been carefully considered to date.

APPLICATIONS TO PUBLIC OPINION

We review above in broad terms several different research perspectives on social influence: studies of group pressure and conformity, research on normative reference groups (both classified here as primarily normative in their focus), social comparison theory, research on comparative reference groups, studies of minority influence, and research on social categorization (each classified as being concerned primarily with informational processes). Our final task is to relate these various perspectives more directly to the processes of public opinion formation and change.

Early theoretical conceptions of public opinion (e.g., Cooley, 1909; see also Blumer, 1946) in fact share many basic features with social–psychological models of group interaction. According to these *discursive* conceptualizations, public opinion is viewed as developing at the societal level out of a communicative reaction to disagreement or ambiguity. As Blumer (1946) described it, public opinion arises when a group of people recognize a state of disagreement over some matter and subsequently engage in discussion and debate over the issue to determine an appropriate way of meeting the problem. An *issue* is thus any matter of conflict, disagreement, or collective uncertainty, while a *public* is the collective entity that organizes, through the give-and-take of debate, into interacting groups and factions representing different viewpoints. The discursive communication process that gives shape to publics in modern societies operates at multiple levels: at the interpersonal level, through face-to-face communication, as well as at the social system level, through mass mediated exchange (Price & Roberts, 1987). In any large and complex community or society, the channels of interaction that may lead to public opinion are myriad. An issue may trigger discussion among groups of citizens as well as coverage in a variety of local and national media. These concurrent forms of communication together shape a public that will ultimately include activists, interest group leaders, and a great many relatively disinterested bystanders. Some people actively discuss the issue and think carefully about it. Some organize around the issue, trying to propagate their views. Many are far less actively interested, occasionally noticing something in the papers or on television. More people yet are likely to ignore the issue entirely, as survey research has amply illustrated (see, e.g., Kinder & Sears, 1985). Although it falls short of truly interactive conversation as one might find in face-to-face groups, this large-scale "discussion" via extensive media coverage and popular expression brings mass attention to bear on common problems.

Face-to-face links between all members of a large public (e.g., the "national public") are, of course, impossible. When we speak of such an entity, then, we mean a complex network of interpersonal groups comprised of people who attend to mass media messages for news and information related to an issue, and who may in turn discuss the matter with local acquaintances (Price & Roberts, 1987). Members of a large public can thus experience two general forms of communication: (1) direct interpersonal contact with other people and groups, and (2) contact through the media with larger collective movements, personalities, and ideas beyond the confines of one's personal associations (Price & Roberts, 1987, p. 795). Social influence processes—both normative and informational in kind—can thus be exercised via either or both levels of communication.

To help us appreciate and better understand the full range of social influences that are operative in the formation of pubic opinion, we can create a simple matrix by crossing two analytic dimensions: (1) the *nature* of the influence, in terms of whether it is primarily normative or informational, and (2) the *communicative setting* that conveys the influence, in terms of whether it involves direct interpersonal contact or indirect exposure to groups or individuals via other media of communication. The resulting two-by-two matrix (see Figure 8.1) can assist us in classifying, and perhaps better integrating, the multiple lines of research in social psychology that can inform our understanding of public opinion. Beginning with the left-hand side of the matrix (the interpersonal context), let us briefly consider each of the cells separately.

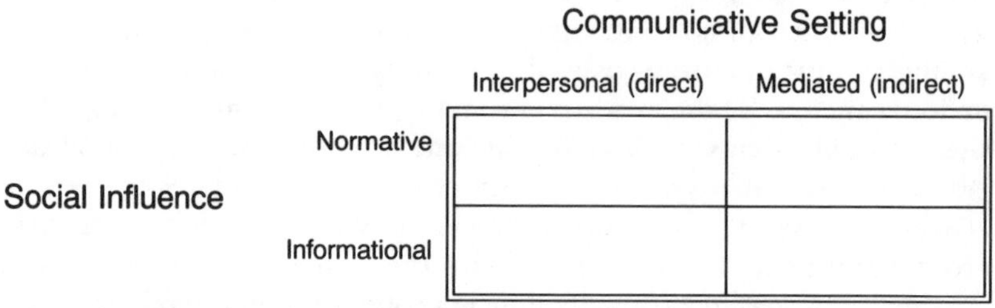

FIGURE 8.1. Four-cell matrix of social influences on public opinion.

The Interpersonal Context

Normative Influences

The interpersonal/normative cell of our matrix represents an area where there has traditionally been a close connection between social–psychological lines of research—particularly on conformity and norm enforcement—and public opinion research. For example, a series of influential election studies carried out in the 1940s and 1950s by Paul Lazarsfeld and his colleagues (e.g., Lazarsfeld, Berelson, & Gaudet, 1948; Berelson, Lazarsfeld, & McPhee, 1954) indicated that interpersonal communication networks comprise a strong mediating "filter" for messages disseminated through the mass media. Moreover, these studies also found that primary groups—family, coworkers, and friends—tended to be very homogeneous in their attitudes and voting behaviors. Drawing from the ongoing laboratory work of Asch and others, Lazarsfeld and his associates (e.g., Katz & Lazarsfeld, 1955) interpreted these findings as evidence of strong normative effects stemming from personal associations. Since that time, the view that interpersonal relations exert considerable normative influence on individual opinions has acquired nearly axiomatic status in empirical research on mass communication and public opinion (Lane & Sears, 1964; see also Rogers, 1983). These results are not so surprising. Given that normative influence stems from desires to meet the positive expectations of groups and is motivated by perceived social rewards or negative sanctions such as social isolation, direct face-to-face encounters with others provide the ideal medium for the its operation (Milgram, 1974).

Nonetheless, there are several important theoretical considerations involved in applying social–psychological research on normative influence to public opinion formation in naturally occurring interpersonal communication contexts. It is important to keep in mind, for example, that normative influence processes, such as conformity in the face of social pressure, theoretically occur *only* when a group already shares a normative or majority response (Hyman, Wright, & Hopkins, 1962; Allen, 1965; Moscovici, 1985). In other words, people become subject to interpersonal normative influence only when primary group norms exist as well-understood, positive expectations of the group (Deutsch & Gerard, 1955). For this reason, the degree of consensus within a group and the extent to which members share an awareness of that consensus become very important in determining whether group pressure and norm enforcement, as opposed to some alternative communicative response to an issue, will ensue.

Only when primary group norms are firmly entrenched and when someone within the group challenges them, then, would the kind of active social pressure similar to that observed in conformity experiments be put into motion. One key difference between normative influence settings in social psychology experiments and in naturally occurring interpersonal discussion contexts rests in the probable source of the uncertainty that triggers communication. In typical experiments, internal division within the group (created by the use of experimental confederates) sparks communication and influence attempts. Yet available evidence indicates that primary groups are generally quite homogeneous in their attitudes and opinions (see, e.g., Rogers, 1983), suggesting that deep group divisions and disagreements would be somewhat unlikely. Thus, very active social pressure aimed at deviants in interpersonal relations may not be all that common a phenomenon.

Beyond such group pressure scenarios, however, other interesting normative processes are also possible. For many public issues, the genesis of uncertainty or ambiguity probably lies outside the proximate social environment itself, arising when people are exposed to novel information that challenges existing local norms from other (e.g., mass media) sources. If primary group norms are well established and people feel a sense of commitment to them, the response at the interpersonal level may well be expressions aimed at reaffirming these norms. On the other hand, if people are somewhat uncertain about socially appropriate forms of behavior and about the probable reactions of others within their interpersonal networks, communication may be aimed at clarifying appropriate norms. In this case, initial interaction may be rather tentative and careful of misstatement, until a clearer understanding of primary group norms is established. In these kinds of tentative communicative forays, a variety of informational as well as normative processes may well occur.

Another set of theoretical issues to consider in applying normative influence models to public opinion contexts concerns the motivations people have for conforming to group norms. As discussed above, rewards such as feelings of social approval or negative sanctions such as social isolation are thought to be the principal forces motivating conformity and the acceptance of norms. Such forces are clearly at work in experimental groups, which are typically closed communication systems charged with resolving an issue internally. But how do these motivations play themselves out in more "open" systems of communication where people can (1) choose not to interact if they wish, as when they simply avoid discussing politics with certain people; (2) selectively interact with different people and groups on different matters; and (3) rely upon supplemental private communication through a wide variety of noninterpersonal sources? The answer to this question is unfortunately not very clear at present. There are certainly situations where people are able to disregard primary group norms on matters of opinion without suffering extreme sanctions. We noted earlier that research on conformity has already identified a wide array of factors that support social dissent, even in direct pressure-group settings. For example, we know that increased levels of information can contribute to confidence in one's opinion and thus support nonconformity. In the mass-mediated stream of information surrounding most public issues, people are able to identify sources of support for opinions that are locally counter-normative, and in this way media use may facilitate nonconformity in personal relations.

Finally, we should note that experimental studies often create task-oriented group dynamics where consensus is highly valued as a means to a necessary end. It is not entirely clear from available evidence how important it is for naturally interacting primary groups to achieve such uniformity. If pressures toward uniformity do exist, they may well stem from very different causes (such as Festinger's hypothesized drive for social comparison, as we discuss below), which might contribute to informational rather normative influence processes. Although interpersonal relations constitute an important medium for normative social influence, then, some of the key conditions that produce group pressure and conformity in laboratory settings may often *not* be present in naturally occurring communication settings. This is not to say that social influence will fail to occur in these situations—the opinion research we cited above clearly indicates that primary groups are very influential—but this influence may very well be primarily informational rather than normative in nature.

Informational Influences

One interesting feature of informational and comparative approaches to social influence is that they may "travel" better between the laboratory and natural opinion formation settings. Even if we are dealing with social networks that lack the task orientation of experimental groups, pressures to communicate may still originate from individual needs for accuracy, cognitive structure, or self-validation (Kruglanski & Mayseless, 1987). These motivations not only stimulate interpersonal communication; they also determine the particular kinds of people sought out for interaction and comparison.

For example, if it is quite important to a person that he or she hold a correct opinion on some matter, then rather extensive information searching could ensue, involving perhaps cross-validation of opinions through comparisons with people who are very different (as well as very deliberate use of mass media sources, as we discuss below). This pattern of behavior may be more the exception than the rule, given ample evidence of minimal levels of interest in public affairs (and with them, presumably, minimal motivations to be accurate). Still, those individuals who are very interested in and follow public affairs closely, such as the opinion leaders identified by the Lazarsfeld research team (e.g., Katz & Lazarsfeld, 1955), may well engage in active social comparison processes of this kind under conditions of ambiguity or uncertainty. For many others possessing far less interest in an issue, the primary motivations for social comparison may be simply a need to locate a suitable answer (i.e., a need for cognitive structure), or to maintain certain pleasing or valued kinds of conclusions. Extrapolating from the experimental work of Kruglanski and Mayseless (1987), we would expect people with these motivations to select for comparison other people who are known to be very similar to themselves. The motivation, in these latter cases, is with validating adequate opinions rather than arriving at correct ones.

Research on comparative reference groups, meanwhile (e.g., Pettigrew, 1964; Runciman, 1966; Rosenberg & Simmons, 1972; Singer, 1981), alerts us to the role of situational characteristics in determining which people and groups serve as points of reference. The workplace, schools, and a number of other settings create the possibility for interpersonal exchanges of opinion with people who are rather *un*like ourselves. Although we may be motivated to seek out people we like (and who think like us), sometimes situations force us to compare ourselves to very dissimilar others.

The application of such an interpersonal/comparative framework to the analysis of public opinion formation seems potentially quite useful. By identifying the motives people bring with them to their consideration and discussion of public affairs, and by identifying the characteristics of the other people and groups who are most salient in their social environment, public opinion researchers could gain a better sense of the constellation of social reference points employed by people in forming their opinions. Such a framework would cast members of the public in a more active role as processors of social information rather than as subjects of social norms. It is interesting to note that a social comparison framework also posits certain pressures toward uniformity of opinion (stemming from individual drives to establishing a validating social reality) that would tend to produce the same general phenomenon—homogeneity in primary groups—often interpreted as evidence of normative influence.

We noted above that interpersonal relationships provide perhaps the ideal communication settings for normative processes such as group pressure to operate. However, it is also useful to consider how *minority* influence may work through interpersonal communication as well. Recall that the process theoretically unfolds when group consensus is disrupted by a minority that adopts and steadfastly maintains a deviant opinion. Over time, the consistent actions of minority members can theoretically introduce enough uncertainty over the issue to force reappraisals of the situation, thus leading to possible conversions to the new position. The process is a very intriguing one for the researcher of public opinion to consider, but here again the translation from experimental group contexts, where most minority influence research is conducted, to actual communication settings requires some care. Given the homogeneity that characterizes most interpersonal relations, for example, the bulk of experience with opinion minorities is likely to come from *outside* the confines of regular acquaintances (e.g., from mass media sources). At some point, however, novel opinions must succeed in overcoming primary group norms if they are going to gain wide acceptance. Research on the diffusion of agricultural and technological innovations, for instance (e.g., Rogers, 1983), indicates that the conversion of people who are centrally located in interpersonal networks is a key step in the diffusion process. Normative primary group solidarity may effectively resist minority opinions from the outside, but this resistance can be shaken when someone within the primary group network converts to and publicly expresses a minority position. At this juncture the interpersonal majority/minority dynamics described by Moscovici would presumably begin to unfold.

Although the foregoing is by no means an exhaustive consideration of social–psychological perspectives on interpersonal communication and opinion formation, it nonetheless illustrates the variety of ways in which face-to-face discussion can provide a medium for both normative and informational social influence. It also points to some of the conceptual and theoretical difficulties involved in extrapolating various group influence perspectives in social psychology to the naturally occurring discussion contexts that help shape public opinion. The matrix helps in another way, by aiding us to identify a few areas deserving of greater theoretical and empirical attention. While there exists a long and well-established tradition of public opinion research concerned with primary groups as normative influences, for instance, the kinds of influence processes identified by the interpersonal/informational cell of our matrix have yet to receive much systematic treatment.

The Mass Communication Context

In considering the role of interpersonal discussion in shaping opinion formation, we must keep in mind several important points. First, there are likely to be many instances in which, due to lack of public interest and involvement (Kinder & Sears, 1985; Neuman, 1986), interpersonal discussion of issues simply does not occur or happens very infrequently. On any given issue, large numbers people in the general population may not engage in *any* of the interpersonal communication processes outlined above, although they may nonetheless become aware of the problem via the mass media and consider it privately to some extent. Second, when interpersonal discussion does occur, it is played out against the broad symbolic backdrop provided by mass communication (Graber, 1982). Discussion of public affairs does not occur in a vacuum: instead it resonates with mass media use (Chaffee, 1981). People are forming their opinions, then, not in isolation, but within the context of a much broader collective process. In other words, members of a public are not just relating to local groups; they are also learning about and adjusting their relationships to broader social groups and national movements that emerge in response to the issue. Third, the fundamental idea underlying the discursive model of public opinion is that social conflict creates collective and individual uncertainty, which results in communicative attempts to alleviate it by restoring or creating consensus. At the small-group level (as observed in experimental settings) interpersonal discussion, social comparison, majority pressure, and other now familiar influence processes unfold. At the societal level, the response plays itself out via mass mediated communication throughout the public—which may involve the reestablishment of an existing opinion norm, the creation of an entirely new consensus, the realignment of structural relationships within a public, or the adoption of an innovative minority position. Although there are important differences between this mass-mediated process of debate and negotiation and the various social influence processes studied in social psychology, there are important theoretical linkages as well. For all of these reasons, we should consider the various normative and informational influences that may accompany the wider mass-mediated "discussion" surrounding public issues.

Normative Influences

The mass-mediated/normative cell of our matrix represents an area that has gained increasing attention in recent years, stimulated in large part by Noelle-Neumann's (1974, 1981, 1984) "spiral of silence" theory. Although we do not describe her theory in any great detail here (see Chapter 10 by Glynn, Ostman, & McDonald in this volume), it represents an interesting and ambitious attempt to apply social–psychological research on conformity, particularly the work of Asch, to mass communication and public opinion. In brief, Noelle-Neumann argues that the mass media provide the major source of information about prevailing social norms in modern societies, and that when people learn through the mass media that the general climate of opinion is turning against their personal views they will refrain from expressing their opinions for fear of social isolation. This "silencing" of opinion, in turn, leads over time to a strengthening of the perceived solidarity of the majority, thus further increasing pressures upon those in the minority to conform, and so on. This process continues, creating a spiral of silence that eventually propels the perceived majority view to dominance and crushes dissenters. Noelle-Neumann further claims that the mass media can (and often do) falsely portray the climate of opinion as supporting a minority view, thus silencing members of the majority and bringing the media-supported opinion to ascendance.

Interesting theoretical attempts like the spiral of silence illustrate a number of key issues that must be addressed in applying normative influence models from social psychology to mass communication contexts. First, what sort of motivations would support conformity to a broad societal climate of opinion, as represented in the mass media? While Asch explained the conformity of his subjects in terms of heightened anxiety and fears of social isolation, it must be remembered that these subjects faced social pressure in the form of majority opinion that was (1) completely unanimous, and (2) encountered face-to-face. The ability of mass media portrayals to exert the same kind of majority pressure, as critics of Noelle-Neumann's theory (e.g., Salmon & Kline, 1985) point out, is certainly open to question. Rarely would public opinion on any given issue seem to be perceived as completely unanimous in support or a particular view. And the mass media (at least, the American media) typically present a variety of viewpoints on social issues rather than a well-articulated portrayal of a single, dominant opinion (Glynn & McLeod, 1985). Even if such an image were projected, the presence of primary groups—generally homogeneous, as noted earlier—would seem to provide a powerful source of social support for resisting societal norms. Second, there is little reason to expect that noninterpersonal communication settings would create the same feeling of anxiety over social isolation that was apparently created in Asch's face-to-face pressure situations. Not surprisingly, then, findings from various recent studies (e.g., Taylor, 1982; Glynn & McLeod, 1985) provide only weak support for the contention that these hypothetical silencing effects are generated by the mass media.

It is also useful to remind ourselves, once again, that the normative pressure directed against minorities in small group experiments arises in part because these groups face tasks that necessitate rather high levels of internal consensus. As we discussed in considering normative/interpersonal cell of our matrix, it is not clear whether the same pressures toward uniformity generalize to naturally occurring groups—in this case to the broad "public at large." The extent of these pressures is probably quite variable, depending upon the nature of the issue at question. During time of war, for example, opposition to a military draft may be seen as intolerable, while in peacetime such opposition may draw far weaker responses from the majority. As Allen (1965) points out, the "weight" of majority pressure is determined not just by its numerical size, but by its internal consensus and the commitment of its members to the normative viewpoint. Thus the normative power of mass-mediated presentations would likely be strongest under system-wide conditions that best approximate those known to foster conformity in small groups: when a clear and well-understood social norm exists, when high levels of commitment are attached to the norm by members of the majority, when these people are motivated to defend the norm actively, and when interdependence among members of the public is very high (as in our wartime example).

There may be other conditions under which social norms conveyed by the mass media prove influential. For example, some evidence suggests that diffuse societal norms may have an impact on expressed opinions when more specific reference group norms are not available or are unclear (e.g., Charters & Newcomb, 1958). Along similar lines, Katz and Lazarsfeld (1955) found that those people who have fewer interpersonal contacts are generally more susceptible to media influence. Thus when interpersonal communication is very limited, or when group norms are not in place, media portrayals may have a greater normative impact.

Also, even if the media do not project a single dominant opinion, they can still prove influential by communicating the opinion norms of different competing groups within the public. The capacity of the mass media to relay information concerning reference group norms (through, for example, coverage of demonstrations, publicity of official group opinions and statements, or broad journalistic descriptions of social conflict between groups) can result in making particular group affiliations salient; and as we noted above, the increased salience of reference groups has been shown to induce more normative group behavior (Sherif, 1953; Kelley, 1955; Charters & Newcomb; 1958). The views of such groups, functioning as both positive and negative points of reference, may indeed provide people with useful normative direction in forming their opinions. However, the operative motivation here would seem to the possibility of certain individual gratifications rather than the avoidance of negative social sanctions. Given that the communication context is private and not interpersonal, such rewards might take the form of increased self-esteem or satisfaction stemming from the reaffirmation of a valued tie with a particular group (Kelman, 1958, 1961). On the other hand, as we discuss below, these kinds of reference group effects can also be understood in more informational/comparative terms as the product of social categorization and social identification (e.g., Turner, 1985).

The normative/mass-mediated cell of our matrix, then, alerts us to the fact that individuals may respond under certain conditions to broader normative climates of opinion and to mass-mediated reference group norms, as well as to local group norms (see, e.g., Katz, 1983). We can conceptualize interpersonal relations as constituting smaller opinion publics that may work in concert with or against the larger, systemic debate over public issues. In such a confluence of many *potential* normative forces, only certain ones will become operative over the course of an individual's social interaction concerning a given issue. An important empirical issue to be sorted out is the determination of which particular norms become salient for various people. As Shibutani (1955) put it, the crucial problem in understanding behavior is that of "ascertaining how a person defines a situation, which perspective he uses in arriving at such a definition." Both structural and motivational variables may determine which norms are brought into play. For example, people isolated from interpersonal discussion but exposed to mediated information may respond primarily to distal reference group norms, while others who rely heavily upon conversation with acquaintances would be responsive to their perceptions of proximate social norms. Predicting the normative response of people exposed to differing viewpoints through *both* interpersonal communication and mass media use would be considerably more complex. Uncertainty is clearly one likely consequence, which may motivate additional communication (via both channels of communication), leading to searches for different viewpoints in an effort to establish an appropriate frame of reference. This latter process, however, may be better understood as an informational process—as social comparison behavior in response to normlessness—than as an instance of normative influence.

Informational Influences

Overall then, normative social influence, resting as it does upon social rewards and sanctions for its power, may best be exercised though interpersonal interaction, and remain somewhat limited in its application to mass communication. Informational and comparative influences, on the other hand, may generalize to mass communication and public opinion contexts more readily. Indeed, the mass-mediated/informational cell of our matrix represents perhaps the most interesting, although unfortunately one of the most poorly developed, areas of public opinion research to consider. Here we focus on just a few interesting possibilities.

First, mass communication can serve as a catalyst for uncertainty. Recall that informational influence processes are theoretically most probable under conditions of increased uncertainty, when social consensus is either not well established or not clearly understood. Our previous discussion of the interpersonal context surrounding opinion formation suggested that uncertainty about public issues may often arise, not from social disagreements within one's primary groups, but rather through exposure to minority arguments and opinions from the mass media. One very important function performed by the mass media is to *publicize* an issue; that is, to broadcast social conflict and in so doing circulate ideas that may challenge existing social norms. Thus while mass communication can sometimes reaffirm social consensus (through the normative processes discussed above) it can also assist in indirectly casting doubt upon them.

Second, and closely related to the first point, mass communication can serve as an extended forum for social comparison processes. The research we reviewed earlier suggests that one natural response to such normative ambiguity is "social reality" testing; and as we discussed above, much of this testing may be done in interpersonal contexts through comparisons with those most proximate in our daily experience (e.g., "Did you hear about this news? What do you think?"). In a very important sense, however, mass media use can supplement and complement these efforts. People are able to select for comparison not only friends and neighbors, but also the Democratic Party, the National Rifle Association, the president, various church officials, and a multitude of other people and groups. Just as with interpersonal communication, a variety of situational and motivational variables will theoretically influence the particular points of opinion comparison. Recent advancements in social comparison theory—in particular the motivational extensions proposed by Goethals and Darley (1977) and Kruglanski and Mayseless (1987)—may provide an excellent theoretical framework for the analysis of patterns of mass media public affairs exposure. The study of media use as a *selective* process has long been a part of research on mass communication and public opinion (e.g., Bauer, 1964; Sears & Freedman, 1967; Frey, 1986). A social–comparative theoretical framework, integrating both motivational and situational bases for the selection of comparison sources, may provide an effective model for better understanding the information search and avoidance strategies used by people in response to public issues.

The application of social comparison perspectives to mass media use is not without its special considerations. Mass-mediated opinion comparison processes likely differ in some important respects from those carried out in interpersonal settings. Miller (1978) argues that interpersonal communication encounters are generally based on *psychological* (i.e., personal) information, while the relationship between interactants in mass-mediated communication is generally *sociological* (i.e., impersonal or group-based) in nature. Although in some cases we may feel as if we "know" public personalities psychologically, the bulk of our experience with the people and groups we encounter through the mass media depends upon social types and categories. Research on social categorization and social identification may thus help us to understand better the ways in which mass-mediated opinion comparisons are made. Evidence suggests, for example, that when outgroups are made salient, people naturally become reminded of their ingroup membership as well (e.g., Wilder & Shapiro, 1984). So reading about actions of prominent Republicans is likely to make one's affiliation with the Democratic Party salient, while seeing the Pope on television is likely to make one's one religious affiliations salient. Much of the comparative information processing that stems from mass media use, then, may be in this way fundamentally social-categorical in nature.

Such group-based processing of mass-mediated information squares very well conceptually with the discursive model of public opinion that we outline above. Given that the public emerges as an organized collective entity through debate in response to an issue, a primary effect of communication surrounding the issue is a clearer perception in people's minds regarding the nature of disagreements, and a more extensive mapping of relationships among social groups with respect to the problem at hand (Price & Roberts, 1987). For members of a large and heterogeneous public, forming and expressing opinions are fundamentally ways of participating in a collective process. Just as subgroups and opinion factions form in smaller groups in response to issues, so do collective movements and social groups organize in response to system-level debate. A primary function of mass communication with respect to the discursive process of public opinion formation is to provide interacting members of the public with a sense of its collective organization—with a view, in other words, of who the opposing "sides" are for particular issues.

In line with this conceptual formulation, there is ample evidence that groups and group attachments figure heavily in political thinking (cf. Converse, 1964; Kinder & Sears, 1985). According to Turner's (1982, 1985) social identification theory, when people define a situation along group lines, they also tend to engage in "self-stereotyping" behavior and adopt prototypical characteristics of their ingroup. Mass media depictions of broader trends in public reaction—their portrayals of the opposing "sides" on issues—may thus have consequential effects on opinion formation. By depicting how various groups of people within the public are crystallizing into opinion factions, the mass media can make certain ingroups and outgroups salient and, through social categorization and social identification processes, elicit more prototypical ingroup opinion responses from their audiences (Price, 1989). Such processes may help to account for the findings of early election studies, which indicated that one major effect of public debate was that it "speeds up the trend of opinion within groups and brings inconsistent minor opinions in harmony with major opinions, thus tending to increase both the consistency within groups or strata and the polarization between them" (Berelson & Steiner, 1964, p. 545).

Finally, the mass-mediated/informational cell of our matrix directs us to consider the ways in which minority influence may be exerted through mass communication. As we noted earlier, the mass media may often comprise the primary source of information concerning minority opinions for many members of the public. The approach to minority influence we have outlined above (viz. Mugny & Pérez, 1991) suggests that the actions of minorities, as portrayed in the media and interpreted by the population at large, can be critical in causing members of the majority to reconsider the validity of their position. Our earlier discussion concerning minority influence in interpersonal communication settings suggests that something like a two-step process of innovation may be at work. Exposure to minority positions via mass communication over time can force reappraisals of the issue under debate, resulting in some internal conversions even though these cannot be outwardly expressed due to prevailing local norms. Eventually, if people become confident enough in their new opinion to speak up for a minority position (or if they are simply willing to risk social censure) interpersonal minority influence processes may be initiated, producing further conversions and considerably accelerating the "diffusion" of a minority opinion. This kind of process might have been at play, for example, during the late 1960s when racial segregation (the prevailing norm in the South) came under attack in the United States. The research of O'Gorman (O'Gorman, 1975; O'Gorman & Garry, 1976) found that Southern whites were actually more favorably disposed toward racial integration than they perceived other whites to be. Such findings of "pluralistic ignorance" may have resulted from private conversions to the prointegration position, which at that time still lacked enough perceived support to be openly expressed.

CONCLUSION

The manner in which public opinion arises out of discussion and debate is both complex and dynamic, and does not yield easily to scientific understanding. Nonetheless, the last half century of systematic inquiry into the workings of social influence offers us a great number of conceptual and theoretical tools to use in our study of public opinion. This chapter has concerned itself with the challenge of putting some of those tools to use. We have outlined a variety of themes in research on social influence, and discussed the ways they may help illuminate the origin and development of public opinion in complex societies.

A proper integration of social–psychological research with the analysis of public opinion faces a number of conceptual and theoretical challenges, only some of which we have tried to address here. There is, we have seen, no single theory available for ready application; and the traditional distinction between normative and informational influence we have employed—while no doubt useful for establishing a certain degree of conceptual clarity—can become quite cloudy when one ponders the complexities of social influence and group reference phenomena (see, e.g., Singer, 1981). Even so, our review of potential research applications has identified a wide range of potential influence phenomena, many of which have yet to receive careful theoretical analysis or empirical attention. More than anything else, our analysis has pointed to the theoretical utility of considering the *full* range of possible social influence phenomena—informational as well as normative processes, in interpersonal as well as mass-mediated communication settings—that may shape public opinion.

Available models and concepts from social psychology can help to flesh out theoretically the intricate dynamics of public communication. We have learned a great deal from 50 years of research about the ways discussion and social negotiation can affect the formation of opinions in small-group settings. Perhaps the lessons learned there, coupled with findings of reference group research and linked conceptually to a larger "discursive" model of opinion formation, will lead us in the next 50 years to more powerful and general theories of mass communication and public opinion.

NOTES

1. As we note here, Asch's experiments have been commonly regarded as path breaking studies establishing the power of conformity. However, in a recent review Friend, Rafferty, and Bramel (1990) point out that these experiments might just as easily be interpreted as having demonstrated the powers of independence. After all, about two thirds of the responses given by Asch's subjects were actually correct (i.e., not influenced by the unanimous and incorrect group opinion).

REFERENCES

Adorno, T., Frenkel-Brunswick, E., Levinson, D. J., & Sanford, R. N. (1950). *The authoritarian personality*. New York: Harper & Row.

Allen, V. L. (1965). Situational factors in conformity. In L. Berkowitz (Ed.), *Advances in experimental social psychology* (Vol. 2, pp. 133–175). New York: Academic Press.

Allen, V. L. (1975). Social support for nonconformity. In L. Berkowitz (Ed.), *Advances in experimental social psychology* (Vol. 8, pp. 1–43). New York: Academic Press.

Allen, V. L., & Wilder, D. A. (1979). Group categorization and attribution of belief similarity. *Small Group Behavior, 10*, 73–80.

Allport, G. W. (1968). The historical background of modern social psychology. In G. Lindzey & E. Aronson (Eds.), *The handbook of social psychology* (Vol. 1, pp. 1–80). Reading, MA: Addison-Wesley.

Asch, S. E. (1952). *Social psychology*. New York: Houghton Mifflin.

Asch, S. E. (1956). Studies of independence and conformity: A minority of one against a unanimous majority. *Psychological Monographs, 70*(9, Whole No. 416).

Baldwin, J. M. (1893). *Elements of psychology*. New York: H. Holt.

Bauer, R. A. (1964). The obstinate audience: The influence process from the point of view of social communication. *American Psychologist, 19*, 319–328.

Berelson, B. P., Lazarsfeld, P. F., & McPhee, W. N. (1954). *Voting: A study of opinion formation in a presidential campaign*. Chicago: University of Chicago Press.

Berelson, B. P., & Steiner, G. A. (1964). *Human behavior: An inventory of scientific findings*. New York: Harcourt, Brace and World.

Berger, J. M. (1987). Desire for control and conformity to a perceived norm. *Journal of Personality and Social Psychology, 53*, 355–360.

Blumer, H. (1946). Collective behavior. In A. M. Lee (Ed.), *New outlines of the principles of sociology*. New York: Barnes and Noble.

Braungart, R. G., & Braungart, M. M. (1979). Reference group, social judgment, and student politics. *Adolescence, 14*, 135–139.

Burnstein, E. & Vinokur, A. (1977). What a person thinks upon learning he has chosen differently from others. *Journal of Experimental Social Psychology, 11*, 412–426.

Campbell, J. D., Tesser, A., & Fairey P. J. (1986). Conformity and attention to the stimulus: Some temporal and contextual dynamics. *Journal of Personality and Social Psychology, 51*, 315–324.

Chaffee, S. H. (1981). Mass media in political campaigns: An expanding role. In R. E. Rice & W. J. Paisley (Eds.), *Public communication campaigns* (pp. 181–198). Beverly Hills, CA: Sage.

Charters, W. W., Jr., & Newcomb, T. M. (1958). Some attitudinal effects of experimentally increased salience of a membership group. In G. E. Swanson, T. M. Newcomb, & E. L. Hartley (Eds.), *Readings in social psychology* (rev. ed.). New York: Holt, Rinehart and Winston.

Converse, P. E. (1964). The nature of belief systems in mass publics. In D. E. Apter (Ed.), *Ideology and discontent* (pp. 206–261). New York: Free Press.

Cooley, C. H. (1909). *Social organization: A study of the larger mind*. New York: Scribner's.

Deutsch, M., & Gerard, H. B. (1955). A study of normative and informational influences upon individual judgment. *Journal of Abnormal and Social Psychology, 51*, 629–636.

Doise, W., Deschamps, J. C., & Meyer, G. (1978). The accentuation of intracategory similarities. In H. Tajfel (Ed.), *Differentiation between social groups: Studies in the social psychology of intergroup relations*. London: Academic Press.

Eagly, A. H. (1983). Gender and social influence: A social psychological analysis. *American Psychologist, 38,* 971–981.

Eagly, A. H. (1987). Social influence research: New approaches to enduring issues. In M. P. Zanna, J. M. Olson, & C. P. Herman (Eds.), *Social influence: The Ontario Symposium* (Vol. 5). Hillsdale: Lawrence Erlbaum Associates.

Festinger, L. (1950). Informal social communication. *Psychological Review, 57,* 217–281.

Festinger, L. (1954). A theory of social comparison processes. *Human Relations,* 7, 117–140.

Frey, D. (1986). Recent research on selective exposure to information. In L. Berkowitz (Ed.), *Advances in experimental social psychology* (Vol. 23, pp. 41–80). New York: Academic Press.

Friend, R., Rafferty, Y., & Bramel, D. (1990). A puzzling misinterpretation of the Asch 'conformity' study. *European Journal of Social Psychology, 20*, 29–44.

Geller, S. H., Endler, N. S., & Wiesenthal, D. L. (1973). Conformity as a function of task generalization and relative competence. *European Journal of Social Psychology, 3*, 53–62.

Glynn, C. J., & McLeod, J. M. (1985). Implications of the spiral of silence theory for communication and public opinion research. In K. R. Sanders, L. L. Kaid, & D. Nimmo (Eds.), *Political communication yearbook, 1984*. Carbondale: Southern Illinois University Press.

Goethals, G. R., & Darley, J. M. (1977). Social comparison theory: An attributional approach. In J. M. Suls & R. L. Miller (Eds.), *Social comparison processes: Theoretical and empirical perspectives*. Washington, DC: Hemisphere.

Graber, D. A. (1982). The impact of media research on public opinion studies. In D. C. Whitney, E. Wartella, & S. Windahl (Eds.), *Mass communication review yearbook* (Vol. 3, pp. 555–564). Beverly Hills, CA: Sage.

Hovland, C. I., & Janis, I. L. (Eds.). (1959). *Personality and persuasibility*. New Haven: Yale University Press.

Hyman, H. H. (1942). The psychology of status. *Archives of Psychology* (No. 269).

Hyman, H. H., & Singer, E. (Eds.). (1968). *Readings in reference group theory and research*. New York: The Free Press.

Hyman, H. H., Wright, C. R., & Hopkins, T. K. (1962). Reference groups and the maintenance of changes in attitudes and behavior. In H. H. Hyman, C. R. Wright, & T. K. Hopkins (Eds.), *Application of methods of evaluation*. Berkeley: University of California Press.

James, W. (1890). *The principles of psychology*. New York: H. Holt.

Janis, I. S., & Field, P. B. (1959). A behavioral assessment of persuasibility: Consistence of individual differences. In C. I. Hovland & I. L. Janis (Eds.), *Personality and persuasibility*. New Haven: Yale University Press.

Kaplan, N. (1968). Reference groups and interest group theories of voting. In H. H. Hyman & E. Singer (Eds.), *Readings in reference group theory and research*. New York: The Free Press.

Katz, E. (1983). Publicity and pluralistic ignorance: Notes on 'The spiral of silence'. In E. Wartella, D. C. Whitney, & S. Windahl (Eds.), *Mass communication review yearbook* (Vol. 4, pp. 89–100). Beverly Hills, CA: Sage.

Katz, E., & Lazarsfeld, P. F. (1955). *Personal influence*. Glencoe, IL: Free Press.

Kelley, H. H. (1952). Two functions of reference groups. In G. E. Swanson, T. M. Newcomb, & E. L. Hartley (Eds.), *Readings in social psychology* (rev. ed.). New York: Holt, Rinehart and Winston.

Kelley, H. H. (1955). Salience of membership and resistance to change of group-anchored attitudes. *Human Relations, 3*, 275–289.

Kelley, H.H. (1967). Attribution theory in social psychology. In D. Levine (Ed.), *Nebraska Symposium on Motivation* (pp. 192–241). Lincoln, NE: University of Nebraska Press.

Kelman, H. C. (1958). Compliance, identification, and internalization: Three processes of attitude change. *Journal of Conflict Resolution, 2*, 51–60.

Kelman, H. C. (1961). Processes of opinion change. *Public Opinion Quarterly, 25*, 57–78.

Kimball, R. K., & Hollander, E. P. (1974). Independence in the presence of an experienced but deviate group member. *Journal of Social Psychology, 93*, 281–292.

Kinder, D. R., & Sears, D. O. (1985). Public opinion and political action. In G. Lindzey, & E. Aronson (Eds.), *The handbook of social psychology* (Vol. 2, 3rd ed.). New York: Random House.

Kruglanski, A. W., & Mayseless, O. (1987). Motivational effects in the social comparison of opinions. *Journal of Personality and Social Psychology, 53*, 834–853.

Lane, R. E., & Sears, D. O, (1964). *Public opinion*. Englewood Cliffs: Prentice-Hall.

Lazarsfeld, P., Berelson, B., & Gaudet, H. (1948). *The people's choice: How the voter makes up his mind in a presidential campaign*. New York: Columbia University Press.

LeBon, G. (1960). *The crowd*. (R.K. Merton, Ed.). New York: Viking. (Original work published in 1895)

Lewis, S. A., Langan, C. J., & Hollander, E. P. (1972). Expectation of future interaction and the choice of less desirable alternatives in conformity. *Sociometry, 35*, 440–447.

Luchins, A. S., & Luchins, E. H. (1955). On conformity with true and false communications. *Journal of Social Psychology, 42*, 283–303.

Mackie, D. M. (1986). Social identification effects in group polarization. *Journal of Personality and Social Psychology, 50*, 720–728.

Marlowe, D., & Crowne, D. P. (1961). Social desirability and response to perceived situational demands. *Journal of Consulting Psychology, 25*, 109–115.

Mead, G. H. (1934). *Mind, self, and society*. Chicago: University of Chicago Press.

Merton, R. K., & Rossi, A. K. (1957). Contributions to the theory of reference group behavior. In R. K. Merton (Ed.), *Social theory and social structure* (rev. ed.). New York: The Free Press.

Milgram, S. (1974). *Obedience to authority*. New York: Harper and Row.

Miller, G. R. (1978). The current status of theory and research in interpersonal communication. *Human Communication Research, 4*, 164–178.

Miller, L. E., & Grush, J. E. (1986). Individual differences in attitudinal versus normative determination of behavior. *Journal of Experimental Social Psychology, 22*, 190–202.

Moscovici, S. (1976). *Social influence and social change*. London: Academic Press.

Moscovici, S. (1980). Toward a theory of conversion behavior. In L. Berkowitz (Ed.), *Advances in experimental social psychology* (Vol. 13). New York: Academic Press.

Moscovici, S. (1985). Social influence and conformity. In G. Lindzey and E. Aronson (Eds.), *The handbook of social psychology* (Vol. 2, 3rd ed.). New York: Random House.

Moscovici, S., & Faucheux, C. (1972). Social influence, conformity bias, and the study of active minorities. In L. Berkowitz (Ed.), *Advances in experimental social psychology* (Vol. 6, pp. 149–202). New York: Academic Press.

Moscovici, S., & Lage, E. (1976). Studies in social influence III. Majority versus minority influence in a group. *European Journal of Social Psychology, 6*, 149–174.

Moscovici, S., Lage, E., & Naffrechoux, M. (1969). Influence of a consistent minority on the responses of a majority in a color perception task. *Sociometry, 32*, 365–379.

Moscovici, S., & Nemeth, C. (1974). Minority influence. In C. Nemeth (Ed.), *Social psychology: Classic and contemporary integrations* (pp. 217–249). Chicago: Rand McNally.

Moscovici, S., & Neve, P. (1972). Studies on group polarization of judgments III. Majorities, minorities and social judgments. *European Journal of Social Psychology, 2*, 221–244.

Mugny, G. (1984). Compliance, conversion and the Asch paradigm. *European Journal of Social Psychology, 14*, 353–368.

Mugny, G., & Pérez, J. A. (1991). *The social psychology of minority influence* (V. W. Lamongie, Trans.). Cambridge, England: Cambridge University Press.

Nemeth, C. J., & Shaw, B. M. (1989). The tradeoffs of social control and innovation in groups and organizations. In L. Berkowitz (Ed.), *Advances in experimental and social psychology* (Vol. 22). New York: Academic Press.

Neuman, W. R. (1986). *The paradox of mass politics: Knowledge and opinion in the American electorate*. Cambridge, MA: Harvard University Press.

Newcomb, T. M. (1943). *Personality and social change*. New York: Holt, Rinehart and Winston.

Newcomb, T. M. (1946). The influence of attitude climate upon some determinants of information. *Journal of Abnormal and Social Psychology, 41*, 291–302.

Newcomb, T. M. (1948). Attitude development as a function of reference groups: The Bennington study. In M. Sherif (Ed.), *Outline of social psychology*. New York: Harper and Row.

Newcomb, T. M. (1950). *Social psychology*. New York: Dryden Press.

Newcomb, T. M. (1962). Persistence and regression of changed attitudes: Long-range studies. *Journal of Social Issues, 19*, 3–13.

Newcomb, T. M., Koenig, K. E., Flacks, R., & Warwick, D. P. (1967). *Persistence and change*. New York: Wiley.

Noelle-Neumann, E. (1974). Spiral of silence: A theory of public opinion. *Journal of Communication, 24*, 43–51.

Noelle-Neumann, E. (1981). Mass media and social change in developed countries. In E. Katz & T. Szecsko (Eds.), *Mass media and social change*. Beverly Hills: Sage.

Noelle-Neumann, E. (1984). *The spiral of silence: Public opinion—Our social skin*. Chicago: University of Chicago Press.

O'Gorman, H. J. (1975). Pluralistic ignorance and white estimates of white support for racial segregation. *Public Opinion Quarterly, 39,* 313–330.

O'Gorman, H. J., & Garry, S. L. (1976). Pluralistic ignorance: A replication and extension. *Public Opinion Quarterly, 40,* 449–458.

Pettigrew, T. (1964). *A profile of the negro American*. Princeton: D. Van Nostrand.

Price, V. (1989). Social identification and public opinion: Effects of communicating group conflict. *Public Opinion Quarterly, 53,* 197–224.

Price, V., & Roberts, D. F. (1987). Public opinion processes. In C. R. Berger & S. H. Chaffee (Eds.), *Handbook of communication science*. Beverly Hills: Sage.

Rogers, E. (1983). *The diffusion of innovations* (3rd ed.). New York: Academic Press.

Rosenberg, M. (1965). *Society and the adolescent self-image*. Princeton: Princeton University Press.

Rosenberg, M., & Simmons, R. G. (1972). *Black and white self-esteem: The urban school child*. Washington DC: The American Sociological Association.

Runciman, W. G. (1966). *Relative deprivation and social justice*. Berkeley: University of California Press.

Salmon, C. T., & Kline, F. G. (1985). The spiral of silence ten years later: An examination and evaluation. In K. Sanders & D. Nimmo (Eds.), *Political communication yearbook, 1984*. Carbondale: Southern Illinois University Press.

Scott, J., & Schuman, H. (1988). Attitude strength and social action in the abortion dispute. *American Sociological Review, 53*, 785–793.

Sears, D. O., & Freedman, J. L. (1967). Selective exposure to information: A critical review. *Public Opinion Quarterly, 31*, 194–213.

Sherif, M. (1935). A study of some social factors in perception. *Archives of Psychology* (No. 187).

Sherif, M. (1936). *The psychology of social norms*. New York: Harper and Row.

Sherif, M. (1953). The concept of reference groups in human relations. In M. Sherif & M. O. Wilson (Eds.), *Group relations at the crossroads*. New York: Harper and Row.

Sherif, M., & Sherif, C. W. (1964). *Reference groups*. New York: Harper and Row.

Sherif, M., White, B. J., & Harvey, O. J. (1955). Status in experimentally produced groups. *American Journal of Sociology, 66*, 370–379.

Shibutani, T. (1955). Reference groups as perspectives. *American Journal of Sociology, 60*, 562–569.

Siegel, A. E., & Siegel, S. (1957). Reference groups, membership groups, and attitude change. *Journal of Abnormal and Social Psychology, 55*, 360–364.

Simon, B., & Brown, R. (1987). Perceived intragroup homogeneity in minority-majority contexts. *Journal of Personality and Social Psychology, 53*, 703–711.

Singer, J. E. (1966). Social comparison: Progress and issues. *Journal of European Social Psychology, 1*, 103–110.

Singer, E. (1981). Reference groups and social evaluations. In M. Rosenberg & R. Turner (Eds.), *Social psychology*. New York: Basic Books.

Snyder, M. (1974). Self-monitoring of expressive behavior. *Journal of Personality and Social Psychology, 30*, 526–537.

Snyder, A., Mischel, W., & Lott, B. E. (1960). Value, information, and conformity behavior. *Journal of Personality, 28*, 333–341.

Stern, E., & Keller, S. (1953). Spontaneous group references in France. *Public Opinion Quarterly, 17*, 208–217.

Stouffer, S. A. (1949). *The American soldier: Adjustment during army life* (Vol. 1). Princeton: Princeton University Press.

Suchman, E. A., & Menzel H. (1955). The interplay of demographic and psychological variables in the analysis of voting surveys. In P. Lazarsfeld & M. Rosenberg (Eds.), *The language of social research*. New York: The Free Press.

Tajfel, H. (1969). Cognitive aspects of prejudice. *Journal of Social Issues, 25*, 79–97.

Tajfel, H. (1982). Social psychology of intergroup relations. *Annual Review of Psychology, 33*, 1–39.

Tajfel, H., & Turner, J. C. (1979). An integrative theory of intergroup conflict. In W. G. Austin & S. Worchel (Eds.), *The social psychology of intergroup relations*. Monterey, CA: Brooks/Cole.

Tajfel, H., & Wilkes, A. L. (1963). Classification and quantitative judgement. *British Journal of Psychology, 54*, 101–114.

Tarde, G. (1903). *Laws of imitation*. New York: Holt. (Original work published in 1890)

Taylor, D. G. (1982). Pluralistic ignorance and the spiral of silence: A formal analysis. *Public Opinion Quarterly, 46*, 311–335.

Turner, J. C. (1982). Towards a cognitive redefinition of the social group. In H. Tajfel (Ed.), *Social identity and intergroup relations* (pp. 15–40). Cambridge: Cambridge University Press.

Turner, J. C. (1985). Social categorization and the self-concept: A social-cognitive theory of group behavior. In E. J. Lawler (Ed.), *Advances in group processes* (Vol. 2, pp. 77–122). Greenwich, CT: JAI Press.

Turner, R. H. (1956). Role-taking, role standpoint, and reference group behavior. *American Journal of Sociology, 61*, 316–328.

Walsh, R. H., Ferrel, M. Z., & Tolone, W. T. (1976). Selection of reference group, permissiveness attitudes, and behavior: A study of two consecutive panels. *Journal of Marriage and Family, 38*, 495–507.

Wheeler, L. (1991). A brief history of social comparison theory. In J. Suls & T. A. Wills (Eds.), *Social comparison: Contemporary theory and research*. Hillsdale, NJ: Lawrence Erlbaum.

Wilder, D. A. (1981). Perceiving persons as a group: Categorization and intergroup relations. In D. L. Hamilton (Ed.), *Cognitive processes in stereotyping and intergroup behavior*. Hillsdale, NJ: Lawrence Erlbaum.

Wilder, D. A. (1984). Predictions of belief homogeneity and similarity following social categorization. *British Journal of Social Psychology, 23*, 323–333.

Wilder, D. A., & Shapiro, P. (1984). The role of outgroup salience in determining social identity. *Journal of Personality and Social Psychology, 47*, 342–348.

9

The Cognitive Revolution in Public Opinion and Communication Research

James R. Beniger
Jodi A. Gusek

Academic research on public opinion and communication, until recently Balkanized in a dozen or more distinct and provincial schools or approaches, has begun to be swept up in a major paradigm shift—already the most far-reaching change in the field since the widespread acceptance of the minimal effects model in the late 1950s and early 1960s. Although most often identified as a "cognitive revolution," the new paradigm transcends cognitive science and social psychology to include political information processing, macrosociology, and much of the traditional subject matter of the humanities.

Succinctly summarized, the paradigm represents a shift in dependent variables from attitudes to cognitions, a shift in independent variables from persuasive communication to less directed media processes ranging from "framing" through "discourse" to the social construction of reality, and a refocusing of interest from simple change (like conversion from one candidate or party to another) to the structuring or restructuring ("structuration") of cognitions and meaning. As a result, stability has become today—in sharp contrast to the heyday of the minimal effects model—no less interesting than change.

New interest also focuses on *process*, which now serves to explain static structure, gradual change, and even revolution. Process includes not only the processing of information inside a respondent's head (the "black box" of behavioral psychology and traditional survey research) but also processes involving the "public" aspects of public opinion formation and change: news coverage and dissemination, public opinion measurement and reporting, interest group advertising and public relations, and public policy debates. All are conducted in public, mostly via the mass media, and all affect public opinion in often complex ways.

Understanding of this dramatic paradigm shift in public opinion and communication research, and appreciation of the change represented by the new information-processing paradigm, must begin with history. This history includes the origins of cognitive science, the rise of cognitive and information-processing models in social psychology, the spread of this cognitive revolution to survey research methodology, and its growing influence on public opinion and communication research over the past decade.

ORIGINS AND EARLY HISTORY

Because large-scale social surveys afforded some of the earliest means of rationalized state control, they owed their development—as might be expected—to the Control Revolution undergone by industrializing nations in the late 19th century (Beniger, 1986; see also Beniger, 1983). Introduced in late Victorian England by Charles Booth (1889), social surveys had by the 1920s begun to depend on psychology for both theory and methods (Converse, 1987, ch. 2). Most useful of these contributions were the concept of *attitude*, introduced in social psychology by W. I. Thomas and Florian Znaniecki (1918), and the methodology of attitude scaling pioneered by psychologists Floyd Allport and D. A. Hartman (1925), Emory Bogardus (1926), L. L. Thurstone and E. J. Chave (1929), and Rensis Likert (1932).

After the U.S. government began to develop large-scale surveys in the mid-1930s, researchers increasingly applied psychological concepts and methods to national cross-sectional studies (Converse, 1987, ch. 1). Many of the pioneers of public opinion and communication research—including George Gallup, Harold Lasswell, and Paul Lazarsfeld—were trained in psychology. Students of public opinion formation and change still contribute to various academic literatures that remain the province of social psychology, including those devoted to interpersonal relations, small-group behavior, attitudes, personality, and quasiexperimental design.

Conversely, social psychologists define their own field—at the most theoretical level—as centered on precisely the same phenomena that public opinion and survey researchers study in more practical and applied contexts. In perhaps the most cited definition of social psychology, for example, Gordon Allport (1968, p. 3) describes his field as "an attempt to understand and explain how thought, feeling, and behavior of individuals are influenced by the actual, imagined, or implied presence of others." Allport's dependent variables of "thought, feeling, and behavior" generalize the cognitions, attitudes, and actions (ranging from questionnaire responses to voting behavior) studied in public opinion research. Allport's general causal variable of "the actual, imagined, or implied presence of others" subsumes the various phenomena of *communication*—from political socialization and interpersonal influence to crowd behavior and mass media effects—of particular interest to survey researchers.

Many of the pioneers of public opinion and communication research were themselves social psychologists: Floyd and Gordon Allport, Hadley Cantril, Dorwin Cartwright, Carl Hovland, Herbert Hyman, Daniel Katz, Kurt Lewin, Rensis Likert, Henry Link, Theodore Newcomb, and Charles Osgood, to name just a few. Among the first national polls of public opinion and consumer behavior were those begun in 1932 by the Psychological Corporation, a consortium of nearly half the members of the American Psychological Association that was organized by James Cattell, the first psychologist to be named to the National Academy of Sciences (Converse, 1987, pp. 107–108). When *Public Opinion Quarterly*—according to Converse (1987, p. 63) the "single most important vehicle for publication in survey research"—was launched in 1937, the six editors, including Cantril and Lasswell, chose Floyd Allport to write the lead article for the first issue (Allport, 1937). Both Hovland and Lewin rank, with Lasswell and Lazarsfeld, among the four "Founding Fathers" of communication research (Berelson, 1959; Schramm, 1983).

Similar symbiotic relationships among social psychology and public opinion, communication, and survey research persisted from the 1920s to the mid-1950s, when shared interests began to wane. In 1955, Bernard Berelson noted that both Paul Lazarsfeld and Samuel Stouffer—then the two leading academic survey researchers—seemed to have abandoned public opinion research altogether (Berelson, 1955), a conclusion later shared by Sills (1987, 1989). Lazarsfeld published his last important book on survey research in 1958 (Converse, 1987, p. 381); the last of his 13 articles in *Public Opinion Quarterly* appeared in 1960 (Meyer & Spaeth, 1984, p. 202). As Converse (1987, p. 381) notes, "By 1960, many in the generation of social scientists that had worked on surveys during the war (e.g., Field, Hart, Stouffer, Cantril, Lazarsfeld, Merton, Likert, and Cartwright) were no longer active in survey work."

In 1958, when Berelson, then director-designate of Columbia University's Bureau of Applied Social Research, delivered his now infamous eulogy for communication research at the annual conference of the American Association for Public Opinion Research (Berelson, 1959), many pioneers of the communication field—including Hovland, Lasswell, and Lazarsfeld—had already left it. Two years later, Joseph Klapper published a revised and expanded version of his 1949 doctoral dissertation as *The Effects of Mass Communication* (1960), a major synthesis of media effects studies that served to minimize their importance relative to that of personal influence—thereby signaling the end of most collaboration between communication and survey researchers. The following year, Berelson himself left the Bureau of Applied Social Research for the Population Council.

The period from the mid-1960s to the late 1970s marked a relative decline in both communication and survey research. According to Kurt and Gladys Lang, by the late 1950s "communication research had come gradually to lose its place as a major concern within the conventionally recognized academic disciplines" (Lang & Lang, 1983, pp. 130–131). As psychologists, sociologists, and political scientists like Cantril, Lazarsfeld, and Lasswell lost interest in communication, the study of mass media effects separated from that of public opinion, while survey research methods—bolstered by the first computer routines for survey analysis—diffused throughout the social and behavioral sciences as a generalized means of data collection (Presser, 1984). Jean Converse, who ends her history of survey research in 1960, cites as the "golden yield" of the era 11 books, all published between 1957 and 1961 (Converse, 1987, p. 382).

In our own 1986 informal mail survey (Beniger, 1987a) of 89 prominent scholars chosen to represent various cohorts, disciplines, and institutions and a wide range of traditions and styles of public opinion and communication research, 73 respondents cited one or more persons or publications as important to the field, naming a total of 379 different books and articles. Of the 40 publications mentioned by five or more respondents—up to 33 for *The People's Choice* by Lazarsfeld, Berelson, and Gaudet (1944)—none appears in the years 1965–1969 and only five during the 15-year period 1965–1979, less than one third the average frequency for the other years since 1944 (Beniger, 1987a, pp. 12–13). The two exceptions from the early 1960s are the first major papers by Philip Converse (1962, 1964), possibly the most influential work in the past quarter century on public opinion as an effect of mass communication (Beniger, 1987b). Although countless other explanations of the study results might be offered, they are nonetheless compatible with the conclusion that public opinion and communication research suffered a relative decline between the mid-1960s and the late 1970s.

This 15-year slump—spanning roughly the period from Berelson's address and Klapper's book to the first notable papers on social cognition, agenda setting, and the spiral of silence—marked a lull before the rebirth of public opinion and communication research under the new cognitive paradigm. During and even before the slump, a period from the mid-1950s to the late 1970s, half a dozen other academic disciplines (psychology, linguistics, computer science, neuroscience, anthropology, and philosophy) were transformed by the cognitive revolution—an interdisciplinary convergence via information-processing models on classical questions concerning human knowledge and its composition, sources, development, and effects (Gardner, 1985). For the origins of this cognitive revolution, which would eventually transform research on public opinion and communication, we must look still further back in time.

COGNITIVE SCIENCE

Most cognitive psychologists trace their philosophical forebears back either to René Descartes or to Immanuel Kant (Flanagan, 1984, p. 180). Descartes (1596–1650), usually regarded as the father of modern philosophy, addressed virtually all of the questions about the mind that define modern cognitive science. He began his investigations with the insight that even though one might doubt all of one's sense experiences, one could not doubt one's own existence as a thinking being, formulating this idea in the famous proposition, "*Cogito ergo sum*" (1637/1968, pt. 4), "I think, therefore I am." On this basis he argued that mind and body are distinct substances, the famous Cartesian dualism that distinguished purposeful, voluntary actions from unintentional, involuntary ones, thereby making free will possible.

Descartes's mind–body dualism led him to devalue the senses and ultimately to attribute ideas not to sensual but to innate causes. This extreme preference for *nativism* over *empiricism* (nature over nurture, preformation over learning) is the main reason some cognitive scientists—notably Noam Chomsky (1966, 1968) and Jerry Fodor (1975)—draw their inspiration from Descartes rather than from Kant. Ultimately, however, Descartes's philosophy undermines the very possibility of a scientific psychology: if the only reliable access to the mind is that of its owner, psychological phenomena are not subject to intersubjective methods, and thereby escape the purview of science altogether.

In contrast to the extreme nativism of Descartes, Kant (1724–1804) held a more moderate position, recognizing two types of *a priori* knowledge: Descartes's *analytic* one, which is innate, and a new *synthetic a priori* which begins with experience (and thus is not analytic) but does not derive from experience (i.e., is not *a posteriori*). In this way Kant (1781) distinguished an *initial* (analytic) cognitive system, innate yet capable of enriching itself, from the *additional* cognitive rules acquired through experience (i.e., synthetic rules) which are nevertheless *a priori* in the sense that they preform subsequent experience.

Kant built his case in response to David Hume, whose empiricism had led him to dismiss concepts like causality as metaphysically uninteresting because they could not be traced back to sensory data. To counter such philosophical skepticism, Kant stood Hume's conclusion on its head, arguing that universally held concepts not traceable to sense impressions must be supplied *a priori* by the perceivers themselves—thereby giving such concepts central importance, making "cognitive psychology as we know it today both possible and respectable" (Flanagan, 1984, p. 184), and destroying radical empiricism in the bargain. Kant himself likened his triumph over Hume to a "Copernican revolution" in epistemology: Just as Copernicus had made "the spectator to revolve and the stars to remain at rest," Kant in his own view had made the mind active relative to sensory data in the construction of knowledge (Kant, 1781/1929, pp. 22–23).

Between raw sense impressions and the *a priori* concepts, following Aristotle's "categories of thought" Kant interposed mental "representations" or *schemata* to mediate between perception and cognition. Introduced in psychology by the British neurologist Henry Head (1926), the concept of the *schema* helped Frederic Bartlett (1932) to explain social and cultural components of memory. Because behaviorism, which rejects all mentalistic terms to focus exclusively on the study of overt behavior, ruled psychology from the late 1910s (Watson, 1914, 1919) until the mid-1950s, cognitive concerns survived in the work of only a few psychologists: investigations by Piaget (1926, 1932, 1936) into the development of Kantian categories in children, for example, or the "cognitive maps" posited by Tolman (1932) to explain the ability of animals to navigate altered mazes.

Howard Gardner (1987, ch. 3) traces the birth of modern interdisciplinary cognitive science to 1956 and the important publications and papers of that year in psychology (Bruner, Goodnow, & Austin, 1956; Miller, 1956), linguistics (Chomsky, 1956), computer science (Newell & Simon, 1956), and anthropology (Goodenough, 1956; Lounsbury, 1956). By the early 1970s, additional work placed two other disciplines, neuroscience (Hubel & Wiesel, 1959, 1962; Lettvin, Maturana, McCulloch, & Pitts, 1959) and philosophy (Putnam, 1960, 1973; Fodor, 1975), among the cognitive sciences.

During the formative years of cognitive science, through 1972, a spate of important books contributed to the rapid rise of the new interdisciplinary field, its increasing scope captured by their titles: Bruner, Goodnow, and Austin, *A Study of Thinking* (1956); Chomsky, *Syntactic Structures* (1957); Lévi-Strauss, *Structural Anthropology* (1958); von Neumann, *The Computer and the Brain* (1958); Miller, Galanter, and Pribram, *Plans and the Structure of Behavior* (1960); Lévi-Strauss, *The Savage Mind* (1962); Fodor and Katz, *The Structure of Language* (1964); Chomsky, *Aspects of the Theory of Syntax* (1965); Neisser, *Cognitive Psychology* (1967); Simon, *Sciences of the Artificial* (1969); Tyler, *Cognitive Anthropology* (1969); Morris, *Writings on the General Theory of Signs* (1971); Pribram, *Languages of the Brain* (1971); and Newell and Simon, *Human Problem Solving* (1972).

For the years since 1972, we now focus on the rise of cognitive models in psychology, the discipline that has most directly inspired the cognitive revolution in research on public opinion and communication.

COGNITIVE PSYCHOLOGY AND SOCIAL COGNITION

Since the 1930s, the development of both survey research and social psychology has been marked by continual shifts of assumptions, interest, and emphasis among five conceptual dimensions concerning cognition:

1. Irrational versus rational respondents;
2. Dynamics versus statics of cognition;
3. Subjective versus objective features of cognition;
4. Complex versus simple stimuli and responses;
5. Causes and effects internal versus external to respondents.

Even as Elmo Roper and George Gallup prepared to conduct the first national surveys based on scientific samples in 1935, Muzafer Sherif completed a study of "social factors in perception" that found human subjects to be less rational than previously thought (Sherif, 1935). The following year, as the new sample surveys eclipsed the *Literary Digest* straw poll by predicting President Franklin Roosevelt's reelection over Alfred Landon, psychologist I. Lorge demonstrated that political and aesthetic judgments could be readily distorted by prestigious labels, thereby establishing the so-called prestige and halo effects (Lorge, 1936). In the same year, Sherif published a major book, *The Psychology of Social Norms*, detailing the vulnerabilities of even the simplest perceptual judgments to group pressure (Sherif, 1936). With further elaboration of Sherif's "reference group theory" in the early 1940s (Hyman, 1942; Newcomb, 1943), cognition itself came to be seen as inefficient and flawed.

Support for the contrary view—that humans are essentially rational and cognitively efficient—also came from research in the early 1940s. Psychologists Helen Block Lewis and Solomon Asch explained away findings like prestige effects as the results of rational efforts to establish meaning through cognitive reorganization (Lewis, 1941; Asch, 1946, 1951). Leon Festinger's pioneering work on informal social communication in the late 1940s also embraced the view of the human subject as fundamentally rational. Individuals communicate, according to Festinger (1950), in order to achieve a most objective "social reality."

Research in the 1940s also inspired psychologists to shift their attention from the structural and substantive properties of cognitions to cognitive dynamics—including motivational as well as structural dynamics. Structural and configurational dynamics, so named because they derive from the structure of objective stimuli that exist independent of their receiver, were first discussed by the European Gestalt and field theorists earlier in the century (Wertheimer, 1912, 1945; Kohler, 1917, 1929; Koffka, 1935). Structural dynamics were introduced in American psychology in the early 1940s by Wolfgang Kohler (1940) and Fritz Heider (1944, 1946), as well as by Lewis (1941) and Asch (1946), to account for interactions and interdependence among cognitions. Motivational or behavioral dynamics, first discussed by the early behaviorists (Skinner, 1938), consist of factors external to structural dynamics that account for the individual's own reconstruction of stimuli, through which they can reinforce or change cognitive processes.

Ironically, Festinger's more notable theory of cognitive dissonance (Festinger, 1957), which dominated social psychological research in the 1960s, had just the opposite effect: It served to reinstate the human subject as essentially irrational—or at least as "rationalizing" rather than rational. According to dissonance theory, correspondence between cognition and "reality" necessarily clashes with each individual's strong inclination to maintain consistency among cognitions themselves. So noxious are inconsistent cognitions, Festinger found, that humans routinely forsake objective reality—adjusting action, motivation, affect, and even perception—in order to maintain their own psychological comfort. This result holds even for phenomena far removed from the psychological laboratory: witness, for example, the behavior of flying saucer cultists (Festinger, Riecken, & Schachter, 1956).

Reaction against the prevailing dissonance view of the individual as fundamentally irrational came with the so-called cognitive revolution of the mid-1960s. The correspondent inference theory of E. E. Jones and Keith Davis (1965), Harold Kelley's theory of causal attribution (1967, 1971), and attribution-theory approaches to achievement motivation (Weiner et al., 1971; Weiner, 1973) all posited the individual as a quasi-scientist who carefully weighs factors in logical fashion. These and similar models of human inference machines, common in the late 1960s and early 1970s, rank among the most rational ever to appear in social psychology.

As research on attribution began to accumulate, however, deviations from the rational model of the individual as "naive scientist" increasingly characterized the more interesting findings. Experimental subjects repeatedly failed to attend to all available information, were highly selective in what they remembered and inferred, and proved inept at impartial evaluation. As early as 1966, E. E. Jones and V. A. Harris had found that even when subjects were told that a debater had been assigned a position (e.g., for or against Fidel Castro), they still associated it with the debater himself (Jones & Harris, 1967), a bias that Lee Ross (1977) came to call the "fundamental attribution error." Similar findings of subjects' distortion, bias, and error increasingly dominated publications on attribution in the 1970s, including those of Jones and Nisbett (1971), Ross, Bierbrauer, and Polly (1974), Miller and Ross (1975), Lerner, Miller, and Holmes (1976), and Ross, Greene, and House (1977).

By the mid-1970s, social psychologists had begun to institutionalize attention to human irrationality and imperfections in the still prominent study of biases and heuristics. Pioneers of the field include cognitive psychologists Philip Johnson-Laird and Peter Wason (Johnson-Laird & Wason, 1970, 1977; Wason & Johnson-Laird, 1972) and Daniel Kahneman and Amos Tversky (Kahneman & Tversky, 1972, 1973; Tversky, 1977; Tversky & Kahneman, 1973, 1974). Between 1972 and 1981, five times as many journal articles documented the "poor" as compared to "good" cognitive performance of research subjects (Christensen-Szalanski & Beach, 1984). Most problems resulting from *biases* (not purposeful) and from *heuristics* (purposeful) have been linked to two countervailing human tendencies of omission and commission: to neglect the logical and statistical strategies of science, on the one hand, and to overutilize intuitive or simplistic inferential strategies on the other (Nisbett & Ross, 1980).

This is not to say that any bias or heuristic problem necessarily results from irrationality *per se*. When studies take extracognitive factors like the subject's intentions and circumstances—particularly social ones—into account, "the picture that emerges is not always that of a misguided creature but often of one who is willing to suffer a few misses and false alarms for the sake of overall greater cognitive efficiency and general adaptation to a capricious environment" (Markus & Zajonc, 1985, p. 196). If work on biases and heuristics does not judge subjects' inferences against rationality in any absolute sense, neither does it routinely investigate whether subjects judge their own performances by the same criteria of validity assumed by experimental measures (Nisbett & Ross, 1980).

The obvious implication is that both sides in the 50-year debate have been correct: Humans are sometimes rational, sometimes irrational. This conclusion supports a more fruitful version of the debate: the current argument about which effects reflect true cognitive biases (irrationality) and which suggest purposeful applications of individual heuristics—heuristics that nevertheless might be considered rational. Outcomes of these arguments will likely include new boundaries between cognitive and social psychology, fields now increasingly indistinguishable, and perhaps new theories about the boundaries separating the essential human cognition from the variety of its social contexts, including those involving public opinion and mass communication.

COGNITION AND SURVEY RESEARCH

Although the cognitive paradigm did not begin to emerge in survey research until the early 1970s, especially through the pioneering collaboration of psychologist Norman Bradburn and sociologist Seymour Sudman (Sudman & Bradburn, 1974, 1982; Bradburn & Sudman, 1979), development of various of its components dates from the very beginnings of the field early in the century. These components include Lippmann's idea of "enlisted interest," which he illustrated with the story-relaying parlor game attributed to Jung (1916, p. 81) that also inspired the adoption by Bartlett (1932) of the concept of schema (Lippmann, 1922, p. 110); the conformity experiments of Sherif (1935) and Asch (1951); reference group theory (Sherif, 1936; Hyman, 1942; Newcomb, 1943); the first report of the forbid–allow asymmetry in question wording (Rugg, 1941); the cognitive balance theory of Heider (1946); and an influential paper by Hyman and Sheatsley (1947) on why information campaigns fail.

Similar contributions to what would become the cognitive paradigm in survey research accelerated after World War II, beginning with work by Hovland, Janis, and Kelley (1953) on the clues audiences use to judge the veracity of speakers, and with the analysis of cognitive dissonance by Festinger (1957). While Festinger's dissonance theory implied that people do not like inconsistency, Heider's balance theory assumed the compatible idea that people prefer consistency, a model generalized in the early 1950s from interpersonal relationships (Newcomb, 1953) to triadic sets of relationships among attitudes of all kinds by Cartwright and Harary (1956).

Growing dissatisfaction with question wording also fed interest in cognitive issues in post-World War II survey research (Cantril, 1944; Payne, 1951). McNemar (1946) found that the inclusion or omission of response alternatives could change both proportions and the rankings of several proportions, while Payne (1951) demonstrated "primacy effects"—that is, greater preference for alternatives presented higher in a list—and Thorndike, Hagen, and Kemper (1952) achieved fuller reports to sensitive or threatening questions using more impersonal methods (self-administered questionnaires as compared to face-to-face interviews). As a result, several early textbooks on interviewing called for a comprehensive "theory of asking questions" (Hyman, 1954; Kahn & Cannell, 1957).

Other components of what would become the cognitive paradigm in survey research that emerged in the 1950s include the demonstration that party labels provide a critical cue for the cognitive filtering of political information (Berelson, Lazarfield, & McPhee, 1954; Campbell, Converse, Miller, & Stokes, 1960), as well as for the pioneering work on television's celebration of General Douglas MacArthur (Lang & Lang, 1953) and on McCarthy era journalism more generally (Breed, 1955). The latter studies showed the mass media to be active framers of social reality even as they are constrained by larger political processes that frame the expectations of both journalists and their audiences.

By 1960, Joseph Klapper could identify 22 studies, completed between 1936 and 1959, that found audiences actively processing mass media messages through selective exposure, perception, and retention, with each individual member thereby maintaining "a protective net in the service of existing predispositions" (Klapper, 1960, pp. 19–26). Through 1960, *Public Opinion Quarterly* had published 20 full-length articles on the subjects of cognition, perception, knowledge and information, and dissonance (Beniger, 1987b, p. S56, using Meyer & Spaeth, 1984).

As we have seen, survey research experienced a relative decline during the following two decades. Of the 40 works mentioned by five or more respondents to our 1986 mail survey of 89 prominent scholars, only five publications appeared during the entire 15-year period from

1965 to 1979—less than one third the average frequency for all the years since 1944 (Beniger, 1987a, pp. 12–13). The peak for cognitive articles published in *Public Opinion Quarterly* through 1982 came during the seven-year period from 1959 to 1965, when 24 full-length articles appeared, 13 on cognition and dissonance alone. The rate fell by one half during the 11-year period from 1966 to 1976, when *POQ* published 23 such articles, only four on cognition and dissonance (Beniger, 1987b, p. S56).

Because this decline occurred simultaneously with the later stages of the cognitive revolution and the birth of cognitive science, it may not be surprising that many of the more notable publications in survey research during the period were comprehensive methodological works well grounded in cognitive theory: Sudman and Bradburn, *Response Effects in Surveys* (1974); Bradburn and Sudman, *Improving Interviewing Methods and Questionnaire Design* (1979); Schuman and Presser, *Questions and Answers in Attitude Surveys* (1981); Hogarth, *Question Framing and Response Consistency* (1982); Sudman and Bradburn, *Asking Questions* (1982); Ericsson and Simon, *Protocol Analysis: Verbal Reports as Data* (1984); and Turner and Martin, *Surveying Subjective Phenomena* (1984). These efforts culminated in the increasingly institutionalized collaboration of survey research methodologists and cognitive psychologists.

INTERDISCIPLINARY COLLABORATION ON SURVEY METHODOLOGY

Collaboration between cognitive psychologists and survey methodologists first became institutionalized in 1978, according to several of the pioneers (Jabine, Straf, Tanur, & Tourangeau, 1984, pp. 1–2; Aborn, 1989; Jobe & Mingay, 1991, p. 176), at a one-day seminar in the United Kingdom jointly sponsored by the Social Science Research Council (U.K.) and the Royal Statistical Society. Discussion centered on problems associated with the collection and interpretation of retrospective and recall data in social surveys; resulting papers were published the following year as *The Recall Method in Social Surveys* (Moss & Goldstein, 1979). Also in 1978, a prominent American cognitive psychologist, Ulric Neisser, called for a shift in research on memory to more naturalistic settings, arguing that those in the field had become overly concerned with theoretical issues at the expense of the "social reality" that ought to motivate their work (Neisser, 1978).

Two years later, the Committee on National Statistics (CNSTAT) of the National Research Council convened a one-day panel in Washington, D.C., on the survey measurement of subjective phenomena.

Participants discussed problems of validity and reliability in subjective measures and recommended an extensive interdisciplinary investigation of the subjective aspects of survey questions. The final report and papers of the panel, *Surveying Subjective Phenomena*, were published four years later in two large volumes (Turner & Martin, 1984). Also in 1980, the nonprofit Bureau of Social Science Research in Washington, D.C., with funding from the U.S. Bureau of the Census and the Bureau of Justice Statistics, convened a two-day workshop on applying cognitive psychology to problems of respondent recall of victimization for the National Crime Survey. The workshop report (Biderman, 1980) concluded that survey design would benefit from the application of cognitive theory and, conversely, that cognitive research would benefit if more surveys were treated as experiments for testing cognitive theory.

The first programmatic effort to foster collaboration between cognitive psychologists and survey researchers came in 1983 when CNSTAT, with funding from the National Science Foundation, convened a six-day "Advanced Research Seminar on Cognitive Aspects of Survey Methodology (CASM)" in St. Michaels, Maryland, with a two-day follow-up meeting in Baltimore in January, 1984. The 22 participants included eight psychologists, eight statisticians, three anthropologists, two sociologists, and one political scientist, a reflection of the new interdisciplinary collaboration on cognitive survey methodology. The CASM report (Jabine et al., 1984) defined cognitive science as "the study of such processes as understanding language, remembering and forgetting, perception, judgment, and inferring causes," expressed surprise that until "a few years ago" cognitive scientists and survey researchers "had little contact," and included an agenda for accelerated collaboration.

With eight years' hindsight, Jobe and Mingay (1991, p. 177) conclude that CNSTAT's CASM seminar

> incorporated two features which set the stage for future developments in highly specific ways. One was the videotaping and subsequent critical analysis of an actual interview. . . . The videotaped interview proved to be a provocative tool in the generation of ideas for future research. The other was the detailing of several specific research undertakings which, if put into practice, would put the issues of collaborative feasibility to the test. . . . Included in the ideas were a series of laboratory studies to explore cognitive processes in survey responding to investigate whether protocol analysis (cf. Ericsson and Simon, 1980, 1984) would be an effective method of studying how respondents retrieve information from memory and answer survey questions, to investigate how the feelings associated with the response to one attitude question may influence responses to later questions, and to investigate cognitive processes and knowledge repre-

sentations that are implicit in responses to many survey questions (see Jabine et al., 1984). All but one of these specific research projects were subsequently supported, mostly by the National Science Foundation (NSF).

Also in 1983, the year of CASM's first meeting, the first publications explicitly attempting to link cognitive and survey research appeared in psychology journals. Work by Loftus and Marburger (1983) on improving the accuracy of retrospective reports using "landmark events" like the eruption of Mt. Saint Helens extended earlier research on memory in natural settings (Bahrick, Bahrick, & Wittlinger, 1975; Linton, 1975, 1982; Keenan, MacWhinney, & Mayhew, 1977; Keenan & Baillet, 1980). Meanwhile, West German scholars had begun to apply theory derived from judgmental research in the field of social cognition to surveys of attitudes and subjective indicators like life satisfaction. An early publication of this new work (Schwarz & Clore, 1983) reported that subjects put in either a good or bad mood tend to judge both specific aspects of their lives and their general life satisfaction as affectively consistent with their prior moods.

In the following year, the West German government-funded Zentrum für Umfragen, Methoden und Analysen (Center for Surveys, Methods and Analysis, or ZUMA) sponsored the International Conference on Social Information Processing and Survey Methodology at the Center's headquarters in Mannheim. Unlike the previous interdisciplinary meetings in the field, according to the resulting volume (Hippler, Schwarz, & Sudman, 1987), "the ZUMA conference was organized so that researchers from both cognitive psychology and survey research, who were already convinced of the value of interaction, could present theoretical and experimental findings to each other." The 14 authors (eight American, four German, two Dutch) included ten psychologists, three sociologists, and one political scientist, but only one attendee of the 1983 CNSTAT seminar: social psychologist, survey methodologist, and statistician Roger Tourangeau. "We would like to be able to present much more richly developed specific theories as well as empirical tests of these theories," the ZUMA conference editors lamented. "Unfortunately, the state of the art does not yet permit that" (Hippler, Schwarz, & Sudman, 1987, p. 2).

Jobe and Mingay (1991, pp. 177–178) compare the ZUMA conference to CNSTAT's CASM seminar held the previous year:

> Both the CNSTAT activity and the ZUMA conference addressed the same collaborative issues and brought together experts from cognitive science and survey research to grapple with them; and both put into motion

> vehicles by which a collaborative venture might be sustained. . . . Both the CNSTAT and ZUMA activities assessed the differences in methodology between cognitive psychology and survey research, the barriers to collaboration, and the benefits to each discipline if these barriers could be surmounted. . . . In West Germany, as a direct result of the ZUMA conference, the German Research Council and the Federal Department of Science and Technology provided research grants. In addition, ZUMA established a research programme (e.g. Hippler and Schwarz, 1986; Schwarz, 1990; Schwarz and Bienias, 1990), and sponsors an annual conference on cognition and survey management. . . . Statistics Canada has also begun a questionnaire design programme (Nargundkar and Platek, 1989).

During the year following the ZUMA conference, the first publications appeared based on U.S. government-funded surveys grounded in cognitive theory and techniques. Lessler and Sirken (1985) published the early "goals and methods" of a National Center for Health Statistics (NCHS) laboratory study of "the cognitive aspects of survey methodology" (see also Sirken & Fuchsberg, 1984). Rothwell (1985) described laboratory and field response studies sponsored by the U.S. Bureau of the Census for the 1980 Census. A preliminary report appeared the following year on work sponsored by the U.S. Bureau of Justice Statistics on cognitive research-based alternative screening procedures for the National Crime Survey (Martin, 1986).

A spate of new theoretical work attempting to integrate the separate approaches and findings of cognitive and survey research began to appear in 1987. Strack and Martin (1987) published a revision of their ZUMA conference presentation on what they called "a process account of context effects in attitude surveys" in the conference's edited volume (Hippler, Schwarz, & Sudman, 1987, pp. 123–148). Bradburn, Rips, and Shevell (1987) introduced their theoretical approach to the effects of memory and inference on surveys—particularly on autobiographical questions—to the broad readership of *Science* magazine. *Public Opinion Quarterly* published a cognitive theoretic account of response-order effects in attitude measurement (Krosnick & Alwin, 1987). The following year, Tourangeau and Rasinski (1988) published their theoretical treatment of the cognitive processes underlying context effects like those described by Strack and Martin (1987).

The explosion of articles integrating cognitive and survey research published after 1987 marks that year as the turning point for acceptance of the new interdisciplinary field. More than two dozen important articles appeared in the four-year period from 1987 to 1990 on a wide range of topics that wed cognitive science and survey techniques, including memory in naturalistic contexts (Schwarz, Strack, Kommer, &

Wagner, 1987; Means, Mingay, Nigam, & Zarrow, 1988; Thompson, Skowronski, & Lee, 1988; Brewer, Dull, & Jobe, 1989; Means, Nigam, Zarrow, Loftus, & Donaldson, 1989; Jobe et al., 1990; Schwarz, 1990); question order, wording, and comprehension (Smith, 1987; Schwarz & Scheuring, 1988; Strack, Martin, & Schwarz, 1988; Ottati, Riggle, Wyer, Schwarz, & Kuklinski, 1989); effects of response alternatives and orderings (Schwarz, Strack, Muller, & Chassein, 1988; Hippler & Schwarz, 1989; Mingay & Greenwell, 1990; Schwarz & Bienias, 1990); and cognitive interviewing techniques (Lessler, Tourangeau, & Salter, 1989; Royston, 1989; Jobe & Mingay, 1990).

Because the institutionalized collaboration of cognitive scientists and survey methodologists has run for little more than a decade, it is obviously too early to assess its lasting impact on the two fields. Judging by the progress to date, however, this interdisciplinary effort would appear to be a major contribution to cognitive research—and perhaps the most significant development in survey methodology since the invention of scientific sampling in the early 1930s.

Whatever the lasting impact of cognitive science on survey research methodology *per se*, the cognitive revolution of the mid-1950s to the late 1970s continues to exert a much more widespread and pervasive influence on the study of public opinion and communication more generally. Not the least of these influences has been the major paradigm shift, introduced in the opening paragraphs of this paper, that includes political information processing, macrosociology, and much of the traditional subject matter of the humanities.

PUBLIC OPINION AND COMMUNICATION RESEARCH

As documented above (see also Beniger, 1987a, 1987b), research on public opinion and communication experienced a relative decline during the 1960s and 1970s, roughly the period from Bernard Berelson's eulogy for communication research (Berelson, 1959) and Joseph Klapper's *The Effects of Mass Communication* (1960) through the cognitive revolution in psychology, linguistics, computer science, neuroscience, anthropology, and philosophy—the interdisciplinary amalgam that constitutes the new cognitive science. The prominent exceptions to the two-decade slump, as we discuss above, are the first major papers by Philip Converse (1962, 1964). Not only did Converse reassert the importance of political ideology and belief systems and reestablish the dynamics of attitude stability and instability, he also raised doubts about the quality of public opinion that might influence election and policy outcomes.

Undoubtedly Converse's work appealed to many communications scholars because it suggested one way to avoid the disheartening implications of minimal effects. If attitudes and belief systems can be allowed to depend on cognitive dynamics and statics involving schema as well as knowledge, then communication that changes "only" cognition may be just as important to public opinion and resulting behavior as communication with more readily measured effects. Indeed, psychological research on attitudinal change contemporary with that of Converse found that credible information can have a more lasting impact on public opinion than do mere persuasive appeals (Kelman, 1961; McGuire, 1969).

Whatever motivated the widespread development, debate, and application of Converse's ideas during the two decades of relative decline in interest in public opinion research among communications scholars, the later years of that period—after the early 1970s—did bring several more directed efforts to circumvent the findings of minimal effects by means inspired by the cognitive revolution. This included work on "agenda setting" begun by McCombs and Shaw (1972), on the "spiral of silence" by Noelle-Neumann (1974), and on "cultivation analysis" by Gerbner and Gross (1976), all efforts based on models of atomized individuals under, at the least, the cognitive influence of the mass media. As seen by cultivation analysis, for example, the public not only has its agenda "loaded" (as in agenda setting), but also receives from infancy a socialization to the "mainstream" of a common symbolic environment that once had come from family, play group, neighbors, and teachers, but now consists mostly of images and messages mass-produced by television.

Similar ideas had been widely discussed throughout the formative decades of public opinion research, the 1920s through 1950s. Major components of the agenda-setting model, for example, can be found in Lippmann's "pictures in our heads" and "enlisting of interest" (1922, chs. 1 & 11), in Merton's "frame of reference" (1945; Merton & Kitt, 1950, based on Stouffer et al., 1949–1950), in the "status conferral" mechanism of Lazarsfeld and Merton (1948), in Festinger's "social reality" (1950), and in the tradition of work in psychology on attention and salience in communication (Broadbent, 1958). Major components of the spiral of silence model appear in the social pattern described by Allport (1924) as "pluralistic ignorance," in Schanck's (1932) treatment of "public opinion" versus "private attitudes," in the "social self" of Mead (1934, pt. 3) that emerges by assuming the attitudes of "significant others," and in reference group theory (Sherif, 1936; Hyman, 1942; Newcomb, 1943), in conformity experiments (Sherif, 1935; Asch, 1951; see also Wheeler & Jordan, 1929), and in bandwagon modeling (Simon, 1954). Allport explicitly described the spiral of silence model in *Public Opinion Quarterly*'s first issue (1937, pp. 14–16).

That these rich lodes of research were not fully mined until the early 1970s can be blamed, at least in part, on the increasingly stifling climate created by behaviorism following Watson's pioneering work in the early 1910s. Behaviorist thinking, which flatly rejected all cognitive concepts in favor of the direct study of overt behavior, dominated much of social science from the late 1910s until the mid-1950s. Not until the cognitive revolution of the mid-1950s to the late 1970s were social scientists progressively freed to pursue the kinds of syntheses of past research represented by agenda setting, the spiral of silence, and cultivation analysis.

To these major components of the cognitive revolution in public opinion and communication research might be added at least seven other recent currents of activity (Beniger, 1987b). Roughly in chronological order of their emergence, these efforts include: uses and gratifications research (Blumler & McQuail, 1969; Katz, Gurevitch, & Haas, 1973; Blumler & Katz, 1974); studies of the knowledge gap (Tichenor, Donohue, & Olien, 1970; Tichenor, Rodenkirchen, Olien, & Donohue, 1973); work on political cognition (Axelrod, 1973, 1976; Becker, McCombs, & McLeod, 1975; Lau, Sears, & Centers, 1979; Sears, Lau, Tyler, & Allen, 1980; Fiske & Kinder, 1981; Iyengar & Kinder, 1987); convergence and coorientation models (McLeod & Chaffee, 1973; Chaffee & Choe, 1980); various approaches to audience decoding (Hall, 1974; Worth & Gross, 1974; Turner, 1977; Bourdieu, 1980; Csikszentmihalyi & Kubey, 1981); hegemonic models (Hall, 1977; Hall, Critcher, Jefferson, Clarke, & Roberts, 1978; Gitlin, 1979, 1980, but see Kinder, 1982); and studies of "media events" (Katz, 1980; Katz, Dayan, & Motyl, 1981; Dayan & Katz, 1992).

Although the many obvious differences within and among these separate theoretical approaches tend to obscure their similarities and convergence, they look surprisingly alike when collectively compared to the older minimal effects model. In sharp contrast to this model, all of the more recent approaches sidestep questions of persuasion and political conversion to concentrate on more complex processes involving information, whether on the individual level as cognitions or on the societal level as culture, ideology, and belief systems.

Consider, for example, work on political cognition, which ordinarily examines small groups using detailed data collection, and on audience decoding, which focuses on individual "negotiations" within the constraints of message and text. Each approach, in its own distinct way, contributes to the microdynamics of a single, more comprehensive information-processing model. Similarly, the various approaches to audience decoding generalize that process to the more macrolevel information exchange within "interpretive communities," which in turn exercise the control of public opinion and culture that plays a central role in, for example, hegemonic models. Such control, in turn, may be fed back to mass audiences, for example, through the "framings" of media elites.

Consider, too, how interrelationships among the various components of an information-processing model are directly reflected in the various distinct theoretical approaches just discussed: Uses and gratifications research, for example, establishes the audience of mass communication as an active processor of information in pursuit of individual needs, so that the mass media might be said to supply information, including schema, with which to think (Katz, 1987). Work on the knowledge gap shows that those people most likely to acquire information are also those most likely to acquire still more, presumably because information creates cognitive structures that require what sociologist William Gamson (quoted in Neuman, 1987) calls "fleshing out," but with the important macrosocietal effect that the knowledge rich get richer while the knowledge poor remain relatively poor. Interpersonal-level convergence and coorientation models emphasize that individuals exchange even mass media information among themselves, thereby converging at least partially on shared schema.

These and many other more recent but similar approaches to public opinion and communication research reflect nothing less than the major paradigm shift described in the opening paragraphs of this paper. Centered on cognitive processing, media framing, and active audience engagement in mass communication, the new paradigm represents a shift in dependent variables from attitudes to cognitions, a shift in independent variables from persuasive communication to less directed media processes ranging from "framing" through "discourse" to the social construction of reality, and a shift in scholarly interest from simple change to the structuring or restructuring of cognitions and meaning (Beniger, 1987b).

These three shifts imply a corresponding shift in research from partisan advocates (like political parties) to more "objective" and therefore at least potentially more influential communicators like professional journalists and columnists (Page, Shapiro, & Dempsey, 1987). These communicators, in turn, will no longer be the passive "gatekeepers" of the agenda-setting model so much as active "shapers" or "framers" of public opinion who might determine what even the most influential political operatives must do to effect attitudinal change. Just such a view of the news media has emerged since the mid-1970s, simultaneously with various other approaches that reflect the new cognitive paradigm, in a spate of empirical studies resulting in books by Epstein (1973), Altheide (1974), Roshco (1975), Schudson (1978), Tuchman (1978), Gans (1979), Gitlin (1980), and Bennett (1983), among others. During the same period, according to Gans (1983, p. 174), "a similar feast has taken place overseas, notably in Great Britain."

SUMMARY AND CONCLUSIONS

After three quarters of a century, the grip of behaviorist thinking on the social sciences—and the accompanying hold of radical positivism—have been broken forever. In their place we have various fruits of the cognitive revolution of the 1960s and 1970s: a cognitive science that embraces at least half a dozen major academic disciplines, the growing convergence of quantitative social science and cognitive theory, increasing collaboration between survey research methodologists and cognitive psychologists, and a sweeping new paradigm shift—away from the 30-year preoccupation with media effects—in both public opinion and communication research.

What lies ahead? Although the paradigm shift to information processing, cognition, and social change is still too new to view with much perspective, we might nevertheless hazard a few tentative predictions: As survey methodology grows more rationalized, gradually forsaking art in the name of science, results of past surveys will increasingly be seen as artifacts of survey methods—of question syntax, semantics, ordering, and the structure of response sets. Although macro-level historical changes—cultural as well as political and social—will draw increasing attention, structural stability resulting from dynamic processes like those of societal control will become no less interesting than change. Not only the harder science disciplines of the new cognitive science but also the humanities, through the study of processes from "framing" through "discourse" to the social construction of reality, will increasingly join collaborative study of public opinion and mass communication.

With all of these changes, already in progress, public opinion and communication research will return more and more to the interdisciplinary arena—to the study of a wide variety of cognitive and other information processes and their complex interactions—the arena in which these two fields first emerged nearly three quarters of a century ago.

REFERENCES

Aborn, M. (1989, January). Is CASM bridging the chasm? Evaluations of an experiment in cross-disciplinary survey research. Paper presented at the American Statistical Winter Conference, Statistics in Society, San Diego, CA.

Allport, F. H. (1924). *Social psychology*. Boston: Houghton Mifflin.

Allport, F. H. (1937). Toward a science of public opinion. *Public Opinion Quarterly, 1*, 7–23.

Allport, F. H., & Hartman, D. A. (1925). The measurement and motivation of atypical opinion in a certain group. *American Political Science Review, 19*, 735–760.

Allport, G. W. (1968). The historical background of modern social psychology. In G. Lindzey & E. Aronson (Eds.), *The handbook of social psychology* (Vol. 1). Reading, MA: Addison-Wesley.

Altheide, D. L. (1974). *Creating reality: How TV news distorts events*. Beverly Hills, CA: Sage.

Asch, S. E. (1946). Forming impressions of personality. *Journal of Abnormal Social Psychology, 41*, 258–290.

Asch, S. E. (1951). Effects of group pressure upon the modification and distortion of judgments. In H. S. Guetzkow (Ed.), *Groups, leadership and men: Research in human relations* (pp. 177–190). New York: Russell and Russell.

Axelrod, R. M. (1973). Schema theory: An information processing model of perception and cognition. *American Political Science Review, 67*, 1248–1266.

Axelrod, R. M. (1976). *Structure of decision: The cognitive maps of political elites*. Princeton, NJ: Princeton University Press.

Bahrick, H. P., Bahrick, P. O., & Wittlinger, R. P. (1975). Fifty years of memories for names and faces: A cross-sectional approach. *Journal of Experimental Psychology: General, 104*, 54–75.

Bartlett, F. C. (1932). *Remembering: A study in experimental and social psychology*. Cambridge, England: Cambridge University Press.

Becker, L. B., McCombs, M. E., & McLeod, J. M. (1975). The development of political cognitions. In S. H. Chaffee (Ed.), *Political communication: Issues and strategies for research* (pp. 21–63). Beverly Hills, CA: Sage.

Beniger, J. R. (1983). The popular symbolic repertoire and mass communication. *Public Opinion Quarterly, 47*, 479–484.

Beniger, J. R. (1986). *The control revolution: Technological and economic origins of the information society*. Cambridge, MA: Harvard University Press.

Beniger, J. R. (1987a). *Public opinion and mass communication: The past half-century*. Unpublished manuscript, Annenberg School for Communication, University of Southern California, Los Angeles.

Beniger, J. R. (1987b). Toward an old new paradigm: The half-century flirtation with mass society. *Public Opinion Quarterly, 51*, S46–S66.

Bennett, W. L. (1983). *News: The politics of illusion*. New York: Longman.

Berelson, B. R. (1955). The study of public opinion. In L. D. White (Ed.), *The state of the social sciences* (pp. 299–318). Chicago: University of Chicago Press.

Berelson, B. R. (1959). The state of communication research. *Public Opinion Quarterly, 23*, 1–6.

Berelson, B. R., Lazarsfeld, P. F., & McPhee, W. N. (1954). *Voting: A study of opinion formation in a presidential campaign*. Chicago: University of Chicago Press.

Biderman, A. D. (1980). *Report of a workshop on applying cognitive psychology to recall problems of the National Crime Survey*. Washington, DC: Bureau of Social Science Research.

Blumler, J. G., & Katz, E. (Eds.). (1974). *The uses of mass communications: Current perspectives on gratifications research*. Beverly Hills, CA: Sage.

Blumler, J. G., & McQuail, D. (1969). *Television in politics: Its uses and influence*. Chicago: University of Chicago Press.

Bogardus, E. S. (1926). *The new social research*. Los Angeles: Jesse Ray Miller.

Booth, C. (1889). *Life and labour of the people*. London: William and Norgate.

Bourdieu, P. (1980). The production of belief (R. Nice, Trans.). *Media, Culture and Society, 2*, 3.

Bradburn, N. M., Rips, L. J., & Shevell, S. K. (1987). Answering autobiographical questions: The impact of memory and inference on surveys. *Science, 236*, 157–161.

Bradburn, N. M., & Sudman, S. (1979). *Improving interviewing methods and questionnaire design*. San Francisco: Jossey-Bass.

Breed, W. (1955). Social control in the newsroom: A functional analysis. *Social Forces, 33*, 326–335.

Brewer, M. B., Dull, V. T., & Jobe, J. B. (1989). Social cognition approach to reporting chronic conditions in health surveys. *Vital and Health Statistics* (Series 6, No. 3). Washington, DC: U. S. Government Printing Office.

Broadbent, D. E. (1958). *Perception and communication*. Oxford: Pergamon.

Bruner, J. S., Goodnow, J. J., & Austin, J. G. (1956). *A study of thinking*. New York: Wiley.

Campbell, A., Converse, P. E., Miller, W. E., & Stokes, D. E. (1960). *The American voter*. New York: Wiley.

Cantril, H. (Ed.). (1944). *Gauging public opinion*. Princeton, NJ: Princeton University Press.

Cartwright, D., & Harary, F. (1956). Structural balance: A generalization of Heider's theory. *Psychological Review, 63*, 277–293.

Chaffee, S. H., & Choe, S. Y. (1980). Time of decision and media use during the Ford–Carter campaign. *Public Opinion Quarterly, 44*, 53–69.

Chomsky, N. (1956, September 10–12). *Three models of language*. Paper presented to the Symposium on Information Theory, Massachusetts Institute of Technology, Cambridge, MA.

Chomsky, N. (1957). *Syntactic structures*. The Hague: Mouton.

Chomsky, N. (1965). *Aspects of the theory of syntax*. Cambridge, MA: MIT Press.

Chomsky, N. (1966). *Cartesian linguistics*. New York: Harper & Row.

Chomsky, N. (1968). *Language and mind*. New York: Harcourt, Brace & World.

Christensen-Szalanski, J. J., & Beach, L. R. (1984). The citation bias: Fad and fashion in the judgment and decision literature. *American Psychologist, 39*, 75–78.

Converse, J. M. (1987). *Survey research in the United States: Roots and emergence 1890–1960*. Berkeley, CA: University of California Press.
Converse, P. E. (1962). Information flow and the stability of partisan attitudes. *Public Opinion Quarterly, 26*, 578–599.
Converse, P. E. (1964). The nature of belief systems in mass publics. In D. E. Apter (Ed.), *Ideology and discontent* (pp. 206–261). New York: Free Press.
Csikszentmihalyi, M., & Kubey, R. (1981). Television and the rest of life: A systematic comparison of subjective experience. *Public Opinion Quarterly, 45*, 317–328.
Dayan, D., & Katz, E. (1992). *Media events: The live broadcasting of history*. Cambridge, MA: Harvard University Press.
Descartes, R. (1968). *Discourse de la méthode*. Reprinted as *Discourse on method and meditations* (F. E. Sutcliffe, Trans.). New York: Penguin. (Original work published in 1637)
Epstein, E. J. (1973). *News from nowhere: Television and the news*. New York: Random House.
Ericsson, K. A., & Simon, H. A. (1980). Verbal reports as data. *Psychological Review, 87*, 215–251.
Ericsson, K. A., & Simon, H. A. (1984). *Protocol analysis: Verbal reports as data*. Cambridge, MA: MIT Press.
Festinger, L. (1950). Informal social communication. *Psychological Review, 57*, 271–282.
Festinger, L. (1957). *A theory of cognitive dissonance*. Stanford, CA: Stanford University Press.
Festinger, L., Riecken, H. W., & Schachter, S. (1956). *When prophecy fails: A social and psychological study of a modern group that predicted the destruction of the world*. New York: Harper & Row.
Fiske, S. T., & Kinder, D. R. (1981). Involvement, expertise, and schema use: Evidence from political cognition. In N. Cantor & J. F. Kihlstrom (Eds.), *Personality, cognition, and social interaction* (pp. 171–190). Hillsdale, NJ: Erlbaum.
Flanagan, O. J., Jr. (1984). *The science of the mind*. Cambridge, MA: MIT Press.
Fodor, J. A. (1975). *The language of thought*. New York: Thomas Y. Crowell.
Fodor, J. A., & Katz, J. J. (Eds.). (1964). *The structure of language: Readings in the philosophy of language*. Englewood Cliffs, NJ: Prentice-Hall.
Gans, H. J. (1979). *Deciding what's news: A study of CBS Evening News, NBC Nightly News, Newsweek, and Time*. New York: Pantheon.
Gans, H. J. (1983). News media, news policy, and democracy: Research for the future. *Journal of Communication, 33*, 174–184.
Gardner, H. (1985). *The mind's new science: A history of the cognitive revolution*. New York: Basic.
Gerbner, G., & Gross, L. (1976). Living with television: The violence profile. *Journal of Communication, 26*, 173–199.
Gitlin, T. (1979). Prime time ideology: The hegemonic process in television entertainment. *Social Problems, 26*, 251–266.
Gitlin, T. (1980). *The whole world is watching: Mass media in the making and unmaking of the New Left*. Berkeley, CA: University of California Press.

Goodenough, W. H. (1956). Componential analysis and the study of meaning. *Language, 32*, 195–216.

Hall, S. (1974). The television discourse: Encoding and decoding. *Education and Culture, 25*, 8–14.

Hall, S. (1977). Culture, the media, and the 'ideological effect.' In J. Curran, M. Gurevitch, & J. Woollacott (Eds.), *Mass communication and society* (pp. 315–348). Beverly Hills, CA: Sage.

Hall, S., Critcher, C., Jefferson, T., Clarke, J., & Roberts, B. (1978). *Policing the crisis: Mugging, the state, and law and order*. New York: Holmes and Meier.

Head, H. (1926). *Aphasia and kindred disorders of speech* (2 vols.). New York: Macmillan.

Heider, F. (1944). Social perception and phenomenal causality. *Psychological Review, 51*, 358–374.

Heider, F. (1946). Attitudes and cognitive organization. *Journal of Psychology, 21*, 107–112.

Hippler, H-J., & Schwarz, N. (1986). Not forbidding isn't allowing: The cognitive basis of the forbid-allow asymmetry. *Public Opinion Quarterly, 50*, 87–96.

Hippler, H-J., & Schwarz, N. (1989). 'No-opinion' filters: A cognitive perspective. *International Journal of Public Opinion, 1*, 77–87.

Hippler, H-J., Schwarz, N., & Sudman, S. (Eds.). (1987). *Social information processing and survey methodology*. New York: Springer-Verlag.

Hogarth, R. M. (Ed.). (1982). *Question framing and response consistency: New directions for the methodology of social and behavioral science, No. 11*. San Francisco: Jossey-Bass.

Hovland, C. I., Janis, I. L., & Kelley, H. H. (1953). *Communication and persuasion: Psychological studies of opinion change*. New Haven, CT: Yale University Press.

Hubel, D. H., & Wiesel, T. N. (1959). Receptive fields of single neurons in the cat's striate cortex. *Journal of Physiology, 148*, 574–591.

Hubel, D. H., & Wiesel, T. N. (1962). Receptive fields, binocular interaction and functional architecture in the cat's visual cortex. *Journal of Physiology, 160*, 106–154.

Hyman, H. H. (1942). The psychology of status. *Archives of Psychology, 38*, 5–94.

Hyman, H. H. (1954). *Interviewing in social research*. Chicago: University of Chicago Press.

Hyman, H. H., & Sheatsley, P. B. (1947). Some reasons why information campaigns fail. *Public Opinion Quarterly, 11*, 412–423.

Iyengar, S., & Kinder, D. R. (1987). *News that matters: Television and American opinion*. Chicago: University of Chicago Press.

Jabine, T. B., Straf, M. L., Tanur, J. M., & Tourangeau, R. (Eds.). (1984). *Cognitive aspects of survey methodology: Building a bridge between disciplines*. Report of the Advanced Research Seminar on Cognitive Aspects of Survey Methodology. Washington, DC: National Academy Press.

Jobe, J. B., & Mingay, D. J. (1990). Cognitive laboratory approach to designing questionnaires for surveys of elderly respondents. *Public Health Reports, 105*, 518–524.

Jobe, J. B., & Mingay, D. J. (1991). Cognition and survey measurement: History and overview. *Applied Cognitive Psychology, 5*, 175–192.

Jobe, J. B., White, A. A., Kelley, C. L., Mingay, D. J., Sanchez, M. J., & Loftus, E. F. (1990). Recall strategies and memory for health care visits. *Milbank Memorial Fund Quarterly/Health and Society, 68*, 171–189.

Johnson-Laird, P. N., & Wason, P. C. (1970). A theoretical analysis of insight into a reasoning task. *Cognitive Psychology, 1*, 134–148.

Johnson-Laird, P. N., & Wason, P. C. (1977). A theoretical analysis of insight into a reasoning task. In P. N. Johnson-Laird & P. C. Wason (Eds.), *Thinking: Reading in cognitive science*. Cambridge, England: Cambridge University Press.

Jones, E. E., & Davis, K. E. (1965). From acts to dispositions: The attribution process in person perception. In L. Berkowitz (Ed.), *Advances in experimental social psychology*, (Vol. 2.). New York: Academic Press.

Jones, E. E., & Harris, V. A. (1967). The attribution of attitudes. *Journal of Experimental Social Psychology, 3*, 1–24.

Jones, E. E., & Nisbett, R. E. (1971). *The actor and the observer: Divergent perceptions of the causes of behavior*. Morristown, NJ: General Learning Press.

Jung, C. G. (1916). *Collected papers on analytical psychology* (C. E. Long, Trans.). London: Bailliere, Tindall, & Cox.

Kahn, R. L., & Cannell, C. F. (1957). *The dynamics of interviewing*. New York: Wiley.

Kahneman, D., & Tversky, A. (1972). Subjective probability: A judgment of representativeness. *Cognitive Psychology, 3*, 430–454.

Kahneman, D., & Tversky, A. (1973). On the psychology of prediction. *Psychological Review, 80*, 236–251.

Kant, I. (1929). *Kritik der reinen vernunft*. Reprinted as *Critique of pure reason* (N. K. Smith, Trans.). London: Macmillan. (Original work published in 1781)

Katz, E. (1980). Media events: The sense of occasion. *Studies in Visual Communication, 6*, 84–89.

Katz, E. (1987). Communications research since Lazarsfeld. *Public Opinion Quarterly, 51*, S25–S45.

Katz, E., Dayan, D., & Motyl, P. (1981). In defense of media events. In R. W. Haigh, G. Gerbner, & R. B. Byrne (Eds.), *Communication in the twenty-first century* (pp. 43–59). New York: Wiley-Interscience.

Katz, E., Gurevitch, M., & Haas, H. (1973). On the use of the mass media for important things. *American Sociological Review, 38*, 164–181.

Keenan, J. M., & Baillet, S. D. (1980). Memory for personally and socially significant events. In R. S. Nickerson (Ed.), *Attention and performance VIII*. Hillsdale, NJ: L. Erlbaum.

Keenan, J. M., MacWhinney, B., & Mayhew, D. (1977). Pragmatics in memory: Study of natural conversation. *Journal of Verbal Learning and Verbal Behavior, 16*, 549–560.

Kelley, H. H. (1967). Attribution theory in social psychology. *Nebraska Symposium on Motivation, 15*, 192–238.

Kelley, H. H. (1971). *Attribution in social interaction*. Morristown, NJ: General Learning Press.

Kelman, H. C. (1961). *Enough already about ideology: The many bases of American public opinion.* Paper presented to the American Political Science Association.

Kinder, D. R. (1982). *Enough already about ideology: The many bases of American public opinion.* Paper presented to the American Political Science Association.

Klapper, J. T. (1960). *The effects of mass communication.* Glencoe, IL: Free Press.

Koffka, K. (1935). *Principles of gestalt psychology.* New York: Harcourt, Brace.

Kohler, W. H. (1917). *The mentality of apes* (E. Winter, Trans.). New York: Harcourt, Brace.

Kohler, W. H. (1929). *Gestalt psychology: An introduction to new concepts in modern psychology.* New York: Liveright.

Kohler, W. H. (1940). *Dynamics in psychology.* New York: Liveright.

Krosnick, J. A., & Alwin, D. F. (1987). An evaluation of a cognitive theory of response-order effects in survey measurement. *Public Opinion Quarterly, 51,* 201–219.

Lang, K., & Lang, G. E. (1953). The unique perspective of television and its effects: A pilot study. *American Sociological Review, 18,* 3–12.

Lang, K., & Lang, G. E. (1983). The "new" rhetoric of mass communication research: A longer view. *Journal of Communication, 33,* 128–140.

Lau, R. R., Sears, D. O., & Centers, R. (1979). The 'positivity bias' in evaluations of public figures: Evidence against instrument artifacts. *Public Opinion Quarterly, 43,* 347–458.

Lazarsfeld, P. E., Berelson, B., & Gaudet, H. (1944). *The people's choice.* New York: Duell, Sloan and Pearce.

Lazarsfeld, P. F., & Merton, R. K. (1948). Mass communication, popular taste and organized social action. In L. Bryson (Ed.), *The communication of ideas: A series of addresses* (pp. 95–118). New York: Institute for Religious and Social Studies, Harper & Row.

Lerner, M. J., Miller, D. T., & Holmes, J. G. (1976). Deserving and the emergence of forms of justice. In L. Berkowitz & E. Walster (Eds.), *Advances in experimental social psychology* (Vol. 9). New York: Academic Press.

Lessler, J. T., & Sirken, M. G. (1985). Laboratory-based research on the cognitive aspects of survey methodology: The goals and methods of the National Center for Health Statistics study. *Milbank Memorial Fund Quarterly/Health and Society, 63,* 565–581.

Lessler, J. T., Tourangeau, R., & Salter, W. (1989). Questionnaire design in the cognitive research laboratory. *Vital and Health Statistics* (Series 6, No. 1). Washington, DC: U. S. Government Printing Office.

Lettvin, J. Y., Maturana, H. R., McCulloch, W. S., & Pitts, W. H. (1959). What the frog's eye tells the frog's brain. *Proceedings of the IRE, 47,* 1940–1951.

Lévi-Strauss, C. (1958). *Anthropologie structurale.* Reprinted as *Structural anthropology* (C. Jacobson & B. Grundfest Schoepf, Trans.). New York: Basic Books.

Lévi-Strauss, C. (1962). *La pensée sauvage.* Reprinted as *The savage mind.* Chicago: University of Chicago Press.

Lewis, H. B. (1941). Studies in the principles of judgments and attitudes: IV. The operation of "prestige suggestion." *Journal of Social Psychology, 14*, 229–256.

Likert, R. (1932). A techniques for the measurement of attitudes. *Archives of Psychology, 140*, 1–55.

Linton, M. (1975). Memory for real-world events. In D. A. Norman & D. E. Rumelhart (Eds.), *Explorations in cognition*. San Francisco, CA: W. H. Freeman.

Linton, M. (1982). Transformations of memory of everyday life. In U. Neisser (Ed.), *Memory observed: Remembering in natural contexts*. San Francisco: W. H. Freeman.

Lippmann, W. (1922). *Public Opinion*. New York: Harcourt, Brace.

Loftus, E. F., & Marburger, W. (1983). Since the eruption of Mt. Saint Helens, has anyone beaten you up? Improving the accuracy of retrospective reports with landmark events. *Memory and Cognition, 11*, 114–120.

Lorge, I. (1936). Prestige, suggestion, and attitudes. *Journal of Social Psychology, 7*, 386–402.

Lounsbury, F. G. (1956). A semantic analysis of the Pawnee kinship usage. *Language, 32*, 158–194.

Markus, H., & Zajonc, R. B. (1985). The cognitive perspective in social psychology. In G. Lindzey & E. Aronson (Eds.), *Handbook of social psychology* (Vol. 1). New York: Random House.

Martin, E. (1986). *Report on the development of alternative screening procedures for the National Crime Survey*. Washington, DC: Bureau of Social Science Research.

McCombs, M. E., & Shaw, D. L. (1972). The agenda-setting function of mass media. *Public Opinion Quarterly, 36*, 176–187.

McGuire, W. J. (1969). The nature of attitudes and attitude change. In G. Lindzey & E. Aronson (Eds.), *The handbook of social psychology* (2nd ed., Vol. 3, pp. 136–314). Reading, MA: Addison-Wesley.

McLeod, J. M., & Chaffee, S. H. (1973). Interpersonal approaches to communication research. *American Behavioral Scientist, 16*, 469–499.

McNemar, Q. (1946). Opinion-attitude methodology. *Psychological Bulletin, 43*, 289–374.

Mead, G. H. (1934). *Mind, self, and society: From the standpoint of a social behaviorist*, (C. W. Morris, Ed.). Chicago: University of Chicago Press.

Means, B., Mingay, D. J., Nigam, A., & Zarrow, M. (1988). A cognitive approach to enhancing health survey reports of medical visits. In M. M. Gruneberg, P. E. Morris, & R. N. Sykes (Eds.), *Practical aspects of memory: Current research and issues: Vol. 1. Memory in everyday life* (pp. 537–542). New York: Wiley.

Means, B., Nigam, A., Zarrow, M., Loftus, E. F., & Donaldson, M. S. (1989). Autobiographical memory for health-related events. *Vital and Health Statistics* (Series 6, No. 2). Washington, DC: U. S. Government Printing Office.

Merton, R. K. (1945). The sociology of knowledge. In G. Gurevitch & W. E. Moore (Eds.), *Twentieth century sociology* (pp. 366–405). New York: Philosophical Library.

Merton, R. K., & Kitt, A. S. (1950). Contributions to the theory of reference group behavior. In R. K. Merton & P. F. Lazarsfeld (Eds.), *Continuities in social research: Studies in the scope and method of "The American Soldier"* (pp. 40–105). Glencoe, IL: Free Press.

Meyer, P., & Spaeth, M. A. (Eds.). (1984). A cumulative index of volumes 1–46, 1937–1982. *Public Opinion Quarterly, 48*, part. A, 1–266.

Miller, D. T., & Ross, M. (1975). Self-serving biases in the attribution of causality: Fact or fiction? *Psychological Bulletin, 82*, 213–225.

Miller, G. A. (1956). The magical number seven, plus or minus two: Some limits on our capacity for processing information. *Psychological Review, 63*, 81–97.

Miller, G. A., Galanter, E., & Pribram, K. H. (1960). *Plans and the structure of behavior*. New York: Holt, Rinehart & Winston.

Mingay, D. J., & Greenwell, M. T. (1990). Memory bias and response-order effects. *Journal of Official Statistics, 5*, 253–263.

Morris, C. (1971). *Writings on the general theory of signs*. The Hague: Mouton.

Moss, L., & Goldstein, H. (Eds.). (1979). *The recall method in social surveys*. Studies in Education (new series) (Vol. 9). Windsor, Canada: NFER Publishing.

Nargundkar, M. S., & Platek, R. (1989). Qualitative methods in questionnaire design. *Proceedings of the International Association of Survey Statisticians, International Statistical Institute*, 453–470.

Neisser, U. (1967). *Cognitive psychology*. New York: Appleton-Century-Crofts.

Neisser, U. (1978). Memory: What are the important questions? In M. M. Gruneberg, P. E. Morris, & R. N. Sykes (Eds.), *Practical aspects of memory* (pp. 3–24). New York: Academic Press.

Neuman, W. R. (1987). Parallel content analysis: Old paradigms and new proposals. In G. Comstock (Ed.), *Public communication behavior* (Vol. 2). Orlando, FL: Academic.

Newcomb, T. M. (1943). *Personality and social change: Attitude formation in a student community*. New York: Holt, Rinehart and Winston.

Newcomb, T. M. (1953). An approach to the study of communicative acts. *Psychological Review, 60*, 393–404.

Newell, A., & Simon, H. A. (1956, September 10–12). The logic theory machine. Paper presented to the Symposium on Information Theory, Massachusetts Institute of Technology.

Newell, A., & Simon, H. A. (1972). *Human problem solving*. Englewood Cliffs, NJ: Prentice-Hall.

Nisbett, R. E., & Ross, L. (1980). *Human inference: Strategies and shortcomings in social judgement*. Englewood Cliffs, NJ: Prentice-Hall.

Noelle-Neumann, E. (1974). The spiral of silence: A theory of public opinion. *Journal of Communication, 24*, 43–51.

Ottati, V. C., Riggle, E. J., Wyer, R. S., Jr., Schwarz, N., & Kuklinski, J. (1989). Cognitive and affective bases of opinion survey responses. *Journal of Personality and Social Psychology, 57*, 404–415.

Page, B. I., Shapiro, R. Y., & Dempsey, G. R. (1987). What moves public opinion? *American Political Science Review, 81*, 23–43.

Payne, S. L. (1951). *The art of asking questions*. Princeton, NJ: Princeton University Press.

Piaget, J. (1926). *The child's conception of the world*. London: Paul, Trench, Trubner.
Piaget, J. (1932). *The moral judgment of the child*. New York: Harcourt, Brace.
Piaget, J. (1936). *The origins of intelligence in children*. New York: International Universities Press.
Presser, S. (1984). The use of survey data in basic research in the social sciences. In C. F. Turner & E. Martin (Eds.), *Surveying subjective phenomena* (Vol. 2, pp. 93–114). New York: Russell Sage.
Pribram, K. H. (1971). *Languages of the brain: Experimental paradoxes and principles in neuropsychology*. Englewood Cliffs, NJ: Prentice-Hall.
Putnam, H. (1960). Minds and machines. In S. Hook (Ed.), *Dimensions of mind*. New York: New York University Press.
Putnam, H. (1973). Philosophy and our mental life. Paper presented to the Foerster Symposium on Computers and the Mind, University of California, Berkeley, CA.
Roshco, B. (1975). *Newsmaking*. Chicago: University of Chicago Press.
Ross, L. (1977). The intuitive psychologist and his shortcomings: Distortions in the attribution process. In L. Berkowitz (Ed.), *Advances in experimental social psychology* (Vol. 10). New York: Academic Press.
Ross, L., Bierbrauer, G., & Polly, S. (1974). Attribution of educational outcomes by professional and non-professional instructors. *Journal of Personality and Social Psychology, 29*, 609–618.
Ross, L., Greene, D., & House, P. (1977). The "false consensus effect": An egocentric bias in social perception and attribution processes. *Journal of Experimental Social Psychology, 13*, 279–301.
Rothwell, N. D. (1985). Laboratory and field responses research studies for the 1980 census of population in the United States. *Journal of Official Statistics, 1*, 137–157.
Royston, P. N. (1989). Using intensive interviews to evaluate questions. In F. J. Fowler, Jr. (Ed.), *Health survey research methods* (pp. 3–7). Washington, DC: U. S. Government Printing Office.
Rugg, D. (1941). Experiments in wording questions: II. *Public Opinion Quarterly, 5*, 91–92.
Schanck, R. L. (1932). A study of a community and its groups and institutions conceived of as behaviors of individuals. *Psychological Monographs, 43*, 2 (195), 1–133.
Schramm, W. (1983). The unique perspective of communication: A retrospective view. *Journal of Communication, 33*, 6–17.
Schudson, M. (1978). *Discovering the news: A social history of American newspapers*. New York: Basic Books.
Schuman, H., & Presser, S. (1981). *Questions and answers in attitude surveys: Experiments on question form, wording, and context*. Orlando, FL: Academic.
Schwarz, N. (1990). Assessing frequency reports of mundane behaviors: Contributions of cognitive psychology to questionnaire construction. In C. Hendrick & M. Clark (Eds.), *Review of Personality and Social Psychology* (Vol. 11, pp. 98–119). Beverly Hills, CA: Sage.
Schwarz, N., & Bienias, J. (1990). What mediates the impact of response al-

ternatives on frequency reports of mundane behaviors. *Applied Cognitive Psychology, 4*, 61–72.

Schwarz, N., & Clore, G. L. (1983). Mood, misattribution, and judgments of well-being: Informative and directive functions of affective states. *Journal of Personality and Social Psychology, 45*, 513–523.

Schwarz, N., & Scheuring, B. (1988). Judgments of relationship satisfaction: Inter- and intraindividual comparison strategies as a function of questionnaire structure. *European Journal of Psychology, 18*, 485–496.

Schwarz, N., Strack, F., Kommer, D., & Wagner, D. (1987). Soccer, rooms, and the quality of your life-Mood effects on judgments of satisfaction with life in general and with specific life-domains. *European Journal of Social Psychology, 17*, 69–79.

Schwarz, N., Strack, F., Muller, G., & Chassein, B. (1988). The range of response alternatives may determine the meaning of the question: Further evidence on information functions of response alternatives. *Social Cognition, 6*, 107–117.

Sears, D. O., Lau, R. R., Tyler, T. R., & Allen, H. M., Jr. (1980). Self-interest vs. symbolic politics in policy attitudes and presidential voting. *American Political Science Review, 74*, 670–684.

Sherif, M. (1935). A study of some social factors in perception. *Archives of Psychology, 27*, 5–60.

Sherif, M. (1936). *The psychology of social norms*. New York: Harper & Row.

Sills, D. L. (1987). Paul F. Lazarsfeld, February 13, 1901-August 30, 1976. In *Biographical Memoirs* (Vol. 56, pp. 251–282). Washington DC: National Academy Press.

Sills, D. L. (1989). Lazarsfeld, Paul F. (1901–1976). In E. Barnouw, G. Gerbner, W. Schramm, T. L. Worth, & L. Gross (Eds.), *International encyclopedia of communications* (Vol. 2, pp. 411–412). New York: Oxford University Press.

Simon, H. A. (1954). Bandwagon and underdog effects and the possibility of election predictions. *Public Opinion Quarterly, 18*, 245–253.

Simon, H. A. (1969). *Sciences of the artificial*. Cambridge, MA: MIT Press.

Sirken, M. G., & Fuchsberg, R. (1984). Laboratory-based research on the cognitive aspects of survey methodology. In T. B. Jabine, M. L. Straf, J. M. Tanur, & R. Tourangeau (Eds.), *Cognitive aspects of survey methodology: Building a bridge between disciplines* (pp. 26–34). Washington, DC: National Academy Press.

Skinner, B. F. (1938). *The behavior of organisms: An experimental analysis*. New York: Appleton-Century.

Smith, T. W. (1987). That which we call welfare by any other name would smell sweeter: An analysis of the impact of question wording on response patterns. *Public Opinion Quarterly, 51*, 75–83.

Stouffer, S. A., et al. (1949–1950). *The American soldier: Studies in social psychology in World War II* (4 vols.). Princeton, NJ: Princeton University Press.

Strack, F., & Martin, L. L. (1987). Thinking, judging, and communicating: A process account of context effects in attitude surveys. In H.-J. Hippler, N. Schwarz, & S. Sudman (Eds.), *Social information processing and survey methodology* (pp. 123–148). New York: Springer-Verlag.

Strack, F., Martin, L. L., & Schwarz, N. (1988). Priming and communication: The social determinants of information use in judgments of life-satisfaction. *European Journal of Social Psychology, 18*, 429–442.

Sudman, S., & Bradburn, N. M. (1974). *Response effects in surveys: A review and synthesis*. Chicago: Aldine.

Sudman, S., & Bradburn, N. M. (1982). *Asking questions: A practical guide to questionnaire construction*. San Francisco: Jossey-Bass.

Thomas, W. I., & Zaniecki, F. (1918). *The Polish peasant in Europe and America: Monograph of an immigrant group*. Chicago: University of Chicago Press.

Thompson, C. P., Skowronski, J. J., & Lee, D. J. (1988). Telescoping in dating naturally occurring events. *Memory and Cognition, 16*, 461–468.

Thorndike, R. L., Hagen, E. H., & Kemper, R. A. (1952). Normative data obtained in the house-to-house administration of a psychosomatic inventory. *Journal of Consulting Psychology, 16*, 257–260.

Thurstone, L. L., & Chave, E. J. (1929). *The measurement of attitudes*. Chicago: University of Chicago Press.

Tichenor, P. J., Donohue, G. A., & Olien, C. N. (1970). Mass media flow and differential growth in knowledge. *Public Opinion Quarterly, 34*, 159–170.

Tichenor, P. J., Rodenkirchen, J. M., Olien, C. N., & Donohue, G. A. (1973). Community issues, conflict, and public affairs knowledge. In P. Clarke (Ed.), *New models for mass communication research* (pp. 45–79). Beverly Hills, CA: Sage.

Tolman, E. C. (1932). *Purposive behavior in animals and men*. New York: Century.

Tourangeau, R., & Rasinski, K. A. (1988). Cognitive processes underlying context effects in attitude measurement. *Psychological Bulletin, 103*, 299–314.

Tuchman, G. (1978). *Making news: A study in the construction of reality*. New York: Free Press.

Turner, C. F., & Martin, E. A. (Eds.). (1984). *Surveying subjective phenomena*, 2 vols. New York: Russell Sage Foundation.

Turner, V. (1977). Process, system, and symbol: A new anthropological synthesis. *Daedalus, 106*, 61–80.

Tversky, A. (1977). Features of similarity. *Psychological Review, 84*, 327–352.

Tversky, A., & Kahneman, D. (1973). Availability: A heuristic for judging frequency and probability. *Cognitive Psychology, 5*, 207–232.

Tversky, A., & Kahneman, D. (1974). Judgment under uncertainty: Heuristics and biases. *Science, 185*, 1124–1131.

Tyler, S. A. (Ed.). (1969). *Cognitive anthropology*. New York: Holt, Rinehart, & Winston.

von Neumann, J. (1958). *The computer and the brain*. New Haven, CT: Yale University Press.

Wason, P. C., & Johnson-Laird, P. N. (1972). *The psychology of reasoning: Structure and content*. Cambridge, MA: Harvard University Press.

Watson, J. B. (1914). *Behavior: An introduction to comparative psychology*. New York: Henry Holt.

Watson, J. B. (1919). *Psychology from the standpoint of a behaviorist*. Philadelphia: J. B. Lippincott.

Weiner, B., Freize, I., Kukla, A., Reed, L., Rest, B., & Rosenbaum, R. M. (1971). *Perceiving the causes of success and failure*. Morristown, NJ: General Learning Press.

Weiner, B. (1973). *Theories of motivation: From mechanism to cognition*. Chicago: Markham.

Wertheimer, M. (1912). Experimentelle studien uber das sehen von bewegungen. *Zeitshrift für Psychologie, 61*, 161–265.

Wertheimer, M. (1945). *Productive thinking*. New York: Harper & Brothers.

Wheeler, D., & Jordan, H. (1929). Change of individual opinion to accord with group opinion. *Journal of Abnormal and Social Psychology, 24*, 203–206.

Worth, S., & Gross, L. (1974). Symbolic strategies. *Journal of Communication, 24*, 27–39.

10

Opinions, Perception, and Social Reality

Carroll J. Glynn
Ronald E. Ostman
Daniel G. McDonald

This chapter integrates recent work in the investigation of perceptions of others' opinions as a component of the public opinion process. It provides a description of theoretical foundations relating communication, perception, and public opinion, and an overview and description of current research in psychology and social psychology relevant to theories of public opinion. It describes six current public opinion perspectives that examine perceptions of others' opinions as a major focus: the spiral of silence, pluralistic ignorance, false consensus, the "looking-glass" perception, impersonal impact–unrealistic optimism, and the "third-person" effect. It also specifies a research perspective by which perceptual mechanisms can be investigated within a common theoretical framework.

THEORETICAL FOUNDATIONS

Today's students of public opinion and human interaction believe, almost as an article of faith, that human communication and behavior are *socially* derived and motivated. Wellsprings of this belief can be traced to late 19th- and early 20th-century scholars, whose writings helped to overcome dominant 19th-century theories concerning human behavior. Those earlier theories argued that instinct, heredity, and social evolution were the deterministic mechanisms that caused humans to tick. In fact, the prevailing explanatory role of instinct as a fundamental turnstile through which human behavior passed persisted well into the 20th century in the works of social psychologist William McDougall and others (Bevis, 1921; Martin, 1920; McDougall, 1917) and still resonates in some contemporary research and thought (Collier, Minton, & Reynolds, 1991).[1] However, while many intellectuals in the early 20th century retained a belief in the basic importance of instinct, others increasingly found a role for effects of environment, particularly culture and the social environment (Irion, 1950).

While John Dewey (1922) pointed to the fundamental importance of "definite, independent, original" instincts such as fear, anger, and sexual desire, he also labeled as "instincts" such human feelings and social reactions as rivalry, love of mastery over others, gregariousness, and envy. Further, while considering these instincts or "impulses" necessary to a discussion of human conduct, Dewey did not find them sufficient explanations, suggesting that "any impulse may become organized into almost any disposition according to the way it interacts with surroundings" (Dewey, 1922, cited in Ratner, 1939, p. 739).

Interactionist theories moved away from instinct- and impulse-based explanations of human behavior, placing greater importance on the role of communication and discussions of the critical nature of symbols.[2] Cooley, in his 1902 book *Human Nature and the Social Order*, argued a sociological evolution, saying that an understanding of humans required knowledge of both a stream and a path running parallel to the stream along its banks. The stream in Cooley's analogy was heredity ("animal transmission"). The path was communication ("social transmission"). The stream was more ancient, but the path, well on its way to becoming a road, increasingly carried a heavy volume of traffic. Cooley said that heredity, (which he thought of largely in terms of potential), interacted on a complementary basis with physical and social environment (process), to produce what a human was and would be (product). Cooley did not believe that humans engaged in automatic, unreflective behavior.

Humans were different from other animals, Cooley argued, because of their greater inherent potential, which was coachable and plastic. Another of his famous concepts was the human capacity for "sympathy" (mental sharing). For Cooley, what was really important about humans was not their physical makeup ("a lump of flesh"), but social and moral realities ("ideas") that existed in their minds and imaginations. These ideas would stimulate motives. And from motives, the reflective observer could gauge behaviors. Thus, to understand Napoleon, for example, we need to examine not his body, but that part of his body which we call "mind" and the quality of his ideas and imaginings, *as well as* the ideas and imaginings of others concerning Napoleon. Napoleon, Cooley argued, did not exist in isolation, as a separate entity. Rather, Napoleon was (and is) a composite of ideas and imaginings which he and his contemporaries recorded, coupled with an amalgam from subsequent persons who have studied, imagined, and reconstructed him.[3] Cooley underscored this in his writing: *self and other do not exist as mutually exclusive social facts*. He wrote that "I" was a term with meaning only insofar as the "I" thought of him- or herself in reference to an "Other." The I required an association with the Other, which in turn made communication both fundamental and critical. In order to communicate, Cooley stated, the I had to enter into and share the minds of an Other or Others. This capacity was called sympathy—the sharing of mental states that can be communicated.

So important was this relationship of the I to the Other that Cooley suggested that the I could not exist without the Other. This symbiosis he called "the looking-glass self."[4] One's conception of the I took into account what that person imagined the Other to imagine concerning the I. In Cooley's words, "A self-idea . . . seems to have three principal elements: the imagination of our appearance [the example under discussion] to the other person; the imagination of his judgment of that appearance, and some sort of self-feeling, such as pride or mortification" (Cooley, 1902, p. 184). The "We" (group self) was born when the I included the Other or Others in an identification that had at its core something held in common. The We was "stimulated by co-operation within and opposition without" (Cooley, 1902, p. 209). This group self, in turn, had its existence only in reference to a larger entity—society—a concept that occupied the central focus of the Progressive intellectual group with which Cooley is identified, because of large-scale disjunctions in the social order during the late 19th and early 20th centuries (Carey, 1989; Peters, 1989).

Perhaps Cooley's greatest contribution to public opinion and social psychological theory was his conception of the primary group (Martindale, 1960). This concept figured prominently in his 1909 book, *Social Organization*. Cooley defined primary groups as those involving intimate, face-to-face association and cooperation. Primary groups fused individuals through mutual identifications, sympathies, and social ideals into common wholes and social unities. Thus, Cooley elaborated on the We described in his previous book. He characterized the We as a means of thwarting the primal and brutal animal passions that sprang from instinct, such as lust and greed. Communication was the primary means by which the primary group formed and endured. Cooley referred broadly to communication as "the mechanism through which human relations exist and develop—all the symbols of the mind, together with the means of conveying them through space and preserving them in time . . . [making possible] fellowship in thought" (1909, pp. 61, 63). Communication is "truly the outside or visible structure of thought, as much cause as effect of the inside or conscious life of men" (1909, p. 64). Cooley included nonverbal forms of communication and forms of travel among his examples of communication.

Of particular notice here is that primary groups and communication, for Cooley, were the basis of public opinion. In keeping with his generous, optimistic view of the world, Cooley further felt that organized public opinion was equivalent to democracy. As such, public opinion was "no mere aggregate of separate individual judgments, but an organization, a cooperative product of communication and reciprocal influence. . . . The minds in a communicating group become a single organic whole" (1909, pp. 121–122). Cooley pointed out that public opinion contains a wide variety of different points of view. He called for serious discussion and consideration of those points of view, leading to mature judgment rather than superficial popular impressions. He believed that group expressions on an issue, duly debated and arrived at, would be superior to the average, separate capacities of individuals within the group. He discussed the notions of effective and specialized public opinion, noting that in an age of complexity and specialization, it should not be unusual to find that particular groups have more opinions, have more intense opinions, and subsequently exert more influence on public actions and decisions regarding certain issues than did the general public. Cooley did feel, however, that actions of effective and specialized groups should be and would be accountable to subsequent review and action by the general public (a corrective response to abuse and misguided action which he called "latent authority"). Cooley appears to have believed that individual involvement in public opinion and in public governance was inevitable: "The fundamental need of men is for self-expression, for making their will felt in whatever they feel to be close to their hearts; and they will use the state in so far and in such a manner as they find it helpful in gratifying this need" (1909, p. 409).

George Herbert Mead, a champion and expander of Cooley's thought (Mead, 1930, 1932, 1934, 1936, 1938), summarized Cooley's doctrine of society in two terse epigrams: it is an affair of consciousness, and consciousness is necessarily social. Mead pointed out that humans were not primarily individuals who "discovered" society, arguing, "The mind itself in the individual arises through communication" (Mead,

1930, p. 699). Moreover, an individual acts, not only in his or her own perspective, but in the perspective of others. Mead established as principle that an individual enters into the perspective of others, so far as he or she is able to take others' attitudes, or occupy their points of view. In fact, one must, according to Mead, be an other before one can be a self. By playing a variety of social roles, one learns to integrate and achieves an understanding of group life, including knowing what to do. Thus, the individual becomes a "generalized other" and is able to address social and community attitudes.

Mead accorded a premier position to verbal and nonverbal communication and communication feedback. Feedback was seen as critical in establishing identical meanings between self and other (true communication). Through communication, establishment of appropriate social behaviors, responses and forms of conduct are possible (1934, 1936, 1938). Repetition of this basic phenomenon permits groups to arise with common perspectives and with important sets of internalized significant symbols. These basic ideas have influenced and even formed the foundation for much of the public opinion theory in symbolic interactionism and the subsequent empirical research that has characterized the latter half of the 20th century (see, e.g., Albig, 1956; Allen & Waks, 1990; Anderson, 1987; Berger & Luckmann, 1966; Denzin, 1981; Faules & Alexander, 1978; Gordon, 1952; Hastorf, Schneider, & Polefka, 1970; Kitt & Gleicher, 1950; Martindale, 1960; Watzlawick, 1976).

CURRENT PERSPECTIVES

The past two decades have seen the development of a number of new approaches to the conceptualization of public opinion. Several of these approaches incorporate a perceptual component—an individual's awareness, assessment or sense of relevant others' opinions. Many of these approaches make use of perceptive "mechanisms" that operate to assess the "climate of opinion," which in turn is seen as a force affecting an individual's own opinions and behavior (e.g., Fields & Schuman, 1976; O'Gorman with Garry, 1976; Davison, 1983; Noelle-Neumann, 1984). The central characteristic of most of this research is the notion that people use reference groups,[5] either explicitly or implicitly, as a guide in constructing their own views on public issues.

Because public opinion theory subsumes a number of academic disciplines, including sociology, social psychology, political science, and communication, scholars in different fields may be investigating similar processes and yet be unaware of the similarities of their own approaches to other contemporary approaches. In addition, because of the amount of work being conducted under disparate labels, few attempts have been made to integrate similar perspectives within one overarching framework of public opinion processes.

Whether the reference group is small, such as a neighborhood or family (e.g., Fields & Schuman, 1976; Glynn, 1983, 1989) or large, such as a city or nation (e.g., Noelle-Neumann, 1977; 1984), the major implication is that individuals care what others think about public issues, form perceptions of what others think, and, to an extent, modify their own opinions and/or behaviors on the basis of those perceptions (Noelle-Neumann, 1977). The roots of this conceptualization of public opinion date to at least the turn of the century, when Cooley (1902) suggested that "imaginary interlocutors," or reference persons, enter the communicator's flow of associations and influence what is communicated. Throughout the century, this perspective has been informed and sharpened by social–psychological work on small group processes, attribution theory, person perception, inter-group perception, assimilation–contrast phenomena, and on research on the "self" versus the "other" (see Price & Oshaygan, chapter 8 in this volume). In addition, these ideas have served as a guide for applied mass communication research concerns such as gatekeeping and agenda setting, whereby a referent audience, existing in the minds of the communicator, has been shown to influence the content and substance of what is being communicated (Bauer, 1958; de Sola Pool & Schulman, 1959; White, 1950).

THE PERCEIVED OBJECT: PUBLIC OPINION

One of the unresolved issues in the area, is, in effect, a challenge to the validity of the entire research agenda: there is no definition of public opinion upon which there has been general agreement. This is an especially acute problem for the field of public opinion because, unlike many research areas in which a relatively small body of academics must decide upon a precise and usable definition, members of the general public are being asked their perception of the key research concept, usually without the benefit of a definition of any sort.

Despite the growing body of research following these public opinion perspectives, relatively few studies have sought to clarify what, exactly, the public is providing its perception about (cf. Glynn & Ostman, 1988). Operationally, public opinion questions typically are asked using scales based on pro/con opinion statements to which respondents indicate direction and intensity of agreement (strongly agree, agree, uncertain, disagree, and strongly disagree). The result is the production of numerous individual responses, each following an idiosyncratic definition, "mapped" by the individual onto a researcher-derived list of opinion statements and questionnaire response pattern. Much analysis is given to investigating these individual perceptions which are aggregated by whole samples and (sometimes) broken out by demographic groupings (e.g., education, socioeconomic status, gender).[6]

The ambiguities in conceptualization and operationalization have led to research findings that report survey respondents' perceptions of "what most people think," "what public opinion is," or "what the average person's opinion is" on particular issues. There is a paucity of information about whether these different approaches are seen as distinct, or even relevant, by the general public (Glynn & Ostman, 1988). Instead, a growing body of recent empirical research on the importance of the public's perceptions of public opinion as a factor influencing public opinion itself has developed from different academic disciplines, each carrying varied hypotheses and theoretical positions.

THE SOCIAL CONTEXT, SOCIAL PERCEPTION, AND PUBLIC OPINION RESEARCH

The recent emphasis on perceptions as a component of public opinion forges distinct links between public opinion theory and several related areas. We are most concerned with research in two of these areas: social perception and the social context. MacLeod (1951) long ago noted that the term social perception itself is commonly used in two senses: the social determination of perception and the perception of the social. Other writers have referred to the former as the social construction of reality, while the latter has been described as the construction of social reality. The social determination of perception is clearly an effect of society on the individual, while perception of the social refers to an individual's perception of society, more of a psychological orientation with emphasis on individual traits impacting upon perception of an otherwise "objective" reality.

The Social Context

Major work on the social determination of perception assumes that human activity seldom occurs in isolation. Individual characteristics, attributes, and personality factors do not entirely determine the extent of human activity. Additionally, the social context is an important factor in assessing the perceptions of others' opinions, such as perceptions of others' voting preferences and opinions on a social issue. People respond to the events, cues, and opportunities that are specific to a given environment. External social factors as well as individually intrinsic factors provide powerful explanations for behavioral outcomes (e.g., Dogan & Rokkan, 1974; Huckfeldt, 1979; Huckfeldt & Sprague, 1986; Jackson, 1969).

While social structure is often defined in terms of environments and contexts, Eulau (1986) noted that context and environment are concepts that should not be mistaken for each other: "*Context* is a compositional phenomenon that *emerges*, and there is nothing deterministic about it as there is likely to be about the environment" (p. 216). An environment is a structured setting that shares one or more common characteristics: spatial boundaries, political functions, political organization, and so on. In contrast, a context is defined in terms of an environment's social composition, and the resulting consequences of social composition for social interaction and the social transmission of information and influence. This distinction is grounded in a tradition whose modern origin traces to Blau's (1957) work on structural effects and on the work of Davis, Spaeth, and Nelson (1961) on compositional effects. Research on the social context tends to follow from either of two different perspectives: (1) the social context as a source of social loyalty and group membership (i.e., identification), and (2) the social context as a structural factor that transforms social interaction (Huckfeldt, 1984; Jackson, 1965). The first perspective focuses on reference group norms: people surrounded by a particular group often come to identify with the group and adopt group norms. The second explanation points toward the pattern and content of social interaction and the manner in which this interaction is structured by the social composition of some population.

These two perspectives might be seen as logical descendants of Kelley's (1952) two functions of reference groups: establishing and transmitting norms, and serving as a basis for social comparison. The first function is integrative: reference groups assimilate and incorporate individuals into the group. The second function may be nearly the opposite, as reference groups produce hostility, intimidation, and exclusion of nonmembers. These explanations have been directed toward explaining political convergence as well as political divergence (Huckfeldt, 1984).

Contextual theories are traditionally grounded in the field of political science and are organized by a variety of social influence arguments that emphasize the consequences of population composition for the behavior of individuals within the population (e.g., Berelson, Lazarsfeld, & McPhee, 1954; Huckfeldt & Sprague, 1986). These explanations typically have been supported by such findings as "blue collar workers are more likely to vote for left-leaning parties if they live among other blue collar workers" or "low status people are more likely to participate in politics if they live among other low status people, and high status people are more likely to participate if they live among other high status people" (Huckfeldt, 1986).

Contextual relationships indicate two main theses. First, the behavior of individuals is affected by various forms of social influence but that the nature and content of that social influence varies systematically across both individuals and contexts. Second, there is a time-oriented process of social influence: an individual is embedded within a particular context, the context structures social interaction patterns, information is conveyed through social interaction, and the individual forms a response based upon this information (Huckfeldt, 1986).

The contextual influence literature thus focuses on actual characteristics of groups and situations. On the other hand, work on perceptions of others' opinions concentrates on group members' perceptions of group and social situations. There is nothing in the contextual influence theory that precludes the use of perceptions as a contextual force. However, from a social context perspective, these perceptions would be included assuming that perceptions are accurate; the "perceptual" influence literature is more concerned with the investigation of the accuracy of those perceptions and in describing the perceptual mechanisms that are operative. Thus, research concerned with perceptions of others' opinions typically does not attempt to integrate contextual influence as an explanatory concept in the process.

Perception of the Social

Much current work in public opinion research fits more clearly under the idea of the "perception of the social": it is concerned with how an individual's perception of various groups in society affect the individual's opinions or attitudes. Recent work in attribution theory, stereotyping, and intergroup perception related to "assimilation" and "contrast" phenomena offers important clues to the operation of perceptual mechanisms (cf. Granberg, 1984; Brent & Granberg, 1982; Rothbart, Dawes, & Park, 1984).

Granberg (1984) and others attempted to build a framework for understanding how people attribute attitudes to group members. They did this by stating theoretical propositions based on balance theory and an extension of the functional theory of attitudes. Briefly, when Granberg and others used balance theory as a theoretical point of departure, they noted, as in Heider's (1958a) P–O–X model, that a person (P) could move toward a generally preferred state of cognitive balance by changing P's attitude toward O (the other person), P's attitude toward X (the object, issue, or question at hand) or P's impression of O's attitude toward X (the attributional element). If there is ambiguity or uncertainty about O's attitude toward X, then an available avenue to achieving cognitive balance would be for P to alter or distort when making the attribution of O's attitude toward X. If the actual difference between P's and O's attitudes becomes underestimated in the attribution process, assimilation has occurred, and if the actual difference is overestimated or exaggerated, contrast has occurred. Thus, it is a straightforward application of Heider's (1958a) theory to expect that people will tend to engage in assimilation when attributing views to a liked other (or group) and contrast when attributing views to a disliked other (or group) (Granberg, 1984; Granberg & Brent, 1974; Sherif & Hovland, 1961; Sherif, Sherif, & Nebergall, 1965).

Granberg (1984) further noted that balance theory implies that people will be motivated to stress, highlight, and exaggerate the similarities between their own attitudes and the predominant view within their ingroup (assimilation) and to exaggerate the differences between their attitudes and the predominant view in an outgroup (contrast), taking into account both membership and reference group ties (whether positive or negative, etc.). The processes themselves are unobservable; the evidence of assuming that assimilation has occurred is the resultant underestimation of differences; if overestimation occurs, the result is taken as evidence for the occurrence of contrast effects (Granberg, 1984). However, there are situations where literal interpretation of balance theory may be inappropriate, for example, when one perceives that members of an outgroup share one's preference not to associate (e.g., segregation).

People may, in certain circumstances, attribute views to an outgroup that are similar to their own attitudes (Glynn & Ostman, 1988). This may be especially true in relation to the matter of how closely and under what circumstances members of two groups ought to associate. Thus, the functional view may lead to the prediction that for some issues, people making attributions will tend to assimilate in their estimates of the views of members of both the ingroup and (perhaps to a lesser extent) the outgroup.

The functional theory of attitudes is also relevant to the study of research concerned with the perception of others' opinions in the sense that it holds that people develop, retain, and alter attitudes for value-expressive, ego-defensive knowledge and social adjustment purposes. To change a person's attitude, it is important to know the function of the attitude for that person (Katz, 1960). It is only a small step to suppose that the impression people form of where others stand on a given issue can also serve a social adjustment or instrumental function. For example, it was often observed on a casual basis that many southern whites in the United States in the 1950s claimed that the blacks in their area liked things the way they were (cf. Granberg, 1984).

These socioperceptual concepts (i.e., assimilation and contrast) have implications for developing public opinion theory. Because much of the recent work in public opinion relies upon such perceptual mechanisms in assessing public opinion of opposing factions (cf. Noelle-Neumann, 1977; Fields & Schuman, 1976; O'Gorman with Garry, 1976; Davison, 1983), the assimilation–contrast phenomena and resultant exaggerated differences appear to be directly applicable to public opinion research. An integration of these perspectives might aid in developing an understanding of the behavior of individuals' perceptions in the face of a changing "climate of opinion."

The Social Context and Perception of the Social: The Social Construction of Reality

The social psychology of everyday life is a rich tapestry of interwoven roles, groupings, and social norms to which the individual continually adapts, obtains information, and provides information for others. The city, state, workplace, school, church, family, and neighborhood each have a particular norm of information flow (type of information, expert sources, etc.), and a particular behavioral system with a given set of values, procedures, and attitudes that may be adopted by the individual member. Within a specific workplace, for example, communication might typically be organized within a hierarchical (top down) fashion, while the geographical organization of a neighborhood might result in a very different communication network structure, in which physical proximity might most affect frequency of interaction.

The second aspect of the social context also is illustrated through behavior within a group in that each group has a particular interaction pattern that is constrained by the type of group, its purpose, and its members. Reference groups may therefore be important in terms of direct information transfer (what enters the group and is transmitted to the individual), and in terms of the norms, attitudes, and values that are held or perceived to be held by other group members. In other words, in some instances, what is not said may be just as important (or even more important) than what is said.

It is not surprising that a myriad of ideas, concepts, perspectives, and hypotheses have developed in connection with individuals and the perception of "self" and of the "other." In social psychology, self-perception and person perception literatures have developed using different methods and different conceptualizations. Most research in social psychology comparing self and other focuses on actor–observer attributional differences or on the mnemonic properties of self- and other representations (Kihlstrom, et al., 1988; Prentice, 1990; Watson, 1982). Considerably less attention has been given to developing a theoretical integration by providing an explanation of self–other differences (Prentice, 1989).

This paucity of social–psychological research integrating self- and other perception stands as a direct contrast to most current public opinion research, which focuses directly on the relationship between own opinion and perceptions of generalized others' opinion to develop public opinion.

Perceptions of Self, Others, and Public Opinion

Given the nature of public opinion theory involving self-perception and other perception as two components of public opinion, it is important to consider research in psychology and social psychology that generally treats these perceptions as two different phenomena. When comparisons of self- and other perceptions have been made, they have tended to be based on actor–observer relationships (e.g., Watson, 1982). Some comparisons indicate that self-perception seems to be formed by direct knowledge of internal states (emotions, cognitions, and memory) while perception of others appears more restricted in that it appears to be based on observable, external features. Several studies have confirmed this general tendency and found differences in the extent to which self- and other perception rely on privileged information about attitudes, thoughts, and feelings. McGuire and McGuire referred to self-perceptions as being formed by covert reactions such as thoughts and feelings, while other perceptions are formed by overt actions, especially social interactions. This is similar to research by Jones and Nisbett (1971), which suggested that people locate causes of their own behavior in the external situation but use personality as an explanation for others' behavior.

Other researchers have described the content of self- and other representations to investigate whether similar criteria are used for both representations. In general, this research suggests that the degree of familiarity with the "other" is important in determining what dimensions and characteristics to use to evaluate information about the other. After a certain degree of familiarity, however, the arrangement of information and dimensions of information about an individual is identical to the arrangement and dimension used to classify information about the self (Prentice, 1989).

For example, Miller and McFarland (1987) found that people believe that they possess more of the traits that produce social inhibition (e.g., bashfulness, hesitancy, self-consciousness) than does the generalized other (Miller & McFarland, 1987). In general, this literature suggests that individuals see themselves as a bit more complex than are generalized others. For example, individuals tend to view traits as more descriptive of others than of themselves (Goldberg, 1978), except that they also see themselves as more extreme on traits than are average others. Thus, an individual can see him- or herself as varying from situation to situation because of the complexity of his or her makeup, but will stereotype the behavior of others based on what are perceived to be particular traits that the individual possesses.

SIX PERSPECTIVES ON PERCEPTION AND PUBLIC OPINION

In public opinion research the investigation of perceptual mechanisms has been subsumed under a number of labels, including (1) pluralistic ignorance hypothesis (cf. Fields & Schuman, 1976; O'Gorman with Garry, 1976); (2) "false consensus" (also known as "egocentric bias" and, in earlier works as "ethnocentrism") (cf. Sumner, 1906; Ross, 1977; Ross, Greene, & House, 1977); (3) "looking glass perception" (Fields & Schuman, 1976); (4) the "spiral of silence" theory (cf. Noelle-Neumann, 1984); (5) the impersonal impact hypothesis (also labeled "unrealistic optimism" and "personal optimism and societal pessimism") (cf. Cook, 1980; Tyler & Cook, 1984; Weinstein, 1982; Culbertson & Stempel, 1985); and (6) the third person effect hypothesis (cf. Davison, 1983).

The six public opinion perspectives and frameworks all include perception of others' opinion in one form or another. What differs between them is how various components of the public opinion process are arranged and which particular components are important in the process. They might be subdivided into two distinct categories: those that see public opinion as a process and provide information and conjecture about how that process works; and those that are most interested in particular products or the end results of specific aspects of public opinion.

For the present chapter, we use "product" as to refer to the end result or descriptive label applied to certain perceptual conditions, with little or no explanation as to how that condition occurred. By "process," we mean to a more elaborate description of a causal system of relationships that describes not only the end result, but how that result occurred. We next describe the major research under each of the six perspectives dealing with self and other.

Pluralistic Ignorance

"Pluralistic ignorance" is one of the more researched concepts in the perceptual influence literature (e.g., Allport, 1924; Schanck, 1932; Newcomb, 1953; Fields & Schuman, 1976; O'Gorman with Garry, 1976; Miller & McFarland, 1987; Taylor, 1982). The term refers to a situation in which the minority position on issues is incorrectly perceived to be the majority position and vice versa. Miller and McFarland (1987) define pluralistic ignorance as what occurs when individuals infer that identical actions of the self and others reflect different internal states. Schanck (1932) originally labeled this phenomenon "misperceived consensus" or "misperceived sharing." The two "classic" studies of pluralistic ignorance, Allport (1924) and Latane and Darley (1970), were both prompted by the situation of a majority of group members' public acceptance and private rejection of a norm.

The literature since Allport (1924) has defined pluralistic ignorance within a number of different approaches. A range of factors, such as fear of embarrassment, social desirability, social inhibition, and so on are said to affect the amount of discrepancy between one's own (cognitive) opinion and one's expressed opinion (or behavior). The pluralistic ignorance hypothesis in relation to public opinion is most concerned with perceptual accuracy, and usually analyzes some aspects of the role of social perception in public opinion. As such, it is a special case of inaccurate perceptions of majority opinion. Pluralistic ignorance may be seen as occurring when individuals either overestimate or underestimate the proportion of others who think, feel, or act as they themselves do (Taylor, 1982). As such, pluralistic ignorance research usually involves analyzing the pattern of people's perceptions of the distribution of opinion.

Pluralistic ignorance is a product, not a process, occurring when there is an issue with divisiveness. The major assumption is that people have a quasi-statistical sense or perception of others' opinions. According to the pluralistic ignorance hypothesis, these conditions result in inaccuracy in perception, or "pluralistic ignorance." These conditions obviously do not explain the process underlying this condition (e.g., how or why perceptions are inaccurate). Pluralistic ignorance merely describes the coincidence of an issue with inaccurate perceptions. Miller and McFarland (1987), investigating why pluralistic ignorance occurs, suggested that fear of embarrassment is one of the key motivating factors behind pluralistic ignorance. They suggested that individuals are inhibited from expressing their true feelings on issues, and that the result is often a case of pluralistic ignorance.

False Consensus

"False consensus" refers to the tendency for individuals "to see their own behavioral choices and judgments as relatively common and appropriate to existing circumstances, while viewing alternative responses as uncommon, deviant and inappropriate" (Ross, Greene, & House, 1977). Operationally, false consensus occurs when a person engaging in a given behavior estimates that same behavior to be shared by a larger proportion of some reference group than is estimated for that reference group by a person engaging in an alternative behavior (Mullen et al., 1985).

Although the parameters of this phenomenon are not fully understood (Mullen et al., 1985), Ross described two possible explanations for false consensus. On the one hand, false consensus could represent a nonmotivational and unintentional perceptual distortion that results from a selective exposure to and recall of other people who are in fact in agreement with oneself. On the other hand, false consensus could represent a motivated and intentional strategy to appear normal, appropriate, and rational. To add further to the complexity, Dawes (1989) suggested that the egocentric bias that is seen as the heart of false consensus effects may also lead to a failure of consensus rather than a false consensus.

Sherman, Presson, and Chassin (1984) suggested three types of explanations for false consensus effects: self-enhancement, motivation to view the other as oneself, and need for social support and validation. Their results indicated a greater likelihood of false consensus when judges were given success feedback (self-enhancement motivations) about their task performance. False consensus is also a product, rather than a process. The conditions for the product are the same as those for pluralistic ignorance, including (1) an issue or behavior that is divisive and (2) the quasi-statistical sense of others' opinions. When these two conditions result in a bias in perception toward exaggerated agreement with oneself there will be "false consensus." There is no way to determine beforehand when pluralistic ignorance will occur or when false consensus will occur.

Looking Glass Perception

A major phenomenon said to structure perceptions of the opinions of others on social issues has been termed the "looking glass perception" (Fields & Schuman, 1976), which hypothesizes that people see significant others as holding the same opinions on issues as they themselves do. The looking glass perception is assumed to operate quite apart from the actual distribution of opinion. Although extensive research has not been conducted on the phenomenon, current findings indicate that in the absence of strong counter forces, a large proportion of people feel that most other people have opinions similar to their own on public issues. An exception was noted by Fields and Schuman (1976), who found a pattern of response that they describe as "conservative bias," where respondents assume that others hold more conservative opinions than their own. Glynn (1989), also found that in some situations there also is evidence of a "liberal bias" where respondents see others as having more liberal opinions than their own. Conservative and liberal biases are thus particular patterns occurring within the data, rather than explanatory concepts. They also could be described as false consensus or pluralistic ignorance, depending upon which phenomenon is being researched.

Looking glass perception typically occurs when (1) there is an issue or behavior that may or may not be divisive and (2) there is a "blockage" of the quasi-statistical sense, resulting in a definition of perceptions of others as "agreement with oneself." Contrary to how it may be referred to in the literature, it appears that the looking glass perception is a product. There are no conditions detailed for when this phenomenon will or will not occur or when it will affect some people and not others. The end product is looking glass perception.

The Spiral of Silence

It is in the context of high public uncertainty combined with an increase in the flow of communication that Noelle-Neumann suggested that the "spiral of silence" (1977, 1984) becomes operative. The spiral of silence theory states that one's perception of the distribution of public opinion motivates one's willingness to express political opinions. This self-expressive act then changes the "global environment of opinion," altering the perceptions of other persons, and ultimately affects the willingness of individuals to express their own opinions (Taylor, 1982). Individuals who notice that their own personal opinions are shared throughout a group will voice these opinions self-confidently in public; those who notice that their opinions are "losing ground" will be inclined to adopt a more reserved attitude and remain silent. The basic premise is that through social interaction, people influence each other's willingness to express opinions. That is, to the individual "not isolating himself is more important than his own judgment" (Noelle-Neumann, 1977).

The major components of the spiral of silence include (1) an issue of public interest; (2) divisiveness on the issue; (3) a quasi-statistical sense that helps an individual perceive the climate of opinion as well as estimate the majority and minority opinion; (4) "fear of isolation" from social interaction; (5) an individual's belief that a minority (or "different") opinion isolates oneself from others, and (6) a "hardcore" group of people whose opinions are unaffected by others' opinions.

The spiral of silence theory evolved as a result of serendipitous research findings from the 1965 West German elections. In Noelle-Neumann's own words, the research "had measured a lot more than we understood" (1984, p. 3). While the two major parties had been locked in a dead heat from December until September, a series of questions ascertaining the public's perception of the election winner was showing a steady, independent movement. During the final days before the election, 3 to 4% of the voters shifted in the direction of the public's perception of the winner.

Noelle-Neumann observed a similar situation in the 1972 election, and began developing the spiral of silence as a theory of public opinion. Since that time, a plethora of research activity has been conducted on the spiral of silence, including work by Glynn (1983, 1989), Glynn and McLeod (1985), Katz (1983), LaSorsa (1991), Price and Allen (1990), Salmon and Kline (1985), Taylor (1982), and Kennamer (1990). This work has sought to clarify and elaborate on Noelle-Neumann's theory, and has centered most specifically on the willingness of an individual to speak out in public. Taylor (1982) found strong support for the idea that those in the majority would be more willing to speak their opinions, although he suggests that fear of isolation may not be the causal factor affecting the willingness to speak out.

Dating back to research by Asch (1952), Sherif (1936) and Milgram (1961), empirical evidence has supported the idea that people may be so affected by their perception of what others think that they feel pressured to conceal their own opinion (Lasorsa, 1991). Lasorsa's research on political outspokenness suggests that the willingness to speak out is associated with political interest and self-efficacy. Taylor (1982) found that expected benefits of opinion expression are the motivating factors, rather than fear of isolation. Similarly, Salmon and Neuwirth (1990) investigated the perceptions of opinion "climates" and the willingness to discuss the issue of abortion. They found that knowledge of the issue and personal concern about the issue played important roles in whether or not individuals were willing to speak out in public. They found only mixed supportive evidence that "fear of isolation" affected willingness to speak out.

The basic ideas behind the spiral of silence are not unique. Kerr, MacCoun, Hansen, and Hymes (1987) investigated what they described as the "momentum effect," the idea that if some members of a group move toward a particular opinion, others will follow. Other researchers have described a similar "gain–loss effect" (Aronson & Linder, 1965) and "bandwagon effect" (Myers & Lamm, 1976). As Kerr et al. (1987) operationalized it, the momentum effect was equivalent to a test of the spiral of silence. They described their results as supporting the idea of an antimomentum effect: subjects were much more sensitive to current levels of support than to changes in the level of support. Kerr (1981), however, found support for a momentum effect in a mock jury. Kerr et al. (1987) suggested that this shift in position among the mock jury members may be spurious and a function of other simultaneous influences on all the members, rather than a true momentum effect.

Of the six "perceptual mechanisms" of import in this chapter, Noelle-Neumann's comes closest to being an actual "theory." The "spiral of silence" can be considered a process because it occurs over time and consists of a series of actions, often resulting in a behavioral outcome (such as a vote). However, as with the other perceptual mechanisms, Noelle-Neuman's model is missing any specified role for communities, organizations, and reference groups in mediating the effects of the larger society. Although Noelle-Neuman did differentiate society to some extent (e.g., by certain demographic groups), she did not make clear whether these groups are inherently more vulnerable (i.e., more anxious about isolation) to the spiral of silence or simply less exposed to the media (cf. Glynn & McLeod, 1984 for a discussion). In addition, even though she relies upon the experimental work of Asch (1951) when discussing the fear of isolation, Noelle-Neuman (1977) did not implement a consistent theoretical thread in her research.

Impersonal Impact/Unrealistic Optimism

Several recent lines of research regarded the perceptual perspective as an independent variable related to vulnerability, or risk perceptions. Accordingly, individuals see themselves as being somehow different from others in terms of the probability of good or bad things happening to them. Research findings suggested that people believe that negative events are less likely to happen to them than to others in society, while positive events are more likely to happen to themselves than to others, across a wide range of topic areas (Culbertson & Stempel, 1985). Tyler and Cook (1984) noted that the hypothesis has a major assumption: that people can and do distinguish between two possible levels of judgment: societal and personal. Individuals' beliefs about the larger community and conditions of community residents in relation to some social phenomenon form a "societal level" of judgment and decisions. Individuals' beliefs about their own condition and risks form a second, "personal" level.

Tyler and Cook (1984) noted that the hypothesis has a second component: that mass mediated messages affect people's perceptions of the prevalence of certain problems or risks within a society, but do not affect their perceptions of personal risks. They later revised this latter component of the impersonal impact hypothesis to develop the "differential impact" hypothesis: for some conditions, issues, and types of people, media impact will be perceived to operate differentially on personal and societal level judgments, while under other conditions media effects will occur on both or neither level of judgment. Major components of the impersonal impact hypothesis include (1) an issue with variance in opinions; (2) a "societal level" judgment and a "personal level" judgment (beliefs about the larger "community" and occurrence of social phenomenon in the community versus belief about occurrence of that same social phenomenon in one's own life); (3) an assumption that these personal and societal level judgments are separate; (4) an understanding that informal social communications are most effective for influencing personal concerns; (5) the assumption that media impact occurs primarily on societal level judgments; and (6) a perception of the effect of media presentations on judgments of oneself and judgments about others. Impersonal impact is clearly a process-oriented phenomenon that describes the various conditions that lead some audience members to be affected in one way by the media, others in another, and still others not at all. Research evidence on the topic has not yet been conclusive, as different mechanisms have been posited to describe inconsistent results. Thus, the literature has seen development of hypotheses related to impersonal impact, unrealistic optimism, unrealistic pessimism, and societal pessimism (Culbertson & Stempel, 1985; Weinstein, 1980).

Third-Person Effect

Working independently from and earlier than Tyler and Cook (1984), Davison (1983) suggested that in general, individuals tend to think that the media will have greater impact on others than on themselves, a phenomenon he labeled the "third-person effect." Culbertson and Stempel (1985) independently suggested several ideas consonant with the idea of greater perceived media impact on others than on oneself. Davison (1983) suggested that an individual's belief that the media will have great impact on others but not on oneself often becomes the basis for action by an individual or organization. Thus, the "third person" may be seen as either the "other" person, who is affected by mass mediated messages, or the original person, who, not affected by the primary media message, but perceiving the probability of the media's effect on others, reacts to the impact that he or she thinks the message will have on others.

This approach contrasts with Tyler and Cook's (1984) "impersonal impact" hypothesis in that Tyler and Cook suggested that individuals are affected by mediated messages primarily in their judgments of societal prevalence of a given problem or risk within society. The third-person effect requires that individuals analyze media presentations, resulting in a perception that others will be more influenced by these presentations than themselves. Characteristics of the third-person effect notion include (1) an issue that has variance in opinion (e.g., degrees of involvement, agreement, etc.); (2) media presentation of the issue; (3) a belief that oneself is less susceptible to media presentations than are others; (4) a description of individuals' perceptions of the impact of media portrayal of an issue on themselves versus others (as opposed to impersonal impact, where individuals project the occurrence of phenomena portrayed in the media onto societal-level judgments about the occurrence of these events in society); and (5) a similarity with impersonal impact in that individuals must separate themselves from others. Third-person effect is a process: it consists of a series of conditions resulting in some action based on perceptions of the effect of media presentations.

A PROBLEM OF ARTICULATION

Taken together, these studies and this perspective suggest a vibrant, growing research area that scientists are convinced is productive. The difficulty for public opinion theory is to untangle the conceptualizations, hypotheses, and measurement issues to get at the major components of all of these perspectives and find the consistent threads and consistent findings. What is sorely needed is a program of research involving scientists from a number of fields, working toward formulation of a systematic perspective on public opinion that can eliminate "pseudoconcepts" from the literature and articulate research attention on those variables that can be shown to be important across different issue content.

These threads of commonality suggest that there might be considerable research integrating these perspectives; so far very little work has examined any combination of these perspectives (cf. Glynn & McDonald, 1989; Rucinski & Salmon, 1990). The common terms alone would suggest comparisons between the perspectives. In the descriptions above we demonstrated that several of the public opinion approaches had common ideas and terms. As a first step toward integration, we advance Figure 10.1, which provides a kind of "map" related to the results of public opinion research, and how those results might be interpreted across several perspectives.

For simplicity in describing the model, we consider an issue in which individuals are either in favor of or opposed to a specific proposal or plan of action. Through the figure, certain relationships between perspectives that have been implied or briefly described become more explicit and predictions may be made or results attributed to certain patterns of individual responses. Several hypotheses can be developed to aid in generating more explicit help.

When the model of Figure 10.1 is examined in terms of the various perspectives (e.g., the looking glass perception, pluralistic ignorance, or false consensus), certain cells of the cross-tabulation become quite specifically tied to particular public opinion product perspectives, sometimes suggesting the need for greater specificity before any data can be evaluated. In fact, several cells are outcomes that may be attributed to more than one process, making evidence in that cell ambiguous at best. Specifically, respondents in a state of pluralistic ignorance can be seen in cells III and VI, where the individuals believe that the majority hold the opinion opposite their own, yet the actual majority holds the same opinion as the individual. When examined in relation to the marginal distributions, this cell could provide information about the extent of

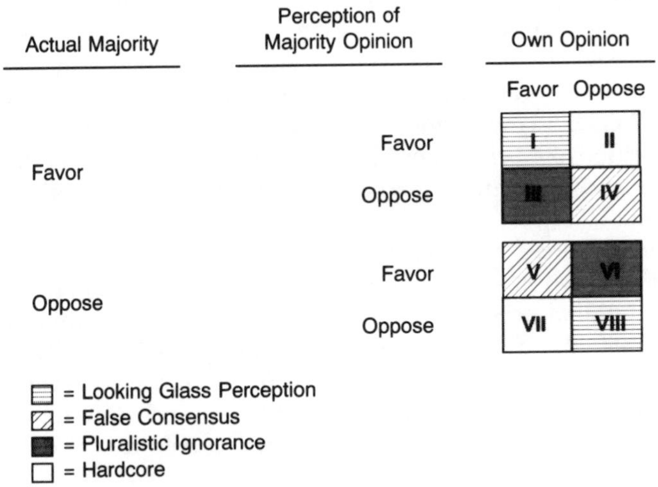

FIGURE 10.1. The distribution of public opinion.

pluralistic ignorance in the sample (e.g., on certain issues are we more likely to find a state of pluralistic ignorance among the majority, or are the majority accurate in their perceptions?).

The state of false consensus can be identified where the individual believes the majority to hold the same opinion as the individual, but the majority actually hold the opinion opposite that of the individual (cells IV and V). These cells might be usefully compared to cells I and VIII, where there is evidence of the looking glass perception: there is no method of distinguishing between respondents of cells IV and V who are there because of the looking glass perception and those who are there because of false consensus. A comparison might be helpful in illuminating various conditions that operate to distinguish the reason for particular patterns of response. Without those reasons, it is fruitless to suggest that one of the processes is operating, for it might just as easily be the other.

Cells II, III, V, and VIII can be used to identify the "hardcore" group according to the spiral of silence—those individuals who either correctly or incorrectly perceive the majority as being opposed to their own views. The spiral of silence suggests that "hardcoreness" is more akin to a trait than to a situation, so there has been no distinction in whether or not perceptions of majority opinion are correct. Alternatively, only those hardcore individuals who are correct in their perceptions are of interest at a given time, because they cause the opinion spiral to reverse. Unfortunately, these two cells are also indistinguishable by theory. What makes them "hardcore" is that they speak their opinions in spite of the perception that they are in the minority. The difficulty in not distinguishing these groups is that the individuals falling into cell IV are not only hardcore, but, as described above, are also pluralistically ignorant. Again, neither perspective has developed far enough to enable a distinction between the two. Conceptually, however, the two reasons for being in cell IV should describe very different kinds of people: the perceptually inaccurate or the unchanging in the face of opposition.

Similarly, there is a problem with distinguishing those in cells I, II, VII, and VIII who are there because they have a correct perception of majority opinion versus those who are there for any other reason. Theoretically, there should be a distinction between holding a looking glass perception, being "hardcore," and being correct in one's assessment of majority opinion. Unfortunately, theoretical development in this area has not given us enough information to distinguish these differences.

Although the figure represents only a first attempt to integrate these diverse perspectives, it does suggest some weaknesses and concerns that have not been addressed in research. It is clear that there is a common ground among researchers in a diverse field. It is equally clear that common perspectives and ideas are moving in a similar direction. That direction is a concern with the difference that public opinion makes in people's lives. Still not clear, however, is what constitutes public opinion. As researchers, we cannot unravel the processes until we have decided what we are studying. That is the task of future research.

NOTES

1. Bevis, in a 1921 paper read before the Washington, D.C. Society for Nervous and Mental Diseases and published that same year in the *American Journal of Psychiatry*, discussed psychological traits of "the Southern Negro" in terms of supposed biological unpreparedness to live in American society. Aside from the assumption that medical doctors like himself were able to rank entire races on intelligence via "blood," the article is notable as a classic piece of unthinking, unabashed racism. The biological examination of genomes, which involves inquiry into human DNA, is more feverish today than at any point in human history. In the U.S., for instance, an estimated $3 billion in federal funds will be spent in the next 15 years on basic research, touted at this time as a means of locating and possibly preventing disease. Concerning a picture of a baby in its March 20th, 1989 cover story, however, *Time* opined, "What will this baby be? Football star? Scholar? Rock guitarist? Although the child's future will be heavily influenced by environment, much of his or her fate may already have been predetermined. Encoded in the genome, the DNA in the infant's 46 chromosomes, are instructions that affect not only physical attributes, but also intelligence, susceptibility to disease, life-span and even some aspects of behavior" (Jaroff, 1989, p. 63).

2. For details on how mass communication figured into Cooley's thought and that of other "Progressives" of the times, see Carey (1989) and Peters (1989).

3. In reference to this social sifting, it is interesting to note that Napoleon himself was reputed to be a great student of public opinion: "Emil Ludwig represents Napoleon as ever on the watch for indications of public opinion; always listening to the voice of the people, a voice which defies calculation. 'Do you know,' he said in those days, 'what amazes me more than all else? The impotence of force to organize anything'" (Bernays, 1928, p. 18).

4. Martindale (1960) argued that Cooley's formulation was not original, but was a neat restatement of James's (1890) description of the "social self."

5. Shibutani (1961) defined "reference group" as "that group, real or imaginary, whose standpoint is being used as the frame of reference by the actor" (p. 257), and "any identifiable group whose supposed perspective is used by the actor as a frame of reference in the organization of his perceptual field" (p. 258). Campbell, Converse, Miller, and Stokes, (1964) extended this notion by noting that a reference group can exert either a positive *or negative* influence

upon the individual's political attitudes and behavior (reprinted in Luttbeg, 1974). For a more recent statement on polarized groups and their effects on individual opinion expression, see Goldner (1991).

6. Goldner (1991) has been critical of public opinion research methods on this point: "the focus on public opinion as a process between the individual and society at large achieved by quizzing individuals and aggregating their responses, has also obscured the role that identity with one group and opposition to another plays in evaluating the effects of expression" (p. 221).

REFERENCES

Albig, W. (1956). *Modern public opinion*. New York: McGraw-Hill.

Allen, R. L., & Waks, L. (1990). The social reality construction of attitudes toward the social roles of women and African Americans. *The Howard Journal of Communications, 2*, 170–191.

Allport, F. H. (1924). *Social Psychology*. Boston: Hougton Mifflin.

Andersen, S. M., & Cole, S. W. (1990). Do I know you? The role of significant others in general social perception. *Journal of Personality and Social Psychology, 59*(3), 384–399.

Anderson, J. A. (1987). *Communication research: Issues and methods*. New York: McGraw-Hill.

Aronson, E., & Linder, D. (1965). Gain and loss of esteem as determinants of interpersonal attractiveness. *Journal of Experimental Psychology*, (1), 156–171.

Asch, S. E. (1952). *Social Psychology*. New York: Prentice-Hall.

Bauer, R. A. (1958). The communicator and his audience. *Journal of Conflict Resolution, 2*, 67–77.

Bauer, R. A. (1964). The obstinate audience: The influence process from the point of view of social communication. *American Psychologist, 19*, 319–328.

Berelson, B. M., Lazarsfeld, P., & McPhee, W. (1954). *Voting: A study of opinion formation in a presidential campaign*. Chicago: University of Chicago Press.

Berger, P. L., & Luckmann, T. (1966). *The social construction of reality: A treatise in the sociology of knowledge*. Garden City, NY: Doubleday.

Bernays, E. L. (1928). *Propaganda*. New York: Liveright Publishing Corp.

Bevis, W. M. (1921). Psychological traits of the Southern Negro with observations as to some of his psychoses. *American Journal of Psychiatry, 1*, 69–78.

Blau, P. M. (1957). Formal organizations: Dimensions of analyses. *American Journal of Sociology, 63*, 58–69.

Brent, E., & Granberg, D. (1982). Subjective agreement with the presidential candidates of 1976 and 1980. *Journal of Personality and Social Psychology, 42*, 393–403.

Campbell, A., Converse, P. E., Miller, W. E., & Stokes, D. E. (1964). The American voter: An abridgement. In N. R. Luttbeg (Ed.), *Public opinion & public policy* (rev. ed., pp. 189–207). Homewood, IL: The Dorsey Press.

Carey, J. W. (1989). Commentary: Communications and the Progressives. *Critical Studies in Mass Communication, 6*, 264–282.

Cohen, J., Mutz, D., Price, V., & Gunther, A. (1988). Perceived impact of defamation: An experiment on third-person effects. *Public Opinion Quarterly, 52*, 161–173.

Collier, G., Minton, H. L., & Reynolds, G. (1991). *Currents of thought in American social psychology*. New York: Oxford University Press.

Cook, F. (1980). The impact of directly and indirectly experienced events. *Journal of Personality and Social Psychology, 39*, 13–28.

Cooley, C. H. (1902). *Human nature and the social order*. New York: Charles Scribner's Sons.

Cooley, C. H. (1909). *Social organization: A study of the larger mind*. New York: Charles Scribner's Sons.

Cronbach, L. J. (1955). Processes affecting scores on 'understanding of others' and 'assumed similarity.' *Psychological Bulletin, 52*, 177–193.

Cronbach, L. J. (1958). Proposals leading to analytic treatment of social perception scores. In R. Tagiuri & L. Petrullo (Eds.), *Person perception and interpersonal behavior* (pp. 353–379). Stanford, CA: Stanford University Press.

Culbertson, H., & Stempel, G., 3rd. (1985). Media malaise: Explaining personal optimism and societal pessimism about health care. *Journal of Communication, 2*, 180–190.

Davis, J. A., Spaeth, J. L., & Nelson, C. (1961). Analyzing effects of group composition. *American Sociological Review, 26*, 215–225.

Davison, W. P. (1983). The third-person effect in communication. *Public Opinion Quarterly, 47*, 1–15.

Dawes, R. M. (1989). Statistical criteria for establishing a truly false consensus effect. *Journal of Experimental Social Psychology, 25*, 1–17.

Denzin, N. K. (1981). The interactionist study of social organization: A note on method. In D. Bertaux (Ed.), *Biography and society: The life history approach in the social sciences* (pp. 149–167). Beverly Hills, CA: Sage Publications.

de Sola Pool, I., & Shulman, I. (1959). Newsmen's fantasies, audiences and newswriting. *Public Opinion Quarterly, 23*, 145–158.

Dewey, J. (1922). *Human nature and conduct*. New York: Henry Holt and Co.

Dogan, M., & Rokkan, S. (Eds.). 1974. *Social ecology*, Cambridge, MA: Harvard University Press.

Doob, L. W. (1935). *Propaganda: Its psychology and technique*. New York: Henry Holt and Co.

Eulau, H. (1986). *Politics, self and society*. Cambridge, MA: Harvard University Press.

Faules, D. F., & Alexander, D. C. (1978). *Communication and social behavior: A symbolic interaction perspective*. Reading, MA.: Addison-Wesley.

Fields, J., & Schuman, H. (1976). Public beliefs about the beliefs of the public. *Public Opinion Quarterly, 40*, 427–448.

Glynn, C. J. (1983). *Perceptions of others' opinions as a component of public opinion and its relationship to communication in the neighborhood: A systems level analysis*. Unpublished Ph.D. dissertation, University of Wisconsin, Madison.

Glynn, C. J. & McLeod, J. M (1984). Public opinion du jour: An examination of the spiral of silence. *Public Opinion Quarterly, 48*(4), 731–740.

Glynn, C. J. & McLeod, J. M. (1985). Implications of the spiral of silence theory for communication and public opinion research. In K. Sanders, L. Kaid, & D. Nimms (Eds.), *Political Communication Yearbook* (pp. 43–68). Carbondale: Southern Illinois University Press.

Glynn, C. J. (1989). Perception of others' opinions as a component of public opinion. *Social Science Research, 18*, 53–69.

Glynn, C. J., & Ostman, R. E. (1988). Public opinion about public opinion. *Journalism Quarterly, 65*(2), 299–306.

Goldberg, L. R. (1978). Differential attribution of trait-descriptive terms to oneself as compared to well-liked, neutral, and disliked others: A psychometric analysis. *Journal of Personality and Social Psychology, 36*, 1012–1028.

Goldner, F. H. (1991). Rhetorical reticence, if you're for it I'm against it, or at least I'll keep my mouth shut: Opinion expression and formation in the context of polarized groups. *International Journal of Public Opinion Research, 3*, 220–237.

Gordon, R. L. (1952). Interaction between attitude and the definition of the situation in the expression of opinion. *American Sociological Review, 17*, 50–58. (Reprinted in D. Katz, D. Cartwright, S. Eldersveld, & A. M. Lee (Eds.), *Public opinion and propaganda: A book of readings*. New York: The Dryden Press, 1954).

Granberg, D. (1984). Attributing attitudes to members of groups. In J. R. Eiser (Ed.), *Attitudinal Judgment* (pp. 85–108). New York: Springer-Verlag.

Granberg, D., & Brent, E. (1974). Dove–Hawk placements in the 1968 election: Application of social judgment and balance theories. *Journal of Personality and Social Psychology, 29*, 627–695.

Granberg, D., & Brent, E. (1980). Perceptions of issue positions of presidential candidates. *American Scientist, 68*, 617–625.

Hastorf, A. H., Schneider, D. J., & Polefka, J. (1970). *Person perception*. Reading, MA.: Addison-Wesley.

Heider, F. (1958a). Consciousness, the perceptual world and communications with others. In R. Tagiuri & L. Petrullo (Eds.), *Person perception and interpersonal behavior* (pp. 27–32). Stanford, CA: Stanford University Press.

Heider, F. (1958b). *The psychology of interpersonal relations*. New York: Wiley.

Huckfeldt, R. R. (1979). Political participation and the neighborhood social context. *American Journal of Political Science, 23*(3), 579–592.

Huckfeldt, R. R. (1980). Variable responses to neighborhood social contexts: Assimilation, conflict and tipping points. *Political Behavior, 2*(3), 231–257.

Huckfeldt, R. R. (1984). Political loyalties and social class ties: The mechanisms of contextual influence. *American Journal of Political Science, 28*, 399–417.

Huckfeldt, R. R. (1986). *Politics in context: Assimilation and conflict in urban neighborhoods*. New York: Agathon Press.

Huckfeldt, R. R., & Sprague, J. (1986). Social order and political chaos: The structural setting of public information. In J. Kuklinski & J. Ferejohn (Eds.), *Information and democracy*. Urbana: University of Illinois Press.

Irion, F. C. (1950). *Public opinion and propaganda*. New York: Thomas Y. Crowell Co.

Jackson, J. (1965). Structural characteristics of norms. In I. D. Steiner & M.

Fishbein (Eds.), *Current studies in social psychology* (pp. 301–309). New York: Holt, Rinehart and Winston.

James, W. (1890). *Principles of psychology*. New York: Henry Holt and Co.

Jaroff, L. (1989, March 20). The gene hunt. *Time*, pp. 62–67.

Jones, E. E., & Nisbett, R. E. (1971). *The actor and the observer: Divergent perceptions of the causes of behavior.* Morriston, NJ: General Learning Press.

Katz, D. (1960). The functional approach to the study of attitudes. *Public Opinion Quarterly, 24*, 113–204.

Katz, E. (1983). Publicity and pluralistic ignorance: Notes on the 'spiral of silence.' In E. Wartella, D. C. Whitney, & S. Windahl (Eds.), *Mass Communication Review Yearbook* (Vol. 4, pp. 89–100). Beverly Hills, CA: Sage.

Kelley, H. H. (1952). Two functions of reference groups. In G. E. Swanson, T. Newcomb, & E. Hartley (Eds.), *Readings in social psychology* (pp. 410–414). New York: Henry Holt and Co.

Kennamer, J. D. (1990). Self-serving biases in perceiving the opinions of others. *Communication Research, 17*(3), 393–404.

Kerr, N. L., MacCoun, R. J., Hansen, C. H., & Hymes, J. A. (1987). Gaining and losing social support: Momentum in decision-making groups. *Journal of Experimental Social Psychology, 23*, 119–145.

Kihlstrom, J. F. (1978). Introduction. *Journal of Personality and Social Psychology, 53*, 989–992.

Kitt, A. S., & Gleicher, D. B. (1950). Determinants of voting behavior: A progress report on the Elmira election study. *Public Opinion Quarterly, 14*, 393–412. (Reprinted in D. Katz, D. Cartwright, S. Eldersveld, & A. M. Lee (Eds.), *Public opinion and propaganda: A book of readings*. New York: The Dryden Press, 1954.)

Lasorsa, D. L. (1991). Political outspokenness: Factors working against the spiral of silence. *Journalism Quarterly, 68*(1/2), 131–139.

Latane, B., & Darley, J. (1970). *The unresponsive bystander: Why doesn't he help*? New York: Appleton-Century-Crofts.

Lemert, J. (1981). *Does mass communication change public opinion after all*? Chicago: Nelson-Hall.

Lewin, K. (1938). The conceptual representation and the measurement of psychological forces. *Contribution to Psychological Theory, 1*(4), 447–458.

Luttbeg, N. R. (Ed.). (1974). *Public opinion and public policy* (rev. ed.) Homewood, IL: The Dorsey Press.

MacLeod, R. D. (1951). The place of phenomenological analysis in social psychological theory. In J. H. Rohrer & M. Sherif (Eds.), *Social psychology at the crossroads* (pp. 215–241). New York: Harper and Row.

Martin, E. D. (1920). *The behavior of crowds*. New York: W. W. Norton.

Martindale, D. (1960). *The nature and types of sociological theory*. Boston: Houghton Mifflin.

McDougall, W. (1917). *An introduction to social psychology*. Boston: John W. Luce.

Mead, G. H. (1930). Cooley's contribution to American social thought. *The American Journal of Sociology, 35*, 693–706.

Mead, G. H. (1932). The objective reality of perspectives. In A. E. Murphy

(Ed.), *Philosophy of the present* (pp. 161–175). LaSalle, IL.: Open Court Publishing Co. (Reprinted in A. Strauss (Ed.), *George Herbert Mead on social psychology: Selected papers*. Chicago: The University of Chicago Press, 1956.)

Mead, G. H. (1934). Mind. Self. Society. In C. W. Morris (Ed.), *Mind, self, and society* (pp. 1–328). Chicago: University of Chicago Press. (Reprinted in A. Strauss (Ed.), *George Herbert Mead on social psychology: Selected papers*. Chicago: The University of Chicago Press, 1956.)

Mead, G. H. (1936). The problem of society—how we become selves. In M. M. Moore (Ed.), *Movement of thought in the nineteenth century* (pp. 360–385). Chicago: University of Chicago Press. (Reprinted in A. Strauss (Ed.), *George Herbert Mead on social psychology: Selected papers*. Chicago: The University of Chicago Press, 1956.)

Mead, G. H. (1938). The process of mind in nature. In C. W. Morris (Ed.), *The philosophy of the act* (pp. 357–420). Chicago: The University of Chicago Press. (Reprinted in A. Strauss (Ed.), *George Herbert Mead on social psychology: Selected papers*. Chicago: The University of Chicago Press, 1956.)

Milgram, S. (1961). Nationality and conformity. *Scientific American, 205*(6), 45–51.

Miller, D. T., & McFarland, C. (1987). Pluralistic ignorance: When similarity is interpreted as dissimilarity. *Journal of Personality and Social Psychology, 53*(2), 298–305.

Mullen, B., Atkins, J., Champion, D., Edwards, C., Hardy, D., Story, J., & Vanderklok, M. (1985). The false consensus effect: A meta-analysis of 115 hypothesis tests. *Journal of Experimental Social Psychology, 21*, 262–283.

Myers, D. G., & Lamm, H. (1976). The group polarization phenomenon. *Psychological Bulletin, 83*, 602–627.

Noelle-Neumann, E. (1977). Turbulences in the climate of opinion: Methodological applications of the spiral of silence theory. *Public Opinion Quarterly, 40*, 143–158.

Noelle-Neumann, E. (1984). *The spiral of silence: Public opinion—Our social skin*. Chicago: University of Chicago Press.

O'Gorman, H., & Garry, S. (1976). Pluralistic ignorance—A replication and extension. *Public Opinion Quarterly, 40*, 449–458.

Peters, J. D. (1989). Satan and savior: Mass communication in progressive thought. *Critical Studies in Mass Communication, 6*, 247–263.

Prentice, D. (1989). Familiarity and differences in self- and other-representations. *Journal of Personality and Social Psychology, 59*, 369–383.

Price, V., & Allen, S. (1990). Opinion spirals, silent and otherwise. *Communication Research, 17*(3), 369–391.

Ratner, J. (1939). *Intelligence in the modern world: John Dewey's philosophy*. New York: The Modern Library.

Ross, L. (1977). The intuitive psychologist and his shortcomings: Distortions in the attribution process. In L. Berkowitz (Ed.), *Advances in experimental social psychology* (Vol. 5, pp. 150–195). New York: Academic Press.

Ross, L., Greene, D., & House, P. (1977). The 'false consensus effect': An egocentric bias in social perception and attribution process. *Journal of Experimental Social Psychology, 13*, 279–301.

Rothbart, M., Dawes, R., & Park, B. (1984). Stereotyping and sampling biases in intergroup perception. In J. R. Eiser (Ed.), *Attitudinal judgment* (pp. 109–134). New York: Springer-Verlag.

Rucinski, D., & Salmon, C. T. (1990). The 'other' as the vulnerable voter: A study of the third-person effect in the 1988 U.S. presidential campaign. *International Journal of Public Opinion Research, 2*(4), 345–368.

Salmon, C. T., & Kline, F. G. (1985). The spiral of silence ten years later. In D. D. Nimmo & K. R. Sanders (Eds.), *Political communication yearbook* (pp. 3–30). Carbondale: Southern Illinois University Press

Salmon, C. T., & Neuwirth, K. (1990). Perception of opinion 'climates' and willingness to discuss the issue of abortion. *Journalism Quarterly, 67*(3), 567–577.

Schanck, R. (1932). A study of a community and its groups and institutions conceived of as behaviors of individuals. *Psychological Monographs, 43*(2) (Whole No. 195).

Sherif, M. (1936). *The psychology of social norms*. New York: Harper.

Sherif, M., & Hovland, C. (1961). *Social judgment: Assimilation and contrast effects in communication and attitude change*. New Haven: Yale University Press.

Sherif, C., Sherif, M., & Nebergall, R. (1965). *Attitude and attitude change: The social judgment involvement approach*. Philadelphia: Saunders.

Sherman, S. J., Presson, C. C., & Chassin, L. (1984). Mechanisms underlying the false consensus effect: The special role of threats to the self. *Personality and Social Psychology Bulletin, 10*(1), 127–138.

Shibutani, T. (1961). *Society and personality: An interactionist approach to social psychology*. Englewood Cliffs, NJ: Prentice-Hall.

Sumner, W. G. (1906). *Folkways*. Boston: Ginna and Co.

Taylor, D. G. (1982). Pluralistic ignorance and the spiral of silence: A formal analysis. *Public Opinion Quarterly, 46*, 311–335.

Tyler, T., & Cook, F. L. (1984). The mass media and judgments of risk: Distinguishing impact on personal and societal level judgments. *Journal of Personality and Social Psychology, 47*, 693–708.

Watzlawick, P. (1976). *How real is real? Confusion, disinformation, communication*. New York: Random House.

Weinstein, N. D. (1982). Unrealistic optimism about future life events. *Journal of Personality and Social Psychology, 39*, 806–820.

White, D. M. (1950). The gatekeeper: A case study in the selection of news. *Journalism Quarterly, 27*, 383–390.

IV

THE MEDIA OF COMMUNICATION AND THE OPINIONS OF PUBLICS

11

Issues in the News and the Public Agenda: The Agenda-Setting Tradition

Maxwell McCombs
Lucig Danielian
Wayne Wanta

A considerable gap exists between what happens in the world each year and the typical person's awareness of those things. The ratio of events to actual knowledge is a tremendously large one. In part, this situation exists because of inevitable barriers in the mass communication process. Plato's allegory of the cave is very much a description of contemporary knowledge and opinions about public affairs. Even simple textbook information, such as the name of one's congressman or the three branches of the federal government, is beyond the ken of a significant number of adults. While interest and motivation are major filters in the diffusion of public affairs knowledge, there also are significant limitations on the information sources used by most citizens. The typical daily newspaper, for example, has room for less than one fifth of the news that is available to it each day from its own news staff, wire and syndicated services, and press releases.

The news media shape this overwhelming flow of information to fit their limited capacity by applying professional news values. These are criteria for deciding what will be used and what will be discarded. This daily sifting and evaluation by the news media of the information from the world out there is a valuable service for each of us individually and, collectively, for our community and nation. While this general role of journalism—what Harold Lasswell (1948) called the surveillance function—long has been recognized, there is a more precise role of the news media that did not receive close attention until the last two decades. This is the agenda-setting role of journalism—the ability of newspapers, television, and news magazines to focus public attention on a few public issues to the virtual exclusion of all others (McCombs & Shaw, 1972). In other words, the news media can set the focus of the public agenda.

Walter Lippmann (1922) defined the public agenda as that array of issues concerning which the well-being of numerous individuals is dependent upon mutual action, cooperation, or, at least, tacit consent. He also noted that this array of issues is largely beyond direct experience:

> For the real environment is altogether too big, too complex, and too fleeting for direct acquaintance. We are not equipped to deal with so much subtlety, so much variety, so many permutations and combinations. And although we have to act in that environment, we have to reconstruct it on a simpler model before we can manage it. To traverse the world, men must have maps of the world. (p. 16)

It is the news media, noted Lippmann, that provide these maps of the world. Through their selection and display of the daily news, journalists provide major cues about what are the important topics of the day. Over time, many of the issues receiving major emphasis in the news become the major issues on the public agenda. Although this agenda-setting role of the news media is a secondary and unintentional by-product of the necessity to select a few issues for attention, it is one of the most significant effects of mass communication. Of course, newspaper editorial pages make an explicit and intentional effort to persuade their readers, but this involves only a tiny minority of the journalists producing the daily news package. The vast majority of journalists eschew any effort at direct persuasion, which makes it all the more important to explicate the agenda-setting role of the news.

This assertion that news coverage influences the salience of issues on the public agenda—or, put more directly in causal terms, determines the salience of issues on the public agenda—can be examined and tested in a variety of ways (McCombs, 1981; Rogers & Dearing, 1988). If the metaphor of an agenda is taken literally, the array of issues on the news agenda is compared with the array of issues on the public agenda. The original empirical test of agenda setting by Maxwell McCombs and Donald Shaw (1972) did exactly that. They matched the rank order of issues according to their coverage by newspapers, television networks and news magazines with the rank order of those same issues among Chapel Hill, North Carolina voters during the 1968 presidential election. These voters' perceptions of the most important issues facing the country correlated very highly with the pattern of news coverage. McCombs and Shaw successfully circumvented an argument ongoing at that time about the minimal effects of the mass media on opinions and attitudes by focusing their theory on the initial steps leading up to opinion change. Public awareness is the first step in the formulation of public opinion.

On the national level, similar comparisons of news coverage with responses to the standard Gallup question, "What do you think is the most important problem facing this country today?," also show a striking level of correspondence. For example, a pioneering examination of the turbulent 1960s by Ray Funkhouser (1973) studied the relationship of news coverage of major issues to public opinion and to the realities underlying those issues. He found that the Vietnam War, race relations, and campus unrest ranked at the top of both the press agenda and the public agenda during that decade. Conversely, issues such as poverty and women's rights ranked low on both agendas. Neither the salience of issues singled out for attention by the news media nor the salience of issues among the general public showed any striking relationship to external events. Coverage of the Vietnam War and campus unrest peaked a year or more before these events reached their historical climaxes. News coverage of poverty and women's rights had almost no relationship to contemporary actualities. Peaks of public concern and news coverage occurred in years that showed no change at all in the underlying situation. In short, the agenda-setting role of the news is exactly that: it is an influence exerted by the news media, not an instance of the mirror theory of journalism.

Both the assumptions involved in the design of Funkhouser's study and his empirical findings, are relevant to the questions recently raised by European scholars about communication and reality:

- Does any objective meaning of a text exist, apart from what the sender of the text intended it to mean and apart from the understandings of the readers of the text (Kleinnijenhuis, 1990)?
- Is mass communication an integral element of society, or are the media just passive transmitters of a reality that has an existence of its own, independent of the communication process (Severin & Tankard, 1992)?

In regard to the first question, the Funkhouser methodology responds in the affirmative. In regard to the second question, his findings support a strong positive response to the first part and a strong negative response to the second part. Although the news agenda is constrained by reality—no one would claim that the daily news is manufactured out of whole cloth—nevertheless, the news media enjoy considerable latitude in sketching our maps of reality.

The consequences of this independent social role played by the news media can be seen most clearly in examinations of the ebb and flow of a single issue over time. A comparison of front-page New York Times content and American public opinion from 1954 to 1976 showed strong agenda-setting effects for civil rights issues (Winter & Eyal, 1981). On the local level, a comparison of the Louisville Times coverage with local public opinion from 1974 to 1981 found agenda-setting effects for three issues: education, crime and the environment. The reverse pattern of public opinion influencing news coverage existed for health care and public recreation; and there was no consistent pattern at all for economic development and local government (Smith, 1987). An intensive year-long national study of German television news coverage of 16 issues found agenda-setting effects on energy, the environment, and European politics. Problem awareness influenced coverage on two other issues. No effects were found for the remaining nine issues. Agenda-setting effects were most likely to occur when coverage was intense (more than 30 stories per month) and when there was large variation in the coverage from month to month (Brosius & Kepplinger, 1990).

Examination of public issues one at a time also is amenable to laboratory experimentation where measures of how salient an issue is for an individual can be made in conjunction with controlled levels of exposure to news coverage on that issue. Experiments have found agenda-setting effects on individuals for such issues as energy, defense, inflation, civil rights, social security and unemployment (Iyengar & Kinder, 1987).

THE AGENDA-SETTING PROCESS

The phenomenon of agenda setting can be examined from a variety of perspectives. A typology of four categories was introduced by McCombs (1981). The substantive dimension of this typology distinguishes between studies focusing on a single issue versus those examining the full array of issues on the media and public agendas. The second dimension identifies the level of analysis, aggregate population measures versus individual measures. The combination of these two dicotomized dimensions yields the four categories in Figure 11.1:

	Measurement of the agenda	
Focus of attention	Aggregate data	Individual data
Set of issues	I Mass Persuasion	III Automaton
Single issue	II Natural History	IV Cognitive Portrait

FIGURE 11.1. A typology of approaches to agenda-setting research.

1. Mass persuasion studies, which focus on sets of issues and on aggregated data describing public agendas at the societal level. Much of the research on agenda setting has been performed at this level and provides strong support for such effects (e.g., McCombs & Shaw, 1972; Funkhouser, 1973; Weaver, Graber, McCombs, & Eyal, 1981).
2. Automaton studies, which examine sets of issues and individual agendas. One study found only moderate support for agenda setting when individuals were asked to rank order six or more issues (McLeod, Becker, & Byrnes, 1974), but there seems little reason to expect an individual to mirror perfectly the rank-ordering of public issues in current news coverage.
3. Natural history studies, which look for agenda-setting effects in aggregated public agenda data, but for single issues. Effects for agenda setting also are strong at this level of analysis (e.g., Winter & Eyal, 1981; Lang & Lang, 1983; MacKuen & Coombs, 1981).
4. Cognitive portrait studies, which investigate single issues and individual agendas. In contrast to the automaton category, there is strong support for agenda setting for most of the cognitive portrait research (e.g., Iyengar & Kinder, 1987; Protess et al., 1991).

Considerable attention also has been placed on the time frame for agenda-setting processes. How long does it take for these agenda-setting effects to appear? The typical time span for the translation of news coverage on an issue into a reasonably high degree of salience for that issue on the public agenda is 5 to 7 weeks. But, as common sense would dictate, there is tremendous variability across issues. The answer also depends on your perspective in terms of the four kinds of studies outlined in Figure 11.1. For "Mass Persuasion" studies, which are focused on the full array of issues on the agenda, it takes at least one or two months to discern significant shifts in the public agenda (Stone & McCombs, 1981; Salwen, 1988). But "Natural History" studies, which follow the rise and fall of a single issue across time, typically find strong effects at much shorter time intervals. Eaton (1989) found almost immediate effects on the public agenda from news coverage of such familiar issues as inflation, poverty, and budget cuts. Winter and Eyal (1981) found that public concern about civil rights between 1954 and 1976 followed news coverage by about eight weeks on the average. It is conceivable that this time lag between news coverage and shifts in salience became shorter once civil rights was established as an enduring public issue. Unfortunately, the published data are silent on this point. But Brosius and Kepplinger (1990) suggest that the time span for new issues may literally be years, while the response time to more familiar issues may be extremely short. In short, public consensus on the key issues of the day may be extremely stable, so that established issues move on and off the public agenda with ease in response to the daily news while new issues must struggle to gain a position on the public agenda.

The time frame also seems to depend upon the medium, newspapers or television. For example, Shaw and McCombs (1977) found that newspapers more strongly influence agendas early in presidential campaigns, but that television proved to have stronger effects as the campaign progressed. In a more general setting outside of an election context, Palmgreen and Clarke (1977) found stronger agenda-setting effects for television, both networks and local, on the public agenda of national issues. However, the local newspaper had an edge on local television in its impact on the public agenda of local issues. Clearly, differences in the agenda-setting power of the media should have something to do with how credibly or legitimately different media channels are perceived by the public and with the different ways in which news itself is presented by different media. For example, Danielian (1989) found that more than half of the network news coverage of citizen action interest groups involved acts of civil disobedience.

Contingent Conditions

The agenda-setting process in its entirety is complex and includes a variety of components ranging from those factors shaping media agendas to variables that mediate the magnitude of agenda-setting effects for public agendas. Most research has focused on the media agenda's impact on public agendas. In general terms, agenda setting can be thought of as a transactional model in which effects are the results of interactions between two active participants, the mass media and the individual

(McCombs, 1981). Thus, at a very basic level, the contingent conditions under which agenda-setting processes are most likely to work can be classified into two general categories based on the two active participants: message variables, for example—the level of conflict depicted in news stories about issues—and audience variables, such as individuals' socioeconomic status.

A few of these variables are obvious. For example, an individual's frequency of exposure to news about issues has been a consistent factor in most studies: more exposure results in the increased susceptibility to media agenda-setting effects. However, several variables are less obvious. MacKuen and Coombs (1981), for instance, found that the level of drama with which a story is portrayed is a better predictor of agenda setting than the mere frequency of exposure to news stories.

Many of the contingent variables studied are complex in nature and have allowed for a sophisticated analysis of the processes at work in the media's setting of the public agenda. It would be difficult to list comprehensively all of the contingent variables examined by agenda-setting researchers. Thus, to illustrate the agenda-setting process, three variables worthy of note are discussed here: the need for orientation, the obtrusiveness of issues (both examples of contingent conditions based on individual attributes), and how issues are framed in news stories (an example of a contingent variable based on characteristics of the message).

The Need for Orientation

McCombs and Weaver (1985) note that the need for orientation has its theoretical underpinnings in cognitive utilitarian theories. These theories view the individual as a problem solver who approaches all situations as an opportunity to acquire useful information for coping with life's challenges (McGuire, 1974). Individuals, then, are active processors of information who seek out information to satisfy perceived needs, and the need for orientation provides a useful bridge between the agenda-setting concept and the uses and gratifications perspective in mass communication research.

The need for orientation can be defined in terms of two concepts: political relevance, or the perceived importance of the problem, and political uncertainty, the perceived existence of a gap or lack of knowledge about a problem. Low relevance and low uncertainty will lead to low need for orientation. Here, individuals do not perceive that a problem is important and do not feel that they are lacking information in this area. Thus, they will not believe an issue is important, will not seek out additional information from the news media, and will not be accessible to agenda-setting effects. High relevance and high uncertainty, on the other hand, will lead to high need for orientation and thus high agenda-setting effects. High relevance and low uncertainty, or low relevance and high uncertainty, will lead to moderate need for orientation. The concept of the need for orientation has been supported by a variety of evidence.

Weaver, Graber, McCombs, and Eyal (1981), for example, found that although levels of motivation to follow the campaign had only minor effects on issue agendas during the spring and summer periods, those groups of voters with a high need for orientation had issue agendas in the fall that were substantially more similar to the newspaper and television agendas than did other voters. Motivation to follow the campaign was most important in the agenda-setting process near the end of the race when the need for information was greatest among the undecided voters.

MacKuen and Coombs (1981) also found that those most interested in politics had group agendas most similar to the various media agendas. Similarly, Erbring, Goldenberg, and Miller (1980) found that increased uncertainty (in the form of weaker political party affiliation) and increased interest in public affairs were positively linked to increases in concern about government credibility.

On the other hand, McLeod, Becker, and Byrnes (1974) found that the less interested voters showed stronger agenda-setting effects than the more interested, but that undecided younger voters also showed stronger agenda-setting effects, suggesting that those with a moderate need for orientation (low interest and high uncertainty) are most affected. Schoenbach and Weaver (1983) also found that those with low interest and high uncertainty were most influenced by media exposure regarding the salience of European issues.

McCombs and Weaver (1985) suggest that the reason for the discrepant findings on the need for orientation is that other variables must be taken into account, including the overall importance of the campaign or subject being studied, the personal experience of people with regard to the issues on the media agenda, and the degree of interpersonal discussion of these issues.

Obtrusiveness of Issues

Issues can be placed on an obtrusiveness–unobtrusiveness continuum. Issues that are obtrusive are those with which the public has independent knowledge or direct experience, such as the issue of inflation. Individuals do not need the news media to explain to them that rising prices are a salient problem; they experience this problem first-hand. At the other end of the continuum, unobtrusive issues are those with which most of the public has little independent knowledge and no direct experience—for example, a foreign war in which the United States is not a participant. Some researchers argue that agenda-setting effects are greater for issues at the unobtrusive end of the continuum because individuals can only learn salience cues through the news media and thus are not exposed to interfering information from personal involvement (Winter, 1981; Blood, 1981; Zucker, 1978).

However, recent research has not supported this conclusion. Experiments by Iyengar and Kinder (1987), for example, produced mixed results on the effects of obtrusiveness of issues. They collected longitudinal data demonstrating the contemporaneous effects of television news on two issues usually considered obtrusive—energy and inflation—and found that the media are stronger predictors of public opinion than indicators of "real" world conditions. But they did not find similar results for the obtrusive issue of employment.

Lasorsa and Wanta (1990), meanwhile, found stronger agenda-setting effects for issues with which individuals had a high level of personal involvement. They conclude that personal involvement with an issue sensitizes individuals to that issue. Individuals then seek out additional information on the obtrusive issue from the news media. This increased exposure to news media messages, in turn, increases the potential magnitude of agenda-setting effects.

Issue Framing

The agenda-setting effect also is contingent upon how reporters and editors choose to frame issues. For example, Shaw and McCombs (1977) found differential agenda-setting effects for the issue of crime. Effects were stronger when the issue was portrayed as a social problem than when the news was presented as a straight crime report. Similarly, Williams, Shapiro, and Cutbirth (1983) found stronger agenda-setting effects when issues specifically were framed as components of an electoral campaign rather than without this crucial frame.

Wanta and Hu (1993) also conclude that how an issue is framed is an important determinant of issue salience. In a longitudinal examination of international problems and their news coverage in four news media, they found that stories with high degrees of conflict and stories with concrete presentations (which included Americans in the stories) had the strongest agenda-setting impact. In addition, two news categories—international trade not involving the United States, and politics not involving the United States—correlated negatively with public concern for two of the news media. This result suggests that press coverage, besides increasing public concern with certain issues, can also decrease concern. Certain categories of news, such as stories dealing with international politics and trade, can give individuals cues that the international arena is functioning quite smoothly.

PUBLIC OFFICIALS AND POLICYMAKERS

While the core of agenda-setting is itself well mapped—that is, the media's effect on the perceived importance of issues among members of the public—less attention has centered on two other points at which agenda setting takes place: factors influencing coverage of issues that reach the media agenda, and the media and public's impact on policy and decision-making agendas. Research at this more macro or sociopolitical level of analysis focuses on questions surrounding what the media agenda itself is, who sets it and why, and how public policy and decision-making are affected by media and public agendas and opinion.

Attention has focused on the agenda-setting influence of newsmakers such as the president and public relations staffs, and on how the media affect each others' agendas. Does the president affect the press agenda or does the reverse process take place, in which the president responds to news media coverage? The media agenda of issues in the news coverage preceding and following the president's annual state of the union address has been compared with the agenda of issues presented in the speech itself (Wanta, Stephenson, Turk, & McCombs, 1989; Gilberg, Eyal, McCombs, & Nicholas, 1980). The findings in these analyses of addresses by Presidents Nixon, Carter, and Reagan are mixed: in two cases the media set the president's agenda of issues and in two other cases the president was able to set the media agenda of issues. A longitudinal analysis of major public issues between 1970 and 1987 also found mixed results on the direction of influence (Wanta, 1989). Page and Shapiro (1984) argue that the popularity of a president may be an intervening variable in the agenda-setting process.

Analyses of public relations' influence on news media agendas provide clearer results. Turk (1986) compared the press releases and other communications produced by six state agencies with newspaper coverage of the agencies and the issues with which they are concerned. She found that 51% of the news releases and other handouts were accepted and used in news stories. And when information originated by the agency was used by reporters, the resulting news stories reflected the issue agendas promoted by the agency—that is, the public information officers were able to set the media agenda. Or, more specifically, news sources can influence the way an issue is framed. The topic's newsworthiness was the most cited factor by journalists when they were queried about the decisions behind their gatekeeping choices, and information framed in a straightforward and nonpersuasive manner made it onto the news agenda more often than information including an agency spin.

The media also set each other's agendas (Reese & Danielian, 1989; Danielian & Reese, 1989). In an analysis of newspaper, television network news, and news magazine coverage of the cocaine issue during 1986, it was found that media not only set each others' agendas, but that more often than not the *New York Times* was in the leading position. The media converged on the drug issue both in amount and type of coverage and the news sources used. Convergence appeared to be strongest when information was supplied by prominent sources, such as national and foreign leaders. Mathes and Phetsch (1989) found a similar leadership role for *Die Zeit* on major German issues.

A team of researchers at Northwestern University explored the news media's agenda-setting effects on the public, decision-makers and public policy through six quasiexperiments. Their research projects range from the issues of corruption in federally funded home health care programs and the reporting and handling of rape in the Chicago area to the disposal of toxic waste and international child abductions (Protess et al., 1991). The findings are mixed. For example, the home health care television news series had stronger effects on the public than the newspaper report on rape, the television report on toxic waste, or the "60 Minutes" segment on child abductions. The toxic waste and child abduction reports resulted in significant changes in the attitudes and actions of decision makers.

The Northwestern researchers conclude that two factors are important for achieving significant changes in public attitudes: (1) news reports that are unambiguous and that include dramatic, convincing, and clear evidence of the problem; and (2) "nonrecurring issues," which are presented as breaking stories that have received little prior attention in the news. Four factors have an impact on the effects of news on policy: (1) the timing of the news report; (2) the extent of collaboration among journalists and decision makers; (3) the level of public and interest group pressure; and (4) the availability of cost-effective solutions.

While the Northwestern projects continue to produce important data about media effects on policy, a more longitudinal approach to these agenda-setting processes is needed. For example, Page and Shapiro (1984) examined the influence of public opinion on policy and found that such influence is strongest when public opinion is large and stable, issues are salient, change is moving in a liberal direction and the policy issue's scope of conflict is wide.

METHODOLOGICAL REFINEMENTS

The initial agenda-setting studies conducted by Maxwell McCombs and Donald Shaw were striking in the simplicity of their data analysis. The number of stories dealing with certain issues was compared to the number of respondents who stated that the issues were "the most important problem facing this country today." Spearman rank-order correlations tested whether the media and public "agendas" were significantly similar. Indeed, the two agendas were highly similar.

Mirroring advancements by social scientists in other disciplines, agenda-setting researchers have begun to utilize increasingly sophisticated data analysis techniques. Wanta and Hu (1994) developed a path analysis model examining three audience contingent conditions: exposure to media messages, reliance on the media for political information, and perceived credibility of the news media. Their findings suggest that individuals who perceive the press as highly credible become dependent upon the media for information, then increase their exposure to media messages, which in turn leads to stronger media agenda-setting effects. Thus, perceived credibility and reliance on the news media were related—though indirectly—to the magnitude of agenda-setting effects.

Two recent studies show the potential fruitfulness of employing time series analysis in agenda setting. Time series analysis, which has been used extensively by economists to predict future market behavior, has had only limited utility to mass communication scholars because of two restrictions: (1) time series analysis requires an extremely large number of time points (McCleary & Hay [1980] argue that 70 to 90 time points are necessary); and (2) time series analysis requires consistent time intervals with no missing data.

Zhu (1992) used a time series analysis to propose a mathematical model of agenda setting. His model suggests that issues must compete with one another for the attention of the public. The salience of an issue on the public agenda is not only a function of the preceding news coverage—the point emphasized by the theory of agenda setting—but also is a function of the existing salience among the public for other competing issues and the existing salience of these competing issues on the news agenda. In short, the public agenda has the characteristics of a zero-sum game. This perspective on the public agenda provides an explanation for the early observation that the public agenda typically consists of no more than five to seven issues (Shaw & McCombs, 1977). While such a limited agenda might seem antithetical to the democratic ideal of diversity in public dialogue, a positive social benefit is a significant degree of consensus about the major priorities of the day.

Wanta and Foote (1993) also used a time series analysis to examine the influence of President Bush on the news media during his first 80 weeks in office. Their findings suggest that the president may influence coverage of issues on which he is an important source, such as international crises, and on which he has a pet interest, such as patriotism and flag burning. For issues on which other sources may provide more accurate or detailed information, such as economic issues, the president has much less influence. Finally, on social problems, such as crime and the environment, the president may use the media as a guide to the importance of issues on which he should respond.

MAPPING THE FRONTIER

Communication is a vast frontier to explore. It is everything from a parent and teacher discussing a child's performance to major public information campaigns designed to restructure our schools. And social scientists are inherently explorers. There are always new topics to examine, new methodologies to develop, and new concepts to explicate. While this exploration can be exciting and fruitful, it also has its downside. In his review of agenda-setting studies, James Winter (1981, p. 240) lamented that "the drive for total innovation has overwhelmed the scientific prerequisite of at least partial replication." New ideas are important, but they are more important when they are developed in detail and subjected to rigorous testing and replication. In recent years, some scholars have heeded this point and abandoned the role of explorer for the role of surveyor. Rather than rushing off into new territory, these scholars have concentrated on the detailed mapping of the agenda-setting process (McCombs, 1992).

This new role of surveyor is especially apparent in the attention devoted to the public agenda. Until recent years, the public agenda largely has been a fixed benchmark in the research literature. Typically, its operational definition is a question used over the decades by the Gallup Poll: "What do you think is the most important problem facing this country today?". While from time to time new research explored the nature of these agenda-setting effects, most of the explorers concentrated their attention on the independent and intervening variables that produced these effects. Recently, an international effort, *Communication and Culture* by Alex Edelstein, Youichi Ito, and Hans Mathias Kepplinger (1988), outlined three distinct agenda-setting effects: (1) thinking; (2) what to think about; and (3) what to think.

This elaboration of the public agenda is based on frequently cited comments by Bernard Cohen (1963) that while the media may not tell us what to think, they are stunningly successful in telling us what to think about. In this new elaboration, thinking is synonymous with awareness and salience, the terms traditionally used to define the agenda-setting effect. As noted, operational definitions of thinking commonly are framed in terms of the Gallup MIP questions. From this perspective the public agenda is a broad set of issues or topics.

When these responses are probed to discover why respondents think the issue is the most important one facing the country or which facet of the issue is most salient, the agenda-setting effect is being framed in terms of what to think about. News media do more than make their audiences aware of general topics. The news of the day directs our attention, suggesting particular aspects of a problem or situation for consideration. This level of analysis can be conceptualized as the attributes of issues. Just as there can be a public agenda of issues, there also can be a public agenda of the attributes or facets of each issue.

A new methodology called cognigraphics (Carter, Stamm, & Heintz-Knowles, 1992) yields creative insights into what people are actually thinking about when they name a particular issue. The starting point for cognigraphics is Freud's word association technique. Whether the focus of the research is a topic designated by the researcher or is the topic named in response to the MIP question, respondents are asked to give the first word that comes to mind for that topic. Then they are asked to describe the relationship that exists in their minds between the topic and the word associate, selecting from a list of six logical relationships. Cognigraphic research has found considerable variation in the portraits that people construct about such public issues as the budget deficit, education, and AIDS. All this is considerably more than an expanded portrait of the public agenda. It is a first step "to understand agenda-setting well enough to suggest what the media might do that would improve the public capability to think together about its common problems" (Carter et al., 1992, p. 870).

A third agenda-setting effect focuses on what people do think. Here, agenda-setting research merges with attitude-change research. The press can sometimes so direct and monopolize our attention that it determines our attitudes. Examination of public opinion polls for 80 different issues over the past 15 years reveals that television news coverage has a major impact on the movement of public opinion (Page & Shapiro, 1992, pp. 339–348).

To date, agenda-setting research has focused on awareness and cognitions about issues as the necessary prelude to attitude and opinion change. Research linking the public agenda to public opinion is an important next step in understanding agenda-setting processes.

Weaver et al., (1981) found that the media not only set the public's agenda, but that the news agenda also affects voter evaluations of candidates and the way in which the public forms its images of candidates. Experiments conducted by Iyengar and Kinder (1987) have determined that television news also has the power to prime the public's judgments. They concluded that by focusing on some issues and ignoring others, news can help determine the way individuals judge governmental and presidential performances, candidates, and policies. And as an example of direct opinion effects, Page and Shapiro (1992) analyzed all network news sources for 80 diverse issues and found direct effects on the public's opinion on issues, but for only three source types: popular presidents, experts, and editorial commentary. Kepplinger, Donsbach, Brosius, and Staab (1989) compared media coverage of Helmut Kohl in seven leading newspapers and magazines with opinions of the German general public between 1975 and 1984. Evaluative shifts in the news media preceded shifts in public opinion with a time lag of about 3 to 6 months.

While discussions of agenda-setting typically have explicitly eschewed attitude-change effects, the ability—indeed, the necessity—of the news media to frame issues (Gitlin, 1980) requires an expanded statement of agenda-setting effects. The news is presented in the form of stories. Telling a story requires the selection of a frame, a theme, for the story. These frames create a perspective for thinking about particular issues in the news. Recall that news stories viewed by subjects in a series of experiments clearly established specific perspectives or criteria that these subjects subsequently used to evaluate presidential performance (Iyengar & Kinder, 1987). One's store of information shapes one's opinions.

This trilogy of agenda-setting effects, outlined in *Communication and Culture*, provide one map of public opinion and communication. Another effort at mapping the agenda-setting process, explication of need for orientation as a psychological explanation for agenda-setting, also has expanded our view of communication and public opinion by linking two discrete communication perspectives, agenda setting and the spiral of silence (McCombs & Weaver, 1985). While agenda setting and the spiral of silence (Noelle-Neumann, 1984) have explored different public opinion outcomes—the salience of issues versus a willingness to state one's opinion publicly—they do share a common psychological basis. Both agenda setting and the spiral of silence arise from the innate curiosity of people regarding the world around them. This curiosity motivates attention to the news media and their cues about the salience of issues (agenda setting) and about the distribution of public opinion on issues (the spiral of silence). While these two traditions share a common base concept, the explorers bearing the flags of these two traditions ventured into different portions of the communication and public opinion domain.

CONCLUSION

The mass media frequently are described as our windows on the world. But two historically prominent observers of mass communication explicated that metaphor in quite opposite terms. Walter Lippmann detailed the gatekeeper tradition in which the media take a highly selective look through the window, while Harold Lasswell detailed the surveillance function, which suggests a broad, sweeping view from the window. Recognizing this contrast, Carter et al. (1992, p. 869) note:

> In both views, the media can be expected to pay attention to things that make a difference and/or to things with which differences can be made, that is, to things of consequence. . . . An agenda is a familiar tool for collective behavior, for a community to think together about matters of shared consequence.

But are these agendas inclusive or exclusive? Whose perspective prevails in contemporary public life? Lasswell's view of an inclusive agenda with its broad, encompassing vista, or Lippmann's view of an exclusive agenda that is tightly focused?

Recent empirical evidence suggests a tightly focused public agenda that is resistant to major change. Shaw and Martin (1992) found a convergence in public opinion about four key issues—education, pollution, housing, and poverty—among persons with disparate demographic characteristics who were highly exposed to the news agenda. The agendas of men and women, whites and blacks, young and old, more educated and less educated, all converged as their exposure to the news increased. In the course of setting the public agenda, the news media also create social consensus.

There also is a significant inertia factor in this consensus process. Implicit in the original, most parsimonious formulation of agenda-setting is the idea of a fluid and shifting public agenda. But Zhu's (1992) recent work shows that the potential for rapid change eminating from the coverage of new issues is braked by the competing news coverage and concern among members of the public for other issues on an agenda that typically can handle no more than five to seven issues at any moment in time.

A growing understanding of the agenda-setting process simultaneously tells us something about the contemporary public life and highlights the implications of contemporary practice for an informed public opinion. This research and discussion also provides an opportunity to reframe our windows on the world.

REFERENCES

Blood, W. (1981). *Unobtrusive issues in the agenda setting role of the press*. Unpublished doctoral dissertation, Syracuse University.

Brosius, H. B., & Kepplinger, H. M. (1990). The agenda-setting function of television news: Static and dynamic views. *Communication Research, 17*, 183–211.

Carter, R. F., Stamm, K. R., & Heintz-Knowles, K. (1992). Agenda-setting and consequentiality. *Journalism Quarterly, 69*, 868–877.

Cohen, B. C. (1963). *The press and foreign policy*. Princeton, NJ: Princeton University Press.

Danielian, L. H. (1989). *Network news coverage of interest groups: Implications for mass media and democracy*. Unpublished doctoral dissertation, University of Texas at Austin.

Danielian, L. H., & Reese, S. D. (1989). A closer look at intermedia influences on agenda-setting: The cocaine issue of 1986. In P. Shoemaker (Ed.), *Communication campaigns about drugs* (pp. 47–66). Hillsdale, NJ: Lawrence Erlbaum.

Eaton, H., Jr. (1989). Agenda setting with bi-weekly data on content of three national media. *Journalism Quarterly, 66*, 942–948, 959.

Edelstein, A. S., Ito, I., & Kepplinger, H. M. (1989). *Communication and culture: A comparative approach*. White Plains, NY: Longman.

Erbring, L., Goldenberg, E. N., & Miller, A. H. (1980). Front-page news and real-world cues: A new look at agenda-setting by the media. *American Journal of Political Science, 24*, 16–49.

Funkhouser, G. R. (1973). The issues of the sixties: An exploratory study in the dynamics of public opinion. *Public Opinion Quarterly, 37*, 62–75.

Gilberg, S., Eyal, C., McCombs, M. E., & Nicholas, D. (1980). The state of the union address and the press agenda. *Journalism Quarterly, 57*, 584–588.

Gitlin, T. (1980). *The whole world is watching: Mass media in the making and unmaking of the new left*. Berkeley: University of California Press.

Iyengar, S., & Kinder, D. R. (1987). *News that matters: Agenda-setting and priming in a television age*. Chicago: University of Chicago Press.

Kepplinger, H. M., Donsbach, W., Brosius, H. B., & Staab, J. F. (1989). Media tone and public opinion: A longitudinal study of media coverage and public opinion on Chancellor Kohl. *International Journal of Public Opinion Research, 1*, 326–342.

Kleinnijenhuis, J. (1990, May). Applications of graph theory to cognitive communication research. Paper presented at the meeting of the International Communication Association, Dublin.

Lang, G. E., & Lang, K. (1983). *The battle for public opinion: The president, the press and the polls during Watergate*. New York: Columbia University Press.

Lasorsa, D. L., & Wanta, W. (1990). The effects of personal, interpersonal and media experience on issue salience. *Journalism Quarterly, 67*, 804–813.

Lasswell, H. D. (1948). The structure and function of communication in society. In W. Schramm (Ed.), *Mass Communication* (pp. 117–130). Urbana, IL: University of Illinois Press.

Lippmann, W. (1922). *Public Opinion*. New York: Macmillan.

MacKuen, M. B., & Coombs, S. L. (1981). *More than news*. Beverly Hills, CA: Sage.

Mathes, R., & Phetsch, B. (1989, May). Spill-over effects of media opinion leadership in the agenda-building process: The rise and fall of counter issues. Paper presented at the meeting of the International Communication Association, San Francisco.

McCleary, R., & Hay, R. A., Jr. (1980). *Applied time series analysis for the social sciences*. Beverly Hills, CA: Sage.

McCombs, M. E. (1992). Explorers and surveyors: Expanding strategies for agenda-setting research. *Journalism Quarterly, 69*, 813–824.

McCombs, M. E. (1981). The agenda-setting approach. In D. D. Nimmo & K. R. Sanders (Eds.), *Handbook of political communication* (pp. 121–140). Beverly Hills, CA: Sage.

McCombs, M. E., & Shaw, D. L. (1972). The agenda-setting function of mass media. *Public Opinion Quarterly, 36*, 176–187.

McCombs, M. E., & Weaver, D. H. (1985). Toward a merger of gratifications and agenda-setting research. In K. E. Rosengren, L. A. Weaver, & P. Palmgreen (Eds.), *Media gratifications research: Current perspectives* (pp. 95–108). Newbury Park, CA: Sage.

McGuire, W. J. (1974). Psychological motives and communication gratification. In J. G. Blumler & E. Katz (Eds.), *The uses of mass communication: Current perspectives on gratifications research* (pp. 167–196). Beverly Hills, CA: Sage.

McLeod, J. M., Becker, L. B., & Byrnes, J. E. (1974). Another look at the agenda-setting function of the press. *Communication Research, 1*, 131–166.

Noelle-Neumann, E. (1984). *The spiral of silence: Public opinion—Our social skin*. Chicago: University of Chicago Press.

Page, B. I., & Shapiro, R. Y. (1984). Presidents as opinion leaders: Some new evidence. *Policy Studies Journal, 12*, 649–661.

Page, B. I., & Shapiro, R. Y. (1992). *The rational public: 50 years of trends in Americans' policy preferences*. Chicago: University of Chicago Press.

Palmgreen, P., & Clarke, P. (1977). Agenda-setting with local and national issues. *Communication Research, 4*, 435–452.

Protess, D. L., Cook, F. L., Doppelt, J. C., Ettema, J. S., Gordon, M. T., Leff, D. R., & Miller, P. (1991). *The journalism of outrage: Investigative reporting and agenda-building in America*. New York: Guilford Press.

Reese, S. D., & Danielian, L. H. (1989). Intermedia influence and the drug issue: Converging on cocaine. In P. Shoemaker (Ed.), *Communication campaigns about drugs* (pp. 29–46). Hillsdale, NJ: Lawrence Erlbaum.

Rogers, E., & Dearing, J. (1988). Agenda-setting research: Where has it been, where is it going? In J. Anderson (Ed.), *Communication yearbook* (Vol. 11, pp. 555–594). Beverly Hills, CA: Sage.

Salwen, M. B. (1988). Effect of accumulation of issue salience in agenda setting. *Journalism Quarterly, 65*, 100–106, 130.

Schoenbach, K., & Weaver, D. H. (1983, May). Cognitive bonding and need for orientation during political campaigns. Paper presented at the meeting of the International Communication Association, Boston.

Severin, W. J., & Tankard, J. W., Jr. (1992). *Communication theories: Origins, methods, uses in the mass media* (3rd ed.). New York: Longman.

Shaw, D. L., & McCombs, M. E. (1977). *The emergence of American political issues: The agenda-setting function of the press*. St. Paul, MN: West Publishing Company.

Shaw, D. L., & Martin, S. E. (1992). The function of mass media agenda-setting. *Journalism Quarterly, 69*, 902–920.

Smith, K. (1987). Newspaper coverage and public concern about community issues. *Journalism Monographs*, No. 101.

Stone, G. C., & McCombs, M. E. (1981). Tracing the time lag in agenda setting. *Journalism Quarterly, 58*, 51–55.

Turk, J. V. (1986). Public relations' influence on the news. *Newspaper Research Journal, 7*(4), 15–27.

Wanta, W. (1989). *The president, press and public opinion: An examination of the dynamics of agenda-building*. Unpublished Ph.D. dissertation, University of Texas at Austin.

Wanta, W., & Foote, J. S. (1993, May). The president-press relationship: A time series analysis of agenda-setting. Paper presented at the meeting of the International Communication Association, Washington, DC.

Wanta, W., & Hu, Y. W. (1993). The agenda-setting effects of international news coverage: An examination of differing news frames. *International Journal of Public Opinion Research, 5*, 250–264.

Wanta, W., & Hu, Y. W. (1994). The effects of credibility, reliance and exposure on media agenda-setting: A path analysis model. *Journalism Quarterly, 71*, 90–98.

Wanta, W., Stephenson, M. A., VanSlyke Turk, J., & McCombs, M. E. (1989). How president's state of the union talk influenced news media agendas. *Journalism Quarterly, 66*, 537–541.

Weaver, D. H., Graber, D. A., McCombs, M. E., & Eyal, C. H. (1981). *Media agenda-setting in a presidential election: Issues, images and interests*. New York: Praeger.

Williams, W., Jr., Shapiro, M., & Cutbirth, C. (1983), The impact of campaign agendas on perceptions of issues in the 1980 campaign. *Journalism Quarterly, 60*, 226–231.

Winter, J. P. (1981). Contingent conditions in the agenda-setting process. In G.

C. Wilhoit & H. de Bock (Eds.), *Mass communication review yearbook 2* (pp. 235–247). Beverly Hills, CA: Sage.

Winter, J. P., & Eyal, C. H. (1981). Agenda-setting for the civil rights issue. *Public Opinion Quarterly, 45*, 376–383.

Zhu, J. H. (1992). Issue competition and attention distraction: A zero-sum theory of agenda-setting. *Journalism Quarterly, 69*, 825–836.

Zucker, H. G. (1978). The variable nature of news media influence. In B. D. Ruben (Ed.), *Communication yearbook 2* (pp. 225–240). New Brunswick, NJ: Transaction Books.

12

Conflict, Consensus, and Public Opinion

Clarice N. Olien
George A. Donohue
Phillip J. Tichenor

One of the enduring themes in the social science literature is the role of mass media in reporting conflict. Media have been alternatively identified with (1) avoiding conflict and stressing consensus (e.g., Janowitz, 1952, Breed, 1958; Edelstein & Schulz, 1963) and (2) playing up conflict (e.g., Key, 1967). An underlying question remains open: What is the role of media in reporting conflict and consensus, and how does this reporting affect those perceptions and outlooks that we call "public opinion?" This is an exploration of conflict as a social process and of the role in media in reporting conflict under different structural conditions. Analysis of media role includes both the question of what content is reported, and the impact of media reporting on formation of public opinion.

Conflict has historically been recognized as a basic and pervasive social process. It was central to the concerns of such early social philosophers as Aristotle, Aquinas, and St. Augustine; to later writers such as Machiavelli and the social contract theorists; and to the analyses of a number of 19th century social theorists, including Marx, Comte, Gumplowicz, and Ratzenhofer (Gumplowicz, 1894; Lichtenberger, 1923; Martindale, 1963; Bernard, 1983).

While these writers stress the ubiquitous nature of conflict, they vary in emphasis upon source of conflict and its implications. Machiavelli saw conflicts between political groups as a problem for management by the ruler, while Marx regarded the primary source of conflict as the class struggle between property owners and propertyless workers. Later writers saw conflict in more generalized terms. Gumplowicz (1894, pp. 125–127) saw much conflict originating in ethnic divisions of Europe, with an alternation of war and peace in which "peace is only a continuous latent struggle" that may or may not lead to increased well-being for both the rulers and the subjected group. Such improvement, in Gumplowicz' view, depended upon social organization and reorganization in postmedieval Europe, following regional conflicts. An example was the interposing of merchants as a middle class between the nobility and the peasantry. This interposition led to immense expansion of human services.

Just as political philosophers have traditionally seen conflict as basic to social change, mass media of all ages have reported conflicts. Even when the "big story" on the world scene is the relaxation of tensions, the relaxation will be seen against the backdrop of struggle and ferment. Political change in Europe from autumn 1989 to early 1990 was less an elimination of conflict than a shift in the nature of conflicts, both among and within nations. Sweeping changes in national governments signaled a sharp realignment of groups and different kinds of power struggles. The problem of global survival was redefined, with fear of nuclear war being gradually replaced or joined by fear of global environmental destruction and regional conflicts, some of which, like the Gulf War, had the potential for being international conflagrations.

SOCIAL CONTROL

The centrality of social conflict arises from its integral role in processes of social control, including the control of information. Social order is a central concern in all societies and conflict is part of the control process. It is not a question of eliminating conflict—however strongly such a wish might be expressed—but of managing it. Containment or even creation of one controversy may serve to ameliorate or constrain another conflict, often a larger and more encompassing one.

The contention that conflict does not necessarily have negative outcomes is a central theme of the later conflict theory literature. Such writers as Georg Simmel (1955), Lewis Coser (1954, 1967) and Ralf Dahrendorf (1959) have provided extensive discussions of the functions of conflict in social processes. The tendency for inner cohesion to develop as a result of an external threat—unity in the face of the enemy—is often cited. Furthermore, conflictual relations may stimulate new insights into social problems, leading to innovative ways of dealing with these problems or of articulating group positions. Conflict is often said to prevent ossification of the structure, and thereby facilitate adaptability. Conflicts energize the production and dissemination of information, which may either intensify or defuse the issue. Schumpeter (1976) makes essentially the same point about competition as an antidote for ossification in industrial and commercial organization. All such outcomes have social control consequences.

The study of public opinion itself may be seen as a way of studying social control. This is evident in at least three closely related senses. The first is that the public affairs issues themselves, as Lippmann (1922) noted, are often about how others should manage their affairs. A second is that public opinion, as noted in the early literature on social control, occurs in a context of social organization and may exert on the system considerable pressure to conform. Thus, the well-publicized reports of public opinion, whether about presidential campaigns, human rights, or gun registration laws, become part of the information resources employed to advance a particular notion of who and/or what rules should prevail. A third is that since mass media themselves are agents of social control, the controls placed upon the media are vital to an understanding of opinion formation processes (Swanson, 1949).

MEDIA AND DEFINITIONS OF CONFLICTUAL PROBLEM

There is considerable evidence that popular definitions of social problems tend to be those carried by the mass media. One interpretation is that media establish *and* report agendas, thereby "setting" these agendas for society. This view is open to considerable challenge on the grounds that media are not independent agencies but are as subject to system controls as are government, the courts, the schools, or education. Media adoption of agency agendas is evident when the Surgeon General calls a press conference to announce a new set of data on the incidence of AIDS or lung cancer. Information emanates from powerful agencies with a purpose and the media transmit purposive information in accordance with agency agendas. Media transmittal of the military definition of the Persian Gulf War is perhaps the most spectacular recent example of this process.

Media organizational arrangements maintain this flow of purposive, conflictual information. Following an extensive analysis of the New York Times and Washington Post, Sigal (1973) noted that the "routine channels for newsgathering . . . constitute the mechanism for official dominance of national and foreign news" in the papers. By "routine channels" Sigal meant those set up by the government and therefore generally under control of governmental officials. Sigal concluded that only 24% of all channels for news in the Times and Post combined could be attributed to reporter "enterprise," such as interviews or the reporters' own analyses, and 4% from other media reports. The remaining 72% were attributed to official proceedings, press releases, press conferences, "background briefings" and other events primarily under governmental control. The implication is that in Sigal's analysis, governmental agencies had extensive control over social agendas in national and international new coverage in these two major newspapers.

Once a problem is defined in a particular way by the major power actors, this definition may take on a life of its own in the media, and become superimposed upon other issues. This superimposition is frequently noted in the conflict literature (Coser, 1954, 1967; Dahrendorf, 1959). Such common terms in the media as "Cold War" and "Iron Curtain" are indicative of this tendency, since both reinforce the notion of two global political systems at odds with each other for control of the will and ways of humanity. For decades, a wide range of international events such as student exchanges, international geophysical research, Olympic competition, and artistic performances by Soviet and Chinese groups in the United States were interpreted within the Cold War framework. Such a definition is functional for many processes within both Eastern and Western nations, including maintaining a particular type of national identity, patriotism, a military establishment, and a rationale for a particular political and economic orientation toward developing nations.

The tendency to maintain an atmosphere of conflict can be seen when there are sudden, dramatic, and unilateral changes in the power relationships from which the older conflict definitions emerged. Soviet Russia's "glasnost" and "perestroika" policies of recent years and the rapid political changes in Eastern Europe in late 1989 are illustrative. A U.S. political campaign specialist said: "At the core of 75 percent of [American] conservative thinking and action is anti-communism; you take that away and you take away the glue that has held the movement together for a generation" (Salholz, Fineman, & Rogers, 1989). A common theme on editorial and "op-ed" pages has been that the very existence of *perestroika* has been a gauge of instability in the Soviet Union, instability that might well lead to a hard-line military dictatorship.

CONFLICT AND THE "GUARD DOG" PRESS

The accusation that media generate conflict for conflict's sake—or for profit's sake—is well known and not necessarily without merit, although it is incomplete as well as based upon a particular value judgement. It is a statement often countered by the view that the First Amendment to the U.S. Constitution guarantees a *watchdog* role in reporting conflict. This watchdog notion harks back at least to the 18th century, when doubts were raised as to whether even elected parliaments could be trusted to serve the common good (Carlyle, 1841; Boyce, 1978). The press was seen in both British and French systems as a "fourth estate," sitting in the galleries in perpetual watch over the nobility, the church, and the popular representatives, goading them to be responsive to their constituent interest.

This fourth estate, or "watchdog" role of the press is open to the same challenge as the "agenda setting" interpretation, in that it presumes press independence and autonomy, which is not feasible in an interdependent society. While media do serve a surveillance role, the question is, what *kind* of surveillance? It may be suggested that the media serve not as watchdogs for the community as a whole, but as guard dogs for groups having the power and influence to create and command their own security systems. This is power support, although not a "lap dog" notion. The press is conditioned, like a guard dog, to be suspicious of all potential intruders, and it sometimes raises an inexplicable howl. This occasional inconvenience is tolerated, since it is better to have a few false alarms than no alarm at all.

Actions of a guard dog are shaped according to who, if anybody, is defined as the intruder or threat. A 19th-century rural newspaper could editorialize robustly against the railroads headquartered in New York, Chicago, or Minneapolis. Raising the sentry alarm about high rail rates set in distant offices was seen as serving the local power groups as well as the community at large. More recent community press reaction to Medicare, to state planning agencies and to state proposals for siting powerlines and waste disposal locations in rural areas are similar situations.

Saying that the media are controlled by dominant powers in business and government might be challenged as not squaring with the occasional disputes that erupt between media and powerful officials. How can one argue that the media are controlled by such powers when the press can so mercilessly hound a well-known senator, presidential candidate or wealthy banker? Actually, this occasional tendency to turn to one of the masters and yet protect their house is fundamental to the guard dog conception of media. A guard dog's conditioning may produce a sentry alarm during internal disputes as well as in the face of clear external threats. The sentry is on guard against all intruders so long as the masters are acting in unison and according to a stable and known power relationship. Media are dependent upon power *relationships*, rather than simply individual agencies or powerful actors. Power relationships tend to maintain themselves, and media are part of this maintenance process. A presidential order to the armed forces to invade Grenada or Panama draws wide support from the bipartisan political leadership and therefore from the media. Media coverage typically looks to legitimizers for clarification of ambiguous situations. Such non-ambiguous figures as Manuel Noriega and Saddam Hussein become almost automatic targets of guard dog attack. On the other hand, if there are challenges to or between power figures that reach a point of destabilization, media will reflect confusion while seeking other legitimizers. When Richard Nixon's fall from the Presidency was imminent in the summer of 1974, much media attention went to the congressional leadership, members of the Cabinet, and Judicial figures whose legitimacy had not been questioned.

Media news is primarily about those at or near the top of the power hierarchies and those low in the hierarchies who threaten the top (Gans, 1979). Media organizations and new gathering routines reinforce this power orientation, through selection of sources that are available, efficient, and authoritative. Military sources in Vietnam and the Persian Gulf wars were generally treated as authoritative and antiwar protests were treated by-and-large as social threats.

Uncertainty occurs when challenging groups raise a realistic possibility that the power relationships may be altered. Watergate and Irangate dominated media attention because in each case the highest position of political executive power in the nation was under challenge—not from the media, but from the established political structure upon which the media depend. Socially weak groups were virtually unheard of through media in both cases. Few if any views about abortion rights or environmental pollution are reported from ethnic minorities, labor unions, farm groups, and other interests low on the political power scale.

A substantial amount of evidence is consistent with the guard dog conception of media as sentries for established groups in social conflict. Coverage of scientific and technological issues typically concentrates on administrative sources (Tichenor, Olien, Harrison, & Donohue, 1970). Shoemaker (1984) and Herman (1985) found media concentrating on powerful groups and "marginalizing" less powerful groups. This support appears to be acknowledged by the established leaders. In a Minnesota study, elected and appointed officials in local government regarded media coverage of issues as helpful and not harmful to their group interests. By comparison, leaders of local groups and farm protest groups were more likely to see media coverage as nonsupportive or even harmful to their outcomes.

Guard dog reporting in social conflict has a sharper focus on role incumbents than on power structure, since structures are what the guard dog role is conditioned to protect. Such controversies as Watergate, Irangate, and corruption in the savings and loan industry seem to gravitate eventually to deviant individuals. When the general welfare of the system is threatened, there is little question that the individual may be sacrificed. The principle is that if the system is not preserved, individual rights will not survive either.

A prime process for conflict control, in which media as guard dogs participate heavily, is ritualistic controversy such as the political campaign. Reporting is less intense when the strategies of powerful actors are confined to the traditional rules of political conflict. Primaries are predictable in length of time, media appearances, political advertisements, occurrence of elections, poll reporting, and types of public events. This ritualistic coverage often ignores strategies for "changing the game," especially if they emanate from nonpowerful groups. George McGovern in the 1972 presidential campaign repeatedly raised questions about the Watergate break-in, but without succeeding in making it a priority news item. Instead, he was labelled as "shrill" and "strident" for repeating the charge of corruption. The major media story about Watergate emerged after the Nixon inauguration, after the FBI launched an investigation and arrests were made. Similarly, reporters in national news media during the late 1980s gave little coverage to growing evidence of a crisis in the savings and loan industry.

CONFLICT AND CONSENSUS IN HOMOGENEOUS STRUCTURES

This guard dog reporting of conflict and consensus is highly constrained by the social structure, which determines the nature of conflict itself. In some structures, the patterns of contact are largely on a primary, face-to-face basis, with a minimum of formally stated rules and a minimum of conflict reporting in mass media. These structures—such as small farming towns and mining communities—are marked by homogeneity in every sector, including religion, family, ethnicity, economy, and political groupings. Individuals encounter each other informally and in multiple capacities. The department store clerk and the insurance salesperson, although otherwise unrelated, will meet each other again and again at the local restaurant, in the supermarket, during religious worship, or at the annual community picnic or high school homecoming game. In this atmosphere, conflicts are difficult to separate and isolate.

While tensions are hardly unknown in such a community, they are relatively unlikely to surface as open intergroup differences. If a citizen has differences with the city council over a change in the land-use ordinance that would allow a fast-food franchise to go up next to the bank on Main Street, those differences may well be settled over the telephone or over coffee before the council proceeds to a vote. Or, if the issue is brought up afresh at a council meeting, a variety of interpersonal techniques may be employed to contain the problem and avoid a confrontation that is seen as disruptive (Hicks, 1946; Vidich & Bensman, 1958). The newspaper then reports the decision for or against the franchise as an orderly and consensual act, with minimal, if any, attention to the other side of the question. Even if the small-town newspaper editorially urges the council to make up its mind quickly, the typical effect is not to foment controversy but to reinforce the prevailing view of homogeneous structures that action is to be favored over lengthy deliberation. This is one of many forms of guard dog reinforcement of a consensus system.

Contrary to what might be assumed, "consensus" in such communities cannot be equated with widespread agreement or active support. There may be little awareness of the initial proposal from the fast-food company and the leadership may expend little effort in consulting widely. Consultation is primarily among the leadership elite, which might well include the would-be managers of a fast-food outlet. A public opinion poll might or might not support the views of the leaders, as has been found in various community studies (Nix & Seerley, 1975; Donohue, Olien, & Tichenor, 1975; Tichenor, Donohue, & Olien, 1977). The decision-making process as it plays out is dependent upon general acceptance of the fact that leadership has the power to decide.

Such acceptance of authority in the small town may or may not include strong convictions in the public at large about the *legitimacy* of the decision or the deciders. Membership on the town board, county board, or city council may be restricted to a small elite, turnout at elections may be meager, and acceptance of council decisions may be based upon popular feelings of resignation rather than popular admiration of the incumbents. "You can't fight city hall" is a well-known community belief. Its frequent expression is symptomatic of a condition of structurally maintained acceptance of authority.

This is not to say that "acceptance of authority" is a characteristic of small towns alone, since it is well known in bureaucratic structures at all levels of society. The difference is that the small, homogeneous structure is typically without mechanisms for effectively challenging authority—no pluralism, no conflict abatement procedures, no organized challenge, and no conflict reporting about the issue.

If this is a typical pattern of media reporting in small town structures, from whence comes the notion of the editorially outspoken small town editor? While that notion may to a certain extent be mythical, much of the conflictual energy in small towns is directed toward what are seen as external threats. The guard dog behavior of the press in a consensus community becomes especially apparent in editorials castigating external acts of higher levels of government that go against the grain of dominant local feeling, such as environmental restrictions that are seen as suppressing economic development in northern Minnesota, or state sanitation requirements that are seen as interfering with a small town's sewer system construction plans (Tichenor, Donohue, & Olien, 1980).

Such "guarding" tends to be ritualistic and reinforcing rather than investigative. Local leadership groups generally have their own contacts with external sources. They learn about federal agency grant programs, education statutes, state health requirements and effects of new tax legislation not from the local press, but from communications emanating directly from metropolitan centers. These may be metro mass media, bureaucratic memoranda, or interpersonal contacts.

Infrequent as public conflicts are in homogeneous communities, those initiated by external agencies may be especially intense. An illustrative case is the opposition to a high voltage powerline across Minnesota in the late 1970s, which arose when groups in a series of contiguous communities mobilized against an energy structure being proposed by a regional utility cooperative, with the tacit support of a state governmental agency that was technically neutral (Olien, Tichenor, & Donohue, 1980). Intensity of such conflicts stems from the fact that the local structure lacks such conflict control mechanisms as mediation agencies and labor–management negotiation procedures.

Conflicts within small, homogeneous communities may also be especially intense during times of major structural change (Gurr, 1972; Gricar & Brown, 1981). A northeastern Minnesota community for more than a decade had two weekly newspapers in direct competition for both readers and advertisers, taking opposing views on a number of local issues. The community was in transition from mining and logging to an economy oriented more heavily toward tourism. A second newspaper was established as a representative of the tourist interests and reflected—at times with considerable acrimony—the tensions between the traditional groups and the challenging tourist groups. During this transitional period, each competing group had its own media sentry.

Structural change and brief periods of intense conflict may also be seen in long-time farming communities that happen to be within the growth region of an expanding metropolis. As the community becomes the residential location of a new population with jobs elsewhere, the "new crowd" may challenge the traditional leadership for control of government, schools, and the churches. In some cases, a new weekly newspaper is established to reach this new audience, and the older one either changes, folds or merges with the new one as the community takes on a more distinctly suburban atmosphere and the power struggle is resolved in favor of the new residents or a coalition that leaves the traditional leadership with no alternative except to join. There comes a point when the leadership accepts the late Sam Rayburn's admonition that "to get along, you gotta go along." When the old guard becomes quiescent, its guard dogs are silent as well.

Similar short-term controversies have occurred between newspapers and cable television systems in a few metropolitan fringe communities, when competition for advertisers opened previously unexpressed animosities between newer and older commercial interests. One would expect these controversies to be resolved as turf becomes tacitly divided and advertisers revert to a predictable pattern of buying media space and/or time.

CONFLICT AND CONSENSUS IN PLURALISTIC STRUCTURES

While conflict does not occur without constraints, the constraints in a more pluralistic structure are quite different from those of the homogeneous community. Pluralism refers to the potential for a wide variety of social power groupings and is typical of metropolitan centers. These structures have a high degree of role specialization, greater differentiation among occupations, more formal bureaucracies in government, more extensively organized education, greater religious and ethnic diversity, and a tendency to evaluate performance on a meritocratic basis rather than on family and other primary group factors. Relationships are more structured and segregated, so that some are secondary for greater efficiency. Such face-to-face interactions as those in department stores, auto service centers and health clinics become highly specialized, limited to those who are part of the action. In the small town hardware store, one may have conversations with the clerk, the manager, and the other customers. In the urban store, the conversations are limited to the clerks or customer service representatives and deal with specific products and prices and little else. One's workaday life and family life are sharply separated, and face-to-face communication is inadequate for communication among groups and individuals. Interest groups and agencies of government, business, education, and religion depend upon secondary communications—including newspapers, television, radio, and magazines—for information about what other groups and agencies are doing.

In this urban structure, the various groups and agencies operate on more of a conflict model than a consensus model. The organization of activity recognizes conflict, the potential for it, and therefore the need to control it. The guard dog role of the media is tacitly acknowledged by leadership. There are extensive formal mechanisms for managing conflict and for "cooling out" groups that mobilize protests. The specialized court system, hearing procedures in governmental agencies, and complex labor–management negotiation procedures may be seen as mechanisms of this type. Each has a formal structure for dealing with grievances and tensions in a rationalized way designed to reduce tensions and coopt the protesting group. The press is one of these "cooling out" mechanisms.

In such a structure, the proposal to establish a fast-food franchise would follow a sequence of events very different from what would be seen in a small town. The metropolitan city council is fundamentally different in structure, being composed of representatives of interest groups rather than elites. The metro council is supported by a more extensive governmental bureaucracy, has more professional expertise available to it, and has developed procedures for dealing openly with conflict while at the same time keeping it within bounds and not threatening system stability.

The request for locating the fast-food franchise is referred initially to that segment of the government bureaucracy that interprets the zoning regulations. If a variance from those regulations is required, the issue is put on the council's meeting agenda and is potentially known to all reporters on the council beat. Should this variance be contrary to the interests of the surrounding neighborhood, there is more likely to be an organized presentation of those interests than would have been the case in the small town. Strategies for organizing protest are better known, there is more professional expertise available for such organization, and the council procedures are designed to take into account the possibility that protests may occur. The protesters, if organized well enough, may attract several media and get an entire hearing covered by prime-time television news. The ensuing council decision is then made in an atmosphere of considerable public attention, and yet has a routine character.

Media reporting and a certain conflictual atmosphere are all part of the routine. Media reporting contributes to management of conflict, even though the participants may criticize the media for either underreporting or overreporting the issue.

Research evidence on media reporting generally supports this structural conception of conflict processes. In an analysis of Minnesota community newspapers in 1965, weeklies in smaller and more homogeneous communities contained a lower proportion of conflict than did dailies in larger and more pluralistic communities. The differences were apparent in absolute amount of coverage as well as in proportion of news space devoted to conflict. It was also clear that the majority of the conflict in that year was in local government rather than in other institutions.

Later analyses, conducted in 1979 and again in 1985 among the same newspapers, pointed to some changes. As expected, the newspapers as a group devoted a higher proportion of space to conflict in later years as the system as a whole became more pluralistic. That is, the two decades after 1965 in Minnesota saw an increase in economic diversity, decreased dependence upon agriculture, increased education, and increased interdependence among communities. Also, the newspapers grew in size, so that the absolute increases in conflict reporting were even greater—amounting to a tripling, from an average of 15 column inches per edition in 1965 to 45 inches in 1979.

In both earlier and later analyses, conflict reporting was greater in the more pluralistic northeast and southeastern sections of the state than in the more homogeneous, rural farm southwest and northwest. However, it was also found that in 1979 and again in 1985, the regional daily newspapers no longer devoted a larger proportion of their news space to local controversy than did the weeklies. Since the dailies are published more frequently, they still had a larger absolute amount.

It appears that this changing orientation toward local conflict among regional dailies can be traced to a combination of factors including the changing nature of regional cities, changes in the media mix, and a shift to corporate ownership among daily newspapers. During the two decades after 1965, nonmetropolitan communities with dailies generally had greater population growth than did smaller ones, and in many cases this growth was in peripheral areas, following a pattern that had occurred earlier in center cities. Secondly, the large daily newspapers of the center cities reduced their circulation sharply in rural areas in response to the changing demographics and heavy "bottom line" pressure to concentrate circulation in the suburban residential areas containing the target populations sought by advertisers. Thirdly, the regional dailies were being bought out one by one by external corporations, so that by 1985 all except two of 19 studied were owned by corporations with multiple newspaper properties.

These factors converge to produce a changing orientation toward local reporting in regional daily newspapers. With an expanded residential population outside the home city boundaries, city council news no longer has quite the same relevance. The circulation pullback by the metro dailies in several cases led to increased circulation by regional dailies and a shift to a higher proportion of nonlocal news. The drop in local conflict reporting was greatest among those regional dailies under corporate ownership, a difference especially apparent in 1979 when roughly half were still locally owned. A further analysis in 1985 suggested that the corporate-owned regional dailies were more likely to concentrate on business news, including external business and economic reports. When editors were asked to name their top stories, those in corporate-owned dailies in 1985 were especially likely to put business reports in that category. This emphasis is consistent with the orientation of large corporations generally, and with the function of media in promoting economic growth and the interdependence between the community and the larger society.

CONFLICT AND KNOWLEDGE

The "stimulation and vitality" principle leads to the expectation that controversy would enhance the distribution, acquisition, and discussion of information. A considerable amount of evidence supports this expectation. Political scientists in early studies noted the relationship between intensities arising from political conflicts and the extent to which adult Americans possess information about political policies and objectives (Key, 1967; Hennessy, 1970; Almond & Verba, 1960; Lane & Sears, 1964). There appears to be more evidence leading to this conclusion than to the opposite one, that communication might be hampered by intense controversies (Lundberg, 1939; Williams, 1972).

Many of these studies employed the individual unit of analysis. A study with communities as analytic units provided evidence of the relationship among media coverage of issues, intensity of issues, and level of knowledge held by individuals within the communities (Tichenor, Donohue, & Olien, 1980). The analysis was based upon surveys in 19 community areas in Minnesota between 1969 and 1978, measuring knowledge about a variety of environmental and political issues that were the subjects of "top stories" of the time. These included allegations of pollution of Lake Superior by a taconite processing plant, mercury toxicity in lakes and rivers, banning certain pesticides, and establishing regional planning centers that were seen as potential threats to local autonomy.

The data provided support for several hypotheses derived from conflict theory. First respondent perception of conflict intensity was clearly higher in those communities where there had been heavier coverage of the issues in the media. The rank correlation between a newspaper coverage index and community perception of conflict, across the 19 communities, was .58 and statistically significant. A second finding was that the higher the perceived conflict about an issue, the more people talked to others in the community about the issue. A third finding was that the more interpersonal communication occurred, the greater the number of persons in the community who were familiar with the issue. The pattern was indirect, in that media coverage by itself was not strongly associated with familiarity. Instead, it appeared that media reinforced a perception of intensity, which led to more discussion and, ultimately, to greater familiarity.

Another analysis of the data from the 19 communities concerned the relationship between conflict intensity and gaps in knowledge between more and less educated groups. Previous research had supported the hypothesis that the heavier the media publicity about an issue, the greater the gap in knowledge between the different educational levels (Tichenor, Donohue, & Olien, 1970). These gaps are a result of both (1) the trained capacities that accompany formal education for seeking and acquiring information from media and (2) characteristics of media reporting and distribution that are designed to appeal particularly to more affluent groups that also have higher levels of formal education. The issues in question, in the earlier knowledge studies, were primarily national in scope. They included familiarity with outer space research and a variety of health issues, such as the question of a link between smoking and lung cancer.

Conflict theory also leads to the reasoning that the more intense a controversy, the more likely all groups in the community are to be attuned to the issues and to follow media reports about it. The data, across the 19 Minnesota communities, supported this reasoning as well as the notion that conflict may produce a certain amount of equalization of acquisition of information. The higher the intensity about an issue, the less the magnitude of the gap that occurred in knowledge about that issue between groups higher and lower in education.

In these particular studies, the highest intensities were in one small town with a long-standing sewage disposal problem and another facing a problem of toxicity in a local lake. Both cases involved a conflict between the local community and state agencies. In the first, the community had for years been under pressure from a state agency to construct a system for treating sewage, and the projected cost and how to finance it were matters of intense local controversy. In the second, the community bordered a large lake that was a popular spot for both fishing and water sports. A federal–state report indicated that fish taken from this particular lake contained high levels of mercury and, therefore, should be eaten in limited amounts, if at all. The report had received heavy local and statewide publicity, and the local newspaper charged that the community was being unfairly "singled out" in the report. The town, the editorial suggested, might lose its reputation as a popular resort area and suffer a drop in seasonal business as a result of the report. While interviews were being conducted in the community, the state health department took the lake off the "mercury danger list," in effect refuting the earlier report.

The first conflict raised questions about property taxes, as well as about the capacity of local government to resolve a problem. The second involved a threat both to local identity and to a major source of local income. In each community, more than a third of the respondents had reported discussing the issue recently with someone else. Familiarity with the issue was nearly universal and, therefore, did not vary appreciably according to education or any other characteristic.

CONFLICT AND PERSUASION

While there is little research evidence that speaks directly to the question, one might inquire whether conflict and conflict intensity bear a systematic relationship to opinions held in the population. One generalization that can be gleaned from the literature is that the more intense respondents are about an issue, the more likely they are to have opinions on those issues and to be involved, such as through political participation. (Key, 1967, p. 226ff.).

Analysis of a powerline protest provided some evidence on the relationship between conflict intensity and opinion holding. In this particular case, respondents who saw the powerline as a "touchy subject" (i.e., regarded it as an intense issue) were more likely to be opposed to the powerline than those who did not recognize the issue as intense.

Data from this analysis also suggest a role of the media in opinion formation. The correlations between use of newspapers as sources and perception of conflict were direct and consistent, ranging from .22 to .52 in the early stages of the protest. Attention to newspapers may have led to greater perception of the issue as a controversy, thereby reinforcing a definition of the situation that highlights the struggle and elicits sympathy for the protestors' arguments. Protest groups may find that achieving public recognition of a conflict through publicity is equivalent to getting some support from the public. In the powerline analysis, the media role in achieving such support appeared to be indirect, in that the zero-order correlations between media use and opinions were low and statistically insignificant. The indirectness of this relationship may well be important, given the lack of relationship in other studies between media consumption and perception of dimensions of social conflicts (Cohen, Adoni, & Bantz, 1990).

CONFLICT CONTAINMENT IN PLURALISTIC STRUCTURES

The tendency of conflict to stimulate thought and communication and even give the community some vitality does not prevent individual actors, including those in pluralistic structures, from preferring consensus. It is the system that maintains the pattern of formal organization and reporting of conflictual issues that is often contrary to individual interests. There is a *recognition* of the conflict mode of operation that characterizes a pluralistic system in which consensual decision making is nevertheless held to as an ideal. President Lyndon Johnson's repeated urging to political leaders to "come reason together," however unrealistic it was, expressed both the wish for consensus and the recognition of conflict during the 1960s, a time of increasing pluralism in the nation as a whole.

Several procedures in pluralistic systems, in fact, are quite explicitly designed to moderate if not eliminate certain kinds of conflict. Leadership insistence upon eliminating the ward system in school districts and cities is illustrative. Metropolitan and suburban school boards often insist that at-large representation is essential to avoid "being pressured by special interest groups" so that elected leaders will be "more concerned about the community as a whole." One consequence is that a neighborhood concerned about an issue such as school bus service has no one board representative to represent their local concerns. The same board may issue statements regretting low turnout at elections, without necessarily recognizing the fact that the existing structure works against high participation. Nevertheless, the widespread existence of at-large representation on boards and councils testifies to its importance in conflict management. This arrangement serves to ward off conflicts involving concerns of groups with marginal power status while concentrating on "legitimate issues" brought up by the major power centers of the community or region. Dismissing a concern as one of "special interests" is often a signal that the protesting group has marginal power.

This analysis of overt conflict limitation may seem to fly in the face of the view that participation adds to legitimation of authority (e.g., Ginsberg, 1982). It might be pointed out that participation is a mechanism for maintaining legitimacy, but not necessarily the only one. Many structures retain high legitimacy for long periods of time without undergoing serious challenge, such as the medical community of the U.S., especially during the first two decades after World War II. There may be a point when an organizational structure falls into an ossifying routine, and challenge from other groups may stimulate innovations in organizational structure. It takes organization to challenge structure, and the challenging groups may be bureaucracies themselves. When that occurs, as with challenges of organized citizen groups before the city council, the council's response is often to strike a compromise that defuses the protest and in the process adds to the council's legitimacy. Media reporting reinforces this legitimacy.

While conflict situations often stimulate communication, interest, and thought, a point of public disinterest and even disgust may be reached in conflicts that are perceived to be without solution, lost causes, or both. "All they do is bicker," is a reason often offered for ignoring an intractable public issue. Existence of such a view, while often decried as apathy, may nevertheless be functional for maintenance of a particular leadership group and containment of conflict intensity.

Structural dependence upon apathy as a form of social control is sometimes noted in the breach. In 1970, the University of Wisconsin campus was the center of intense antiwar demonstrations that included widespread student strikes, graffiti on classroom walls and, eventually, some violent encounters with law enforcement officers. The institution's President in a faculty meeting that year noted with a tone of both candor and irony: "Remember the 1950's, when we urged students to get involved? Well, they took our advice" (Tichenor, 1970).

CONFLICT FUNCTIONS AND STAGES OF PROTEST

Conflict theorists such as Simmel, Coser, and Dahrendorf noted various functions of conflict, such as the increasing vitality it yields, but did not contend that conflict *invariably* has such consequences. A hypothesis suggested by recent investigations is that the specific consequences may depend upon the stage of the conflict process and the nature of the conflict management procedures employed at a given stage. The Minnesota powerline dispute occurred over a period of years and according to different stages, which were defined as problem definition, bureaucratic confrontation, and demonstration confrontation.

That is, the initial year or more was a period when various protesting groups organized in opposition to construction of the powerline. The second stage, that of bureaucratic confrontation, included a period of governmentally sponsored hearings for adjudication of the line location. These hearings, patterned after judicial procedures, typify the formal conflict management procedures that keep controversy at a moderate level without involving intense interpersonal contacts.

Such conflict management procedures are not universally admired. The powerline protest entered a third phase of demonstrations when protesting groups concluded that the "neutral" public agencies in fact favored the powerline project. The protest demonstrations reached crescendo intensity *after* the State Supreme Court had ruled that the project could proceed and work proceeded at construction sites. By this time, however, the protest was a lost cause and was symbolic of this defeat.

Surveys were conducted during each of these phases, and analysis of both media content and measures of audience knowledge revealed a shift over time in what media reported and what information the public possessed. In the initial stages, the reporting centered around the technical questions of line location, voltage, line spans, and problems of potentially harmful energy transmission from the 400-kilovolt direct current lines to human beings and animals. The audience surveys indicated considerable awareness of these issues.

As the protest moved to a demonstration phase, the issue became one of conflict resolution and the coverage shifted from newspapers alone to domination by television. In fact, in the final year, the powerline protest was named by television announcers as the "top story" in Minnesota. Both the coverage and the responses of individuals tended to concentrate on the conflict itself and the particulars of the confrontations, such as the various (and innovative) picketing strategies employed. These strategies included demonstrators spraying the construction sites with gaseous fertilizer, putting flowers in the buttonholes of police officers, and smearing themselves with animal feces while inviting the highway patrol officers to arrest them.

At this stage, responses to the knowledge measurement questions among audience members were dominated by these events, while questions of technical characteristics of the line and the possibility of negative health effects were mentioned with decreasing frequency. This appeared to be a result of both the stage of the process and the powerful role of television, which concentrates on visualized events rather than on in-depth knowledge. Along with an awareness primarily of the confrontations, survey responses indicated increasing distaste for the controversy—in spite of a continued majority belief that the "farmers were right" in opposing the line.

This analysis suggested a hypotheses for further testing, that the "knowledge-stimulation" effects of conflict occur primarily during periods of initial mobilization and that popular distaste for conflict becomes increasingly likely with protracted disputes. If supported in further research, this hypothesis would have extensive theoretical import and practical implications for information campaigns. The implications might well be complex, since creation of popular distaste may or may not be in the interests of various groups counterpoised to each other in a conflict. As indicated above, popular aversion to a controversy may in some cases work to the advantage of established groups who are waiting for a protest group's energy and public support to dwindle. This is what occurred in the powerline controversy. On the other hand, popular disaffection may work to the advantage of a labor union on strike if the disaffection is directed toward absence of consumer goods that might become available again if the strike were to be settled.

CONFLICT AND PUBLIC OPINION

We return here to a question posed at the outset: what is the role of media in reporting conflict and consensus, and how does this reporting affect those perceptions and outlooks we call "public opinion"? From the preceding discussion, a few summary generalizations may be offered.

1. *Conflict, as a major element of media reporting, is an aspect of social control*. Reporting conflict is part of the process of conflict management, which, while often functional for the ends of advocacy groups, often has the consequence of "cooling out" these groups.

2. *Conflict reporting further serves system maintenance by concentrating on relationships between the major powers in the system*. When a president and Congress disagree on a foreign policy question, that conflict constitutes major news, while a disagreement between politically marginal groups gets little attention. Such attention to disputes among the major powers serves to reinforce those powers.

3. *The notion that media play a watchdog role in reporting conflict is a myth*. The metaphor of "guard dog" is more appropriate, since this label recognizes dependence of the media on dominant powers and relationships among them. A principal characteristic of guard dog reporting is focus on role incumbents rather than structural features of the system.

4. *Conflict reporting is constrained in different ways, depending upon community structure*. The more pluralistic the structure, the more likely it will operate on a conflict model and the more likely it is that the media will report conflict in public life.

5. *Conflict is a major stimulator of knowledge formation*. The more intense the conflict about an issue, the greater the amount of information generated and reported, and the more likely media audiences are to be knowledgeable about the issue.

6. *Conflict is a stimulator of opinion formation*. The more intense the public controversy, the more likely members of the public are to hold and express opinions on the issue.

7. *Conflicts may have a legitimizing function for specific public opinions*. Under some conditions, creation of a controversy may be instrumental for attaining public sympathy or support for one side of an issue. This appears to occur through the tendency of a conflict situation to legitimize the sheer existence of the issue. Conversely, dominant groups seeking to ward off challenges will typically downplay the elements of controversy, thereby withdrawing legitimacy from alternative views.

8. *Whether conflict has a legitimizing function for public opinion may depend upon the stage of the controversy*. During a period of initial mobilization, the stimulating aspects of controversy may work to the advantage of challenging groups. If the issue wears on and appears irresolvable, however, a sense of public aversion to the entire issue may develop, leading to withdrawal of attention and support and pressure to settle.

Most if not all public opinion is about conflictual issues and how they should be resolved. Information may be both generator and outcome of conflict, a result of the tendency of media to report those issues that have either the potential of conflict arousal or have already achieved that status. The basic conditions and processes involved in this media reporting, and audience reaction to it, remain as a central concern for social science research.

REFERENCES

Almond, G., & Verba, S. (1960). *The civic culture: Political attitudes and democracy in five nations*. Princeton, NJ: Princeton University Press.

Bernard, T. J. (1983). *The consensus-conflict debate: Form and content in social theories*. New York: Columbia University Press.

Black, G. S. (1974). Conflict in the community: A theory of the effects of community size. *American Political Science Review, 68*, 1245–1261.

Boyce, G. (1978). The fourth estate: The reappraisal of a concept. In G. Boyce, J. Curran, & P. Wingate (Eds.), *Newspaper history: From the 17th century to the present day* (pp. 19–40). London & New York: Constable/Sage.

Breed, W. (1958). Mass communication and sociocultural integration. *Social Forces, 37*, 109–116.

Carlyle, T. (1963). *On heroes and hero worship*. London: Oxford University Press. (Original work published in 1841)

Cohen, A. A., Adoni, H., & Bantz, C. R. (1990). *Social conflict and television news*. Newbury Park, CA: Sage.

Coser, L. (1954). *The functions of social conflict*. New York: Macmillan.

Coser, L. (1967). *Continuities in the study of social conflict*. New York: Macmillan.

Dahrendorf, R. (1959). *Class and class conflict in industrial society*. Stanford, CA: Stanford University Press.

Donohue, G. A., Tichenor, P. J., & Olien, C. N. (1975). Mass media and the knowledge gap: A hypothesis reconsidered. *Communication Research, 2*, 3–23.

Edelstein, A., & Schulz, J. B. (1963). The weekly newspaper's leadership role as seen by community leaders. *Journalism Quarterly, 40*, 565–574.

Gans, H. L. (1979). *Deciding what's news: A study of CBS evening news, NBC Nightly News, Newsweek and Time*. New York: Pantheon.

Ginsberg, B. (1982). *The consequences of consent*. Reading, MA: Addison-Wesley.

Gricar, B. G., & Brown, L. D. (1981). Conflict, power, and organization in a changing community. *Human Relations, 34*, 877–893.

Gumplowicz, L. (1894). *The outlines of sociology* (F. W. Moore, Trans.). Philadelphia: American Academy of Political and Social Science.

Gurr, T. S. (1972). The calculus of civil conflict. *Journal of Social Sciences, 28*, 1, 27–47.

Hennessy, B. (1970). *Public opinion*. Belmont, CA: Wadsworth.

Herman, E. S. (1985). Diversity of news: Marginalizing the opposition. *Journal of Communication, 35*, 3, 135–146.

Hicks, G. (1946). *Small town*. New York: Macmillan.

Janowitz, M. (1952). *The community press in an urban setting*. New York: Free Press.

Key, V. O. (1967). *Public opinion and American democracy*. New York: Alfred A. Knopf.

Lane, R. E., & Sears, D. O. (1964). *Public opinion*. Englewood Cliffs, NJ: Prentice-Hall.

Lichtenberger, J. P. (1923). *Development of social theory*. New York: The Century Company.

Lippman, W. (1962). *Public opinion*. New York: Macmillan.

Lippmann, W. (1925). *The phantom public*. New York: Harcourt, Brace and Company.

Lundberg, G. A. (1939). *The foundations of sociology*. New York: Macmillan.

Martindale, D. (1963). *Community, character, and civilization*. New York: Free Press.

Nix, H. L., & Seerley, N. R. (1973). Comparative views and actions of community leaders and nonleaders. *Rural Sociology, 38*, 4, 427–438.

Schumpeter, J. A. (1976). *Capitalism, socialism and democracy*. London: George Allen and Unwin, Ltd.

Shoemaker, D. (1984). Media treatment of deviant groups. *Journalism Quarterly, 61*, 66–75.

Simmel, G. (1955). *Conflict and the web of group affiliations*. Glencoe IL: Free Press.

Swanson, C. E. (1949). Midcity daily: The news staff and its relation to control. *Journalism Quarterly, 26*, 20–28.

Tichenor, P. J. (1970). Personal notes from an October, 1970 faculty assembly, University of Wisconsin, Madison.

Tichenor, P. J., Donohue, G. A., & Olien, C. N. (1970a). *Community conflict and the press*. Newbury Park, CA: Sage.

Tichenor, P. J., Donohue, G. A., & Olien, C. N. (1970b). Mass media flow and differential growth in knowledge. *Public Opinion Quarterly, 34*, 159–170.

Tichenor, P. J., Olien, C. N., Harrison, A., & Donohue, G. A., (1970). Mass communication systems and communication accuracy in science news reporting. *Journalism Quarterly, 47*, 673–683.

Tichenor, P. J., Donohue, G. A., & Olien, C. N. (1977). Community research and community relations. *Public Relations Review, 3*(4): 96–109.

Vidich, A. J., & Bensman, J. (1958). *Small town in mass society*. Princeton, NJ: Princeton University Press.

Williams, R. M., Jr. (1972). Conflict and social order: A reserach strategy for complex propositions. *Journal of Social Issues, 28*, 1, 11–26.

13

Origins and Consequences of Mediated Public Opinion

Klaus Schoenbach
Lee B. Becker

"OPINIONS" AND "PUBLIC OPINION"

Every day there are hundreds of "public opinion" polls under way. Opinions about products, about institutions, and about advertising campaigns are gauged. Governments and political parties keep market research companies busy: every single week since 1950, for instance, the (West) German government has received a report about its image, about the issues the people believe to be the most important, and about the public's satisfaction with how the economy runs (Schmidtchen, 1965, 220 ff.).

But do these surveys really describe the state of "*public* opinion"? First of all, what is an "opinion"? Opinions, as they are measured in "public opinion" surveys, are both "beliefs" and "attitudes." According to Fishbein and Ajzen (1975, p. 12), beliefs are cognitions that link attributes to objects; they are "pictures in our heads," as Lippmann (1922) put it. Objects can be persons, groups, institutions, behaviors, events, and so on. Attributes of these objects comprise qualities, characteristic features, causes, consequences, but also other objects related to the one to be described. One special case of "beliefs" are "images"; images link persons, institutions, groups, or products as objects to character traits, aims, and other qualities. An "attitude," according to Fishbein and Ajzen (1975, p. 6) is "a learned predisposition to respond in a consistently favorable or unfavorable manner with respect to a given object."

As to the *objects* of "opinions" in everyday "public opinion" research, their range reaches beyond mere *public* images of persons and institutions and also does not only contain *political* beliefs and attitudes. Such a wide definition of "opinion" is in accordance with how the objects of "public opinion" have been defined early on. A review of the literature shows that the earliest definitions of "public opinion" (e.g., by Locke or Rousseau) subsume opinions about people, institutions, values, norms, and even lifestyles and fashions (see Noelle, 1966).

Now, what makes an opinion—be it belief or attitude—"public"? Is public opinion—as the survey technique suggests—(1) simply any opinion held by a *majority* of citizens (one of the definitions of public opinion suggested by de Sola Pool in 1973)—a "volonté de tous," as Rousseau called it in the 18th century? Or is it rather (2) "public reasoning," the opinion of those who either have the intellectual capabilities to arrive at socially useful beliefs and attitudes and to discuss them publicly (see, e.g., Habermas, 1962), and/or have the power and the instruments to make their views publicly known? Examples of such "publics" are TV commentators, professors, bishops, politicians, newspaper publishers, and interest groups (Hennis, 1957). Or is it, finally, (3) any opinion concerning *public affairs* (de Sola Pool, 1973)?

The first definition regards public opinion under a democratic perspective, where every single opinion counts; the number of people sharing a specific opinion is important, and surveys intended to find out this number are useful. The second definition clearly is an elitist one: only the opinions of certain persons, legitimized either by their expertness or their power, are really significant. The public may share these opinions or may not. Since these opinions come from people supposedly with insight into and responsibility for the complicated mechanisms of a community, the "common" people are *expected* to share them. Given this definition of public opinion, representative surveys of the population in order to find out what is public opinion are not only superfluous, but simply wrong (see, e.g., Hennis, 1957). The third definition, finally, is a topic-centered one; it does not say anything about those who hold "public" opinions.

A variant of these three definitions is put forward by Graber (1982). She defines public opinion as (4) a consensus about a matter of political concern, as opposed to public pseudo-opinions, which are politically relevant opinions expressed by different sub-publics. Pseudo-opinions lack a sound information base and the honing that comes from dialogue and debate. Similarly, Price and Roberts (1987) define public opinion in terms of a *public process*, not as a summation of individual opinions. This means that there is a process by which the public becomes aware of, seeks to understand, and develops policy toward issues. From the point of view of the individual, this is fundamentally a learning experience. We learn from personal discussions, from our own thinking about the issues, and from the information we encounter in the mass media.

Noelle-Neumann (1977, p. 205) identifies "public opinion" as (5) any opinion that everybody can "make public," that everybody is allowed to openly express without fear of being socially isolated. For Noelle-Neumann, public opinion definitely has to do with *all* people, similar to what the first definition mentioned above suggested. However, public opinion is not only a matter of numbers, it is a matter of visibility. It even can be the opinion of a minority. What counts is that this minority speaks up and behaves as if it were a majority or soon would become one. Noelle-Neumann believes that, in most cases, it is fairly easy to find out which opinion can be expressed openly without any negative sanctions—the "public opinion"—and which cannot. She argues that humans, as social beings, have a "quasi-statistical sense" making them aware of which opinion is fashionable and which is not. This fifth type of public opinion works as an institution of social control. Public opinion, in Noelle-Neumann's sense, exercizes pressure on the members of society; they keep silent, if they believe themselves to be in the minority. In democratic cultures, it puts leaders under pressure, too. Public opinion as an institution of society controls the state and the elites, forcing them to act in specific ways.

De Sola Pool (1973) argues that if public opinion is opinions *publicly expressed*, we can talk about the emergence of public opinion in society and contrast societies in terms of existence or absence of public opinion. In this way, the change in Europe in the quiet revolution of 1989 and 1990 (Echikson, 1990) was a change reflected in the emergence of public opinion for the first time ever. At first, people uttered their opinions through their feet, an old way of such expression of opinion in Europe. Before long, however, these subdued but unmistakable expressions of public opinion were followed by opinions articulated through placards and speeches, often amplified through the voices of the newly freed or newly confident media. Finally, of course, the societies allowed for a free expression of the public's opinions.

DIFFERENT WAYS MASS MEDIA IMPACT PUBLIC OPINION

All the definitions of public opinion outlined above, except for the first, share one important communality: the element of publicity. And here, the mass media come into play. In large, complex societies opinions very often only become *majority ones* because they are disseminated via television, radio, newspapers, and magazines. And even if we regard public opinion as the result of a discourse of the intellectual and the powerful, media—for example, certain elitist journals—are the conveyor belts of public opinion.

In this sense, then, the study of public opinion necessarily involves consideration of the role the media play in publicizing, shaping and creating that public opinion. Public opinion analysis is necessarily also media analysis. There are at least three ways by which the media may influence public opinion:

1. The first one may be called a direct method: the media communicate events, arguments, and opinions that change the minds of their audience about the importance or the structure of specific topics.
2. The two other ways are more subtle and indirect. Here, the audience is not necessarily presented with good arguments for accepting something as public opinion, but is confronted with indications of what already seems to be public opinion. The media convey impressions of how accepted an opinion may be and whether a minority opinion may be successful in the future. Thus the media help the individual find out what can be expressed openly.
3. In addition, the media claim to mirror society, and journalists claim to be representatives of the common interests of society. In this fashion, there is the suggestion that the media contains indication of what others besides the editors and reporters think and are concerned about.

There are three different ideal–typical ways in which mass media can provide us with information that might become the material for public opinion in most of the definitions described above (see also Ronneberger, 1973):

1. Mass media can serve as mere conveyor belts. New or different beliefs and attitudes to be dispersed into the public are defined by elite persons or groups. Mass media simply offer them to their mass audience without any alterations. This process may work the other way round as well. The mass media take up what is of popular concern, publish it—acting in the "mirror role" of the media—and thus pass it on to the elite.
2. Mass media use elite or mass opinions as raw material, but feel

free to *select* and to *emphasize* those views they believe to be worthy of being published.

3. Mass media professionals and organizations themselves *create* images and find issues. In this case, they take a role as "molders" of public opinion.

At all times, and in all societies, the mass media may have been trying to be *both* molders and mirrors of public opinion (Rosengren, 1972). It is not very probable that they have ever been a mere "forum," a pure transmission instrument of opinions in society, as the first role described above suggests; The pressure of being selective in what to publish is too great. It is thus reasonable to assume that in Western societies today the primarily second and third roles described above apply. The press, television, and radio select, sometimes even push, opinions that they see as worthwhile to become "public." They do so not necessarily by offering beliefs and attitudes explicitly. Rarely in any Western newspaper report or television program would we find phrases like, "This is a new opinion about foreign policy that we urge you to accept as your own." Instead, the media most often present events as if they were mere depictions of what happened in the world. They describe events, they picture people, they quote what prominent persons say. Audience opinions and, at least sometimes, public opinion may follow implicitly, by interpreting the images offered by the media. We thus have to look primarily to news and entertainment as the main sources for opinions about oneself and the world, rather than at special "opinion" articles or programs, such as editorials or commentaries.

If the media are not mere conveyors of opinions stemming either from the elite or the mass public, questions such as the following become important: who determines which views of the world are published? According to which criteria does that happen? We must ask these same questions for news and for entertainment.

NEWS AND MEDIA ENTERTAINMENT AS DETERMINANTS OF PUBLIC OPINION

For more than 40 years, research results have shown that not every opinion has the same or even any chance to be published. The criteria journalists use when they select and create views of the world are obviously not as haphazard or idiosyncratic as one might suppose or even hope for (see also Schoenbach, 1983a). There is enough evidence that—despite freedom of the press and the nominal pluralism of mass communication—the media create a surprisingly consonant image of important issues, in both their news reporting and their entertainment sections.

In a Norwegian study, Galtung and Ruge (1970) suggested that some criteria of news selection and presentation are common to all media in a specific culture, in fact, some even to all media of the world. The greater the cultural proximity of an event is, they wrote, the more probable that it gets published. Perceived relevance for one's own group or country is another important criterion. Consonance with what is expected—plus a certain amount of surprise within this consonance—also helps information to enter the media, as do other characteristics, such as the short duration of an event, or its simple structure. Schulz (1982) goes even further: the mere perception, the isolation of specific events that may be selected for later publication, is guided by structural principles of the social *construction* of reality. These principles are very similar to the ones that the psychology of perception has found as anthropological constants.

The two Norwegian authors assumed furthermore that four specific selection criteria apply to Western Europe and North America better than to other regions: events and opinions related to "elite nations" (those with great political and economic power) and to "elite persons" (prominent and/or powerful figures) have a good chance to be published. "Personalization" (opinions that can be ascribed to specific people) and negativism (indications and warnings of dangers, disasters, crises) are the two other characteristics of opinions and events enhancing their publication.

The selection of newsworthy information, according to Galtung and Ruge (1970), is not a sinister conspiracy of some journalists and their powerful sources. It is guided by mostly subconcious ideologies. Basic philosophical assumptions of a culture are represented in it (see also Schoenbach, 1983a):

- Personalization, for instance, can be derived from cultural idealism; human beings are regarded as masters of their destinies.
- Negative news is worth reporting in societies that take for granted an inevitably positive evolution.
- A basic notion of Augustinian philosophy is to assume a linear and persistent movement of society toward an ultimate and positive goal. Thus in Western societies unambiguous, literally "straightforward," occurrences have a better chance of becoming news than "slow-moving historical circles" or "indeterminate or fluid" situations (Rock, 1973, p. 77).

Schulz (1976) speculated about the purposes for which Western cultures maintain the guidelines for news that Galtung and Ruge (1970) hypothesized. Using the system-functional perspective, he argues that to be highly selective in news making is functional in a system that tries to make sure its members are able to take common action by sharing perceptions—which constitutes a *public* opinion—of what is at stake. Since society can pay only a limited amount of attention to events, *negative* occurrences threatening the order of a system must be dealt with extensively. Functional in this sense is everything that stabilizes the system. Concentration on elite actions, for instance, assures members of society that there is sufficient continuity in political and social life: the same people make news all the time.

Several content analyses have shown that news indeed tends to offer uniform views about ourselves and the world around us. For example, as early as 1960, Guback (1968) found that 15 different radio stations framed an important speech by John F. Kennedy about the U.S. Cuban policy as an election campaign event, even though Kennedy had dealt in his speech with his rival Richard Nixon only for a few minutes. The result was that the listeners did not learn anything about Kennedy's stand on Cuba. Three British researchers (Halloran, Elliott, & Murdock, 1970) found that in spite of both ideological and qualitative differences of the media, the news coverage of a 1968 anti-Vietnam War demonstration in London had been focusing on the same limited aspect of the upcoming event: it was reported as necessarily violent. After the demonstration was over and only a handful of the 60,000 marchers had had a short scuffle with the police, the media nevertheless maintained the violent image they had constructed of the march by putting the rare violent scenes at the center of their reporting.

The Glasgow University Media Group (1976) found an amazing similarity in the images that the two British TV networks BBC (a public TV company) and ITN (a commercial one) depicted of industrial life: "It is like looking at the synoptic gospels, and facing the almost irresistible question: what is their common source?" (p. 203). Similarly, based on a study of almost 6,000 news items in ten different West German media, Schulz (1976) confirmed that news heavily concentrates on elite persons, elite nations, negative events, and actions of individuals. Differences among the media observed were small; their consonance was striking. Similar results were reported by Schatz (1980), and Lange (1981).

In the international coverage of Swedish newspapers, orientation toward clearly structurable *events* is overwhelmingly more frequent than the description of *processes* (Hedman, 1981). The results of Schoenbach and Schulz (1980) are very similar: West German media depict an image of third world countries that strips reality down to a limited number of event types (mainly wars, catastrophes, crimes, etc.), locales (primarily the capitals) and persons (leaders, prominent people). Meier and Schanne (1983) reveal that Swiss newspapers uniformly focus on economically powerful nations: 27% of international news refers to only four countries. Schoenbach (1978) was able to show that negativism and elite action are common criteria even for the selection of local news in newspapers. Kepplinger (1989) found that negative reporting continues even when the problem becomes less pronounced.

The above-cited studies, undertaken largely by European scholars, underscore the observation that news is highly patterned, and that, as a consequence, not every opinion has the same probability of being represented in the mass media. Examples of relevant American research leading to this same conclusion can be found in Paletz and Entman (1981). Also, recent reviews of this literature appeared in Shoemaker (1987) and Shoemaker and Reese (1991).

Of course, there is some variety within the above-described general framework: the media may be elite-centered, but they may report about *different* elites. They may be negativistic, but they definitely choose between murders (tabloids) and bankruptcies (prestige papers). Nevertheless, it looks as if there is an elitist bias in the image of the world offered by Western media. Prominent people and organized pressure groups definitely have better access to the mass media. Their opinions are more often presented as, if not "public," then at least published. This is not necessarily done in a direct, manipulating way, but simply (1) because news values are favourable for them, and because journalists in leading positions are part of the elite themselves, sharing its views anyway (see, e.g., Hoffmann-Lange & Schoenbach, 1979; McQuail, 1983, p. 356).

There is *manifest* evidence of the elite's image-defining power in a study by Noelle-Neumann and Kepplinger (1978). They found that in the German city of Mainz, the local newspaper mirrored quite well the issues the local *elite* had called important in surveys conducted during the same period of time. Thus workers in Mainz learned from their newspaper what problems the elite had in mind, whereas the elite itself had only a very vague impression of what workers found important.

George Gerbner and his colleagues offer the most evidence about how mass-media *entertainment* depicts us and our environment (see a summary of this research in Signorielli & Morgan, 1990). Television entertainment particularly is middle-class centered and very violent (see also Bouwman's [1982] analysis of violence in Dutch television entertainment). Earlier work by Adorno (1967), Scheuch (1971), and Holzer (1971), among others, had already speculated about a uniform picture of the world that mass-media entertainment, particularly that of television, offers in Western societies: it was assumed to be conservative and slightly elevated (i.e., with some, but not too many improbable and exotic features). Traditional roles were said to be confirmed, the order of society not questioned. Luck was assumed to play an important role in rewarding or punishing the actors. After some trouble, conflicts seem always to be resolved; there is usually general harmony in the end (see also Greenberg, 1980; Cantor & Pingree, 1983). Turow (1984) argues that these media entertainment biases result from the needs of the various media organizations themselves.

While an exhaustive review of this literature is beyond the scope of this chapter, it is clear that media entertainment content is highly patterned. As was true for news content, the presented entertainment content selectively presents opinions and the raw materials in which opinions can be based.

MEDIA EFFECTS ON THE FORMATION OF PUBLIC OPINION

What do the results we present here about the media's picture of the world mean for the formation of public opinion? First of all, they simply indicate that mass publics are permanently confronted not with a totally pluralistic, but with a specifically focused picture of their environment. Of course, this picture does not necessarily influence the views people themselves have of what is going on. They could simply reject media contents and declare them unreal. They usually do not, because the media image has an impact on them. This is not only highly plausible, but there also is evidence for it.

The impact of the mass media's picture of the world on the mass public is particularly plausible in large and complex societies. Where else should most of our images come from—images about what is going on in national and international politics, in cultural life, in fashion and in customs and mores—if not from the media? Kepplinger (1975) even assumes that the "real culture" is replaced by a "media culture" that is as real for most of the people as reality itself. Studies showing that media coverage does directly influence public opinion include the early work of British researchers Trenaman and McQuail (1961), who reported at least a correspondence between media coverage and what people think. These authors found that the way the electorate rank ordered the importance of seven national issues was fairly similar to that ordering in the media coverage. This was an early indication of an "agenda-setting" effect. Convincing empirical results suggest that this correspondence between media and public is caused by the media themselves; they *shape* their audience's picture of the world rather than *reflect* it.

Examples primarily from the United States of "agenda-setting" research can be found in Protess and McCombs (1991). Less well known is the European work on this topic. For example, in a panel study, Schulz (1978) demonstrated an amazingly clear causal relationship between media coverage and the political events that the audience declared important. Schoenbach (1983b), also in a panel survey, of the West German electorate in 1979, showed that media use led to increased salience of a specific issue: European politics (see also Schoenbach, 1982).

An interesting result can be found in a multinational study about the media's role in the first European election campaign in 1979 (Thoveron & Sauerberg, 1983). All over Western Europe, there was a strong correlation between which political issues television was emphasizing (European integration and agricultural policy) and the notions of *heavy viewers* of television campaign coverage. But this agenda-setting effect is confined to that group alone. The largest portion of the voters—those having encountered TV information about the election only occasionally—kept insisting on issues closer to their everyday lives, such as the economy or energy politics. Quite similar results are reported in Buss and Ehlers' (1982) study of the 1980 national election in West Germany.

People's serious concerns about the energy supply in West Germany and hysterical behaviour during the first so-called oil crisis in 1973 were, according to Kepplinger and Roth's (1978) study, a consequence of media coverage alone. They maintain that the actual oil supply did not justify the term "crisis" at all. In a study of the long-term impact of television news, Kepplinger, Brosius, Gotto, and Haak (1989) found both clear-cut agenda-setting effects of the news for some topics and a complete ignorance of other topics also covered by television, depending on how relevant the audience felt these issues to be for their everyday life. Schoenbach (1987) found that an AIDS campaign by the German tabloid "BILD" had a tremendous short-term impact on the public salience of that issue. Within a month, the proportion of people regarding AIDS as one of the most important problems rose from two to 22%.

The evidence that the media alter the public's picture of the world is not limited to the area of agenda setting. For example, Noelle-Neumann (1977), in her study of voters' opinions about which party might win the 1976 West German national election, found that heavy viewers of political programs on television revealed a slightly different estimation of the potential winner. Hildebrandt (1984), in his analysis of issue diversity in West German counties, found that people living in an area with only one local newspaper named fewer important national issues than those in areas with more local newspapers. During the 1972 national election campaign, the media obviously altered the image characteristics of leading West German politicians (Noelle-Neumann, 1980).

Gerbner and his collaborators maintain that not only is the assumption of entertainment uniformity true, but that this uniformity also has a significant impact on the ways people view reality. "Commercial populism," for instance, is assumed to be a picture of the world distributed by U.S. television entertainment (Gerbner, Gross, Morgan, & Signorielli, 1982). Gunter and his colleagues' analyses of cultivation effects of TV programs in Britain belong to the rare European examples of studies in this area (see, e.g., Gunter, 1987; Gunter & Wakshlag, 1988). The studies show that the perceived risk of being involved in crimes does depend on TV entertainment viewing.

Ambiguous evidence on the cultivation power of television was found by Winterhoff-Spurk (1989) in Germany. He investigated the impact of watching television on the perceived temporal and spatial dimensions of events and on the stereotyping of persons. In Sweden, Rosengren and Windahl (1989) investigated long-term effects of the media's portrayal of reality on children and adolescents and showed that there is at least a mutual effect between the amount of watching television and the viewers' perspective of the world.

In most of the studies mentioned above (see Kepplinger & Holicki, 1987, for additional examples), we cannot discern whether public opinion was created by the media themselves or generated by their mere support of a specific opinion or climate that existed beforehand, initiated by other persons or groups in society. What can be stated, however, is that in any case, the media play an important role as sources of public opinion in mass publics.

Certainly we may suspect that the strength of the media's impact depends on several factors—for instance, the credibility of a medium itself and of the sources it may quote. Mass communication research has suggested a third, and probably the most, important catalyst of media effects on mass public opinion: the needs and motives of the audience (see, e.g., Weaver, 1980). In fact, many studies of agenda setting and of the transmission of images revealed that political interest of audience members, their needs for orientation, for surveillance, "vote guidance," and so on, amplify the media's capability of passing their views of the world on to the public.

MEDIA INFLUENCE THROUGH PUBLISHED POLLS

Polls published by the media are the first of the two more indirect ways of influencing the audience's opinion mentioned above. We call these indirect, because the message recipient is not responding to the content of the media on explicit merits of the contents, but rather is using that content to make *inferences* about public opinion. The effect comes about as a result of those inferences. The techniques of polling, with its direct contact with the public, developed after about 1933. In the United States Gallup and Harris have always enjoyed a close relationship to the media, with each providing columns used by newspapers around the country. The situation is not dissimilar in Europe, where the media often commission or conduct polls for use in their news operations. The influential German newsmagazine *Der Spiegel*, for example, periodically reports on public opinion, as do the public television stations in that country. The same applies in France, where the weekly magazine *L'express* commissions public opinion surveys.

The influence of media-reported polls per se on *individuals* is open to debate. There is evidence that newspaper reports of polls, however, are read in significant numbers (Glynn & Ostman, 1988), and an effect of such polls reporting can be expected, given what we know about how the audience responds to other indicants of public opinion.

THE IMPACT OF OTHER MEDIA INFORMATION ABOUT MAJORITY OPINIONS

There also is evidence for the second more indirect way of influencing public opinion: the use of the *routine* content of the media as an inference of public opinion. Such content is not explicitly labeled as indicants of public opinion, but it can be interpreted as such either because it reflects opinion or because it is expected to shape opinion. De Sola Pool (1973) notes that until 1935, the only way to judge public opinion was through media content. McLeod, Becker, and Byrnes argued, as early as in 1974, that voters may be sensitive to media reports of issue saliences in part because they see these reports as indicants of what other people in the relevant public arena regard as important (McLeod, Becker, & Byrnes, 1974). In other words, the audience is using the media content as an indicator of public opinion. If this is true, such an effect would be an indirect one rather than a direct one, as it is often viewed.

The idea of the spiral of silence (Noelle-Neumann, 1984) is particularly explicit in arguing that most audience members are sensitive readers of the media in order to learn of majority opinion. Readers and viewers, as noted earlier, search for indicants of "majority" opinion in the mass media. These indicants can be public opinion polls, but they also are likely to be such indicants as interviews with opinion proponents or—even more simply—the attention paid to one set of arguments or perspective rather than to another. Readers are even encouraged to treat this content as an indicant of public responses to the issues facing the community. This does not necessarily lead to the "persuasive" effects of media contents described above: people do not have to accept an opinion in order to assume that it is a majority one or a fashionable one.

While this central idea in the spiral of silence theory has not been seriously challenged so far, there is significant criticism of other aspects of the theory. For example, Salmon and Neuwirth (1990) report, based on a 1986 survey of Madison, Wisconsin residents, only limited support for the assertion that individuals who perceive that their opinion is congruent with that of the majority will be more willing to engage in conversations about the issue with a stranger who holds an opposing viewpoint. There was no significant influence of climate of opinion on willingness to talk with a television reporter. There is no evidence, either, that a local opinion climate exerts a greater influence over willingness to express opinions than does a more distant (national) climate. Scherer (1990), using a five-wave panel survey in West Germany, shows that perceptions of majority opinions do not precede the attitudes toward an issue accordingly, as Noelle-Neumann argues. Instead, perceptions follow one's attitudes: people in favor of an opinion tend to see their view as the majority one, and not that much the other way round.

INDIRECT MEDIA IMPACT ON THE "ELITE"

To this point, we have spoken about the impact of the mass media on the populace in general. We turn our attention now to the impact of the media on elite or specialized groups in society. We see these responses as coming about in part as a result of these elites making inferences about public opinion from media content. Because these elites care about public opinion for a variety of reasons, they treat all such indicants as important and often modify their own behavior as a result of what they learn about public opinion from the mass media. We believe, once again, that elites, like the mass audience, respond to two different indicants of public opinion. The first is public opinion polls.

Sussman (1988), in his personal recounting of his experiences as director of polls for the Washington Post, makes a particularly compelling case in this regard. While one of the themes of Sussman's book is that leaders often ignore public opinion for a variety of reasons—including their own interests and powerful vested interests that counter public opinion—he makes a strong case for the extent to which they monitor it. Others do as well. Sussman says that in 1968 early polls by Gallup and Harris showed Nixon far ahead of Hubert Humphrey, and one result was that financial contributions to Humphrey dried up, making it impossible for him to buy television time in the crucial final weeks of the campaign. Humphrey ended up losing by one percentage point.

Sussman also reports that a poll he conducted on Jerry Falwell showing that only half of the people even recognized the name of the televangelist, coupled with other similar polls, minimized the power in Washington of Falwell and his type. According to Sussman, Ronald Reagan while president changed his tax plans as a result of public opinion, as well as his plans on Medicare and Medicaid. Sussman argues that the polls even have impact on the media themselves. According to Sussman, the media are somewhat deferential to powerful presidents, and very tough on presidents who are low in popularity. The media read the polls to determine the tone of their coverage.

Yet another example of this effect on elites of public opinion poll reports in the media can be found in the work of Mauser and Fitzsimmons (1991), who show that polls carried by the media affected the exchange rate of the Canadian dollar. As the likelihood of electoral success of those more favorable to the United States–Canadian trade agreement increased, the exchange rate became more favorable to Canada. The elite groups that determine exchange rates through their market activities were reading the polls as indicants of public opinion and behaving accordingly. The impact of polling in U.S. presidential elections is discussed by Lavrakas and Holley (1991).

A certain amount of caution is in order here: it should not be inferred from the data above that the media polls alone create these governmental responses. Governmental leaders—at least at the national level—also have access to their own polls. But the media polls are publicly released, and that can force the leaders to act where private polls might not. Sussman (1988) implies that this was the case with the Falwell polls. At the level of smaller communities, in addition, private polls, as well as media polls, become less common (McBride, 1991). Government leaders must then rely on other cues to assess public opinion.

We also believe elites respond to other indicants of public opinion in the mass media, such as the routine coverage of day-to-day events, because they, like the audience members in general, use this routine coverage to learn about public opinion. Perhaps more than the general audience member, however, these elites infer that the routine media coverage has affected audience members in some way. In this sense, the elite is using the media as an indicant of public opinion because it is inferring a media effect that *may* or *may not* even take place.

It is, in fact, our view that the "ordinary people's" responses to media content that implicitly indicates public opinion may be even much less significant than responses of the political and governmental elite, who either feel the content is an indicant of already formed public opinion or an indicant of public opinion about to be formed as a result of the influence of the media themselves. There is some—although limited—evidence already at hand of this media effect on the elite. Research about the impact of public opinion published in the mass media on leaders is unfortunately rare. Elite persons often cannot be interviewed and many probably would not admit that their actions were influenced by media information. But there are some hints that this may nevertheless happen.

We know from Weiss (1974) that elites, in the United States at least, are very attentive to the mass media. A national sample of 545 members of America's elite were interviewed in 1971–1972. Included were corporations, labor unions, Congress, federal departments and agencies, political parties, voluntary associations, and the mass media. Weiss found that most leaders say that they get most of their information about national issues that concern them from sources within their business and industrial sector. But overall, the mass media still are the dominant source, since not all sectors of the elite have alternative channels. Weiss also says that the media serve as a link among members of different sectors, reporting news, ideas, and opinions that members of one sector need to understand the world outside their own sector. Very similar results can be found in Puhe and Wuerzberg's (1989) study of the information behavior of German members of parliament.

We also have evidence that elites are sensitive to the issue agendas of the mass media because they anticipate that those agendas will become the agendas of their constituents. For example, Cook et al., (1983), in a field study of the effects on policy elites of a national newscast dealing with health care, found that governmental leaders changed their own salience evaluations as a result of the newscast. They also changed their perceptions of how the public saw these as important as a result of simply watching the program, which said nothing of public opinion on the topic.

Pritchard (1986) has investigated the effect of publicity on the decision of prosecutors to plea bargain rather than go to trial with a case. Case records in Milwaukee, Wisconsin were studied for an 18-month period, focusing on 90 homocides, and compared with media coverage of these cases. He found that press behavior was the strongest predictor of whether prosecutors engaged in negotiations with the accused. The shorter the average story, the more likely the prosecutor was to negotiate. In a second study, Pritchard, Dilts, and Berkowitz (1987) dealt with actions of prosecutors in areas of pornography. The data come from a survey of prosecutors in Indiana. They were asked about action taken against pornographers as well as perceptions of the importance of pornography to themselves, to their constituents, and to the local newspapers. Their own agenda was negatively related to the prosecutor's activity against pornography. The best predictors of action, instead, were the perception of the citizen's agenda and the perception of the newspaper agenda.

Bunn (1970), in his analysis of the so-called Spiegel-affair, points out that a critical "public opinion" in most of the West German newspapers caused a serious crisis of the West German government. Some ministers resigned. The government had closed down the weekly magazine *Der Spiegel*, accusing it of having betrayed national security secrets. This event soon became an issue of freedom of the press.

Several political events are described by Seymour-Ure (1974), demonstrating that, in Great Britain, mediated public opinion influenced political leaders and shaped British politics. An important role of the mass media during the West German–Polish negotiations in the early 1970s ("Ostpolitik") becomes obvious in Wittkaemper's (1986) comprehensive study of political actors, journalists, and media coverage. The press definitely furthered the treaty between the two countries by depicting a mainly positive public opinion toward a peaceful coexistence.

One of the clearest examples of political actors responding to media coverage and the *presumed* effect of that coverage on others is the activity of Gary Hart in 1987 (Newsweek, 1987). Five days after *The Miami Herald* reported a weekend rendezvous with model Donna Rice in his Washington townhouse, Gary Hart withdrew from the race for the Democratic nomination for the presidency. At the time, Hart was the frontrunner in the polls. The final decision to withdraw was made as Hart was learning that the *Washington Post* was about to publish a story that he was involved with yet another woman. *Newsweek* wrote that Hart's "poll ratings fell by the day," but the magazine reports no direct evidence to support that conclusion. The magazine also revealed that 64% of the people surveyed in a Gallup poll thought the media were being unfair to Hart in their treatment of marital infidelity, 52% said the private lives of candidates should be "off limits to the press," 70% disapproved of the use of "stakeouts" by the media to uncover such activities (as the *Miami Herald* had done), and 69% said the media were focusing on the Hart story "because they know such stories attract large audiences." *Newsweek* reported that Hart's fundraising was drying up and his staff was in turmoil. As Mutz (1989) reports, Hart later attempted to reenter the presidential race after realizing that the *voters* had not abandoned him, but he was too late. He could not recover the delegates and financial support he had lost.

The Hart story was replicated several years later on the local level in Columbus, Ohio, where the mayor, involved in two scandals that raised questions about his character, announced that he would not stand for reelection, only to waver later before deciding finally to retire from office. The first series of news stories resurrected an old charge of sexual imposition on a minor; the second detailed an affair between the mayor and one of his administrators, who held her position at his will, and who, along with the mayor, was married. The mayor denied the affair and was forced to change his story only after a television station in town tracked him and his administrator to a liaison in another city. The media were relentless in pursuit of both stories, and the story dominated the news for several weeks. Independent polls, however, showed that the electorate rallied around the mayor, who had generally enjoyed very high approval ratings, during the time of attack. There certainly was no evidence in the poll-data trend that warranted the mayor's decision to retire. Obviously, the mayor, like Gray Hart, believed sympathetic media coverage was essential for his effectiveness. Presuming the negative effect of the media on electorate opinion, he acted accordingly.

Klingaman (1987) provides anecdotal evidence that this is hardly a new phenomenon. British representatives at the Paris Peace Conference in 1919 were considering a proposal to recognize formally Bolshevik Russia. But the conservative newspapers in London got wind of this and indicated their horror. Prime Minister David Lloyd George is reported to have said, "As long as the British press is doing this kind of thing, how can you expect me to be sensible about Russia?"

On the other hand, there are always examples of politicians acknowledging the presumed power of the media by *resisting* it. In Germany, for instance, several top politicians involved in scandals told the surprised audience that they planned to "withstand" the pressure they felt by "the press." Other examples of this phenomenon are recounted by Molotch, Protess, and Gordon (1987).

Davison (1983) has labeled all these effects as "third-person effects." Such an effect occurs whenever person one sends a message, which persons two and three receive, and person two estimates the effect of this message on the third person. Davison acknowledges that some people (second persons) will use this perceived effect on the third party as a basis for action. Any such effect is predicated on the actual inference by person two of an effect on person three, and this psychological process of inferring dominates most of Davidson's manuscript.

Mutz (1989, pp. 4–6), however, gives considerable attention to the potential consequence of the assumption of a media effect:

> Based on assumptions of substantial media effects on the electorate, candidates and campaign managers organize entire campaigns around maximizing media coverage. . . . Despite the more restrained conclusions of academic researchers, campaign managers perceive media coverage to be highly influential in persuading voters. Thus whether media content actually influences political attitudes and behaviors or not, it has a substantial impact on the conduct of elections as a result of . . . perceptions of media influence. . . . The existence of laws regarding the print or broadcast of libelous statements, media censorship, and the entire advertising industry are all testimony to the idea that assumptions about media effects have definite behavioral consequences at an institutional level. . . . The third-person effect involves more . . . than . . . a psychological tendency to assume that others are more easily influenced than oneself; this hypothesis also suggests that people may take significant actions based on these perceptions.

THE THIRD-PERSON INFERENCE

Davison (1983) produced only limited evidence that individuals really do make inferences about media effects on others. The published studies that followed Davidson's piece document Davison's finding and offer a clearer picture of this psychological process, which we presume plays such an important role in the response of elites discussed above. Cohen, Mutz, Price, and Gunther (1988) confirmed the existence of the third-person phenomenon in an innovative study that provided a linkage between the attribution of a third-person effect and libel law deliberations in the United States. Cohen et al. found that students in their experiment judged the effect of a libelous story to be greater for others than for themselves. The effect was magnified as the "others" became progressively more distant from the student. When the defamation was attributed to a negatively biased source, the effect was accentuated.

Mutz (1989), in a survey of a university community, found that people estimated that media reports on campus protest regarding university investment in South Africa and on rioting in South Africa had more effect on other people than on themselves. She also found that issue salience influenced the gap in perception. That is to say, those persons for whom the issue was important showed a larger gap between "own" estimate of influence of the media and estimates of influence on "others" than did other persons.

Lasorsa (1989) found evidence for the third-person inference in a panel study conducted before and after the television broadcast of the "Amerika" series about life in the United States following a Soviet takeover. The study showed no evidence of an effect of the program on concern about a Soviet threat, about the United Nations, or about civil defense. It also found, consistent with that result, that viewers were unlikely to report an effect of the program on themselves. On the other hand, viewers felt the program would affect others. This tendency to report greater effects on others than on oneself was more pronounced among viewers who considered themselves to be experts on political affairs. There was evidence that the better educated and the strongly interested were more likely to show this effect.

Perloff (1989) reports on two experiments that, taken together, show that subjects estimated media effects that exceeded actual effects. He also found that the subjects' initial position on the issue covered by the experimental television newscast determined the nature of estimation of its effect. Subjects, regardless of the position held, were always pessimistic: they estimated that a news program would produce movement away from their own position on the part of "neutral" subjects. The partisans also believed that neutral subjects would recall facts that supported the position opposite that held by the subject.

Based on a study of responses to the 1988 presidential election, Rucinski and Salmon (1990) report that people estimated campaign effects greater for others than for themselves across five media content categories: news, political advertisements, negative political advertisements, political debates, and polls. They again found that the better educated respondents were more likely to estimate effects on others. Gunther (1991), in another experimental study using libel decisions as the context, asked his subjects to read a newspaper story that made negative assertions against a police chief. Again, he found strong evidence of a third-person effect. Trustworthiness of the source played a role. The more trustworthy source produced less of a gap between estimated effect on self and others than the untrustworthy source. Tiedge, Silverblatt, Havice, and Rosenfeld (1991), in surveys conducted in Milwaukee, Wisconsin and St. Louis, Missouri, asked respondents about general effects of the media: whether the media stifled independent thought, whether the media distracted users from other, more beneficial behavior. Differences between effects on oneself and the public in general were found across all three areas. The gap was greater for the better educated and for the older respondents.

Together, the studies document quite convincingly, across a variety of topics, the phenomenon of attributing greater effects to another than to oneself. Wherever investigated, better educated people and those who claimed to be experts revealed a greater third-person effect than others. This points to a plausible explanation of third-person effects: the concept of "social desirability." At least in Western societies, many people believe it socially undesirable to be affected by media messages, particularly by those of an everyday and "trivial" nature, such as those on television, radio, and film. They rather project their own impregnability onto the other members of the audience. Because being influenced "only" by, for example, a television program is considered "undignified" particularly among those with a higher formal education, it is not surprising that third-person effects show up more frequently in that group.

The third-person effect studies reviewed above deal only indirectly with the consequences of this attribution of effects. Rucinski and Salmon (1990) expected, but did not find, a link between perceptions of differential effects and tolerance for various forms of media control and censorship. Gunther (1991) found no effect of a self–other discrepancy on awards of damage for the defamatory story. However, the finding in several of the studies that the better educated respondents are more likely to attribute greater effects on others than on themselves, and Mutz's (1989) argument that this comes about because they feel some special expertise in this regard, is consistent with the idea that elite actors in the public opinion arena might take action because of the expectation of media effects. That there is no relationship between perception of effects and subsequent action in the two studies cited immediately above may reflect the social desirability of the "no-effect-on-self" response.

CONCLUSIONS

"Public opinion" has been defined in several different ways. Virtually all definitions, however, have one element in common: *publicity*. In complex societies, this publicity is provided mainly by the mass media: they distribute, further, or even create opinions that become "public" because they are convincing or at least attractive. They also convey impressions of those issues with which public opinion is presently concerned. And even if they do not influence public opinion itself, they may be the instruments of the public discussion that is regarded necessary in some definitions of public opinion.

Whatever images of public opinion the media transport, they do so obviously in a fairly uniform way—even in pluralistic societies. The audience does not encounter a choir of very many different voices from which to choose opinions, which then may become "public" ones because they are so reasonable and convincing. Instead, by selecting and interpreting reality in a more or less restricted fashion and with fairly clear-cut priorities the mass media exert considerable impact on public opinion.

The mass media may not, however, be the molders of public opinion because they suggest convincing evidence and, thus, plausibility, for one opinion or another. Their power may rather consist of their ability to serve as *indicants* of public opinion for their audiences. Those media indicants of public opinion obviously are differently important for mass and elite audiences. It seems as if their impact is even more dramatic on the elite. Politicians, for instance, have shown strong, sometimes even anticipatory, reactions to what the media depicted or created as "public" opinion. Although most of the evidence that we have for those elite reactions is based on personal accounts, we feel that this evidence should not be dismissed as nonscientific. The so-called third-person effect may be strongest on prominent and powerful people—people who fall through the gaps of regular scientific data-gathering methods.

In this paper, we tried to incorporate examples from European research on public opinion and the media's role. We were able to show that research in Europe often replicates, sometimes even precedes, comparable studies in the United States. Since the late 1980s, Eastern and Central Europe provide us with precious insights into emerging public opinion. Opinions became public first by face-to-face ways of communication and then were picked up by the media, exerting pressure on the powerful but also on every citizen. Perhaps never before in such a dramatic way has public opinion emerged. The role of the media in transmitting that opinion can be understood, however, in the context of research literature reviewed in this chapter.

REFERENCES

Adorno, T. W. (1967). *Ohne Leitbild*. Frankfurt: Suhrkamp.

Bouwman, H. (1982). Cultural indicators. *Rundfunk und Fernsehen, 30*, 341–356.

Bunn, R. F. (1970). The Spiegel affair and the West German press: The initial phase. In J. Tunstall (Ed.), *Media sociology* (pp. 439–451). London: Constable.

Buss, M., & Ehlers, R. (1982). Mediennutzung und politische Einstellung im Bundestagswahlkampf 1980. *Media Perspektiven, 4* , 237–253.

Cantor, M. G., & Pingree, S. (1983). *The soap opera*. Beverly Hills, CA: Sage.

Cohen, J., Mutz, D., Price, V., & Gunther, A. (1988). Perceived impact of defamation: An experiment on third-person effects. *Public Opinion Quarterly, 52*, 161–173.

Cook, F. L., Tyler, T. R., Goetz, E. G., Gordon, M. T., Protess, D., Left, D. R.,

& Molotch, H. L. (1983). Media and agenda setting: Effects on the public, interest group leader, policy makers, and policy. *Public Opinion Quarterly, 47*, 16–35.

Davison, W. P. (1983). The third-person effect in communication. *Public Opinion Quarterly, 47*, 1–15.

de Sola Pool, I. (1973). Public opinion. In I. de Sola Pool, F. Frey, W. Schramm, N. Maccoby, & E. B. Parker (Eds.), *Handbook of communication* (pp. 779–835). Chicago: Rand McNally College Publishing Company.

Echikson, W. (1990). *Lighting the night: Revolution in Eastern Europe*. New York: William Morrow and Company, Inc.

Fishbein, M., & Ajzen, I. (1975). *Belief, attitude, intention and behavior*. Reading, MA: Addison-Wesley.

Galtung, J., & Holmboe Ruge, M. (1970). The structure of foreign news. In J. Tunstall (Ed.), *Media sociology* (pp. 259–298). London: Constable.

Gerbner, G., Gross, L., Morgan, M., & Signorielli, N. (1982). Charting the mainstream: Television's contribution to political orientations. *Journal of Communication, 32*(2), pp. 100–127.

The Glasgow University Media Group. (1976). *Bad news* (Vol. 1). London: Routledge & Kegan Paul.

Glynn, C. J., & Ostman, R. E. (1988). Public opinion about public opinion. *Journalism Quarterly, 65*, 299–306.

Graber, D. A. (1982). The impact of media research on public opinion studies. In D. C. Whitney, E. Wartella, & S. Windahl (Eds.), *Mass communication review yearbook 1982* (pp. 555–564). Beverly Hills, CA: Sage.

Greenberg, B. S. (1980). *Life on television: Content analyses of U.S. TV drama*. Norwood, N.J.: Ablex.

Guback, T. H. (1968). Reporting or distorting: Broadcast network news treatment of a speech by John F. Kennedy. In H. J. Skornia, & J. W. Kitson (Eds.), *Problems and controversies in television and radio: Basic readings* (pp. 347–358). Palo Alto, CA: Stanford University Press.

Gunter, B. (1987). *Television and the fear of crime*. London: John Libbey.

Gunter, B., & Wakshlag, J. (1988). Television viewing and perception of crime among London residents. In P. Drummond, & R. Paterson (Eds.), *Television and its audience: International research perspectives* (pp. 191–210). London: BFI Books.

Gunther, A. (1991). What we think others think: Causes and consequence in the third-person effect. *Communication Research, 18*, 355–372.

Habermas, J. (1962). *Strukturwandel der Oeffentlichkeit*. Neuwied: Luchterhand.

Halloran, J. D., Elliott, P., & Murdock, G. (1970). *Demonstrations and communication: A case study*. Harmondsworth, Middlesex: Penguin.

Hedman, L. (1981). International information in daily newspapers. In K. E. Rosengren (Ed.), *Advances in content analysis* (pp. 197–214). Beverly Hills, CA: Sage.

Hennis, W. (1957). *Meinungsforschung und repraesentative Demokratie*. Tuebingen: J. C. B. Mohr.

Hildebrandt, J. (1984). *Zeitungswettbewerb und Themenvielfalt*. Unpublished master's thesis, University of Munich, Munich.

Hoffmann-Lange, U., & Schoenbach, K. (1979). Geschlossene Gesellschaft. In H. M. Kepplinger (Ed.), *Angepasste Aussenseiter* (pp. 49–75). Freiburg, Munich: Karl Alber.

Holzer, H. (1971). *Gescheiterte Aufklaerung?* Munich: Piper.

Kepplinger, H. M. (1975). *Medienkultur und Realkultur*. Freiburg, Munich: Karl Alber.

Kepplinger, H. M. (1989). *Kuenstliche Horizonte: Folgen, Darstellung und Akzeptanz von Technik in der Bundesrepublik*. Frankfurt: Campus.

Kepplinger, H. M., Gotto K., Brosius, H. B., & Haak, D. (1989). *Der Einfluss der Fernsehnachrichten auf die politische Meinungsbildung*. Freiburg, Munich: Karl Alber.

Kepplinger, H. M., & Holicki, S. (1987). *Der Einfluss des Fernsehens auf die oeffentliche Meinung: Annotierte Bibliographie empirischer Forschungsergebnisse 1980–1986*. Bonn: Bundesministerium fuer Forschung und Technologie.

Kepplinger, H. M., & Roth, H. (1978). Kommunikation in der Oelkrise des Winters 1973/74. *Publizistik, 23*, pp. 337–356.

Klingaman, W. K. (1987). *1919: The year our world began*. New York: Harper & Row.

Lange, K. (1981). *Das Bild der Politik im Fernsehen*. Frankfurt: Haag & Herchen.

Lasorsa, D. L. (1989). Real and perceived effects of "Amerika." *Journalism Quarterly, 66*, 373–378, 529.

Lavrakas, P., & Holley, J. (Eds.). (1991). *Polling and presidential election coverage*. Newbury Park, CA: Sage.

Lippmann, W. (1922). *Public opinion*. New York: Macmillan.

Mauser, G. A., & Fitzsimmons, C. (1991). The short-term effect of election polls on foreign exchange rates: The 1988 Canadian federal election. *Public Opinion Quarterly, 55*, 232–240.

McBride, F. (1991). Media use of preelection polls. In P. Lavrakas & J. Holley (Eds.), *Polling and presidential election coverage* (pp. 184–199). Newbury Park, CA: Sage.

McLeod, J. M., Becker, L. B., & Byrnes, J. E. (1974). Another look at the agenda-setting function of the press. *Communication Research, 1*, 131–166.

McQuail, D. (1983). The election functions of television. In J. G. Blumler (Ed.), *Communicating to voters* (pp. 345–358). Beverly Hills, CA: Sage.

Meier, W., & Schanne, M. (1983). Die Schweiz und ihre 'Next-Door-Giants.' In U. Saxer (Ed.), *Politik und Kommunikation* (pp. 42–49). Munich: Oelschlaeger.

Molotch, H., Protess, D., & Gordon, M. (1987). The media-policy connection: Ecologies of news. In D. L. Paletz (Ed.), *Political communication research* (pp. 26–48). Norwood, NJ: Ablex.

Mutz, D. C. (1989). The influence of perceptions of media influence: Third person effects and the public expression of opinions. *International Journal of Public Opinion Research, 1*, 3–23.

Newsweek. (1987, May 18). The sudden fall of Gary Hart. (International Edition), pp. 8–14.

Noelle, E. (1966). *Oeffentliche Meinung und soziale Kontrolle*. Tuebingen: J.C.B. Mohr.

Noelle-Neumann, E. (1977). Das doppelte Meinungsklima: Der Einfluss des Fernsehens im Wahlkampf 1976. *Politische Vierteljahresschrift, 18*, 408–451.

Noelle-Neumann, E. (1980). *Wahlentscheidung in der Fernsehdemokratie*. Freiburg, Wuerzburg: Ploetz.

Noelle-Neumann, E. (1984). *The spiral of silence: Public opinion—Our social skin*. Chicago: University of Chicago Press.

Noelle-Neumann, E., & Kepplinger, H. M. (1978). Journalistenmeinungen, Medieninhalte und Medienwirkungen. In G. Steindl (Ed.), *Publizistik aus Profession* (pp. 41–68). Duesseldorf: Droste.

Paletz, D., & Entman, R. (1981). *Media power politics*. New York: Free Press.

Perloff, R. M. (1989). Ego-involvement and the third person effect of televised news coverage. *Communication Research, 16*, 236–262.

Price, V., & Roberts, D. F. (1987). Public opinion processes. In C. R. Berger & S. H. Chaffee (Ed.), *Handbook of communication science* (pp. 781–816). Newbury Park, CA: Sage.

Pritchard, D. (1986). Homicide and bargained justice: The agenda-setting effect of crime news on prosecutors. *Public Opinion Quarterly, 50*, 143–159.

Pritchard, D., Dilts, J. P., & Berkowitz, D. (1987). Prosecutors' use of external agendas in prosecuting pornography cases. *Journalism Quarterly, 64*, 392–398.

Protess, D. L., & McCombs, M. E. (Eds.). (1991). *Agenda setting: Readings on media, public opinion, and policymaking*. Hillsdale, NJ: Lawrence Erlbaum Associates.

Puhe, H., & Wuerzberg, H. G. (1989). *Lust & Frust: Das Informationsverhalten der deutschen Abgeordneten*. Koeln: informedia.

Rock, P. (1973). News as eternal recurrence. In S. Cohen & J. Young (Eds.), *The manufacture of news* (pp. 73–84). Beverly Hills, CA: Sage.

Ronneberger, F. (1973). Leistungen und Fehlleistungen der Massenkommunikation. *Publizistik, 18*, 203–215.

Rosengren, K. E. (1972). Ten points about moulders and mirrors. In Deutsche UNESCO-Kommission (Ed.), *Forschung und Massenmedien* (p. 72). Munich: Dokumentation.

Rosengren, K. E., & Windahl, S. (1989). *Media matters: TV use in childhood and adolescence*. Norwood, N.J.: Ablex.

Rucinski, D., & Salmon, C. T. (1990). The 'other' as the vulnerable voter: A study of the third-person effect in the 1988 U.S. presidential campaign. *International Journal of Public Opinion Research, 2*, 345–368.

Salmon, C. T. & Neuwirth, K. (1990). Perceptions of opinion "climates" and willingness to discuss the issue of abortion. *Journalism Quarterly*, 67, 567–577.

Schatz, H. (1980). *Fernsehnachrichten in demokratietheoretischer Sicht*. Unpublished manuscript, Duisburg.

Scheuch, E. K. (1971). Unterhaltung als Pausenfueller. In G. Prager (Ed.), *Unterhaltung und Unterhaltendes im Fernsehen* (pp. 13–46). Mainz: v. Hase & Koehler.

Scherer, H. (1990). *Massenmedien, Meinungsklima und Einstellung: Eine Untersuchung zur Theorie der Schweigespirale*. Opladen: Westdeutscher Verlag.

Schmidtchen, G. (1965). *Die befragte Nation*. Frankfurt, Hamburg: Fischer.
Schoenbach, K. (1978). Die isolierte Welt des Lokalen. *Rundfunk und Fernsehen, 26*, 260–277.
Schoenbach, K. (1983a). News in the western world. In L. J. Martin & A. G. Chaudhary (Eds.), *Comparative mass media systems* (pp. 33–43). New York: Longman.
Schoenbach, K. (1983b). *Das unterschaetzte Medium*. Munich: Saur.
Schoenbach, K. (1987). Medienberichterstattung als Indikator oeffentlicher Meinung. In BVM (Ed.), *Marktforschung fuer Entscheidungen* (pp. 195–210). Duesseldorf: BVM.
Schoenbach, K., & Schulz, W. (1980). *The image of the U.S.A. and Latin American countries in West German media*. Paper, XXX International Communication Association, Acapulco, May.
Schulz, W. (1976). *Die Konstruktion von Realitaet in den Nachrichtenmedien*. Freiburg, Munich: Karl Alber.
Schulz, W. (1978). *Mass media and the image of political reality*. Paper presented at the IAMCR Congress, Warsaw, September.
Schulz, W. (1982). Ein neues Weltbild fuer das Fernsehen? *Media Perspektiven, 1* (1982), 18–27.
Shoemaker, P., with Kay Mayfield, E. (1987). Building a theory of news content: A synthesis of current approaches. *Journalism Monographs*, 103.
Shoemaker, P., & Reese, S. (1991). *Mediating the message: Theories of influence on mass media*. New York: Longman.
Seymour-Ure, C. (1974). *The political impact of mass media*. London: Constable.
Signorielli, N., & Morgan M. (1990). *Cultivation analysis: New directions in media effects research*. Newbury Park, CA: Sage.
Sussman, B. (1988). *What Americans really think and why our politicians pay no attention*. New York: Pantheon Books.
Thoveron, G., & Sauerberg, S. (1983). Did voters get the message? In J. G. Blumler (Ed.), *Communicating to voters* (pp. 284–298). Beverly Hills, CA: Sage.
Tiedge, J. T., Silverblatt, A., Havice, M. J., & Rosenfeld, R. (1991). *Journalism Quarterly, 68*, 141–154.
Trenaman, J., & McQuail, D. (1961). *Television and the political image*. London: Methuen.
Turow, J. (1984). *Media industries*. New York: Longman.
Weaver, D. H. (1980). Audience need for orientation and media effects. *Communication Research, 7*, 361–376.
Weiss, C. H. (1974). What America's leaders read. *Public Opinion Quarterly, 38*, 1–22.
Winterhoff-Spurk, P. (1989). *Fernsehen und Weltwissen: Der Einfluss von Medien auf Zeit-, Raum- und Personenschemata*. Opladen: Westdeutscher Verlag.
Wittkaemper, G. W. (Ed.). (1986). *Medienwirkungen in der internationalen Politik*. Muenster: Lit.

14

Making News and Manufacturing Consent: The Journalistic Narrative and Its Audience

Gertrude J. Robinson

THE MEDIA AND PUBLIC OPINION FORMATION

Public opinion scholarship has traditionally assumed that the media are "neutral" distribution networks funneling assorted types of information to diversified mass publics. These publics, in Charles Wright's (1959) terminology, are viewed as anonymous and undifferentiated by message producers. Such a model fails to account for two important components in public meaning creation: the role of the media as narrators of public events, and audience expectations, which also affect the production of the journalistic discourse. Reception theorists have begun to address these issues. They argue that meaning does not reside "out there" in words on a page or dots on a television screen, but comes about as a result of an interaction between viewer and image, reader and text. Reception theorists note that these interactions, which occur so frequently that we hardly notice them, are furthermore embedded in particular institutional, historical, and cultural contexts that themselves condition the production of public meaning (Allen, 1987, p. 5).

Recent scholarship has identified three different types of media involvement in public meaning creation. Among these are the media's selective construction of social knowledge, which provides a frame of reference through which different social groups come to understand their own and others' "lived reality." A second type of ideological labor is involved in presenting an inventory of values, goals, and lifestyles that are currently available in a particular modern industrial society. A third and even more difficult function of the media is the fashioning of public consensus on major issues of the day (Hall, 1977, pp. 341–342). By fashioning this consensus the media provide the essential preconditions for democratic public opinion formation, which is based on the opportunity to reconcile disputes through discussion rather than through confrontation or violence (Hall, 1980, p. 56).

The media's most important political role is thus to make the consensus view of society *visible* as a feature of everyday life and to convince viewers that as citizens they are part of a "public" that shares a common stock of knowledge. Developing such a consensual viewpoint has two important political implications for Western democratic society. It suggests that the multiplicity of subgroups share roughly the same interests and have roughly the same power in political life. The ideological labor of public opinion creation is thus reflexive. It helps both to *constitute* the notion of "society" as an ordered public stage on which legitimate teams of protagonists and antagonists play out their political roles, and it *demonstrates* this order symbolically to its audience through the structure of the news narrative. How media narratives convince and "reframe" descriptions of political occurrences and thus create public consensus on divisive political issues is not yet well understood. Nor is it clear what role the audience plays in this complex process of meaning creation.

To clarify these issues, the process of public opinion formation in the context of Quebec's highly divisive referendum on "sovereignty–association" was studied. This referendum campaign, which proposed a new constitutional arrangement with the rest of Canada, began with the November 1, 1979 tabling of the Parti Québecois' *White Paper* (D'égal à égal) in Quebec's National Assembly. In it the blueprint for a sovereign Quebec and its entente with the remaining nine Canadian provinces was for the first time made public. Of course, the sovereignty–association proposal on which citizens were to vote May 20, 1980 engendered intense debate not only among those opposed (English speaking and immigrant minorities), but also among Quebec's French majority, who were evenly split on the sovereignty issue. The *White Paper* tabling reportage by Montreal's four French and English stations provided an excellent example for analyzing both the narrative and the rhetorical strategies that the stations constructed for their respective audiences. For political life to continue, the potentially explosive issue of secession had to be naturalized and the Parti Québecois' political program had to be interpreted in such a way that *both* its Montreal supporters on the Francophone YES side and its opponents on the English and immigrant NO sides could continue to feel part of the Canadian political system.

The analysis of the *White Paper* narrative is based on the total one-week (November 1–7, 1979) Montreal sample of all local and national news casts, of which there are eight. Three of these were presented in French (*Ce Soir, le Dix*, and *Telejournal*) and five in English (*City at Six, City Tonight, Pulse, CBC National, CTV National*). Since meaning creation in television news is the result of a coded set of audiovisual utterances, we use three units of analysis: the segment, the item, and the story. Most of the observations are recorded at the segment level, a unit of analysis defined in terms of a change either in role or in visual mode (Connell, 1980, p. 140; Robinson et al., 1983). Such a unit captures the interplay between narrative (audio) and presentational (visual) characteristics that have previously eluded researchers. Two larger units of analysis, the "item" and the "story" are associated with only a few observations. We view "items" as a semantic and syntactic category that includes segments and is defined in terms of an anchor introduction and a news angle. The most inclusive category, the news "story," is a purely semantic category, which is defined in terms of coherence of subject matter related to an identifiable event (Robinson, 1989). The variables measured at these two levels are suited to comparisons of French and English *White Paper* news narratives, because they record duration over a number of segments.

NEWS STORIES: COMPONENTS OF CONSTRUCTION

All attempts at treating "public opinion" formation by the media as a process that can be directly "read off" from the content, as agenda-setting and other research approaches did, overlook the fact that television programming is more than content. It is a complex sign system collectively created by referendary news dramas that were conjointly created by Montreal's English and French language stations and their audiences. Because the sign system is audience based, it helps to pinpoint the narrative *communalities* and *reflexivities* between journalistic encodings and audience decodings. Such an analysis also demonstrates that significance arises from both textual and narrative configurations. In the news drama public actors *create* the order and consistency that *constitutes* the notion of "society" in which public opinion rests. Consensus gets built up about heroes and villains, and policy can be made because the moral and rational grounds of authority are assumed to be discoverable (Gusfield, 1981, p. 22). Public opinion creation and sense making are consequently constructions, at times fragile and elusive, which are dependent on preexisting viewer knowledge and expectations that were very different for Montreal's English and French viewers.

Three sets of cognitive framework's, an earlier study showed, help to mesh audience and journalistic understandings of what the referendum was about (Robinson & Charron, 1989, p. 148). On the pragmatic level, they included a series of journalistic conventions about what classes of people are legitimated players in the political process. North American political reporting recognizes four: politicians, journalists, experts, and the public. Available political knowledges furthermore framed what the referendum campaign was assumed to be *about*. They classified what side of the debate—"YES," "NO," or "undecided"—the actors were on. A third set of frameworks emerged from the ongoing "nationalistic" debate about Quebec's special role in the Canadian federation. These were codified for the "YES" side by the Parti Québecois *White Paper* (Fraser, 1984, p. 373). We called these frameworks "canonical formulas" and found that they structured the salient *issues* of the referendum debate on the semantic level. Finally, there were the already mentioned journalistic frameworks that define the "proper" televisual rendition of occurrences in the referendary campaign. These helped English- and French-speaking professionals to sift out the *topics* and *arguments* that were advanced by different actors and to narrate them in the proper format for their respective news programs.

Narrator roles in the television discourse can be roughly divided into two major classes. There are the intrastation news presenter roles, which are filled by journalistic personnel, and the extrastation roles, which use legitimated political players as contributors to the *White Paper* discourse. The four intrastation roles—anchor, reporter, commentator, and interviewer—provide what John Hartley calls the "institutional voice" of the station. Previous studies have shown that the institutional voice frames the ways in which the story is to be interpreted and thus provides the general meaning context for its respective audience group (Hartley, 1982, p. 47; The Glasgow University Media Group, 1976, p. 298). Our comparative analysis discovered that the French and English stations fashioned their discourses quite differently. In the French stations only two intrastation roles, the anchor and the reporter, contextualize the news discourse, appearing in 69% of all segments. The English stations, in contrast, use four roles to construct their news accounts, privileging the reporter role (45% of segments) over the anchor (24% of segments) and adding commentators (11%) and interviewers (10%) to create greater visual and verbal variety in their news programs.

In spite of playing an important role in democratic politics, the politician's ability to speak directly to the public has diminished over the years. This shift is reflected in politicians' renditions in the news programs. Though they appear in almost as many segments as anchors (English, 26%; French, 20%) in the English language newscasts, newsmakers and politicians are rarely permitted to tell their own stories. Typically they are used to introduce a new story angle or to make explicit a point that the producer has in mind. This supporting role in the news discourse is visually reinforced by "front and level" camera treatment (78% of segments), which is different from the "face to camera" presentation modes used for the journalistic roles. Together these role and visual characteristics indicate that the journalists are in command of the *White Paper* narrative and thus set the crucial meaning contexts for their varied Montreal audiences. The inability of newsmakers and politicians to subvert this ongoing journalistic discourse has become a major bone of contention in public opinion creation during the 1980s; it is dealt with in greater detail in the final section of this essay.

POLITICAL EVENTS FEATURED

All political dramas feature a set of events in which party leaders and their followers battle over political ascendancy. Because "events" refer to the kinds of happenings that the stations featured as a referendary item/story, the variable is conceptually related to what journalists consider "newsworthy." Eleven different types of events can be distinguished for the referendary narrative, including such things as meetings, tablings, speeches, and polls. These, according to Roland Barthes, are ordered and mark out different levels of intelligibility in the news narrative (Barthes, 1977, pp. 117–119). It is revealing to compare the CBC's *City at Six* and the *Ce Soir* coverage of the *White Paper* document in the Quebec National Assembly, of the day-long walkout by Quebec civil servants contesting a wage proposal, of the disruption of a closed door briefing, of the opposition members' inability to read the document, of their anger, and so on. The English and French stations' narratives link and integrate these event reconstructions in very different ways and thus provide the skeleton for radically different interpretative contexts.

Our verbatim transcript demonstrates that English journalists, who knew that their viewers were against secession, made an event selection that acknowledged the audience's deep suspicion of the Parti Québecois' intentions. The CBC's *City at Six* on November 1, 1979 (story 2; item 1) provided this account of the *White Paper* tabling:

> *Anchor* (Stan Gibbons): It was a *miserable* day for a lot of people in Quebec City, certainly for anybody that had anything to do with distribution of the *White Paper*. The government planned to hand out copies early this morning to reporters at the Quebec City Convention Centre, but striking civil servants had a plan of their *own*, as Mervin McLeod reports.
>
> *Reporter* (Mervin McLeod): It was *such* a well planned event. But when the hundreds of reporters showed up to read the long awaited *White Paper* at 8:30 this morning they found hundreds of striking civil servants blocking the entrance to the hall. Outside waited several thousand more. Then, suddenly a door was smashed, and in they poured into the hall the government has *so carefully* prepared for the journalists to digest the *White Paper*. The room quickly became a shambles as strikers milled around singing union songs and throwing around the foolscap that was supposed to hold the words of wisdom about sovereignty-association. (emphasis in original)

The English stations' event selection, linking, and emphasis on the negative themes of "chaos" and "instability" provide a context for the audience's negative assessment of the Parti Québecois' *White Paper* tabling event that is quite different from and never raised by the French stations' account.

In contrast, the French coverage of *Ce Soir* (story 1; item 1) contextualized the *White Paper* tabling in a neutral discourse that stressed that the strike inconvenienced the journalists who were to read the document, but *not* the government that presented the document in the National Assembly at 14:00 hours, as planned.

> *Reporter* (Gilles Morin): L'opération *Livre Blanc*, planifié depuis plusieurs semaines par le gouvernement, a été dérangé par des fonctionnaires mécontents. Au nombre de deux à trois milles, ils sont arrivés au Centre Municipal des Cóntres ce matin avant les journalistes. Tous ses derniers devraient prendre connaissance à l'avance du contenu du *Livre Blanc*. Les manifestants ont brisé une porte vitrée et une fois à l'intérieur ils ont neutralise des machines à écrire en leur enlevant les rubans, fait voler les papeteries, bref, c'était sans dessus-dessous. Cette manifestation a d'avantage dérangée les journalistes que le gouvernement. Le *Livre Blanc* a été déposé comme prévu à 14:00 heures à l'Assemblée Nationale sans autres incidents.

(*Transl.*) The release of the *White Paper*, planned for weeks by the government, was disrupted by disgruntled civil servants. Between two and three thousand of them arrived this morning at the Municipal Convention Centre before journalists who were to arrive to be briefed on the contents of the document.

The protesters broke a glass door and, once inside, incapacitated typewriters by stealing their ribbons and scattering papers—in short, they turned the place upside down. This protest inconvenienced journalists more than the government. The *White Paper* was tabled, as planned, at two o'clock P.M. in the National Assembly with no further incident.

Alhough the two stations' accounts in this instance reconstruct the same set of events, Table 14.1 indicates that the *overall* event reconstruction of the *White Paper* tabling and subsequent General Assembly debate were reconstructed quite differently by the Anglophone and Francophone stations. Table 14.1 shows that the event selection for the English news narrative privileges speeches (30%) and parliamentary discussions (22%) *about* the controversial *White Paper*, while downplaying the document's content (11%), which is known to be disapproved of by the viewers. Disapproval is also the reason why so much attention is paid to the civil servant strike (10%), which was clearly a nonreferendary event. The French stations' event reconstructions cover both speeches (23%) and the *White Paper*'s content (20%) about equally, while ignoring the parliamentary discussion (11%). In such a narrative format the political values of both the pro-and antireferendary audiences are acknowledged. French stations were also more evenhanded in providing the same amount of coverage (16%; 15%) to responses from other sources, parties, governments, and opponents of the document.

TABLE 14.1. Event Reconstructions in the Anglophone and Francophone *White Paper* Discourse (% of Duration)

Events	Anglophone	Francophone
Speeches	30 (1)	23 (1)
Parliamentary discussion	22 (2)	11 (4)
Document content	11 (4)	20 (2)
Sources' response	16 (3)	15 (3)
Revolts, demonstration	10 (5)	5
Public response	3	7
Reports presented	—	9 (5)
Tabling	3	4
Meetings	—	5
Public debate	—	3
Others	—	1

The differing English and French news discourses demonstrate that viewer values not only affect a station's event selection but also the ways in which station personnel construct the notion of "balance." In the English programs negative events like the civil servant strike were selected and highlighted to illustrate and reinforce the *existing* negative public opinion attitude toward the Parti Québecois' *White Paper* document. In the French programs a sense of narrative "balance" was achieved by featuring positive and negative responses from a wide range of different sources, among them other Canadian parties, federal and provincial government agencies, and national and international markets. Such a construction of "balance" would make the reports acceptable to both the "YES" and the "NO" voters in Quebec's referendary campaign.[1]

THE CAST OF CHARACTERS ON THE PUBLIC STAGE

While different event selections set the broad context for English and French audience interpretations of the *White Paper* tabling, the cast of characters constitutes another important narrative element that clearly distinguishes the two news discourses. The characters or sources of referendary news stories are divided into the "YES" and the "NO" sides, representing the two identifiable political positions in the campaign. The "YES" forces include Mr. Lévesque, the Premier of Quebec, and Parti Québecois (PQ) spokespersons who were in favor of Quebec secession. The federalist "NO" forces were led by Prime Minister Trudeau and other federal politicians and by Mr. Ryan, the head of the provincial Liberal party. Other characters not readily identifiable with either side of the referendum debate were not included in the analysis. They appear in about one third of the total news segments (English 36%; French 38%). Characters and events are intimately interconnected and modify the values that will be attached to news stories. Our comparative analysis documents that both sets of stations take their audience's presumed political preferences into account and present and highlight different sets of characters. In the English narrative the "NO" forces arguing against the sovreignty option are featured in 73% of all segments, while French station narrations highlight the "YES" forces (61%). Although this is a surprising and seemingly disproportionate overrepresentation of the "NO" and "YES" forces in their respective discourses, we see later that journalistic argumentation strategies cancel out these quantitative disproportions and produce a sense of narrative "balance" at a higher level of interpretation.

NEWS STORIES: NARRATIVE STRATEGIES OF CONSENSUS BUILDING

All attempts to analyze the media's role in public opinion formation must account for their *active* participation in this process. Reception theorists argue that this "activity" goes beyond the media's selection of the events to be narrated and the cast of characters to be covered. From the audience's point of view this activity refers to a particular narrative process that creates unique news program scripts with their own plot laws. As "scripts" news stories implicitly contain explanations and normative dimensions that project for the audience how things work in their society, as well as rules about how to live. As a symbolization of the social order, the story world of the television news program thus transmits metadramatic understandings of the political and the social worlds. The "scripting" of news stories and the discourses in which they are embedded have received increasing attention in the 1980s, because they permit us to gain a better understanding of how news narratives "persuade" their viewers through both presentational devices and logics of argumentation. As demonstrated below, the news narrative makes use of three important presentational devices to *direct* implicitly the meanings that Montreal audiences were able to attach to the events of the *White Paper* tabling. These devices can be categorized as special styles of speech, special linking devices, and special story formats. Each of these will now be analyzed in greater detail.

Styles of Speech and Modes of Address in "News Talk"

The institutional voices of the Montreal television stations "speak" to us in a particular style that is recognizable and familiar to French and English audiences. As viewers we do not seem to have any difficulty in understanding the news language's special form, fluency, and uninterruptedness. This is because any language is a code based on cultural understandings that are *shared* by journalists and audiences alike and that involve common frameworks of knowledge and meaning structures (Hall, 1980, pp. 130–131). Speaker and hearer roles, though separate, are thus united by a reflexive commitment to honor the other's existence and point of view, otherwise the talk makes no sense.

In television new programs the news talk as a language system is highly structured, formal, and polite. Many have therefore characterized it as being "rational and bureaucratic" (Dahlgren, 1985a, p. 358; Altheide, 1985, p. 12). Such a description is at best partial since it fails to illuminate the "persuasive" quality of this language system, which visually clues the viewer in to the same space and time continuum with the station. Studio personnel thus become "stand-ins" for us as viewers and are framed in such a way as to imitate conversation: we could be talking to them across our coffee table. All of these pictorial sign renditions also reinforce the "opaqueness" (windowpane) metaphor that anchors the "unvarnished," "brute fact" narrative the newscast seeks to create. Stories on English and French local and network news, like other narratives, presuppose the existence of a storyteller, a subject who does the telling and orchestrates the voices belonging to all other characters. Irving Goffman (1983, p. 236) provides an important clue when he notes that anchors are different from conventional storytellers. They "announce" another's text and merely give the *impression* that they have authored what is being said. The viewer addressed is also restricted by the announcing mode: although he or she is visually recognized as a "phantom" participant in the communicational encounter, there is no opportunity for response. This does not, however, imply total viewer passivity, as Todd Gitlin suggests (Gitlin, 1977, p. 788). Viewers respond actively and interpret the three different types of faultless speech announcing in quite discriminating manners.

Our comparative analysis demonstrates that in both the English and the French news discourses, the "direct" mode of announcing is the preferred style of news speech. Combined with what we have called "face to camera" imagery, it simulates a two-person telephone conversation in which the news personnel ostensibly speak to each audience member individually. In the *White Paper* reconstruction a full 100% of all anchor interactions, and 98% of all reporter statements utilize the "direct" mode of address. In this mode the narrator quotes a spokesperson or "speaks for self." The "indirect" modes of address, in contrast, are found in such mediated situations as interviews, speeches, press conferences, and editorials. They are overwhelmingly the setting in which the statements of "extrastation" personnel appear. Newsmaker/politician statements are heavily inflected (98%), as are those of experts (83%). Both are rendered primarily in the "interview" mode, where only a *portion* of their statements are reproduced verbatim. People in the street are never allowed to speak directly; their opinions are always elicited in the "interview" mode (100%).

Much less frequently anchors and reporter/interviewers are engaged in two other types of "announcing," which Goffman calls "three way" and "fresh talk" announcing. The first occurs when the anchor hails one of his own "team" such as the reporter, or the sports and weather persons. "Fresh talk" announcing is practiced by reporters and commentators when they provide more voice-over detail about a particular news event (Goffman, 1983, pp. 336–441). Although these occur more rarely, all three types of "announcing" share the same communicational characteristics, treating the remote audience as a visually ratified participant while verbally denying the viewer access. Public opinion formation in such a setting will also be one-way, legitimating those who can talk in their own voice over those who cannot. Through the "indirect" mode of address, extrastation voices become "characters" in the station's narration. Rhetorically this means that they are in an *indirect relation* to what is being said (Nichols, 1976, p. 39). They are turned into subordinate "NOminees" that are called upon to illustrate a point, introduce a news angle, or present an alternative point of view. Although there is variation in televisual news styles in Europe, our evidence indicates that both the English and French Canadian stations utilize the *same* modes of address. Such a finding testifies not only to the unifying influence of professional training across language groups in North American journalism, but also to the fact that there are different stylistic manners for rendering "objectivity" in the European and the North American news discourses, which require further investigation.

English and French Linking Devices

Since the "modes of address" of our English and French stations' *White Paper* accounts were the same, other narrative devices must account for their differing argumentation strategies. Chief among these are the narrative "linking" functions that are performed by the station personnel and the "story formats" that result from these functions. Five linking processes can be distinguished. They are "linking," which provides the textual function of guiding the viewer through the news story; "framing," which establishes the topic and its relevance; "focusing," which determines the angle of the story; "NOminating," which clues the audience in to the identity of the newscast participants; and "summing up," which draws together the main threads of the news items, so that the relevance and the context into which the story is to be placed can be assessed by the viewer (Brunsdon & Morley, 1978, pp. 58–59). All of these strategies clarify the points at which argumentation enters the supposedly "neutral" journalistic discourse. The linking processes thus act as a skeleton of persuasion.

Our comparison indicates that the anchor person's segments involve four narrative strategies: linking (22%), framing (29%), focusing (27%), and nominating (20%). Each of these is utilized almost equally. Because they are involved in almost all presentational devices, anchors have the greatest influence on the "audiencing" function—that is, the ways in which viewers will interpret a news story's meaning (Ang, 1987). Commentator and reporter roles follow with three and two presentational devices each. Commentators primarily link (32%), frame (32%), and focus (29%) arguments. Reporters most frequently focus (41%) or frame (32%). Newsmaker/politician's voices, in contrast, can only rarely affect the interpretation of a news segment: they speak in their own voices in only 10% of the segments, and are otherwise slotted into the "NOminee" position (90%).

Examples of the ways in which these presentational devices were used and affect the reconstruction of the *White Paper* tabling come from the CBC's *City at Six* program on November 1, 1979 (story 1, item 1).

> *Anchor* (Stan Gibbons): The *White Paper* on sovereignty–association has been tabled; but it was almost upstaged by an invasion of civil servants into the room where the document was supposed to be released. We have the full story tonight on the *City at Six*. [linking]
>
> Good evening. I'm Stan Gibbons. George Finstadt is in Quebec City. [nominating]
>
> Just after two this afternoon Premier Lévesque stood in the National Assembly and tabled the *W.P.* on sovereignty–association, a document called "Quebec–Canada, a New Deal." [linking/framing]
>
> Don McPherson has spent most of the afternoon reading it and he reports there is nothing in it that is substantively news. But it is different. It's the first time a government of Quebec, not just a party, has outlined a position for negotiating a new relationship with Canada. Here's his report. [nominating/focusing]

The evidence shows that through the five-stage linking process, in which identifiable speakers explicitly address the audience, journalistic control determines how external voices are allowed to enter the narrative and how their telling is going to be evaluated. According to Genette, the stations' narrative voices not only define the types of knowledge that will become available to the viewers, but also the legitimacy of all voices within the narrative logic itself (Genette, 1982). These narrative devices help the journalistic voices to affect the strategy and structure of the news story itself. In Brunsdon and Morley's words (1978, p. 61):

> The structure contains (in both senses: includes and holds within limits) the independent–authentic contributions of the extra-programme participants. . . . The discursive work of linking and framing items binds the divergent realities of . . . varied news accounts into the . . . one "reality for the program."

From an interpretive standpoint the stations' voices provide the "metalanguage" of the news program. They are in charge of the meanings a news story will convey, not only through the rhetorical subordination of other voices, but also because this narrative subordination implies that what politicians, experts, and the public say, is rhetorically *less believable*. Although these three groups are legitimated political actors in the democratic contest for public opinion formation, the narrative evidence confirms that the media personnel have "usurped" these actors' interpretive capacities. It is thus no wonder that there is a growing critique on the part of politicians that their messages to the public are being intercepted and quoted out of context.

Special Story Formats

The "story format" refers to the narrative pattern in which a news item is couched. There are special types of journalistic narrations through which the journalistic requirements for "balance" and "neutrality" are *stylistically* represented. Michael Schudson notes that it is precisely through observing these statutory obligations that the ideological affectivity of the media is achieved (Schudson, 1989, p. 267). Our analysis identifies eight of these: report, description, commentary, narration, opinion, points of view, opinion poll, and fact (Kline, 1982, pp. 28–31). Story formats provide insight into the "rhetorical"—that is, the persuasive—strategies embedded in the narrative structure of the news program itself. Of these eight story formats only two can be called "neutral" or "factual" (descriptions and reports), while the six others all incorporate varying degrees of interpretation (opinion, points of view, commentary, and narration). *Descriptions* in our analysis refer to stories that are couched in the "you are there" presentational style and are without commentary, while *reports* contain only a bare outline of the news event.

Table 14.2 corroborates the strikingly different story formats that English and French journalists utilized in recounting the *White Paper* tabling. English stations, knowing of the skepticism of their viewers toward the document, rendered fully one half (50%) of their stories in the heavily inflected *opinion* format. Because these stories evaluate an external source (employing a view, opinion, speech, or report as the pivot of the story) the format lends itself to representing ideas with which one is not in agreement. English stations also made use of the *commentary* format, which assesses an event in relation to its causes or consequences in another 13% of all stories. More than two thirds (67%) of English language stories were thus heavily interpreted, as one would expect in a political situation in which the majority of Anglophone viewers had already made up their minds.

Table 14.2 indicates further that the French stations' news dis-

TABLE 14.2. Comparison of Anglophone and Francophone Newscasts by Story Format (% Duration)

Story Format	Anglophone	Francophone
Opinion	50	28
Points of view	17	33
Commentary	13	13
Description	9	12
Narration	11	5
Report	1	10

courses, which had to appeal to audiences on both sides of the referendary debate, used the *points of view* format most frequently (33%). This format makes conflict the center of the story and thus lends itself to the rendition of "balance" in the polarized referendary debate through the juxtaposition of opposing views. French stations were also much heavier users of the more "neutral" *description* and *reports* story formats, which constituted an additional quarter (22%) of their story accounts. Even in this news discourse, however, 28% of all stories were narrated in the *opinion* format, corroborating the thesis that all journalistic reconstructions are heavily inflected.

Together, these comparisons show that public opinion formation proceeds through at least four interlocking narrative processes: the exclusion of the viewer as an *active* participant in the communicational encounter; the subjugation of the politicians' and other outsider's voices in the news narrative; the "linking" devices that contextualize the subject matter; and the unique story formats in which the narrative is couched. Each of these "adds" narrative elements to the journalistic recounting of events. Editorialization is thus a very complex process that enters the news discourse not only through the selection and reordering of events, but also much more forcefully, yet less visibly, through the narrative process of "dramatization" itself. These dramatization processes *create* the meaning contexts into which the audience's interpretive hypotheses must ultimately fit. The processes are therefore often called "propagandistic" because they help to "manufacture" public consent by quietly rearranging the meaning context through rhetorical means (Herman & Chomsky, 1988, p. xi). "Dramatization" creates a sense of an orderly political process in connection with the *White Paper* tabling, which "naturalizes" the news personnel's version of what happened. The naturalization process central to the functioning of "persuasive" communication, creates public opinion through the presentation of an "institutional order of power [that] is projected as one of consensus and legitimacy, *as if* it were compelling and beyond the argument of rational people" (Gusfield, 1981, pp. 75–76).

RHETORICAL SUBSTANCE: THE "WHATNESS" OF THE WHITE PAPER DEBATE AND ITS TYPES OF APPEAL

What is this institutional order of power that the English and French Montreal stations create concerning the *White Paper* tabling? To get at these questions, story formats have to be correlated with the cast of characters involved in the political debate as voices and as actors. If each television news program renders politics as a "theater of public life" how were the "YES" and "NO" sides rendered? Election coverage in North American television follows well-established narrative strategies, which we have described elsewhere as using game metaphors and polar oppositions to add dramatic impetus to the ongoing stories (Robinson, 1989, p. 150). Leader descriptions enter this narrative as audiovisual *dramatis personae*, while diverse social groups, provincial and federal party representatives, business men, and others become unified and stereotyped into the polarized "YES" and "NO" forces. In the Quebec referendary debate these leaders' *personae* became stereotyped into the smoke-surrounded, populist orator Lévesque, signified by the blue "fleur de lis" flag, and the stern, intellectual adversary Claude Ryan, signified by the red "maple leaf." Although we expected that the English stations would not support the "YES" team, we were not prepared for the very critical semantic inflections that *both* news narratives attached to the "YES" side of the debate. Why were these surprising contextualizations undertaken by the two station groups? And how did their appeals reflect and structure preexisting audience knowledges?

As indicated above, the "sympathetic" "NO" characters made up an overwhelming three quarters (73%) of the characters mentioned in the English news coverage, leaving only about one quarter (27%) of the news attention for the coverage of the "YES" side. The French news narrative, in contrast, focused its narrative attention on the "YES" side, privileging it by a two-thirds margin (61%) over the other actors (39%) on the political stage. This seeming disproportionate importance accorded to only one side of the referendary debate by both sets of stations is, however, counterbalanced by the ways in which the two news narratives insert the "NO" and "YES" characters' voices into their discourses. In both station groups this is accomplished through *indirection*. This means that both the English as well as the French stations did not let the different *dramatis personae* speak for themselves, but recontextualized their statements through three narrative strategies. The journalistic narrator either uses the statement in a straight commentary; articulates it as part of a news analysis; or quotes the source indirectly by paraphrasing the statement. The major difference between the English and the French stations' narratives is that the French contextualize the "YES" side more heavily than they do the "NO" side. Our comparison showed that 81% of the "YES" side's statements are indirectly presented, versus 63% of those offered by the "NO" opposition. In the English narrative both the "YES" (66%) and the "NO" (60%) sides are about equally interpreted. This, then, is the first argumentation strategy that explains both language stations' more empathetic account of the "NO" side in the political debate.

Our comparison of the *use* to which English and French stations put a character's statements provides insight into a second argumentation strategy. Here again it appears that the "NO" side has a better chance of maintaining interpretive independence for its claims than the "YES" side. This is evidenced by the fact that Premier Lévesque's statements were generally used as a basis for interpretation, while those of Claude Ryan were left completely uninterpreted. Although both of these characters spoke for themselves, the statements of the "YES" side's Lévesque were recontextualized by the station personnel, while those of the leader of the "NO" side were left in his own voice. The Parti Québecois spokespersons were also treated to the same pattern of differential interpretation, while the statements of the federalist Provincial Liberals were left uninterpreted. Again, the statements of the "YES" side were voiced over while those of the "NO" were rendered verbatim. Because the news personnel of *all* stations not only paraphrased the "YES" side's statements more frequently, but additionally used them to further their own narrative goals, we can say that "YES" side statements were *doubly contextualized*. Such a double contextualization rendered these "YES" side statements less creditable to the viewer. They did not carry the same force precisely because they had been translated into the more rational bureaucratic news language used by the station voices.

A third and final argumentation strategy that was used particularly by the French stations also exercises differential control over the statements of the "YES" versus the "NO" sides in the referendary debate. It is achieved through the *explanatory context* into which a character's statements are placed. Table 14.3 shows clearly that more of the "YES" side statements (38%) than those of the "NO" side (9%) are interpreted, which means that the narrator interprets the significance of the statement, document, or event. More "NO" (35%) than "YES" (24%) side's statements are also used as the source for interpreting, or in the "quote as proof" mode—a format in which 30% of the "NO" and only 14% of

TABLE 14.3. Comparison of the "Explanatory Context" of YES and NO Side Statements in Anglophone and Francophone News Programs (% Segments)

	Anglophone		Francophone	
	NO	YES	NO	YES
Source as basis	25	21	35	24
Quote as proof	23	27	30	14
Interpretation	19	24	9	38
Introduction	10	7	22	22
Uninterpreted	17	14	4	3
Diminishes	5	7	—	—
Evaluation	1	—	—	—

the "YES" side's statements appear. A second interesting point revealed by this table is that the English news discourse seems to treat the "NO" and the "YES" sides of the debate more evenhandedly, making no significant distinctions in the explanatory strategies used for the two sides.

One can conclude from these findings that the French stations had to work harder to keep their narratives "balanced" than the English stations, which were reporting to audiences who were homogeneously of the "NO" point of view. This "working harder" of the French stations, the table indicates, means that they had to do more interpreting and use more strategies than their English counterparts. Only a negligible 4% of their character's statements were left uninterpreted, as compared to the English stations' 17%. Furthermore, in order to satisfy their politically polarized audience groups, two very different kinds of explanatory strategies had to be developed for the "YES" and the "NO" side's arguments: an *indirect* interpretation strategy using the "source as basis" and "quote as proof" modes for the "NO" side's statements, and a *direct* interpretation strategy for the "YES" side's statements. In the English news discourse no such differences in interpretive strategies for the two sides' arguments are needed, because the political outlooks of their audience groups were homogeneous.

POLITICAL CONSENSUS BUILDING AND "IMAGE POLITICS"

Alvin Gouldner (1976, p. 96) has argued that the relation between the media and the public is so close that they are mutually constitutive concepts: "A public consists of persons who habitually acquire their news and orientations from impersonal mass media." The styles in which mass communications are rendered are therefore of central significance because they offer differential opportunities for ordinary citizens to participate in the politics of decision making. David Chaney notes that the interdependence of public opinion and the mass media clarifies a common feature of them both: "They are ways of talking about society that are to a significant extent governed by the interests of metropolitan administrative elites" (Chaney, 1981, p. 116). There is, as our study has demonstrated, never *a* public, but a potentially *large set* of publics. In Montreal's referendary campaign these publics organized themselves by language and ethnic origin. English Canadians and immigrants from Italy, Portugal, and Greece, who constituted the majority of ethnic Quebecers, aligned themselves with the antisecessionist "NO" side in the campaign. French-speaking Quebecers, in contrast, constituted publics that ranged along the political continuum from those approving the province's sovereignty, to those who were neutral or against it.

The different ways in which Montreal's English and French speaking stations, as consensus builders for their particular publics, narrated the *White Paper* tabling, show furthermore that "public opinion" is an evocative concept describing a rhetorical process through which authorities and pressure groups categorize beliefs in a way that marshals support or opposition to their interests (Edelman, 1977, p. 50). The differing narrations arose out of differing event selections, differing casts of characters, and the use of differing argumentation strategies. While the English stations focused on the "NO" side of the debate, the French stations overwhelmingly covered the "YES" side's characters. *Both* sets of stations, however, treated the "NO" side's arguments differently within their news programs and contextualized them less heavily. They used the "NO" statements as a "source" for interpretation or in the "quote as proof" mode, where a character can speak in his or her own voice. In the case of the "YES" side statements, the narrator contextualized 38% of all statements directly, paraphrasing or voicing-over what had been said.

The analysis has also demonstrated the active role of the audience in meaning creation, which has been overlooked by much research. Although the different Montreal audiences were spatially "phantoms" in the mass-mediated television situation, they were temporally acknowledged in the rhetorical construction of the news programs. Even though the differing audience segments could not talk back to the announcer/reporters, their "points of view" were acknowledged in the *White Paper* narrations. Audiences, this evidence shows, have an important role to play in public opinion formation. They supply the various "common stocks of knowledge" and the "logics of argumentation." Michael Schudson (1982, p. 98) correctly observes that "narrative conventions function less to increase or decrease the truth value of the message they convey, than to shape and narrow the range of what kinds of truths can be told" in a particular historical time and place.

We have argued elsewhere (Robinson & Charron, 1989, p. 161) that the rise of consumer culture has had an impact on politics in a variety of ways. Recent scholarship argues that between 1920 and 1970 the marketplace itself gradually absorbed the functions originally performed by diverse and separate cultural institutions, among them political parties. In consumer culture, which cuts across income and wealth strata, class and ethnicity are superseded by the market. The latter provides affinity groups who share a similar lifestyle with guideposts for personal and social identity. The major image diffusers within free enterprise society are the media, whose advertising-sponsored flow of symbols crosses all social groups. Advertising's "democracy of consumption," which promises the *symbols* of status and influence to everyone, now mediates and stands between the traditional social institutions, which embody the uneven distribution of wealth and power in society. We contend that in such a setting the advertising model of persuasive communication becomes the norm and also penetrates politics as the preferred rhetoric for addressing the voter. What has been called "image politics" is the symptom of this penetration, and refers to the style and rhetoric of contemporary media campaigns that have increasingly become expressions of advertising and marketing techniques and are especially since the 1980s increasingly indistinguishable from product advertisements (Leiss, Kline, & Jhally, 1986, p. 311).

Joshua Meyrowitz (1985) explores the sources of "image politics" and locates them not only in advertising practices, but also in the changed communications environment that provides all public officials with an *overabundance* of media exposure. The camera eye and the microphone ear can now probe both the previously "private" backstage and the "public" onstage behavior of politicians, in what he calls a "sidestage" or "middle region" view (Meyrowitz, 1985, p. 270). With invasive electronic coverage, politicians, as performers of social roles, lose part of their rehearsal time, as well as their previously private rehearsal space. Consequently, their performances become more spontaneous and extemporaneous. While contemporary politicians therefore try hard to structure the *content* of the media coverage they receive, the *form* of the coverage itself is changing the kinds of political image they are able to express. The revealing nature of television's expressive presentational style cannot be fully counteracted by manipulation, practice, and/or high-paid consultants, because the political ritual itself has changed.

When the means of communication and the forms of interaction change, so must the "characters" that are portrayed. This study demonstrates that media personnel by means of their idiosyncratic narrative rules cocreate political "scripts" with and for their particular viewer groups. As such, they not only generate meanings about public happenings in the "real world" but also represent politics as a "theater of public life." This scripting has, of course, also affected politicians' behavior. To begin with it has heightened the "expressive" dimension of a politician's *persona,* as does the juxtaposition of the stylized renditions of the "mobile," chain-smoking and rumple-suited Lévesque to those of the "stolid," academic, and carefully dressed Ryan. It has also made election campaigning much more hazardous, because political drama is more highly "ritualistic" than everyday social behavior. A single inappropriate act can disqualify a political performer from completing the ongoing election ritual. Edmund Muskie's public shedding of tears, and Brian Mulroney's "dice rolling" remark during the recent constitutional debate, are but two examples of "contaminating" acts that sent these performers' popularity scores plummeting instantaneously.

"Image politics" involves much more than a surface change in style, because political reality and political ritual are closely intertwined. According to Lance Bennett, political campaigns serve two interrelated purposes. One is the politician's short-term pragmatic purpose to be elected. The other and perhaps more important function of campaigns is social ritual: the creation of "the backdrop against which the public can work out its tensions and satisfy its needs for security, order, leadership, and control over the future" (Bennett, 1977, pp. 219–220). The referendum evidence has demonstrated that the pragmatic and ritualistic elements of campaign discourses cannot be separated. It is therefore incorrect to say that there is a real (efficient, useful) politics that is masked by an unreal (superficial) sham show called "image politics." Denying the ritualized nature of politics is itself part of the ritual in which, as is detailed above, those who purport to report on politics, have themselves become deeply enmeshed. Journalists themselves have become "actors"—although *unlegitimated*—actors on the political stage, where through their role as "narrators" they have usurped political power, which, according to democratic theory, is not theirs to exercise. Far from playing a merely "recording" role, media personnel and media institutions today threaten to shatter the delicate system of checks and balances that was supposed to circumscribe the powers of the legislative, the executive, and the judicial branches of government against those of the "fourth estate."

ACKNOWLEDGMENTS

Funds for this project were received from the Social Science Research Council of Canada (#410-81-0398-R1) and from McGill University's Faculty of Graduate Studies and Research. They are herewith gratefully acknowledged.

NOTE

1. To unravel the relationship between explanation and narrative in news stories our dramaturgical analysis interrelated narrator roles, cast of characters, events and "components of argumentation." Seven *narrator roles* are divided into two major groups: newspresenter roles (anchorperson, reporter, commentator, and interviewer) and three outside sources (newsmaker, expert, and person in the street). Each of these is situated in a particular relationship to the camera. *Characters* or sources of news stories are divided into the "YES" and "NO" forces. Characters and *events* are intimately related and therefore handled separately in our analysis. Components of story construction include seven *story formats* (report, description, commentary, narration, opinion, points of view, opinion poll, fact). *Presentational devices* characteristic of specific narrator roles are: linking; framing; focusing, nominating, and summing up. *Presentation of voice* and context code the source and manner in which news personnel utilize outside sources. They are *indirect* or *direct*. *Audience links* refer to anchorperson's use of direct references to the audience through use of personal pronouns. SPSS-X subprograms were used to compute the results of this analysis. BREAKDOWN was used for analyses in which the dependent measure was the length of the segment in seconds. Where the dependent measure was the number of presentational devices used, the MULT RESPONSE subprogram was employed. The CROSSTABS subprogram was used for analyses where the number of segments was the dependent measure.

REFERENCES

Allen, R. C. (1987). Introduction: Talking about television. In R. C. Allen (Ed.), *Channels of discourse* (pp. 1–16). Chapel Hill: University of North Carolina Press.

Altheide, D. L. (1985). *Media power*. Beverly Hills, CA: Sage.

Ang, I. (1987, August 4). *Stereotyping the audience: And how to avoid it.* Paper presented at the ICA Conference, Montreal, Canada.

Barthes, R. (1977). *Image, music, text.* Glasgow: Fontana/Collins.

Bennett, W. L. (1977). The ritualistic and pragmatic bases of campaign discourse. *The Quarterly Journal of Speech, 63*, 219–238.

Brunsdon, C., & Morley, D. (1978). *Everyday television: "Nationwide."* London: British Film Institute.

Chaney, D. (1981). Public opinion and social change: The social rhetoric of documentary and the concept of news. In D. Chaney (Ed.), *Mass media and social change*. Beverley Hills, CA: Sage.

Connell, I. (1980). Television news and the social contract. In S. Hall, D. Hobson, A. Lower, & P. Willis (Eds.), *Culture, media and language* (pp. 139–156). London: Hutchison.

Dahlgren, P. (1985a). *Tuning in the news: TV journalism and the process of ideation*. Stockholm: Journalisthogskolan Skriftserie.

Edelman, M. (1977). *Political language*. New York: Academic Press.

Fraser, G. (1984). *P.Q.: Rene Lévesque and the parti Québecois in power*. Toronto: Macmillan.

Genette, G. (1982). *Figures of literary discourse*. New York: Columbia University Press.

Gitlin, T. (1977). Spotlights and shadows: Television and the culture of politics. *College English, 38*(8), 787–801.

The Glasgow University Media Group. (1976). *More bad news*. London: Routledge & Kegan Paul.

Goffman, I. (1983) *Forms of talk*. Philadelphia: University of Pennsylvania Press.

Gusfield, J. R. (1981). *The culture of public problems*. Chicago: University of Chicago Press.

Hall, S. (1977). Culture, the media, and the ideological effect. In J. Curran, M. Gurevitch, & J. Wollcott (Eds.), *Mass communication and society* (pp. 315–348). London: Edward Arnold.

Hall, S. (1980). Encoding and decoding the television discourse. In Stuart Hall *et al.* (Eds.), *Culture, media, language* (pp. 128–139). London: Hutchison.

Hartley, J. (1982). *Understanding news*. London: Methuen Co. Ltd.

Herman, E. S., & Chomsky, N. (1988). *Manufacturing consent*. New York: Pantheon Books.

Kline, S. (1982). *The rationality of the reel: The structure of interpretation in television news*. Toronto: York University.

Leiss, W., Kline S., & Jhally, S. (1986). *Social communication in advertising*. Toronto: Methuen.

Meyrowitz, J. (1985). *No sense of place: The impact of electronic media on social behavior*. New York: Oxford University Press.

Nichols, W. (1976). Documentary theory and practice. *Screen, 17*(4), 34–48.

Robinson, G., Bloom, M., & Sullivan, D. (1983). Visual presentation and representation: Stylistic differences in French and English TV news coverage. (French Version) *Communication et Information, 4*, 63–85.

Robinson, G., & Charron, C. Y. (1989). Television news and the public sphere: The case of the Quebec referendum. In M. Raboy & P. Bruck (Eds.), *Communication for and against democracy* (pp. 147–163). Montreal: Black Rose Books.

Schudson, M. (1982). The politics of narrative form: The emergence of news conventions in print and television. *Daedalus, 3*(4), 97–113.

Schudson, M. (1989). The sociology of news production. *Media, Culture and Society, 11*, 263–282.

Wright, C. R. (1959). *Mass communication: A sociological perspective*. New York: Random House.

V

PUBLIC OPINION AND THE PROMISE OF DEMOCRACY

15

The Press, Public Opinion, and Public Discourse

James W. Carey

> The vast growth of the social, steadily encroaching on both public and private life, has produced the eerie phenomenon of mass society, which rules everybody anonymously, just as bureaucracy, the rule of no one, has become the modern form of despotism.
>
> —MARY MCCARTHY (1958)

At this late date in the history of the American republic it may be impossible to recover a useful and usable conception of public opinion and public discourse, despite notable attempts to do so. Since there is more than a hint of the romantic in the verb "recover," I should explain my use of it. Phrases such as "the recovery of the public sphere," used rather often these days, do not necessarily imply that there was once, long ago, in some pristine past, an era in which the public reigned, in which our ancestors lived a free and uncoerced life of communal bliss, and that we, now armed with spiritual travellers' checks, can haul back to the present and reestablish. To paraphrase Gertrude Stein, "Back there there is no there there." The "recovery of public life" is not an attempt to recapture a period, historical moment, or condition but, instead, to invigorate a conception, illusion, or idea that once had the capacity to engage the imagination, motivate action, and serve an ideological purpose. Public life refers to an illusion of the possible rather than to something with a given anterior existence. To place public life in the past is merely to situate it in a context where it can be thought, rather than in a landscape where it was real.

The reason why contemporary politics and with it the press and public opinion often seems so meaningless is that they have been severed from any imagination of a possible politics that can serve as a basis of action and motivation. Gripped by what C. Wright Mills called "crackpot realism," we have pretty much concluded that "public life" is not only an illusion and a species of the pastoral but an undesirable objective of both politics and everyday life. We may still hold to some notion of democracy as a desirable state of affairs, but it is, to appropriate the title of Robert Entman's (1989) book, a "democracy without citizens," a democracy without a public or a public life.

This evacuation of the public realm, a feature of both contemporary theory and practice, is driven, of course, by the ruthlessly privatizing forces of capitalism, which often make such a life unthinkable. However, the evacuation of the public realm is also a product of progressive thought. Most ideological positions, Left and Right, actively struggle against the notions of the public, public discourse, and public life. In short, whatever political allegiances obtain, they are in agreement on one point: a modern political community must be, empirically, theoretically, and normatively, a community of power not of discourse, an arena of naked and manipulative struggle between interest groups, another item in the culture of consumption and coercion. This is the way the world works and, in truth, the only way it can and ought to work. There is simply no conceivable alternative. Because modern political culture was formed as a reaction formation to totalitarianism, we are convinced that the only alternative to the omniscient state is an elite and managed democracy conducted as a propaganda contest in which the public is a spectator and ratifier of decisions made elsewhere. Why are we so imaginatively impoverished?

A sense of conceptual loss, then, will pervade this chapter—a loss of, to paraphrase some lines of Lawrence Levine (1988), a rich, shared public culture. American culture was from the outset deeply divided by race, ethnicity, class, and, above all, religion. Nonetheless, it was also typified by a shared culture, less hierarchically organized, not adjectivally divided by labels such as high, mass, and popular, and not, strictly speaking, the property or province of any one group. Today our only shared culture is a commercial one, a substitute for a political culture, and what exists of politics is formed as a metaphor of commerce and an imperative of markets. While that culture, with its commitment to markets, can do many things, it cannot produce a politics, or it can produce nothing more than a politics of interests.

The object, then, of this reconsideration of the press, politics, and public opinion is to move toward a shared political culture, particularly in terms of our understanding of the First Amendment and, therefore, our understanding of what have come to be thought of as the "rights" of assembly, speech, and the press. To defend free speech so that people may be unfettered in forming their own opinions and choosing their own ends is a rather different matter than defending it on the grounds that a life of political discussion is inherently worthier than a life unconcerned with public affairs, worthier than a life merely self-absorbed and self-interested. (Sandel, 1984) These questions have been raised anew by the spectacle of recent presidential politics.

HAVE WE REACHED A WATERSHED?

The parenthesis enclosing the 1988 and 1992 presidential primaries and elections may turn out to be—although the wish is certainly father to the thought—a watershed period in American politics and in the history of public opinion. In the aftermath of the 1988 election there was widespread disgust with American politics and with the press itself, a disgust that muted the normal happiness of political victory and the end to yet another endless season of campaigning (Rosen, 1992). It was a monumentally smarmy campaign, reduced to a few slogans and brutal advertisements that produced yet another record low in voter turnout. A predictable round of seminars and symposia followed decrying the "degradation of democratic discourse" and the immiseration of the press in horse-race and gossip-column journalism. The theatrical and hermetically sealed quality of the campaign was caught by Joan Didion (1992):

> When we talk about the process, then, we are talking increasingly, not about "the democratic process," or the general mechanism affording citizens of a state a voice in its affairs, but the reverse: A mechanism seen as so specialized that access to it is correctly limited to its own professionals, to those who manage policy and those who report on it, to those who run the polls and those who quote them, to those who ask and those who answer the questions on the Sunday shows, to the media consultants, to the columnists . . . to the handful of insiders who invent, year in and year out, the narrative of public life. . . . What strikes one most vividly about such a campaign is precisely its remoteness from the actual life of the country. (pp. 49–50)

The widespread disenchantment of the public with the spectacle of politics—with what Ms. Didion called "Insider Baseball," a game only for the players, not even for the fans—was evident not only in low voter turnout but in the large (9%) decline in the audience for the political conventions. The conventions were saved only by commercial demography: as one advertising specialist put it, "the upscale target audience was there" (Didion, 1992). Following the election there were renewed calls for the press to reconstruct its approach to politics, including an exhortation from one of the most distinguished practitioners of the craft, David Broder (1990). Cries of "never again," were heard in some newsrooms around the country and a few, most notably the Charlotte *Observer*, laid plans for radically altered forms of election coverage in the future. Despite that, the 1992 primary season opened pretty much as a reenactment of the worst of the lessons learned in 1988. The differences that initially obtained came largely as a result of matters outside the control of either press or politics. Tom Harkin's favorite son status lowered the visibility of the Iowa caucus, giving a long run-up to the New Hampshire primary. With abundant time and an initial primary in a small and accessible state with a strong tradition of town meeting governance, the campaign managed to escape the confines of television and spread out into towns and hamlets. Driven by the absence of a significant Republican contest, and by the unusual candor of Paul Tsongas, the primary was direct and intimate and produced an unusually high level of issue-oriented political discourse. Voter interest and turnout was up as the campaign fanned out from New Hampshire to the multiple primaries of Super Tuesday. At that point, political hope dissipated; the campaign reentered the simulated world of journalism: Bill Clinton's character moved to the forefront, his dalliance with Gennifer Flowers became an obsession, his Vietnam draft status an easy and never-ending story. Feeding-frenzy journalism reigned, and voter interest declined such that by the New York primary voter turnout was down by almost one third over 1988. Everything journalists and politicians promised to avoid post-1988 was again the norm as the campaign swung into summer.

But then something began to change. In part, it was a spontaneous movement among voters to reclaim the campaign for themselves, symbolized by the second debate in Richmond, in which the candidates directly faced voter questions. In part it was the gravitation of the campaign into the talk show circuit—Larry King, Arsenio Hall, Tabitha Soren, Rush Limbaugh. It was also partly the use of e-mail, partly the use of computer bulletin boards, partly the fax machine, partly the use of 800 numbers, partly call-in radio, and partly private satellite hookups that signaled a shifting of ground. The phrase that caught on to describe this shift was the "new news": new technological forms eroding historic relations of press and politics, and the emergence of a new public opinion as a altered force in political campaigns (Katz, 1992). To many traditional journalists and some politicians, this was disaster, for it displaced a cozy and predictable game into a new, uncertain, less manageable landscape. The traditional power and influence of the press evaporated, displaced by the entertainment industry, celebrities impersonating journalists, and new, less mediated, contact between citizens and candidates. The broadcast networks, a bastard by-product of the Fairness Doctrine and a vaudeville tradition that had, against all odds, created exceptional moments of electronic journalism, were particularly threatened by the migration of political discourse out of the news room and into a new electronic highway of chattering classes and masses.

This is a story that, like all good stories, had a villain: Ross Perot. Perot's campaign, totally electronic, had circumvented party organization and presidential primaries. Perot even avoided a national convention, as volunteers got him on the ballot in state after state. Consequently, he did not have to campaign in the states, ignored local newspapers, radio and television, and in effect told the national press "I can win without you and against you." This was not a third-party candidate but a no-party candidate. Perot demonstrated that it was possible to run with one's own money and avoid restrictions on federal matching funds. He laid down new rules for presidential politics: avoid specifics, stay away from journalists, hold as few press conferences as possible, stay off the serious interview programs, cultivate electronic populism by exploiting call-in radio. Who needs Sam Donaldson if you can speak directly to a disorganized mass?

All this gave rise to the worst fear of journalists formed by the experience of World War II: the new media had greased the wheels of modern politics for demagogues and demagoguery. The electronic revolution had created mass politics and mass society; only the technical words were missing. Journalists had encountered the postmodern form of politics and public opinion, and it left them little role in campaigns. If, as Joan Didion (1992) put it, campaigns "raise questions that go . . . vertiginously to the heart of the structure" of the press and politics, what then, was the future of journalism and the meaning of public opinion?

Even if some of this seems completely wrong, we ought to begin on a note of empathy for journalists. Journalists, like the historians they in some ways resemble, have always been prey to false dawns, and to eras artificially defined as having ended. The journalist and historian alike inhabit the same world as politicians, even if they are a step away from the action and, like politicians, they absorb an inexhaustible supply of beliefs in Nirvana and Armageddon. The politician needs to believe that the events in which he or she is taking part belong to a sequence that is nearing its heroic or—when the dawn is dimmest—its craven and predestined conclusion. The language of blurred continuity, with which we understand and describe our own lives, most of the time, is anathema to the political leader, and often to the journalist and historian as well (Young, 1989).

Journalists are genetically marked—the phrase is not too strong—by the characteristic struggle and fear of this century, particularly one imprinted by World War II and its aftermath. Journalistically the 20th century can be defined as the struggle for democracy against propaganda, a struggle inevitably waged by an "objective" and "independent" press. That struggle culminated in the seizure of the means of communication by the demagogues of the 1930s and 1940s—Hitler and Stalin—and their Cold War reincarnation Joseph McCarthy, whose ghost haunts American journalism (Bayley, 1981). Perot's eruption into American politics recalled, if only implicitly, this episode. However, for those on the other side of the post-war divide, that struggle no longer seems apposite: the fear of demagoguery seems a curious hang-over of a forgotten age, and its reoccurrence improbable. Similarly, the quest for independence or objectivity seems to a younger generation a curious absence of passion and commitment, a deliberate sitting out of history.

This historical divide, which is also a generational one, is the mobile reference point of the hyperbolic division between the modern and the postmodern. If a medium implies and constitutes a world, then the world of modern journalism, a particular world of communication, democracy, and public opinion, a world built on the model of the modern newspaper and later network television, seemed to be running to the sea in red ruin. But, for the moment, the important lesson is this: all terms of the political equation—democracy, public opinion, public discourse, the press—are all up for grabs. All such terms are historically variable even as they define one another in mutual relief. Whatever democracy as a way of life may be, it is constituted by particular media of communication and particular institutional arrangements through which politics is conducted: speech and the agora, the colonial newspaper and pamphlet in the taverns of Philadelphia, the omnibus daily in the industrial city, the television network in an imperial nation. Similarly, a medium of communication is defined by the democratic aspirations of politics: a conversation among equals, the organ of a political ideology, a watchdog on the state, an instrument of dialogue on public issues, a device for transmitting information, the tool of interest groups. In addition, the meaning of public opinion gravitates between the abstract and concrete, between public sentiment and public judgment, between references to a concrete way of life, a mode of political action, and the statistical concatenation of individual desires and sentiments (Marcus & Hanson, 1993).

To belabor the point: what we mean by democracy depends on the forms of communication by which we conduct politics. What we mean by communication depends on the central impulses and aspirations of democratic politics. What we mean by public opinion depends on both. None of these phenomena is natural, none of the terms transcendent, all are found only within history. They exist only within language, within the particular historical conjunctures in which we define them.

However, something is afoot in modern societies that seems peculiarly tied to communications, to the decline of certain media that have defined the context of communications and democracy since the end of World War II and perhaps longer. The media have decisively changed in the last 20 years, both as technologies and as institutions. But democracy has changed also, as the ends of political life have been conceived in recent years. For example, there is a widespread desire for less *pro forma* political representation—whether by the press or by elected officials—and for more real political participation; there is more demand that the state act like a corporation, solving problems by producing new solutions on demand rather than muddling through difficulties (Barber, 1984).

What is changing is not some preternatural form of journalism, some transcendent form of democracy and public opinion, but rather a useful social arrangement, now in rather deep trouble, that was a modern invention. Modern journalism and modern democracy came into being around the 1890s and have had a pretty long run. But there was democracy before modern journalism; there will be democracy after it, although there are difficult and dangerous transitions to be negotiated. If only for the sake of argument, I contrast two ideal types of public opinion, journalism and democracy, which we can call journalism in a public society—constituting our original understanding of the press and the First Amendment—and journalism in a national society, the modern phase, which now seems to be coming to an end. This serves as a prelude to a brief conclusion on the dangerous and hopeful potentials of journalism, democracy, and public opinion in the years ahead.

THE EVOLUTION OF THE PUBLIC

Our basic understanding of journalism, politics, and democracy emerged in the public houses, the taverns of colonial America, although it was powerfully controlled by images of Greece and Rome and the language of republican political theory. Pubs were presided over by publicans who were often publishers as well. Publicans picked up information from travellers who often recorded what they had seen and heard on their journeys in log books stationed at the end of the bar, and from conversations in the pub. They recorded them and printed them, in order that they might be preserved and circulated. To these they added speeches, orations, sermons, offers of goods for sale, and the political opinions of those who gathered in public places—largely merchants and traders. In other words, the content of the press was by and large the spoken word, the things being said by public men in public places. In turn, conversation and discussion, public speech, was animated by what was read in the newspapers that circulated in the same public houses. As a French diplomat described it in 1783, "They have printed the news at once; they are read avidly in the Circles, the taverns and public places. They dispute the articles; they examine from all sizes, since all the individuals without exception take part in public affairs and are [therefore] naturally talkers and questioners."

Journalism reflected speech, and was largely made up of speech—the ongoing flow of conversation, not in the halls of state and legislature, but in public houses. This gives us our original understanding of the public: the public was a group, often of strangers, who gathered to discuss the news (Gouldner, 1976). Describing Philadelphia on the eve of the Revolution, Sam Bass Warner (1968) observes,

> Gossip in the taverns provided Philadelphia's basic cells of community life. . . . Every ward of the city had its inns and taverns and the London Coffee House served as the central communication node of the entire city. . . . Out of the meetings at the neighborhood tavern came much of the commonplace community development . . . essential to the governance of the city . . . and made it possible . . . to form effective committees of correspondence. (pp. 19–20)

Lest we be swept away by romanticism, the tragic flaw in this conception of the public should be noted, a flaw that had something to do with the decline of the public sphere—at least in concept. It was a public effectively restricted by race, class, and gender; that is, the public consisted of middle-class men who had an interest and stake in public affairs, commerce, business, or trade. Later, when public space began to fill with workers and artisans of another class, these merchants retreated into private space, into the men's clubs that are still a feature of large cities (Gouldner, 1976; Habermas, 1989). However, these fatal imperfections do not diminish the historical importance of the public as it was then defined, or the power of the concept in illuminating politics.

The public, in this phase, was not a fiction or an abstraction: a group of people sitting at home watching television or privately and invisibly reading a newspaper, or numbers collected in a public opinion poll. The public was a specific social formation: a group of people, often strangers, gathered in public houses to talk, to read the news together, to dispute the meaning of events, to join political impulses to political actions. The public was brought into existence by the conditions of the 18th-century city and by the printing press itself. The public was activated into a social relation by the news and, in turn, the primary subject of the news was the public: the opinions being expressed in public by merchants, traders, citizens, and political activists of the time. The emphasis on the public as a society of strangers does not imply that those who gathered to discuss the news were in fact strangers, but that the discussion occurred in an open context, in a place that was open to strangers and whose presence had to be taken into account.

In our time, the public is pretty much an abstraction, a term of exhortation and reflection. "The public's right to know" is the worn and unintelligible slogan of modern journalism. That press justifies itself in the name of the public, it exists to inform the public, to serve as the extended eyes and ears of the public; the press protects the public's interest and justifies itself in its name. The power of the term public comes from the fact that while the Constitution and the Bill of Rights are silent on the matter, it is the deepest and most fundamental concept of the entire liberal tradition. Liberal society is formed around the notion of a virtuous public. For John Locke, to be a member of the public was to accept a calling.

But the historical public is of a rather more humble origin. The public is a group of strangers that gathers to discuss the news, as well as being a mode of discourse among them. For the public to form, urban life had to develop sufficiently for strangers to be regularly thrown into contact with one another, and there had to be newspapers and pamphlets to provide a common focus of discussion and conversation. The public, then, was a society of conversationalists or disputants, dependent upon printing for the dissemination of their ideas.

However, for the public to gather, there had to be a public space, places where strangers could gather to discuss the news and where there were expectations, however imperfectly realized, of a rational, critical discourse among everyone involved. Public space, in turn, depended on public habits, manners, and talents: the ability to welcome strangers, to avoid intimacy, to wear a public mask, to shun the personal, to clamp some control on affect, and, in general, to achieve some psychological distance from the self. As such, the public was taken to be critical and rational—critical in the ordinary sense that nothing in public was to be taken for granted, everything was to be subject to argument and evidence, and rational, again in the ordinary sense, that the speaker was responsible for giving reasons for believing in any assertion, so that there was no intrinsic appeal to authority. "Critical" and "rational" are terms that in contemporary discourse have become transcendental, to be debated as abstract and essential qualities, present or absent in the self. However, the terms must refer to ordinary human practices: a willingness to answer questions, to be forthright, to disclose hidden motives, and to avoid dragging in notions like God or Science to save an argument when it begins to weaken.

Looked at from another angle, the public was more than a group of people or a mode of discourse, it was a location, a sphere, a sector of society. The public sphere was a seat of political power, which was thus not exclusively located in the State or its representatives nor in the private sector—the household and the company. Power was located, as well, in the world between the State and the private sector, in the public and in public discourse. And it was only in this sphere that power could wear the face of rationality, for it was the only sphere in which private interest might, even in principle, be transcended (Habermas, 1989; Robbins, 1993).

For our purposes, the critical factor was that the press, journalism—its freedom and its utility—was not an end in itself, but was justified in terms of its ability to serve and bring into existence an actual social arrangement, a form of discourse and a sphere of independent, rational, and political influence, its ability to provide one mode in which public opinion might form and express itself. The press did not so much inform or educate the public or serve as a vehicle of publicity or as a watchdog on the state—the roles it would assume in a later period. Rather, it reflected and animated public conversation and argument. It furnished material to be discussed, clarified, and interpreted, which constituted information in the narrow sense; but the value of the press was predicated on the existence of the public and not the reverse. Freedom of the press was an individual right, to be sure, but the right was based on the unspoken premise of the existence of the public.

Today, we generally read the First Amendment as a loose collection of clauses: religion, assembly, speech, and press. These clauses in turn contain separable rights exemplified by Supreme Court decisions that we can understand as free speech cases, free press cases, and so on. When read against the background of public life, however, the First Amendment is not a loose collection of separate clauses, but a compact description of a desirable political society. In other words, the amendment is not a casual array of clauses or high-minded principles, and it does not deed freedom of the press as a property right to journalists or any particular group (Carey, 1992). On this reading, the First Amendment describes the public and the ground conditions of public debate, rather than merely enumerating rights possessed by groups. It was only in the modern period that we developed the notion that the First Amendment protected rights and that the doctrine of rights could be used as a trump card to depress debate. On my reading, the First Amendment was an attempt to define the nature of public life as it existed at the time or as the Founders hoped it would exist. To put it in an artlessly simple way, the First Amendment says that people are free to gather together, free to have public spaces, free of the intrusion of the state or its representatives. Once gathered they are free to speak to one another and to carry on public discourse, freely and openly. They are further free to write down what they have to say and to share it beyond the immediate place of utterance. The religion clause, which might seem to be a rather odd inclusion, is at the heart of this interpretation. Religion was the fundamental social divide of the 18th century. In a society that still spoke a religious language in public and private, heresy was the major sin, as is clear, for example, from Milton's *Aeropagitica*. It was, therefore, the major reason for exclusion from the public realm and excommunication from public life. The religion clause merely says that people may not be excluded from public space and discussion, even on the basis of religion. Today religion is less problematic and the vexing exclusions are based on race, property, and gender. However, it was the religion clause that established the dynamic for further dismantling the boundaries and exclusions of public life.

Despite our contemporary disengagement from public life, the public remains the implicit term of the First Amendment and the "God term" of liberal society and the press alike—the term without which neither the press nor democracy makes any sense. This originalist conception of a public, a conversational public, a public of discussion and disputation independent of both the press and the State, has pretty much been eviscerated in our time. It has a philosophical existence and, because with us law feeds on the corpse of philosophy, it continues to be present in the language of Supreme Court cases.

Public life stands for a form of politics in which, in Jefferson's phrase, "We could all be participants in the government of our affairs" (Smith, 1985). Political equality in its most primitive mode simply meant, to rephrase Smith (1985), the right to be seen and heard—to have a public life. When the life of a people is dominated by a few public figures become political celebrities, the rest of us, denied the opportunity to be seen or heard, abandon the possibility of public joy and satisfy ourselves with private pleasures. Only when we can speak and act as citizens and have some promise that others will see, hear, and remember what we say will an interest in public life grow and persist. Therefore, the object of our politics remains the creation and restoration of what deTocqueville called the "little republics within the frame of the larger republic" (Smith, 1985). This is an imperative task if we are to aggregate an authentic public opinion and sustain political discourse. Without it all "political objects must remain indefinite and transient and political action short-lived and ineffective" (Smith, 1985, pp. 268–269).

THE MODERN ERA OF JOURNALISM

The transition from the original understanding of the press and politics to journalism in the modern era was slow and tortuous. Throughout the 19th century, the public sphere increasingly split into regional and class-based warring factions, organized around political parties and a partisan press. Journalism became an organ of such parties or, however independent, nevertheless ideologically aligned with political parties. Journalism expressed and reflected a bifurcated public sphere, as individuals joined in politics through party and press. Participation still occurred through party and press, and through the demonstrations, street parades, and street life that were expressions of both. As the franchise was extended, legal participation rose to unprecedented and unrepeated levels. Voter turnout averaged 77% in the last quarter of the 19th century. Popular politics, as Michael McGerr (1986, p. 5) puts it, "involved more than suffrage rights and record turnouts." Elections required visible support mobilized through popular journalism and political parties. Thus, the transformation to a separation between politics and the public had begun.

The modern era of journalism stretches from the 1890s to the 1970s. It begins with the birth of the national magazine, the development of the mass urban newspaper, the domination of news dissemination by the wire services and the creation of early, primitive forms of electronic communication. It culminates in the network era of television, when the entire nation could be assembled by three commercial networks, and on certain high holy days of politics—the Kennedy assassination, the quadrennial political conventions—the nation was so assembled (Dyan & Katz, 1992). The nation sat down to be counted as citizens of a continental, 24-hour-a-day republic.

In the United States truly national media and a national audience displaced from a local public did not emerge until the 1890s with the creation of national magazines and a national network of newspapers interconnected via the wire services. Such media were eventually supplemented by motion pictures produced in Hollywood and distributed nationally, and by radio in the 1920s. The rise of national or mass media, first via print and then the air waves, created "the great audience": a new collectivity in which we were destined to live out a major part of our lives. These media cut across the structural divisions in society drawing their audience irrespective of race, ethnicity, occupation, region, or social class. This was the first national audience and the first mass audience and, in principle, it was open to all. Modern communications media allowed individuals to be linked, for first time, directly to the "imaginary community of the nation" (Anderson, 1983, p. 6)—at least for nations as large as the United States—without the mediating influence of regional and other local affiliations. Such national media laid the basis for a mass society, understood in its most technical and least ideological sense: the development of a form of social organization in which intermediate associations of community, occupation, and class did not inhibit direct linkage of the individual and primary groups to the state and other nationwide organizations through mass communications.

The rise of national media represented a centripetal force in social organization. Such media greatly enhanced the control of space by reducing signally time (the gap between the time a message is sent and received as a function of distance) in communication, by laying down direct lines of access between national centers and dispersed audiences, and by producing a remarkable potential for the centralization of power and authority.

The period from 1890s onward saw the creation of a variety of social and cultural movements that were reactions against and impulses toward the formation of a national society through a national system of communication. Progressivism, populism, nativism, the know-nothings, women's suffrage, temperance, the Grange, and, indeed, the formation of modern ethnic and racial groups were all attempts to master, tame, and direct the currents of social change. A new class structure organized around a newly dominant class—the plutocrats—a structure Henry Adams lamented and Charles Beard described, was also created. These movements—some modern, some antimodern, some even postmodern—expressed a restless search for new identities and for new forms of social and cultural life. Taken together these movements offered new ways of being for a new type of society. These were movements organized by the new media, defined by media, commented upon by media, formed within media or at least as a response to new conditions of social life brought about in part by new media.

Our images of democracy and the press, to summarize, were formed within the structure and ideology of community life. As late as the turn of the century, democracy was seen as confined to small geographic areas and small populations. The New England town meeting was the icon of democracy and the newspaper and journalist gave life, meaning, and dignity to the local community—to the classical form of the public. This image of the pub, the publican, and the publisher all rolled in one, presiding over the meeting house where the public gathered to discuss the news, representing in his person the public interest, and publishing a public newspaper that summarized and reprinted public opinion—that is, what people were saying in public—this was the classic conception of democracy and the press, derived from ancient political theory and realized in the local and decentralized life of the republic in its first century. This bucolic notion of democracy and the press was transcended by the forces of industry and expansion, and with both came the need in this century to form both a new conception of democratic action and a new conception of the press within democracy. Both were born within what was, at least from the standpoint of journalism, the most important social movement of the turn of the century, the progressive movement, which both redefined the past and projected a new democratic future.

The progressive movement contained three separable but closely connected moments. First, it was an attack upon the plutocracy, upon concentrated economic power, and upon the national social class that increasingly had a stranglehold over wealth and industry. The economic dimension of the movement, however, also included the struggle by middle-class professionals—doctors, lawyers, journalists, social workers, and so on—to become a national class, to find a place in the national occupational structure and the national system of class influence and power. The national class of progressive professionals was, in many ways, merely a less powerful imitation, the shadow movement, of the national class of plutocrats, the new titans who ran and controlled industrial America.

Journalists were central to this new progressive class of professionals. They formed themselves into national groups and lobbied to professionalize their standing through higher education. They sponsored histories of their profession and a new reading of the First Amendment along with ethical codes of conduct to justify their new-found status in the new middle-class professional world. They tried to figure out new ways of reporting on and commenting about this new world—a new professional ideology in other words—that justified their place in the new order of things.

Progressivism was also a movement of political reform at the national level and, even more, an attempt to reclaim the cities from the political bosses and the urban machines. In many cases this was an attempt to uproot the political influence of ethnic working-class groups who had earlier on seized city politics from local commercial and cultural elites. Progressivism was devoted to "good government" (read honest, middle-class government) and created the chain of Better Government Associations that one still finds in major American cities. Progressivism was for merit and against patronage, for science and against tradition, for middle-class politics and against working-class privilege.

Journalists were usually allies of the movement for better government. That is, they were committed to certain middle-class ideals of honesty and uprightness. They warred against the machines if only because the machines did not need the press to govern. It did quite well with patronage and ward organization, whereas reform movements were dependent upon the publicity only the press could give and thus assiduously courted and flattered the new journalists. But journalists were aligned with the reform and progressive movements by ideology and conviction, by certain beliefs about modernity and the role of the press in a movement that was at once economic, political, and cultural.

Progressivism, in another guise, was a cultural movement that sought to define new styles of life, patterns of child rearing, modes of family life, taste in art, architecture, urban planning, and personal conduct. Progressive education, progressive child rearing, progressive art, progressive science, and progressive taste were as important in this movement as progressive economics and politics. Progressivism in culture became, in general, part of the outlook of the new journalists who took up residence in the new national media that formed the discourse of the nation.

The three wings of progressivism were joined to one common desire: a desire to escape the merely local and contingent, an enthusiasm for everything that was distant and remote, a love of the national over the provincial. The national media of communication—particularly magazines and books but including as well newspaper journalists, who found themselves pursuing a career that took them from city to city and paper to paper, assignment to assignment—were the arena where the progressive program was set out and the place where the struggle for its legitimation occurred.

The initial impact of the progressive movement on journalism was the rise of "muckraking," which in its initial stages directed its attack against the "plutocracy" and the business class. Muckraking arose within magazines rather than newspapers, since these new national media had no affiliation with politics—let alone with a given political party. While they owed, as Michael McGerr (1986) has pointed out, something to the crusading tactics of newspapers, muckraking magazines, like sensational newspapers, did not dwell long on any topic. They were "hit-and-run artists" who could expose corruption in an institution and lead to the passage of something like the Pure Food and Drug Act, but they did not have the shape and persistence to constitute a tradition of journalism or to sustain a continuous politics. What muckraking did do was to further a tradition of journalism that took as its task the unmasking of power, to serve as a watchdog not only of the state but of the full range of interest groups. For much of the 19th century political parties served as the principal means of influencing the distribution of economic resources and government privileges. When interest groups and pressure groups developed late in the century as a new vehicle for affecting governments increasingly involved in regulation of the economy, voting for party candidates in elections became less important. Muckraking gave rise to propaganda analysis: the unmasking of attempts by interest groups to control and manipulate the press. Both muckraking and propaganda analysis were attempts to unmask the power, privilege, and special interests that stood behind the presumed general beneficence of both private and public institutions. This was an American version of what became known in Europe as *Ideologiekritik*. However, muckraking was framed within the language of American democracy: muckrakers, first of all, took themselves to be representative of the people—protectors of the people's interests and not an independent intellectual class. Second, muckraking was straightforward, descriptive, and aimed at provoking public action rather than theoretical reflection. Third, while they aimed their efforts at unmasking the power of the business class, economic institutions, and business ideology, muckrakers examined concentrated power and propaganda in all its forms: labor unions as well as manufacturers' associations, universities as well as businesses. A paradigmatic figure in all this was Upton Sinclair, who in three significant volumes exposed the power and privilege of corruption of the meat-packing industry in *The Jungle,* higher education in *The Goose Step,* and even the press itself in *The Brass Check*.

What muckraking demonstrated and turned into an operative principal for the press was that democracy was no longer competition between political parties bearing explicit programs and ideologies but competition between interest and pressure groups who used the state, political parties, the press—indeed any apparatus available—to control the distribution of economic rewards and social privilege. By definition, interest groups operate in the private sector, behind the scenes, and their relation to public life is essentially propagandistic and manipulative. When interest groups arrive upon the scene, the public ceases to have a real existence. Moreover, the struggle among interests groups turns language into "public relations"; that is, an instrument in a struggle for advantage rather than a vehicle of the truth. All appearances become unreliable, all language suspect, all appeals to the public interest a sham move in the struggle for private advantage.

It was in this situation that the traditions of modern journalism and the particular conceptions of the media and democracy came into being, throwing each other into mutual relief. The press, in effect, broke away from politics. It established itself, at least in principal, as independent of all institutions: independent of the state, independent of political parties, independent of interest groups. It became the independent voter writ large; its only loyalty was to an abstract truth and an abstract public interest. This is the origin of objectivity in journalism, as Michael Schudson (1978) has shown. Objectivity was a defensive measure, an attempt to secure by quasi-scientific means a method for recording the world independent of the political and social forces that were shaping it. In this rendition, a democratic press was the representative of the people, of people no longer represented by political parties and the state itself. It was the eyes and ears of a public that could not see and hear for itself, or indeed talk to itself. It went where the public could not go, acquired information that the public could not amass on its own, tore away the veil of appearances that masked the play of power and privilege, set on a brightly lit stage what would otherwise be contained offstage, in the wings, where the real drama of social life was going on unobserved. The press seized hold of the First Amendment and exercised it in the name of a public that could no longer exercise it itself. The press became an independent profession and a collective institution: a true Fourth Estate that watched over the other lords of the realm in the name of those unequipped or unable to watch over it for themselves. The press no longer facilitated or animated a public conversation for public conversation, had disappeared. It informed a passive and privatized group of citizens who participated in politics through the press. What conversation remained was orchestrated by the press in the name of a superior knowledge and superior instruments of inquiry into just what was going on.

But, paradoxically enough, this new role of representative of the public was contained within a sentiment that was increasingly antipopulist and antipublic. One of the principal architects of this new understanding was the major American journalist of this century, Walter Lippmann. Lippmann's *Public Opinion* (1922), which is the founding book of modern American journalism, was an extended reflection on his experience as a member of Woodrow Wilson's staff at the drafting of the Treaty of Versailles. His conclusion was a dour one: it is impossible to get out of drift and achieve mastery by relying on the public or the press. There is no such thing as informed public opinion; therefore, public opinion cannot master events. Voters are inherently incompetent to direct public affairs: "They arrive in the middle of the third act and leave before the last curtain, staying just long enough to decide who is the hero and who is the villain" (Rossiter & Lare, 1963, p. 111). Lippmann concludes: "The common interest in life largely eludes public opinion entirely and can be managed only by a specialized class. I set no great store on what can be done by public opinion or the action of the masses" (1922, p. 111). The road away from drift and toward mastery, toward a sustainable democracy, was not through the public, not through public opinion, and not through the newspaper. The only hope lay in taking the weight off the public shoulders, recognizing that the average citizen had neither the capacity nor the interest and competence to direct society. Mastery would come only through a class of experts—a new order of samuri—who would mold the public mind and character: men and women dedicated to making democracy work for the masses, whether the masses wanted it or not.

Lippmann, in effect, took the public out of politics and politics out of public life, depoliticizing the public sphere. He turned the public over to private and specialized interests, albeit interests regulated by his new samuri class. Scientists were Lippmann's model for that class because he wrote in the heyday of science—an innocent age when science could be taken to be the exemplar of culture as a whole. He assumed that scientists were a transcendent class, without interests or objectives beyond the securing of truth, philosopher kings of the new world. The actual work of the world he turned over to the "interests":

> The burden of carrying on the work of the world, of inventing, creating, executing, of attempting justice, formulating laws and moral codes, of dealing with the technic and substance, lies not upon government but on those who are reasonably concerned as agents in the affair. Where the problems arise, the ideal is a settlement by the particular interests involved. They alone know what the trouble really is. (Rossiter & Lare, 1963, p. 111)

But what is the role of journalism in a world ruled by interests and regulated by science, a world in which the public fades to a spectator? It is not the task of journalism to tell the truth, for journalism has nothing to do with the truth. News is a blip on the social radar, an early-warning system that something is happening—nothing more. Otherwise, journalists primarily serve as conduits relaying truth arrived at elsewhere, by the experts—scientists in their laboratories, bureaucrats in their bureaus. The truth is not a product of the conversation or debate of the public or the investigations of journalists. Journalists merely translate the arcane language of experts into a publicly accessible language for the masses. They transmit the judgments of experts, and thereby ratify decisions arrived at by that class, not by the public or public representatives.

But journalists perform one other vital function: the chief function of news is publicity. News kept the experts honest; it kept them from confusing the public interest with the private interest by exposing them to the bright light of publicity. Lippmann had more faith in publicity than in the news or an informed public: "The great healing effect of publicity is that by revealing man's nature, it civilizes him. If people have to declare, publicly, what they want and why they want it, they won't be able to be altogether ruthless. A special interest openly avowed is no terror to democracy; it is neutralized by publicity" (Rossiter & Lare, 1963, pp. 226–227).

The central weakness of the tradition of independent journalism, the kind of journalism espoused by Lippmann and practiced in the craft, is this: while it legitimized a democratic politics of publicity and experts, it also confirmed the psychological incompetence of people to participate in it. Again, it evolved a political system of "democracy without citizens" (Entman, 1989). While preserving a valuable role for the mass media, it evacuated the role of political parties and citizens. Political parties, weakened by independent journalism, were decimated by television, which reduced parties to devices for raising money for television advertising and turned politics toward the cult of personality without party. Citizens, denied a public arena, became either consumers of politics or escapists from it.

In other words, the dissolution of the public theoretically was but a prelude to dissolving it practically. In the spot occupied in democratic theory by the public, Lippmann and others inserted interest groups and the cadres of experts in their employ. This reduced the public to a phantom, and created the situation in which citizens are the objects rather than the subjects of politics (Ginsburg, 1986). It turned the First Amendment into a possession of the press and of interest groups with whom the press engaged in both combat and accommodation. Towards that combat citizens stood largely as spectators and ratifiers. In truth, the conversation of the culture was taken outside the public realm and into private spaces. It became increasingly a scientistic journalism devoted to the sanctity of the fact and of objectivity, but one in which the bright light of publicity invaded every domain of privacy. We developed a journalism that was an early-warning system, but one that kept the public in a constant state of agitation or boredom. It is a journalism that reports a continuing stream of expert opinion but because there is no agreement among experts, it is more like observing talk-show gossip and petty manipulation rather than bearing witness to the truth. It is a journalism of fact without regard to understanding, through which the public is immobilized and demobilized and merely ratifies the judgments of experts delivered from on high.

It is, above all, a journalism that justifies itself in the public's name but in which the public plays no role, except as an audience—a receptacle to be informed by experts and an excuse for the practice of publicity. The issue could no longer be one of the First Amendment protecting public debate, for there was no longer any public debate to protect. For example, public opinion no longer refers to opinions being expressed in public and then recorded in the press. Public opinion is formed by the press and modeled by the public opinion industry and the apparatus of polling. Today, polling—a word that comes, interestingly enough, from the old synonym for voting—is an attempt to simulate public opinion in order to prevent an authentic public opinion from forming. With the rise of the polling industry our entire understanding of the public went into eclipse. The public was replaced by the interest group as the object of analysis and as the key political actor. In interest group theory, the public ceases to have a real existence. It fades into a statistical artifact, an audience whose opinions count only insofar as individuals refract the pressure of mass publicity. In short, while the word "public" continues in our language as an ancient memory and pious hope, the public as a feature and factor of real politics has disappeared.

The media and democracy increasingly reduced itself to a game in which, at its best, sources erected ever more complicated veils of appearance over events and journalists tried ever more assiduously to pierce the veil. But the mystery behind the mystery was that there was no mystery at all. It was a dialectic of appearance and demystification that tied the state, interests groups, and the press together in a symbiotic relationship against the fragmented remains of the public. Sometimes the press had the upper hand in the dialectical struggle; at other times, interests groups dominated and the press did little more than serve as their extension. As Entman (1989) has described it, the game was played because each had something the other side needed. Interest groups and sources had newsworthy political information that had been subsidized to ease its collection and presentation, the indispensable raw material needed to construct the news. Journalists could "provide publicity slanted favorably or unfavorably" (p. 19). Elites sought to "exchange a minimal amount of potentially damaging information for as much positively slanted coverage" (pp. 19–20), as could be obtained. Journalists sought to "extract information for stories" that would bring "acclaim or acceptance from editors and colleagues" (p. 20). Elites and journalists, in other words, mutually manipulated one another to mutually shared ends. However, the public stood in relation to this game as an increasingly bored and alienated and, above all, cynical spectator, learning most of all to distrust all appearances whether mounted by elites or journalists and, most damagingly, to distrust all language, to look at all language as a mere instrument of interest and obfuscation. And, in this context, journalism could no longer link up political impulses with political action; it could produce publicity, scandal, and drama, but it could not produce politics.

Today, Americans have lost interest in politics. Indeed, the title of E. J. Dionne, Jr.'s book, *Why Americans Hate Politics* (1991) expresses a more active alienation from public life than is revealed merely by the low voter turnouts that have progressively marked the entire modern period. The absence of participation is evidenced, as well, by active disengagement from political parties—the rise of the independent voter, more often, the independent nonvoter—and by declining levels of political knowledge. There is active opposition to public life and an absence of public spirit in favor of a private and apolitical existence.

The best evidence for this was the long-term decline in political participation as measured by voting and shadowed by knowledge of and interest in politics. Political participation declined throughout the period of national journalism, with temporary blips and recoveries in certain periods such as the depression and World War II. But the trend line has been clear, and no attempts to reverse it bureaucratically—extension of the franchise, easing voter registration restrictions, democratizing the candidate selection process through primaries—has reversed it (Congressional Quarterly, 1991; Scammon & McGillivray, 1989). The decline has been even sharper than revealed by the conventional measures of voting in presidential elections. Those measures ignore the even more precipitous declines in primary, local, and off-year congressional elections. The steepness of the decline also has been masked in recent times by the greater participation of African-Americans, particularly in the South, as practices which artificially restricted voting among racial minorities have been removed.

Above all, the press lost credibility and respect; it was no longer believed. As poll after poll showed, journalists had earned the distrust of the public and were increasingly seen as a hindrance to rather than avenue of politics and political reform. The watchdog press, the adversarial press was exposed to greater skepticism during the period of its greatest success—namely during the Vietnam War and Watergate. While the press dismissed the rising tide of criticism during these episodes as merely reactionary politics, the problem went deeper. In the public's eyes, the press had become the adversary of all institutions, including the public itself. "My newspaper" of older usage became "the newspaper"; it had severed its contact and allegiance with the public. As the press sought greater constitutional power for itself and greater independence from the state, as it sought to remove all restrictions on its activities and its newsgathering rights, it was forced to press the legal case that it was a special institution with special rights—rights that were independent of the rights of free speech and rights that were different than, and often opposed to, the rights of ordinary men and women. In a series of court cases in the 1960s, the press sought special privileges and powers and developed a view of the First Amendment that would secure them. Justice Potter Stewart (1975, pp. 633–634) developed a constitutional theory justifying an adversarial and watchdog press:

> The primary purpose of the constitutional guarantee of a free press was . . . to create a fourth institution outside the government as an additional check on the three official branches. . . . The relevant metaphor is of the Fourth Estate.
>
> The Free Press guarantee is, in essence, a *structural* provision of the Constitution. Most of the other provisions in the Bill of Rights protect specific liberties or specific rights of individuals. . . . In contrast, the Free Press Clause extends protection to an institution.

Ultimately this view creates a passive role for the public in the theater state of politics. The public is an observer of the press rather than "participators in the government of our affairs" and in the dialogue of democracy. The role of the citizen is not to participate in the formation of politics but to become a member of a veto group restraining decisions once they pass a certain boundary. The vision of an active and continuous involvement by citizens not only fails to describe the reality of American politics but even the end, object, or desirable state of its politics. It is the media that must be protected rather than the citizens' ability to participate in politics. The individual citizen was seen as remote and helpless compared to the two major protagonists—government and the media.

The Fourth Estate view supported the press in its news gathering cases. It focused on the activities of the journalists rather than the activities of the public. Under this view, journalists would serve as agents of the public in checking an inherently abusive government. To empower it to fulfill such a role, the press had to possess special rights to gather news. Thus under the Fourth Estate model a free press essentially was equated with a powerful press, possessing special privileges of news gathering (Bollinger, 1991). The view of the press as the representative of the public could only be sustained if the following conditions were met: the public had to believe that the press was authentically their representative and therefore in a responsible and fiduciary relation to it; the public had to believe that the press was not in cahoots with the state, with the most powerful of interest groups or both; and the public had to believe that the press was capable of representing the world, that is, of rendering a reasonable, unbiased, true, and factual account of it. In all these senses of representative, the press has been found wanting.

It is time to betray this argument, however, for despite the criticism one can bring to bear on modern journalism, the truth is also that the press has been a bulwark of liberty in our time and that no one has come up with a better arrangement. The watchdog notion of the press, a press independent of all institutions, a press that represents the public, a press that unmasks interest and privilege, a press that shines the hot glare of publicity into all the dark corners of the republic, a press that searches out expert knowledge among the welter of opinion, a press that seeks to inform the private citizen—these are ideas and roles that have served us well through some dark times. Not perfectly, not without fault, but well, and they have formed the accepted notions of democracy and the press in our time. But, as the century has progressed, the weaknesses of modern journalism have become increasingly apparent and debilitating. The press, in the eyes of many, increasingly got in the way of democratic politics rather than serving as a supporting institution. As a result, modern journalism is now under assault by technology, by the distemper of the times and by social changes the modern press has been unable to master.

JOURNALISM ENCOUNTERS THE POSTMODERN

I opened this chapter with an image of dismay brought on by the campaigns of 1988 and 1992. In that period we started to feel the force of something underway for close to two decades. Sometime in the early to mid-1970s, the entire pattern of communication, the existing structure of the media, of modern journalism and the press, started to break up. The causes were technological and economic and only later were they processed through politics and transformed to an ideology. The symptoms and symbols of the change were two technologies—satellites and computers—the consequences of which, in combination with other devices, reconfigured the map of communications and social relations. Satellite broadcasting put everyone in the same place for purposes of communication or, inversely, eliminated distance as a cost factor in communication. Computer technology not only altered all the parameters of numerical calculation, but through miniaturization, widely diffused large-scale capacity for information processing, storage, and retrieval. The radiant arc of a communication satellite 22,300 miles above the earth synchronizes time and ingests the globe into one homogeneous space. The computer abstracts geography into the galaxy and miniaturizes the clock of awareness to the pico second. The conquest of time and space, the dream of 19th-century Romantics, explorers, and imperialists (often the same people) has now been realized. The creation of this homogenous time and space led both governments and private firms to realize that they were entering a new phase in the political economy of the world, one in which trade no longer follows the flag but the communications system; in which knowledge, always a source of power, has been bleached into information, adapted to a new technology of digital encoding and made lighter and more transportable to enhance the capacity to manipulate and control human activity. The world of work and commerce is subject to shocks from disturbances reverberating from the most distantly imaginable financial and commodity markets. The world of politics and culture is shaped by Time Warner's announcement, "The World is Our Audience," and the realization that the aggressive transformation of publics into audiences, which in the late 19th century created the "imaginary community of the nation," is now a global process.

Economic activity, political sovereignty, and cultural production changed shape and consequences within a reconstituted social world: not the city, the nation, or the empire but the globe became the habitus of these processes. Both fragmentation and homogenization became two contradictory trends within a single global reality: a splitting in which social life simultaneously expanded and contracted, the stage of human activity enlarged to the globe and collapsed to the village all at once (Appadurai, 1990).

While cable and satellite have enlarged the scale and scope of communications, they have also, and paradoxically, narrowed and limited it. Cable television, a product of satellite and computer, has radically expanded channel capacity, the variety of television services available, and the capacity to segment the television audience. Cable is practically as old as television, for it was the last mile of the network system relaying over the air signals to remote hamlets where topography created signal disturbance. Wedded to satellites, cable now penetrates to 60% of American homes, and multichannel systems fragment the audience into narrow niches based upon taste, hobbies, avocations, race, ethnicity—indeed, a potentially limitless world of work and leisure. Even politics is turned into a hobby. When cable is combined with other innovations, some actual some still potential—the growth of super stations, direct satellite broadcasting, interactive teletext and video text, VCR's—two consequences follow. The "great audience," the audience assembled by newspapers and television, is splintered and dissolved, and newspapers and network television, which reached their peak of profitability and influence in the 1970s, recede as both economic and political forces.

Everywhere the scale and meaning of these changes is sought through metaphors such as the "global village," "spaceship earth," and, the favorite phrase, the "information society." But these reassuring metaphors contrast sharply with the disorder and chaos of real life. Out on the streets one encounters ceaseless and disorderly flows of new people and new things moving outward to new places along new routes: flows of migrants, guest workers, tourists, entrepreneurs and itinerants; new flows of capital, factories, messages, products, ideas, images, and currencies. New things flowing from new places to new places, upsetting established patterns of geography, trade, and communications, imploding and exploding at the same time. The information society turns out to be an unstable and in many ways an unfriendly place in which ethnic and other kinds of nationalisms again occupy the center of the stage. Everywhere state and nation are pitted against one another; "primordia have been globalized" and identity politics are practiced on a world scale (Appadurai, 1990, p. 285). A new information class, along with a new technology, has brought us to, in the title of the former chairman of Citicorp, Walter Wriston's book (1992), *The Twilight of Sovereignty,* since that class has the skills to write a complex software program that produces a billion dollars of revenue and yet to walk past any customs officer in the world with nothing of "value" to declare.

The consequences of technology are never clear until they are processed through politics, and the consequences of satellites, computers, and cable television did not emerge until, to take but two examples, they were wedded to the ideology and policies of the Reagan and Thatcher administrations in the United States and Great Britain. The general name for these policies is privatization: deregulation of broadcasting, the cultivation of high-tech industry, and the fostering of renewed competition in telecommunications. In the United States, restrictions on cable were removed, network broadcasting was hamstrung, the public interest and the fairness doctrines dismantled, the Bell System broken up and private competition in telecommunications encouraged. The notion that there was a public interest in broadcasting or in the press generally was simply set aside. Private competition was deemed adequate because in the absence of a viable notion of a public, a public interest was simply inconceivable within the ideological frameworks that ruled politics. Since 1934 American broadcasting lived under the fairness doctrine, which attempted to make a public interest articulate by requiring broadcasters to examine issues of public importance and to reflect all sides of political issues. In effect, the fairness doctrine was an attempt to create a public space within an essentially commercialized system of broadcasting. The doctrine led to the creation of first-class journalism organizations within television networks that were ruled, even more than newspapers, by heavy capital requirements and commercial imperatives toward entertainment and profit. In 1986 the Federal Communications Commission (FCC) threw out the fairness doctrine and with it the entire notion of broadcasting as a public space. As Mark Fowler, the FCC chairman under Reagan, put it, "Television is just another household appliance, a toaster with a picture." (Brown, 1992)

This view is now beyond controversy; it has bipartisan support, which is to say all resistance has collapsed into the notion that communication is exclusively a private activity. The only dispute concerns which private industry will gain the largess of government support: cable or broadcasting, Hollywood producers or the telephone companies. Public broadcasting comes under increasing attack for political bias and, even more, for being inefficient and unnecessary given the imperatives of the market. As a result, proposals are entertained either to sell it off to private interests or to merge it with the Radio Free Europe and the United States Information Agency (USIA) into a super propaganda agency.

In Europe public broadcasting systems are being turned into private commercial enterprises or becoming subject to new competitive pressure from the private sector. Once satellites were available it was a foregone conclusion that some firms, most likely American, were going to invade the television space of European countries and siphon off the mass market. To prevent this, or alternatively, to preserve a European "high culture" tradition, country after country has either given up state-run television or permitted the growth of private networks. In short, we have neither a public sphere within politics or a public sphere within broadcasting.

With the progressive weakening of public broadcasting around the world, communications is seen more uniformly as a matter of private market transactions. In turn, as the costs of television increase, as state systems are faced with declining revenues, as global communications companies such as Time Warner straddle the globe, the phenomenon of coproduction takes on a new importance. News and culture are increasingly made by joint operations that cut across national and linguistic boundaries. That is, the production of culture, including most importantly the news, becomes disarticulated from existing national societies and polities. Pastiche cultures, postmodern cultures assembled by a cross-national production process, turns the world into an audience for homeless communications.

These economic changes were congruent with developments on a much wider plane. In the 1970s governments all over the industrialized world were becoming more conservative. The first leap of oil prices in the mid-1970s meant that inflation was becoming the great enemy of stability and antiinflationary strategy dominated the thinking of all governments. This led to monetary control and the first attempts to expand high-tech telecommunications industries. Even such socialist governments as were elected—in France, Australia, and New Zealand, for example—adopted highly conservative economic policies and encouraged the further privatization of journalism and communications. That was the zeitgeist. The movement toward privatization, which is global in scope, encompasses the deregulation of telecommunications and the constriction of public space, the elimination or decline of public or state-run broadcasting, the simultaneous fragmentation of audiences into narrower and narrower segments, their reassembly into transnational markets of news and entertainment, and the creation of pastiche cultures that originate without regard to national traditions. The connection of a fragmented structure of production to a fragmented structure of home reception results in a further emptying out of the public sphere: the entire notion of public communication and a common culture of politics evaporates in the "new Balkans," where groups and individuals occupy political space outside a common arena of discourse and communication. The notion of citizens of a common polity who participate in a common political tradition becomes increasingly difficult to imagine. The release of market forces in telecommunications that affected everything, including newspapers and the print press, was fueled not only by purely economic considerations but by the firmly entrenched belief that there was no longer a public interest or a public sphere. All that was left were acquisitive individuals and their interests. The very starkness of this notion and its inability, therefore, to create a sense of community constituted not a safeguard but a threat to political freedom.

These complex and interrelated changes in the world of journalism and democracy emerged in the new technology of politics in the 1992 election. Many of the most troubling phenomena—citizen councils, call-in radio, public debates with public questioners, spontaneous grassroots nominating movements—represented attempts, however dangerous, by a fragmented and dispersed public, one that had not completely lost and forgotten the image of a truly public life, to use the new technology and new media, designed purely for commercial purposes, to re-form themselves, outside the journalistic establishment, as a public and to reassert both a public, interest and public participation in the sphere of national politics.

This movement does not, at the moment, have much theoretical support because of the commitment of all segments of the political spectrum to an ideology of rights-based liberalism. That position begins from the claim, to paraphrase Michael Sandel (1982, 1984), that we are separate, individual persons, each with his or her own aims, interests, and conceptions of the good. It seeks a framework of rights that will enable us to realize our capacity as free moral agents, consistent with a similar liberty for others. Alas, to challenge this view one must question the claim of the priority of the right over the good, the picture of the freely choosing individual it embodies, and the Hobbesian state it must inevitably create.

As Michael Sandel (1982, p. 175) puts it, "The priority of the self over its ends means I am never defined by my aims and attachments, but always capable of standing back to survey and assess and possibly to revise them." This is what it means to be a free and independent self, capable of choice. And this is the vision of the self that finds expression in the ideal of the state as a neutral framework. On the rights-based ethic, it is precisely because we are essentially separate, independent selves that we need a neutral framework, a framework of rights that refuses to choose among competing purposes and ends: "If the self is prior to its ends, then the right must be prior to the good" (Sandel, 1982, p. 175).

But what can journalism, the First Amendment, and public opinion mean under this tyranny? Unless we are willing to entertain the possibility, again paraphrasing Sandel, that we are defined, at least in part, by the communities we inhabit—indeed that we are the animals that are forever creating and destroying communities—and that we participate in and are formed by the purposes characteristic of those communities, I see no possibility of recovering a meaningful notion of public life or public opinion. Unless we can see the story of our lives as part of a narrative of a public community, a community of general citizenship rather than one restricted by class, race, gender, and so on, while simultaneously believing that our lives are also embedded in communities of private identity—family, city, tribe, nation, party or cause—can journalism and public opinion, the press generally, make a moral and political difference serve not merely as a vehicle of "effects."

I would hope we have learned by now, after 20 years or more of painful struggle, that the expansion of individual rights and the erosion of common identifications, the growth of entitlements and the erosion of common judgment, is not a recipe for social progress. The result has been the movement of politics from smaller forms of association to larger, more comprehensive structures in which political participation is reduced even as it seems to expand. While some contemporary ideologies worship the private market and some the liberal state, both end up concentrating power in the corporate economy and the bureaucratic state; both evacuate those intermediate forms of social life that can sustain a more vital public life.

Some liberals argue that an emphasis on the common good and public life creates prejudice and intolerance. They remind us that the modern nation is not the Athenian polis and that such a vision of democracy is both nostalgic and dangerous. Modern government cannot embody a conception of the good except as a path to totalitarian temptations.

This is the argument for diversity made by those are already deracinated, and who wish nothing more than to deracinate others. The plea for diversity is simply a plea for sameness or a plea for those identities invented by and confirmed in the state. Minorities who thereby seek protection from the liberal state will be extinguished or turned into instruments of state power without an independent cultural life. It is for this reason, rather than for the sake of some senseless nostalgia, that we need to recover public life.

REFERENCES

Anderson, B. (1983). *Imagined communities: Reflections on the origin and spread of nationalism.* New York: Verso Books.

Appadurai, A. (1990). Disjuncture and difference in the global cultural economy. In M. Featherstone (Ed.), *Global culture* (pp. 295–310). Newbury Park, CA: Sage.

Barber, B. (1984). *Strong democracy: Participatory politics for a new age.* Berkeley: University of California Press.

Bayley, E. F. (1981). *Joe McCarthy and the press.* Madison: University of Wisconsin Press.

Bollinger, L. (1991). *Images of a free press.* Chicago: University of Chicago Press.

Broder, D. (1990, January 30). Democracy and the press. *Washington Post,* p. A15.

Brown, L. (1992). *Les Brown's encyclopedia of television* (3rd ed). Detroit: Visible Ink.

Carey, J. W. (1992). A Republic, if you can keep it: Liberty and public life in the age of Glasnost. In R. Arsenault (Ed.), *Crucible of Liberty: 200 Years of the Bill of Rights* (pp. 108–128). New York: Free Press.

Congressional Quarterly (1991). *Presidential elections since 1789* (5th ed.). Washington, DC: Congressional Quarterly.

Didion, J. (1992). *After Henry.* New York: Simon & Schuster.

Dionne, E. J., Jr. (1991). *Why Americans hate politics.* New York: Simon & Schuster.

Dyan, D., & Katz, E. (1992). *Media events: The live broadcasting of history.* Cambridge, MA: Harvard University Press.

Entman, R. (1989). *Democracy without citizens.* New York: Oxford University Press.

Ginsburg, B. (1986). *The captive public: How mass opinion promotes state power*. New York: Basic Books.

Gouldner, A. (1976). *The dialectic of ideology and technology*. New York: Oxford University Press.

Habaermas, J. (1989). *The structural transformation of the public sphere*. Cambridge, MA: The MIT Press.

Katz, J. (1992, March 5). Rock, rap and the movies bring you the news. *Rolling Stone,* pp. 33, 36–37, 40, 78.

Levine, L. W. (1988). *Highbrow/Lowbrow: The emergence of cultural hierarchy in America*. Cambridge, MA: Harvard University Press.

Lippmann, W. (1922). *Public opinion*. New York: Macmillan.

Marcus, G. E., & Hanson, R. L. (1993). *Reconsidering the democratic public*. University Park, PA: Pennsylvania State University Press.

McCarthy, M. (1958, October 18). Philosophy at work. *The New Yorker,* p. 202.

McGerr, M. (1986). *The decline of popular politics*. New York: Oxford University Press.

Robbins, B. (Ed.). (1993). *The phantom public sphere*. Minneapolis: University of Minnesota Press.

Rosen, J. (1992). Politics, vision and the press. In S. Charlé (Ed.), *The new news v. the old news* (pp. 3–33). New York: The Twentieth Century Fund.

Rossiter, C., & Lare, J. (Eds.). (1963). *The essential Lippmann*. New York: Random House.

Sandel, M. (1982). *Liberalism and the limits to justice*. Cambridge, England: Cambridge University Press.

Sandel, M. (1984). *Liberalism and its Critics*. New York: New York University Press.

Scammon, R. M., & McGillivray, A. (1989). *American voter 18*. Washington, DC: Election Research Center.

Schudson, M. (1978). *Discovering the news*. New York: Basic Books.

Smith, B. (1985). *Politics and remembrance*. Princeton, NJ: Princeton University Press.

Stewart, P. (1975, January). Or of the press. *Hastings Law Journal, 26* ,633–634.

Warner, S. B. (1968). *Private city: Philadelphia in three stages of its growth*. Philadelphia: University of Pennsylvania Press.

Wriston, W. B. (1992). *The twilight of sovereignty*. New York: Charles Scribner's Sons.

Young, H. (1989). *The Iron Lady: A biography of Margaret Thatcher*. New York: Farrar, Strauss & Giroux.

16

The Influence of Rationality Claims on Public Opinion and Policy

Murray Edelman

RATIONAL CHOICE AS SYMBOL AND FETISH

The frequency and optimism in the late 20th century of claims that decision makers and researchers have invented techniques that maximize efficiency, "rational choice," and benefit–cost ratios has coincided with an unprecedented and apparently growing incidence of disastrous policy decisions, governmental actions that fail to accomplish their purposes, and policies that prove counterproductive. In pursuing international peace and security, waging war, designing weapons systems, fighting poverty, combating racism and other forms of social discrimination, reducing economic and social inequalities, and accomplishing other goals that are frequently proclaimed and widely supported, successes have been rare and often temporary, and failures dramatic and recurrent (Janis, 1982; Edelman, 1977).

The policies that fail and the words that succeed are systematically linked. They create each other in ways that throw light on the mystified workings of contemporary public and private bureaucracies, the political functions of language, and the construction of public opinion. This chapter explores those dynamics. More specifically, it examines the effects of rationality and efficiency claims on how people interpret the political spectacle and on their inclination to remain quiescent or to resist established policies.

Whatever else it is, the focus on efficiency and rationality in the language of administrators, public officials, and academic students of public policy is a response to the pervasiveness of inefficiency and malfunctioning in news reports about governmental and corporate actions: a revealing instance of Kenneth Burke's (1969, p. 39) insight that political rhetoric serves to "sharpen up the pointless and blunt the too sharply pointed." The language of "linear programming," "cost–benefit analysis," and similar recipes for managerial effectiveness, together with reliance upon complex technologies to minimize "human error," (and upon claims of human error to absolve technologies that fail) have become the hallmarks of bureaucratic public relations and self-assurance.

They inculcate fetishism into policy formation, for they create symbols that then dominate the thinking and actions of their creators and of a large part of the interested public; and the fetishism is effective even when the policies are not. Such displacement of failed or controversial action by reassuring language has become a central attribute of contemporary government because failures are frequent and serious, because the tests of success or failure are largely ideological, and because the likelihood of failure or ineffective action is built into the political system. The failures typically serve the economic and status interests of powerful groups of people, so that disparities in resources and the language that rationalizes the disparities construct each other.

Although this language does not describe the process of policy formation and assessment, it does serve a significant political purpose: it creates a spectacle that helps marshal public support for policymakers and academic analysts who justify themselves in the language of rational choice theory or other claims to a recondite formula for success that the general public must accept on faith. Like all political texts, this language constitutes a political weapon, not a description. It is itself a potent form of political action, for it creates a world in which biases can be erased, ideological differences objectively evaluated, the consequences of policies both predicted before the fact and rigorously appraised afterward, and costs and benefits expressed in comparable terms and their balance calculated. By the same token it creates a world in which administrators and academics who use rational choice theory are accorded high status and influence.

CONFUSIONS ABOUT POLITICAL GOALS

In several ways the language of rational choice generates confused assumptions about political goals. It assumes, incorrectly, that goals are unambiguous, that conflict about them is not an integral part of their implementation, and that means and ends are separable from each other.

The definition of public problems to be solved and governmental goals to be achieved is a response to widespread ethical and patriotic sentiments. It reassures the public that we aspire to achieve peace and prosperity, eliminate poverty, reduce unemployment, promote public health, increase economic productivity, eliminate racism and discrimination against minorities, provide decent housing, increase national security, and so on. Such names for goals reassure the public that officials and aspirants for public office are decent people and that accepted ethical standards and patriotic sentiments are being pursued.

Yet such basic goals are never achieved; and with respect to some of the most crucial ones, public policy has brought regress rather than progress. The enormous expenditures for defense and the vast amount of talk and planning about national security since World War II have produced a less secure world, in which wars are more frequent and fear of aggression more intense than before. Poverty and unemployment are higher than the levels that were regarded as acceptable in the early years of the century, and seem to be increasing. Racism and discrimination based on religion, ethnicity, and sexual preference remain widespread and seem to be increasing as well, with recurrent virulent flare-ups. It is evident that the language that defines social problems and promises efficient and rational solutions for them does not set an agenda to be followed, but does reassure those who want to be persuaded that the political system reflects their moral beliefs.

The fact is that such language grossly misstates the political agenda and the issues that engage the energies of policymakers in their everyday actions. It is evident that in practice—if not in the political spectacle that rhetoric creates—each widely supported "goal" constructs a political battleground, a site for in-fighting, rather than a moral consensus. The "social problems" governments claim they want to solve provide welcome opportunities for some. Continuous threats of wars and occasional shooting wars are opportunities for business contracts, as well as for marshalling public sentiment behind regimes and often against expenditures for social programs. Unemployment and poverty mean lower wages and a more docile work force. Discrimination against minorities means increased opportunities for majorities. The consistent pattern in these cases is that the moral consensus that most people share to a greater or lesser degree is not compatible with the economic and status interests of groups of people who already command large resources and influence. Public policies that attack these problems rhetorically but never solve them in actuality have proven psychologically and politically compatible with a public opinion that empathizes with the victims of these problems but also with the economic interests of the elites who benefit from the persistence of the problems. The elites doubtless sympathize with the suffering too; the assumption that sentiments shape actions is a tidy example of misleading clarity and reductionism in political rhetoric (Edelman, 1988).

The metaphor that underlies the terms "efficiency" and "rationality" clouds the nature of public policymaking in such a way as to insure that proclaimed goals will be achieved only imperfectly, even while it reassures the public. These words imply that there is an unambiguous goal to be achieved, for only in that case does it make sense to search for the least costly and most effective methods of achieving it. But by definition political goals are always either ambiguous or in conflict with other widely supported objectives. To state ends in language that speaks of a "public interest," "the public welfare," or a general virtue like "happiness" is to avoid conflict by maximizing ambiguity. To state ends in specific terms, on the other hand,—"make discrimination against homosexuals a crime," "double the minimum wage," "ban handguns," "cut the defense budget 20%"—is to take it for granted that opposition and conflicting positions will also be put forward as goals. What, then, is the efficient or the rational course?

These concepts, just like "the public interest," become ambiguous containers into which actors and onlookers place divergent policy proposals. And, like the phrase "the public interest," the words "rationality" and "efficiency" are revealed as polemical weapons for whatever policy their users favor, rather than as the scientific or technical terms they pretend to be. But because they rationalize different and conflicting ends, the actions they justify are certain to be compromises in order to make them politically feasible, insuring that no such proclaimed goal will be pursued resolutely or effectively achieved.

When a social problem hurts elites rather than disadvantaged groups, public policy is likely to attack it resolutely. As a case in point, contrast governmental actions respecting inflation with those respecting poverty and unemployment. The latter, as noted earlier, often insure exacerbation of the very social problems they purport to combat because poverty and unemployment bring financial and political advantages for some elite groups.

The Reagan administration deliberately created the deep recession of 1981 and 1982, and there is always pressure from influential conservatives to avoid monetary and fiscal policies that would cut unemployment too effectively. The unemployment level fluctuates, but the level that is accepted as "normal" has grown substantially in this century, still another example of the ideological character of language purporting to be value-free.

Inflation, by contrast, helps debtors and hurts creditors, while usually reducing unemployment and poverty. The Federal Reserve Board, the Treasury Department, business groups, and central banks in industrialized countries accordingly define it as a more serious problem than unemployment and adopt measures to keep it low, even though these policies create suffering for the working population and the poor. It is not the existence of a damaging condition or the numbers who are hurt that chiefly determines whether policymakers regard decisive action to attack it as rational, but rather who benefits and who suffers.

It is evident that beliefs about rationality and efficiency incorporate controversial value assumptions and that their meanings change with the values and ideologies of those who use them. These concepts are the constructions of capitalism and bureaucracy in the countries affected by the industrial revolution. More often than not they reflect the values upon which those institutions are built, notably the assumptions that human beings, natural resources, and planning are instruments for the production of profits from capital resources and that everyone benefits in the measure that this goal is realized.

IMPLICATIONS FOR THE EXALTATION AND DEBASEMENT OF PEOPLE

The methodological and explicit emphasis of systematic policy planning is on choosing means to achieve ends at the lowest cost; but the substantive and implicit emphasis that gives this worldview its motivational force often depends on the definition of people as means rather than ends. More specifically, workers, and consumers are regarded as instruments for making the economy productive and profitable, a postulate that is all the more powerful because it is tacit, usually masked by some variation of Adam Smith's metaphor of the unseen hand and by discourse about helping the unfortunate. This central assumption is therefore rarely examined or criticized.

The focus upon rational choice embraces some related premises as well. It encourages a focus on leadership or, more precisely, on followership: the equation of hierarchical position with effective planning, competence, expertise, status, level of reward, and level of sacrifice; the penalizing of gratifications that divert attention from hierarchical roles; the premise that damage to groups of people defined as unworthy is irrelevant to the calculus of costs; and the assumption that inequality is a prerequisite of efficiency and rational action.

Policy planners and managers responsible for administering policies are likely to be even more susceptible to this kind of reassurance about their competence than their critics and the general public. From the perspective of involved officials systematic decision making offers a way out of a difficult thicket. It suggests that those who use it are competent and professional and that their critics are dilettantes, a posture that generates unjustified confidence in one's decisions and in one's own talents, and discourages self-criticism and self-reflection.

Such evocation of hubris and dogmatic self-assurance is a hallmark of a great deal of administrative decision making, and it is especially pervasive and damaging in organizations operating in areas in which the pursuit of dubious policies brings severe harm to many people. As Irving Janis (1982) has shown, criticism from people defined as outsiders or dilettantes is likely to reinforce determination to pursue the very policies that evoked the criticism and the failures, as such remarkable and frequent foreign policy fiascoes as the Bay of Pigs, Vietnam, the stationing of marines in Lebanon, and the support of the contras in Nicaragua illustrate. Domestic fiascoes often illustrate the point just as well: consider the creation of homelessness in recent decades through housing and economic policies.

Just as this kind of language augments the power and the self-assurance of officials, it encourages humility and acquiescence in deprivation among the population hurt by particular policies. It teaches them that they are unable to understand or criticize the actions of the authorities, who are uniquely qualified to determine what will serve the public interest. What is expected of them is support for competence, and the rational and patriotic course is to offer such support. The formal procedures that provide democratic influence and access for the public in principle are accordingly nullified by language that discourages public involvement, challenges, or resistance, even when people are required to accept deaths in wars whose purpose is unclear, homelessness, poverty, inadequate educational facilities, and a growing disparity in quality of life between the rich and the middle class and the middle class and the poor. The narcotizing effect of language about rational procedures provides the ultimate evidence that such language is divorced psychologically from public hopes that government will assure a decent quality of life and remedy blatant inequalities in advantages and in sacrifice.

The language of rational choice serves quite often to justify actions that powerful groups or public officials favor but of which much of the public disapproves. More and more, public policy is divorced from what majorities want while it is justified as the rational way to accomplish an ambiguous abstract goal. Majorities have long favored gun control, abortion rights, a higher minimum wage, and many other specific objectives that legislatures and administrative bodies have often rejected. Other governmental actions like the military invasions of Korea, Vietnam, Grenada, and Iraq at least temporarily create popular support because they evoke problematic beliefs about the goals they serve. The focus on rationality muddles discussion of goal priorities while helping to rationalize the specific actions of bureaucracies.

As noted earlier, the implicit though seldom acknowledged value of maintaining inequalities and existing advantages in resources and status remains central, masked by promises of well-being for everyone in a future that never arrives.

THE IDEOLOGICAL DEFINITION OF BENEFITS AND COSTS

As a rationalization the language of systematic decision making is bound to justify courses of action that chiefly reflect the demands of the most powerful groups, for only those policies are politically viable. In both subtle and crude ways calculation of the benefits and costs of alternative or contrary demands is likely to reflect the anticipated opposition of influential interests and the costs of changing established institutional arrangements.

Substantially enlarging the number of firms awarded arms contracts will predictably entail the cost of hiring inexperienced technicians and scientists and the loss of economies of scale; but the long-term and less readily calculable social advantages of wider geographical and social dispersion of federal money is likely to be ignored or given much less weight. Requiring welfare recipients to work or undertake job training entails obvious economic benefits if the workfare plans function as it is assumed they should. But the added opportunities for waste and cheating by trade schools, the long-term injuries of children whose parents cannot take adequate care of them, the social costs that flow in the long run from the increased opportunities for employers to pay low wages, and the likelihood that in areas of high unemployment the newly trained welfare recipients will still be without work are likely to be discounted or ignored.

The language in which the identification of benefits and costs is conventionally discussed can be understood as an inversion of the cognitive process that actually takes place. The writings on policy studies postulate that after a goal is stated, planners calculate the benefits and costs of alternative ways of achieving it. But, as we have already seen, the publicized "goal" is selected from a set of conflicting objectives; and it is not so much "given" as "taken" by people with a particular value orientation or ideology, or by a public influenced by questionable governmental action and talk.

The act of choosing a goal goes a long way toward predetermining which costs and benefits will be emphasized and which minimized or ignored. To focus upon avoiding price inflation, for example, is to highlight the benefits that will accrue to creditors and business groups while minimizing the costs to workers and the poor of higher unemployment, and the costs to debtors of money with a high value. A focus upon the goal of minimizing unemployment reverses these priorities.

This tactic also distorts or erases ethical priorities among benefits and among costs. Until rational choice theory became fashionable, industrial health and safety laws rested on the premise that protection of workers from maiming or death in the course of their employment was self-evidently worth the costs of the administration of such laws, and the same priority of life and health over increased profits justified unemployment compensation, workmen's compensation, child labor, and other kinds of protective legislation. The emphasis in recent years, by contrast, has been upon highlighting the monetary costs of administering such laws, thereby providing a rationale for eliminating or weakening them. If the benefits of treating injured workers or compensating surviving spouses are not significantly greater than the costs of administering the laws or of an arbitrary determination of the money value of a life, it follows that the rational course is to let people get hurt or be killed. An arithmetic calculation based on a masked ideological premise supplants respect for life and health, an impressive tribute to the power of language to construct reality.

The conviction that quantitative calculations of benefits and costs enhance rational choice and efficiency is all the easier to sustain because the success or failure of a controversial public policy is itself not a matter of fact, but is always dependent on interpretation. When an automobile mechanic is asked to repair faulty brakes, there is an obvious empirical test of his or her success or failure. But that model is not at all applicable to judging the success or failure of governmental actions, even though the language of election campaigns and ideological arguments typically imply that it is. Advocates of a challenged policy construct tests that show success, while opponents construct other tests that show failure, so that both are likely to persevere in their opinions, regardless of experience with the policy. Many decades of experience with welfare laws, abortion laws, increases in the arms budget, economic and military interventions in Third World countries, and countless other controversial policies have failed to produce any consensus on which courses of action have succeeded and which have failed. The argument of this chapter should have made it clear why that kind of ambiguity and continued political contention is inevitable. The language of "rationality" and "efficiency" constructs an illusory, grossly simplified model of how policies are formulated, administered, and evaluated; but it is a model that anxious publics are likely to find reassuring.

This kind of language, moreover, erases premises as impressive as those it constructs. It obliterates the central role of debatable values in policy choice, and it often minimizes attention to the relative benefits of alternative objectives. As already noted, it deletes from the analyst's and the observer's calculations the overriding importance of some values, regardless of how much it costs to achieve them. It wipes out the knowledge that every decision that a claim is a "fact" is based upon some theoretical orientation (Wolin, 1969), because a fact never has a self-evident meaning but rather requires interpretation.

The language of rational choice eradicates awareness that every course of action gives rise to proliferating, never-ending waves of consequences that are different for diverse groups of people and for disparate time periods. It eliminates the distinction between reason and rationalization, defining the latter as if it were the former.

THE IDEOLOGICAL DEFINITION OF "RATIONALITY"

The terms "efficiency" and "rationality" carry the connotations already noted when they appear in the context of technical and professional discussion. But they generate wider and more ambiguous connotations as well, and the confusion between their narrower and broader meanings is central to their potency as political weapons. In popular discussion we deploy a number of ambiguous terms to connote desirable policy and win wider support for whatever courses of action are linked to these concepts. Among the more common terms that serve this essentially propagandistic purpose are "the national interest," "the public interest," "democracy" ("communism" in the former Eastern bloc countries), "rational," and "efficient." When used in this way these concepts are close to interchangeable, for they all combine wide ambiguity with strong favorable affect. Their lack of specificity gives them their political power, so that any policy can be sanctified by inculcating the belief that it is "rational," "democratic," or "in the public interest." The practice draws upon psychological projection for its potency. It encourages people with a personal reason to favor a policy to transform their self-serving inclinations into justifications imbued with patriotism, altruism, logic, or fashionable ideology. Such performative language is critical to political discourse.[1] By the same token, all political language is performative, helping to create beliefs and realities; and language is most potent as a political weapon when it purports to refer to an objective reality in a clear, rigorous, or precise way.

THE ANALYTIC USES OF RATIONAL CHOICE

My discussion so far has focused upon the ways in which the language of rationality and efficiency undermines itself and distorts opinion, contributing to ineffective realization of announced policy objectives. But no social process is straightforward; there are always multiple and conflicting consequences. It is therefore important to consider as well just how the efforts of policy analysts to specify the benefits and costs of alternative courses of action can sometimes make some contribution to "efficiency" in the conventional sense and educate the public as well.

First, there is always a chance that some costs and some benefits not apparent to most observers will be identified, although that advantage, as already suggested, is likely to be diluted by the strong incentive to define costs and benefits in order to justify existing disparities.

Second, the effort to be specific in identifying advantages and disadvantages and, when possible, to quantify them, may encourage policy planners to enlarge the scope of their thinking or to see links that are not immediately evident. Detailed attention might be directed, for example, to the relative effects upon employment and the gross national product of arms spending and of spending for the manufacture of civilian goods.

But that example also partly undermines itself, as every example would, because it calls attention to the endless ramifications of every policy, and therefore to the arbitrary nature of efforts to highlight particular consequences and limit benefit and cost calculations to those. Analysts or planners may claim that it is "reasonable" to confine attention to the immediate or direct consequences of a policy or to those they define as the major ones, but the claim is bound to be self-serving, even if not always intentionally so. Costs and benefits that justify the policies the analyst favors are likely to be accepted as the direct and major ones, still another instance of the propensity to define issues in a manner that rationalizes a preferred outcome. Opponents of a proposal to use public funds to pay for abortions see the destruction of life as its direct and major consequence, while advocates see fairness to poor women and a woman's right to control her own body as the direct and major consequence. Is the major result of widening eligibility for welfare benefits the prevention of suffering and hunger, or is it tax increases and the encouragement of dependency? Is it "reasonable" to take account of the likelihood that a rise in interest rates will enlarge unemployment and poverty and thus increase crime and the costs of prisons? As soon as we move from the level of abstract concepts to consider specific policy proposals, it becomes evident that the calculation of costs and benefits does not avoid bias in analysis, but rather incorporates it in a new, typically concealed, form.

It is an implicit assumption of the emphasis upon rationality and efficiency that the ambiguities, irrelevancies, and confusions of metaphors and other tropes are eliminated by a focus upon demonstrable causes and effects; but the language of rationality reduces them to a particular set of tropes while minimizing the chance that the metaphorical nature of the argument will be recognized for what it is (McCloskey, 1985).

The tropes this kind of discourse stresses pervade the culture of industrialized societies: leadership, expertise, specialization, means and ends, differences in personal worth based upon wealth or hierarchical position, an idealized future springing from the acceptance of sacrifice in the present. The metaphors and the premises they embody permeate popular science, popular art (notably television news and television sitcoms), popular recreation, pedagogy, psychological counseling, and everyday discourse. In short, the focus upon efficiency reinforces, and is reinforced by, the prevailing social and political spectacle (Edelman, 1988).

Many of these observations make it clear that rational choice models offer a rationalization for decisions rather than a formula for arriving at them. Their formulation flows from complex and conflicting political pressures respecting controversial policies, mutually incompatible objectives of concerned interest groups, uncertainties regarding the relative power of those groups, the sanctions at their disposal, their probable reactions to future developments, and consequent confusions and disputes regarding what concrete measures to adopt. The rational choice model assumes a never-never land in which none of these perplexing complications exist. But they always exist for planners and administrators, although individuals differ widely in their sensitivity to them, their personal sympathies with particular interests, and their skill in coping with them. The least risky way of coping is to respond to the group interests that wield the strongest clout.

It is hardly surprising, then, that the hallmarks of difficult administrative decisions are vacillation, confusion, and a more sensitive regard for short-term political rewards and sanctions than for long-term consequences. In this milieu the calculation of benefit–cost ratios or some other means of achieving rationality or efficiency can win support for dubious past decisions from legislators and part of the public, not because the calculations themselves are persuasive, studied, or widely known, but because the claim that a decision was made rationally and the language in which the claim is couched become potent condensation symbols. As symbols they reassure people who know that policies are often misconceived, wasteful, or disastrous, and who want to believe that there is a facile resolution for a disturbing dilemma.

AMBIGUITY AND CONTRADICTION IN POLICY MAKING

Advocates of these methodologies assume that they reduce or eliminate the ambiguities and uncertainties that pervade conventional policy planning; but, as already suggested, they simply transfer the ambiguities to new locales and mask them. Ordinary language about dealing with social problems dwells upon uncertainties about causes, the relative influence of a range of contributing determinants, the comparative feasibility of diverse courses of action, and the role of accident and the unexpected. Uncertainties, contradictions, and oppositions are recognized and tentativeness in choosing and assessing solutions encouraged. When people have faith in "systematic" methods, by contrast, these complications are covered over, repressed, or simplified to make them fit rational choice premises. Adoption of one of the systematic formulas reassures its user that the influences systematically taken into account are the only pertinent ones, and that the quantitative values assigned to them guarantee precision, although guesses and arbitrary determinations inevitably play a large part in shaping both of these procedures. Recognition of errors and reassessment of policies accordingly become much less likely, because misleading clarity and simplicity create tempting paths to distortion and to masked ideology. To put it another way, understanding depends upon avoiding the certainties that flow from a constricted conceptual framework. James March (1986) recognized this danger when he wrote, "Where contradiction and confusion are essential elements of the values, precision misrepresents them."

There is an even stronger argument against schemes that cover over ambiguities, confusions, and contradictions: these latter properties of public discourse make valuable contributions to understanding. First, they do so because they accurately reflect the ambivalence or multivalence with which people are likely to view policy dilemmas. To accept them as intrinsic characteristics of the problem to be addressed rather than as irritants to be arbitrarily erased helps planners and the public to take advantage of the potentialities of the mind and the situation, as such seminal 20th-century social theorists as Freud, Wittgenstein, Derrida, and Foucault demonstrated in their diverse ways. In dealing with political issues a focus upon the contradictions and ambiguities that are always there helps us to recognize as inherent complexities, dilemmas, and unexamined or ideologically motivated premises in policy planning. To be effective, administrators have to take them into account in their everyday actions, even if they justify those actions in terms that sound more politic. In this light rational choice and similar schemes for "systematic" decision making look like public relations devices, whether or not those who deploy them recognize them as such.

The well-known models of policy formation that are based on a rationality premise, such as those by Downs (1957) and Olson (1971) illustrate the tendency to rationalize acquiescence or compromise with power, even when they are ostensibly critical of the established order. This result flows from their efforts to find generalizations or covering laws rather than focusing upon the concrete experiences of people in specific social situations. As already suggested, the generalization inevitably becomes a form of reductionism, ignoring benefits, aspirations, costs, and ambiguities other than those that constitute the constructed model.

Both of these models are carefully conceived, provide some nonobvious insights, and seem to point to important criticisms of existing institutions. Downs sees it as irrational to support candidates or parties that espouse policies one does not favor. But millions of voters do exactly that, and a case can easily be made that they are acting rationally because their votes are means to further a different end from the one to which Downs reduces the question. These voters may want public officials who employ the symbols they like, who present a physical appearance they like, who take a congenial stand on one issue that they see as more important than all the others combined, or who can be counted on to elevate the status of their ethnic, racial, or religious group. What is really at issue is the arbitrariness of a particular definition of rationality or of the goal to be achieved efficiently.

The same problem arises with Olson's model, which purports to show that it is irrational to contribute to or join an organization if one can reap the benefits that organization seeks as a "free rider." If the goal is to achieve those benefits at the lowest immediate cost, Olson's conclusion is self-evident. But even though they certainly recognize it as such, millions of people pay to show support for causes they can enjoy whether or not they pay for them: listener-sponsored and public radio and television, civil rights organizations, organizations seeking social or political change, and many others. If they want to enhance the chance of achieving one of these goals, paying rather than remaining a free rider is hardly irrational.

The focus upon rationality in discourse about public policy, in short, is a form of politics that claims the authority of science. Like many political actions, it is most potent when it masks its ideological nature from the officials who practice it as well as from the public whose lives they affect.

NOTE

1. John Austin (1962) called attention to the fact that language is often a form of action that changes the world.

REFERENCES

Austin, J. (1962). *How to do things with words*. Cambridge, MA: Harvard University Press.

Burke, K. (1969). *A grammar of motives*. Berkeley: University of California Press.

Downs, A. (1957). *An economic theory of democracy*. New York: Harper & Row.

Edelman, M. (1977). *Political language: Words that succeed and policies that fail*. New York: Academic Press.

Edelman, M. (1988). *Constructing the political spectacle*. Chicago: University of Chicago Press.

Horkheimer, M., & Adorno, T. (1972). *Dialectic of the enlightenment*. New York: Herder and Herder.

Janis, I. (1982). *Groupthink. Psychological studies of policy decisions and fiascoes*. Boston: Houghton Mifflin.

March, J. (1986). In J. Elster (Ed.), *Rational choice*. New York: New York University Press.

McCloskey, D. (1985). *The rhetoric of economics*. Madison: University of Wisconsin Press.

Olson, M. (1971). *The logic of collective action*. Cambridge, MA: Harvard University Press.

Wolin, S. (1969). Political theory as a vocation. *American Political Science Review, 62*(4), 1062–1082.

17

Public Opinion as Public Judgment

Harry C. Boyte

During the anxious days of Revolutionary ferment in 1776, John Adams expressed his conviction that the citizenry of the nation would be able to act wisely on the great challenges before them. "Time has been given," he wrote to his wife Abigail, "for the whole People, maturely to consider the great Question of Independence and to ripen their Judgments, dissipate their Fears, and allure their Hopes, by discussing it in News Papers and Pamphletts, by debating it, in Assemblies, Conventions, Committees of Safety and Inspection, in Town and Country Meetings, as well as in private Conversations" (Mathews, 1988, p. 5)

Adams voiced a rendering of public opinion as public judgment that was widespread during the Revolution and that continued throughout the 19th century: the concept of the outcome generated by a body of people ("the whole People") who came together through a process of discussion, debate, and dialogue about current affairs. Like the view of later editors and reporters, publishers and educators, lecturers and creators of study circles who championed a similar notion, Adams invoked what he had observed in a process of public discussion with distinctive characteristics. He was also a fervent advocate of such discussion as essential for the "ripening" of judgment.

Today, we have become consumers of endless reports on "public opinion." We learn what our neighbors and our coworkers think, as well as the views of those we have never met, by reading about the distillation of their ideas in polls. Polling has become a significant industry, as indispensable to corporate planners as it is to political professionals.

All of this purportedly illustrates the triumph of liberal democracy. In countries across the world in the advent of communism's collapse, leaders' invocations of public opinion is a staple of political rhetoric. Yet a closer look at the shifting meaning in the term dramatizes democracy's dilemmas. If public opinion has seemingly triumphed, it is far different than the idea advanced by John Adams. The "whole People" has become a phantom. Meanwhile, few, indeed, speak any longer of the "ripening of Judgment."

Public opinion in common parlance today is the snapshot collection of our undigested views, our private "takes" unshaped by any process of discussion and give-and-take with other perspectives outside our immediate lives. Snippets of public opinion in the newspaper *USA Today* capture this state of affairs pictorially. At the bottom of the editorial page, individuals with their pictures in separate boxes respond to the "question of the day." There is no discussion whatsoever.

The notion that private opinions are what the citizen has to contribute lies at the center of the crises in politics in our time. The problems facing the nation, from decaying bridges and inadequate schools to teen pregnancy, racial conflict, and environmental degradation, are of such a scope and complexity that they cannot be met without substantial civic involvement. Solutions require richer insights than experts can produce. Problems need the perspectives that grow from diverse points of view; they require the involvement of those most affected. They demand a citizenry sufficiently engaged that it is capable of creating structures of accountability.

All these forms of involvement are dependent upon judgment. Yet even as public opinion reigns supreme, judgment is precisely what has been lost. This loss grows from the erosion of any sense of *public* as more than a collection of individuals or special interests. Politics has been taken over by a professional class who have little use for substantial public involvement, at least as politics is now practiced (Ehrenhalt, 1991).

Exploration of how the original concept of public opinion as public judgment developed and what might be done to prompt its reemergence challenges more than voting provisions, campaign finance, and television advertising. Retrieval of the concept of judgment points toward a different understanding of politics and citizenship, unlike technocratic rule by experts and professionals. Such retrieval also provides an alternative to the characteristically moralized and ideological forms of citizen activism on the Left and Right that constitute the main alternatives, in which partisans of an issue or cause claim their righteousness and portray their opponents as depraved and evil. Public judgment is the specter haunting concentrated power and totalizing ideology of every sort.

The following begins with a discussion of the connection between the modern concept of public opinion and the concept of "public," understood both as political space and political agency, with certain types of ends. It argues that "public" carried overtones of location—especially the associational networks of civil society—standing between the private and domestic realm and the state, a location that had a relatively open, diverse quality. "Public" also suggested groups of people joined together for deliberative, insurgent, and pragmatic ends that connected their specific concerns to larger public issues. The association of public opinion, public space, and public action embodied in the concept of public judgment created patterns of communication with identifiable characteristics: lasting over time, invoking norms of inclusivity and pragmatic conceptions of the public welfare across the boundaries of specific communities, expressing relatively horizontal relationships of power.

This conception of public opinion *as* public judgment came to political expression in the diverse, variegated populist movement that emerged in the last decades of the 19th century, a movement that sought to adapt concepts of active public life and public citizenship to modern society. Today as well, prospects for the revival of public judgment are contingent upon the spread of political education that teaches the skills, arts, and concepts of public deliberation and public action to ordinary people and professionals alike.

THE RISE OF PUBLIC OPINION AS PUBLIC JUDGMENT

> By "the public sphere" we mean first of all a realm of our social life in which something approaching public opinion can be formed. . . . A portion of the public sphere comes into being in every conversation in which private individuals assemble to form a public body [and] behave neither like business or professional people transacting private affairs, nor like members of a constitutional order subject to the legal constraints of a state bureaucracy. Citizens behave as a public body when they confer in an unrestricted fashion . . . about matters of general interest. (Habermas, cited in Calhoun, 1992, p. 9)

The strong connection between "opinion" and "politics" was illustrated in the shifts of meaning in late 18th-century France. Thus, in 1765, the article on "Opinion" in the *Encyclopédie* defined the word in terms of the classically rationalist distinction between *knowledge*, which was based on science ("a full and entire light which reveals things clearly, shedding demonstrable certainty upon them") and *opinion*, which was seen as shifting and unreliable ("but a feeble and imperfect light which only reveals things by conjecture and leaves them in uncertainty and doubt") (Baker, 1987, p. 238).

By 1789, the "Opinion" entry had disappeared from the *Encyclopédie Méthodique*. Instead, under politics, "opinion" had become "public opinion." Moreover, its resonances had been radically transformed. "Public opinion," said Jacques Nicker, former minister to Louis XVI, was "an invisible power that, without treasure, guard or army, gives its laws to the city, the court, and even the places of kings" (Baker, 1987, p. 238). Or, as editor Jacques Peuchet elaborated in the same work, public opinion was the highest form of political knowledge, designating "the sum of all social knowledge . . . [the] judgments made by a nation on the matters submitted to its tribunal. Its influence is today the most powerful motive for praiseworthy actions" (Baker, 1987, p. 240).

Opinion in this sense was an integrative process. One's views were understood to become *expanded*, more multidimensional, fuller by engagement with the perspectives of others, the history of the community, the facts with which one had not previously been acquainted. Immanuel Kant captured this distinction in his contrast between the *sensus privatur*—views that are only formed through privatized or narrow experience—and the *sensus communis*—common or public sense. The former he also called "cyclopean thinking," based on the Cyclops, the character in Greek mythology who had only one eye.

For Kant, it was entirely possible to be a learned cyclops, "A cyclops of mathematics, history, natural history, philology and languages" (Tyson, 1988, p. 1). But without the "enlarged thought" or public judgment that comes from engagement with a diversity of other viewpoints and perspectives, the learned person fails to think "philosophically"—in Kant's terms, as a member of a living human community (Tyson, 1988). Indeed, Kant argued that the most severe form of insanity was that defined by *sensus privatus*—those cut off from *sensus communis*, who had radically lost touch with any public process (Tyson, 1988, p. 1; Beiner, 1983; Biskowski, 1990).

As Jurgen Habermas has observed, there was in the development of the modern concept of public opinion an interplay between political aspirations and reformers' demands, on the one hand, and far-reaching transformations in the social and economic relationships of European society, on the other. This interaction led to the emergence of concepts such as "public opinion," "public judgment," and the concept of "the public" itself.

Trends toward long-distance trade and commercialization undermined the household economy and created pressures toward a commodity market that reworked political relations and also created new "public knowledge" across communal and even national boundaries. A politicized and self-conscious language of public location, public action, and public opinion was closely connected, moreover, to the development of a vibrant urban culture that formed a spatial environment for the public sphere: lecture halls, museums, public parks, theaters, meeting houses, opera houses, coffee shops, and the like. Associated with such changes was an emergent infrastructure of new social information created through institutions like the press, publishing houses, lending libraries, and literary societies.

Finally, the explosion of voluntary associations in the 18th and 19th centuries created a social setting in which a sense of a disparate, far-ranging, but self-conscious "public" could take shape. Politicized associations of debate and discussion, such as the new reading and literary societies and their associated institutional networks like the press, publishing houses, libraries, clubs, and coffee houses were especially important. These formed a context in which older hierarchical principles of deference and ascribed social status gave way to public principles of "rational" discourse, and emergent professional and business groups could nourish and assert their claims to a more general social and political leadership. In such public spaces, patterns of communication emerged that were characterized by norms of inclusivity, the give-and-take of argument, and a relatively horizontal experience of power. Arguments were judged by their suitability, by pragmatic considerations of anticipated consequences, by excellence of logic, and so forth—not by the social status of the speaker.

By the close of the 18th century and the beginning of the 19th, a public sphere "was casting itself loose as a forum in which the private people, come together to form a public, readied themselves to compel public authority to legimate itself before public opinion. The *publicum* developed into the public, the *subjectum* into the reasoning subject, the receiver of regulations from above into the ruling authorities' adversary" (Habermas, 1989, pp. 25–26).

American educational and media institutions have their roots in this understanding of public action as involving deliberation about political issues of the day and public spaces as forums for inclusive, open communicative exchange. Thus, newspapers commonly described their mission as creating informed public discussion of current issues. In the 19th century, the expansion of public education came about often largely through the efforts of voluntary citizen organizations, and was seen as essential to a well-informed, deliberative citizenry. Similarly, public libraries were created through citizen efforts, and justified as "arsenals of democracy."

The view of the citizenry as a deliberative body produced large civic education movements. In the early 1830s, John Holbrook's Lyceum Movement created adult learning centers in order to provide forums for citizens to discuss public affairs. By 1837, the movement included an estimated 3,000 towns. After the Civil War, the Chatauqua Assembly movement continued this legacy, eventually including 15,000 "home study circles" for discussion of public affairs, as well as artistic performances and public lectures. University extension programs, adopted from England in the 1880s, were designed to promote better rural citizenship, as well as improved farming. In poor and immigrant communities, institutions like the Workmen's Circle and Settlement Houses sought to educate citizens to learn about and discuss public issues.

Yet a singular focus on the public created through deliberation, characteristic of Habermas's approach, is too bounded by the experiences and cultures of white, middle-class, male Protestants of the 19th century to describe the real world of political turbulence and change. A more dynamic understanding of public areas historically comes from looking at "public" as a series of diverse publics, created through a provisional and open-ended process of struggle, change, and challenge (Ryan, 1992; Eley, 1992; Fraser, 1992).

The 19th century was replete with decentered publics of street corner politics, popular discussion clubs, and insurgent organizations, far removed from the reading rooms and clubs of polite society. These illustrated the ways in which political judgment and citizenship, far from abstract and universalist categories, are always infused with interests and points of view. Public judgment is not the search for objective "truth" in pursuit of the "public good." In living politics, judgment and public engagements are dependent on context and perspective, always suffused with power relations.

This context-dependent, provisional, open-ended quality of public involvement and public judgments is dramatized by particular attention to the pragmatics of much public action. For the Greeks, public judgment was conveyed by the concepts of *phronêsis*, or practical wisdom. Practical wisdom involved the insight and practical theory accumulated through collective work around common issues in the space of public life. Questions of justice and processes of deliberation were integral parts of this process, but *phronêsis* involved, as well, an ongoing experience of actual governance around questions of ongoing community survival and maintenance—from moral legislation to sewage control (Boyte, 1991).

When common action is separated from public debate, the processes through which citizens learn crucial dimensions of public life are lost, because reason is separated from experience of the consequences of action. Citizens inevitably become mainly observers, spectators, and audience. What is left is "objective" and critical knowledge, on the one hand, especially as logic and analytic thinking. Education in our schools today emphasizes this sort of knowledge. Or, on the other hand, what is stressed is subjective, intuitive, and emotional knowledge, of the sort found in artistic endeavors and "personalized politics." But the sharpness of these divisions between ways of knowing— and their separateness from political capacity—have grave political consequences.

A conceptual severance of debate from responsible action corresponds to formal political experience in modern republics, where political representatives make the formal decisions about public affairs, and political authority is delegated, not practiced directly by, the citizenry as a whole. (Conservatives regularly invoke "citizen responsibility," but tend to ignore the structural and institutional relations that strip citizens of power and authority.)

Yet neglect of the active dimension of judgment means that the citizen is inevitably a spectator. In contrast, the concept of practical judgment highlights the largely pragmatic, problem-solving motives that often move people in the public sphere, in both formal and informal contexts. Communitarian theorists of democracy, such as Habermas, in separating out "instrumental reason" from "communicative action" create an idealized—and thus marginalized—public theater for ordinary citizens, removed from the interplays of power and interest and practical concern that characterize real politics.

American politics has historical spaces for formal direct democracy, such as the New England town meeting, but the traditions of practical public problem solving were mainly embodied in the multiple voluntary traditions of civil society. These, in turn, had roots in the European experiences of most immigrants (Bertoff, 1982; Boyte, 1989; Evans & Boyte, 1986; Keane, 1988). When the French observer Alexis de Tocqueville traveled across the country in the 1830s, he was struck by the role of citizens as agents: "Americans of all ages, all stations in life, and all types of disposition are forever forming associations . . . at the head of any new undertaking, where in France you would find the government or in England some territorial magnate, in the United States you are sure to find an association" (Tocqueville, 1969, p. 523).

Attention to the experiences of problem solving by women's groups, for example, highlights a process of judgment formation that involves not only deliberation but assumption of responsibility for a variety of practical tasks. Through welfare organizations and other associational activities—educational institutions, religious groups, moral reform organizations of all kinds—women learned a series of public skills, capacities, and sensibilities such as the exercise of power, judgment tied to action, listening, negotiation, and practices of accountability. The Women's Christian Temperance Union (WCTU) of the late 19th century, for instance, combined decades of problem-solving effort and reform agitation in its slogan, "Do Everything." Historian Ruth Bordin conveyed the scale: by 1889 WCTU Chicago's activities included "two day nurseries, two Sunday Schools, an industrial school, a mission that sheltered four thousand homeless or destitute women in a twelve month period, a free medical dispensary that treated over 1,600 patients a year, lodging for men that had to date provided temporary housing for over fifty thousand men, and a low-cost restaurant" (Bordin, 1980, p. 98).

Experiences of power wielding and problem solving lent 19th-century social movements an idiomatic style that unmistakably combined three elements of public agency: public as critic and public as insurgent force was wedded to an understanding of public as responsible and powerful actor. As Frances Willard, the WCTU's guiding force, put it, the temperance crusade gave women a transformed sense of their own agency, whether or not they understood themselves to be in political opposition:

> Perhaps the most significant outcome of this movement was the knowledge of their own power gained by the conservative women of the Churches. They had never even seen a "women's rights convention," and had been held aloof from the "suffragists" by fears as to their orthodoxy; but now there were women prominent in all Church cares and duties eager to clasp hands for a more aggressive work than such women had ever before dreamed of undertaking. (Epstein, 1981, p. 100)

As a consequence, popular movements of groups excluded or marginalized by the dominant terms of politics and citizenship used republican language while they gave it new vibrancy through wedding civic responsibility to struggles around power and justice. Thus the Common School Movement, for example, organized around the demand that education be available to poor and working-class communities. In this view, public school education was both an instrument of democracy—the means for educating common people to be full citizens—and itself, increasingly, a new form of social property. The very possession of an "education" in schools was seen as a foundation for independence and civic virtue, the condition for active participation in public affairs (Greer, 1972).

During Reconstruction, the black population undertook a crusade whose twin goals of education and land challenged America's racially restrictive commonwealth. "It was a whole race trying to go to school," recalled Booker T. Washington about those years in his autobiography, *Up from Slavery*. "Few were too young, and none too old, to make the attempt to learn. As fast as any kind of teachers could be secured, not only were day-schools filled, but night-schools as well. The great ambition of the older people was to try to learn to read the Bible before they died" (Kluger, 1977, p. 51). The Freedmen's Bureau in 1865 opened more than 4,000 schools across the South and, in the next five years, almost a quarter of a million people attended them. Throughout the South, those with education became leaders during the years of Reconstruction (Foner, 1988).

POPULISM AND PUBLIC JUDGMENT

American populism drew upon this legacy of public life and democratic insurgency for its central images and vocabulary as it developed into a massive farm movement in the latter years of the 1880s. Desperate to retain their land, escape tenantry, and maintain their independence, farmers devised a new method of cooperatively marketing their crops and purchasing their supplies. When the very existence of their cooperatives was threatened by the refusal of banks to extend credit, they created the People's, or Populist, Party to challenge government policies. Ultimately the party could not break the hold of the two party system for a number of reasons: the racism of whites, the cultural chasm between largely Protestant farmers and the growing Catholic immigrant population in northeastern cities, and fierce loyalties to party and party machine. But populist language nonetheless shaped decades of subsequent reform (Goodwyn, 1976).

At the heart of the Populist movement was a conception of citizens as responsible agents in the public world, whose sovereignty was threatened by the crop lien system and by the growing concentration of financial and monopoly interests in the nation. The wedding of the language of civic responsibility with the demand, as the Populist Party platform put it, "to restore government of the republic to the hand of the 'plain people' with whom it originated," (Goodwan, 1976, p. 265) had several dramatic effects.

In the first instance, it allowed the movement to challenge concentrated property by recalling the "commonwealth" theme of the social nature of property. The cooperative commonwealth that the Populists envisioned was not hostile to enterprise or private ownership. Rather, the thrust of the Populist platform proposed ways to hold accountable basic elements of the nation's economy—those things like transportation, money supply, and land policy seen as essential to independence and small-business survival.

This kind of language created the rhetorical repertoire for 20th-century reformers who challenged the social irresponsibility of concentrated economic power by means of standards of public judgment that applied the concepts of a larger public good. Thus, for instance, Theodore Roosevelt in his famous New Nationalism speech challenged the "sinister influence or control of special interests," which he identified with ancient threats to democracy:

> Exactly as the special interests of cotton and slavery threatened our political integrity before the Civil War, so now the great special business interests too often control and corrupt the men and methods of government for their own profit. . . . The true friend of property, the true conservative, is he who insists that property shall be the servant and not the master of the commonwealth. . . . The citizens of the United States must effectively control the mighty commercial forces which they themselves called into being. (Roosevelt, 1981, p. 334)

Populists not only called for renewed civic responsibility for large property, along with ways to hold property accountable. They also applied the rhetoric of civic responsibility and public judgment making to themselves as well by establishing extensive programs of self-education.

Building on old traditions in the South and Midwest, parades and rivals, Alliance schools and lecture circuits, developed to "educate the people." An Alliance Press numbered something like 1,000 newspapers, with names like the *Advocate*, the *American Nonconformist*, *Progressive Farmer,* and *Appeal to Reason*. "The suballiance is a schoolroom," as one lecturer put it (Goodwan, 1976, p. 3). This educational process, in turn, made visible progress in democratizing political culture in often striking ways. The movement encouraged a measure of women's participation in public roles unprecedented in the 19th-century social environment. Its leadership was more ethnically diverse than any other political institution. It even raised questions about the bedrock premise of the white South, racial superiority (Goodwyn, 1976; Jeffrey 1975).

Over the past century, populist language has maintained its rhetorical effectiveness in politics, but the actual experiences of everyday power that nourished the movement have weakened. This resulted in what Lawrence Goodwyn, Populism's historian, has termed "shadow movements" in place of democratic politics—movements of demagogic protest in grievance, rather than serious efforts at democratization.

THE EROSION OF JUDGMENT

In enormous cities, many scarcely knew their neighbors, much less those on the other side of the tracks. Waves of immigrants brought new customs, traditions, and languages. Mass communications technologies weakened the ties between the press and the citizenry. The locus of civic involvement gradually shifted from voluntary association and community activity to government itself, though many mediating institutions, from unions to neighborhood schools, continued to have strong civic dimensions. In the view of many Progressive reformers, through various public agencies and electoral reforms—regulations, direct election of senators, referenda, initiative, and the like—citizens would shape the "great community" of the state.

Yet the reality proved different. Aside from a new rising professional class, most Americans continued to identify with their locales, traditions, and cultures. But their worlds seemed increasingly shaped by distant forces over which they had little control. Corner grocers slowly gave way to chain stores; local decisions over education were removed to state or national bureaucracies; local businesses were bought out by global corporations.

By the last decades of the 19th century, the public sphere had begun to atrophy. The growing replacement of a competitive capitalist economy with a monopolized economy dominated by large industrial and financial interests undermined the power and authority of the commercial and professional middle classes. The state itself increasingly took on the role of social regulator of conflicts, and the public began to break apart into a myriad of special interests. Meanwhile, in cultural systems from the arts to the communications media, developments over the last century have progressively eroded voluntary, interactive, and associational environments, recreating "the public" as a passive mass of individualized consumers (Habermas, 1989).

As large government agencies and corporate structures came to predominate, a new generation of managers and technical specialists developed who drew their basic metaphors and language from science. A culture of professionalism detached knowledge from local communities in field after field, emphasizing rationality, methodical processes, and standards of "objectivity" in place of public deliberation. Kant's "learned cyclops" multiplied in every setting (Bledstein, 1976; Lasch, 1977).

Even a generation ago in settlement houses, 4-H clubs, schools, unions, and the like, citizens learned practical arts of public life like negotiation, accountability, granting of public recognition, and exercise of power and authority from a continuing practice of community action in voluntary and informal community institutions and in small-scale business, farming, and artisanal and craft professions. The public world, either formally construed as politics or informally experienced as the civic sphere, was not seen as radically separated from everyday life. In turn, the erosion of this dimension of a pragmatic, problem-solving public weakened the daily experiences of popular agency and public capacities for judgment.

Against this background, the Left made a Faustian bargain. Socialists and welfare state liberals alike said, in effect, that if democracy understood as participation in governance is impossible in the modern world, they would settle for a more equal distribution of resources and incomes instead, to be accomplished primarily through the state. This theme, expressed as the singular focus on questions of justice (both distributive and procedural) on the liberal Left, was also given institutional foundations in the growing bureaucracies and large scale organizations of reform: enormous unions, political parties, professional associations, and so forth. All of these progressively detached popular participation and agency from politics. As a consequence, justice—not power and the exercise of public judgment about its uses—increasingly formed the axis of political debate in welfare state politics (Evans & Nelson, 1989).

Such historical experience has shaped the language of modern politics, reflected in the approaches of elites and their critics and opponents alike. But whatever phenomenological plausibility there is to a one- or two-dimensional construction of the public sphere, there is also considerable political cost. The very division between life world and system world, between making life and making history, as obvious and natural as it first appears, obscures the actual living agency of ordinary people along the borders between the everyday and the systemic, the fashion in which power never operates simply in a monochromatic and unidirectional fashion but always is a complex, interactive ensemble of relationships.

Without attention to and cultivation of the experiences and education that produce *phronêsis*, or the practical judgment and common sense developed through communal reflection on action over time, political thought ineluctably tends toward an ideological and dogmatic quality of public opinion. An excessively sharp contrast between the institutional world and the lived experience of the people lends itself to a romanticized and Manichean politics, where forces of light and good battle forces of dark and evil.

Such a pattern increasingly characterized the protest politics of the 1960s, turning the crusade between "Free World" and "Iron Curtain" into its moral obverse—a battle between "flower children" and "Amerika." Subsequently, such an understanding of issue conflicts has come to characterize virtually every popular dispute, on both the Left and the Right, from prayer in the schools to abortion, from garbage incinerators to AIDS. Despite the participatory flavor of the most grass-roots activism, the result has been a restriction of any possibility for a genuine public sphere ever since. Seeing controversies as the clash between innocents and monsters severely constricts the possibilities of engagement with one's opponents.

PUTTING "PUBLIC" BACK IN PUBLIC OPINION

Public judgment includes the deliberative activities that Adams suggested, the kind of civic office occupied when people learn to think broadly about public questions. Today this sort of judgment continues in the jury system, where citizens regularly rise to the occasion of determining justice and adjudicating conflicting claims. The League of Women Voters has continued a valiant effort to sustain concepts of public deliberation, against the grain of the political culture. And new efforts to revive study circle and Chatauqua traditions, such as the 3,500 groups involved in the Kettering Foundation's National Issues Forums, suggest intimations of a widespread interest in a different chemistry of political talk. But these remain exceptions.

Public judgment also entails a larger perspective on social change and reform that involves ethical questions of justice. It also means, crucially, public engagement in actual governance that puts the public into politics as more than critic, audience, or deliberator. This conception of judgment suggests a theory of political communication with certain transcommunal principles, such as the ideal of the general welfare or "commonwealth," understood as an open-ended and pragmatically determined location where groups with varying interests and values negotiate their differences and contribute their distinctive perspectives in the interest of large-scale problem solving. It also involves basic ground rules of discourse, such as open and inclusive communication, interactive exchange, and attentiveness to different points of view.

The project of retrieving public judgment has populist dimensions: the entrance of "the people" into decision making. Populism revolves around the theme of power. On both the Right and the Left, the call to "return power to the people" can easily shape a politics of grievance and demagoguery. Demagogic populism is, again, Manichean, extolling the innocence of "the people" against nefarious elites. As the current fashion in radio talk shows illustrates, it undermines the possibility of judgment as surely as do the politics of television soundbites and political consultants.

Yet a far different sort of populist politics animated the movements by that name in the late 1880s and the 1890s. In the 19th century Populists challenged restrictive and centralized power while they also cultivated the political potential of ordinary women and men. They wedded struggles for power and justice with a strong sense of public responsibility and the cultivation of public judgment.

This marriage, resulting in a civic impulse of liberal and democratic inclination, has a renewed relevance today. It offers important resources for moving beyond the contemporary crisis in politics, in which a cacophony of claims for rights and assertions of prerogatives threaten to drown out any concern for the refurbishing of the civic capital upon which we all depend. It brings citizens to center stage at a time when certain political functions characteristic of the citizenry as a whole—political deliberation and problem solving that involves widespread change in behavior, values, and outlook—have a growing importance.

The loss of a strong language of public life has colored recent debates around renderings of a politics or of "ordinary people." Political theorists and social critics like Christopher Lasch, Robert Bellah, Jean Bethke Elshtain, Michael Sandel, Alasdair MacIntyre, and others have made trenchant criticisms of the "thinness" of politics as expressed in technocratic, modernist, and therapeutic languages. They call for a politics that reflects communal traditions and "values of ordinary Americans" such as family, place, and religion (Lasch, 1991; Bellah, Madsen, Sullivan, Swidler, & Tipton, 1985; Elshtain, 1981; Sandel, 1982; MacIntyre, 1981).

These arguments have helped importantly to retrieve a sense of political communication as always emerging from human narrative—particularities of place, time, and history. Yet this approach also has clear limits. The politics of community neglects the bitter divisions and prejudices that often structure everyday experience. Local communities in American history have contained many cultural resources, but they have also been rent by hierarchies along lines of gender, race, and culture. Moreover, today many of the neighborhood building blocks of community action, such as ethnic groups, religious congregations, extended family networks, and political party organizations have weakened. In recent years, neighborhood action has tended toward a parochial "not in my backyard" stance. Moreover, community politics fails to connect local problems and community efforts with larger arenas to public policy, power, and change. As a result, proposals for "communitarian" politics sound idealized and nostalgic. For example, Sandel's argument that the Democrats should adopt a community-based language was illustrated by a cover story in *The New Republic* in 1988 with the image of a 19th-century small town. Without mechanisms and political spaces to engage the world beyond community lines, opportunities for cultivation of public judgment are limited (Sandel, 1988).

POPULISM, PUBLIC LIFE, AND PUBLIC JUDGMENT

Populism of liberal spirit—a populism of public judgment—cannot collapse politics or the public world into community, any more than politics can be formulated as simply electoral activity and expert advice, as protest or service. Rather, such politics needs a transcommunal understanding of political space and communication, beyond shared understandings and ways of life. The challenge is to generated a different sort of politics that teaches the concepts and arts of a turbulent, diverse, and variegated public world stretching across particular community lines. What gets lost today in institutional politics and in the dominant forms of citizens activism—protest, service, and community action—is precisely this public arena, and the sense of the public as a strong agent that can act within it.

An understanding of the public as responsible agent teaches the moral ambiguity and open-ended, provisional quality involved in the pragmatic tasks and communicative process of the public life, where the search is not for personal closeness, "truth," final vindication, or normative communal consensus, but rather for appropriateness, fit, and provisional if sound resolution of concerns. In private life, one looks mainly for intimacy and similarity of outlook, value, and background. In a problem-solving public, in contrast, the point is not bonding experiences or self-revelation. Personal interests often bring people into the public world (witness the insight in the 1960s slogan, "the personal is the political"). But neither an intimate and personalized style nor communal principles like trust, loyalty, familiarity, and friendship are very effective or productive for action in larger public settings. Rather, the public arena is best structured by principles like accountability, strategic actin, respect, and recognition. Politics involves a pragmatic interplay and bargaining among a variety of interests, values, and ways of looking at experience. Knowledge is not simply divided between categories like "objective" and analytic or "subjective" and emotional. Different ways of knowing and perspectives are valued because they are helpful and create more power, in just the sense suggested by the Jainist fable of the 12 blind men surrounding an elephant, who only know "the truth" by pooling their knowledge.

In a public sphere of actors as well as protestors, no one is simply a victim or an innocent. The development of minimal agreement about ethical standards for public life becomes essential, but everyone bears a measure of responsibility. The reward is an experience of public *creation* and public *freedom*, where ordinary people learn that they can help shape the world around them according to their interests and aspirations.

To revive this sense of public life in which judgment plays a crucial part, civic education needs self-consciously to combine particular interests with attention to the wider welfare. This approach located interests of specific groups in relation to the public interest. For some years, this has been especially the contribution of public interest leaders like Ralph Nader and groups like Common Cause. Recently, arguments for universal, as contrasted with targeted entitlement programs of the sort advanced by *The American Prospect* illustrate such a strategy.

Similarly, a public-spirited citizen politics would draw upon the legacy from the original Populists by making civic education a central project. Today, authentic efforts at democratization are far more complicated than 19th-century challenges to "the monied interests." Effective political pedagogy for our time necessarily involves teaching concepts of public life itself, including the simple concept that there is such a thing as the public world, different from private or community experience. Such political education connects local efforts with strategies for larger changes in many institutions and in public policy—not simply with the economy.

In this vein, Project Public Life at the University of Minnesota's Humphrey Institute of Public Affairs has shown how the concepts and skills of public life, defined as a distinctive, diverse arena of practical action and deliberation, can be used to reengage citizens in the politics of settings as varied as government, education, health care, and the workplace. Creating a mapping of public concepts—frameworks for analyzing the interactions among varying interests, viewpoints, and power relations in the public arena—forms a foundation for political reengagement and judgment, since it allows people to put themselves back into the political world as responsible moral agents, rather than remain as spectators. As one 4-H agent in Minnesota put it, "Looking at situations in terms of concepts like public life and power adds another dimension, like putting on 3-d glasses in the movies" (Project Public Life, 1991, p. 6).

For instance, Project Public Life's Public Achievement initiative, undertaken with St. Paul Mayor Jim Scheibel and Minnesota 4-H, challenges teenagers to reclaim politics as everyday problem solving around issues in which they feel a stake. Public Achievement begins with discussions in which teens react to the word "politics." Out of more than a thousand teenagers, a handful had any positive reactions—and those were mainly involved in student government. Most define "politics" as sleazy politicians lying about each other on television. Teenagers have positive reactions to the word, "public," however, with associations from parks and concerts to "ordinary people" like themselves. Moreover, they identify a multitude of problems in which they see themselves as having a direct stake, from school governance to day care for teenage mothers and race relations.

Public Achievement creates opportunities for teams of teenagers, working with coaches from community organizations, local college campuses, and schools, to develop an action plan around such problems, a plan relevant to their lives and communities. The art of Public Achievement is to open space for teens to "own" their effort—designing and implementing strategies for action, creating public forums where they deal with diverse groups of teenagers from other communities—but also to have adults in relationship with them, challenging but not dominating, teaching them the cultures and maps of their institutional environments.

Such a process stands in stark contrast to other forms of public engagement they have seen, from service to protest. Its public language differs sharply from one-on-one service involvements, for instance, which characteristically stress the personal growth themes that reflect the ascendancy of psychology in recent years as the disciplinary touchstone of kindergarten through 12th-grade education. Students have learned "Care Bear" politics—how to "express their feelings." Even sophisticated high school service curricula stress self-esteem, personal discovery, and bonding with others. "Politics" is entirely absent. Young people have also been raised on a diet of consciousness raising about social problems, from race conflict and global warming to falling SAT scores. What they have not seen are many practical solutions. A solution for the 1990s thus needs to differ from both encounter-group experience and 1960s-style protest politics.

Public Achievement stresses pragmatic public action, reflection, and relationships with others whom one many not necessarily "like" or agree with on many issues, but with whom one can work on concrete issues of concern. "This allows me to do something I want, not just something the teachers tell me to do," explained Tracy Veronen, an eighth-grader at St. Bernard's Catholic school in St. Paul (*Catholic Bulletin*, 1991, p. 1). In counterpoint, Jeff Mauer, a teacher in the school, says the trick is to guide instead of lead: "Adults feel like they have to jump in an fix everything," explained Maurer (*Catholic Bulletin*, 1991, p. 1). "I have developed a new appreciation and respect for my students as I watched them identify issues, devise strategies to deal with them and evaluate their own progress." Such a process vividly illustrates that teenagers are not so much apathetic or unconcerned about politics as they are usually unaware of any ways it might be productive or accessible. Teams from diverse cultural and economic backgrounds show enthusiasm, seriousness, creativity, and capacities for judgment in public problem-solving work, where the point is not bonding or learning to "care for another" but rather having an impact, gaining visibility and engaging effectively in politics. Politics stops being an unpleasant spectator sport, and becomes something that is interesting, challenging, and rewarding.

Similarly, the Solomon Project of Project Public Life is built around strategies for teaching low-income communities to develop ongoing, practical public relationships with educators around school problems. The affiliated Lazarus Project has brought concepts and skills of public discussion, debate, and action into nursing home settings and educational programs of health care professionals, where previously a therapeutic language of care had rendered themes of interest and power invisible.

Today, growing numbers of citizens feel disengaged from the political process and from public affairs. Voting levels have declined precipitously. Citizens voice common complaints: the political process rewards posturing and hype. There is little serious discussion of the problems that the country faces. Lacking widespread involvement, politics is dominated by extremes.

The problems with politics have not simply been inflicted *upon* the citizenry, however. No matter how much complaint, or how many reforms are proposed, politics is unlikely to get much better until citizens reclaim their public roles as deliberators and actors.

Neither a narrowly technocratic politics nor a moralized politics nor a politics of intimacy nor an invocation of community is enough. To meet the challenge of citizenship and effective reform, we need something larger: a liberal outlook that reengages the American people in democratic participation, and a civic activism that shows the connections between people's everyday lives and interests and the realm of formal politics and public affairs. This revitalization of a robust citizenship, long overdue, is essential for America's political and social renewal. It is from this synthesis that we can imagine revival of a public world in which citizens once again become subjects and creators of history rather than history's objects, and public judgment returns to the field of public opinion.

ACKNOWLEDGMENTS

This piece benefits from initial collaboration with Frances Moore Lappe, the research efforts and discussions with Kathryn Stoff Hogg, and the comments of Ted Glasser.

REFERENCES

Baker, K. (1987). Politics and public opinion under the old regime. In J. Censer & J. Popkin (Eds.), *Press and politics under the old regime* (pp. 204–246). Berkeley: University of California Press.

Beiner, R. (1983). *Political judgment*. Chicago: University of Chicago Press.

Bellah, R., Madsen, R., Sullivan, W., Swidler, A., & Tipton, S. (1985). *Habits of the heart: Individualism and commitment in American life*. Berkeley: University of California Press.

Bertoff, R. (1982). Peasant and artisan, Puritans and Republicans. *Journal of American History*, *69*, 579–598.

Biskowski, L. (1990). Political rationality and citizenship. Unpublished Ph.D. dissertation, University of Minnesota.

Bledstein, B. (1976). *The culture of professionalism: The middle class and the development of higher education in America*. New York: Norton.

Bordin, R. (1980). *Women and temperance: The quest for power and liberty, 1873–1900*. Philadelphia: Temple University Press.

Boyte, H. (1989). *CommonWealth: A return to citizen politics*. New York: Free Press.

Boyte, H. (1992). The pragmatic ends of popular politics. In C. Calhoun (Ed.), *Habermas and the public sphere* (pp. 340–355). Boston: MIT University Press.

Catholic Bulletin. (1991, January). St. Paul, MN: Archdiocese of St. Paul.

Ehrenhalt, A. (1991). *The United States of ambition*. New York: Times Books.

Eley, G. (1992). Nations, publics, political cultures. In C. Calhoun (Ed.), *Habermas and the public sphere* (pp. 289–339). Boston: MIT University Press.

Elshtain, J. B. (1981). *Public man, private woman*. Princeton, NJ: Princeton University Press.

Epstein, B. (1981). *The politics of domesticity: Women, evangelism and temperance in nineteenth century America*. Middletown: Wesleyan University Press.

Evans, S., & Nelson, B. (1989). *Wage justice: Comparable worth and the paradoxes of technocratic reform*. Chicago: University of Chicago Press.

Evans, S., & Boyte, H. (1986). *Free spaces: The sources of democratic change in America*. New York: Harper & Row.

Foner, E. (1988). *Reconstruction: America's unfinished revolution: 1863–1877*. New York: Harper & Row.

Fraser, N. (1992). Rethinking the public sphere. In C. Calhoun (Ed.), *Habermas and the public sphere* (pp. 109–142). Boston: MIT University Press.

Goodwyn, L. (1976). *Democratic promise: The populist movement in America*. New York: Oxford University Press.

Greer, C. (1972). *The great school legend*. New York: Basic Books.

Habermas, J. (1989). *The transformation of the public sphere*. Boston: MIT University Press.

Jeffrey, J. (1975). Women in the Southern Farmers Alliance. *Feminist Studies, 3*, 75–87.

Keane, J. (Ed.). (1988). *Civil society and the state*. New York: Verso.

Kluger, R. (1977). *Simple justice: The history of Brown v. Board of Education and black America's struggle for equality*. New York: Vintage.

Lasch, C. (1977). *Haven in a heartless world: The family besieged*. New York: Basic Books.

Lasch, C. (1991). *The true and only heaven: Progress and its critics*. New York: Norton.

MacIntyre, M. (1981). *After virtue*. Notre Dame: University of Notre Dame Press.

Mathews, D. (1988). *The promise of democracy*. Dayton, OH: Kettering Foundation.

Project Public Life. (1991). *Teaching politics: Annual report*. Minneapolis: Humphrey Institute.

Ryan, M. (1992). Gender and public access. In C. Calhoun (Ed.), *Habermas and the public sphere* (pp. 259–288). Boston: MIT University Press.

Roosevelt, R. (1981). New nationalism. In S. Hyman (Ed.), *Law, justice and the common good: Readings for leadership* (pp. 334–335). Minneapolis: Hubert H. Humphrey Institute.

Sandel, M. (1982). *Liberalism and the limits of justice*. Cambridge, England: Cambridge University Press.

Sandel, M. (1988). The Democrats and community. *New Republic*, pp. 20–23.

Toqueville, A. de (1969). *Democracy in America*. New York: Doubleday.

Tyson, R. (1988). Odysseus and the Cyclops. Dayton, OH: Kettering Foundation.

18

The Politics of Polling and the Limits of Consent

Charles T. Salmon
Theodore L. Glasser

"Blumer was wrong."

With these three unambiguous and uncompromising words, so began the introduction to the fifty-year anniversary issue of *Public Opinion Quarterly*, a compendium of the major intellectual currents collectively comprising the torrent of public opinion scholarship since 1936 (Singer, 1987). Consider the incredible magnitude and range of historical events which had provided the fertile learning laboratory for the infant field of public opinion research and which might have served as alternative points of departure: the social reforms of the Roosevelt era, World War II, polling fiascos in political elections, the Cold War, political assassinations, *Roe v. Wade*, Vietnam, the Civil Rights movement, Watergate, and AIDS; startling innovations in computer technology and quantitative research methodology which would forever alter sampling procedures, interviewing techniques and strategies for data analysis; and the dozens of books, monographs, articles, and soundbites from the pioneers of the modern era of public opinion research: George Gallup, Elmo Roper, Paul Lazarsfeld, Angus Campbell, Herbert Hyman, Harold Lasswell, and countless others. That the editor chose to introduce this commemorative issue with a rebuke to a then recently deceased sociologist who had devoted but a solitary article to the topic of public opinion and who had never even been published in the *Quarterly* is truly a remarkable testament to the power of an idea.[1] In its own way, it simultaneously represented an ironic legitimation of Herbert Blumer's incisive diagnosis of, and prescription for, what he regarded as a conceptually and methodologically infirm institution of public opinion polling.

Our goal is to examine the latent conception of democracy inherent in the practice of polling and to assess the implications of polling for the practice of journalism. We begin with reference to two seminal figures in the development of the modern era of public opinion, James Bryce and George Gallup. We then turn to a comparison of competing perspectives on public opinion and communication, drawing particularly on Blumer's 1948 critique. We conclude with a discussion of the implications of these perspectives for a press committed to preserving the conditions for public debate and democratic participation.

TACIT ASSUMPTIONS OF PUBLIC OPINION POLLING

Too many social scientists, Blumer observed in 1948, had adopted a strictly operationalist view of public opinion, a hopelessly tautological position rooted in the belief that "public opinion consists of what public opinion polls poll." Though this criticism may appear excessively harsh, it is at least fair to say that the application of polling and survey research to the study of public opinion is so commonplace, so widespread that it constitutes a prime example of what Kuhn (1970) has described as a dominant paradigm. As Ginsberg (1986, p. 60), among many others, has observed, "poll results and public opinion are terms that are used almost synonymously." Converse (1987, p. S14) implicitly concurs, acknowledging that "it is exactly this kind of 'one person one vote' tally of opinions as routinely reported today by polls and surveys which has now become the consensual understanding the world around as to a baseline definition of public opinion." Indeed, one social science dictionary has as its first definition of public opinion, "The prevailing and predominant attitudes and judgments of the members of a community on given issues of general controversy *as determined by public opinion polls* [italics added]" (Theodorson & Theodorson, 1969, p. 325).

And yet, something so taken for granted, from Blumer's perspective, constitutes a "logically unpardonable" blurring of the distinction between *what* is being studied and *how* it is being studied, as though a technique or procedure (i.e., the operation of polling) could somehow constitute, seemingly intrinsically, the very object it presumed to study.[2]

One might be reluctant to accept, for example, a definition of "communication" as that phenomenon determined by "communication-ometers," and yet that is precisely the type of acceptance that has long gone unstated in the preponderance of mainstream public opinion research.

What has led to so uncritical an acceptance of polling and survey research as an appropriate vehicle for assessing public opinion? The answer is rooted in two specific premises serving as the foundation of the modern era of public opinion research: (1) that the preferences of individuals, rather than special interest groups, should dictate public policy; and, (2) that a public opinion "situation" is an individual behavior analogous to voting in an election or purchasing a tube of toothpaste.

Bryce's Democracy and Gallup's Legacy

These conceptual underpinnings of the dominant paradigm of modern public opinion research can be traced to the seminal writings of James Bryce, who, in *The American Commonwealth* (1895), offered his observations about the quintessential elements of the American philosophy and practice of democracy. In his view, "Every man knows that he is himself a part of the government, bound by duty as well as self-interest to devote part of his time and thoughts to it. He may neglect this duty, but he admits it to be a duty" (Bryce, 1895, p. 269). Bryce contended that a central assumption of "orthodox" democratic theory is "that every citizen has, or ought to have thought out for himself certain opinions, i.e., ought to have a definite view, defensible by arguments, of what the country needs, of what principles ought to be applied in governing it (p. 250)." At the same time, he was enough of a realist to admit that this assumption probably was not a viable one because of the typically low priority "public questions" assumed in the lives and leisure-time thinking of the great mass of citizens.

Underlying Bryce's conceptualization of democracy was his belief, based upon his analysis of historical events, that the judgment of the "common," uneducated man repeatedly had proven to be the equal of that of the elites. As a result, he advocated a form of democracy in which the opinion of the common man would carry the same weight as that of the elite. The democratic ideal would be achieved "if the will of the majority of the citizens were to become ascertainable at all times, and without the need of its passing through a body of representatives, possibly even without the need of voting machinery at all" (Bryce, 1895, p. 258)

The impact of Bryce's writings on George Gallup, a pioneer of public opinion research, cannot be overstated; in fact, Bryce has been described as the "patron saint" of the pollsters in the vanguard of the modern era of public opinion research (Rogers, 1949), a moniker which seems apt, given the frequency with which they alluded to his writings on the topic. George Gallup, the leading figure of this era, frequently drew on Bryce's (1895, p. 354) maxim that "the obvious weakness of government by public opinion is the difficulty in ascertaining it" as a way of legitimizing his technique. Finally, Bryce's idealized democracy could be achieved because political decision makers could now scientifically ascertain the preferences of individuals on any issue (Gallup, 1972).

Gallup, however, clearly put his own unique spin on his extension of Bryce's political philosophy by drawing on his background in researching consumer preferences. In his master's thesis completed at the State University of Iowa a decade before the presidential election that would catapult him into fame, Gallup (1925) had considered two different approaches to evaluating salesclerks in a local department store: the complaints and praises of customers and the ratings by the employment manager. Both were problematic, he reported, but the former was especially so because a few customers might "have an ax to grind." What was needed, therefore, was a way of assessing what all customers felt, not just the vocal few. Similarly, in his doctoral thesis, a study of newspaper readership, Gallup (1928) had described the problem editors faced when newspaper readers complained about news selection and features: Were they merely an "articulate minority" or the actual majority of readers? In both cases, Gallup's primary concern had been that the preferences of a loud minority might be misinterpreted as the preferences of the silent majority.[3]

Gallup reiterated this same concern when promoting the use of his commercial technique for the study of public opinion. He commented that "in this day of pressure groups, telegram barrages, and other forms of protest, the worried legislator must cope with such techniques and therefore may mistakenly identify all the noise and clamor with public opinion" (Gallup & Rae, 1940, p.25). The reported ability of his technique to neutralize the power of pressure groups was particularly salient in the specific historical and ideological contexts of the time. Citing the 1940 report of the Dies Committee on un-American activities, Gallup and Rae (1940, p. 11) decried pressure groups and powerful interests "... who speak in the name of democracy while abusing its freedoms to destroy its structure." Reminiscent of the language used in primitive World War I propaganda efforts, Gallup and Rae (1940, pp. 8–9) asked:

> Signor Mussolini insists that Fascism has "thrown on the dump heap" the "lifeless theories" of democracy; Comrade Stalin decries the democratic way as a sham and a delusion ... Herr Hitler scoffs at the "foolish masses. . . ."
>
> From this challenge spring two fundamental questions to which an

> answer must be given. *Is democracy really inferior to dictatorship? Can democracy develop new techniques to meet the impact of this strange new decade?*

Gallup's "new technique," rooted in commercial marketing research, called for "refuting the claims of pressure groups" and, in the process, bringing about a "truer democracy" (Gallup, 1966, pp. 548–549). In other words, although Gallup recognized that special interest groups had substantial involvement in the arena of public opinion, he made the value judgment that this involvement was undesirable, indeed, antithetical to his vision of how a democracy should operate. This view was not peculiar to Gallup, but was shared by other pioneers of the modern era of polling, most of whom, according to Converse (1987, p. S15), hoped to make the "voice of the people" successfully "compete with the few voices in the ears of power. . . ."

This is the crux of the paradox which Blumer would so insightfully capture in his essay. That is, Gallup and his contemporaries would use empirical research procedures not to study the democratic process as it actually existed, but as they would have preferred it to exist. Opinion which was actually public and often exercised by organized groups—in the form of lobbying efforts, telegrams, and protest—would be viewed as potentially threatening to democratic principles and hence would be excluded from mainstream studies of public opinion (i.e., polls). On the other hand, opinion which was actually *not* public, i.e., the private opinions of individuals, would become the exclusive focus of mainstream research and would, in the process, artificially be made "public." The mantle of objectivity and science would serve as the legitimizing cloak for this program of social activism. Blumer (1948, p. 548) elaborates:

> If one seeks to justify polling as a method of studying public opinion on the ground that the composition of public opinion *ought to be* different than what it is, he is not establishing the validity of the method for the study of the empirical world as it is. Instead, he is hanging on the coat-tails of a dubious proposal for social reform.

PUBLIC OPINION, VOTING, AND CONSUMER PREFERENCES

The polling technique proved to be useful for predicting consumer preferences for store clerks, voting behaviors, and the like, all situations in which individuals confront a fixed set of known alternatives and possess equal power to express a choice. Given these parameters, it should not be surprising that the pollsters achieved a certain measure of accuracy in predicting individual acts of behavior. While it is certainly true that the voting intentions of individuals often are related to their opinions on issues, transferring the use of a measurement technique appropriate for assessing the former to an assessment of the latter assumes an equivalence between the two which does not exist (Blumer, 1948, p. 547). To do so would be analogous to transferring the technology of measuring heat, i.e., a thermometer, to the measurement of light, a phenomenon which often accompanies heat but which is conceptually distinct.

First of all, public opinion situations do not involve an individual venturing into a "voting booth" or store to express one preference from among a fixed set of alternatives. As Fred Goldner (1971) has observed: "The public does vote and it does consume; but what does it 'do' with regard to issues such as Vietnam, the S.S.T., or the economy?" There is no standard, agreed-upon action, analogous to a vote in a formal election or purchase in a store, that an individual performs in a public opinion "situation." Neither is there a location—no "booth"—in which public opinion is to occur, as is the case, for voting and shopping for consumer goods.

Further, public opinion "situations," unlike elections, do not occur at fixed time intervals such as every two or four years. They are often spontaneous, capable of occurring in a variety of forms, settings, and contexts at any point in time. Finally, in a voting situation, each individual's expression of a preference counts the same as any other's, hence the fundamental principle of "one person, one vote." Such is not the case with public opinion. Even a cursory familiarity with American politics is sufficient for one to realize that the opinions of such organizations as industrial trade associations, labor unions, corporations, and churches, to cite just a few, often "count" more in public policy decision making than do the opinions of unorganized individuals (see Blumer, 1948; Namenwirth, Miller, & Weber, 1981). The success of one trade association, the National Rifle Association (NRA), in formulating policy incongruent with the opinions and preferences of a majority of individuals is an obvious example of this point. Further, this disparity is not restricted to the case of organized groups versus individuals, but is found within collectivities of individuals themselves. Some persons' opinions "count" more than others; this is the basis of the notion of opinion leadership described by Katz and Lazarsfeld (1955) a half-century ago and recently illustrated with the proliferation of the talk radio format. As Wiebe (1953, p. 350) observed:

> An arbitrary value of 1 assigned to each opinion is simply poor mathematics in attempting to predict on issues where the researchers know with practical certainty that one person's decision to behave (opinion) is at least 100 times as important as that of another person on the same issue.

And yet mainstream public opinion research ignores these obvious discrepancies and persists in adhering to a paradigm (i.e., one person, one vote) which is inherently unsuited for studying the empirical nature of the phenomenon.

Regrettably, Blumer's critique of public opinion polling is as timely today as it was in 1947 when he spoke to members of the American Sociological Society. For while the techniques of polling may be more reliable today than they were a few decades ago, their validity—or lack thereof—remains essentially unchanged.

In many ways, Blumer's critique is of greater significance today, because public opinion polls and the public opinion they depict have become a staple of American life. Due largely to the journalist's propensity for empirically incontrovertible "facts" (Tuchman, 1978; Gans, 1979), polling organizations have found among members of the press a ready outlet for their polls. For in keeping with the increasingly fashionable view of journalism as an applied social science (Meyer, 1973; McCombs et al., 1976; Ismach, 1979), public opinion polls represent an appropriately objective and thus self-evidently legitimate source of news. To be sure, so enamored are journalists of polls that large numbers of news media regularly publish or broadcast syndicated polls, and many now sponsor—and some even conduct—their own polls. In the rush to accommodate the day's data, publication of the results of public opinion polls are rivaled only by publication of the Dow Jones Industrial Average and the Consumer Price Index.

THE PRESS, PUBLIC OPINION, AND DEMOCRATIC IDEALS

It should come as no surprise that Gallup's conception of public opinion has received a warm reception in the newsroom, for Gallup's decision to treat public opinion as the opinions of individuals rests on many of the same democratic assumptions as a press committed to personal autonomy and individual self-determination. Just as assessing public opinion means little more than assessing a fair representation of the opinions of individuals, securing public expression means little more than securing individual expression for a reasonably large number of individuals. What is "public" and "shared" is not, therefore, conceptually distinct from what is "private" and "personal"; indeed, *public* opinion and *public* expression are "public" only by virtue of their weight or amount: a little or a lot.

Assessing public opinion principally in terms of its quantity benefits pollsters and journalists alike, but especially the latter, in four important and related ways. First, knowing public opinion as a calculable occurrence brings to it the aura of science and the prestige of scientific measurement; it adds precision and specificity to what otherwise would be an inexact and ephemeral phenomenon. The rise of polling in the 1930s coincided with the rapid professionalization of journalism, which in turn, Hallin (1985, p. 129) reminds us, "paralleled the rise of science as a cultural paradigm against which all forms of discourse came to be measured."[4]

Second, a numerical expression of public opinion transforms the subjectivity of opinion into the objectivity of fact; journalists' stories can be filled with opinion and at the same time defended as factual and impartial. The use of polls provides an easier defense against charges of bias than the justification journalists can offer for using the opinions of the prominent and elite. Opinions gleaned from polls enjoy more of a populist appeal, and decidedly more credibility, than the opinions of unsung individuals—interviews of "people-on-the-street"—whose lack of credentials presumably qualifies them to serve as surrogates for "the public."

Third, the use of poll data enables journalists to evade the difficult question of the *quality* of public opinion. Just as scientists embrace the rigor of their "methods" but distance themselves from the "results" of their investigations, journalists and pollsters can endorse the logic of polling while they remain professionally "disinterested" in what polls reveal.

Fourth, the quantification of public opinion appeals to, and simultaneously affirms, journalists' faith in a free and enlightened electorate; it vivifies the political authority of the citizenry and underscores the viability of each individual, separate and sovereign, as the locus of democratic power. By recognizing the value of individual opinion and by granting everyone, at least statistically, an opportunity to be heard, public opinion polls foster what appears to be an entirely open and egalitarian form of democracy. Accordingly, public opinion polls serve to legitimize a view of politics and democracy that resonates with journalism's enduring commitment to personal freedom and individual autonomy, a commitment to a freedom *from* the state intended to protect *self*-determination, *self*-expression, and *self*-interest.

Public Opinion and the Ideal of the Marketplace

The negative view of freedom that characterizes the preponderance of free press theory today—the "central image" of the First Amendment, as Bollinger (1991) puts it—presupposes a private sphere independent of the state, a metaphorical "space" where individuals, unencumbered by obligations, demands and other "public" pressures, are free to pursue their own ends. This is the ideal of the "marketplace of ideas," to use the metaphor that has been in vogue since Oliver Wendell Holmes popularized it in 1919,[5] a vision of society wedded to the Darwinian proposition that truth, beauty and goodness cannot be known independent of, or prior to, their test for survival in an open and unfettered competition.

The marketplace metaphor takes commerce as its conceptual resource. Self-governance works as "free trade"—democracy, that is, amounts to freedom of choice, whether the selections involve competing products, competing policies or competing politicians. Community, in turn, exists as a means to unknown ends; it succeeds, ideally, as a voluntary association aimed at advancing each member's needs and interests. As Held (1987) puts it, the marketplace metaphor envisions a model of democracy focused "on the legitimate pursuit by individuals of their interests and on government as, above all, a means for the enhancement of these interests" (p. 65); it views society as a fundamentally utilitarian arrangement "in which individuals have unlimited desires, form a body of mass consumers and are dedicated to the maximization of private satisfaction" (p. 69).

The principles of *laissez-faire* that inform a marketplace perspective require protection for the individual-as-producer, which in traditional First Amendment jurisprudence means freedom for *individual* expression. This protection, ordinarily articulated as a speaker's right to be heard, seldom extends to the *content* of expression, which would amount to a listener's right to hear (cf. Norris, 1976). Producers serve consumers (i.e., speakers serve listeners) through the demands and dynamics of the marketplace; any a priori requirement for content would violate the principle of individual autonomy. Freedom of choice exists, then, but only as marketplace forces dictate: No one can demand what the marketplace cannot deliver.

Likewise, no one can demand that the marketplace transform rights into opportunities, which is to say the *right* of expression must be kept separate from the *opportunity* for communication. To recycle an argument developed elsewhere (Glasser, 1991), in a society steeped in the principles of a free and open marketplace, individuals enjoy only the right to speak *in* public. To speak *to* the public requires "communication"; and communication, like other aspects of commerce, is not a public right but a private privilege.[6] Whereas self-expression can flourish in the absence of suppression by the state, communication will flourish only as it succeeds in the marketplace.

This separation of expression from communication—arguably one of the enduring legacies of Locke and the Enlightenment (Peters, 1989)—accounts for the marketplace's peculiarly psychological orientation to public opinion. Opinions themselves are taken to be personal, subjective and idiosyncratic; they are possessions, personal property. Within a marketplace framework, opinions *belong* to the individual; like meaning itself, they are matters of the mind. Communication, by contrast, serves as the mechanism for making opinion public—ergo "*public*ity," the noun we use to denote the process through which we publicize the private.

From a marketplace perspective, it follows, communication exists principally as a mode of delivery; the model of communication is one of transportation (Carey, 1989, pp. 3–88), where opinion is to communication what freight is to a train: One merely transports the other. Individual opinions—typically a mélange of personal preferences, interests, inclinations, wishes, convictions, and the like—become, ipso facto, public opinion once they are grouped together and their configuration receives some "official" designation from pollsters or the press.

As the metaphor implies, the marketplace *displays* politics and invites consumers *qua* citizens to express their preferences by choosing among competing policies, platforms, and politicians. Political discourse in this context functions as advertising. Whether they appear as themselves in purchased space (or time) or are disguised as news and information, these advertisements appeal to an audience understood more in terms of group psychology than political authority. To be sure, the goal of political advertising, whatever its form, is not participation, but identification; rather than reminding citizens of their power, their political opportunities, and their obligation to contribute to public debate, political advertising aims to create what Calhoun (1992) aptly describes as "occasions for consumers to identify with the public positions or personas of others" (p. 26).

Under these conditions, Calhoun (1992) observes, public opinion amounts to the equivalent of brand loyalty. Public opinion in the arena of the marketplace confers consent, of course, but it is consent of the kind that is characteristically weak, uncritical, and tentative. Existing as it does mainly through the polls that measure it and which give it its public appearance, public opinion in the tradition of Gallup conceives consent as a sign of allegiance; the public is allowed to respond by acclamation—or by withholding acclamation—but the public is not expected to respond substantively and discursively.

Public Opinion and the Ideal of the Public Sphere

The idea of a "public sphere" is conceptually and politically distinct from the idea of a marketplace, at least insofar as the former presupposes a "free space" as free from the whims of the marketplace as it is free from the demands of the state. But to understand the two in dichotomized terms, as we have in Table 18.1, is not to deny the historical conditions for their convergence. In the early 1800s, in the United States and elsewhere, a marketplace of "petty commodity producers," as Habermas (1989) describes the circumstances, gave rise to a "bourgeois public sphere" that operated as a political forum through its "transmission and amplification of the rational–critical debate of private people assembled into a public" (p. 188). It was a time of "relatively widely and evenly distributed ownership of the means of production," Habermas observes, which meant that most "citizens"[7] could readily "attain the status of property owner" and thereby "acquire" private interests worthy of public attention (pp. 86–87).

But with the disappearance of the preindustrial market economy that characterized the U.S. marketplace in the early decades of the 19th century, participation in the public sphere became more difficult and less overtly political. The new barriers to the marketplace, exacerbated by an escalating concentration of ownership of the means of production, including the means of communication, transformed political interests into commercial interests—and transformed "a journalism of conviction

TABLE 18.1. Comparing the Marketplace with the Public Sphere

	Marketplace	Public sphere
Freedom is	Negative	Positive
Protection aimed at	Individual expression; the right to be heard	The content of expression; the right to hear
Communication is	Privately controlled	Publicly protected
Public opinion	Is the "property" of each individual	Is the consequence of public debate and deliberation
Goal of the First Amendment	To protect individual self-expression	To protect the conditions for public discourse
Freedom of expression	Fosters individual self-determination	Fosters collective self-determination
The press functions as	A source of information	A catalyst for conversation
Access rights?	No	Yes
Consent emerges	Through competing ideas and freedom of choice	Through argumentation and consensus

into one of commerce" (Habermas, 1974, p. 53). There were now more consumers than producers, a ratio that meant most citizens played the role of customer whose private interests were expressed "in public" only through purchases in the marketplace.

Neither nostalgia nor naivete, however, accounts for the growing interest in studying the conditions for participation that characterize the ideal of the public sphere; for no one anticipates the restoration or recreation of the particular confluence of circumstances that prevailed more than a century ago. Rather, across the social sciences and throughout the humanities, the idea of a public sphere, understood normatively but also empirically, represents a renewed interest in revitalizing the practice of democracy. What animates this discussion, and no doubt what underscores its importance, is, as Post (1993, p. 654) suggests, "the disreputable state of contemporary democratic dialogue."

While Post's assessment of "The Quandary of Democratic Dialogue" is but one of scores of recent commentaries on the importance of promoting "a rich and valuable public debate" (p. 654), his analysis usefully defends the "positive" freedom of the public sphere as an adjunct to, rather than as a repudiation of, the "negative" freedom of the marketplace. That is, while Post recognizes the value of subordinating "individual rights of expression to collective processes of public deliberation" (p. 654), he will not accede to abandoning the "axiomatic and foundational principle" of First Amendment law, namely the "ascription of autonomy" (pp. 672–673).

What Post rejects, then, is the standard libertarian view—and very much the prevailing view, according to Bollinger (1991)—of a government utterly incapable of not abusing its authority over the press, a government basically "untrustworthy when it comes to regulating public debate" (Bollinger, 1991, p. 20). But what he also rejects is the "managerial authority" of the state when used to "suppress speech within public discourse for the sake of imposing a specific version of national identity" (p. 665). The compromise Post sketches, consistent in principle with Emerson's (1981) "affirmative" theory of the First Amendment, calls on the state to preserve "the pervasive indeterminacy of public discourse" while at the same time taking on the responsibility, when needed and where appropriate, to "coordinate and facilitate expression" (p. 665). Autonomy "can be negated," Post concludes, but only in "discrete and local ways where First Amendment presumptions of autonomy have come to seem merely 'fictions' masking particularly intolerable conditions of private power and domination" (p. 673).

By inviting the state to combat private abuses of power—by having the state play the role of "executor" of the public sphere, as Habermas (1974, p. 49) proposes—Post implicitly acknowledges the folly of separating expression from communication. Self-expression evolves through communication; the public sphere, unlike the marketplace, offers an opportunity to discover or create a common good—a *general* interest—that can be known only through public deliberation. As Fraser (1992) explains, the notion of a public sphere

> does not assume that people's preferences, interests, and identities are given exogenously in advance of public discourse and deliberation. It appreciates, rather, that preferences, interests, and identities are as much outcomes as antecedents of public deliberation, indeed are discursively constituted in and through it. (p. 123)

Communication, it follows, does not convey consent but actively fashions it. "Communication in this context," Calhoun (1992) writes, "means not merely sharing what people already think or know but also a process of potential transformation in which reason is advanced by debate itself" (p. 29). It is a transformation of the kind Taylor (1989, p. 167) has in mind when he refers to the *power* of communication to take individuals over a certain threshold and into a universe of discourse in which meaning is not simply shared but *established*. What is at stake when communication operates this way, Taylor points out, is not you and me but *us*; communication establishes a sense of "our" that is something greater than a mere aggregation of "yours" and "mine." Public opinion, therefore, denotes a critical agreement—ideally a consensus—on *common* goods and *general* interests. It confers consent of the strongest kind by expressing a distinctively public point of view arrived at through an open and unfettered debate.

THE OPINIONS OF PUBLICS AND THE POWER OF THE PRESS

Even at our contentious best, we would not suppose that polls of opinions could—or even should—disappear. Survey research can add considerably to our knowledge of political processes. When used to simulate the outcome of an election, for example, surveys of samples of likely voters can yield interesting and usually reliable results.

When used as a gauge of "public opinion," however, polls not only miss the mark but shift the target. As we have noted, polls offer at best a naive and narrow view of democracy; they posit a conception of participation that confuses a plebiscitary system with a democratic one. Moreover, polls defy the "publicness" of public opinion; by operationally defining public opinion as a compilation of individual opinions, polls in effect disclaim any requirement for individuals to stake a *public* claim for their opinions and the reasons for them.

Basically, Blumer was right.

The Opinions of Publics

From Blumer (1948) to Bourdieu (1979), academic critics have argued for decades that public opinion polls provide a misleading and potentially oppressive account of public opinion: If the "substance of political life is public discussion," as Eliasoph (1990, p. 465) and countless others contend, polls not only fail to capture it but in many ways serve to inhibit it. Remarkably, ordinary citizens, unschooled in the academic literature and unfamiliar with its technical terms, share a strikingly similar perspective; they, too, find that polls ignore the dynamics of public opinion and impede its formation. As Herbst (1993a) found in her small but telling study of "citizens' construction of political reality":

> the quantitative data polls . . . make certain public discussions irrelevant or extremely difficult to stimulate. Polls are believed to suppress critical thinking, and to dictate the questions a society asks itself as well as the range of possible answers. The people I spoke with seemed to understand just how polling restricts debate on their *own* issues of concern. (p. 450)

Through a series of hour-long interviews with a politically diverse group of "informants," activists and non-activists alike, Herbst probed the "lay theories or connotations of 'public opinion' "; she sought to discover, phenomenologically, "how people understand public opinion processes" (pp. 449, 442). What Herbst found among the Chicago-area residents she studied was skepticism and cynicism about "how public opinion is measured and how it is discussed by elites," which in turn underscored a widespread sense of alienation: "There was a general feeling . . . that public opinion formation processes were somehow *out of their hands*—that *they* were not part of 'public opinion' " (p. 449).

One important way in which polls foster a sense of alienation is the way in which they *dislocate* the individual citizen. By focusing on the individual and on individual opinion, polls accentuate the "privateness" of opinion and neglect the importance of collective processes of deliberation aimed at reaching a publicly accepted consensus. Individuals are effectively isolated from the very feature that makes public opinion distinctively public. Pollsters seem to forget, or ignore without acknowledgement, the origins of the phenomenon of "public opinion" and a requirement that dates to the 18th century: "Public opinion can by definition only come into existence when a reasoning public is presupposed" (Habermas, 1974, p. 50).

The requirement of a "reasoning public" offers at once both an historically realistic account of how democracy works and a normatively provocative critique of the conditions necessary to bring about and preserve the kind of civic culture that self-governance demands. It not only invites theorizing about the importance of "an institutionalized arena of discursive interaction," to use Fraser's (1992, p. 110) Habermasian definition of "a public," but recognizes as well the particular and peculiar needs of modern societies. This is no small challenge, Fraser demonstrates, in light of the complexities associated with a large, diffuse "welfare state mass democracy" of the kind that exists today in the United States.

Fraser's analysis of publics and public opinion begins with the recognition that "stratified societies," by which she means "societies whose basic institutional framework generates unequal social groups in structural relations of dominance and subordination," do not—and arguably should not—operate under the assumptions of "a single, overarching public sphere" (p. 122). While Fraser does not rule out the possibility of a unitary public arena, just as she does not rule out the possibility of an egalitarian *and* multicultural society, the "ideal of participatory parity" is better achieved by recognizing and dealing with enduring inequalities rather than by theorizing them away (cf. Pollock, 1976). Fraser's goal, then, is not to postulate the conditions for "full parity of participation in public debate and deliberation"; that is not, she believes, "within the reach of possibility." Instead, Fraser asks, "What form of public life comes closest to approaching that ideal? What institutional arrangements will best help narrow the gap in participatory parity between dominant and subordinate groups?" (p. 122).

The model Fraser proposes is one of a multiplicity of publics, an arrangement better suited to different cultural groups and the means for their participation in the larger society. These various publics—"subaltern counterpublics," as Fraser describes them—provide alternative venues for individuals whose identities, needs, and interests have been deliberately or unwittingly slighted in the "structured setting" in which day-to-day life unfolds. They are opportunities for what Fraser calls "discursive contestation," opportunities for other voices—other idioms and styles—to make themselves heard in a forum where they can be taken seriously.

But counterpublics do not exist for the sole purpose of inventing and circulating counterdiscourses; they are not *only* "spaces of withdrawal and regroupment." Counterpublics also function as "bases and training grounds for agitational activities directed toward wider publics" (p. 124); they exist to widen the range of discourse, to expand the terms of debate, and to enlarge the opportunities for participation. Fraser thus intentionally complicates the issue of separatism. She wants separate publics, each with their own set of issues and concerns, but she also wants these publics to feed into successively larger publics; the aim of this "tier of publics," as it might be termed, "is to disseminate one's discourse into ever widening arenas" (p. 124).

It is not difficult to discern in Fraser's plan for a "plurality of competing publics," even as we have crudely sketched it here, a rejection of the singularity of public opinion. It is also clear that Fraser's plan eschews procedures that, as Pollock (1976) puts it, "enumerates and appraises all individuals as having equal rights, as dots without qualities so to speak, ignor[ing] the real differences of social power and social impotence" (p. 231). Within Fraser's framework, publics have opinion*s*, which is to say "public opinion" ought to be understood not as the "opinions of individuals," but as the "opinions of publics."

The Power of the Press

From Fraser's perspective, and from the perspective of much of the recent work in response to Habermas's recently translated dissertation (Habermas, 1989), the press plays a vitally important role in the processes of self-governance not as a provider of information but as a facilitator of public opinion. The difference can be overdrawn but the point is this: Public opinion requires a forum for its development, a "free space" where nothing but the power of a good argument can prevail, and more often than not "the press"[8] is all that is available for this purpose.

Recent critiques by Carey (1987), Rosen (1991), and Lasch (1990), drawing more from Dewey (1927, 1958) than from Habermas, develop the theme that the press can better meet the needs of public opinion by recalling its earlier commitment to debate and argument, a commitment all but abandoned by the turn of the century. Changing conditions in journalism, particularly the rise of the disinterested and impartial "reporter," ended up reversing the relationship between argument and information. By today's conventional wisdom, information feeds argument. But, Lasch suggests, information might be better understood as the by-product of debate, not as its precondition: "We do not know what we need to know until we ask the right questions, and we can identify the right questions only by subjecting our own ideas about the world to the test of public controversy" (p. 1).[9]

Rosen strikes a similar tone in his cautious celebration of the prospects for a more "public journalism," a journalism "more supportive of a realm of meaningful public discussion" (p. 268). He argues for—and indeed provides an illustration of—a shift from a "journalism of information" to a "journalism of conversation," to use Carey's competing models of press performance. Like Lasch and Rosen, Carey is hopeful that the "public will begin to reawaken when they are addressed as conversational partners and are encouraged to join the talk rather than sit passively as spectators before a discussion conducted by journalists and experts" (p. 14). Whereas a journalism of information commodifies public opinion by accentuating its final form, even when it is acknowledged to be only a "snapshot in time," a journalism of conversation focuses on the conditions for public discourse by creating and preserving opportunities for debate and discussion: Reporting on public opinion is comparatively less important than accommodating it.

Public opinion polls fit comfortably within the tradition of a journalism of information. Polls always produce opinion; indeed, they *seduce* opinion, which is what Pollock (1976, p. 229) means when he observes that much of what passes for "public opinion" are crude and unsupported stereotypes for which the individual "respondent," questioned anonymously, is seldom held accountable: "The contradiction between the compulsion to have an opinion and the incapacity to form an opinion leads many people to accept stereotypes which relieve them of the thankless task of forming their own opinions and yet enable them to enjoy the prestige of being in touch with things." The additional risk, as Miller (1991) found in his study of the 1990 Nicaraguan election, is that polls will report unheld opinions which protect individuals from public scrutiny of their *real* opinions.

A journalism of conversation, by contrast, views public opinion as the consequence of a social and public inquiry into common goods. It is the type of journalism that pays attention to the subtleties of language and to the diversity of expression (cf. Eliasoph, 1990). It avoids, whenever possible, the "circumscribed choices" (cf. Salmon, 1994) that polls unavoidably impose on the citizenry. A journalism of conversation seeks a publicly tested consensus; reachable or not, it is the goal of a free and robust press.

NOTES

1. Though he devoted only one article to the concept of public opinion, he referred to it in several other works. See especially "The Mass,the Public, and Public Opinion," in Alfred McClung Lee's *New Outline of the Principles of Sociology* (Blumer, 1946). See also several of Blumer's works contained in a *festschrift* devoted to his political philosophy (Lyman & Vidach, 1988).

2. Blumer's (1948) critique of polling can be summarized in a series of six points: (a) Public opinion must be viewed as a phenomenon of society; its form and function emanate from a particular social fabric. If it is to be studied empirically, it must be studied in a way that is faithful to its actual nature and role in society. (b) Society is not merely an "aggregation of disparate individuals," as implied by the methodology of polling. It is instead comprised of organized, functional groups—corporations, trade associations, unions, ethnic groups, etc.—which pursue different and often conflicting interests, possess differing degrees of prestige and power, and, as a result, vary in their ability to translate private interests into public policy. (c) These functional groups attempt to influence the outcome of various social issues, problems, and disputes by bringing to bear pressure on those individuals or groups who have the power to make decisions. (d) These key decision makers must sift through the various influences, claims, and demands and decide which ones "count" as "legitimate." (e) Public opinion is formed and expressed not through an interaction of autonomous individuals sharing equally in the process but instead through the interaction of unequally powerful functional groups. (f) realistically speaking, public opinion consists of those views that reach the attention of decision makers. It is important to recognize that since the days of Blumer's critique, polls have become fully integrated into the political process so that they now regularly *do* reach the attention of decision makers. In other words, by Blumer's own definition, polls have become an integral component, but still not an exclusive determinant, of what constitutes public opinion (see Lemert, 1981; Converse, 1987).

3. As such, it can be argued that Gallup was implicitly hypothesizing spiral of "noise," in which a minority faction, through its expression of opinion, essentially drowns out the voice of the majority. This perspecitve is an interesting contrast to that of Elizabeth Noelle-Neumann, whose "spiral of silence" model (described in several other chapters in this volume) of the public opinion process focuses on the implications of the expression of majority opinion drowning out the voice of the minority.

4. As Herbst (1993b, pp. 89–111) found in her study of a few dozen journalists asked to recall their treatment of public opinion in the 1930s and 1940s, newsrooms at the time were increasingly drawn to the "instrumental benefits" of a numerical description of public opinion. Even before the widespread use of the survey technique developed by Gallup, newspapers found a variety of ways to rationalize and routinize their treatment of public opinion: counting telegrams and telephone calls, monitoring letters-to-the-editor, tabulating canceled subscriptions and drops in circulation, categorizing editorial comment, and so on. If they weren't yet convinced of the accuracy of polls, journalists in the early years of polling were, Herbst concludes, "quite taken by the authoritative nature of quantitative techniques" (p. 90).

5. In *Abrams v. U.S.* (1919), in one of the Supreme Court's most remembered dissenting opinions, Holmes wrote: "When men have realized that time has upset many fighting faiths, they may come to believe even more than they believe the very foundations of their own conduct that the ultimate good desired is better reached by free trade in ideas—that the best test of truth is the

power of the thought to get itself accepted in the competition of the market, and that truth is the only ground upon which their wishes safely can be carried out" (p. 630).

6. Kairys (1982, p. 166) makes precisely this point when he observes that individuals in a marketplace democracy are protected only in their "displays of displeasure": picketing, demonstrating, distributing leaflets, etc. The more effective opportunities for public expression almost always require control of, or at least access to, the *means* of communication—namely the press and other mass media—and these are generally available only to individuals or groups with considerable wealth, power, and prestige. "[T]he ordinary person or group of ordinary persons," Kairys concludes, "has no means, based in the Constitution or elsewhere, to engage meaningfully in that dialogue on the issues of the day that the First Amendment is so often heralded as promoting and guaranteeing."

7. Only select groups of individuals, however, qualified for citizenship. Race and gender, for example, excluded many from their role as citizens. While it is true, then, that "during the period from 1830 to 1900 . . . [e]ighty percent of the eligible voters went to the polls in presidential elections," it is a little misleading to conclude from this, as Lasch (1990, p. 2) does, that early voting data offer evidence of "popular participation in politics."

8. By "the press" we mean to include a full range of media dedicated to the exchange of opinion. This is a rapidly expanding category that at a minimum includes newspapers of all kinds, magazines, newsletters, radio and television, electronic bulletin boards, and so on. There are, of course, nonpress venues for the exchange of opinion—for example, town halls, salons of one kind or another—but in this section we are interested in exploring the power of the press.

9. For an interesting assessment of a forgotten pioneer in this area, see Katz's (1992) tribute to Gabriel Tarde, whose essay on "Opinion and Conversation" (Tarde, 1969), originally published in 1898, anticipated much of what is being said today.

REFERENCES

Abrams v. U.S., 250 U.S., 250 U.S. 616 (1919).

Blumer, H. (1946). The mass, the public, and public opinion. In A. M. Lee (Ed.), *New outline of the principles of sociology* (pp. 185–193). New York: Barnes and Noble.

Blumer, H. (1948). Public opinion and public opinion polling. *American Sociological Review, 13*, 542–554.

Bollinger, L. C. (1991). *Images of a free press*. Chicago: University of Chicago Press.

Bourdieu, P. (1979). Public opinion does not exist. In A. Mattelart & S. Siegelaub (Eds.), *Communication and class struggle* (pp. 124–130). New York: International General.

Bryce, J. (1895). *The American commonwealth* (Vol. 2, 3rd. ed.). New York: Macmillan.

Calhoun, C. (1992). Introduction: Habermas and the public sphere. In C. Calhoun (Ed.), *Habermas and the public sphere* (pp. 1–48). Cambridge, MA: MIT Press.

Carey, J. W. (1987, March/April). The press and public discourse. *The Center Magazine*, pp. 4–16.

Carey, J. W. (1989). *Communication as culture*. Boston: Unwin Hyman.

Converse, P. (1987). Changing conceptions of public opinion in the political process. *Public Opinion Quarterly, 51*(4, part 2), S13–S24.

Dewey, J. (1927). *The public and its problems*. New York: Henry Holt.

Dewey, J. (1958). *Experience and nature*. New York: Dover Books.

Eliasoph, N. (1990). Political culture and the presentation of a political self: A study of the public sphere in the spirit of Erving Goffman. *Theory and Society, 19*, 465–494.

Emerson, T. I. (1981). The affirmative side of the First Amendment. *Georgia Law Review, 15*(Summer), 795–849.

Fraser, N. (1992). Rethinking the public sphere: A contribution to the critique of actually existing democracy. In C. Calhoun (Ed.), *Habermas and the public sphere* (pp. 109–142). Cambridge, MA: MIT Press.

Gallup, G. (1925). *A study in the selection of salespeople for Killian's department store, Cedar Rapids, Iowa*. Unpublished master's thesis, State University of Iowa, Iowa City.

Gallup, G. (1928). *An objective method for determining reader interest in the content of a newspaper*. Unpublished doctoral thesis, State University of Iowa, Iowa City.

Gallup, G. (1966). Polls and the political process—Past, present and future. *Public Opinion Quarterly, 29*, 544–549.

Gallup, G. (1972). *The sophisticated poll watcher's guide*. Ephrata, PA: Science Press.

Gallup, G., & Rae, S.F. (1940). *The pulse of democracy: The public-opinion poll and how it works*. New York: Simon & Schuster.

Gans, H. (1979). *Deciding what's news*. New York: Random House.

Ginsberg, B. (1986). *The captive public: How mass opinion promotes state power*. New York: Basic Books.

Glasser, T. L. (1991). Communication and the cultivation of citizenship. *Communication, 12*, 235–248.

Goldner, F. (1971, May). *Public opinion and survey research: A poor mix*. Paper presented at the annual meeting of the American Association for Public Opinion Research.

Habermas, J. (1974). The public sphere: An encyclopedia article (1964). *New German Critique, 1*(Fall), 49–55.

Habermas, J. (1989). *The transformation of the public sphere*. Cambridge, MA: MIT Press.

Hallin, D. C. (1985). The American news media: A critical theory perspective. In J. Forester (Ed.), *Critical theory and public life* (pp. 121–146). Cambridge, MA: MIT Press.

Held, D. (1987). *Models of democracy*. Stanford, CA: Stanford University Press.

Herbst, S. (1993a). The meaning of public opinion: Citizens' constructions of political reality. *Media, Culture and Society, 15*, 437–454.

Herbst, S. (1993b). *Numbered voices: How opinion polling has shaped American politics*. Chicago: University of Chicago Press.

Ismach, I. (1979, March 9). *Precision journalism: Coming of age* (ANPA News Research Report No. 18). Reston, VA: American Newspapers Publishers Association.

Kairys, D. (1982). Freedom of speech. In D. Kairys (Ed.), *The politics of law* (pp. 140–171). New York: Pantheon.

Katz, E. (1992). On parenting a paradigm: Gabriel Tarde's agenda for opinion and communication research. *International Journal of Public Opinion Research, 4*, pp. 80–85.

Katz, E., & Lazarsfeld, P.F. (1955). *Personal influence*. Glencoe, IL: The Free Press.

Kuhn T. (1970). *The structure of scientific revolutions* (2nd ed.). Chicago: University of Chicago Press.

Lasch, C. (1990). Journalism, publicity and the lost art of argument. *Gannett Center Media Studies Journal, 4*(2), 1–11.

Lemert, J. B. (1981). *Does mass communication change public opinion after all? A new approach to effects analysis*. Chicago: Nelson-Hall.

Lyman, S. M., & Vidich, A. J. (1988). *Social order and the public philosophy.* Fayetteville, AR: University of Arkansas Press.

McCombs, M., Shaw, D.L., & Grey, D. (1976). *Handbook of reporting methods.* Boston: Hougton Mifflin.

McDonald, D. (1962). Opinion poll interviews. [One of a series of interviews on the American character]. Center for the Study of Democratic Institutions.

Meyer, P. (1973). *Precision journalism.* Bloomington: Indiana University Press.

Miller, P. V. (1991). Which side are you on? The 1990 Nicaraguan poll debacle. *Public Opinion Quarterly, 55*, 281–302.

Namenwirth, J.Z., Miller, R.L., & Weber, R.P. (1981). Organizations have opinions: A redefinition of publics. *Public Opinion Quarterly, 45*, 463–476.

Norris, S. E. (1976). Being free to speak and speaking freely. In T. Honderich (Ed.), *Social ends and political means* (pp. 13–28). London: Routledge & Kegan Paul.

Peters, J. D. (1989). John Locke, the individual, and the origin of communication. *Quarterly Journal of Speech, 75*, 387–399.

Pollock, F. (1976). Empirical research into public opinion. In P. Connerton (Ed.), *Critical sociology* (pp. 225–236). New York: Penguin Books.

Post, R. (1993). Managing deliberation: The quandary of democratic dialogue. *Ethics, 103*, 654–678.

Rogers, L. (1949). *The pollsters: Public opinion, politics and democratic leadership*. New York: Alfred A. Knopf.

Rosen, J. (1991). Making journalism more public. *Communication, 12*, 267–284.

Salmon, C. T. (1994). The circumscribed choice: Editor's introduction. *Argumentation, 8*, 325–326.

Singer, E. (1987). Editor's introduction. *Public Opinion Quarterly, 51*(4, part 2), S1–S3.

Tarde, G. (1969). Opinion and Conversation. In T. N. Clark (Ed.), *Gabriel Tarde on communication and social influence* (pp. 297–318). Chicago: University of Chicago Press.

Taylor, C. (1989). Cross-purposes: The liberal-communitarian debate. In N.L. Rosenblum (Ed.), *Liberalism and the moral life* (pp. 159–182). Cambridge, MA: MIT Press.

Theodorson, G.A., & Theodorson, A.G. (1969). *A modern dictionary of sociology*. New York: Thomas Y. Crowell Co.

Tuchman, G. (1978). *Making news*. New York: Free Press.

Weibe, G.D. (1953). Some implications of separating opinions from attitudes. *Public Opinion Quarterly, 17*(4), 328–352.

Author Index

C

P

R

Subject Index

DATE DUE

DEC 17 1995		JUL -7 2000	
DEC -9 1996			
DEC 16 1996			
APR 30 1997			
OCT 14 1997			
DEC 17 1997			